Northern California

Golf GETAWAYS

S0-BUB-269

Northern California

Golf GETAWAYS

Sensational Weekend Escapes On and Off the Links

AVALON
TRAVEL
publishing

Susan Fornoff & Cori Kenicer

Northern California *Golf* **GETAWAYS**
Sensational Weekend Escapes On and Off the Links

Please send all comments, corrections, additions, amendments, and critiques to:

NORTHERN CALIFORNIA GOLF GETAWAYS:
Sensational Weekend Escapes On and Off the Links
AVALON TRAVEL PUBLISHING
5855 BEAUDRY ST.
EMERYVILLE, CA 94608, USA
email: info@travelmatters.com
website: www.travelmatters.com

Cori Kenicer and Susan Fornoff

Published by
Avalon Travel Publishing, Inc.
5855 Beaudry St.
Emeryville, CA 94608, USA

Printing History
1st edition—February 2001
5 4 3 2 1

Text copyright© Cori Kenicer and Susan Fornoff, 2001.
All rights reserved.
Illustrations and maps copyright© Avalon Travel Publishing, 2001.
All rights reserved.

ISBN: 1-56691-247-4
ISSN: 1531-4235

Editors: Karen Bleske, Marisa Solís
Copy Editor: Deana Shields
Index: Sondra Nation
Illustrations: Bob Race
Graphics Coordinator: Erika Howsare
Interior and Cover Design: Amber Pirker
Production: Amber Pirker
Map Editor: Mike Ferguson
Cartography: Bob Race

Front cover photos: Lincoln Park Golf Course, San Francisco ©George Kenicer, 2001; Napa Valley ©Index Stock Photography, Inc., 2001

Distributed in the United States and Canada by Publishers Group West

Printed in U.S.A. by R.R. Donnelley

All rights reserved. No part of this book may be translated or reproduced in any form, except brief extracts by a reviewer for the purpose of a review, without written permission of the copyright owner.

Although every effort was made to ensure that the information was correct at the time of going to press, the author and publisher do not assume and hereby disclaim any liability to any party for any loss or damage caused by errors, omissions, or any potential travel disruption due to labor or financial difficulty, whether such errors or omissions result from negligence, accident, or any other cause.

Contents

Go With Golf 1

1 Up, Up, and Away: Little River and Sea Ranch 5
Itinerary 8 ■ Courses 14 ■ Lodging 15 ■ Dining 17 ■ Straying
Off Course 19 ■ Details, Details 20

2 Blow Me a Birdie: Bodega Bay 23
Itinerary 26 ■ Courses 29 ■ Lodging 31 ■ Dining 33 ■ Straying
Off Course 34 ■ Details, Details 36

3 Some Pars with That Wine? Sonoma Valley 39
Itinerary 42 ■ Courses 49 ■ Lodging 52 ■ Dining 56 ■ Straying
Off Course 57 ■ Details, Details 59

4 Don't Whine, Wine! Napa Valley 63
Itinerary 67 ■ Courses 75 ■ Lodging 79 ■ Dining 82 ■ Straying
Off Course 85 ■ Details, Details 87

5 A Capital Idea: Sacramento and the Foothills 91
Itinerary 94 ■ Courses 99 ■ Lodging 103 ■ Dining 105 ■
Straying Off Course 107 ■ Details, Details 108

6 For Riders and Billy Goats: North Lake Tahoe 111
Itinerary 114 ■ Courses 118 ■ Lodging 122 ■ Dining 124 ■
Straying Off Course 127 ■ Details, Details 128

7 The Right Left Turn: Plumas County 131
Itinerary 134 ■ Courses 139 ■ Lodging 142 ■ Dining 144 ■
Straying Off Course 146 ■ Details, Details 147

8 Gambler's Windfall: South Lake Tahoe and Carson Valley 151
Itinerary 1: South Lake Tahoe 154 ■ Itinerary 2: Carson
Valley 160 ■ South Lake Tahoe Courses 165 ■ Carson Valley
Courses 167 ■ South Lake Tahoe Lodging 171 ■ Carson Valley
Lodging 173 ■ South Lake Tahoe Dining 174 ■ Carson Valley
Dining 176 ■ Straying Off Course 178 ■ Details, Details 181

9 Thar's Golf in Them Thar Hills: Calaveras County 185
Itinerary 189 ■ Courses 194 ■ Lodging 197 ■ Dining 199 ■
Straying Off Course 200 ■ Details, Details 201

10 In the Shadow of Diablo: Livermore Valley 205
Itinerary 208 ■ Courses 214 ■ Lodging 217 ■ Dining 219 ■
Straying Off Course 220 ■ Details, Details 221

11 For Golfers Only: The Central Valley 225
Itinerary 229 ■ Courses 235 ■ Lodging 236 ■ Dining 237 ■
Straying Off Course 238 ■ Details, Details 239

12 Golden Gate Golf: San Francisco **243**
Itinerary 246 ▪ Courses 253 ▪ Lodging 256 ▪ Dining 259 ▪
Straying Off Course 262 ▪ Details, Details 264

13 Coast is Clear: Half Moon Bay **267**
Itinerary 270 ▪ Courses 275 ▪ Lodging 277 ▪ Dining 279 ▪
Straying Off Course 281 ▪ Details, Details 282

14 Chips Galore: Silicon Valley **285**
Itinerary 288 ▪ Courses 295 ▪ Lodging 298 ▪ Dining 300 ▪
Straying Off Course 302 ▪ Details, Details 303

15 Where the Sun Usually Shines: Santa Cruz **307**
Itinerary 313 ▪ Courses 318 ▪ Lodging 321 ▪ Dining 323 ▪
Straying Off Course 324 ▪ Details, Details 326

16 Mission Possible: Hollister and San Juan Bautista **329**
Itinerary 332 ▪ Courses 336 ▪ Lodging 338 ▪ Dining 339 ▪
Straying Off Course 341 ▪ Details, Details 341

17 Almost Heaven: Monterey Peninsula **345**
Itinerary 1: Penultimate 347 ▪ Itinerary 2: Budget 351 ▪
Penultimate Courses 355 ▪ Budget Courses 357 ▪ Penultimate
Lodging 360 ▪ Budget Lodging 363 ▪ Penultimate Dining 365 ▪
Budget Dining 368 ▪ Straying Off Course 369 ▪ Details,
Details 370

18 Golf Heaven: Pebble Beach **373**
Itinerary 376 ▪ Courses 381 ▪ Lodging 383 ▪ Dining 385 ▪
Straying Off Course 386 ▪ Details, Details 388

APPENDIX: Top Itineraries for Special Interests **390**

INDEX **392**
Golf Courses 392
Lodging 393
Dining 394
General 397

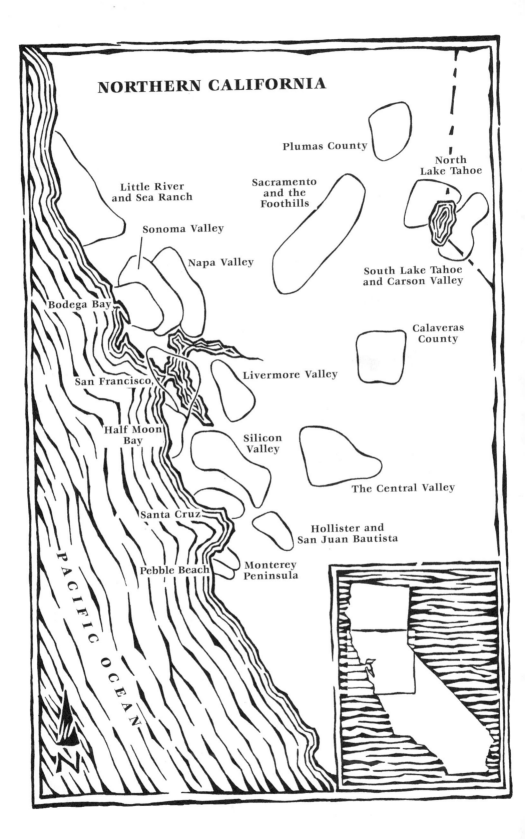

NORTHERN CALIFORNIA

Plumas County

North
Lake Tahoe

Little River
and Sea Ranch

Sacramento
and the
Foothills

Sonoma Valley

Napa Valley

South Lake Tahoe
and Carson Valley

Bodega Bay

Calaveras
County

San Francisco

Livermore Valley

Half Moon
Bay

Silicon
Valley

The Central Valley

Santa Cruz

Hollister and
San Juan Bautista

Pebble Beach

Monterey
Peninsula

PACIFIC OCEAN

Our Commitment

We are committed to making *Northern California Golf Getaways: Sensational Weekend Escapes On and Off the Links* the most accurate, thorough, and enjoyable golf guide to the region. With this first edition, you can rest assured that every recommended golf course and lodging property in this book has been carefully reviewed and accompanied by the most up-to-date information.

However, with every new golf season, it is inevitable that many of the fees will have increased, and so the prices we've listed are best used as benchmarks, for comparison from course to course. If you have a specific need or concern, it's a good idea to check with the golf course on fees and conditions when you make your tee time. And with lodging and dining, changes in ownership or chef cannot be predicted and may result in a change in quality.

The map in this book highlights our chapters and is not necessarily useful as a road map. Please consult maps designed for that purpose if necessary.

If you would like to comment on the book, whether it's to suggest a region or golf course we overlooked or to let us know about any noteworthy experience—good or bad—that occurred while using *Northern California Golf Getaways* as your guide, we would appreciate hearing from you. Please address correspondence to:

Northern California Golf Getaways
1st Edition
Avalon Travel Publishing
5855 Beaudry St.
Emeryville, CA 94608
U.S.A
email: info@travelmatters.com

ACKNOWLEDGMENTS

Thanks to Emmy Moore-Minister of the NorCal PGA and former Bodega Harbour head pro Dennis Kalkowski for planting the seeds of this project by creating the first wonderful escape, and to the many golf course professionals and hotel and restaurant publicists who have assisted us along the way.

Then there were those who actually schlepped us around and found an answer for every little niggly question. We thank you: Linda Beltran of Woodside Hotels & Resorts, Judy Bennett of Del Webb, Norm Blandel at The Dragon, Donna Brady of the Women's Golf Association of Northern California, Suzi Brakken of the Plumas County Visitors Bureau, Bob Buck and the staff at Million Air Monterey, Betsy Cooper of Ironstone Vineyards, Malei Jessee of the Santa Cruz County Conference and Visitors Center, George Kelley of Stevinson Ranch, Bruce Lewis at San Juan Oaks, Chris Lynch at the Resort at Squaw Creek, Dan Marengo of the Fontayne Group, Val Ramsey at Pebble Beach, Rhonda Richards at Twelve Bridges, Bob Trinchero of Greenhorn Creek, Kathy Wake at Ridgemark, Jack Wolf of the Sonoma County Golf Group, and Phil Weidinger of many clients in Carson City and South Lake Tahoe.

When it came to actually maneuvering the book into this form, the folks at Avalon Travel Publishing pulled out all stops on creativity and energy. We thank them all, especially our editors, Karen Bleske and Marisa Solís.

From Susan: I could not have completed this book without taking a flying leap if not for the support of Glenn Schwarz, Larry Yant, and all my understanding associates at the *San Francisco Examiner.* And I would never have started it without Marc Squeri, who not only refrained from dumping me while I was crankily finishing this project, but married me!

From Cori: I would like to thank my husband, George, for keeping me and the computer up and running during the writing of this book. I also want to thank the following people for their support in the different areas in which our lives interfaced around the book: Angelica Chiong, Sarah Colby, Maureen Corrigan, Connie and Larry Easterling, Colleen Horn, Judy and Chuck Kimball, Calvin Murasaki, Judy Oppenheimer, Scott Sommer, Connie Watson, Joanne Wolfeld, Julie Wong, and Charlie Young. Many thanks to Bruce Whipperman and the Bay Area Travel Writers for their support and encouragement.

A Note from Cori

Writing this book has been both a trip back into my past and a journey of discovery. I have enjoyed revisiting golf courses in Northern California where I played as a junior golfer, representing Diablo Country Club.

Growing up, I watched my father, Larry Curtola, build the strong foundations that Diablo Country Club and Castlewood Country Club stand on today, and I still remember him signaling to the tractor driver where to carve the golf holes for Auburn Valley Country Club. My father instilled in me a love of golf at an early age, and he passed away during the writing of this book.

Coming from a childhood immersed in Northern California golf, it has been equally joyful to discover golf where there was none before, and to watch my adopted hometown of San Francisco become a golf destination.

The old threads link up with new ones to weave a tapestry rich with all that represents the best in Northern California golf. I am grateful to be part of its past and its future.

Go With Golf

We believe golf is good. Any golf is better than no golf. Certainly, any day golfing is better than the best day working. So you know we had a lot more fun researching this book than we did writing it. And you know we don't have a lot of nasty things to say about any golf course or any golf hole. That's not why we wrote *Northern California Golf Getaways*.

This book is here to help you make the most of your precious golf getaway time. You're busy, we're busy, but every now and then a faraway golf course beckons, calling us away from the daily routine and offering us fresh scenery, new friends, and unexpected challenges. Sometimes it's hard to answer the call. Maybe you just don't have time to do the thinking such a trip requires. Or you have a nongolfer—maybe two or three—whining, "Well, what am I going to do while you're out there chasing that stupid little white ball?" So now, instead of making some clever reply you'd like to immediately take back, instead of stressing out over where to go, what to do, you open one of the 18 chapters in this book and select one of the 20 itineraries we've lovingly researched.

How to Use This Book

In these pages, within 18 chapters arranged somewhat geographically from the North Coast destination of Mendocino inland and then south to the ultimate golf destination of them all, Pebble Beach, you'll find 20 itineraries for three days of golf and two nights' lodging, all within about a four-hour drive of the greater Bay Area, including Sacramento and San Jose. Use the map following the table of contents and the Appendix, Top Itineraries for Special Interests, to choose the right one at the right time. Then follow the instructions in Warming Up, which offers hints on taking along a nongolfing partner or family; read the chapter introduction in the days you're anxiously awaiting that first tee shot; see Details, Details; and before you know it, you're golfing, smiling, and relaxing—and your companions are happy, too, at being part of your plan.

And if you're really a lucky golfer, someone who loves you has bought the book with the intention of surprising you with one wonderful golf escape after another. Heck, you must be one of those people who gets a hole-in-one now and then too.

As avid, experienced golf travelers ourselves, lucky enough to have golfing spouses, we set up all of the itineraries around our favorite game. We aren't going to urge you to take a 10-mile hike in the morning before you play Edgewood Tahoe, or send you out bar-hopping the night before you play Pebble Beach. Tee times came before dinner reservations, and when we were choosing lodging, we gave major points to the properties either on or very near one of our recommended golf courses. (Presumably you've done some driving to reach your destination escape, and we don't see why you'd want to do a great deal of that once you're there.) We're recommending the very best three-day, two-night golf escape in the region, without much consideration of expense—although we do make note of bargain options along the way.

How did we choose our golf courses, especially in areas rich with options? We tried to choose the three most special or most famous or most unusual courses in the area, but sometimes we'll urge you to play more than 18 holes in a day, just so that you don't miss a fourth equally special field of green. And sometimes we will offer you an option, usually based on your golfing acumen. For instance, in the case of rather expensive and difficult Pasatiempo, the famous old Santa Cruz course, we suggest that if you're not feeling great about your game, you may save money and aggravation by enjoying one of the three other wonderful, less expensive, and less difficult courses nearby.

And if three days of golf are not quite enough, pay close attention to the Alternatives that follow the detailed description of the Itinerary Selections in each chapter. Also, check "Good Company" in the Appendix to see which chapters and itineraries (there are two itineraries in the South Lake Tahoe and Monterey Peninsula chapters) can be easily combined for a one-week vacation. If you're really ambitious, take two months off, do them all, and call us in the morning.

Chapter 1

Up, Up, and Away:
Little River and Sea Ranch

Are you in the mood for golf, adventure, and romance? Just dial 888/INN-LOVE and reserve an ocean-view room with fireplace and hot tub at the Little River Inn. This classic resort boasts the only golf course on the rugged Mendocino coast, which stretches for 80 miles from Gualala north to Westport. The coast is dotted with small villages that reflect a colorful history as lumber and fishing ports. Today's visitors come to enjoy the innovative restaurants, art galleries, boutiques, and cozy country inns, perfect for a romantic weekend. If you're looking for a relaxed golf getaway within four hours of San Francisco, read on.

State parks along the Mendocino Headlands and other seaside areas offer easy access for beachcombing and walks along secluded shores. There are also miles of hiking and biking trails, and beaches and tidepools, to discover at Sea Ranch, an internationally famous second home community extending about 10 miles along Highway 1 just south of Gualala. Sea Ranch has earned a reputation for blending architecture with nature in a simple and scenic environment. The Sea Ranch motto is "living lightly on the land." Although this planned development contains more than 2,300 homesites set on about 4,000 acres, the dominant impression is of natural beauty. Much of the community is not visible from Highway 1. While there is no town center to encourage visitors to stop, the Sea Ranch Lodge, just off Highway 1, offers a full service restaurant and guest rooms. Roads follow the contour of the land with interconnected walking and biking trails. Nature predominates in the landscape, and you see few formal gardens.

The architecture of Sea Ranch represents environmentally sensitive design, but Mendocino is a dead ringer for a New England village, thanks to the East Coast lumbermen who in the late 1800s created buildings just like what they had left behind. Mendocino so resembles a New England seaside town that the popular television series *Murder She Wrote* was filmed there as the setting for the fictitious Maine town of Cabot Cove. Blair House, an antiques-filled bed-and-breakfast inn, was used as the home of amateur detective Jessica Fletcher (played by star Angela Lansbury). The area's dramatic shoreline and quaint towns have provided Hollywood crews with ideal locations for some 60 films and numerous television specials. Nominated for four Academy Awards, *Same Time Next Year* used the elegant Heritage House in Little River as the set for Alan Alda and Ellen Burstyn's annual trysts. Some classic films include *Johnny Belinda* (1948), for which Jane Wyman won best actress; *East of Eden* (1954); *The Russians Are Coming* (1966 Oscar winner); and *The Summer of '42* (1971 Oscar winner).

The north coast might be a postcard-perfect setting, but the golf can be challenging and demanding. The nine-hole Little River Inn Golf Course is a fun trip on narrow fairways through dense redwoods and pines. It makes its way through 2,712 yards of hilly terrain, with some ocean views from elevated tees. Holes number seven and number nine have two separate greens on each hole, with significant yardage difference between them, so you could say the course actually has 11 holes. When playing 18 holes, play the first round from the blue tees and the second nine from the white tees. Longtime golf director Bob Fish said it's best to be conservative off the tee, because although a lot of the holes are reachable for big hitters, they are well guarded and there are lots of trees.

Like most things at Little River, there's a story attached to the building of the nine-hole course. Little River Inn founder Ole Hervilla realized what a potential draw golf would be for the inn, and after talking to golf course architects, he decided to lay out the course himself on heavily forested land that had been in the family since the 1850s. The course opened in 1957. Fish says, "They brought in bulldozers and just did it, without the benefit of traditional golf course designers. That's why it's such a quirky, interesting design."

Sea Ranch Golf Links rounds out your golf experience for this getaway. The championship links course is built along the ocean headlands of the wild

Sonoma Coast and calls for accuracy to offset the prevailing winds that will even chase the ball on the putting green. As former head golf professional Skip Manning used to say, "Save the airfare to Scotland and just come to Sea Ranch Golf Links." The course has ocean views from every hole.

The entire course was designed by Robert Muir Graves in 1973, but the second nine holes were not built until 1996. In 1999 the two nines were switched around, primarily so that the three finishing holes would not be into the wind, as they were originally. As you might expect, there's a difference in playability between the older back nine and the newer front nine, which doesn't have the mature trees that would provide windbreaks. Because the newer front nine greens are younger than the greens on the back, they tend to be a bit quicker, and it's best to try to stay below the pin for most holes on the front nine. Also, the ball will not stop as quickly on the newer greens, so some extra thought is needed on where to land your approach shots.

Most folks who come to Sea Ranch want to "get away from it all" and they rent a house. But the Sea Ranch Lodge also makes a great getaway, especially with its upcoming plans to expand beyond the existing 20 rooms. The lodge was recently purchased by Coastal Hotel Group, which owns nearly 70 upscale hotels nationwide. Coastal's network has introduced the Sea Ranch to more golf vacationers, increasing business for the hotel as well as for the golf course, which pleases Fred Bernadotti, owner of the Sea Ranch Golf Links. He says that up to now, most visitors were at the golf course because they were already at Sea Ranch. However, with the two- and four-day golf clinics being offered by the new pro (PGA Class A head professional Tom Nelson), golf, lessons, and lodging can all be packaged together.

An expanded lodge would mean more rooms for golfers. Architect Lawrence Halprin, considered the "father of Sea Ranch," has been brought in to design the lodge expansion, and the review process is slowly proceeding. Halprin did the original design and layout of the community and masterminded the unique way the houses would blend in with open spaces. In summer 2000, the expansion was still in the talking stages.

When the golf course was originally developed, owners had the choice of building a great nine-hole course and doing another nine later, or building just an average 18 holes. The resulting course received many accolades as an outstanding nine-hole layout. However, when it came time to implement the second nine holes of Robert Muir Grave's original design, things had changed. Environmental issues had become a big concern, and the process plodded along until finally, 22 years later, the course opened with a full 18 holes. Hopefully, approval of the lodge expansion won't take that long.

Some changes are already under way at Sea Ranch, such as the new recreational complex that includes a second pool with changing facilities, which opened Memorial Day weekend 2000. The new 25-meter swimming pool with six lanes is 50 percent larger than the original main pool, still in operation. It's designed in the stunning "rim-flow" style, so that the water flows to the extreme edge of the pool.

You won't find large-scale resort development anywhere along the far Northern California coast. The rugged terrain mandates circuitous, narrow roads that limit access and maintain the remoteness. As Mel McKinney, owner of Little River Inn, says, "The road that people have to travel to reach us practically guarantees that we won't be inundated." Hairpin turns are rewarded with spectacular ocean views and a desire to reach one's destination as soon as possible.

Itinerary

WARMING UP

This itinerary takes you on a long driving trip along windy coastal roads. The scenery is spectacular, but you can't rush it, so allow enough time to stop when you feel like it and just enjoy the relaxed pace. That's why we suggest that the first day be a driving day, to get accustomed to the pace of Mendocino. By the way, if you find that windy roads make you carsick, then you should do the driving. It's amazing how maneuvering along the edge of a steep cliff tends to push all other concerns to the back of your mind.

As you might have gathered from the introduction, we think this is a romantic getaway, one that will be enjoyed by a couple or several couples if you like company. Serious golfers will enjoy Sea Ranch and probably find Little River to be fun. Nongolfers will like the town of Mendocino and the Spa at Little River Inn. At Sea Ranch, the main activity, aside from golf, is hiking or settling in with a good book, which sounds like a pretty good idea.

Since there aren't a lot of choices, you wouldn't want to go all the way up there without hotel reservations and tee times made in advance. As we've advised in other chapters with coastal golf courses, morning tee times are generally best if you want less wind. The popular restaurants get busy on weekends, so make your plans ahead. You might want to make a massage appointment at the Third Court Salon and Day Spa, especially welcome after your golf game at Little River. It's so convenient to the golf course and then an easy walk to your room.

day 1 The ideal—indeed the only—golf getaway in Mendocino is the Little River Inn, a destination well worth the drive to get there. Actually the drive is part of the getaway.

Day 1 is a leisurely driving day designed to let you wind down, anticipating the next two days of north coast golf. Driving time is just under four hours from the Golden Gate Bridge to Little River, depending on how many stops you make. Before the first hour is past, you've left the city behind and entered the bucolic Sonoma County wine country. But if you start wine-tasting here, it will be a long day. Hold off until you reach the Anderson Valley—more on that later.

Stop for a break in the town of Healdsburg at one of the cafés around the shaded main square, or sit outdoors at the trendy Oakville Grocery at Matheson Street, just off Main Street. Take Main down to the intersection of Dry Creek Road, turn left, and head for Highway101 north, toward the town of Cloverdale. Vineyards and wineries begin to appear on either side of the highway. The terrain gets more rural as you reach the "Welcome to Cloverdale" sign, which also reads, "Where the Vineyards Meet the Redwoods." This quiet, nontouristy town doesn't even have parking meters.

Now the adventure begins. Take Highway 128 west from Cloverdale. The two-lane road is well maintained but can be devilishly twisting and windy. It goes through farmland, e.g., "Johnson Ranch, gourmet lamb delivered nationwide," and small towns like Yorkville, population 146. Unless you're behind an unrelenting recreational vehicle, you could be in Boonville in about 40 minutes, where the Anderson Valley Brewing Company and Buckhorn Saloon provides a welcome rest stop. Try the house specialty, Boont Amber Ale. The Anderson Valley Brewing Company has won medals at the World Beer Championships.

Boonville is the main town in the Anderson Valley, Mendocino's winegrowing area, designated as a "Region 1 growing area," or the coolest climate in which grapes may be commercially grown with any success. You'll find mainly chardonnay, gewürztraminer, white riesling, and pinot noir. There are about a dozen wine producers between the towns of Philo and Navarro. Wine-tasting in this area is less crowded and more relaxing than in the more well-known wine regions of Napa and Sonoma. Most wineries don't even charge tasting fees, and they are welcoming and easily accessible, even on a weekend afternoon. Stop at the famous French champagne house, Roederer Estate, for a bottle of bubbly to celebrate your weekend. By the way, the road straightens out as you leave Boonville and head for the coast.

From here it's a beautiful 30-minute drive through a forest of towering redwoods, lacy ferns hugging their trunks, to reach the Pacific Ocean and your destination, the Little River Inn. The gabled Victorian inn has 65 rooms and cottages near the cliffs, with sweeping ocean views. It was one of the first inns on the coast, built in 1853 by settler Silas Coombs; it became the Little River Inn in 1939 when Cora Coombs Hervilla and her husband Ole decided to turn the stately family home into an inn. Wisteria vines climb up the post along the white railing at the front porch entrance. The reception area has a comfortable, old-fashioned atmosphere, with the Emerson grand piano that came around the Horn in 1850.

These folks know how to make guests feel at home. They've been doing it for four generations of family ownership. Dedicated family members maintain the tradition of friendship and hospitality that permeates all facets of the operation. Ole's daughter, Susan McKinney, and her husband, Mel, are owner-managers. As Mel says, "It's still a family operation. Cousin Connie Reynolds runs the inside and her sister, Carrie Clements, does the outside." Ole's Famous Whale Watch Bar is filled with photos and artifacts from the family's and the inn's history, intertwined throughout the years. The homemade ollalieberry cobbler is on the menu for every meal and available in the bar. Insiders know that at 6 P.M. you can get it warm, just out of the oven. Flower gardens and pathways with white wooden gates weave throughout the property.

Most recent additions to the inn (1994) were 12 new guest rooms and the Abalone Conference Room, a reference to the featured item on the inn's menu for many years. Abalone was a rare treat, provided to grateful diners by Ole's weekly forays into Little River Bay with his glass-bottomed boat and hooked bamboo pole. The owners consider possible expansion to the conference facilities, guest rooms, or to the golf course. Mel comments, "My instincts tell me golf is probably the best idea." But they haven't broken ground for a new nine yet and might just leave that for the next generation to tackle.

Upon arrival, your challenging drive will be rewarded with a spacious, ocean-view room and a deep, bubbling hot tub. Dine at the inn's own restaurant (make a reservation for dinner when you make your room reservation) and be prepared for a treat. The sophisticated dining room is set with white table linens, and a mellow guitar player serenades diners on the weekends. Ask ahead for the chef's special seafood appetizer. Local wines from the Anderson Valley complement the meal. After dinner, light up the cozy fireplace in your room and unwind from the day.

day II An early tee time is no problem when you're fortified by a hearty breakfast of Ole's Swedish Hotcakes, from his mother's recipe. Call room service and you'll reach the front desk person, whose cheery response is, "I'll take your order—we do everything here." It's a short walk from your room to the pro shop, with plenty of time to practice on the range or putting green. Next to the golf course are two lighted tennis courts, open to the public and charging $10/hour for singles and $20/hour for doubles. A nongolfing companion could enjoy the tennis or take the trail to Van Damme State Park, choosing either the forest route or the beach route.

The course grabs your attention by the third hole, a 444-yard uphill par-5 to a beautiful green with a heavily wooded backdrop. The path to the fourth tee winds through a shaded glade of tall redwoods, dappled sunlight peeking through the dense foliage. The fourth hole, a 485-yard par-5, is a dramatic dogleg left, and probably the most interesting hole on the course. If you're approaching the green from the right side of the fairway, watch out for stray tee shots from the fifth tee, just a slice away. Hole number 7 is a 203-yard par-3 over a barranca bristling with thick brush, and should you play 18, on the second nine it shortens to 141 yards playing to a smaller green on the right. Sweeping ocean views await you at the eighth and ninth tees. Hole number 9 is a 177-yard par-3 on the front nine and a 273-yard par-4 on the back nine.

The most exciting innovation at the golf/tennis complex was the 1999 opening of the Third Court Salon and Day Spa, offering a full range of facial, body, and beauty treatments to inn guests as well as the general public. It's just steps away from the pro shop. Meet up with any nongolfing companions at the spa or afterward, for a trip into Mendocino for lunch and a chance to browse the shops and galleries. Much of the merchandise is handcrafted by local artists.

Ask a local person where the best 19th hole is, and the answer will usually be "Patterson's." Pewter mugs hang on the overhead rack, each one engraved and numbered, earned by customers who have imbibed more than 100 beers. Baskets of peanuts accompany drinks, and it's okay to toss the shells on the floor.

By the way, many businesses use post office boxes rather than street addresses, so directions aren't always straightforward. Apparently, in the nearby small town of Caspar, an old truck has been parked there so long that nasturtiums are growing out of it and people use it as a reference point for directions. "We're just down from the flower truck."

Then it's back to Little River Inn to watch the glorious sunset from a front-row seat at Ole's Whale Watch Bar or from the "Cigar Porch" outside, if you are so inclined. See any whales out there? During the winter months, majestic gray whales migrate down the coast, easily visible from shore. The bar at Little River is a great hangout for locals as well as visitors.

Lucky you. Dinner reservations tonight are at Stevenswood, where manager William Felder says, "We can offer hand-crafted cooking because our dining room has only 36 seats." The romantic, intimate Stevenswood was voted "Best Restaurant for a Special Occasion" by *MendoScene* in May 1999. Co-owner Bill Zimmer contributes the museum-quality paintings and sculptures that adorn the buildings and grounds from his well-known William Zimmer Gallery in Mendocino. You can even buy one to take home as a memento of this evening.

day III Depart Little River and follow the signs to Highway 1, on your way to Sea Ranch Golf Links, about a 90-minute drive. The awesome coastal highway winds along craggy cliffs overlooking large rock formations sitting in the sea, forming a sort of archipelago. You'll pass intriguing inns and cottages and small restaurants tucked away. Gated driveways lead to houses set in heavy woods and mostly not visible from the road, with an occasional glimpse of a majestic home perched on an ocean cliff. In an hour you should reach the Point Arena Lighthouse and Museum.

The next town, Gualala, population 585, is where Sea Ranch residents go to shop, just over the Sonoma County line. There are some wonderful restaurants and a few art galleries and shops. Sea Ranch Golf Links comes up pretty quickly, and as you are driving south, it will be before the lodge. The unpretentious pro shop has the typical sea-weathered look of Sea Ranch buildings. Warm up at the all-grass driving range and be prepared to enjoy this championship links course. The course has four sets of tees and plays 6,596 from the back tees.

Ever since head professional Tom Nelson arrived in August 1999, things have been happening at the Sea Ranch Golf Links. For starters, work commenced on cart paths to be completed around tees and greens. This is quite an innovation because, following the Sea Ranch philosophy to "go with the land," there have never been cart paths on the course. But players complained about the dust in the summer, and replacing broken axles got expensive, so it was time for a change. The first hole was lengthened by 50 yards. Look for a new entrance with the Sea Ranch logo emblazoned on a large bronze plaque.

It's a fact: local knowledge saves you strokes at Sea Ranch. *Tom's Cheat Sheet* will tell you how to play all those blind shots. Just read "The Golf Professional's Hints on How to Play the Course." In general, Nelson says, "Be sure to warm up first, and when you're out there on the course, let the deer pass by." On this Scottish links-style course, accuracy is more important than distance.

The course can play differently depending on the weather, and Nelson advises on how to play the holes with and without wind. Check out the new lake on the second hole, which mainly affects the back tee. One of the most difficult holes is the 479-yard, par-5 fourth hole, which plays mostly downhill but usually upwind, and includes a wetlands starting 100 yards from the standing dead tree, as well as a lateral water hazard along the entire right side. Nelson advises that before you leave the third green, walk to the west side and look at hole number 4 to see the landing area for your next tee shot, so you know it's going to be tough. Aim to the right of the snag, but not too far right because of the lateral hazard.

Hopefully, the new paths will have better signage to guide players around the course; it's not always clear. Stop a minute to appreciate the panoramic view up and down the coast from the sixth green, before heading for the tunnel under Highway 1 that takes you to the seventh tee. If the wind is in your face, carrying the wetlands could be a problem.

The 162-yard par-3 17th hole over the canyon to an uphill green is the most scenic hole on the course, a real "photo op" with a spectacular ocean setting. The best advice is to not underclub. A new set of forward tees was added downhill and to the left. Hole number 18 is a two-tiered hole with a layup tee shot—rated one of the toughest in Northern California. Water hazards, trees, wild rough, and bunkers combine to create a memorable finishing hole. Overall, Sea Ranch is a challenging links-style course, though not carefully manicured, perhaps in order to represent the untamed Sea Ranch style.

Fred Bernadotti says, "If somebody plays our course for three days and then returns to play their home course, they will play three to five strokes better. They'll learn to get better at certain shots, like low shots into the wind, and how to lay up effectively." He says it's like Scotland and Ireland, where there are blind holes and sometimes you have no idea where the green is.

According to Bernadotti, "This is a links-style course, but it's not true links. We don't have links courses here. The Scots and the Irish defined the term: it includes sand and wind, so trees cannot grow; natural rough as high as it can go; shots that are forced carry, maybe 150 yards to find a fairway, or you must carry rough at the end of the landing area. Links golf is not hitting the ball, it's making shots."

After your "links-style" experience, you can have a quick snack at the pro shop or head down to the restaurant at Sea Ranch Lodge for a full meal. If you find yourself at a romantic window table watching a glorious sunset over the ocean, it may be difficult to leave.

NOTES

Extended Stay at Sea Ranch. The lodge has 20 comfortable rooms, so here's a good opportunity to extend your getaway for another night.

If You Have Only One Day and One Night. Sea Ranch is closer to San Francisco than Little River for a short getaway—a 2.5-hour drive instead of four hours.

Extended Stay and Play. Combine this itinerary with the Bodega Bay chapter or the Sonoma County chapter.

Courses

ITINERARY SELECTIONS

Little River Inn Golf Course
7901 Highway 1
Little River, CA 95456
707/937-5667

The course opened in 1957, with Ole Hervilla the unofficial golf course architect. Doug Howe Sr., head golf professional in the '50s, still holds the course record of 59. Walking is allowed. Carts must stay on paths. Soft spikes are not required. Attire is casual, but no tank tops allowed. Rain checks are issued if rain cancels play, although with golf course superintendent Terry Stratton's new drainage project underway, the course is much better at surviving winter storms. Weekend green fees are $20 for nine holes and $30 for 18 holes, with an additional $16/24 for carts. Inn guests receive a 10 percent discount.

SCORECARD

Architect: Ole Hervilla, 1957
Course Record: 59, Doug Howe Sr.
Men's: Par 71, 5,458 yards, from whites, 67.3 rating for men, 120 slope
Ladies': Par 70, 5,020 yards, 68.6 rating for women, 121 slope
Call 707/937-5667 for tee times. You can call several months in advance.

TEE TIDBITS | There's a small driving range and putting green for practice, and a snack bar at the pro shop. What is so relaxing about Little River is not only the slower pace but the easy convenience of walking from your room to play golf and/or enjoy a spa treatment.

The Sea Ranch Golf Links
P. O. Box 10, 42000 Highway 1
The Sea Ranch, CA 95497
707/785-2468; website www.searanchvillage.com
or www.888searanch.com

Walking is allowed; carts on fairways are okay. They're building new cart paths around the tees and greens. Soft spikes not required. Collared shirts are required for men; no T-shirts or tank tops allowed, although "Sea Ranch is a Levi's kind of place."

Weekend green fees are $65 and carts are $12.50 per rider before twilight, $10 per rider after. Twilight will be at least five hours before sunset, starting on the hour (2, 3, or 4 P.M.) depending on the time of sunset. A nine-hole rate (same as twilight) is available

SCORECARD

Architect: Robert Muir Graves, 1973, 1996
Course Record: 70, Isaac Jimson
Blue: Par 72, 6,596 yards, 73.2 rating for men, 136 slope
White: par 72, 6,226 yards, 71.9 rating for men, 130 slope
Gold: Par 72, 5,494 yards, 68.7 rating for men, 120 slope
Red: Par 72, 4,837 yards, 70.2 rating for women, 120 slope
Call 707/785-2468 for tee times up to 30 days in advance. When the shop is closed, EZ Links takes over, so you can call 24 hours. Check the website to make tee times online.

before the twilight rate. Juniors play for one-half the published rate. Multi-play passes are available at the pro shop.

> **TEE TIDBITS** | Practice facilities include an all-grass driving range with 45 tee stations, a chipping green, two bunkers, and a putting green. Tom Nelson offers a variety of golf instruction programs, from individual sessions to clinics to nine-hole playing lessons. The two- or four-day Golf School will get your game back on track.
>
> Nelson revamped the pro shop to more clearly separate the food service from the merchandise area. He says, "We don't want to be a Scottsdale, we just want to have an efficient shop so people can get the services they need." On weekends they intend to have an outdoor barbecue going. "It won't be fancy fare, but what you would have when you're on vacation . . . just to sit there and have a burger and a beer and watch the whales go by."

Lodging

ITINERARY SELECTION

The **Little River Inn** sits on a bluff overlooking the sea and surf and has the feel of a New England lodge. Built in 1853, it's still owned and operated by the same family. Pathways lined with flowers meander through the grounds, and small white wooden gates lead to the dining room and main building. The 65 rooms and cottages include standard rooms in the main building, larger rooms with hot tubs and fireplaces, plus the four luxurious Van Damme units and next door Coombs Cottage on the ocean side of the highway. The secluded White Cottage is a mile down the road close to the cliffs, with a hot tub on a spacious private deck.

Little River Inn's golf package includes one night in a standard room plus unlimited golf with use of a golf cart, Sunday through Thursday nights only, except holidays. Based on double occupancy. From July to October the rate is $199 a night, which includes tax. Golf and Spa packages include spa treatments and unlimited golf with an ocean-view room, for $310 a night. ■ HIGHWAY 1, LITTLE RIVER, CA 95456; 707/937-5942 OR 888/INN-LOVE (466-5683), FAX 707/937-3944; WEBSITE WWW.LITTLERIVERINN.COM, EMAIL LRI@MCN.ORG

GOLF PACKAGE OPTIONS

At the **Sea Ranch Lodge,** the natural, rustic elegance perfectly suits the solitude of the coastline it fronts. All 20 rooms have ocean views except for the garden room, which has its own hot tub in a private garden. The outside world is held at bay temporarily because there are no televisions in the rooms. You won't even miss it. Have a drink in the windowed solarium before dinner. Sea Ranch Lodge's Golf Package is offered Monday–Thursday, based on double occupancy, and includes 18 holes of golf with cart for two. From April to June, rates range $244–380, depending on the type of room, and from July to November it's $265–418. ■ 60 SEA WALK DR. ON HIGHWAY 1, THE SEA RANCH, CA 95497; 707/785-2371 OR 800/732-7262, FAX 707/785-2917; WEBSITE WWW.SEARANCHLODGE.COM

The **Gualala Country Inn** is near Sea Ranch and has 20 rooms with ocean views and/or Gualala River views, furnished in a warm country atmosphere. Rates include continental breakfast. Room rates are $89–159. The inn offers a special rate for golfers at Sea Ranch Golf Links. Golf and lodging are paid separately. Sunday through Thursday, excluding holidays, it's 20 percent off the room rate and golf is $35 per person with cart. Friday and Saturday the golf is $45 per person with no room discount. ■ 47955 CENTER ST., GUALALA, 95445; 800/564-4466

Sea Ranch Escape handles vacation home rentals, all privately owned, from cottages to five-bedroom houses. Rates range from $225 (for two nights) for a one-bedroom cabin with partial ocean view to a four-bedroom oceanfront home with hot tub and barbecue that would be $625 (for two nights) for four persons, $835 for eight persons. Each house is different, and sometimes you can save money by bringing your own linens. From November 1 to April 30, if you stay two nights you get the third night free. Also, when you rent a home from Sea Ranch Escape and buy two rounds of golf, you receive a transferable coupon for a third round free. ■ SEA RANCH ESCAPE IS IN THE SEA RANCH LODGE; 888/732-7262

ALTERNATIVES

The **Stanford Inn by the Sea** is a two-story, natural wood building where all of the 33 rooms have a view, many with wood-burning fireplaces or four-poster beds, furnished in country antiques. There's a glass-enclosed swimming pool and spa area amid the inn's ornamental and organic gardens, which provide fresh organic produce for The Raven's, Stanford Inn's elegant vegetarian restaurant. Breakfast is included, as are daily afternoon tea and evening reception. This inn is pet-friendly, so bring Fido. ■ COAST HIGHWAY 1 AND COMPTCHE UKIAH ROAD, P. O. BOX 487, MENDOCINO, CA 95460; 707/937-56156 OR 800/331-8884; WEBSITE WWW.STANFORDINN.COM

When the hit movie *Same Time Next Year* came out in 1978, **Heritage House**'s secret was out: it's a great romantic hideaway. The main building houses some guest rooms and the wonderful restaurant, which has three separate dining areas with ocean views, but most of the lodging is

scattered over 37 acres of spectacular gardens that run along the rugged cliffs above the Pacific. No two rooms are alike; you can have old-fashioned and comfy or a luxuriously furnished suite. Most have fireplaces or wood-burning stoves. Heritage House celebrated its 50th year in 1999. Rate plans including meals are available. Room rates range $125–350.
■ 5200 N. HIGHWAY 1, LITTLE RIVER, CA 95456; 800/235-5885 OR 707/937-5885; WEBSITE WWW.HERITAGEHOUSEINN.COM

Vacation Home Rentals: Achieve the ultimate in privacy with a vacation home rental, where you can choose the setting and amenities that suit your tastes. Homes are fully furnished and equipped. Both Mendocino and Sea Ranch offer rental homes.

Mendocino Coast Reservations ■ 1000 MAIN ST., P. O. BOX 1143, MENDOCINO, CA 95460; 707/937-5033 OR 800/262-7801, FAX 707/937-4236; WEBSITE WWW. MENDOCINOVACATIONS.COM, EMAIL MCR@MCN.ORG

Rams Head Realty ■ 1000 ANNAPOLIS RD., P. O. BOX 123, THE SEA RANCH, CA 95497; 707/785-2427 OR 800/785-3455; WEBSITE WWW.RAMSHEAD-REALTY.COM

Dining

ITINERARY SELECTIONS

Before you dine at the **Little River Inn Restaurant,** stop in at Ole's Whale Watch Bar for a cocktail or to watch the sunset. It's rustic and casual, whereas the dining room is sophisticated, with white tablecloths, brass chandeliers, and mellow guitar music on weekends. The special appetizer is a fresh seafood platter heaped with mussels, prawns, and clams. Seafood entrées are interspersed with filet mignon and other meat dishes, plus a wonderful crispy herb-roasted chicken. Entrées come with soup or salad and range $20–28. The homemade ollalieberry cobbler is the best dessert. Breakfast and dinner. Ole's Whale Watch Bar opens daily at 4 P.M. for lighter fare. ■ HIGHWAY 1, LITTLE RIVER; 707/937-5942, 800/INN-LOVE

Patterson's is the local hangout in downtown Mendocino, offering a full bar with more than 100 different beers and good pub fare. You can get fish and chips, shepherd's pie, and such for under $10. Don't be shy about tossing the peanut shells on the floor—everybody does. Patterson's is open daily 10 A.M.–1 A.M. and serves food except 3–6 P.M. ■ 10485 LANSING ST., MENDOCINO; 707/937-4782

The intimate **Restaurant at Stevenswood Lodge** has only 36 seats, so the service is especially attentive and the cooking can be "hand-crafted." The cozy yet sophisticated dining room usually has the fireplace going.

Executive chef Marc Dym's menu presents Mediterranean cuisine, with dishes like smoked tuna niçoise, bouillabaisse with Maine lobster claw, osso bucco, and zabaglione with fresh berries. Main courses are $24–32. Breakfast, dinner, and brunch on the weekends. ■ HIGHWAY 1, THREE-EIGHTHS MILE NORTH OF VAN DAMME STATE PARK, MENDOCINO; 800/421-2810 OR 707/937-2810, FAX 707/937-1237; WEBSITE WWW.STEVENSWOOD.COM

If you stop in at the **Sea Ranch Lodge Restaurant** after golf, say around sunset, just plan on staying the night. The view is so drop dead gorgeous, the open, woodsy design so serene, that you'll be too relaxed to tackle those windy roads. Local, fresh seafood tops the menu, and the lamb is very good too. The restaurant presents special Winemaker's Dinners, five courses including a cheese selection, for $75. Main menu entrées range $17–23. Breakfast, lunch, dinner, and Sunday brunch. ■ 60 SEA WALK DR. ON HIGHWAY 1; 800/SEA-RANCH (800/732-7262) OR 707/785-2371, FAX 707/785-2917; WEBSITE WWW.SEARANCHLODGE.COM

ALTERNATIVES

Mendocino
Café Beaujolais (961 Ukiah St., Mendocino; 707/937-5614) started out in the 1970s serving breakfast in its quaint yellow Victorian, and is still known for imaginative dinners even after founder Margaret Fox sold the cafe in mid-2000. The **Moosse Café** (Kasten and Albion Streets, Mendocino; 707/937-4323) is in the Blue Heron Inn, a white New England–style cottage, and serves casual bistro-type food for lunch and dinner. The fireplace is usually going or guests can relax in the garden setting at the cozy **MacCallum House Restaurant** (45020 Albion St., Mendocino; 707/937-5763; website www.maccallumhouse dining.com).

Sea Ranch
Gualala is the place to go for dinner when you're at Sea Ranch. The new owners of the popular **Pangaea Restaurant** (250 Main St., Point Arena; 707/882-3001) promise to carry on the tradition of fine organic California cuisine and local wines. At **Ocean Song** (39350 S. Highway 1, Gualala; 707/884-1041) in a scenic spot where the river meets the ocean, Renee Sueg adds an international touch to the wide range of items from burgers to filet mignon. Stop by **The Food Company** for gourmet items you can reheat or freeze, in addition to a beautiful array of salads (corner of Highway 1 and Robinson Reef Dr., Gualala; 707/884-1800).

Straying Off Course

MENDOCINO

Parks in the north coast provide biking trails, and they're paved at Van Damme State Park (three miles south of Mendocino) and Russian Gulch State Park (800/444-7275), two miles north of Mendocino. Rent bikes from Catch A Canoe & Bicycles Too, which is at the Stanford Inn by the Sea. It also rents canoes and kayaks (Highway 1 and Comptche-Ukiah Road, Mendocino; 707/937-0273).

From January to late March, the gray whales return to the waters off the north coast. You can take guided whale-watching walks at MacKerricher State Park, just north of Fort Bragg, Mendocino Headlands State Park, and the Point Cabrillo Lightstation. Charter boats leave from Noyo Harbor on whale-watching and fishing excursions. Contact Telstar Charters (32450 N. Harbor Drive, Fort Bragg; 707/964-8770).

Maybe you'd like to catch something instead of just look. In that case, join a party boat from Noyo's Fishing Center in Fort Bragg (3245 N. Harbor, Noyo; 707/964-7609).

We hope you take some time on that drive up Highway 128 to enjoy the wineries along Mendocino's Anderson Valley. Family-operated Navarro Vineyards (5601 Highway 128, Philo; 707/895-3686) only sells directly to customers and select restaurants, and its chardonnay has earned a gold medal. Taste at Greenwood Ridge (5501 Highway 128, Philo; 707/895-2002) in its octagonal tasting room made out of redwood. Husch Vineyards (4400 Highway 128, Philo; 707/895-3216) is comfy and rustic, and the wines are excellent. Roederer Estate Winery (4501 Highway 128, Philo; 707/895-2288) produces sparkling wines befitting its French connection, in a sophisticated tasting room. Not that beer should be left out of this tasting trip. Don't miss a stop at the Anderson Valley Brewing Company and Buckhorn Saloon in Boonville (14081 Highway 128, Boonville; 707/895-2337).

If all the golf, biking, fishing, and wine-tasting has worn you out, head for the Third Court Salon and Day Spa at the Little River Inn (7751 N. Highway 1, Little River; 707/937-3099), which offers full beauty and body treatments.

Garden lovers will want to attend some of the annual garden shows in Mendocino held in the spring. Most of these have a long tradition. The John Druecker Memorial Rhododendron Show (707/964-0994) represents the favorite coastal flower in full bloom. The Mendocino Coast Garden Tour (800/653-3328) showcases eight varied gardens and also hosts a walking tour of gardens in the historic district. The Art in the Gardens (707/965-44352) is held at the Mendocino Coast Botanical Gardens in Fort Bragg.

SEA RANCH

Hiking is the most popular recreational activity at Sea Ranch, with more than 15 miles of trails along the bluff-tops and through the forest. Trail maps also identify bird and flower species. The bike path meanders over the 10-mile length of the Sea Ranch. Rent canoes and kayaks from Adventure Rents (39175 Highway 1, Gualala; 707/884-4386 or 888/881-4FUN; website www.adventurerents.com).

The Point Arena Lighthouse and Museum (707/882-2777) was built in 1870 and restored in 1908 after being destroyed by the 1906 earthquake that devastated San Francisco. It's one of the more interesting sights on the coast. If you're in a meditative mood, visit the Sea Ranch Chapel, a stunning design of wood, glass, stone, and metal intended as a spiritual commune with nature.

Details, Details

SUITCASE

The weather along the north coast can be unpredictable, so always dress in layers. When the fog rolls in, often in July and August, the warmest summer day suddenly becomes overcast. Mendocino has more severe weather than Sea Ranch, but both areas enjoy temperate spring and fall, the best seasons to visit the northern coastal areas. Even in November and December, it can be calm and beautiful. Part of Mendocino's charm is its remoteness and limited access, but that can mean isolation during heavy winter storms.

Miles of spectacular shoreline may beckon, but be aware that the ocean waters are cold year-round. Up north, beaches are for beachcombing, not swimming.

The coast is a casual place. Levi's and khakis are fine during the day, and dressy casual attire is appropriate for dining at even the nicest restaurants. You won't need soft spikes on this itinerary. Dress in layers with a warm jacket and bring comfortable shoes for hiking or walking the beaches.

GETTING THERE

To reach Mendocino from the south, take Highway 101 to Cloverdale. Take the last Cloverdale exit (Fort Bragg/Mendocino, Route 128 west). After you come down the off-ramp, turn left, heading back toward Cloverdale, and follow the signs. You will make a right turn onto 128 very soon. From there, it's about 90 minutes to Little River. When you reach the coast, Route 128 merges with Highway 1. Go north; the ocean will be on your left. It's about eight miles to Little River.

From the east, take Highway 20 from Williams to Highway 101. At this point you can go north to Willits, taking Route 20 to the coast as above. Or you can go south to Ukiah and take Route 253 to Boonville, which is the southernmost Ukiah exit from the freeway. When Route 253 ends, turn right onto Route 128 and continue as above.

Little River Inn is on the east side of the road, opposite the ocean. There is a post office, market, and gas station across the street, on the ocean side of the road.

The Little River Airport (707/937-5129) accommodates private planes. Call ahead (707/937-1224) if you want a rental car.

From Little River to Sea Ranch: Follow the signs to Highway 1 south and continue for about 90 minutes until you see the town of Gualala. Sea Ranch Golf Links is just past Gualala on the right side of the road.

The private Sea Ranch Airport is only for overnight guests of the lodge or rental homes, and arrivals must be cleared in advance. More convenient is the Ocean Ridge Airport in Gualala (707/884-3573). The larger Charles M. Schulz Sonoma County Airport, north of Santa Rosa, honoring the famous cartoonist, is served by United Express and Sky West. Car rentals are available, and it's a scenic 90-minute drive along the Russian River (Highway 116) to the coast.

CONTACTS

- **California Department of Tourism** P. O. Box 1499; Sacramento, CA 95812-1499; 800/862-2543
- **Fort Bragg/Mendocino Coast Chamber of Commerce** P. O. Box 1141, Fort Bragg, CA 95437; 707/961-6300 or 800/726-2780; website www.mendocinocoast.com

- **Sonoma County Tourism Program** 2300 County Center Dr., Santa Rosa, CA 95403; 707/565-5383; website www.sonomacounty.com
- **Redwood Coast Chamber of Commerce** P. O. Box 338, Gualala, CA 95445; 800/778-5252; website www.redwoodcoastchamber.com, email: info@redwoodcoastchamber.com

Chapter 2

Blow Me a Birdie: Bodega Bay

This book got its start in the clubhouse bar at the Bodega Harbour Golf Links. Four couples had just finished the last hole of a wonderful three-day, two-night getaway that was more glorious than they'd been led to expect of the area, and the theme of the last cocktail was, "Why didn't anybody tell us? Somebody oughtta write a book." And here you have it.

Bodega Bay isn't your typical golf destination. There's only one course in town. And, as for the town, well, "It's a community to those who live here, but not a town to those who visit," says local hotelier Cyrus Griffin. "It's such an odd strip of land in that it's two miles long and there's really no center of town—or, as visitors say, 'There's no place to park.'"

That's the fallout from Highway 1, which at Bodega Bay veers away from its inland course to the coast and runs right through the center of, uh, town. There's been talk for years of putting in a bypass behind the, uh, town, thus creating the side streets and cross streets that make a real town, but it's a point of controversy and finance that hasn't yet been resolved. On weekends, the through traffic can be heavy, but during the week it's a peaceful, easy destination. Most anytime, though, Bodega Bay is an escape, not an adventure. Nongolfers who will most enjoy a visit here will—unless they're drawn to the horses at Chanslor Ranch—be the type who are happy with a comfortable chair, a spectacular view, and a book, or perhaps a stroll along the beach at low tide. There are luscious meals to be swallowed, leisurely walks to be taken, and great views to be appreciated. If none of this sounds appealing, perhaps the Silicon Valley chapter is more your speed.

That's not to say that Bodega Bay is some podunk outpost. With a population of 1,250, expected to grow by 50 percent within 10 years, it's becoming an idyllic bedroom community to the rapidly growing Santa Rosa–Petaluma area, with an average home price of more than $300,000 in surroundings that range from lush in spring to wet and wild in winter. Fishing remains the main industry, with about 300 commercial boats that make Bodega Bay the biggest fishing port north of San Francisco and south of Fort Bragg, and there's agriculture (especially dairy, sheep, and cattle) and now tourism.

The first tourists arrived in the neighborhood of the longtime resident Miwok Indians in 1775, when Lt. Francisco Bodega y Cuadra put an anchor in the bay. Russian settlers followed in 1812, using the bay as a port for boats bound for Alaska. It was later a whaling station and then a fishing village, which it remains today. But the area is probably most famous for its place in Alfred Hitchcock's 1962 thriller *The Birds*. He featured many landmarks in Bodega Bay and nearby Bodega, including the Old Potter Schoolhouse. Film buffs still like to look at Bodega Bay through Hitchcock's eyes as they wander around the area's small towns, perusing antiques and looking for a good piece of fish for dinner.

The coming of the Bodega Harbour Golf Links beginning in 1977 also deserves some of the credit for building up the tourism base—as well as the population base. There are some 750 lots on the course, with 650 or so tastefully designed homes already housing mostly local residents. At one time, there were many, many rental units on the golf course, but those are diminishing as the housing values increase and commuters continue to retreat from the high prices of homes in Northern California's urban centers. The golf course was originally built to serve the residents, with a promise to the Coastal Commission that it would always be open to the public at reasonable rates. So far, it's been win-win. The members pay about $130 a month, and visitors' $85 fees pay their bills. Not such a bargain for the visitors, except on weekdays or at twilight, when it becomes a steal. Those weekday specials further help offset the members' low fees and compensate for the remoteness of the course, which does only about 30,000 rounds a year.

"If that golf course were 60 miles closer to San Francisco, holy smokes," said Dennis Kalkowski, who was the head pro at Bodega Harbour from opening until 1999.

Kalkowski opened Bodega Harbour's original nine holes (now the back nine) in 1977. The signature belongs to Robert Trent Jones Sr. and Jr.; supposedly, Senior did the back (original) nine and Junior added the front (new) nine in 1984, but there are reports that the actual work was done by Kyle Phillips of their firm. "The idea was to hire Junior's firm (in 1984) to get continuity, but the funny thing is you couldn't get two more different nines," says Kalkowski.

Neither of the nines opened to rave reviews, either in 1977 or in 1984, and in fact the design for the first hole of the new nine was not accepted; the hole was regraded before it was even seeded. Many of the comments amounted to, "Why would you design a thing like that? Why don't you level it off?" The course was hilly and winding and, particularly the newer front nine, narrow and confounding. Over the years, work has been done to soften the harshness of Bodega Harbour, which is made difficult enough in the first place by its nakedness in the face of Mother Nature, with fog and ocean breezes coming into play. Bunkers were regraded or filled in, and greens were redone.

"For years I've heard it called a love-hate course," said hotelier Griffin. "Some people just can't stand to play hilly, bumpy, windy, foggy courses. I don't understand it. . . . The people who enjoy it play against the course. The people who take out the driver on the first hole just don't understand."

"Number 1 is still a tough way to start your day," agrees Kalkowski of the intimidating, uphill par-4. "But number 5 for the first-time player is the most controversial hole. It's a strategic par-5. But most players equate par-5 to driver, and a lot of unwelcome surprises go with the wrong club selection on that tee shot."

Hole number 5 is a double dogleg, downhill twister with trouble all around. So, the yardage guide calls for a conservative tee shot, of no more than 215 yards from the blue tees, 183 from the whites and 143 from the reds. If you succeed in reaching the aiming stick, you can then risk cutting the corner to the green. And one of the worst things about hole number 5 is that it follows hole number 4, a downhill-way-uphill par-4 that the yardage guide theorizes "may be the longest 400 yards in golf." Hole number 4 is full of hanging lies—feet above the ball, feet below the ball, feet upside down over the ball—and the approach shot is so steep, it's blind. After all this, players often forget to turn around and admire the vast and heavenly view, which is probably the best on the course at this point.

So much for the worst holes. They are Junior's, but so are the wonderful back-to-back par-3s at 6 and 7. Then there are Senior's holes down at "The Pit," where 16, 17, and 18 border on the sand dunes and take players to sea level.

"From a pure golf standpoint, most people prefer the back nine," Kalkowski says. "It sort of makes up for the front nine in a lot of people's minds. You have to hit it long and not necessarily straight, and by the time you get through the back nine you've almost forgotten about the front nine."

But it's unlikely you will ever forget Bodega Harbour once you've played the golf course, which reminds some of Scotland for its wildness, others of Hawaii for its views. And it's our bet that you'll want a second go-round at the golf course, which is why this is the only chapter in this book where you are urged to play a golf course twice on the same getaway.

Itinerary

WARMING UP

This is the perfect gang escape—and the accommodations will be affordable and inviting to both couples and singles. So start planning now for what may become an annual or seasonal outing to beautiful Bodega Bay. That's not to say it isn't a great spur of the moment overnighter—as long as there are tee times to be had on the course, there are most likely rooms to be found in the town.

So, seven days before you want to play, make a morning tee time at Rooster Run for Day 1 and at Bodega Harbour for Day 2. Make a late-morning, post-checkout time at Bodega Harbour for Day 3.

Call Vacation Rentals U.S.A. or Bodega Bay and Beyond to reserve your house on the golf course for at least two nights. Be specific about what you're looking for—check out the pictures and descriptions on the websites, or do some faxing back and forth with the rental companies.

Make a Day 2 dinner reservation at the Duck Club.

If anyone in your group is planning to visit Osmosis or go horseback riding or have a massage, schedule it now.

day 1 You'll depart for the coast via Highway 101 and take the Bodega Bay turnoff at Washington Street in Petaluma. Only instead of heading toward Bodega Bay right now, you're turning east on Washington and parking at Rooster Run.

Rooster Run is one of the finest municipal golf complexes anywhere, perhaps because it is a private-public partnership with everyone's best interests plus profitability in mind. You'll arrive to a friendly greeting in a big, well-stocked pro shop, with a full-service restaurant across the breezeway and two putting greens and a grass driving range out back. You probably won't notice the scenery right away; hopefully you're walking and you'll take the time to look around and enjoy the fact that there aren't houses lining the course, or really even in sight, and that the most action off the course is coming from the airport next door to the back nine.

Fred Bliss was the architect who directed the earth movers around this strip of flat pastureland in 1997, and he designed a fast-draining course that measures more than 7,000 yards from the very back tee but offers four options that allow the course to play as short as under 5,200 yards. There's water in play on several holes, and on a typical day it is the four finishing holes that present the greatest challenge. That's because they generally play into the wind and are difficult to start with.

The first hole immediately lets players in on the overall challenge of Rooster Run, however. It's a fairly short par-5 (well, that's 481 from the "regular" tees) with mounds on the right to punish first-tee slicers, leading to a fairly large green. Large and undulating green. Large, undulating, and fast green. Rooster Run was the first golf course in Northern California to plant G-6 bent-grass greens, which require a mowing height of no more than one-eighth inch. And this course goes one better by hand-mowing the greens five days a week to keep them smooth and fast. It's fun getting to the greens at Rooster Run, but nowhere near as fun as trying to putt them. Even high-handicappers will enjoy this challenge; let's face it, everyone can roll a decent putt now and then. And the approaches to most of the greens are accessible, though the par-5 hole number 11, with a tree-filled barranca fronting the green, glares as an exception.

The finishing hole is a standout, 606 yards from the very back tee, bending around a lake to another of those sharply undulating and fast greens, this one with water in front and sand in back. Hopefully you'll enjoy a happy ending to your round and have something to celebrate, because the Rooster Grill is worth a stop for lunch before you go on your way.

From Rooster Run, it's a straight shot out Washington west to Bodega Bay, and you should be unlocking the door of your house on the golf course within the hour. Take some time to unwind, get your bearings, and rest up for dinner at the Tides Wharf, which is on the bay side of Highway 1. If you time it right, you'll enjoy the sunset from the big windows at bay level, maybe even watch some otters playing alongside you. If drinks are now in order, this is the place; there's not much nightlife in Bodega Bay, and anyway, tomorrow there's golf to be played.

day II This morning you're hoping to finish 18 holes before the wind stirs, as it usually does in the afternoon in Bodega Bay. Maybe you'll start so early, the fog will add an element of mystery, which you really don't need if you've never played this course. The best advice for enjoying your first round here is to follow the advice in the yardage guide, even when you don't believe it, and remember to take in the great vistas. If you've got the right house, you can quickly pop in for a beverage to go—there's no drink cart on the course, and the shack at the turn isn't always open. You can always go into the bar, however, before you venture onto the more open and windswept back nine.

We can recommend lunch at the clubhouse; the food here is good most any time of day, especially the soups. And then it's time to see a little bit of the area. First-timers ought to drive north on Highway 1 up to Jenner, where the Russian River meets the sea, and stop frequently for photographs or exploration. From here, you can take Highway 116 inland along the river to Guerneville, take the River Road fork to the left, and stop at the beautifully landscaped Korbel champagne cellars for a look around and a tasting. There's also a wonderful deli here, in case you didn't have lunch at the course. Afterward, head back to 116 the way you came, turning left onto Main Street toward Occidental and continuing south toward Freestone, picking up Highway 12 west and then Highway 1 back to your house.

A second option would be to head north on Highway 1 from the golf course, turning left onto Eastshore Road to Westshore Road, driving past the Spud Point Marina to Bodega Head, where you can park and stroll some of the five miles of hiking trails among the dunes. This is a great spot for whalewatching in season (November–April).

On your way back to the house, consider a stop at Gourmet au Bay (913 Highway 1 [bay side]; 707/875-9875), a harborfront wine shop that sells tastings and glasses of wine that you can enjoy on the back deck, indoors or out. Owners Ken and Connie Mansfield have collected premium and boutique wines, some of which you can taste and any of which you can buy and take back to the house for a little happy hour in the hot tub.

Tonight you're off to the Duck Club at the Bodega Bay Lodge (you've seen this by now, right next to the golf course development) for as fine a meal as you're bound to have on any of our golf getaways, in a serene, cozy room that most likely will be full of both travelers and locals. We'd recommend something off the menu, but we've never seen anyone go wrong ordering whatever they liked and letting the kitchen do it up.

You've got to be feeling pretty good by now. Light that fire and ponder how you'll do better at Bodega Harbour tomorrow.

day III This morning you've got to take a walk at the beach; just follow the signs for the homeowners, since you temporarily are one of them. Or if you didn't make it out to Bodega Head on Day 2, take a little extra time to do so this morning. Then after checkout, you can have a late breakfast at the clubhouse—maybe fortify yourself before your second encounter with the Bodega Harbour Golf Links. Have you figured out how to play hole number 5 yet? And has that measly little par-3 hole number 6 gotten the better of you again? If not, you can always come back to Bodega Bay again. For now, your time is up.

 NOTES

Money Savers. Make this escape midweek and your third night of lodging in the house may be on the house!

Nongolfers. If you enjoy beachcombing, hiking, horseback riding, wine-tasting, and/or browsing for antiques and collectibles, you will be glad to have to yourself those five hours when others are golfing.

Couples. This is a good escape for couples galore; just add more houses to the itinerary.

Time Savers. Rooster Run is an easy day trip from the Bay Area; Bodega Bay is a better one-nighter because once you get there it's extremely hard to leave. A stay-and-play at the Bodega Bay Lodge and Spa would be the package of choice if you have one night only.

Low-Handicappers. These golf courses are much more difficult than you may think from looking at the scorecards.

Extended Stay. Bodega Bay is such a place unto itself, and the Bodega Harbour Golf Links such a test, you probably will be content to stay and play for two days. Really, when you see your house on the course—the hot tub, the inviting chairs on the deck—it's unlikely you'll want to venture farther. If you do, take a look at the Sea Ranch and Little River Inn course listings in Chapter 1, and the Sonoma courses detailed in Chapter 3, for some alternatives. Heck, you just might want to stay in your house on the course for a week.

Courses

ITINERARY SELECTIONS

Rooster Run Golf Club
2301 E. Washington St.
Petaluma, CA 94954
707/778-1211, fax 707/778-8072
website www.roosterrun.com

You may want to move to Petaluma once you find out about the resident rates at Rooster Run. Locals can play twilight rounds here for $15, and at that price on this course who minds a little darkness? Nonresidents will pay around $26 on a weekday, $32 on a Friday, and $42 on a Saturday or Sunday, plus a $24 cart fee. It adds up to a weekday of golf with cart for under $40, a solid bargain in Northern California. And the course is very walkable. Remember, there was nothing but Kansas-flat meadow here before the dirt movers arrived in 1997.

SCORECARD

Architect: Fred Bliss, 1998
Course Record: 68, Jeff Bricker and Mike Piver
Black: Par 72, 7,001 yards, 73.9 rating, 128 slope
Blue: Par 72, 6,462 yards, 71.2 rating, 124 slope
White: Par 72, 5,889 yards, 68.5 rating for men, 116 slope; 73.0 rating for women, 126 slope
Red: Par 72, 5,139 yards, 69.1 rating for women, 117 slope
Tee times may be made up to seven days in advance.

TEE TIDBITS | Metal spikes were never allowed at Rooster Run, where the feature attraction is the G-6 bent-grass greens. There's a big driving range just behind the pro shop with grass stations, and do not pass the putting greens without taking a few strokes. Putting is the order of the day at Rooster Run. The pro shop carries everything you need, and the apparel has a contemporary edge that many shoppers will appreciate. The course has good drainage and generally plays well long into the winter. If you are playing on the right day, bring your sense of humor. One of the marshals at Rooster Run has a penchant for entertaining players waiting for the green to clear with his best and worst and silliest and golfiest jokes. There's no friendlier service to be found at a municipal course than at Rooster Run. The food at the Rooster Grill makes it worthwhile to plan to finish before the kitchen closes at 3.

Bodega Harbour Golf Links
21301 Heron Dr.
Bodega Bay, CA 94923
707/875-3538, fax 707/875-3256
website www.bodegaharborgolf.com

SCORECARD

Architects: Robert Trent Jones Sr. (1977), Robert Trent Jones Jr. (1988)
Course Record: 64, Trevor Beard
Blue: Par 70, 6,267 yards, 72.4 rating, 134 slope
White: Par 70, 5,656 yards, 69.3 rating for men, 125 slope; par 71 for women, 74.6 rating, 132 slope
Red: Par 69, 4,749 yards, 69.7 rating for women, 120 slope
Call as far as 90 days in advance for your tee time.

The $55 weekday and $85 weekend green fees include carts, and these must stay on the paths. If you enjoy walking but are intimidated by the big ups and downs within your immediate line of sight, consider ditching the cart at the turn and walking the gentler back nine. Those who know the course well try to play in the morning, before the wind has too much chance to stir, and so Bodega Harbour offers twilight and premium twilight rates that are good values if you're willing to take your chances on Mother Nature. Weekend tee times can be elusive, so plan ahead: Tee-time reservations are taken 90 days in advance if secured by a credit card.

TEE TIDBITS | Bodega is a private course that's open to the public, so if you meet any members along the way, thank them. Co-author Susan Fornoff was married on the seventh tee in May 2000. She and new husband Marc Squeri, a lefty, teed off together after the kiss. Yes, they had better things to do than finish off the hole. The clubhouse has a

TEE TIDBITS continued | pool and locker rooms for the members, and a small pro shop and cozy restaurant and bar are open to the public. The food's good, and there are some killer hot adult beverages on the drink list to quickly thaw your windchilled ears. The course logo is a NorCal favorite—it will be hard to resist taking home a shirt or visor. There's no range, but you can warm up in cages or at the chipping/putting greens, free of charge. Try not to hit too many houses as you make your way around the front nine.

Lodging

ITINERARY SELECTION

Two rental companies want to put you in a wonderful, luxuriously appointed house along the golf course. We've dealt with both **Bodega Bay and Beyond** (800/888-3565, fax 707/875-2447; website www.sonomacoast. com) and **Vacation Rentals U.S.A.** (800/548-7631; website www. vacationrentalsusa.com), and frankly we can't tell much difference between the two. The difference lies more between the houses within each company, and that's a matter of the owners' individual tastes. We've walked into some and said, "Ooh, aah." We've walked into others and walked right out. An owner with cheesy taste is going to have a cheesy house. An owner who thinks vacation tenants are going to wreck the place furnishes it cheaply. An owner who wants you to come back every year is going to add all of the touches—CD player, iron and ironing board, blender, TVs in the bedrooms—that will have you asking for that place again.

The best thing you can do is tell the rental companies how many beds you need and what amenities you'd like (hot tub? fireplace? ocean view? linens?) and request a property that opens out to the golf course. We've seen some properties along the course that offer virtually no golf course view whatever. Be specific; there are so many houses, you are bound to find the right one(s) for your group.

GOLF PACKAGE OPTIONS

Bodega Harbour partners with several hotels in the area, and even a Holiday Inn Express in Sebastopol, but there's not much financial gain in this for golf travelers. If you're going to book one of these hotels for a golf package, check the golf course website for the latest specials and make sure you can't do better by simply booking the room and the golf separately.

The Bodega Bay Lodge and Spa is certainly a worthy destination, even for nongolfers. With Doran Beach Park just down the street, and with well-appointed rooms (all have fireplaces) that all have terraces or decks overlooking the ocean, Bodega Bay Lodge scores in every category—plus, it's right next to the golf course. A new addition is a full-service spa that's for guests only; there's also a pool and a glass-enclosed hot tub that serves as an inviting 20th hole. You can stroll out in the bathrobe the lodge thoughtfully supplies. There's no bar here, but the hotel offers a daily complimentary wine hour with nibbles, and dinner at the Duck Club is not to be missed. The overall feeling of privacy makes this the place for you and your special someone. Rooms start at around $200 but can be had for as low as $129 for a quiet off-season weeknight. ■ 103 COAST HIGHWAY 1, BODEGA BAY, CA 94923; 800/368-2468; WEBSITE WWW.WOODSIDEHOTELS.COM

The Inn at the Tides is similar to the lodge but different. Guest rooms are built into the hillside, and a few of the finer ones have terraces offering expansive views. A big draw is the well-sheltered indoor/outdoor pool. There's a workout room, sauna, and whirlpool, and you can have a massage in your room. The Bayview Restaurant is the fine dining option here, and at the bottom of the hill is the Tides Wharf and Restaurant, a complex with a market (featuring fresh fish) and the highly recommended waterside restaurant and bar, probably the liveliest night spot in this sleepy town. Rooms start at around $150. ■ 800 HIGHWAY 1, BODEGA BAY, CA 94923; 800/541-7788; WEBSITE WWW.INNATTHETIDES.COM

For a little bit more than $100 per person, two people can stay at the **Bodega Coast Inn** on a Sunday through Thursday night and golf Bodega Harbour. The Bodega Coast Inn has nice oceanfront rooms starting at about $100 a night for a standard king or queen, going up in price for deluxe rooms with fireplaces. All have views, VCRs, coffeepots, and hair dryers. And there's a spa in the garden. ■ 521 COAST HIGHWAY 1, BODEGA BAY, CA 94923; 800/346-6999, FAX 707/875-2964; WEBSITE WWW.BODEGACOASTINN.COM

The Lok family has two hotels that offer golf packages with Bodega Harbour and Adobe Creek, a resort-style course in Petaluma, starting at around $70 per person per night. Nearer to Bodega Harbour is the relatively new **Holiday Inn Express Hotel and Suites** in Sebastopol (1101 Gravenstein Hwy. S, Sebastopol, CA 95472; 707/829-6677). Nearer to Adobe Creek but only about 35 minutes from Bodega Harbour is the **Quality Inn** in Petaluma (5100 Montero Way, Petaluma, CA 94954; 800/228-5151). There's information about both properties at website www.lokhotels.com.

ALTERNATIVES

Just a mile or so inland, the **Sonoma Coast Villa** offers a Mediterranean-style retreat to guests in search of privacy. The Griffin family has built a country estate with swimming pool and indoor whirlpool, where guest rooms have private patios, wood-burning fireplaces, and unique furnishings. Golfers, there's also a nine-hole putting green to tune you up for the challenge of Bodega Harbour, and owner Cyrus Griffin, a Bodega Harbour member, plans to build a nine-hole course someday, just for guests. Rates start at around $200 and include a hot breakfast each morning. ■ 16702 COAST HIGHWAY 1, BODEGA, CA 94922; 888/404-2255; WEBSITE WWW.SCVILLA.COM

A relative bargain in these parts is **Branscomb Gallery,** where sculptor Ruth Branscomb lets out rooms with original art, king beds, and private baths starting at around $85 during the week. Some of the rooms overlook the water. ■ 1588 EASTSHORE RD., BODEGA BAY, CA 94923; 888/875-8733; WEBSITE WWW.BRANSCOMBGALLERY.COM

There's also the 63-site **Bodega Bay RV Park** just off Highway 1 near the harbor (707/875-3701; website www.campgrounds.com).

Dining

ITINERARY SELECTIONS

The Tides Wharf is a great place to get into the spirit of things, because you'll be sitting harborside, eating all of the good things that came out of those fertile waters in front of you. The menu here is huge, beginning with a long list of seafood appetizers and including pastas, sandwiches, fish, and shellfish entrées—even vegetarian and meat selections. Dinner entrée prices start at around $15 and include soup or salad, delicious sourdough bread, vegetable, and starch of the day. There's also a full bar and kids' menu. ■ 835 HIGHWAY 1, BODEGA BAY; 707/875-3652; WEBSITE WWW.INNATTHETIDES.COM

The **Duck Club**'s reputation is much bigger than the Duck Club itself, thanks to the work of chef Jeff Reilly. His kitchen may put out the world's best crabcakes, and we wouldn't steer you away from the filet mignon, the sea bass, or of course the duck. Entrées start at around $20 and you'll want to add at least an appetizer to that. ■ INSIDE THE BODEGA BAY LODGE, 103 COAST HIGHWAY 1, BODEGA BAY; 800/368-2468; WEBSITE WWW.WOODSIDEHOTELS.COM

ALTERNATIVES

The Duck Club has some things going for it the **Bay View** (800 Highway 1, Bodega Bay; 707/875-2751) does not—beginning with that it's open every morning and every night, while the Bay View opens only Wednesday through Sunday nights. But this Inn at the Tides fine dining establishment similarly puts a mouthwatering local spin on all the traditional favorites—for instance, we wouldn't dare miss the Filet Mignon Hitchcock (stuffed with Dungeness crab with Madeira and béarnaise sauces) were it in season. The view is heavenly, but prices are of the more devilish variety (entrées mostly in the $20 and up range). Unlike the Duck Club, the bar is complete.

If the Tides Wharf was more to your taste, you may also enjoy **Lucas Wharf Restaurant and Bar** (595 Coast Highway 1, Bodega Bay; 707/875-3522; website www.lucaswharf.com), which is just a few doors away from the Tides Wharf and shares a similar ambience, menu, and price range. Lucas Wharf has a fresh fish market and deli for stocking up on picnic supplies, and there's a seafood bar outdoors in good weather.

A more casual and moderately priced restaurant with delicious food, a bay view, and cheerful atmosphere is the **Breakers Cafe** (Pelican Plaza, Bodega Bay; 707/875-2513). All of the local seafood specialties are here, including fish and chips and corn crabcakes. Lunch and dinner are served daily, with dinner entrées starting at around $14 and remaining close to that figure, and breakfast is served until 2 P.M. on weekends.

A local favorite, open for casual dining at breakfast, lunch, and dinner, is the **Sandpiper Dockside Cafe and Restaurant** (1410 Bay Flat Rd., Bodega Bay; 707/875-2278). More seafood specialties served here, plus the glorious bay view. Follow the sign off Highway 1 to Marina and Bodega Head.

You'll stumble across additional dining options if you stroll through the towns of Occidental and Duncans Mills. The **Union Hotel** in Occidental seems like a particularly lively spot, with a long list of pizzas and pastas in the restaurant, drinks in the saloon, and morning goodies in the bakery. And if it's just pizza you want, pick one up with a video and ice cream for dessert at **Pelican Pizza and Video** (1400 Highway 1, Bodega Bay; 707/875-3245).

Straying Off Course

Being so close to the water, it's natural that you may want to take home some fresh rock cod, salmon, Dungeness crab, or halibut. You can catch them yourself off a number of boats, including those at Bodega Bay Sportfishing Center (707/875-3344) and the Boat House (707/875-3495). You can also fish off the Bodega Bay pier without a license.

Wil's Fishing Adventures offers fishing trips and also three- to four-hour whale-watching cruises from January through April. There's even an

evening harbor tour (1580 Eastshore Rd., Bodega Bay; 707/875-2323; website www.bodegabayfishing.com).

If you enjoy the sea without the motion, the Bodega Bay Marine Labora-
tory (707/875-2211), which studies the tidal flats, salt- and fresh-water
marshes, and rocky shores, opens to the public on Fridays 2–4 P.M.

In the village of Freestone, about 15 minutes from Bodega Bay inland,
there's an unusual refuge called Osmosis (209 Bohemian Hwy.,
Freestone; 707/823-8231). The specialty here is the enzyme bath, a
Japanese form of heat therapy that takes place in the midst of Japanese
gardens. Treatments include a blanket wrap or massage and start at
around $60.

Horseback riding on the beach is hugely popular, and the Chanslor
Guest Ranch (2660 Coast Highway 1, Bodega Bay; 707/875-3333) can show
the way with a variety of two-hour, half-day, or all-day trips.

On the north end of Bodega Bay, on the ocean side of Highway 1 a
little more than a mile north of the Visitors Center, stands a unique
monument to a unique story. In 1994, seven-year-old Nicholas Green
was shot and killed when his family was vacationing in Italy, and his
parents donated their son's organs to seven Italians. Nicholas is remem-
bered today at the Children's Bell Tower, a structure of three towers with
130 bells.

Lined up from Doran Park to the north of Bodega Bay are a string of
beautiful and in some cases dangerous beaches: Pinnacle Beach in Bodega
Harbour, Campbell Cove at the end of Bodega Head, Salmon Creek Beach,
Wright's Beach (where you'll see Death Rock), and Goat Rock Beach. The
folks at the Visitors Center can tell you which one bests suits your mood
for the day.

If your idea of a day at the beach includes surfing, kayaking, or biking,
the Bodega Bay Surf Shop can provide you with all of the equipment and
guidance you'll need—and lessons too (1400 Coast Highway 1, Suite E,
Bodega Bay; 707/875-3944; website www.bodegabaysurf.com).

The Russian River meets the Pacific Ocean just up the coast at Jenner;
travel Highway 116 inland and consider stopping to rent a canoe or take a
tour of Russian River wineries before winding back to Bodega Bay. Contact
the Russian River Wine Road for a map (800/723-6336 in California or
707/433-6782).

And if after all this you really need some nightlife, head over to the
town of Bodega, where the Casino stands ready and waiting to feed your
hunger, thirst, and craving for a game of pool (17050 Bodega Hwy.,
Bodega; 707/876-3185).

Details, Details

SUITCASE

Some people think it's always foggy in Bodega Bay. Other people think it's always windy. It's bound to be one or the other, except on the rare, perfect, calm, and sunny day. And for your Day 1 round at Rooster Run, you can expect the weather to be warmer, maybe even hot. So you will want to bring lots of layers and give yourself the option of shorts should the weather turn perfect in Bodega Bay. Evenings will be cool and casual—golf attire may feel dressy here, even at the Duck Club—and perfect for hot tubbing. Metal spikes are not a bad idea for the ups and downs at Bodega Harbour, particularly if it's been raining.

And if you're spending a couple of nights in a house on the golf course, pack some beverages (beer, wine, soda), snacks (cheese and crackers, chips and salsa), and some breakfast goodies (bagels, cream cheese, small packets of coffee, milk).

GETTING THERE

From all points, take Highway 101 to the East Washington exit and head east toward the airport. You'll see Rooster Run on your left.

If you're flying in commercially, either San Francisco International or Oakland International is about a 60-minute drive from Rooster Run.

Pilots will find the Petaluma Municipal Airport (707/778-4404) convenient, without restriction or curfew. Its 3,600-foot runway is right next to Rooster Run, and Hertz and Enterprise deliver rental cars.

CONTACTS

- The **Bodega Bay Area Chamber of Commerce** has launched a fantastic website (800/905-9050; www.bodegabay.com).
- The **Visitors Center** (850 Coast Highway 1; 707/875-3866) is right next to Inn at the Tides, and you can pick up all sorts of maps and tidbits here. You can also call for any information that didn't make it into these pages.

- The **Russian River Chamber of Commerce and Visitors Center** will be helpful if you are interested in exploring the river and the area wineries (16209 1st St., Guerneville; 24-hour information line 707/869-9000; website www.russianriver.com).
- Its people are passionate about Bodega Bay, and you'll see that at the website of Sonoma Coast Villa

proprietor Cyrus Griffin. He has established a user-friendly guide to **Bodega Bay "Best Picks"** that will be most congenial to the nongolfers in your party who think there's nothing to do here (website www.bodegabayvisitors.com).

■ For information on camping at Wright's Beach and Bodega Dunes State Parks, call the state park headquarters at Salmon Creek at 707/875-3483. For information on the county parks, call the office on Doran Beach at 707/875-3540.

Chapter 3

Some Pars with That Wine? Sonoma Valley

Sonoma might be "the road less traveled" when compared to flashy neighbor Napa, but discover the delights of a Sonoma golf escape and you'll be hooked. Take time to discover boutique wineries and secluded inns along backcountry roads. Wine-makers, cheese-makers, and food growers invite you to slow down and enjoy Sonoma's rich agricultural bounty.

A certain bohemian influence permeates Sonoma Valley, continuing the legacy of its colorful past. "Unconventional" best describes some of Sonoma's early citizens, like Hungarian Count Agoston Haraszthy, who founded Buena Vista Winery in 1857 in Sonoma and is called the father of California's wine industry. The prized *vitis vinifera* grapevines he brought from Europe established Buena Vista as California's first premium winery. Haraszthy's stone winery and underground cellars remain today.

And who could forget dashing Jack London, the passionate and contro-versial author who made his home in Glen Ellen? London wrote more than 50 books and was known worldwide. He and his wife, Charmian, designed and built their 26-room dream house, called *Wolf House*, but just before they were to move into it in 1913, it burned down in a mysterious fire. The remains of Wolf House rest within the 800 acres of the Jack London State Historic Park, which also has hiking trails and horseback riding trails, up the hill from the town of Glen Ellen. Sonoma Valley became known as the Valley of the Moon after London's novel of the same name.

Sonoma County is slightly larger than the state of Rhode Island, so for this itinerary we're concentrating on the eastern portion, the golf-rich Sonoma Valley, and including some courses north on Highway 101. You'll be glad to know (or maybe not) that "unconventional" doesn't apply to the golf in Sonoma Valley. There are a number of very solid courses that are challenging and fun. On the top of the list is the classic Sonoma Mission Inn Golf and Country Club, established in 1926. The course has four tee boxes and ranges from 7,087 yards to 5,511 yards. Head professional August Thompson says, "It's a traditional, old-fashioned course where players are not penalized that badly for an errant shot; rather it's the yardage that matters. If you can't hit driver, you won't score well. It's not a miniature-golf-style course."

The golf course was originally part of Sonoma Mission Inn, but owners sold it during the Depression in the 1930s. Thompson says that during World War II, golf legend Sam Snead was stationed in Oakland, and owners wanted him to play the course, so they offered him free golf balls, which were difficult to obtain during wartime because of the rubber shortage. Snead fell in love with the course and played it often during the war years. The course went through several owners until the Sonoma Mission Inn bought it back in late 1998, becoming Sonoma County's only complete destination resort.

The golf course is just a few miles away from the inn (a free shuttle is available), where golfers will find the elaborate spa to be the perfect antidote to a tough day on the course. Relaxed spa-goers glowing from luxurious treatments walk the landscaped pathways between the spa and the hotel swathed in comfy white terry robes and flip-flops. At first you wonder if they all got locked out of their rooms by mistake when they went to get the paper. But then you settle in and quickly become accustomed to the relaxed, easygoing style of the place. It has the atmosphere of a European health spa, where feeling good and being good to yourself are considered part of good health and not simply an indulgence.

Sonoma Mission Inn's new spa, opened in 2000 after a $20-million expansion, centers around the underground artesian mineral springs, which Native Americans considered sacred for their healing, restorative powers. The thermal mineral waters, pumped up from 1,100 feet below, are used in the signature Bathing Ritual. That sounds like something that should be conducted in private, but in fact the Bathing Ritual is a coed activity at the Sonoma Mission Inn, since, as the spa receptionist says, "We are couples-oriented." Swimsuits are required, and they are rather pricey in the Spa Shop, $80–160, so don't leave yours at home. Clothing-optional was briefly considered and just as quickly discarded.

Sonoma Mission Inn derives its name from the nearby Mission San Francisco Solano de Sonoma, founded by Father Jose Altimira in 1823. From this settlement came the design for the town of Sonoma around a central plaza, implemented by Mexican general Mariano Vallejo. The eight-acre Sonoma Plaza is the biggest town plaza in California.

General Vallejo was charged with protecting Mexico's far northern territory, which lasted until 1846 when a band of settlers seized Vallejo and declared California an independent republic. He surrendered peacefully, thus ending the so-called Bear Flag Revolt. Several weeks later the United States claimed California during the war against Mexico, but the statue in the middle of the plaza commemorates the rebels who raised the Bear Flag. Sonoma State Historic Park consists of the mission, General Vallejo's house, and the area of historic buildings around the plaza. You can wander about at your own pace or take a walking tour of the plaza with lively host Marv Parker.

Leaving Sonoma behind, you'll be ready to try the region's other wonderful golf courses. Semiprivate Fountaingrove Resort & Country Club is just north of Santa Rosa, convenient from Highway 101. The course opened in 1985 and underwent extensive renovations in 1998 by original designer Ted Robinson. John Theilade, operations director during renovation, said, "We wanted to make a good course great." Existing lakes were enlarged and all the greens and tees were redone, among other innovations. Although some think the course is now more difficult, Theilade says the NCGA rating did not change. It's still a hilly layout with lots of trees, requiring accuracy. The impressive three-story clubhouse was also remodeled and features a wrap-around deck and great views over the valley.

You can't miss the big old "Round Barn" on your left when driving up Fountaingrove Parkway to the golf course. The historic barn was reportedly part of a Utopian community built in the late 1800s by the followers of mystical leader Thomas Lake Harris. His disciple and right-hand man, Japanese Kanaye Nagasawa (who went by the title "Baron"), kept the commune going with wine-making under the Fountain Grove label and commissioned the barn to be built. Although it has been unoccupied for some time, insiders say plans have been approved to turn the Round Barn into a brewpub.

Only about five miles up Highway 101 from Fountaingrove, Windsor Golf Club is an exceptional public course, reasonably priced, with interesting holes, several lakes, and mature oak trees. Even though houses are being built along the 18th fairway, the rural setting is intact. Windsor hosted six Nike Tour events in the early '90s. David Duval holds the course record, and Tom Lehman, Ernie Els, and John Daly have all played at

Windsor when on the Nike Tour. As golf operations manager Mike Folden says, "You're walking the same fairways as the pros did." Director of golf Charlie Gibson is a former Tour player. The tees were moved on hole number 10 in the summer of 1998 to accommodate Charlie's Grill, the new 19th hole, a popular addition for both golfers and nongolfers.

Windsor is the gateway to the far-flung regions of Sonoma County: the northern towns of Healdsburg and Geyserville, the Russian River area to the west, and the coastal towns of Jenner, Fort Ross, and Bodega Bay. Any of these would make a wonderful extended getaway to your golf escape in Sonoma Valley.

Itinerary

WARMING UP

As you have probably gathered, this is suggested as an adult escape. It would be a good romantic getaway and would also be great for a few couples. Nongolfers will find plenty to keep them occupied near each of the golf courses on the itinerary. Plan on a relaxed country weekend. It's an indulgent kind of escape, i.e., what tastes good and what feels good. Be aware that some small wineries are open by appointment only.

Since we're suggesting dining at the excellent restaurants at our itinerary hotels, make your dinner reservations when you reserve your room. Book tee times as far ahead as possible and spa appointments as well, especially at the popular Sonoma Mission Inn. Be aware that Sonoma Mission Inn is a popular conference spot, so if you'd rather not be there when a large group is in residence, you might ask when you make your reservation.

day 1 On your way to Windsor Golf Club, our first course, we suggest you stop at the Sonoma County Wineries Association Wine and Visitors Center for a good introduction to Sonoma's wine country. It's in Rohnert Park, about 50 miles north of San Francisco off Highway 101, and it is open 9–5 daily. The comprehensive center has wine-tasting, a demonstration vineyard and model wine production facility, and a retail store full of Sonoma products. In addition, California Welcome Center volunteers provide free information and maps on where to go and places to stay.

It's about 15 miles from Rohnert Park to Windsor. Arriving at Windsor Golf Club you'll see the attractive Charlie's Grill first, but that's not where you check in. If you're late, park your car and heft your clubs across the small bridge to the pro shop. Or walk over, sign in, and bring the cart back to your car to load up your clubs. The all-grass driving range is adjacent to Charlie's Grill, so you may want to practice there before heading over to the first tee, which is near the pro shop across the bridge. The 10th tee is adjacent to Charlie's Grill.

Once you figure out where you're going, Windsor turns out to be a fun and challenging golf experience. It all starts with the friendly folks in the pro shop. Manager Mike Folden explains, "As our director of golf says, in this technological era, people get frustrated with automated messages, so if we're here, we answer the phone and field all the questions personally." This is a public course staff that cares.

On the front nine, hole number 2 is a tough par-4 with a creek on the left and trees on the right. The third fairway is defined from the tee by two silver silos along the left side. In driving over the hill to the blind green, you want to draw it around the silos or skirt them, but if it kicks right you may end up in the bunker. Vineyards stretch across the road behind the green. Hole number 4 is a long double dogleg par-5 with an oak tree grove and a bunker in front of the green. Mike Folden suggests laying up in front of the trees on the second shot. Or go left, which leaves a clearer but longer approach. Hole number 7 is a tough uphill par-3 into the wind with bunkers left and right and an undulating green.

By now you've gathered that the course has a lot of personality and character and is not boring. Four lakes come into play, so think about adding a club for insurance to carry the water.

The back nine seems to have more elevation. From par-3 hole number 13, considered the signature hole, you can see wide valley views, as well as from the uphill green on hole number 14. Hole number 17 is a challenge, especially from the white tees. Since the trees on the left have grown bigger, you have to hit a strong draw around them or lay up. With the fairway bunkers and two creeks to cross, it's tempting to play hole number 17 from the neighboring second fairway, but they're way ahead of you. It's out of bounds to do that. Hole number 18 has new home construction on the left, which might mean a future change in the tee box.

Nongolfers could go up to the town of Healdsburg, just 15 minutes away, for a few hours to visit the shops around the square. Healdsburg Carriage Company's horse-drawn carriages can take you on an afternoon of wine-tasting or a tour of the historic downtown or Victorian homes. Some wineries have tasting rooms in the square, like Windsor Vineyards, whose popular personalized wine labels commemorate special occasions. Create a special message to be put on the wine bottles, perhaps for a wedding, and have a case of wine sent to your recipient.

After golf, have a quick bite at Charlie's Grill and you'll see why it's a popular local spot. Then it's off to the Kendall-Jackson Wine Center. Return to Highway 101 south, take the Fulton Road exit and make a quick right into the center. Kendall-Jackson pours wine from its own label and from other wineries it owns around the state as well. Take your glass of wine and wander through the 2.5-acre organic demonstration garden or join one of the tours, given three times a day.

Of particular interest are the Red Wine Sensory Garden and the White Wine Sensory Garden. Within each section are planted the herbs or plants that are generally associated with particular grapes. For instance, the cabernet area would include plantings of cherry, black currant, or tobacco, while a flowery gewürztraminer is associated with jasmine, honeysuckle, or rose. Visitors are encouraged to pick a few leaves, rub them together, and inhale the aroma. Now you know where wine writers get all those descriptive adjectives.

Now you'll be going to Fountaingrove Inn. Drive down Highway 101 south until you reach Santa Rosa. Take the Mendocino/Hopper Avenue exit. Make a left at the stoplight. Hopper changes into Cleveland. Get in the left lane and stay on Cleveland until you come to the first stoplight. Make a left turn and go over the freeway to the next stoplight. Stay in the rightmost left turn lane. Make a left at the stoplight and an immediate right into the Fountaingrove Inn driveway. You'll be happy to eat right there at Equus, so convenient and actually one of the best restaurants in the area. Fountaingrove Inn is comfortable and tranquil, convenient to your next day's golf.

day II Included with the room is a generous breakfast buffet served in Equus Restaurant that includes fresh fruit, muffins and pastries, and hot and cold cereal. Containers are provided to take breakfast back to your room, or you can eat there. You'll have to check out, a minor inconvenience, but we didn't want you to miss that sybaritic spa experience at Sonoma Mission Inn. Nongolfers can go into Santa Rosa for a day of shopping and sightseeing around historic Railroad Square.

From the inn, turn left onto Fountaingrove Drive as it goes uphill past the Round Barn on the left. The Fountaingrove area used to be a ranch, but now it encompasses high-end homes, office buildings and a business park, and a new retirement community by Marriott for assisted living. At the top of the hill turn left to reach the covered entryway to the golf course.

Fountaingrove Resort and Country Club's hilltop setting yields dramatic views and a challenging layout. Its rugged contours were enhanced in 1998 with an expansive renovation by original course designer Ted Robinson Sr. The course closed down for nine months for the work, which reportedly cost more than $6 million.

Major innovations included a fourth set of tees and an improved drainage and irrigation system, which has created what PGA head professional Byron Cone calls Fountaingrove's most outstanding feature, year-round playability. Longtime players and members had to forget everything they knew about the greens, because the rebuilt bent-grass greens displayed undulations that weren't there before. Robinson's well-known genius with waterscapes is evident in the cascading waterfalls starting at the back left of the ninth green, meandering in front of the green and across the 18th fairway to the enlarged lake between holes 10 and 18.

Par-5 hole number 4 makes up for the string of bunkers with a quiet green tucked into the woods. The redone seventh green is defended by water across the front, and you also want to stay away from the water to the left of the green on hole number 9. Hole number 11 is a long dogleg right with a blind second shot you'll catch up with when you get over the hill and see the big oak tree blocking the green. It's deceiving, but there is actually more room than you think, if you approach right of the tree. Cone advises first-timers to strive for accurate tee shots and accurate shots into the green to score well.

The restraint to lay up on some of these long holes, e.g., numbers 4, 8, and 11, will pay off. For instance, on hole number 15, John Theilade suggests hitting an iron off the tee to reach the top of the hill and have a clear second shot on this narrow approach. Par-3 hole number 17 isn't long but memorable, as you must clear a lake rimmed with tall reeds to reach the green. Hole number 18 with the new green and expanded water features is now a dramatic finishing hole. Fountaingrove is semiprivate and encourages club membership. There is even talk of a resort hotel being built at the site sometime in the future. For now, Bogey's Bar & Grill provides a good place for a casual meal with its open deck overlooking the new lake and finishing hole.

When you are done playing golf, we suggest a leisurely drive along a scenic road that will eventually lead you to Highway 12 and the Sonoma Mission Inn. From the course, turn left onto Fountaingrove Parkway until it becomes Montecito Boulevard, and stay on Montecito until it dead-ends at Calistoga Road (about five miles). On this route you'll be in the hills overlooking all of Santa Rosa. Turn right onto Calistoga Road, a quick one-mile drive to Highway 12. Turn left on Highway 12. Following are some suggestions of places to stop along the way to Sonoma Mission Inn. You can do all of them or none of them. Maybe you just want to skip the whole thing and head right for the Spa at Sonoma Mission Inn.

Stop at North Eagle Gallery, a working studio that features original handmade pottery and paintings and a bonsai nursery. Several Kenwood wineries are worth a stop, and you won't need an appointment. Chateau St. Jean's fine reputation and elegant chateau with surrounding gardens and 80 acres of wine grapes make a favorite destination. Family Wineries of Sonoma Valley lets you sample wines from seven different family-owned wineries in one place. Taste hard-to-find handmade wines from wineries with small production capacity and meet the wine-makers, as the tasting room is staffed by the actual winery owner or wine-maker. Kunde Estate Winery has been producing fine wines in Sonoma Valley since 1904 and allows visitors to explore its large aging caves.

Turn right on Arnold Drive (also Highway 116) to reach the tiny town of Glen Ellen. Turn right on London Ranch Road and head up toward Jack London State Historic Park, stopping on the way at Benziger Family Winery. Several times a day the winery takes visitors for a "tram tour" into the terraced vineyards, stopping at exhibits to learn about the vines, then returns to the Tasting Room (which doubles as an art gallery), with a more educated palate to taste the wines.

Continue up London Ranch Road to the 800-acre park, site of Jack London's Beauty Ranch. The House of Happy Walls contains memorabilia of London's home, and it's a short hike to the remains of Wolf House. Returning to the town of Glen Ellen, stay on Arnold Drive (which runs parallel to Highway 12) and about a mile down the road stop at the Olive Press, where extra virgin olive oil is produced and sold.

Olive-oil tasting is a switch from wine-tasting, although the adjectives are similar, and you use French bread rather than drinking it straight. Flavors range from buttery to fruity to pungent to bold. These are "condiment" oils, to be used on cooked, prepared foods, not for cooking. During the harvest season, October–March, visitors can view the pressing from the tasting room.

From the Olive Press, it's only a few miles to the Sonoma Mission Inn. You'll see the golf course on your right, then turn left on Boyes Boulevard. The inn will be less than a mile on your right. We suggest scheduling your spa appointments for 6 P.M. (the last appointment is 8 P.M.) and arriving at least an hour earlier to enjoy the Bathing Ritual, where you progress at your own pace through a warm pool, a hot pool, a cooling shower, then herbal steam room and sauna. The spa treatments that follow will be more effective when you're this relaxed, and you'll be taking full advantage of what this elaborate spa has to offer. The spa is open 6 A.M.–10 P.M., including the indoor and outdoor pools. Treatment hours are 8 A.M.–8 P.M.

Before the spa renovation, the managing director, the marketing director, and the spa director went to Europe for six weeks to research innovative spa treatments. Sounds like a tough assignment, doesn't it? They came back with a giant solid brass tub from Hungary big enough for two, Kur treatment baths, a Vichy shower, and a flotation wrap treatment. For this, patrons are massaged with therapeutic creams, wrapped up, then gently lowered into the special Soft Pack table, which feels like being suspended in a warm waterbed. It's too hard to describe; you just have to try it.

After the spa, you won't want to go any farther than the Restaurant at Sonoma Mission Inn, just off the main lobby, where dinner is served until 9:30 P.M. It's the inn's signature restaurant, previously the Mission Grille, and it re-opened in spring 2000 after renovation. For more casual fare, you can walk over to the Big 3 Diner, just across from the spa. Then your room will be waiting for you, and, if you're lucky, it will have a fireplace to cap off a perfect day.

day III You have several options in the morning. You can sleep in, always a good choice. Or take a morning swim in the inn's swimming pool, which is behind the lobby. Or head over to the spa, which opens at 6 A.M., where you can swim and/or use the fitness facility and even schedule another treatment. All the outdoor pools and hot tubs, and the pools in the Bathing Ritual, are filled with the artesian mineral water that made the inn and the town of Boyes Hot Springs famous in the 1920s. In 1993, the inn brought the underground hot springs to the surface, thus reviving a celebrated tradition. You might pack up and take your clothes to the spa with you (they have lockers) so you can be ready to check out and head for the golf course.

If you use the spa area without a treatment, there is an additional charge.

There are several choices for breakfast. Try room service, coffee and pastries in the inn lobby, or the casual Big 3 Diner across from the spa on Highway 12. Also, the Spa Juice Bar is open 8–4 and offers juices, smoothies, breakfast pastries, and lunch items. You could also go early for your tee time and have breakfast at the Sonoma Mission Inn's golf course. Non-golfers can request a late checkout or go over to the spa to enjoy the pools and facilities.

The Sonoma Mission Inn Golf and Country Club presents a traditional course layout that consistently draws rave reviews. It's used as a qualifying course for the U.S. Open. Designed in 1926 by Sam Whiting and Willie Watson, architects of San Francisco's renowned Olympic Club, the course was rebuilt in 1991 by Robert Muir Graves to bring it up to modern standards. The course was originally part of the inn but went through several ownership changes until 1998, when it was reacquired and reunited with the spa resort.

Hotel guests can take the complimentary shuttle to the course, less than a mile away. The scenic course is set against the Mayacamas Mountains and runs through 177 acres of mature oaks and redwoods, three lakes, and a rushing creek. For all that, it is wide open, and there's a feeling of space, enhanced by the vineyards and rural environs around it and the lack of houses. Sheep are peacefully grazing in the pasture adjacent to the sixth tee. The course looks relatively flat, but in fact there are lots of subtle uphills that you encounter early on, in holes 2 and 3, which make it play longer than you may think. Par-3 hole number 4 is actually an upslope, perhaps not really obvious until you see the cart rolling backward on the cart path.

Signage is not very obvious, except the distances marked on the cart paths. Head professional August Thompson says this is actually deliberate, to maintain the traditional feel of the course, and partly in reaction to the previous owners' abundance of signs on the course. Thompson strives for a high standard of personalized service, saying, "We want to be your country club for a day." He is starting a caddie program, which he sees as an opportunity to help juniors. Rates for an experienced caddie would be about $40.

When Sonoma Mission Inn purchased the course in 1999, it added forward tees, at about 5,500 yards, which had been laid out by Robert Muir Graves but never implemented. Thompson says that signature hole number 7 remains just as it was when Sam Snead called it his favorite hole, with bunkers and oaks on the left and a green with several ridges. This par-3 also has a lake behind the tees that leads into a creek running down the right side and behind the green. Big greens are the biggest challenge throughout the course. Women's Golf Academy instructor Christie Smith says players commonly want to read more break into them, but they really roll true. One of the toughest holes is hole number 15, an uphill dogleg right where you want to stay left.

When you finish playing golf in the early afternoon, head into the town of Sonoma. Visit the historic Buena Vista Winery, then stop at Sonoma Cheese Factory, where you can taste varieties of house-made cheeses. If you haven't had lunch, buy picnic fixings there, including fresh bread from the Sonoma French Bakery down the street, and have a picnic in the plaza, before you visit the mission and other historic sites. If you already ate at the golf course, sightsee during the afternoon and dine in town at the General's Daughter, so named because it's the remodeled home of General Vallejo's daughter, Natalia.

 NOTES

Extended Play for Romantics. Head for the Russian River and stay at Applewood Inn & Restaurant in Guerneville. Don't miss a round of golf at the superb, nine-hole Northwood Golf Course in Monte Rio, among the tall trees. Nongolfers can visit the giant redwoods at Armstrong Redwoods State Preserve or go to some of the beaches along the Russian River in nearby Monte Rio.

Extended Play in Jack London's Back Yard. Stay in one of the country inns along Highway 12 and play golf at Oakmont's West Course or the shorter East Course, or both. This is your chance to visit those places along Highway 12 that you might have missed on Day 2.

Extended Stay for Townies. Head for Santa Rosa, Sonoma's county seat, and stay at family-owned Hotel La Rose, which has earned a place on the National Register of Historic Places. It's a convenient location for walking to shops and restaurants.

Extended Stay for Foodies. Sign up for Ramekins Cooking School in Sonoma, which is also a B&B with six beautiful guest rooms upstairs.

Money Savers. Consider playing golf at off-peak times and using golf packages where available. Also, you may be able to get a good deal at a B&B for a weekday stay. The Sonoma County Golf Group offers a free winter golf discount card good for two-for-one rounds through March 31 at certain courses. Call 800/464-5800 to order.

Traffic. Plan ahead to avoid encountering traffic tie-ups. During peak vacation periods, i.e., summer and weekends, the traffic on both directions of Highway 101 through Santa Rosa is going to be slow even during noncommute hours. Ballot measures to widen 101 didn't pass, so the bottleneck remains. Take those scenic backcountry roads instead.

If You Have Only One Day and One Night. Play golf at Fountaingrove, then tour and wine-taste along scenic Highway 12, check in at Sonoma Mission Inn for spa treatments, dine at the Restaurant at Sonoma Mission Inn or in Sonoma. Stay overnight at the inn, play golf there the next day, then drive back, stopping at the plaza on the way.

Courses

ITINERARY SELECTIONS

Windsor Golf Club
1340 19th Hole Dr.
Windsor, CA 95492
707/838-7888

Golf shop approval is required to play from the championship tees, but you'll find plenty of challenge from the other choices and be pleasantly surprised at how reasonable the green fees are at this well-maintained course. Weekends and holidays are around $45, and the course is walkable, so few will need carts. However, they are $22 and pull carts are $2. Twilight, senior, and junior rates expand the options available. Windsor Golf Club offers $4 off your round when you bring in a water bill from Windsor Water Company. The course is on Windsor Water District land.

TEE TIDBITS | Standard cart policy is on the fairways at 90 degrees. Soft spikes are required, and although it's pretty casual, golf attire is appreciated. The Windsor Golf Club Teaching Center opens in 2000 with two full-time instructors, offering Swing Solutions, a computerized video swing analysis system, and a Ping club-fitting system. The practice facilities are good, with an all-grass range, putting green, chipping green, and practice bunker. Leave yourself time, though, to get from there over the bridge to the first tee. It can be a little confusing the first time.

Charlie's Grill is a great 19th hole, designed from the beginning to be a really great restaurant that happens to be at a golf course. It's spacious with open views to the course, and the food is very good. Full breakfast is served on weekends, in addition to Sunday brunch, where Bloody Marys and Ramos Fizzes are only $3.25. Lunch specials might be trout amandine or chili and cornbread, and the regular menu always includes five or six innovative pizzas under $10. The sophisticated dinner menu includes baby-back pork ribs, wood-oven-roasted half duck, or grilled salmon, generally under $20.

SCORECARD

Architect: Fred Bliss, 1988
Course Record: 63, David Duval
Tournament: Par 72, 6,650 yards, 71.7 rating for men, 127 slope
Championship: Par 72, 6,169 yards, 69.4 rating for men, 122 slope
Regular: Par 72, 5,628 yards, 66.6 rating for men, 116 slope
Forward: Par 72, 5,116 yards, 69.3; 69.1 rating for women, 125 slope
Tee times are accepted one week in advance at 6:30 A.M. by calling 707/838-7888.

Fountaingrove Resort & Country Club
1525 Fountaingrove Parkway
Santa Rosa, CA 95403
707/579-4653

Fountaingrove is semiprivate with a private-club feeling. Green fees did increase after the course reopened in 1998, which made some locals unhappy but resulted in a less crowded golf experience, which suits the members just fine. It's a beautiful course that only got better.

Green fees are $75 on weekends including cart. Carts are mandatory and must stay on paths. Twilight, junior, and senior rates are available. Soft spikes are required, as are collared shirts for men, and no denim or tank tops are permitted. The expanded practice area includes grass tees and a chipping green.

SCORECARD

Architect: Ted Robinson Sr., 1985, 1998
Course Record: 69, Brad Robinson
Tournament: Par 72, 6,940 yards, 73.3 rating for men, 135 slope
Championship: Par 72, 6,439 yards, 71.5 rating for men, 131 slope
Club: Par 72, 5,951 yards, 69.1 rating for men, 126 slope; 74.5 rating for women, 131 slope
Forward: Par 71, 5,424 yards, 71.0 rating for women, 125 slope
For tee times call 707/579-4653 seven days in advance.

TEE TIDBITS | Consider the privileges of membership, which include making tee times 30 days in advance. The spacious clubhouse is open to the public with meeting rooms and sitting rooms and well-appointed locker rooms. Bogey's Bar & Grill serves lunch and dinner daily, with full bar, and breakfast on weekends. Dine inside or out on the deck in a casual atmosphere from a varied menu with prices under $15.

Sonoma Mission Inn Golf & Country Club
1170 Arnold Dr.
Boyes Hot Springs, CA 95476
707/996-0300, fax 707/996-5750
website www.sonomamissioninn.com

This beautiful course seems so walkable, but that won't save you any money on the green fee, and they don't allow pull carts. Carts must stay on paths. Also, the green fees are the highest in the area, approaching $100 on weekends including the cart. Play during the winter for $75. Sonoma County residents get a break midweek, and if it's your birthday, you get to play for $40 including cart. Twilight rates available in full season. The dress code is collared shirt, no jeans, and soft spikes are mandatory.

SCORECARD

Architects: Sam Whiting and Willie Watson, 1926; Robert Muir Graves, 1991
Course Record: 62, Tim Bogue
Black: Par 72, 7,087 yards, 74.1 rating for men, 132 slope
Blue: Par 72, 6,637 yards, 71.1 rating, 130 slope
White: Par 72, 6,123 yards, 69.4 rating for men, 125 yards; 75.2 rating for women, 133 slope
Red: Par 72, 5,511 yards, 71.8 rating for women, 125 slope
Tee times can be made by calling 707/996-0300 or 800/956-4653 one month in advance. Friday, Saturday, and Sunday reservations require a credit card number.

TEE TIDBITS | The course is a little pricey on its own, but if you stay at the inn, the total package makes for a wonderful upscale getaway, considering the spa treatments and the delight of not having to drive anywhere. The shuttle even takes you to the golf course. The practice area is a little weak with only eight stations and two additional spaces on grass in the summer. The Golf Academy, under the direction of Kris Moe, and the Women's Golf Academy, under Christie Smith, offer sophisticated video learning equipment and instruction at the opposite end of the range. The restaurant in the clubhouse serves breakfast and lunch until 3 P.M. in a comfortable setting around a stone fireplace.

ALTERNATIVES

Northwood Golf Course is a classic Alister MacKenzie nine-hole regulation course, par 36, amidst the majestic redwoods of the Russian River Valley. The 1928 design takes you through a narrow chute between the towering redwoods, and the sound of balls hitting the trees will serenade your round. Triangular flags of varying colors are on the trees on certain holes where needed, so you can discern near which trees lies your errant shot. MacKenzie was hired by the elite Bohemian Grove members to build it for them. It's a memorable nine-hole track, three miles west of Guerneville on Highway 116. Green fees are $35 on weekends for 18, $20 for nine, and carts are $20 for 18, $12 for nine. The restaurant, including outdoor deck, is open for breakfast, lunch, and dinner from about May through October, and it serves lunch and dinner only during winter.

■ 19400 HIGHWAY 116, MONTE RIO, CA 95462; 707/865-1116; WEBSITE WWW.NORTHWOODGOLF.COM

In 1992 the **Oakmont Golf Club** purchased the two golf courses from the developer, and the thriving adult community just south of Santa Rosa became a worthy golf destination. Both courses were designed by Ted Robinson Sr. (the same designer as Fountaingrove). The West Course is wide open and walkable, with eight lakes and a waterfall on the 18th hole. The new pro shop and restaurant, The Quail Inn, opened in 2000 as part of the Vision 2000 Program. The Quail Inn has floor-to-ceiling windows in the bar and restaurant area, which has spacious booths lining the wall, and makes the most of the golf course view with mountains in the backdrop.
■ 7025 OAKMONT DR., SANTA ROSA, CA 95409; 707/539-0415

Stone Tree Golf Club is approximately 30 minutes north of San Francisco along Highway 37 in northern Marin, an easy stop on your way to Sonoma. Former USGA president Sandy Tatum and golf legend Johnny Miller collaborated on this 7,000-yard layout amidst oak-forested hills. The new daily-fee club was not open at press time but promises to be a winner.
■ 1410 RENAISSANCE RD., NOVATO, CA 94948; 415/209-6090

If you can only play nine, the **Sonoma County Fairgrounds Golf Center,** which sits inside the fairgrounds racetrack, is ideal to practice your short game. Also, the range is lit at night and has a good chipping facility with bunker. Green fees range $5–12. ■ 1350 BENNETT VALLEY RD., SANTA ROSA, CA 95404; 707/577-0755

Lodging

ITINERARY SELECTIONS

The **Fountaingrove Inn**'s low-rise, understated honey-colored buildings are finished in native redwood, oak, and stone, yet the interiors are almost Oriental in their simple, uncluttered furnishings. There are 90 well-equipped rooms in the main building and 30 deluxe suites in the new conference center a short walk across the parking lot. The small pool and hot tub area provide a welcome respite. Special touches more akin to B&B-style hospitality are included, like the complimentary buffet breakfast served in Equus Restaurant. Fresh cookies appear in the lobby every afternoon. Room service is also available.

The golf course is just a short drive up the hill. Packages include 18 holes of golf with a shared cart, overnight stay in deluxe accommodations, complimentary cocktails in Equus Lounge, welcome gift, morning newspaper, and breakfast. Weekday rates Monday–Thursday are $99 per person, weekends $149 per person, double occupancy. Also, Fountaingrove will offer four days/three nights of Wine Country Golf Camp for $725 per person, including lodging, golf, lessons, and all meals. ■ 101 FOUNTAINGROVE PARKWAY, SANTA ROSA, CA 95403; 707/578-6101 OR 800/222-6101, FAX 707/544-3126; WEBSITE WWW.FOUNTAINGROVEINN.COM

The soft pink **Sonoma Mission Inn Golf and Country Club** is the Sonoma wine country's only complete destination resort. It has luxurious accommodations, an elaborate 40,000 square foot spa, and a classic golf course. The inn's early California Mission–style architecture was enhanced in 2000 with a $20 million renovation that included the new spa, new entryway, and 30 new Mission Suites. Historic Inn Rooms, in the main building, reflect old-style design from 1927 and are the best value, while Wine Country Rooms (some with fireplaces), Wine Country Suites, and the new Mission Suites are in adjacent buildings, amid wildflower gardens and pathways. The Restaurant at Sonoma Mission Inn serves fine dining and the Big 3 Diner offers more casual fare. The Unlimited Golf Package includes guest room, valet parking (standard charge is $10 per night), and unlimited golf for two people per room, per day. Package rates vary, but generally the rate for a Historic Inn Room ranges $360–536, while the One Bedroom Suite package would range $589–820. ■ 18140 HIGHWAY 12, SONOMA, CA 95476; 707/938-9000 OR 800/862-4945; WEBSITE WWW.SONOMAMISSIONINN.COM

GOLF PACKAGE OPTIONS

You can't miss the nine-foot high pink flamingo atop the obelisk-like tower in downtown Santa Rosa, the historic landmark of the **Flamingo Resort Hotel,** built in 1957. In addition to 170 modern rooms and suites, plus the 34-room Courtyard wing especially for business travelers, the Flamingo offers several restaurants, a large heated swimming pool, and access to the Health & Racquet Club. This would be another good place for nongolfers to hang out while the golfers take advantage of the golf packages with three different courses: Oakmont, Fountaingrove, and Bodega Harbor. Packages include a round of golf with cart, one night's lodging, breakfast buffet, use of hotel facilities including Olympic-size pool, whirlpool, and full fitness facility. Prices start at $115 per person, double occupancy, on weekends. Choices of golf courses may change. ■ 2777 4TH ST., SANTA ROSA, CA 95405; 707/545-8530 OR 800/848-8300, FAX 707/528-1404; WEBSITE WWW.FLAMINGORESORT.COM

ALTERNATIVES

Applewood Inn & Restaurant is in Guerneville, nestled on six acres in the Russian River Valley. The California Mission–style villa is surrounded by redwoods and fruit trees. It's relaxing and luxurious, with 16 rooms in separate buildings, which include fireplaces and balconies. Gardens surround the heated pool and spa. The owners remodeled the restaurant in 1999, and the beamed-ceiling main dining room has two rock fireplaces. Rooms range $165–275 and include a bountiful breakfast. ■ 13555 W. HIGHWAY 116, GUERNEVILLE, CA 95446; 800/555-8509 OR 707/869-9093, FAX 707/869-9170; WEBSITE WWW.APPLEWOODINN.COM.

Along Highway 12 in the Kenwood and Glen Ellen area are a number of attractive inns. **Kenwood Inn and Spa**'s 12 suites each have a fireplace and queen-size feather bed. The four Mediterranean-style villas sit around a courtyard with pool and fountain, surrounded by gardens and nestled into a secluded hillside. The spa offers a variety of massages and body treatments in a dedicated space off the lobby. Summer weekend rates range $325–$425, including full breakfast. ■ 10400 SONOMA HWY., KENWOOD, CA 95452; 707/833-1293; WEBSITE WWW.KENWOODINN.COM

Gaige House Inn is a Victorian inn transformed into a sophisticated retreat with modern, sleek Asian decor, yet sumptuously comfortable with king and queen beds and several rooms with whirlpool baths. Some of the 15 rooms have outdoor decks. The pool area is surrounded by lawn, full breakfast at your own private table is included, and the restaurants of Glen Ellen are within walking distance. Summer weekend rates range $230–395. ■ 3540 ARNOLD DR., GLEN ELLEN, CA 95442; 707/935-0237 OR 800/935-0237, FAX 707/935-6411; WEBSITE WWW.GAIGE.COM

The Glenelly Inn is a quaint B&B with six suites in the main building and two in the "owner's cottage," which feature private verandas, country-style furnishings, queen beds, down comforters, and clawfoot tubs with showers. There's a hot tub in the rose garden under a gazebo among lovely gardens. Breakfasts are so good, cookbooks are for sale with the recipes. It's only a few miles from the Sonoma Mission Inn golf course and one mile from Glen Ellen. Prices range $135–160, without seasonal or weekend fluctuations. ■ 5131 WARM SPRINGS RD., GLEN ELLEN, CA 95442; 707/996-6720; WEBSITE WWW.GLENELLY.COM

The Jack London Lodge is the budget choice lodging in this area, with 22 large rooms featuring cable TV, in-room coffee, and small refrigerators. The two-story building has 11 rooms upstairs and 11 rooms downstairs, a swimming pool, and a hot tub. All rooms are the same and the price is about $120 on summer weekends. Call when the office is closed and the recording says, "If you need a room for tonight, please see a bartender at the Jack London Saloon." The saloon and the popular Bistro at Glen Ellen are adjacent to the inn. ■ 13740 ARNOLD DR., GLEN ELLEN, CA 95442; 707/938-8510; WEBSITE WWW.JACKLONDONLODGE.COM

The historic **Hotel La Rose** is in downtown Santa Rosa's Railroad Square, convenient to restaurants, antique shops, and Macy's. It's owned and operated by two generations of the Neumann family. The hotel was built in 1907, renovated and enlarged in 1985, and brought up to date again in 1998; it's on the National Register of Historic Places. Fine dining is featured in Josef's Restaurant. The 49 guest rooms include 20 Carriage House rooms with balcony or patio. Complimentary continental breakfast. Rates range $179–295. ■ 308 WILSON ST., SANTA ROSA, CA 95401; 707/579-3200 OR 800/LAROSE-8, FAX 707/579-3247; WEBSITE WWW.HOTELLAROSE.COM, EMAIL RESERVATIONS@HOTELLAROSE.COM

One of the best choices within walking distance of Sonoma Plaza, **MacArthur Place** offers comfortable, big, well-equipped rooms in an 1850s main house and cottages spread around old-fashioned boxwood-lined gardens with a swimming pool and whirlpool. Upstairs rooms with wisteria climbing up the balcony posts are most desirable. The full-service spa was doubled in size and new treatments added in fall 2000. The inn's steakhouse, called Saddles, is in an adjacent restored 100-year-old barn. Weekend rates range $245–425. ■ 29 E. MACARTHUR ST., SONOMA, CA 95476; 800/722-1866, FAX 707/933-9833; WEBSITE WWW.MACARTHURPLACE.COM, EMAIL INFO@MACARTHURPLACE.COM

El Dorado Hotel is right on the plaza, with 27 rooms and a garden patio defined by an ancient fig tree. Rooms have French windows and terraces, some overlooking the hotel's private courtyard, where complimentary continental breakfast is served; others face the town. There is a heated outdoor pool. Piatti Restaurant is on the property. Rates range $180–$195. ■ 405 1ST ST. W, SONOMA, CA 95476; 707/996-3030, FAX 707/996-3148; WEBSITE WWW.HOTELELDORADO.COM

The intimate **Cottage B&B** has three rooms, entered through either a main courtyard or a private courtyard, and the Mission B&B next door also has three rooms, all with private entry. Each room is provided with fresh breakfast supplies in the refrigerator, and baked goods are delivered to each room in the morning. There is a spa for six and some two-person whirlpools. Each room is very private and self-contained. Weekend rates range $135–265. ■ 302 1ST ST. E, SONOMA, CA 95476; 800/944-1490 OR 707/996-0719, FAX 707/939-7913; WEBSITE WWW.SONOMABB.COM/THECOTTAGE.HTM

The Inn at Cedar Mansion is an 1876 Italianate Victorian residence just off Sonoma Plaza that completed a $1.5 million dollar renovation in 2000. It includes five private suites on beautifully landscaped grounds with a swimming pool and tennis court. Gourmet breakfasts and afternoon hors d'oeuvres are prepared by the in-house chef as well as private evening dining by advance request. Rates range $336–445. ■ 531 2ND ST. E, SONOMA, CA 95476; 800/409-5496; WEBSITE WWW.CEDARMANSION.COM

Dining

ITINERARY SELECTIONS

Equus Restaurant in Fountaingrove Inn offers fine dining in a sophisticated setting with the Gallery of Sonoma County Wines, an extensive wine list. Starters include local oysters on the half shell, and entrées feature local specialties like Sonoma lamb or coastal salmon. Prices range $20–30 for entrées. The attractive dining room has redwood carvings, etched glass, and expansive murals with an equestrian theme. The Equus Lounge offers complimentary hors d'oeuvres Monday–Friday, piano music Friday and Saturday nights, and a full menu. Lunch and dinner. ■ 101 FOUNTAINGROVE PARKWAY, SANTA ROSA; 707/578-0149

When the **Restaurant at Sonoma Mission Inn** opened in 2000, some of the old favorites from the Mission Grille remained, like the creamy pan-seared Sonoma foie gras and house-cured gravlax appetizers, and the medallions of ostrich and two presentations of liberty duck. Tasting bar items are prepared with Eastern herbs and spices, evidenced in the sushi sampler, dim sum, and tandoori flatbreads. Appetizers run about $14 and entrées are just under $30. Sommelier Perry Croft's carefully crafted wine list is arranged by category to describe the wines from light to robust, from dry to fruity. Dinner. ■ 18140 SONOMA HWY., SONOMA; 707/938-9000

The Big 3 Diner at Sonoma Mission Inn is in a separate building from the inn. The casual café has wide menu selections for every meal, and some items are designated for the spa-goers, with detailed nutritional information provided. Try the lowfat Bircher muesli for breakfast. Even some of the pizzas are so designated, and the braised tofu with fresh pasta is an obvious low-cal choice. Breakfast, lunch, dinner. Prices are under $15. ■ CORNER OF BOYES BLVD. AND HIGHWAY 12, SONOMA; 707/939-2410

ALTERNATIVES

The Girl & the Fig (110 W. Spain St., Sonoma; 707/938-3634), formerly in Glen Ellen, recently moved to the Sonoma Hotel, on the Plaza. It's the same "country food with a French passion." The innovative menu offers steamed mussels with Pernod, a cheese course, liberty duck confit, and a dreamy lavender crème brûlée. Prices are under $20. Dinner.

Syrah (205 5th St., Santa Rosa; 707/568-4002) is intimate bistro-style dining with cozy indoor or courtyard seating. The menu emphasizes Sonoma County cuisine but also includes Asian rice rolls, Chinese chicken salad, or niçoise sandwich. Crabcakes are a favorite. The dinner menu offers a few specialties, including pan-roasted chicken or squab, ahi tuna, or grilled T-bone steak. Don't miss the pastries. Entrées range $17–25. Lunch and dinner.

Prominently situated on a corner, **Mixx** (4th and Davis Streets, Santa Rosa; 707/573-1344) is also bistro-style but with a wider menu selection, imaginatively blending local produce and regional items. Lunch is mostly under $15 with the smoked seafood niçoise salad and seafood risotto popular items. Entrées or "large plates" range $16–25 and include Sonoma rabbit and liberty duck breast. The menu indicates several heart-healthy selections and offers to customize dishes to please vegetarians. Mixx has won the "Best of Show Desserts" at the Sonoma County Harvest Fair several years in a row, so bring your sweet tooth. Mixx Pastry is a little bakery counter adjacent. Lunch and dinner.

The Quail Inn (7035 Oakmont Dr., Santa Rosa; 707/539-9215) at Oakmont West Course opened in spring 2000 as part of Oakmont's Vision 2000 renovation, which included the new pro shop. The clean, crisp look includes floor to ceiling windows that take full advantage of the golf course view with mountain backdrop. The Quail's Nest is the bar, which serves breakfast, lunch, and "19th Hole" refreshments until 9 P.M., with a covered patio as well. The Quail Inn features fabric-covered booths and rattan chairs, and the menu showcases Sonoma County's best, with a "Provence in Sonoma" selection that allows you to enjoy a three-course meal from the freshest Sonoma products. Entrées include oven-roasted halibut, pancetta-wrapped filet mignon, and wild mushroom ravioli, and the prices are under $20. Sunset dinners 4 P.M.–6:30 P.M. are popular at a price of $12.95 including soup or salad, entrée, and dessert.

The General's Daughter (400 W. Spain St., Sonoma; 707/938-4004, fax 707/938-4099) is in a renovated Victorian built in 1864 for General Vallejo's daughter, Natalia. The restaurant opened in 1994 after extensive renovation by local builder-designer Suzanne Brangham, winning an award from the Sonoma Historical Society. Whimsical paintings and the photos of local wine-makers in the bar add a personalized touch. Dinner entrées include pan-seared pork tenderloin with port reduction, grilled salmon with a teriyaki glaze, and grilled New York steak. It's hard to resist the warm herb and cheese bread. Entrée prices range from $13 for pasta to $27 for the New York steak. Brunch, lunch, dinner.

Straying Off Course

The Sonoma County Wineries Association Wine and Visitors Center is a great introduction to the area (5000 Roberts Lake Rd., Rohnert Park; 707/586-3795, fax 707/586-1383; website www.sonomawine.com).

The Russian River Wine Road Association represents more than 75 wineries and 36 lodgings in northern Sonoma County. Call 800/723-6336 for information and a map.

The Kendall-Jackson Wine Center at 5007 Fulton Rd. in Fulton (707/571-8100) will give you a deeper sense of wine flavors. Here's the info on suggested stops for the drive along Highway 12 from Fountaingrove to Sonoma Mission Inn: North Eagle Gallery (6191 Sonoma Hwy., Santa Rosa; 707/538-2554); Chateau St. Jean (8555 Sonoma Hwy., Kenwood; 707/833-4134); Family Wineries of Sonoma Valley (9200 Sonoma Hwy., Kenwood; 707/833-5504); and Kunde Estate Winery (10155 Sonoma Hwy., Kenwood; 707/833-5501).

In Glen Ellen, we suggest The Benziger Family Winery (1883 London Ranch Rd., Glen Ellen; 707/935-3000), just down the road from Jack London State Historic Park (707/938-5216). Also in Kenwood is Sugarloaf Ridge State Park, which offers hiking and horseback riding (Adobe Canyon Road; 707/833-5712). For horseback riding in the wine country call Sonoma Cattle Company & Napa Valley Trail Rides in Glen Ellen (707/996-8566). And we don't want you to miss The Olive Press (14301 Arnold Drive, Glen Ellen; 707/939-8900).

A great idea for hassle-free wine-tasting is to take a wine tour and have your own designated driver. Call California Wine Tours (707/939-7225) or Valley Wine Tours (707/975-6462). Another way to visit wineries is by bike. Take a designated tour with Goodtime Bicycle Company (18503 Sonoma Highway in Sonoma; 888/525-0453). And what about a hot air balloon ride above the vineyards? You can call Balloons Above the Valley (800/GO HOT AIR or 707/253-2222).

Learn what food to pair with those wines with cooking lessons at Ramekins (450 W. Spain St., Sonoma; 707/933-0450, fax 707/933-0451; website www.ramekins.com, email info@ramekins.com).

After wine-tasting, shopping and sightseeing are probably the next most popular optional activities in the wine country. For this itinerary, we've concentrated on three areas: Healdsburg, Santa Rosa, and Sonoma. The Healdsburg Carriage Company will take you on vineyard, downtown, or Victorian home tours (707/838-3927). Taste wine and send a personalized wine gift at Windsor Vineyards tasting room (308B Center St. in Healdsburg; 707/433-2822).

When shopping in Santa Rosa around Railroad Square, you might also want to see the Sonoma County Museum (425 7th St. in Santa Rosa; 707/579-1500, fax 707/579-4849). Also in Santa Rosa are the Luther Burbank Home and Gardens (on Santa Rosa Avenue at Sonoma Avenue; 707/524-5445). The famous horticulturist lived in Santa Rosa in the early 1900s, and the gardens are in full bloom in spring and summer.

Browse the little shops around the Sonoma Plaza and don't miss the mission and other historic sites, which altogether make up the Sonoma Historic State Park. You may want to take a Sonoma Plaza Walking Tour with Marv Parker (707/996-9112).

Details, Details

SUITCASE

Bring swimsuit and soft spikes and workout clothes. You won't need a coat and tie or fancy clothes; this is a relaxed country kind of escape. Balmy spring days are idyllic, and you can taste new wines amid the green hills. Summers are hot in the wine country, so bring a hat and sunscreen, but evenings can be cool. Indian summer sometimes extends into the crush season in the fall, when the vines change color to vibrant reds and oranges. Harvest time is an exciting time to visit the wineries. If you go during the cool winter months, you'll be rewarded with an unhurried pace, but dress warmly.

GETTING THERE

If you're going to stop at the Wine Center in Rohnert Park, here are the directions: From northbound Highway 101, exit at Golf Course Drive and bear left at Commerce Boulevard. At the first stop light, turn right on Golf Course Drive. Proceed to Roberts Lake Road and turn left. Take the first right into the parking lot.

From southbound Highway 101, exit Wilfred Avenue/Golf Course Drive. At the first stoplight, turn right onto Redwood Drive. Proceed to the next stoplight and turn right at Commerce Boulevard. Proceed underneath Highway 101 to the stoplight at Golf Course Drive and turn left. Proceed to Roberts Lake Road and turn left. Take the first right into the parking lot.

To reach Windsor Golf Club from points south, take Highway 101 north through San Francisco across the Golden Gate Bridge. Exit at Shiloh Road and go west of the freeway about one-half mile to Golf Course Road, turn right, then left on 19th Hole Drive. From Sacramento take Highway 80 west to Vallejo, then take Highway 37 west to Highway 101 north.

Sonoma County Airport, north of Santa Rosa, was recently renamed Charles M. Schulz Sonoma County Airport, honoring the *Peanuts* creator, one of Santa Rosa's favorite citizens. The airport is served by United Express and Sky West and can accommodate private jets as well.

CONTACTS

- **Sonoma County Visitor Info** (800/576-6662) will send an official *Sonoma County Visitors Guide.* For information online, visit www.sonomacounty.com.
- A Sonoma County calendar of events is online at www.visitsonoma.com. Check the website for a complete list of events held in different regions of Sonoma County, like wine-tastings, offered at restaurants or wineries and often combined with food pairings. You'll also find seasonal festivals held throughout the year and musical performances held at the **Luther Burbank Center for the Arts** in Santa Rosa (707/546-3600).

Chapter 4

Don't Whine, Wine!
Napa Valley

Nearly five million visitors saunter into the world's most popular wine country destination every year, and most of them do not play golf. It's a good thing, too, because those who do love the game and wouldn't think of traveling without their sticks packed in the trunk can't help but whine a bit when they arrive in the Napa Valley.

Where are all the golf courses, they ask? Here's this grand tourist destination, with beautiful vistas for miles around, and not an 18-hole championship course that welcomes public play to be found in the valley proper. The 18-holers—Chardonnay's two courses, Napa's municipal course, and even Silverado's more centrally located but guests-and-members-only resort courses—are all at the very southern end of the valley. There's an afterthought of a nine-holer on the Silverado Trail (Chimney Rock), an exquisite but members-and-guests only nine at Meadowood Resort, and a first-rate new nine (Vintners Golf Club) next to Domaine Chandon in Yountville. But efforts to make Chardonnay pay off by building houses around the course failed due to zoning restrictions, and an ancient nine next to a crumbling historic resort over the hill from St. Helena is always rumored to be about to close. One airport golf course and resort project already had been given thumbs down, while another, Montalcito, developed by the owners of the Resort at Squaw Creek, was proceeding also in the valley's southern end near Napa Muni.

Take our advice to heart here: Wine and don't whine. Grapes, not golf, are what this Napa Valley wine country—a.k.a. Adult Disneyland, a.k.a. Dine Country—is all about. Get with the program, have some bubbly with your breakfast, a chardonnay at the turn, a merlot at the 19th, and try not to think about what great golf holes you could design on that hillside vineyard in the distance.

"Vineyard land is going for up to $100,000 an acre," says Jack Barry, president of Chardonnay Golf Club. "How can you afford that for a golf course?"

Terry Sullivan, who was the director of golf when the relatively new Yountville nine opened, says the course owners inquired about buying the vineyards next door to make nine more holes. "There's no way green fees could support paying the price he wanted," Sullivan said.

Of course, the traditional way to support paying that price would be to build homes around the course. But not in Napa Valley. In 1990, voters here designated the heart of the valley "agricultural preserve," or "ag-preserve," as they cozily call it now. That halted development in the heart of the valley, and even where one might be able to build a home, there must be 40 acres of land per single-family development. So you'll see many homes around Silverado, which was first developed nearly 50 years ago, and none at Chardonnay, which opened in 1987.

"From a financial perspective it just kills me," says Barry. "But from a golf perspective, I love it. My partner thought back in '89 that the vineyards here would be homes, but he couldn't do it and had a rough time. Now we're leasing out the land—Grgich has 200 acres, Hess has 200 acres—and the hillsides are covered in vineyards. So it's truly one of the prettiest facilities I've ever seen."

If you can't beat 'em, join 'em. Barry and friends even have their own label, Talon, which ties into their plans for a new project they're calling Eagle Vines. Eagle Vines will combine nine new holes with the 10 "best" holes (holes 6–15 in case you're wondering) from the mostly private Shakespeare Course, where Michael Jordan and Joe Montana are among the famous members, and which the Secret Service has recommended to the likes of the president of Singapore and the Japanese ambassador. This will make a new 7,000-yard, mostly private course designed by Barry and Johnny Miller. (Yes, we know nine plus 10 equals 19; one of the charms of Chardonnay is the 80-yard 19th hole of the Shakespeare Course, and that will remain in some form.) The leftover holes on the Shakespeare Course will be merged into Chardonnay's Vineyards Course to make three nines and, eventually, it is hoped, a full 36. In the meantime, the focus at Chardonnay is on bringing the public Vineyards Course up a few notches, so it won't pale by comparison to its sister course as it has with the much more manicured and fascinating Shakespeare Course.

The whole project seems quite an extravagant venture in a place where houses couldn't be sold, but the two 300-room hotels under construction on Kelly Road, virtually across the street from Chardonnay, are the basis for such optimism at Chardonnay, which is not nearly as busy on off-season afternoons as operators would like.

At least the off-season in the Napa Valley is brief. The smog-free climate is generally moderate all year—yes, Sherlock, *that's* why the grapes like it so much here—although we did play Chardonnay's Shakespeare Course once during a cold spell, and golf balls were like superballs on the greens. (That was the day Mary at the turn opened up a whole new world of hot chocolate and brandy.) And we did awaken one Christmas morning to a winter wonderland at Silverado, but the frost had melted away by late morning and we were able to celebrate the holiday just the way we like to, with 18 holes on a great golf course in a beautiful setting.

For golfers, indeed, the time to visit is after the crush of the grapes in October and before the crush of tourists from April and beyond. Autumn, in fact, may be the worst time to visit the valley, with winery workers on 24-hour shifts and grape gondolas clogging the already congested roads that won't be widened any time soon, not at the price of that land that could otherwise be used for growing more grapes. The traffic gets worse every day, the locals don't have any place to live, but the local ordinances decree, like a Californian Marie Antoinette, let them eat grapes.

But let's not belabor that point. There is golf to be found here, and quite a range of golf, from parkland course to modern design, from busy, run-down track to exquisitely cared-for walkers-only resort. Beyond Chardonnay, the first courses you'll pass on your way into the valley, is Napa Golf Course, a 1968 Jack Fleming–Bob Baldock design that has matured beautifully over the years into one of the better challenges in Northern California—and a bargain at any price compared to the rest of the neighborhood. Napa Muni was undergoing renovations in summer 2000—nothing too drastic, we're hoping—to offer more reasonable distance options from the tees and a bit more forgiveness around some of the greens, and to jazz up the clubhouse a bit. In the meantime, its proximity to the Napa River makes for a soggy experience in winter, and often rain closes the course for a period in January. But by spring, when the tourists come to town again, there'll be flowers blossoming around the tee boxes and a whole new set of golfers attempting to make their way around all 18 holes with just one golf ball. And we're not saying the course is ridiculously tough, just that there's a high risk-reward ratio that makes it enjoyable.

Just north of Napa Muni is the Silverado Country Club and Resort, which sounds a lot more formal and chichi than it really feels, thank goodness. There are two courses here, the older North Course and the South, which is the one that the PGA Senior Tour uses each October for the Transamerica tournament. Golfers often want to play the South because that's where the pros play, but remember that the PGA Tour used to visit the North Course from 1967 to 1980. Director of golf Jeff Goodwin has this to say about the differences: "The North, from the back tees at least, is longer, and the greens are flatter. The South is shorter but the greens are more undulating. I can't reach the par-5s in two on the North, but on the South there are two that I can. From the regular tees, though, I might score better on the South. And the North, if you play the front nine from the back tees and then played it again from the white tees, you wouldn't even know you were on the front nine again because each hole looks different."

Translation: Since you probably won't have a choice anyway (the members-only course alternates daily), just be assured that you will have fun on either course; they are both just so mature, well designed, and well kept. And Silverado is a good destination even in winter; the courses here were among the first to begin the practice of sanding their fairways to improve conditions in wet weather, and you probably won't mind if the greens are a tad slower than in summer.

Just north of Silverado on the Silverado Trail—and now, look around, you are well into the wine country—is Chimney Rock, once an 18-hole course before it was shrunk to nine to make more room for grape fields. Chimney Rock does great business, having a monopoly of sorts on the golfers at this side of the valley, and is adjacent to the Chimney Rock winery, which is no doubt kept up much better than the golf course. That's just the way it is here. There have even been recent rumors that the remaining nine would be turned into vineyards as well, so don't be surprised if you drive up one day and the fairways are planted.

West of Chimney Rock is the Yountville nine, and considering that nearby residents were successful in their efforts to get the driving range to turn off its lights, we're not sure how the course even came to be. It is far beyond any comparisons with Chimney Rock, and it has a clubhouse that feels both cozy and upscale, with a deck and tables overlooking the first tee and adjacent lake, so it's awfully tempting to make the turn a long-lasting one. The course itself is a par-68 played twice, which most people gladly do if only for the opportunity of rethinking the way they approached the holes the first time. There's not much land here, of course, and the highway borders the course to the east, but there's a surprising feeling of nature and tranquillity. "Enjoyability" is the key word here—it's not ever going to be a U.S. Open site and it doesn't try to be. And Vintners Golf Club definitely has location, location, location, with Domaine Chandon and the charming hotel-filled town of Yountville just on the other side of the highway.

And from here, you're not golfing again unless you're staying at Meadowood—lucky you, you'll get to enjoy nine holes in a valley behind the Restaurant and Grill in relative privacy. This small course isn't easy, what with all the trees lining the narrow fairways and several challenging par-3s, but it is a well-maintained and pretty amenity on a magnificent piece of property.

Just over the hill east of Meadowood is or was Aetna Springs, a nine-hole course that began in 1890 as a five-hole resort course. The rich and famous used to vacation and weekend here, but the historic resort has been standing empty for years and crumbling, all because of local resistance to development. Voters rejected a measure in 2000 that would have allowed private developers to restore the resort to house some 200 visitors; the measure would also have led to a restoration of the deteriorating old course, where wildflowers put on a distracting color show in the adjacent meadow and oak trees crop up in the middle of a fairway when you least expect it. By the time you're reading this, Aetna Springs may have become just another meadow full of flowers.

This is growing country, not golfing country, and if that makes you sad, you'll just have to make your way to a few of the 240 or so area wineries and forget about it. And if that doesn't do it, you can find a memorable meal somewhere here in foodie heaven, and no doubt a comfy bed with a gourmet breakfast and maybe even a hot tub at one of the more than 100 inns in the region. You can have mud baths, go hiking, and peruse art collections or shop for some for your own. No chain stores, though, uh-uh, that's against the rules. Napa Valley is sticking to the plan and dancing to the wine-induced song that brought it there. And that's not so painful, is it?

|tinerary

WARMING UP

For this particular itinerary, you may want to round up a few golfing buddies or a group of social and golfing friends, or maybe just your significant other, and leave the kids with Grandma and Grandpa. Wintertime is especially ideal for a group escape, because lodging rates are lower and tee times more plentiful. On the other hand, if you time it right for Silverado's "Golfer's Dream" your twosome may be able to stay overnight and golf for less than the usual price of two green fees—the only caveat being you won't get a refund if it's too wet to golf. At any rate, book a room, suite, or two-bedroom cottage at Silverado for two nights, requesting Cottage Drive so that you'll be on the golf course. This may put you at some distance from the restaurant and pro shop, but a bellman will pick you up if you do not wish to drive. And go ahead and make your dinner reservations for the evening of Day 1 at the Royal Oak at Silverado. Also, it is recommended that you reserve any spa services at this time; Silverado's new spa, across the street from the main property, is beyond compare.

Call Bistro Jeanty for a Day 2 dinner reservation.

Make a mid-morning Day 1 tee time for Napa Golf Course, an early-morning Day 2 tee time for either course at Silverado, and a Day 3 early-morning tee time for Chardonnay, inquiring about availability on the more private and expensive Shakespeare Course if you prefer.

Call to schedule a late-afternoon Day 3 visit to the di Rosa Preserve, if your Day 3 tee time allows.

And, finally, consider scheduling a visit to one of the wineries that take visitors only by appointment for the afternoon of Day 2. Schramsberg, just south of Calistoga, is highly recommended for its tasting and tours, and if David Nelson is your host you'll be talking golf as well.

day 1 Our escape begins at the foot of Napa Valley, on a golf course that probably came to be to provide a buffer around the occasionally demonic Napa River, and so the best times to visit Napa Golf Course (also known as Kennedy for its location inside the John F. Kennedy Memorial Park, and also known as The Lagoons for reasons we shall discuss) are between April (or even May, if the spring has been wet) and November. The course has a history of shutting down for periods of time when it gets really saturated, so if you want to go play in winter, call and ask about the conditions—the friendly staff won't steer you wrong.

By the time you find your way into the parking lot, you've probably already been cheered up by the sight of all that traffic out on I-80 going other places. Hopefully you're a little early, because Napa has excellent practice facilities, and it would be a good idea to do some chipping and putting. "Face the fact you'll be chipping and putting a lot," says head pro Monte Koch, who describes the greens as "upside-down teacups," not unlike those to be seen at far more hoity-toity places like Pinehurst No. 2. That, of course, means the greens are usually swift, because upside-down teacups don't hold much water.

Most of the players here walk, and you should too. The classic parkland design features mean that the next tee is probably adjacent to the green where you're putting, and the riverside location promises little in the way of elevation changes. Take time to enjoy the variety of pine, sequoia, and oak trees, and imagine what the course must have looked like when Jack

Fleming and Bob Baldock finished it in 1958. Enjoy the lovely landscaping, and see what flowers are blooming around the tee boxes. (Keep in mind that bees like it here too.) Feel the breeze off the bay on the fifth–sixth and 13th–14th holes. Or is that fourth–fifth and 14th–15th?

By the time you visit, the nines most likely will have been reversed, and by the time you get to hole number 10 you'll see why. It's not a very long par-4, but it was a tough hole for openers, with a nasty little lagoon to the right and a big old oak tree between the landing area of all but the longest drives and the green. Then there's the lateral hazard land off to the left, and much potential for disaster, which is not the way that Donald Ross (designer of Pinehurst No. 2) would start off the unsuspecting golfer out for a good time. The old hole number 10, a gentle dogleg right to an elevated green, isn't easy either—in fact, it's rated the toughest hole on that side—but as long as you keep your golf ball out of the driving range to the right chances are good you will make it from tee to green with one ball. Not many players, however, play 18 holes here with one ball—there's water on 12 or so holes, and the pro shop does a good business in used golf ball sales at the turn.

Switching the nines also makes sense because the old hole number 9 makes for a magnificent finishing hole leading up to the old (we hope soon to be refurbished) 1960s clubhouse. (Can it be we will someday think of a building erected in the '60s as a historic landmark in need of protection? Not this one.) And if CourseCo, the management company running the show at Napa, does the job right, you'll be ready to sit on a comfortable deck, have a delicious lunch and wet beverage, and reflect on your round while watching other players start theirs.

After lunch, pull out of the parking lot and head out to the Napa Vallejo Highway and turn left. This becomes Soscol Avenue. Take the 121 fork, which you'll see off to the right—this becomes the Silverado Trail—and turn right at Trancas Street (the Lake Berryessa sign). Go about one mile to Atlas Peak Road, turn left, and follow the signs to check in at Silverado.

Check-in at Silverado is one of the high points. Just pulling into the long driveway and cruising past the tennis courts up to the old, 1870s Miller Mansion hollers, "You're on vacation!" The Miller Mansion, by the way, isn't related to Johnny Miller, the former PGA Tour star now broadcaster who is among the members here (he owns a house on a hill overlooking the course and valley). It was General John Franklin Miller, a Civil War hero, who sought refuge here in the mid-19th century and bought a 1,200-acre property christened La Vergne in memory of one of his battles. The mansion's great living room is now the lounge, and legend has it that an old Spanish adobe is concealed within the walls of the first story because it would have been bad luck to destroy it.

By the 1950s, the mansion was part of the 1,199 acres sold to the

Silverado Land Company (owner Vesta Peak Maxwell kept an acre for her own home) and developed as a resort. The mansion, now a gracious memorial to days gone by, houses meeting rooms and restaurants and gets new arrivals into the spirit of things.

If you've arrived before 4 P.M., you now have a couple of hours to indulge yourself in a spa service, a little time by the swimming pool (the quietest of these is bound to be the spa, where children are not allowed) or a quick winery visit. A good choice for the latter might be Mumm Napa Valley, an easy ride north on the Silverado Trail—you'll see it on the left at 8445. Mumm stays open until 5 in winter, 6 in summer, and there's a self-guided tour through an art gallery with ever-changing exhibits that will make you feel like you deserve the reward of a sparkling tasting on the terrace. It's a great place to spend a restful hour.

This evening, you're in for a treat: dinner at the Royal Oak at Silverado. You should hope it's still light when you sit down, because as golfers you'll appreciate the view of the South Course at twilight. The formality of the mahogany-trimmed dining room may put you off at first—or it may invite you in if you've dressed up—but rest assured that we dined here après golf on one occasion and were warmly greeted by the staff and never felt out of place. Chef Peter Pahk is a magician in the kitchen and a pretty darned good golfer too; you might get him to come and say hello and tell you about his latest round at Silverado if the room hasn't yet gotten too busy. Appetizers are mouthwatering, and if you're a Caesar salad fan here's your chance to enjoy tableside preparation. In fact, to enjoy your meal to the hilt, consider sharing the porterhouse so that you'll have room for dessert and the liqueur cart that will land at your table at the end of it all.

And now it's time for you to end it all so that you'll make it to the first tee on time tomorrow.

day II Your morning tee time should get you around the course—North or South, whichever is in play today for resort guests—in little more than four hours. Whichever course you're playing, long-time head pro Jeff Goodwin promises you a good time. "My whole theme here is to have fun and enjoy yourself," he says. "Golf is supposed to be fun, and we've got a traditional design here that allows you to do that. It's not one of those courses they were building in the '80s, when the theme seemed to be to make the course as difficult as you could, every place like Carnoustie, where the average player wouldn't even be able to finish."

If you didn't have breakfast in the Clubhouse Bar and Grill, you may want to have a quick lunch here now. If you're full of energy and ready to go exploring Adult Disneyland, put your clubs away and drive immediately to V. Sattui—north on the Silverado Trail, left on Zinfandel, right on

Highway 29, and it's there on your right. Your first mission is to taste some of the wines, which are available for purchase only here and never to be found on any menus, and choose a bottle that you can drink right now, with lunch. Then proceed to the deli, pick up some bread, pâté, cheese, pasta salad, whatever strikes your fancy, find a table under a tree, and picnic. There are prettier spots in the valley, better wines, less busy wineries, but no place that offers the V. Sattui complete package with as much convenience. And from here, you'll have easy access to those other wineries with better views or wines or ambience.

A few words about wine-tasting and winery touring here. There are two extremes of experiences in the Napa Valley and everything in between. There is the place that makes great wines and is selective about what they'll pour for you (probably charging you a fee), and the place that makes lots of wine and will freely pour you everything starting with the orange juice they served for breakfast (perhaps charging a fee for some of their reserve wines). In between are places of real character that are proud to show off their facilities along with a select tasting, most likely at a price; smaller, family wineries off the beaten path that will welcome your visit warmly if you would just call ahead; and wineries that offer some special treat such as a restaurant (Domaine Chandon) or tram (Sterling) or art collection (Clos Pegase, Hess) or gardens (Chateau Montelena) that will break up the red-and-white monotony for the wine-challenged in your party. The real wine lovers might enjoy a series of touring-and-tasting trips, each of them focusing on a particular varietal (one for cabernet sauvignon, one for chardonnay, another for sparklers), but they're probably not going to have any time for golf, are they?

But the rest of you want *us* to suggest the perfect wine-tasting itinerary for *you?* What, you say, that's what we're here for? Well, within the context of golfing and lodging at Silverado, and considering that you're setting aside this one afternoon for tasting and touring rather than torturing yourself on another go-round of the links, here's a possible itinerary for an afternoon of some fun in the wine country.

First stop is one of the friendliest tasting rooms around, with excellent wines: Merryvale, just a fraction of a mile north of Sattui on Highway 29. From here, travel north on 29 into Calistoga and turn right at Dunaweal Lane for a stop at Clos Pegase, on your left. Clos Pegase specializes in cabernets, and it offers a "Reserve Room," where you can taste its most special wines for a fee. The layout of the building and grounds invites strolling among paintings and sculptures. From here, proceed to Sterling, just across Dunaweal, for a true Adult Disneyland experience, a tram up a 300-foot knoll to the winery. Here you can take a self-guided tour or go immediately to the winery's roof deck picnic area for a snack and flight of vintage wines. Or, skip the tour and go directly to the tasting room, on your left as you come out of the tram, and hope you can sit at a table amid the trees outside. Sterling is the winery even nondrinkers appreciate.

If you've booked the last tour of the day at Schramsberg, now's the time to truck on over there. Go back to Highway 29, go north to Peterson Road, and make a left, following the narrow tree-shaded road up the hill to the winery. Jacob Schram established this 200-acre estate in 1862; today it produces some of the valley's finest sparklers, which have been a favorite of U.S. presidents. The walls of the reception room are covered with lots of old photos, and the caves are just behind the cozy tasting room, where a fee is charged but pours are premium and ample. There are four tours every day, by appointment only, so call ahead at 707/942-4558.

From here or from Sterling, cut across Dunaweal to the Silverado Trail and head south. En route, you might see if Rombauer (3522, on the right) or Oakville Ranch (7850, on the left) is still open and pouring; both wineries have pretty views, and Rombauer makes a killer chardonnay.

When you reach the Yountville Cross, turn right and proceed to Washington Street in Yountville, turning right and stopping at Bistro Jeanty for dinner. You'll immediately be in the front dining room, which has a bar; there are more tables, and a more intimate atmosphere, in the back. Romantics will want the deuce by the fireplace.

Here you'll find what's described as regional homey French cuisine, which means you might start with any of three or four pâtés that are offered, and perhaps the smoked salmon carpaccio style, or the endive and pear salad with stilton cheese. Then it's sole meunière with mashed potatoes and lemon caper butter, or steak tartare with pommes frites, or maybe the entrecôte grille—a rib-eye steak with french fries and béarnaise sauce. Do try to save room for dessert. We ordered the vanilla ice cream with chocolate sauce and couldn't understand what was taking so long. When it arrived, we realized someone had just made the chocolate sauce. Heaven.

Back to Silverado now. How about a nightcap in the lounge?

day III You're up early and most likely checking out to head for Chardonnay Golf Club, though if there are nongolfers in the group they probably will want to stay at Silverado for the morning for tennis, massage, brunch, or absolutely nothing at all. Or, the nongolfers could leave the golfers at Chardonnay for the morning and visit the di Rosa Preserve nearby. Our plan here calls for golf and then di Rosa, energy willing.

Not that the golf will be physically wearing. Chardonnay discourages walking on the private Shakespeare Course, and good sense rules it out on the public Vineyards Course. There are elevated tees on both courses that make for awkward green-to-tee transitions while creating breathtaking views you'll enjoy most when you're cruising along and not panting up the hill lugging your golf bag. And the cart's included in the daily fees.

We're going to assume you're playing the Vineyards Course, particularly since the Shakespeare Course may have by now been swallowed up by the new Eagle Vines project. To get there, leave Silverado the way you came and make a left turn onto Jamieson Canyon Road (Highway 12 toward Fairfield), turning right at the stoplight that marks the course turnoff.

You'll be treated to Chardonnay's premium service from the time you stop at the bag drop to the time your clubs are cleaned. If you're early, the practice facilities can keep you busy—and if you're racing to the tee, there's a small practice green way up on the hill that serves as the Vineyards Course launching pad.

There's a 1,600-yard difference between the most forward of the five sets of tees and the back, and the course seems to have been made interesting from any of them. There aren't forced carries off most of the tees, but there are some barrancas and creeks that create risk-reward situations on par-5 fairways and on approach shots. A good guide for selecting tees at Chardonnay might be the par-3s—there are three per side, and if you're looking at the scorecard thinking you'll need 5-iron or more to reach them all, consider stepping up.

There have been many changes on the Vineyards Course since it opened. Jack Barry says the previous owners made the Shakespeare Course their pet at the expense of the Vineyards, and so renovations have been beautifying the course and dramatizing the views. Surrounded as they are by vineyards and without too many mature tall trees, these are big-sky courses on the order of Pebble Beach in the way they showcase Mother Nature's doings overhead. The first hole provides an appropriate introduction: you stand up there overlooking vineyards and golf holes, eyeing Mount Tamalpais and the San Pablo Bay and miles and miles of sky, then take a deep breath and swing away. As narrow as are many of the fairways on the Shakespeare Course, the Vineyards is more inviting, with greens that are larger and less undulating but still smooth and quick. Barry's favorite hole is the par-3 fourth, which sweeps from between 132 to 216 yards from a towering tee complex down to a 22,000-square-foot green with three tiers, descending down from the left. You may well be on the green and want to chip; local rules allow you to do that, but please move the ball off the green first.

Head pro Ray Graziani is a big fan of the Vineyards par-5s, particularly the third, a double dogleg with a creek guarding the left side of the fairway and then cutting across it to set off an elevated green that's on the small side for a 545-yard hole—or did it just seem small? Well, you decide. "It's fun to see how many ways the hole can be played," Graziani says. The par-3s and par-5s are certainly the more memorable holes here, and it's a treat to have six of each.

After your round, which should have moved fairly quickly, the staff will clean and pack your clubs. Then you can retire to the Sand Trap, where the best club selection you've made all day might be the club sandwich. Soups and pastas are also delicious here, and there's a solid list of wines by the glass.

Once you've rested, it's probably time to head for your appointment at the di Rosa Preserve, where art and nature have embraced on a 200-acre estate that once was home to art collector Rene di Rosa. You'll want to backtrack a little, following the Highway 12/121 signs toward Sonoma. The preserve, at 5200 Carneros Highway 121, will be on your right. The former home is now a gallery of contemporary, eclectic, some might say funky works that spill out into the fields and lake outside. The 2.5-hour tours (the only way to visit) are by reservation only. None are offered on a Sunday, so if your escape is a weekend jaunt, adjust the itinerary accordingly. If it's Sunday, you might just have to go home after your round of golf at Chardonnay. Oh well, it happens to the best of us.

NOTES

Money Savers. The El Bonita is the budget lodging choice in the Napa Valley—though budget in this chapter means only that you *might* get a room for under $100. Plan a budget escape for midweek, checking the Internet and local golf guides for coupons to play Chardonnay and Napa, and substitute the fine Yountville nine for Silverado.

Nongolfers. You will want to take the Wine Train for lunch while your partner is playing on Day 1. The spa at Silverado—or a mudbath up in Calistoga—can keep you busy on Day 2. And there's shopping to be done on Day 3.

Big Spenders. Meadowood and L'Auberge du Soleil are two of the most wonderful resorts in the world (the former gets the nod here for its beautifully manicured, wooded nine-holer); make sure you take your sweetie.

Time Savers. Silverado offers overnight golf-and-stay packages all year; add a treatment at the spa and dinner at the Royal Oak, and you've crammed a great escape into 24 hours.

Low-Handicappers. Don't miss Napa Golf Course just because it is a muni. It is one of the most challenging, yet still fair, courses in Northern California, and the upgrades under way make it a worthwhile destination.

High-Handicappers. You may have more fun in the Napa Valley by playing just nine holes a day, conserving the rest of your hours for wine tasting and touring.

Extended Stay. Bring lots of money.

Courses

ITINERARY SELECTIONS

Napa Golf Course at Kennedy Park

2295 Streblow Dr.
Napa, CA 94558
707/255-4333
website www.playnapa.com

This municipal course has been one of Northern California's best bargains for years, with green fees that start at a little more than $20 during the week on a course where few would need a cart. After noon, the rates drop in a hurry, first at noon and again at 2. Senior and student discounts are available, and players should also check the website and any local golf publications for coupons.

> **SCORECARD**
>
> (pre-renovation)
> **Architects:** Bob Baldock and Jack Fleming, 1968
> **Course Record:** 65, Jerry McGee
> **Blue:** Par 72, 6,730 yards, 72.3 rating for men, 123 slope
> **White:** Par 72, 6,506 yards, 71.2 rating for men, 120 slope; 76.8 rating for women, 137 slope
> **Red:** Par 73, 5,956 yards, 73.6 rating for women, 130 slope
> **Tee times** may be made up to two weeks in advance.

Another nice feature is "The Lunch Bucket" range program, which gives range visitors 70 balls, lunch, and a soft drink for $6 or so. Tournament packages are also bargain basement at Napa, and, at least while construction has been under way, carts have not been required.

TEE TIDBITS | You can wear just about anything that's legal on head, body, and feet here. The clubhouse is rather old and shabby, but a new restaurant and bigger pro shop were in the works with course renovations. The course redesign isn't likely to change one unfortunate fact some locals refer to as "The Lagoons." That is, it tends to flood when the winter rains arrive in full force and generally isn't back in primo condition until April. An estimated 65 percent of the players walk, and pace of play is generally surprisingly good for such a busy, difficult course. There's a chipping practice area near the range, and you will want to spend a few minutes on the putting green at the first tee. At nearly 6,000 yards, this has been by far one of the longest courses anywhere from the red tees.

Silverado Country Club

1600 Atlas Peak Rd.
Napa, CA 94558
800/362-4727, golf shop 707/257-5460, fax 707/226-6829
website www.silveradoresort.com

Silverado is a relatively busy private course, so try to make a tee time when you reserve your room. Without a golf package, green fees will run at around $120 per player, including a cart. But without a room, the reciprocal fee for country club members and outside players who call the morning they want to play is even higher. There's no walking allowed at Silverado except for members; it's a security problem more than anything, and a darned shame for resort guests who would enjoy strolling the relatively flat grounds here. And carts are paths only.

TEE TIDBITS | A golf package is the way to go at Silverado. The best of these starts every December. Jeff Goodwin's pro shop is one of the best and biggest anywhere. Wear your country club clothes. Metal spikes are still permitted. The big range has a wonderful, bunkered short game practice area. Generally, one of the courses alternately is members-only on any given day. Though most of the regulars have a favorite, there's no difference between the North and South that makes one appreciably better than the other. The South is used in the Senior PGA Tour's Transamerica every autumn primarily because it sets up better for spectators. The North is reminiscent of the original 1955 18-holer. The Silverado Bar and Grill serves breakfast and lunch daily, but a far better setting for your 19th hole would be the Patio Terrace of the Main Lounge, overlooking the 18th green of the South Course.

SCORECARD

Architect: Robert Trent Jones Jr., 1955
North Course Record: 62, Lon Hinkle
South Course Record: 62, J. C. Snead
North Blue: Par 72, 6,854 yards, 73.4 rating for men, 131 slope
North White: Par 72, 6,331 yards, 70.9 rating for men, 126 slope
North Red: Par 72, 5,857 yards, 68.7 rating for men, 121 slope; 73.3 rating for women, 128 slope
South Blue: Par 72, 6,663 yards, 72.4 rating for men, 129 slope
South White: Par 72, 6,254 yards, 70.5 rating for men, 124 slope
South Red: Par 72, 5,642 yards, 67.7 rating for men, 117 slope; 72.7 rating for women, 127 slope

Chardonnay Golf Club

2555 Jamieson Canyon Rd. (Hwy. 12)
Napa, CA 94558
707/257-1900, ext. 2263 for tee times, ext. 2244 for golf shop, fax 707/257-0613
website www.chardonnaygolfclub.com

You can make tee times up to a month in advance for the public access Vineyards Course. If you would like to play the Shakespeare Course and do not have a country club membership, you might try calling and checking on availability on the day you want to play. Or, you can stay at one of the many hotels and inns on Chardonnay's preferred lodgings list, which is regularly updated on the website. Regular weekday rates on the Vineyards Course start at about $50, depending on the season, and include a cart, so few players walk. Weekday rates on the Shakespeare Course, with cart and range balls, start at about $90, and hardly anyone walks though carts generally are to remain on the

SCORECARD

Architect: Algie Pulley, 1987
Course Record: NA
Vineyards Black: Par 72, 6,816 yards, 73.8 rating for men, 129 slope
Vineyards Blue: Par 72, 6,450 yards, 72.1 rating for men, 126 slope
Vineyards White: Par 72, 6,022 yards, 70.3 rating for men, 123 slope
Vineyards Gold: Par 72, 5,584 yards, 72.7 rating for women, 129 slope
Vineyards Red: Par 72, 5,223 yards, 70.7 rating for women, 124 slope
Shakespeare Gold: Par 72, 7,001 yards, 74.4 rating for men, 138 slope
Shakespeare Black: Par 72, 6,593 yards, 72.3 rating for men, 132 slope

paths. Lodging packages are good for discounts of 30 percent weekdays and 25 percent weekends—and you can reserve these up to a year in advance.

TEE TIDBITS | Many courses could learn a thing or two from the superior service at Chardonnay. From the time you arrive at the curb until your cleaned clubs are returned to your trunk, you are undeniably the guest of a gracious host. Note this local rule, which tells you something about the shape of the greens at Chardonnay: "If the apron of the green intersects the line of play between your ball and the hole, you must move your ball off the green if you choose to chip or pitch." Dress code is country club—no jeans, cutoffs, or short shorts. There's a range with grass stations and a short-game practice area. Both courses are wonderful, but naturally playing the more exclusive and expensive Shakespeare is a more luxurious and relaxed experience. When it's been dry, both courses play shorter than their distances would suggest, which means it's often okay to be cocky in your tee selection. John Jacobs Golf School comes here every summer and remains into October. The pro shop is full of exquisite merchandise, and though Vineyards Course players may not use the Member Bar and Grille, the Sand Trap Bar and Grill's diverse menu and cozy atmosphere should suffice for anyone looking for a quick breakfast or more leisurely lunch.

SCORECARD — *continued*

Shakespeare Green: Par 72, 6,147 yards, 70.5 rating for men, 126 slope; 75.9 rating for women, 136 slope

Shakespeare Cream: Par 72, 5,463 yards, 72.3 rating for women, 128 slope

Vineyards course tee times are taken a month in advance on the website, 14 days in advance by phone, although with lodging packages you can book times on either course up to a year in advance.

Vintners Golf Club
7901 Solano Ave.
Yountville, CA 94599
707/944-1992 tee times, fax 707/944-1993

Green fees may seem high for a nine-hole course at around $18 Monday through Friday, $24 weekends, but the 18-hole rate of $6 more is a bargain considering the immaculate conditions and pretty setting. Carts are $24 for 18 holes, but it's hard to see where you'd need one; the course is laid out so tightly that it may be peerless when it comes to walker-friendliness. There are discounts on junior, senior, twilight, and resident green fees.

SCORECARD

Architect: Casey O'Callaghan, 1999
Course Record: 63, Rodney Wilson and Kane Lack
White: Par 68, 5,140 yards, 62.8 rating for men, 134 slope
Gold: Par 68, 4,302 yards, 62.8 rating for women, 108 slope
Tee times can be reserved up to 30 days in advance.

TEE TIDBITS | Bring your nonmetal spikes to Yountville, where you're otherwise welcome to dress as you please. The classy and simple course logo will tempt you to buy something in the pro shop, where reasonable prices seem to prevail. The Lakeside Grill, inside the small but attractive clubhouse, has been attracting area nongolfers for its low prices, delicious food, large beer selection, and pretty terrace. There's a 36-station covered driving range with target greens. Some of the pads are even on natural grass. You'll want to manage your pace of play to make the turn two hours after you start, since that nine-hole tee time is blocked out in advance for your foursome. Play the back white tees and then the front white tees; shorter hitters may want to play the golds, in the same order.

ALTERNATIVES

On the way to or from Napa, an absolute must to play is **Hiddenbrooke Country Club,** one of the most wonderful daily fee courses anywhere. In the fall of 2000, the LPGA brought one of its premier events here to test its top money winners of the year. It's an Arnold Palmer course that's so sprawling, virtually no one walks this course, but cart and range balls are covered in the green fees, which start at around $75 nonprime time. No parallel fairways and, once upon a time, no houses, though that sadly has begun to change—and, eventually, so might Hiddenbrooke's daily fee status. It's a tough, tough layout, so definitely do not be cocky and definitely do consider conditions when you select your tee (there are five choices, beginning with the Palmers, rated at 72.8 and 142 slope, down to the reds, 66.4 and 117). It can be very windy here in the afternoon. A huge new clubhouse adds a touch of class to the experience, so wear your country club clothes and soft spikes. Nonmembers can call seven days in advance for tee times. ■ 2708 OVERLOOK DR., JUST OFF I-80, VALLEJO, CA 94591; 707/557-8181

There are three other nine-hole courses worthy of mention in the Napa Valley area, and each one is bound to have its fans.

On the upscale end of the spectrum is **Meadowood**'s 2,001-yard par-31 course, which the resort describes as an "executive walking course." The only kind of carts allowed here are pull carts, which makes the round feel so much like a walk in the park. The course is set on a narrow ribbon of a tree-lined valley, and there are five par-3s and four par-4s. Playing time should be no more than an hour and 45 minutes, which leaves plenty of time for wine-tasting, croquet, or a massage, and golf shoes are not required. The course, however, is open only to members and hotel guests, and the green fee for hotel guests is $35. That's a whopper for such a tiny course, but it is private and it is delightful. ■ 900 MEADOWOOD LANE, ST. HELENA, CA 94574; 707/963-3646; WEBSITE WWW.MEADOWOOD.COM

If you'd like to stop and golf in the middle of an afternoon of wine-tasting and winery touring, **Chimney Rock** is your stop. On the Silverado Trail and owned by the Chimney Rock winery, this was once an 18-hole course. Remember, though, there's more money in grapes than golf. Now there are nine holes, but at least they're of major-league length, with the course playing to 3,412 yards from the tips. There are two par-5s and two par-3s, and the highlight is the short sixth hole that leads to the winery's door. Conditions here tend to be rough—we couldn't help but think how great it *could* have been—but the place draws throngs of locals, and it would be wise to have a reservation. ■ 5320 SILVERADO TRAIL, NAPA, CA 94558; 707/255-3363

Finally—and the end seems a somewhat odd place for the oldest course in California—there's **Aetna Springs Golf Course.** At least, we hope there is. A proposal to renovate the crumbling 1892 resort was defeated in 2000, and operators were uncertain the course would be able to survive. Well, it's not surprising, because one of the special things about the course is its remote location (but only 25 winding minutes or so from St. Helena), which leads to relatively low usage. Aetna Springs is only 2,690 yards long, but, oh boy, decisions, decisions. There are some ancient oaks in the middle of the course, and a creek forces one to think carefully before pulling out the driver. You can play all day for $15 or $20, and the friendly folks who work, or worked, here make you feel like staying all day. They say it's at its best in the spring, when the wildflowers in the adjacent meadow put on their color show. ■ 1600 AETNA SPRINGS RD., POPE VALLEY, CA 94567; 707/965-2115

Lodging

ITINERARY SELECTION

With so many lodging options in and around the Napa Valley—covering the range from no-tell motel up to the most secluded and exclusive resort properties—it was difficult to choose a home base for a golf escape, considering you'll be doing more than just golfing or you'd probably have stayed home. The **Silverado Country Club and Resort** was simply the natural choice for anyone who wants to play as many of the county's championship courses as possible, because it is difficult and expensive to play here unless you are a guest of the resort or of a member.

That said, well, Silverado isn't a bad escape destination for anyone who wants to get away. With 350 rooms, 17 tennis courts, nine pools, and a topnotch spa, Silverado appeals to conferences, foursomes, and parties of two and does business accordingly. The rooms can be differently configured—bedroom, suite, and two-bedroom cottage are among the possibilities—and many of them are right on the golf course. In fact, you should request Cottage Drive accommodations if you'd like to see birdies and not just birds from your patio. At the right time of year, you can get a room and golf for two for less than $200; in-season rates soar, but there's usually some sort of overnight package offering golf at nonpeak hours for well under $200 per person. ■ 1600 ATLAS PEAK RD., NAPA, CA 94558; 707/757-0200; WEBSITE WWW. SILVERADORESORT.COM

The only other way to be sure of playing golf at Silverado is to stay at the **Fairway Condominiums,** a separately managed group of 14 two-bedroom, two-bathroom units on the North Course. These condos have full kitchens and entitle you to access to Silverado's facilities, though you probably will have to spring for the green fees. Rates start at $250 a night at slow times. ■ 100 FAIRWAY DR., NAPA, CA 94558; 707/255-6644

GOLF PACKAGE OPTIONS

Chardonnay Golf Club partners with a long list of accommodations, in all budget categories and ranges of ambiance, to offer discounted golf and pre-ferred tee times. Call the golf course or check its website for the complete and current list.

And then there's **Meadowood,** which is much, much more than a mere golf package option, but we didn't want to create a new heading just for this exclusive and secluded hideaway just off the Silverado Trail at St. Helena. Meadowood is surely the most famous property in the valley, and for one-bedroom units that start at around $350 it carries a reputation for service that is everything you want it to be: competent, friendly, discreet, complete. There are 250 acres, comprising the charming nine-hole "executive walking course" that is reserved for members and guests of the resort, an adjacent croquet course, tennis courts, a spa, swimming pools, outdoor hot tubs, and even a wine center. Guest quarters are all over the place, so be sure to ask if you'd like to overlook the golf course or be near the spa. The Restaurant is not as well known a special occasion destination as it should be, and The Grill is an excellent option before and after golf, which will cost you an extra $35, but then, if you're staying at Meadowood money is most likely not an issue. ■ 900 MEADOWOOD LANE, ST. HELENA, CA 94574; 707/963-3646; WEBSITE WWW.MEADOWOOD.COM

ALTERNATIVES

You want alternatives, Napa Valley is the place for you. The only option that often seems to be closed is the one in the budget category, so we'll start right there with **El Bonita,** absolutely the best bargain in the wine country and not to be found in most of the guidebooks because it doesn't need to shill to writers to fill its 41 units. Rooms here start at around $85, but if you're passing by on a weekday and have no reservation but cash is in your pocket, don't be shy about bargaining. The rooms are nice and rather large, all of them with refrigerators and microwaves, and there's a pool and hot tub. Avoid the poolside rooms, however, because it can be noisy. Much nicer are the garden units in the rear. ■ 195 MAIN ST. (HWY. 29), ST. HELENA, CA 94574; 800/541-3284; WEBSITE WWW.ELBONITA.COM

Napa Valley's wine glass overflows with sweet little bed and breakfasts, and also the lavish, posh kind where you want to whisper. The competition is fierce enough; you're not about to go wrong with any of the establishments listed with the Napa Valley Conference and Visitors Bureau, or with Bed and Breakfast Inns of Napa Valley. Here, we'll just make note of two of the newer and two of the established candidates.

New to Yountville is **Lavender,** one of the famous Four Sisters Inns, distinguishable by the teddy bears they keep and sell. Lavender's location is prime: it's barely a block from French Laundry, and a quiet and peaceful few blocks away from the action on Washington Street. Six of the eight rooms are in cottages, with lots of privacy seldom to be found in places like this. The cottage rooms have private patios with hot tubs, and bathrooms are as big as many bedrooms. The two rooms in the house (one is actually a suite; another is ideal for wheelchair access) are more in keeping with the style of the oldest house in town (1858). A full breakfast and daily hors d'oeuvres service come with the $175 and up price tag, and you should inquire about golf packages. ■ 2020 WEBBER AVE., YOUNTVILLE, CA 94599; 800/522-4140

Also inquire about golf packages at another wonderful new property, **Villagio Inn and Spa.** This is the little sister of the Vintage Inn, just down Washington Street, but it's a little sister only in age, not in size and grandeur. There's a feeling of Tuscany, helped along by the vineyards outside the lobby terrace, where a champagne continental breakfast is served every morning for guests. Villagio has a variety of accommodations among its simply furnished 112 rooms, all with fireplaces and coffeemakers, starting at $180 or so. There are fountains and water courses, two tennis courts, and a pool that looks fit for Hollywood (in a good way). The location, service, and style of Villagio (just across Highway 29 from the Vintners Golf Club) make it ideal for a Napa Valley golf escape. ■ 6541 WASHINGTON ST., YOUNTVILLE, CA 94599; 800/351-1133; WEBSITE WWW.VILLAGIO.COM

Another larger inn that, like Villagio, avoids cookie-cutter room styles is the **Harvest Inn,** which offers 54 elegant, antique-filled cottages, many with wet bars and fireplaces. The Harvest Inn's St. Helena location puts it in the heart of the wine country, and though rooms start at more than $150 in the best of times, coupons are worth watching for in area tourist publications. ■ 1 MAIN ST. (HWY. 29), ST. HELENA, CA 94575; 800/950-8466; WEBSITE WWW.HARVESTINN.COM

Then there's **Auberge du Soleil,** which you are urged to visit for cocktails on the deck at the end of a winery touring session. Be forewarned: You may take one look around at the vineyard views, the lovely gardens, the huge sun-drenched pool, and the charming cottages and decide to stay. Be forewarned again: The rooms start at about $300 high season, the cottages at about $450. For this, Auberge du Soleil promises peace and pampering (children are discouraged) along with tennis and workout facilities. ■ 180 RUTHERFORD HILL RD., RUTHERFORD, CA 94573; 707/963-1211; WEBSITE WWW. AUBERGEDUSOLEIL.COM

Dining

ITINERARY SELECTIONS

The **Royal Oak** at Silverado serves up dinner and a view of the golf course (hole number 18 South) nightly 6–11, and reservations are required. Entrées start at about $20, and the wine list is impressive. Suggested dress code is "smart casual." A sample menu is displayed at Silverado's website. ■ 1600 ATLAS PEAK RD., NAPA; 707/257-0200, EXT. 5363; WEBSITE WWW.SILVERADORESORT.COM

V. Sattui opens every day at 9 A.M. and stays open longer than most valley wineries, 6 P.M. in summer and 5 P.M. in winter. You'll find some 200 cheeses most any time, but for the widest selection of fresh deli salads, pastas, and daily specials, arrive early in the lunch hour. ■ 1111 WHITE LANE (HWY. 29), ST. HELENA; 707/963-7774

Bistro Jeanty is open all day from 11:30, with entrées starting at about $15 and ranging up to the fillet au poivre at about $25. Reservations are recommended for dinner. ■ 6510 WASHINGTON ST., YOUNTVILLE; 707/944-0103

The **Sand Trap Bar and Grill** at Chardonnay Golf Club is open every day into the late afternoon for breakfast and lunch. Most of the customers prefer traditional American golf course food like burgers, nachos, and salad, so the world's best crabcake made only a brief appearance on the menu. We've especially enjoyed the pork spring rolls and every salad or sandwich we've had. Service is friendly—or you can pick up the phone at the ninth tee and pick up your lunch before you go to the 10th. ■ 2555 JAMIESON CANYON RD. (HWY. 12), NAPA; 707/257-1900

ALTERNATIVES

You should hope someone in your escape group is willing to research what's the latest and greatest on the Napa Valley restaurant scene. (Try the message boards at website www.napavalley.com for the latest reviews by regular diners like us.) With the CIA (no, not that one but the Culinary Institute of America) right there on Highway 29 training chefs to prepare food, and everyone around making wine to go with food, it's no wonder that there are more selections than a golfer needs to worry about, what with having to putt the speedy greens and all. Here's the longest list of options you'll find in any of the chapters of this book, just because they're there. But before you start perusing, if you're on a budget we must advise you to fill yourself up at the golf courses after your round, pick up picnic food at St. Helena's Dean and DeLuca gourmet grocery or the deli at V. Sattui winery, and/or do some cooking in the rarely used kitchen in your suite at Silverado.

But the food nuts will have made reservations at **French Laundry** (6640 Washington St., Yountville; 707/944-2380) 60 days in advance. It is probably the most world-renowned restaurant, with by far the most world-renowned chef (Thomas Keller), in foodaholic Northern California, which explains why you can't get a table at a restaurant where fixed price meals start at $80, not including wine. Cuisine is French-California-country, and the atmosphere is lovely, in a stone building in Yountville that was once, yes, a laundry.

If you're intrigued by French Laundry but would prefer a simpler meal with a smaller bill, then you may like **Bouchon** (6534 Washington St., Yountville; 707/944-8037), a very French bistro owned by Keller and operated by his brother Joseph. Here are the French classics like soufflés and quiches, a warm spinach salad, and a California (remember where we are now) wine list, all presented in a large space with an intimate feel. Bouchon is also a worthy stop for a nightcap; it is open until 2 A.M.

You can sample the cuisine of whichever chef is likely to be the next to open up his own French restaurant in Yountville at **Domaine Chandon** (next door to the Yountville nine, at 1 California Dr., Yountville; 800/736-2892). The restaurant at the winery is excellent, with its offerings of olive-crusted salmon, caramelized scallops, and of course pâté and carpaccio for starters. Domaine Chandon serves lunch and dinner; we recommend a leisurely, expensive lunch (entrées start at around $15, and you'll want more than that) on the trellised patio. Reservations suggested in season.

Though the name is French, the menu at **Auberge du Soleil** (180 Rutherford Hill Rd., Rutherford; 707/967-3111) is more eclectic, closer to California Mediterranean with an Asian touch; witness the seven sparkling sins appetizer selection and the tempura ahi-salmon sashimi. You also may find ostrich, sterling salmon, duck, and lamb. And the "five senses meal," with wines to match, paired with the spectacular view from the hillside terrace, will make you forget that you procrastinated about calling French Laundry until 59 days ahead and couldn't get a rezzie. You may spend almost as much here, with entrées running in the $30s, so perhaps you might prefer to visit for breakfast. Reservations urged in any case.

If talking big spending hasn't moved your eye off the page, we must urge you to visit **The Restaurant at Meadowood** (900 Meadowood Lane, St. Helena; 800/458-8080), just off the Silverado Trail in St. Helena. In a beautiful setting above the golf course, you'll find dreamy dishes like an heirloom tomato salad of vine-ripened tomato sorbet, balsamic reduction, and basil; a sweet white corn bisque; and grilled ahi tuna with crispy ravioli, ratatouille, and tomato coulis. The advice here is do not pass up the day boat scallops if they are on the menu, and save room for dessert. Every night a vintner menu is offered, four courses with four wines paired, and the service is sublime. It's special, it's romantic—not the place for your rowdy post-tournament party—and even though it's expensive you will not feel cheated. A better place for a casual meal of similar quality is The Grill below, which offers an even better view of the golf course in an intimate setting and serves breakfast, lunch, and dinner.

The **Wine Train** (1275 McKinstrey St., Napa; 800/427-4124; website www.winetrain.com) would be listed under Straying Off Course if the food didn't have such a fine reputation. You get on the train in Napa, and it takes you up and down the valley for a three-hour ride that includes lunch, dinner, or brunch. Including meal, but not wine, the ride starts at about $60. Special trips are occasionally offered—a visit to a winery and a murder-mystery dinner theater top the current list—and it is possible to ride the train at a reduced rate at lunchtime without a meal. But who would forgo the achiote pork tenderloin, or Patrick's Chicken Chow Chow, or the rail mixed grill, if one could have it? Reserve to eat during the second seating; visit the wine-tasting car while the early diners chow down.

If zuppa, bruschetta, insalatta, and risotto are your things, then **Tra Vigne** (1050 Charter Oak Ave., St. Helena; 707/963-4444) is your place—and you won't have to blow your whole wine country budget if you choose carefully. Naturally there are the pricey options under the entrées heading, ranging into the $20s, but you can have a delightful meal out on the terrace, under oak trees strung with tiny white lights, by opting for an appetizer (can't go wrong with the calamari), salad, pasta, and dessert. Chef Michael Chiarello has acquired quite a following, and if you want more details about Tra Vigne's cuisine, you'll be able to buy his cookbook. Reservations essential at most times of the year.

Do not visit our next selection if you just want "a little something" or are dieting. At the **Rutherford Grill** (1180 Rutherford Rd./Hwy. 29, Rutherford; 707/963-1792; website www.napavalley.com), you're going to get a big something, no matter what you order. Oh, wait, they do have something called the "nice little house salad." But the roasted chicken, the prime rib, the ribs, the leg of lamb, the appetizers, and all the other salads are ample and filling and fattening and there's bound to be a lot of permissive poaching at your table. The atmosphere is fun, not stodgy, with big, dark leather booths and a lot of shiny brass inside, and a fireplace and umbrellas on the large patio outside. The Rutherford Grill has become a bit of a local favorite because its prices are not outrageous (entrées can be less than $20, and you won't need much more), and it's a respite from the French-Italian-Continental niche that so many other restaurants have filled.

When you've had enough of the restaurant scene (and please don't stop with our suggestions—go and explore and report back to us) you may want to visit **Dean and DeLuca** (607 South St. Helena Highway/Hwy. 29, St.

Helena; 707/967-9980), the West Coast outpost of the famous New York gourmet grocery and deli. Here you'll find everything essential for an in-room dinner by the fireplace or a picnic lunch under a tree. The first thing you'll notice on the way in is the large selection of cheeses and breads. Keep going. There are condiments and packaged specialty foods all over the store, and in the back is the counter where you can buy fresh soups, salads, pastas, and whatever's particularly special today. The adjacent wine hall can augment your menu.

If you're staying in the town of Yountville, you might enjoy taking a walk, looking at menus, and peering in windows before deciding where to dine this evening. Washington Street is full of wonderful, reliable choices. The same is true of Lincoln Avenue in Calistoga, a wonderful wine country destination to which we've given short shrift only because the golf is concentrated to the south of the valley and it's just not convenient for our purposes.

Straying Off Course

Napa Valley is the Adult Disneyland, but if the kids are coming along you will have to stop at Six Flags Marine World Theme Park (495 Mare Island Way, Vallejo; 707/643-6722), on the way to Napa Valley from any direction but north. Marine World is probably a full day of activity, with roller coasters and food booths among the more natural attractions from the sea.

A favorite on-arrival activity of many of the adults who visit is the mud bath. To many, the idea of sitting in a tub of hot mud sounds totally gross. To many who have tried it, it is the ultimate unwinder, an experience that says, "I'm not working now." It's a great stress releaser, particularly with the full package of bath, steam, and massage. A great post-golf activity, but it can take hours. The mud baths are all in Calistoga, up and down and around Lincoln Avenue. That's far from the 18-hole courses, but, hey, that's where the mud is. There's a list of these at website www.napavalley.com; also check Spotlight's *Wine Country Guide,* a free publication listed under Contacts, for coupons.

Naturally there's lots of shopping in the wine country. Many of the wineries have extensive gift shops: Beringer, Sutter Home, and Hess are among the bigger and busier. There's a big outlet mall on Highway 29 in Napa and a smaller one farther north in St. Helena. And the main streets of Napa (1st Street), Yountville (Washington Street), St. Helena (Main Street) and Calistoga (Lincoln Avenue) are great for strolling and spending. Yountville's Vintage 1870, an old brick winery restored into a gallery of art, book, and gift shops, is a popular attraction on Washington Street.

A popular off-season event is the Mustard Festival, which is actually a series of events that run during mustard season, February and March. You'll know if it's mustard season by the yellow of the seed covering the valley, but you can call ahead to check the calendar (707/938-1133).

Bicycling is a popular alternative means of transportation in Napa Valley, especially for wine-tasting, and there are companies that offer excursions that stop at wineries and take riders off the beaten path for picnic lunches and views. The Conference and Visitors Bureau (see Contacts) is the place to start for information. It has a valleywide map identifying Class 1, 2, and 3 routes and listing local resources.

If walking is your thing, there are some great trails in the region, or you can do a winery tour by foot. The best hike, especially in winter, is Mount St. Helena, with views that run up near 200 miles. The Robert Louis Stevenson State Park (707/942-4575) can help with information. Or, if you prefer your hike to be escorted, consider Napa Valley Tours and Trail Hikes (800/964-4142).

One way not to get around, but to get aloft, is hot air ballooning. Napa Valley is the most heavily traveled hot air balloon corridor in the world, and flights operate only in the early, early morning hours—highly weather dependent. A typical flight lasts about an hour, but then there's champagne brunch at the end, so the whole process takes about three hours and $175 or so. Try Adventures Aloft (707/255-8688) or Balloons Above the Valley (800/464-6824), and keep an eye out for discount coupons as you travel the valley.

While we're on the subject of transportation, we mentioned the Wine Train in the Dining section, and now there's the Wine Plane. Jim Higgins and wife Kim will make your party of two or three comfy in a stretch BMW en route to their high-wing sightseeing aircraft, then serve you wine as you buzz the grape fields, all for as little as $100 per person. Tell 'em you read it here and want the special Grapes and Golf flight tour (888/779-6600; website www.wineplane.com).

Another way to get around is by antique car. You can rent one from Antique Car Rentals (707/944-1106; website www.napacars.com) in Yountville.

Of course the best way to get around the Napa Valley is to let someone else do the driving, and there are several companies offering tours by limo or van, often with easy access to private winery tours and tastings. See the suggestions under Contacts for a place to start investigating.

It's always difficult to decide where to start when wine-tasting. The Napa Valley CVB website groups wineries by various categories, so you can get rolling with the information there. And new in 1999 was the Carneros Center, a joint venture by the wineries in this southernmost part of both Sonoma and Napa Valleys, where a concierge could create a personalized itinerary based on wine preference and length of stay (Artesa Vineyards and Winery, 1345 Henry Rd., Napa; 707/224-1668).

Napa Valley is a cultural center, too, and so there are museums. Newest of these is the American Center for Wine, Food, and the Arts, which was established on 12 acres along the Napa River to explore all of the favorites of visitors with a passion for living well. A fall 2001 opening is planned; call or check the website for more details (707/256-3606; website www.theamericancenter.org).

In Yountville, near the nine-hole golf course, you can learn all about wine-making or just take a break from the grape and enjoy some art at the Napa Valley Museum. It's open every day except Tuesday (55 Presidents Circle, Yountville; 707/944-0500; website www.napavalleymuseum.org).

Details, Details

SUITCASE

Weather that's good for grapes is wonderful for golfers too. Temperatures average around 85 degrees in summer and around 50 degrees in winter, but that's not to say you couldn't run across a very hot or very cold day. We've awakened to frost on the course at Silverado in winter and longed for even more trees on tree-filled Napa muni in summer. So the best advice is to be prepared for extremes if you are not visiting in spring or fall. (But even on a hot summer day, you may want to have a sweater or windshirt handy for winery touring and tasting.)

Golf attire is casual at Napa muni, Chimney Rock, and Aetna Springs—they won't kick you out as long as you are dressed—but leans toward the country clubbish at Chardonnay, Silverado, Meadowood, and even to some extent Yountville. Golf attire also is appropriate for most of the area restaurants, though we did see jackets and ties on Christmas Eve. Don't forget your swimsuit, as we have all too many times!

Metal spikes may still be permitted at any and all courses—be sure to inquire—and if it's wet you may be glad you have them.

If you love wine, bring a cooler to protect your inevitable purchases.

GETTING THERE

From Sacramento and points east, take I-80 west to Highway 12 west (Napa exit) and follow Highway 12 past Chardonnay to Highway 29. Turn right at 29 and bear right at the split marked Lake Berryessa. You'll see the signed turnoff to Kennedy Park and the golf course just a couple of miles down on your left.

From San Francisco and points west, and San Jose and points south, you will have to get onto I-80 heading east, exit at Highway 12, and follow the same directions.

The Napa airport, which is practically next to Napa Golf Course and just down the road from Chardonnay, has no restrictions on private planes, and the tower is open 7 A.M.–9 P.M. Car rentals can be arranged through Bridge Ford (800/229-6272).

CONTACTS

- The **Napa Valley Conference and Visitors Bureau** (1310 Napa Town Center, Napa, CA 94559; 707/226-7459, fax 707/255-2066; website www.napavalley.com) produces an annual guide that is the most complete and up-to-date source of lodging information, and you can order it plus a complete and current winery tour map for $10. And you might want to pick up some brochures if you're passing through.

- An excellent, objective, yet insider source of information on current events and entertainment in the valley—plus lots of restaurant reviews—can be found at the *Napa Valley Register's* guide to living and visiting in the Napa Valley (website www.insidenapa.com). For a change of pace, you can also find articles on where to hike and where to see wildflowers.

- And Spotlight's *Wine Country Guide,* while on the ugly and cramped side of things, is an easy-traveling, free, and surprisingly complete guide to all of Northern California's beautiful wine countries. It has maps and a comprehensive listing of winery offerings and hours. You can check out its website or call to order an issue (415/898-7908; website www.winecountryguide.com).

Chapter 5

A Capital Idea: Sacramento and the Foothills

The treasure in the Sierra Nevada foothills these days isn't gold, but golf. The 1850s brought riches beyond imagination to those who toiled to extract the shiny metal from the deep mine shafts or gravelly river beds of towns like Grass Valley, Nevada City, and Auburn, the oldest gold-mining town in the west.

Old Town Auburn retains storefront facades and some original buildings from the gold rush days. Shops and restaurants reflect the historic character. The majestic domed Placer County Courthouse sits atop a hill at 101 Maple St. in Old Town and is a highly visible landmark. Black-and-white photographs of early pioneer days grace the walls, and the first floor houses the Placer County Museum.

Today's visionaries compete for upscale green fees in the foothills along the Interstate Highway 80 corridor, particularly in South Placer County. Towns like Lincoln, Loomis, Rocklin, and Roseville used to be just exit signs on the Interstate, gone by in a flash. Now Lincoln has an upgraded airport that accommodates private jets. Hotels have sprung up along I-80 from Taylor Road to Sierra College Boulevard, big names like Marriott and Hilton. While they mainly serve business travelers to nearby companies like Oracle, Hewlett-Packard, and NEC, golf packages are being developed to attract vacationers on the weekends.

Retirement giant Del Webb Corporation chose the foothills for its first developments outside of the Sunbelt and in the early 1990s opened the retirement community Sun City Roseville with 27 holes of golf called the Sun City Golf Club. So successful was that project that several years later, Sun City Lincoln Hills was developed, which exceeded projections on home sales, and the Lincoln Hills Club opened in spring 2000. Billy Casper and Greg Nash designed both courses.

In addition to techies and seniors, celebrities seeking privacy behind the high walls of gated communities have quietly located in the foothills. Eddie Murphy, Sylvester Stallone, and Jim Carrey have homes near Folsom Lake. When John Travolta was on location during the 1996 filming of *Phenomenon* in Old Town Auburn, he grew enamored of the area and purchased property nearby. Old-timers sitting at sidewalk tables in Old Town call out to docents leading walking tours going by, "Tell 'em about when they did the picture here." Although film crews covered fronts of buildings, changed names of stores, and even paid some businesses to close up shop for a few weeks, Old Town Auburn was still recognizable in the movie.

This golf escape is for those who like to be on the cutting edge, play the newest courses, and experience a destination in the making. Dynamic growth is occurring in the foothills, and golf courses are opening to serve the players who have come to the area to enjoy the moderate climate, reasonable prices, and small town friendliness that remains in what has always been a "country" kind of place. Thousands of homes are being built, new shopping centers are opening, and tourism attractions are being developed. There is an energy of vitality and enthusiasm. And the courses are very good.

However, like anything new, there are some rough edges. Recently opened hotels and restaurants may lack some polish, their employees not yet seasoned. For golf visitors, the synergy between golf, lodging, and dining is in its infancy. A collaborative effort to centralize marketing of the area's golf programs, spearheaded by the Sacramento Convention & Visitors Bureau, is expected to get the ball rolling.

The golf courses included in this itinerary are all upscale daily-fee courses. As yet, there is not a golf resort in the area, i.e., with lodging and golf together. The most exciting courses are in the area northwest of I-80 around Lincoln: Twelve Bridges, Turkey Creek, Whitney Oaks, and Lincoln Hills. Currently golfers who want to play those courses on a golf package can choose between overnight lodging at the upscale Rocklin Park Hotel or at the Holiday Inn in Auburn, about 25 minutes away. Or they can stay in one of the chain hotels along I-80, which are reasonably priced and convenient options. Keep in mind that these hotels cater to business people, generally weekday visitors, so the weekend rates are cheaper.

Twelve Bridges Golf Club is the best-known course in the area and the most dramatic example of the swift transformation occurring in the foothills from ranch land to golf destination. It's still a somewhat remote location. Carved out of the 22,000-acre Joel Parker Whitney ranch of the late 1800s, the course flows with the natural land contours, encompassing huge granite outcroppings. Alongside the 18th tee, a rock wall several feet high remains from the early days. Imagine the arduous task of lifting and placing the heavy, various-sized stones one by one, especially during the hot summer months. Twelve Bridges' superb design and facilities are on display each spring when it hosts the LPGA Tour for the Longs Drugs Challenge. For the event the two nines are reversed to better accommodate spectators, and the players start on the very tough 10th hole, which the LPGA rates as the fourth hardest hole on tour.

Nearby Whitney Oaks Golf Club opened one year after Twelve Bridges. It is part of a burgeoning planned community, and the area around it is booming too. Sunset Drive, the main drag leading to Whitney Oaks, is lined with huge subdivisions and signs announcing the developments and model homes. Golfers marvel at the houses that have sprung up around the course "just since the last time we played here." The entire development at Whitney Oaks comprises 1,075 acres, with 2,000 home-sites planned.

Whitney Oaks shares similar terrain to Twelve Bridges and the distinction of also being part of the vast Joel Parker Whitney ranch. On the path between hole number 11 and hole number 12, moss mostly covers the heavy stone of the pyramid-shaped mausoleum built by old Mr. Whitney as a family memorial. The narrow course with many undulations demands accuracy and length to carry the canyon and wetland areas. To keep the pace of play, the scorecard recommends the range of handicaps that should play each tee.

Turkey Creek Golf Club is on Highway 193, which used to be a quiet country road connecting the small towns of Lincoln and Newcastle. Now the growth of Del Webb's Sun City Lincoln Hills community and other developments along Highway 65 have forced the widening of roads to meet increasing demand. Turkey Creek is managed by ClubCorp, the world's largest owner and manager of country clubs and resorts. ClubCorp also operates the private Granite Bay Country Club, a classic Robert Trent Jones Jr. design about 30 minutes away near Folsom, and Teal Bend Golf Club, a moderately priced daily fee course that opened in 1997 close to downtown Sacramento.

Both Turkey Creek and Teal Bend were designed by Brad Bell, who typically puts the middle tees at about 6,000 yards and forward tees at just under 5,000 yards. Turkey Creek's Director of Golf and General Manager, Jeff Wilson, says that the shorter yardage gives shorter hitters the opportunity of hitting a green in regulation with an iron, instead of using all woods, which makes for a more varied golf experience. Wilson wants Turkey Creek to be recognized as the leader in high-end daily courses.

You may see wild turkeys and even hear goats bleating along the back nine, but don't let the rural environs fool you. This is a smooth and sophisticated golf experience. Such contrasts are part of the golf experience on this itinerary and will continue to delight and surprise golf visitors to the foothills.

Itinerary

WARMING UP

Be prepared for lots of driving around between the golf courses, lodging, and other activities until this emerging golf destination is centralized. While most of the hotels have swimming pools, in deference to the hot summers, you won't find a full-service resort where a spouse or family could have a choice of resort activities while the golfers spend the day on the links. Non-golfers would probably enjoy other itineraries more than this one. It would ideally suit one or more couples, or a group of golfing friends.

Make your tee times as far ahead as possible as these are popular courses. We thought you would want to make a day of it at Twelve Bridges, and maybe even take a lesson at the well-equipped Learning Center, so schedule that ahead as well. If you are using one of the golf packages at the Rocklin Park Hotel or the Holiday Inn at Auburn, ask if they can also make tee times for you.

You may need dinner reservations, especially on Saturday night, so plan accordingly. In the summer months there are often county fairs or music festivals in the foothills towns. Inquire at the hotel or call one of the contact numbers if you are interested in knowing about events occurring during your stay. Reservations would be needed for the paddlewheeler cruises in Old Sacramento.

day 1 We think Twelve Bridges is such an enjoyable golf experience, you'll want to make the most of the day, so any stops along the route will probably be of the fast-food variety. The long flower-lined entryway leads to the dramatic clubhouse, where, after that long drive, you might want to have a quick bite in Chadwick's, which overlooks the ninth and the 18th greens. Or wait until after your round when you can linger and enjoy its clubby atmosphere and excellent service. Be sure to leave time to warm up before your round at the spacious Learning Center. Twelve Bridges' impressive clubhouse and challenging course befit its stature as an LPGA Tour venue.

A sense of natural beauty prevails at this beautiful layout, set in a 335-acre valley with mature oak trees and winding streams, its rolling hills still open space. As part of the Joel Parker Whitney ranch of the late 1800s, Twelve Bridges is named for the 12 granite bridges Whitney built on his property. Three of the original bridges remain on the golf course today, which is in an uninhabited part of the growing town of Lincoln.

Twelve Bridges is scenic and rewards good play; it is not "tricked up" or contrived. The 10th hole becomes the starting hole for the Longs Drugs Challenge, and LPGA players have to deal with its difficult green. Depending on the pin placement you almost have to putt behind you and uphill just to get the ball to roll near the hole and not off the green entirely. Try to stay below the pin. The golf holes are named, some helpfully so, as in hole number 6, "Hidden Creek"; the creek is not visible from the tee. The course goes from "Starting Gate" to "Stonewall."

After golf, head to the Rocklin Park Hotel by retracing your steps back to Highway 65. Turn left onto 65 and follow signs to Interstate 80 east. It will be about one mile on I-80 to the Rocklin Road exit. Turn right onto Rocklin Road, right onto Aguilar, and right onto China Garden. You can see the hotel from the freeway. The attractive double doors open up to Susanne Restaurant and Bakery, a spacious, open layout with high ceilings, all white with crossed beams and appealing patio seating. To your right is a small bar and, through another door, the registration desk for the hotel. It's quiet and comfortable and attractive. We suggest you dine at Susanne tonight. It's excellent and favored by locals for special occasions.

day II Enjoy the generous breakfast buffet offered next to the bakery in the lobby, including hot and cold items that you can bring up to your room on a tray or eat at the small tables. Then drive to Turkey Creek Golf Club. From the Rocklin Park Hotel, go right on China Garden, left on Aguilar, then right on Rocklin Road and left on Sierra College Boulevard. Follow Sierra College until it dead-ends (about seven miles) on Highway 193, and make a left onto 193. The course is about a mile on the right side.

Head for the driving range, where you can hit off grass, with three levels alternated to maintain the surface. The course's dominant feature is a former rock quarry converted into a lake, which comes into play on several holes.

The helpful starter advises you to select the best tee for yardage, and says that on hole number 2, if you hit more than 240 yards, do not use driver. The green has a steep slope in front, and if you don't hit far enough back, the ball picks up speed and careens off the green, sometimes past where you are standing. You'll encounter a similar green on hole number 7, but don't let your frustration let you overlook the spectacular ridge view behind the green.

Hole number 3 is almost all carry over a rock-lined lake that looks like rocks broke through the waterfalls to the left. The lake was formerly used as a rock quarry and comes into play again on hole number 18. Hole number 3 and hole number 9 both come into the clubhouse. Signature hole number 14, "Ursula's Pond," has a lovely, shaded wooded green over water and rocks. The big boulder at the tee of hole number 18 foretells that this hole is laden with obstacles to be overcome, namely carry over water from the tee and over the quarry lake to reach the green on the second shot. You'll want to try this hole again. Finish off your round with a quick stop at the 19th hole and you're off for an afternoon of sightseeing and shopping in Old Town Auburn.

If 4,800 yards seems like not enough of a challenge, short hitters can probably handle the white tees at 6,000 yards until they reach hole number 18 and face carrying the water hazard in front of the tee.

Drive east on I-80 to the exit for Old Town Auburn. From the freeway you can't miss the large stone statue of a kneeling gold panner, Claude Chana, a Frenchman who discovered gold nearby in 1848. Stroll through the quaint stores, antique shops, and historic buildings, like the oldest post office in continuous operation in the west, established in 1848.

Shanghai Restaurant and Bar, opened in the early 1900s and still owned by the Yue family, is a colorful historic saloon that served as the town bar in *Phenomenon.* Oddball memorabilia such as mounted elk and deer antlers, a bicycle, and ancient posters crowd the walls of the narrow bar. The old wooden floor creaks. It's authentic, frequented by locals, and you'll either love or hate its gritty funkiness. The restaurant operation occupies a larger space next door and serves up decent Cantonese food. Stay for dinner if you're in the mood for Chinese, or, for a different experience, go a few doors down to the popular Bootleggers Old Town Tavern & Grill, where hometown boy and Culinary School of America graduate Ty Rowe has created a sophisticated menu and upscale dining experience in a restored brick building that dates from the 1870s. After dinner, it's only a 20-minute drive from Old Town back to the Rocklin Park Hotel.

day III Check out of the Rocklin Park Hotel, maybe taking a muffin or some fruit with you from the breakfast buffet for a later snack. It's time to tackle Whitney Oaks. Make a left turn on Rocklin

Road, then a left turn onto Pacific, a right turn on Sunset Boulevard, and a right turn on Park Drive; turn left onto Whitney Drive, turn right onto Clubhouse Drive, and make a left turn into the parking lot.

Whitney Oaks Golf Club is a beautiful course but not for sissies. Whitney Oaks is close to Twelve Bridges, only 15 minutes away, so they share similar terrain—the rolling hills, oaks, and granite outcroppings—and the distinction of being part of the original Joel Parker Whitney ranch. An early proponent of the game, Whitney had a nine-hole course on his ranch in the late 1800s. Unlike Twelve Bridges, Whitney Oaks is surrounded by housing developments.

As part of an upscale, growing community, Whitney Oaks delivers a first-class golf experience. The front nine is more wide open with wetlands whereas the back nine plays through a narrow canyon with numerous rock outcroppings. Johnny Miller's design was too tough for average players, who came away demoralized and disgruntled, so course improvements were implemented in 1999, consisting of widening fairways, filling in bunkers and ponds, clearing rough, and relieving the complaint of blind shots to narrow landing areas. Bill Falik, one of the owners, says, "We have softened and refined the front nine, making it more playable for all levels of golfer without compromising the integrity of Johnny Miller's design." Purists believe the course shouldn't have been touched, its challenges left intact, but owners felt that pleasing the average player was a high priority.

Although it is more forgiving, Whitney Oaks is still known for narrow fairways, hilly lies, and hazards that sit just short of the green, requiring perilous carries. The fairway undulations that create hilly lies throw your swing off balance, resulting in missed shots that tend to elevate your score. Aiming stakes help, but if you have doubt about your driver on the tee, put it away. For instance, on hole number 5, players with low handicaps using a driver will find that it is better to choose perhaps a 5-wood and aim left of the aiming stake so you can lay up and have 175 yards left to the green.

After your round, retire to the splendid new clubhouse overlooking the 18th green to share your triumphs and defeats on the spacious wraparound deck. Whitney Oaks Bar and Grill makes a fine 19th hole and even offers dinner, so plan to return and sample the full meal service.

Head back toward the Bay Area on I-80 west, then take I-5 toward Los Angeles and take the J Street exit off I-5, which will bring you to Old Sacramento, or "Old Sac," as it's fondly called. During the gold rush days, Old Sacramento was a booming supply town on the banks of the Sacramento River. Today dozens of shops and restaurants fill the roughly three-block area of restored western buildings, considered one of the best concentrations of historic gold-rush-era buildings in the West. The main attraction is The California State Railroad Museum, the largest railroad museum in the United States. It houses a collection of more than 20 restored locomotives. Climb aboard a swaying sleeping car or a 1930s replica dining car.

From Old Sacramento you can take a riverboat cruise on an old paddle-wheeler, the *Spirit of Sacramento*. There are several choices of dinner cruises, including an early evening sunset dinner cruise, if you want to drive home before it gets too late. Gliding along the river on a balmy summer night is a pleasant way to end a golf excursion.

 NOTES

Extended Play for History Buffs Stay overnight in Old Sacramento at the Delta King Hotel, a beautifully restored riverboat transformed into a hotel, where you can dine aboard at the Pilothouse Restaurant. The next day go to Haggin Oaks Golf Course and play the classic Alister MacKenzie Course (1932). Restoration began in 2000, several holes at a time. Leave enough time to browse in the Haggin Oaks Super Shop, one of the largest golf merchandise stores anywhere. Another Sacramento golf option on the way back to the Bay Area would be Teal Bend Golf Club, designed by Brad Bell in a tranquil marshland setting.

Extended Play for Romantics. Go to Auburn and play The Ridge Golf Course, a Robert Trent Jones Jr.–designed course that opened in 1999, then head for Nevada City. Take the Broad Street exit to reach the center of town. The entire downtown area has earned a place on the National Register of Historic Places, so strict guidelines ensure that the quaint, old-fashioned ambience will remain intact. Settle into a cozy Victorian B&B with lace curtains and a four-poster bed.

Money Savers. Play golf in Grass Valley, just three miles from Nevada City, at Nevada County Country Club, where the weekend green fees are the same as the power cart fees, $18. All play is first-come, first-served for visitors, but call first (530/273-6436) to see what is scheduled for that weekend before you show up. It's a little rough around the edges, but the price is right and the folks are friendly. The closest driving range is Quail Valley Golf Course (530/274-1340), where the range is lit until closing at 10 P.M. For $5 you can play the nine-hole course, which the owners built from a flat hay field that was already irrigated.

Newcomers. Play the foothills' newest course, The Lincoln Hills Club, near Twelve Bridges in Lincoln.

If You Have Only One Day and One Night. Play Turkey Creek, dine at Horseshoe Bar Grill in Loomis, stay at Rocklin Park Hotel, then play Twelve Bridges the next day and stop in Old Sacramento on the way home.

Courses

ITINERARY SELECTIONS

Twelve Bridges Golf Club
3070 Twelve Bridges Dr.
Lincoln, CA 95648
916/645-7200 or 888/TWELVEB,
fax 916/645-6729
website www.twelvebridges.com

LPGA Master Professional Noni Schneider is director of golf. She's particularly proud of the Learning Center, which offers an extensive instruction program with both LPGA and PGA qualified instructors, four practice greens and practice bunkers, and video swing analysis. In addition to clinics and individual lessons, Twelve Bridges offers junior camps, parent/child camps, and a women's golf school.

Peak rates are about $60 plus cart fees of $15, and range balls are additional. Special rates are available for twilight, nine holes, and juniors. In addition to the usual weekday/weekend rate structure, Twelve Bridges maintains seasonal rates: off peak is December–February and peak is March–November. Walking is permitted if you carry your bag or rent one of the pull carts offered for a nominal fee. Don't bring your own pull cart. Carts must stay on the path. The course suits varied skill levels with tee boxes ranging from 7,150 yards to 5,310 yards. Soft spikes are required, as is appropriate golf attire, i.e., collared shirts for men and no denim.

SCORECARD

Architect: Dick Phelps, 1996
Course Record: 64, Tom Johnson
Black: Par 72, 7,150 yards, 74.6 rating for men, 139 slope
Green: Par 72, 6,706 yards, 72.6 rating for men, 131 slope
White: Par 72, 6,174 yards, 69.9 rating for men, 123 slope; 76.2 rating for women, 135 slope
Gold: Par 72, 5,310 yards, 71.0 rating for women, 123 slope
For tee times call 916/645-7200, seven days out; for reservations up to 60 days ahead call The Golfer.com at 888/236-8725 and pay an additional charge of $5 per player, payable by credit card when you make the tee time. Green fees are paid at the pro shop when you check in.

TEE TIDBITS | Each aspect of the operation shows depth and professionalism. Twelve Bridges is known for its friendly staff throughout the facility. The beautifully designed clubhouse contains a well-stocked pro shop, which was named one of the top 100 golf shops in the country by *Golf Shop Operations Magazine.* Chadwick's restaurant is worth a stop before or after your round and would be a good place to meet someone and linger. Breakfast and lunch are served until 3 P.M., and a modified bar menu is available after that until dark, with a full bar. Chadwick's has high ceilings, big windows overlooking the course, and a big outdoor patio. Omelets, salads, and burgers are all under $10 and as good as any upscale restaurant.

Turkey Creek Golf Club
1525 Highway 193
Lincoln, CA 95648
916/434-9100

Carts are equipped with the Proshot GPS Yardage System, eliminating the need for a yardage book. However, sometimes neither the layout nor the hazards are clearly displayed. Players may take carts 90 degrees onto the fairway.

Green fees are $65 on weekends, including golf cart and range balls. Walking is allowed, but manager Jeff Wilson says few do because the green fee includes the cart, and besides it's a hike between a few of the holes and not really walker-friendly. Pull carts are not for rent but you can bring them.

SCORECARD

Architect: Brad Bell, 1999
Course Record: 68, Brian Adamson
Black: Par 72, 7,012 yards, 136 slope
Blue: Par 72, 6,617 yards, 71.3 rating for men, 131 slope
White: Par 72, 6,003 yards, 68.8 rating for men, 121 slope; 73.9 rating for women, 134 slope
Gold: Par 72, 4,887 yards, 67.3 rating for women, 121 slope
Make tee times by calling 916/434-9100 up to seven days out; for up to 30 days advance reservations call The Golfer.com at 888/236-8725.

TEE TIDBITS | The 19th hole is open from sunup to sundown, with a casual, sports bar atmosphere, and during the season they show all the games on the big-screen TVs. You order and pick up at the counter, no table service, but the food is better than typical grill fare, with lighter items like chicken Caesar salad in addition to sandwiches and hamburgers, all under $10. Beer and wine are available.

Whitney Oaks Golf Club
2305 Clubhouse Dr.
Rocklin, CA 95765
916/632-8333
website www.whitneyoaks.com

Greens are typically tiered. Try to play with someone who knows the nuances of the course and can tell you where to aim. Carts are allowed 90 degrees on certain holes. Whitney Oaks is a soft-spike facility and requires a collared shirt. Green fees of $70 include cart and range balls, but walking is half as much. Players don't usually walk, the biggest detriments being the long walk between holes 11 and 12 and uphill to the 13th tee.

SCORECARD

Architect: Johnny Miller, 1997
Course Record: 69, Craig Ballard
Black: Par 71, 6,793 yards, 73.7 for men, 132 slope
Gray: Par 71, 6,395 yards, 71.7 for men, 125 slope
Beige: Par 71, 5,940 yards, 69.5 for men, 123 slope; 76.1 for women, 138 slope
Gold: Par 71, 5,480 yards, 67.7 for men, 118 slope; 73.6 rating for women, 132 slope
Green: Par 71, 4,983 yards, 70.9 for women, 127 slope
For tee times call 916/632-8333 seven days ahead.

TEE TIDBITS | Whitney Oaks is semiprivate and various memberships are available. It may even become a fully private country club in the near future. For now, member benefits include preferred tee times and rates and a separate practice area. The impressive new clubhouse is already country club quality. Natural stone and rich wood are used throughout, with floor to ceiling windows facing the ninth and 18th holes.

Whitney Oaks Bar and Grill serves breakfast, lunch, and dinner. Appetizers, sandwiches, and salads are under $10. In addition, a more upscale meal is offered when the dining room opens at night. Entrées range $15–25 and include stuffed pork chop and mustard and rosemary crusted lamb rack. Executive chef Mark Powell was previously at the Sacramento Capitol Club. This is a first-rate 19th hole that immediately gained favor with local residents who aren't even golfers.

ALTERNATIVES

Haggin Oaks is home to the Alister MacKenzie Course (1932), which is considered the jewel of the six Sacramento city courses under the banner of "Capitol City Golf." Purchase of a Capitol City Golf Card allows preferred tee time reservation access and certain discounts. Mature trees line the Alister MacKenzie Course, which is flat and walkable. Hole number 9 is the farthest hole from the clubhouse. Course renovations that took place in 2000 somewhat altered the original layout. The Arcade Creek Course gets a lot of play, especially after work, and offers a reduced rate for only nine holes.

Leave time to browse in the 8,600-square-foot Super Shop, which has one of the largest selections of golf apparel and equipment, plus gift items like shoe bags, golf wrapping paper, etc. Haggin Oaks director of golf Ken Morton Sr. has twice won the National PGA Merchandiser of the Year Award and was named the 1999 National PGA Golf Professional of the Year. Haggin Oaks offers numerous junior golf programs through SAY GOLF, the Sacramento Area Youth Golf Association, which Morton founded in 1983. The Learning Center offers 100 hitting stations, which stay open 24 hours during the summer, plus club-fitting services. Haggin Oaks is an excellent value with a lot to offer. ■ 3645 FULTON AVE., SACRAMENTO, CA 95821; 916/264-TIME (CAPITOL CITY GOLF CENTRAL RESERVATIONS), 916/575-2525 (ALISTER MACKENZIE COURSE—FOR THE SAME DAY), 916/575-2515 (ARCADE CREEK COURSE—FOR THE SAME DAY)

The Ridge Golf Course sits in the rolling hills north of Auburn with vistas of distant ridges that will be snow-covered in winter. It is the closest 18-hole public course to Lake Tahoe, with convenient access off I-80 in Auburn. You could play the Ridge on your way to Tahoe to go skiing. Auburn Municipal Airport is a half mile away.

The Ridge has five sets of tees, three of which are rated for women. *Golf for Women* magazine named the Ridge one of its "Top 100 Fairways" for 2000. Many mature oaks remain on the course, but Placer County mandated that for every one that was removed 10 more had to be planted.

The course is fairly narrow with a lot of undulations and bunkers. Adjust club selection for the approach shots to the uphill greens, of which there seem to be many. Many greens feature false fronts and bowls. It's a peaceful setting without houses around it, but you do hear road noise on the back nine where holes border Bell Road and New Airport Road. A circular driveway leads up to the impressive new clubhouse, which opened in spring 2000 and has a library, meeting rooms, and a full-service restaurant called Lanterns, which is open from breakfast through dinner. Sunday brunch is an all-you-can-eat buffet. ■ 2020 GOLF COURSE RD., AUBURN, CA 95602; 530/888-7888; WEBSITE WWW.RIDGEGC.COM

Teal Bend Golf Club borders Sacramento International Airport on some holes, and you do see and hear the planes sometimes, but the peaceful marshland setting overcomes any intrusiveness. Many environmentally sensitive areas come into play particularly from the back tees. A plaque at the first tee explains that this was once a vast seasonal wetland until reclamation transformed the region into some of California's most productive agricultural lands. Waterbirds frequent the marshes. Teal Bend is known for its large multitiered greens. Green fees include a cart although walking is allowed. It is only 15 minutes from downtown Sacramento and attracts corporate members. Carts are equipped with the Proshot GPS computer yardage system. ■ 7200 GARDEN HWY., SACRAMENTO, CA 95837; 916/922-5209

"Concierge golf" is what it's all about at **The Lincoln Hills Club.** Golfers receive fresh fruit on the first tee, complimentary club cleaning before and after each round, and a free sleeve of balls, among other things. All this for green fees between $40 and $50. The course is part of the 2,300-acre Sun City Lincoln Hills master-planned adult community and is open to the public. Residents receive discounted green fees. The 6,985-yard course designed by Billy Casper and Greg Nash has four tee settings and includes lakes and waterfalls. ■ 1005 SUN CITY LANE, LINCOLN, CA 95648; 916/434-7454

If you have time to play only nine holes, **Black Oak Golf Course** in north Auburn is an attractive choice. It's a well-run family-owned course that's no pushover, especially with its 130/70.0 slope rating from the blue tees. Large oak trees typical of the area shade the fairways, deer wander and nibble throughout, and it's set in a peaceful little valley. Head pro Brent Perkins says, "It's a hookers course," because players benefit by drawing the ball around the doglegs. Hole number 4 is a scenic par-3 over a pond, visible from the parking lot when you drive in. Black Oak is a great value for the price and a fun round. ■ 2455 BLACK OAK RD., AUBURN, CA 95602; 530/878-1900

Try to find a way to visit one of the foothills' best private courses, **Auburn Valley Country Club.** It's a long, hilly, and mature course, its surrounding hillsides dotted with oaks, and the craggy face of Bald Rock Mountain looms over the back nine. Weeping willows line the fairways and 11 lakes, creeks tumble over rocks, and wildlife is abundant with wild turkeys, deer, waterfowl, and migrating geese. It's well laid out and challenging. There are some upscale homes near the entrance, but it retains the rural feel of north Auburn with cows often grazing nearby. The ranch-style clubhouse sits on a hill overlooking the back nine. Auburn Valley allows reciprocal play with other private clubs. ■ 8800 AUBURN VALLEY RD., AUBURN, CA 95602; 530/269-1837

Lodging

ITINERARY SELECTION

Rocklin Park Hotel is 20 miles east of Sacramento off I-80. It offers 67 oversized rooms equipped with upscale amenities and nightly turndown service as well as fitness center, sauna, and business center. An elaborate complimentary breakfast includes hot and cold entrées, with all pastries baked on site by Susanne Restaurant and Bakery. Susanne is open for lunch and dinner and serves room service to hotel guests. Rocklin Park is attractive and comfortable. It offers stay-and-play packages with Whitney Oaks, Twelve Bridges, Turkey Creek, and the Ridge. The golf courses report that Rocklin Park can be counted on to treat their guests well. Package rates range $225–345, double occupancy, and include room, 18 holes of golf with cart, and range balls. ■ 5450 CHINA GARDEN RD., ROCKLIN, CA 95677; 916/630-9400 OR 888/630-9400, FAX 916/630-9448; WEBSITE WWW.ROCKLINPARK.COM, EMAIL HOTEL@ROCKLINPARK.COM

GOLF PACKAGE OPTION

Holiday Inn Auburn is a 96-room full-service hotel conveniently located at the intersection of I-80 and Highway 49. Rooms overlook the pool/patio area, and the adjacent Marie Callender's restaurant offers room service to guests. Old Town Auburn is only one mile away. It is clean and well equipped yet somewhat sterile, and it's a long walk from the front desk to the elevators. The Holiday Inn offers golf packages with the Ridge Golf Course ($99 per person on weekends) and Turkey Creek Golf Club ($109 per person on weekends). ■ 120 GRASS VALLEY HWY., AUBURN, CA 95603; 530/887-8787 OR 800/814-8787, FAX 530/887-9824

ALTERNATIVES

Spend the night at the **Delta King Hotel,** a 1927 riverboat restored and converted to a hotel and permanently moored in Old Sacramento. It's about as long as a football field and five decks high; you can't miss it. Cross the gangplank to enter the floating hotel with 44 smallish wood-paneled staterooms, equipped with cable TV, telephones, and brass beds. A deluxe continental breakfast is included, served in the Pilothouse Restaurant, which is also open to the public for Sunday brunch, lunch, and dinner. ■ 1000 FRONT ST., OLD SACRAMENTO, CA 95814; 916/444-5464

The Marriott Hotels in Roseville, "Official Hotel Complex for the Longs Drugs Challenge," consist of the **Residence Inn** (1930 Taylor Rd., Roseville, CA 95661; 916/772-5500); **Courtyard by Marriott** (1920 Taylor Rd., Roseville, CA 95661; 916/772-5555); and **Fairfield Inn** (1910 Taylor Rd., Roseville, CA 95661; 916/772-3500), which share a common parking lot and are only 15 minutes from Twelve Bridges. The Residence Inn offers suites with full kitchens and grocery shopping service, the Fairfield Inn serves the budget client, and the Courtyard is geared to business travelers. Something for everyone. The rooms are for the most part simple and adequate. Complimentary breakfast is served. Prices hover around $100, with the Fairfield being the least expensive, and all three offer weekend rates of about $30 off weekday rates, typical of the hotels in this area.

The most attractive of the chain hotels along Taylor Road is the **Larkspur Landing Home Suite Hotel,** an all-suite custom-designed hotel whose motto is "home suite hotel for the LPGA." It offers upgraded furnishings and services in its studio and one-bedroom suites, like extra-thick towels and plush leather executive chairs. Studio suites run $104 on weekdays and $94 on weekends. ■ 1931 TAYLOR RD., ROSEVILLE, CA 95661; 916/773-1717, FAX 916/773-1765

For something more romantic, try **Grandmere's Bed and Breakfast Inn,** a luxurious white Victorian mansion built in 1856 by Aaron A. Sargent, U.S. senator and publisher, and restored in 1985. Some of the grand, high-ceilinged guest rooms have four-poster beds and claw-foot tubs. Walk to the shops and galleries of Nevada City's historical district. Full breakfast and afternoon cookies are included. Prices range from $110 for an upper room facing the quiet street to $230 for the Susan B. Anthony Suite. ■ 449 BROAD ST., NEVADA CITY, CA 95959; 530/265-4660, FAX 530/265-4416; WEBSITE WWW.NEVADACITYINNS.COM

Downey House Bed and Breakfast Inn is a charming yellow and white Victorian built in 1869, with smallish but attractively furnished rooms and a garden with a lily pond and waterfall. Four of the rooms have queen-size beds and run $120 on the weekends. It's one block from the downtown area. The rate includes full breakfast and wine and cheese in the afternoon. ■ 517 W. BROAD ST., NEVADA CITY, CA 95959; 800/258-2815; WEBSITE WWW.DOWNEYHOUSE.COM

Dining

ITINERARY SELECTIONS

The Rocklin Park Hotel is one of the favored hotels in the area because of **Susanne Restaurant and Bakery** in its lobby. The attractive open-beam high-ceilinged room is spacious and airy with outdoor seating. A buffet breakfast is served in the lobby to hotel guests only. Lunch items are under $10 and include innovative sandwiches, salads, and pastas. Dinner entrées are mostly under $25 and include soup or salad. Grilled meats, salmon with crab ravioli, and a vegetarian selection reflect a wide variety of menu choices. Early bird specials 5:30–6:30 P.M. offer a three-course dinner for around $15. The in-house bakery makes all the yummy breads, pastries, and desserts. Specials include "Tuesday night half off a bottle of wine," "Wednesday night kids eat free," and "Thursday night seafood buffet." On weekends, live music accompanies dinner, occasionally a harpist, and Sunday is a jazz brunch. Lunch, dinner, Sunday brunch. ■ 5450 CHINA GARDEN RD., ROCKLIN; 916/630-0400

The kooky bar scene and authentic gold-rush ambience of **Shanghai** is really more interesting than the food, and you can't pass it up. The saloon conjures up images of the Wild West, bar brawls and the like, and garage-sale junkies will love the paraphernalia decorating the walls. The restaurant claims to be the only local Chinese restaurant that serves cocktails, and it offers a mean 15-ounce Shanghai Tai served in a souvenir glass. Cantonese-style family dinners for two or more are a good value, ranging in price $9–15 per person. Shanghai also serves as an off-sale liquor store 6 A.M.–2 P.M. Lunch and dinner. ■ 289 WASHINGTON ST., OLD TOWN AUBURN; 530/823-2613

Bootleggers Old Town Tavern and Grill is across the street from the old firehouse in what was Auburn's first city hall (1870). Brick walls, a hand-rubbed solid dark oak bar, and a double fireplace that separates the bar and dining areas set the mood for relaxation. Auburn native and owner Ty Rowe is also a graduate of the prestigious Culinary Institute of America in New York, and his eccentric menu features such diverse items as escargot, juicy baby-back ribs, Korean skirt steak, and Mom's old-fashioned meatloaf. Entrées are around $15. Bootleggers offers a large selection of bottled and tap beers and a wide choice of wines by the glass. Cheesecake and tiramisu are the best desserts. Here's a bit of *Phenomenon* lore: rumor has it that John Travolta frequented Bootleggers while filming was going on and often took home "care packages" on the weekends. Now don't you want to try it? ■ 210 WASHINGTON ST., OLD TOWN AUBURN; 530/889-2229/FAX 530/889-9138

ALTERNATIVES

No, there's not an "&" missing between Bar and Grill in the **Horseshoe Bar Grill** (3645 Taylor Rd., Loomis; 916/652-2222; website www. horseshoebargrill.com). The restaurant is named for its location, at Horseshoe Bar Road and Taylor Road in Loomis, just up I-80 from Rocklin. This is a sophisticated restaurant with rich dark wood paneling, well-chosen art pieces, old-fashioned fixtures, fireplace, and lace curtains in the windows. Theme nights, wine-makers dinners, and wine-tastings keep it a happening place. The food is very good. Entrées include green salad or Caesar salad or soup, and are under $25. The pan-seared brandy-flavored rib-eye steak is a favorite, but so is the coconut shrimp. Sister restaurant Beerman's, in Lincoln, is a steakhouse and brewpub. Lunch and dinner.

Friar Tuck's (111 Pine St., Nevada City; 530/265-9093) just may be the closest thing Nevada City has to a "scene." There's musical entertainment, and the cook-your-own hot oil fondues and cheese fondues provide plenty of entertainment right at your table. In addition, the broad menu includes salmon or filet mignon, with prices under $25. Friar Tuck's offers a warm atmosphere with hearty food, a large wooden bar, and oak booths in the dining enclaves. Dinner only.

The **Nevada City Grill** (401 Commercial St.; 530/265-6138) is a more casual dining experience serving lighter fare. Sit outside under the big tree and enjoy fresh, flavorful salads in generous portions, nine types of hamburgers, and specials like chicken teriyaki stir-fry, most under $10. There are eight tables inside. Specials include New York steak and scampi for about $15. Lunch and dinner.

By far the most interesting dining in Old Sacramento is aboard one of the restored riverboats. The *Spirit of Sacramento* is a large paddlewheeler that plies the river, offering tours as well as dine-aboard lunch, brunch, and dinner cruises, which run about three hours (call 916/552-2933 or 800/433-0263 for reservations and catch the boat at 110 L St.). For a more elegant dining experience on the river, try the **Pilothouse Restaurant** (1000 Front St., Old Sacramento; 916/444-5464) in the Delta King Hotel, which is permanently anchored. In the intimate, wood-paneled dining room with 20 tables, everyone has a river view through the expansive picture window. It's a traditional menu with a seafood emphasis and most entrées under $20 except for the yummy filet mignon and scampi-style prawns combination. It's the ideal dining choice if you're staying at the Delta King.

Straying Off Course

Sightseeing in the quaint gold country towns is a must. Grass Valley and Nevada City are three miles apart and about 25 miles from Auburn on Highway 49. Take a walking tour of Old Town Auburn, led by a docent from the Placer County Department of Museums (530/889-6500), or use the self-guided map. In Grass Valley, the most interesting site is the 780-acre Empire Mine State Historic Park (10791 E. Empire St.; 530/273-8522), which tells the story of the Empire Mine in wonderful displays. It was one of the richest hard-rock gold mines. Mine owner William Bourne's spacious stone cottage has been restored, and living history programs are held there. Hiking, biking, and picnicking are available in the park. An interesting Bay Area connection is that the Bourne family also built the beautiful Filoli mansion and extensive gardens in Woodside.

The entire downtown of Nevada City is on the National Register of Historic Places, so you'll get the feel of what a 19th-century town must have been like. Take a carriage ride through downtown or the Victorian homes to see it all (530/265-8778). Nevada City offers more of an intellectual environment and attracts artists and writers. Visit Broad Street Books (426 Broad St.; 530/265-4204), where the specialty is travel books. The classical music festival, Music in the Mountains (800/218-2188 or 530/265-6124) is held for three weeks in the summer.

The Railroad Museum is the main attraction of Old Sacramento (916/445-6645, daily except holidays). Guided tours of Old Sacramento can be arranged by calling the Visitor Center (916/442-7644). From Old Sacramento, you can tour the nearby State Capitol, in a 40-acre landscaped park and restored to its former grandeur with a soaring rotunda and shiny gold dome, crystal chandeliers, and marble mosaic floors. Free tours run daily (10th St. between L and R Streets, Capitol Mall; 916/324-0333).

Golf artist Jim Fitzpatrick's paintings hang in the most prestigious clubhouses and resorts in the country. At his gallery you'll find original paintings (which he calls "golfscapes"), limited edition prints, golf memorabilia, and perhaps even the artist at work (4208 Douglas Blvd., Suite 200, Granite Bay, CA 94746; 916/624-1487).

The American River offers a variety of rafting adventures, from beginning to advanced. You may contact Tributary Whitewater Tours (20480 Woodbury Dr., Grass Valley; 530/346-6812) and Whitewater Connection (800/336-7238 or 530/622-6446, fax 530/622-7192; email raft@whitewaterconnection.com).

Folsom Lake Recreation Area encompasses 17,718 acres and is two miles northwest of the town of Folsom off Highway 50. Activities include waterskiing, windsurfing, horse rental, and nature trails. Folsom also is home to 70-plus factory outlet stores (13000 Folsom Blvd., Suite 309; 916/985-0312).

Details, Details

SUITCASE

The foothills region is described as "above the fog and below the snow." Low-lying fog frequently lingers around Sacramento in the winter months, threatening visibility, its dampness penetratingly cold. Dress accordingly. On the other hand, summer temperatures can climb to more than 100 degrees, and rattlesnakes occasionally slither through the dry grassy areas, so don't venture into deep rough and be sure to bring sunscreen and a hat. The payoff is balmy evenings, ideal for outdoor dining. Folks dress casually in the foothills so leave the coat and tie at home. In spring the hills are green and wildflowers abound. At the higher elevations, you'll find vibrant fall colors, and Nevada City gets a dusting of snow on its Victorian buildings in winter.

GETTING THERE

From San Francisco, San Jose, or Sacramento, take Interstate 80 to Rocklin, where you will take the exit to Highway 65, crossing over the freeway. Drive several miles toward Lincoln until you see the sign for Twelve Bridges Drive, a new road as of 2001. Take that exit and it is about five miles to Twelve Bridges.

Commercial flights are available from Sacramento International Airport, served by major airlines. The closest small airport is Lincoln Regional Airport (916/645-3443), which has been upgraded with longer runways to accommodate jet aircraft.

CONTACTS

- **Old Sacramento Visitor Information/ Sacramento Convention and Visitors Bureau** 1421 K St., Sacramento, CA 95814; 916/264-7777, fax 916/264-7788; email cvb@sacto.org
- **Old Sacramento Visitor Center** 916/442-7644
- **Old Sacramento Event Hotline** 916/558-3912
- **Grass Valley/Nevada County Chamber of Commerce** 248 Mill St., Grass Valley, CA 95945; 530/273-4667, 800/655-4667; website www.gvncchamber.org, email info@gvncchamber.org
- **Nevada City Chamber of Commerce** 132 Main St., Nevada City, CA 95959; 530/265-2692, 800/655-NJOY; website www.ncgold.com, email ncchambr@oro.net

■ **Auburn Area Visitor and Convention Bureau** 601 Lincoln Way, Auburn, CA 95603; 530/885-5616, fax 530/885-5854

■ **Auburn Visitor Center** 13464 Lincoln Way, Auburn, CA 95603; 530/887-2111, 800/427-6463

Chapter 6

For Riders and Billy Goats: North Lake Tahoe

M ountain golf is a precious commodity, the courses carved out of treacherous terrain, buried under snow for months at a time, and expertly restored to peak condition for a few glorious months of play each year. North Lake Tahoe offers some of the best mountain golf.

Surrounding snowcapped peaks soar as high as 10,000 feet, and the lake sparkles an intense sapphire blue. The largest alpine lake in North America, Lake Tahoe measures 22 miles long and 12 miles wide. It straddles the California-Nevada border at more than 6,000 feet in elevation. Tall fragrant pines tower above lush fairways nurtured with pure snowmelt that rushes over boulders in adjacent streams. This getaway promises to keep you busy with a variety of recreational options, ideal for family vacations: water-skiing, boating, fishing, horseback riding, hiking or mountain biking, and, of course, golf.

From lakefront shopping at Tahoe City to the classy casinos of posh Incline Village, the communities of North Lake Tahoe occupy the northern half of the 72-mile scenic drive around the lake. The shoreline of sandy beaches and rugged cliffs may tempt swimmers, but the water temperature hovers between 65 and 70 degrees, even in midsummer, so few venture in without a wetsuit. Just five miles from the lake, Squaw Valley USA's high-speed tram whisks sightseers to the steep mountain peaks that challenged the world's best skiers at the 1960 Winter Olympics.

North Lake Tahoe offers eight golf courses within a 45-mile radius. Come spring, eager players can't wait for the snow to melt and golf season to begin. Courses typically open in stages, offering whatever holes are playable (i.e., not under snow) as soon as possible. Lane Lewis, owner of the nine-hole Old Brockway Golf Course in Kings Beach, says, "We're usually the first course to open for the season. By April we can usually open 'Whiskey Loop,' which is holes 1, 2, 3, 8, and 9." That particular layout was named for singer Dean Martin, who regularly performed at nearby Cal-Neva Lodge in the '50s. It seems that by hole number 3 Martin's legendary drinking had dulled his golf skills and he was ready for the finishing holes.

A round of golf on any mountain course yields breathtaking scenery and, inevitably, uneven terrain. Expect downhill, sidehill, and uphill lies. Also, elevation changes will play tricks with distance, so don't always believe the yardage markers. Downhill par-3s usually play shorter than indicated, and a shot from the fairway to an uphill green will play longer. As the starter said at one course, "You're playing on the side of a mountain, so you know which way the ball goes." That goes for putts too. The saving grace of all this is that the ball flies noticeably farther because the air is thinner at the high altitude.

Choices abound for a golf vacation in North Lake Tahoe. It's a destination replete with other things to do besides golf, because the short season mandates that all the warm-weather activities be packed into a limited time frame, and you won't want to miss a thing. That's also what makes it a terrific family destination with something for everyone.

An all-inclusive resort such as Northstar-at-Tahoe makes for an ideal family getaway, offering lodging choices ranging from fully equipped studio condominiums to five-bedroom houses and hotel-style rooms in the Village. Complimentary shuttles operate daily, taking guests around the resort to the Village shops and restaurants, to the Swim and Racquet Club, and to the golf course. The Robert Muir Graves–designed golf course offers two distinctly different experiences. The wide-open front nine sprawls over an open meadow, while the back nine twists and turns in a tight layout through dense forest. Some holes play through a grove of aspen trees, whose shimmering small leaves move in the breeze like fluttering wind chimes. Players complain that the back nine has too many blind holes, and on hole number 12, it's difficult to avoid the clump of trees just 170 yards from the blue tees. On hole number 17, you can lay up at "chicken flats," to the right of the creek, but it's still a decent carry over the creek on the second shot.

The luxurious Resort at Squaw Creek boasts a starkly modern six-story hotel, framed by the granite peaks of Squaw Valley USA, site of the 1960 Winter Olympic Games. Golf tops the long list of summer sports and activities available at the resort. Robert Trent Jones Jr. designed a course that opened in 1991 to immediate accolades. *Golf* magazine named it one of the "Top Ten Courses You Can Play." Since it is situated in the Tahoe National Forest, the course adheres to strict environmental regulations imposed by the Army Corps of Engineers, to preserve the existing wetlands and wildlife. Recognized as an Audubon Cooperative Sanctuary Course, Squaw Creek is maintained without chemical pesticides.

Placement of tees, landing areas, and greens creates long carries over protected areas where ball retrieval is not allowed. Think Spanish Bay. It's target golf at its best, with narrow fairways snaking through marshland and meadows, connected by long wood-planked cart paths. Most of the course is laid out on the valley floor, surrounded by the awesome ski mountains. Opinions are all over the map. The course design is widely praised, yet recreational players find it difficult due to the long carries and environmentally restricted areas, often not discerned until it's too late. Head golf professional Chris Lynch has said he supports efforts to make the course more forgiving for resort guests. On the other hand, low-handicappers decry any alterations that would spoil the integrity of a great course. You gotta play it at least once.

If resorts aren't for you, you could stay at your choice of lodging and still play the resort courses, as well as others. There are numerous home and condominium rentals available in North Lake Tahoe, either on or off the lake, and a variety of hotels to choose from. However, you'd have a better choice of tee times and better green fees at Squaw Creek or at Northstar with a stay-and-play package.

Stay-and-play packages are not available at the other 18-hole courses in the area, which you won't want to miss: The Golf Courses at Incline Village and Tahoe Donner Golf Course. Since they are part of residential communities, tee-time priorities are given to homeowners, so it can be difficult for visitors to book a tee time at these popular courses during peak season. The other three courses in the area are nine-hole courses—Tahoe City Golf Course, Ponderosa Golf Course, and Old Brockway, enjoyable for a short round or to play twice for a full 18.

Be sure to leave time for enjoying the lake. Boating and water sports abound. You can dine lakefront and watch the pink sunset glow gradually spread across the still lake waters. Lake Tahoe's original settlers were the Washoe Indians, more than 2,000 years ago. The Washoe word for "lake," *da ow ga,* is thought to be the source for "Tahoe." Maintaining the lake's famed clarity is of great concern, as some studies show that oxygen levels are declining at the bottom of the lake, contributing to algae growth. Organizations like the League to Save Lake Tahoe educate the public about the urgency of protecting the lake, and the Coast Guard advises boaters on how to prevent gas and oil spillage into its pristine waters.

As the season winds down, usually by late October, extensive measures are taken to prepare the courses for winter. John Hughes, director of golf at Incline Village, says they clear snow and ice off the greens, put covers on them, and rope off the greens and tees for the winter. Al Bailey, general manager at Ponderosa Golf Course, says it takes three weeks to prepare the greens for winter by treating them and covering them for protection during the long, cold months.

Some courses allow cross-country skiing. Incline allows use of its driving range for sledding. Others believe that when the deep snowpack becomes frozen and then pressed down by heavy equipment, e.g., to make cross-country tracks, it will take longer to thaw out in spring, thus delaying opening day. Chris Lynch says "Mother Nature is my co-pilot." Even with all the proper preparation, late-season snowstorms can postpone opening date until well into June. While early season conditions can be less than perfect, with areas of water kill and melt off, eager players are usually willing to overlook temporary inconveniences. Squaw Creek and Tahoe Donner are often the last to open fully.

North Lake Tahoe is an ideal place to bring the kids for a family vacation. With the plethora of activities available, everyone can do what he or she wants during the day and gather together at dinnertime. The resorts offer half-day or full-day programs of supervised play for small children, so you can play golf knowing your children are being looked after. Nongolfing members of the family will have plenty to do, and no one will feel left out.

Itinerary

WARMING UP

Gather your energy; this will be an active vacation. Make all your tee times before you go, as far ahead as possible. Try to book tee times when you make lodging reservations. Also, ask to reserve the children's supervised play programs for the same time as your golf game for a worry-free round. If you choose to stay in a condo, ask for a unit with a deck and a barbecue. Also, shop before you leave home and bring food with you so you won't have to take time away from your vacation to go to the store.

Future visitors to North Lake Tahoe will have a new destination to explore when Vancouver-based Intrawest opens a four-season alpine-style resort village at the base of Squaw Peak. Intrawest plans to have 80-plus shops, restaurants, and lodging in a village described as "European-style but High Sierra in spirit," which will cover 13 acres of the upper parking lot area near the lifts and the tram at Squaw Valley. When completed (in phases) in 5–7 years, the village is expected to resemble Intrawest's other successful mountain resorts, such as Whistler/Blackcomb in British Columbia, Mt. Tremblant in Quebec, and Stratton in Vermont.

day 1

Both winter and summer, heading up to Lake Tahoe for the weekend is a time-honored tradition in northern California. Bay Area folks envy those in Sacramento or the foothills who got a head start on the freeway. Auburn is the last sizable town before the ascent into the mountains and offers two popular stops for motorists, Ideka's Fruit Stand and Awful Annie's. Tahoe Donner Golf Course, our first stop on this itinerary, is about an hour east of Auburn off I-80. Take the Donner Lake exit and go left over the freeway.

Occasionally a pudgy brown bear will wander across the fairways at Tahoe Donner, causing more alarm than harm. The densely wooded setting makes for splendid isolation, and even the houses (mostly second homes) are set far enough back to not be intrusive. Accuracy is key on these narrow fairways. Although Tahoe Donner doubles as a ski area in winter, it's not a resort with a central village like Northstar or Squaw Valley. There is no lodging on the premises; rather the emphasis is on the activity, whether skiing or golf.

To reach your Northstar condo after golf, go back to Truckee and take Highway 267 south for six miles to Northstar Drive. It is well marked. Turn right at the big Northstar sign, and the registration office is on your immediate right. Cheerful clerks will give you a map and directions to where you are staying. The accommodations are all individually owned and decorated. You'll find that there are no elevators in the condo buildings, and you may be carrying your luggage from the parking lot down a mountain path and up to a second floor unit. Suggestion: Leave the golf clubs in the car. Take a moment to relax into the quiet pristine setting and the exhilarating mountain air.

You probably won't feel like cooking dinner. So get out the map you were given at check-in and head for the Village, just minutes away by car, or, depending on where you are located, you could walk. Dine at Timbercreek Restaurant, near the big wooden bear statue, where you can sit at an outside table while the kids run around the Village area. As you walk back to the car afterward, the stars are so bright and there are so many of them, it doesn't look real.

day II

Take the kids to Minors Camp when it opens at 9 A.M. Reservations are strongly recommended. Minors Camp is a licensed child care center that offers a day camp for children ages 2–10. Programs may include art, singing, swimming, climbing wall, pony rides, nature walks, and many other activities. The cost is $45 per child for all day, $27 for half day, but resort guests are entitled to one free half day for each child. Minors Camp is in the Village Clocktower Building. The center gives the parents beepers and requests that they stay on the premises; fortunately, the golf course is within acceptable limits.

Then you can go to your tee time at Northstar, just minutes away, and turn your attention to the challenging course before you. Be prepared for mountain streams and ponds on 14 holes and the twists and turns of the back nine. Order your lunch at the turn or grab a sandwich off the beverage cart.

In the afternoon pick up the kids and there's still plenty of daylight left to enjoy swimming together at the Swim and Racquet Club. An outdoor grill offers lunch until midafternoon. Lifeguards carefully monitor the pool area, which is so big that part of it is set aside for diving, part of it is for laps, and part of it is shallow for younger children. There's also water basketball and other activities announced during the day, like "2 P.M. Treasure Hunt."

The Swim and Racquet Club has a junior Olympic-size pool and two outdoor hot tubs plus a lap pool and another hot tub in the secluded "Adult Quiet Area," where no one under 18 is allowed. Ah, the serenity. The bright and airy Fitness Center is equipped with cardio equipment and weights, and its large windows look out on the adult pool area.

Long summer days leave time for more activities. In addition to the golf course, the resort offers 10 tennis courts, horseback riding, fly-fishing, and an Adventure Park with a climbing wall and ropes course. The ski lifts serve as transport to the resort's mountain biking and hiking trails, although hikers sometimes say the trails are dominated by bikers who stir up too much dust in their wake.

The shaded glen off the poolside lawn area has picnic tables and barbecues that you can reserve ahead by calling the Swim and Racquet Club. If you planned it well, meal fixings are already in a cooler in the car, and you're ready for an outdoor dinner. If you forgot something, walk over to the Village Food Company or, for more selection, go to the Safeway in Truckee. The Game Room or Teen Center stays open until dark or close to 10 P.M., and you just might be able to sneak away to one of the hot tubs, which also close around 10 P.M. The hot tub in the adult pool area is especially tranquil.

day III

Check out in the morning and head for Kings Beach because, after all, you want to see the lake, and here's an opportunity to play golf together as a family at Old Brockway Golf Course. Exit

Northstar Drive and turn right onto Highway 267 south for six miles to Kings Beach. Old Brockway Golf Course will be your right at the intersection of Highway 267 and Highway 28/North Lake Boulevard.

Nine-hole Old Brockway appears rather nondescript when you drive by it because only the first and second holes are visible from the road, but it is beautiful when you get back into the other seven holes, quiet and serene with few houses, steeped in ponderosa pines and redwoods. It's challenging too. When you're done, stay and have lunch out on the deck at the Moose's Tooth Café, which overlooks the putting green and pond. You can even see the lake across the road.

 NOTES

Serious Golfers. Sign the kids up for Minors Camp or bring the nanny.

Extended Play. Stay an extra night or two at Incline Village, on the Nevada side of North Lake Tahoe. Play the Championship Course and/or the Mountain Course. Stay at the Hyatt Regency Lake Tahoe, which has a wonderful beach just across the street where you can recline on a chaise lounge under your own beach umbrella, sip a cool drink brought right to you, and watch the boats crisscross the lake. While there is no connection between the Hyatt and the Incline golf courses, hence no golf packages, the Hyatt concierge can make tee times for guests, which can be paid for in the lodging package. Dine at Hyatt's Lone Eagle Grille, which fronts the beach with big picture windows. The Hyatt's Lakeside Cottages are considered some of the best lodging on the lake.

North Lake Tahoe's Nevada side offers the excitement of nonstop action at local casinos. In addition to Hyatt's 24-hour lobby casino, check out the cluster of casinos at the state line, of which the most noteworthy is historic Cal-Neva Resort, where Frank Sinatra and the "Rat Pack" used to hang out. Nevada has no state income tax, and if gaming revenues continue to feed the state's coffers, this probably won't change.

Health. The high altitude and dry climate can cause dehydration and a sort of "altitude sickness," which shows up as fatigue, dizziness, and even fainting. Chris Lynch says Squaw Creek's course marshals are trained to observe players with these symptoms and offer assistance. Your legs may feel like lead. Drink a lot of water and give yourself a few days to adjust to the altitude change.

Parents. In addition to Northstar's Minors Camp, The Resort at Squaw Creek offers Mountain Buddies and the Hyatt Regency Lake Tahoe offers Camp Hyatt, with similar day programs for children.

Romantics. Reserve a table on the deck at Sunsets on the Lake or Gar

Woods so you can watch the moon rising over the mountains to cast a golden path across the lake's glassy surface.

Money Savers. The best way to save money in a resort area like Tahoe is to either go with a stay-and-play package, where available, or stay at an inexpensive motel and avail yourself of twilight rates for golf at the courses you want to play. Also, try to go in the off season.

If You Have Only One Day and One Night. Play golf at Tahoe Donner on the drive up, then check into the Resort at Squaw Creek and enjoy the new spa, which includes fitness center, massage, and salon services. Dine at a restaurant overlooking the lake. The next day play the Resort at Squaw Creek and leisurely drive home.

Nongolfers. The resorts offer many activities on property, or if you're staying in a motel or condo, you can avail yourself of water activities on the lake, horseback riding, hiking, mountain biking, or relaxing.

Courses

ITINERARY SELECTIONS

Tahoe Donner Golf Course
11509 Northwoods Blvd.
Truckee, CA 96161
916/587-9440, fax 916/587-9496

A short distance north of Truckee, Tahoe Donner is known for tight, narrow fairways lined on both sides with trees. There are no out of bounds and no parallel fairways, so the course often employs spotters to help players locate shots and speed play. It's a beautiful, forested layout with undulating fairways, well-maintained with good signage and on-course facilities.

> **SCORECARD**
>
> **Architect:** Joseph B. Williams, 1976
> **Course Record:** 66, John Fought
> **Championship Blue:** Par 72, 6,917 yards, 72.4 rating for men, 133 slope
> **Regular White:** Par 72, 6,587 yards, 71.2 rating for men, 128 slope
> **Forward Red:** Par 74, 6,032 yards, 73.1 rating for women, 138 slope
> **For tee times** nonresidents can call 530/587-9440 10 days in advance.

Tahoe Donner's first hole, an uphill par-4, is also the number one handicap hole, and it doesn't get any easier as long, narrow par-4s seem to proliferate. From the elevated tee on par-3 hole number 7, the majestic Sierras stand out and you can see the ski lifts that dominate this area in the winter. Hole number 18 is a great finishing hole, it's all downhill over a creek and a pond. Tahoe Donner is a relaxed golf experience, not big and fancy, just good golf.

The course is walkable but not an option for visitors since the $100 green fee includes cart. Residents may walk. Dress is mid-thigh shorts and collared shirts. Soft spikes are recommended but not required because of potential liability if someone slips. Cart access is typically 90 degrees.

TEE TIDBITS | This semiprivate course is owned by the Tahoe Donner Association. Head professional Bruce Towle says the amount of play has increased in the years he's been there even though the development is not fully built out yet. They are actively selling houses and finished homes. The property owners "season's pass" provides unlimited golf and preferential tee times 12 days in advance. Property owners' guests pay green fees of about half the regular rate. It's not easy for nonresidents to get good tee times, and Towle says morning tee times are rarely available to the public, but it's still worth it to play a round in the afternoon.

Northstar-at-Tahoe Golf Course
P. O. Box 129 (1680 Basque Dr. in Northstar)
Truckee, CA 96060
530/562-2490

You can see Northstar's front nine from Highway 267. It's wide open with views of Truckee's Martis Valley, several ponds, and frequent bunkers. Before new scorecards combined the nines, it was known as "the Meadow Nine." No one knows the course better than PGA professional Jim Anderson, who recently retired after serving as Northstar's head pro since 1977. He suggests, "Hit below the greens on the front nine." The back nine features tight fairways lined with pine and aspen trees. Because there are several blind holes, forecaddies spot balls on the back nine, especially in the canyons on holes 14 and 16, and on hole number 17. Snow remains longer on the hilly back nine holes because of the higher elevation, and carts are restricted to the paths during the early season, otherwise not. The complimentary yardage guide is helpful.

SCORECARD
Architect: Robert Muir Graves, 1975
Course Record: 72, Jim Anderson
Gold: Par 72, 6,897 yards, 72.4 rating for men, 137 slope
Blue: Par 72, 6,337 yards, 69.5 rating for men, 129 slope
White: Par 72, 6,015 yards, 68.3 rating for men, 125 slope; 73.8 rating for women, 142 slope
Red: Par 72, 5,470 yards, 70.8 rating for women, 136 slope
Call 530/562-2490 for tee times no more than 21 days in advance, with the exception of lodging package guests or groups.

Green fees of $85 ($74 for lodging guests) include shared cart and a bucket of range balls, but walking is allowed and pull carts are available. Think twice about walking the back nine. Afternoon, twilight, and "nine before 9 A.M." rates are attractive. There is a driving range and putting green. Northstar prefers collared shirts, no cutoffs or tank tops. Soft spikes are required.

TEE TIDBITS | Northstar is usually one of the first local courses to open and offers discounted rates until mid-June. It's an attractive mountain golf experience from the moment you enter the shaded parking lot, peaked-roof clubhouse, and pro shop, conveniently next to the practice range and first tee. Wind down on the big deck at The Clubhouse at Martis Valley Grille after your round, and it's a short walk to your car. The pro shop has been recognized as Merchandiser of the Year several times and is usually named in the top 100 golf shops. You'll find the latest fashions, equipment, and accessories.

Old Brockway Golf Course
7900 North Lake Blvd.
Kings Beach, CA 96143
530/546-9909

Old Brockway was built in 1924 and was a favorite of Frank Sinatra, Bob Hope, and Judy Garland. In 1934 the course was the site of the first Bing Crosby Open, because Crosby would invite friends for a week of fun and golf when he was entertaining at Cal-Neva. After Brockway, Crosby moved his tournament to Rancho Santa Fe and eventually to Pebble Beach. The opening scene of the TV series *Bonanza* was filmed on the second fairway.

SCORECARD

Architect: John Duncan Dunn, 1924
Course Record: NA
Championship: Par 72, 6,628 yards, 69.8 rating for men, 125 slope
Regular: Par 72, 6,054 yards, 67.6 rating for men, 116 slope
Forward: Par 72, 4,924 yards, 66.9 rating for women, 113 slope
For tee times call 530/546-9909, up to 30 days in advance.

Owner Lane Lewis has diligently maintained the original 1920s feel of the course, with its tight fairways and small greens, while making changes that include creating a new ninth hole that is primarily wetlands with a pond surrounding the green, renovating the first tee and driving range, and expanding the putting green. Lewis says Old Brockway is the only nine-hole course west of the Mississippi to be Audubon certified, and it has seven acres of wetlands restoration that treats runoff for environmental compliance.

The first and second holes play along the road, then by the third hole it becomes more serene with only a few houses tucked away off the fairways, immense trees, and lots of birds. When you reach hole number 9, it's almost surprising to hear traffic noise and see cars again.

In peak season, you can walk nine holes for $35 or ride for $52. Play a second nine and the rate goes down. Walking is easy but carts are available and allowed on fairways since there are no cart paths. It's pretty casual at Old Brockway, so no dress code is enforced and soft spikes are not required.

TEE TIDBITS | Old Brockway is one of those hidden secrets. Lewis added a new log cabin–style clubhouse and added the Moose's Tooth Café, which has quickly become a popular local spot.

ALTERNATIVES

The **Resort at Squaw Creek** winds along the valley floor through and around wetlands, surrounded by the awesome ski mountains of Squaw Valley USA. Robert Trent Jones Jr. designed a serious test of target golf. Some of those who call the course "unfair" undoubtedly contributed to the plethora of golf balls resting in the shallow ponds, irretrievable due to environmental constraints. Look but don't touch. Golfers bemoan the lengthy carries required on this course, but if you feel compelled to take up another sport, the Squaw Valley horse stables run along the left side of hole number 16. And of course there's always fishing. Chris Lynch says the pond at hole number 18 is stocked with trout (catch and release) and recommends the resort's High Mountain Fly-Fishing Program.

The towering mountains striped with ski lifts surround the valley and cast a long chilly shadow as soon as the sun goes down. Walking is allowed, but golf carts are included in the $115 green fees. Carts must stay on paths. Caddies are available. The resort makes for a convenient 19th hole, with several restaurants and bars to choose from. Tee times can be made up to a year in advance. ■ 400 SQUAW CREEK RD., SQUAW VALLEY, CA 96146; 800/327-3353; WEBSITE WWW.SQUAWCREEK.COM, EMAIL SQUAWCREEK@THEGRID.NET

The **Golf Courses at Incline Village** are the only North Lake Tahoe courses with views of Lake Tahoe. The Championship Course, designed by Robert Trent Jones Sr. in 1964, runs through pine forests to an elevation of 6,500 feet, with narrow fairways, bunkered greens, and water hazards. Director of Golf John Hughes says that fully 68 percent of tee times are reserved for Incline Village residents and, in addition, the course hosts a lot of outside events. Green fees of $115 include shared cart (90-degree rule applies), which contrasts with the residents' rate of $35.

Save some time for shopping in the pro shop. The Northern California section of the PGA named John Hughes Merchandiser of the Year for resorts in 1999. For tee times call 888/236-8725 for The Golfer.com or go online, two weeks in advance. You can reserve more than two weeks ahead by paying a nonrefundable advance charge of $15 per player. ■ P. O. BOX 7590, INCLINE VILLAGE, NV 89452 (955 FAIRWAY BLVD.); 775/832-1144, FAX 775/832-1141; WEBSITE WWW.GOLFINCLINE.COM

The **Mountain Course** is an executive par-58 course that is unexpectedly challenging, featuring four par-4s and the rest par-3s. Designed by Robert Trent Jones Jr. in 1969, it sits at a 500-foot higher elevation than the Championship Course, so it offers more peeks at the lake and opens 2–4 weeks later in the season, after the snow has melted. John Hughes says it is one of the top five of its type in the country, "not a pitch and putt." Green fees are $50 for visitors.

The Mountain Course hosted the National Championship of Executive Courses. It's fun to play, well-maintained, and easier to get on than the Championship Course. There are only two tee settings. For tee times call 775/832-1150. ■ 690 WILSON WAY, INCLINE VILLAGE, NV 89451; 775/832-1144

Be the first on your block to play North Lake Tahoe's newest course, **Coyote Moon,** which opened in 2000. It's in Truckee near Tahoe Donner. The course is designed by Brad Bell and ranges from 7,177 yards to 5,022 yards. The spectacular par-3 13th hole starts from a dramatically elevated tee. Look for the clubhouse to open in 2001. Green fees are $125. ■ 10685 NORTHWOODS BOULEVARD, TRUCKEE, CA 96161; 530/587-0886

This private course is so special, try to find someone who is a member to take you. **Lahontan Golf Club** is North Lake Tahoe's only private, gated golf club community, across from the Tahoe/Truckee Airport on Highway 267, but you can't see any of it from the highway. No expense has been spared in the design of the Tom Weiskopf course or quality of materials used, although it has a natural, park-like feel with no tee markers or out-of-bounds. Most players walk with caddies. Surrounding homes are massive wooden structures built in the "Old Tahoe" style. ■ 12700 LODGE TRAIL DR., TRUCKEE, CA 96161; 530/550-2400 OR 800/582-9919; WEBSITE WWW.LAHONTAN.COM

If you only have time for nine holes at North Lake Tahoe, here are some suggestions. **Ponderosa Golf Course** is a good nine-hole layout for practice or for beginners. It is wide and flat, great for walking, with close parallel fairways, so watch for errant shots. It's privately owned and is one mile south of Truckee on Highway 267, not far from Northstar. It is 3,018 yards, par 36, and has no lessons or range, but there is a pro shop. Green fees are $25 to walk and $42 to ride, for nine holes. ■ 10040 REYNOLD WAY, TRUCKEE, CA 96160; 530/587-3501, FAX 530/587-8463

Tahoe City Golf Course originally opened with six holes in 1917. It is relatively short at 2,570 yards from the middle tees, has alternate tees for 18 holes, and is par 66. The first hole is a 485-yard par-5, the only par-5, and the second hole par-3 features open lake views. It is behind the Bank of America in Tahoe City, thus extremely convenient for visitors and usually crowded. It offers lessons and a driving range. Green fees are $30 to walk and $46 to ride, for nine holes. ■ 251 NORTH LAKE BLVD., TAHOE CITY, CA 96145; 530/583-1516, FAX 530/583-8163; WEBSITE WWW.TCGC.COM

Lodging

ITINERARY SELECTION

Northstar-at-Tahoe offers more than 260 accommodations ranging from studio condominiums to five-bedroom homes. Over the next several years, Northstar plans to double the number of lodging units and remodel the Village. The condos are in clusters of low-rise wooden buildings with a rustic, ski-lodge feel. All units are individually decorated and can vary in amenities, but hotel-style rooms in the Village do not have kitchens. You can request a location close to the pool or close to the Village or close to golf, and ask for amenities that are important to you like a barbecue. Resort guests have complimentary use of the Swim and Racquet Club. Rates for the stay-and-play package are as low as $49.50 per person per night, double occupancy, and include one round of golf per person after noon, per stay,

shared cart, and lodging in a studio condo, Sunday–Thursday only. Two-night minimum stay. Morning tee times are an additional $35 per person.
■ P. O. Box 129, Truckee (Highway 267 at Northstar Dr.), CA 96160; 800/GO-NORTH (800/466-6784) or 530/562-1010, fax 530/562-2215; website WWW.SKINORTHSTAR.COM

GOLF PACKAGE OPTION

The **Resort at Squaw Creek** offers 405 luxurious hotel rooms and suites, three restaurants, three pools, room service, and a brand-new spa. All facilities, including shopping and the golf pro shop, are easily accessible within the convenient hotel complex, but it can be a chilly trek along the uncovered walkway from the lobby to the guest room elevators. The hotel's sophisticated shiny black exterior and stark design look more "downtown" than mountain. Rates for the "Play All Day" golf package are $143 per person per night, double occupancy, including accommodations, unlimited golf or $55 per person worth of FlexiPlan vouchers to use on other resort activities like the spa, and bag storage. ■ P. O. Box 3333 (400 Squaw Creek Rd.), Olympic Valley, CA 96146; 800/327-3353; 530/583-6300, fax 530/581-6632; website WWW.SQUAWCREEK.COM

ALTERNATIVES

Hyatt Regency Lake Tahoe is a 485-room lakefront resort with a 12-story hotel, a 24-hour lobby casino, swimming pool, restaurants, and a private beach across the street behind the hotel's restaurant, the Lone Eagle Grille. Water-sports rentals and bar service are available on the beach. Stay here if you want to be centrally located in Incline Village with the services of a first-class hotel and convenient gambling. The Incline golf courses are a few miles away. For some of the best lodging on the lake, stay at one of the 24 Lakeside Cottages. Hotel rooms start at $205 per night and Lakeside Cottages at $675. ■ Country Club at Lakeshore, Incline Village, NV 89451; 800/553-3288 or 775/832-1234, fax 775/831-7508; website WWW.HYATT-TAHOE.COM

Cal-Neva Resort is a beautifully restored historic casino with 200 guest rooms and cottages at Crystal Bay, straddling the borders of California and Nevada. The Indian Room displays historic Washoe Indian artifacts. Cal-Neva sits above the lake with expansive views and offers a gazebo, popular for weddings, and a European spa that features massage ($60), herbal wraps ($40), and other body and skin-care treatments. Pampering with a view. Room rates are $139–269. Spa packages available. ■ P. O. Box 368 (2 Stateline Rd.), Crystal Bay, NV 89402; 800/CAL-NEVA or 775/832-4000, fax 775/831-9007; website WWW.CALNEVARESORT.COM

Sunnyside Resort is the place if you want to stay right on the lake in Tahoe City, in a comfortable pine lodge with fireplaces and a good restaurant. It has a casual, cozy atmosphere with only 23 rooms and some suites. Everyone loves the huge expansive deck that juts out over the lake, where the restaurant serves lunch, dinner, and Sunday brunch. Rates are $165–205 per night and include continental breakfast. ■ 1850 W. LAKE BLVD., P. O. BOX 5969, TAHOE CITY, CA 95730; 530/583-7200 OR 800/822-2SKI; WEBSITE WWW. SUNNYSIDERESORT.COM

River Ranch Lodge is a historic rustic lodge with a good restaurant, outdoor grill, and attractive rooms that sits on the banks of the Truckee River, just minutes from Squaw Valley. River rafters careen by on the rushing water. It was originally called the Deer Park Inn and completed in 1888. Many rooms have private balconies overlooking the river. The restaurant serves breakfast, lunch, and dinner at tables by the rock fireplace or cantilevered over the rushing river, and there's outside patio dining during summer months. Summer rates range $85–125, including continental breakfast. ■ HIGHWAY 89 AT ALPINE MEADOWS ROAD, P. O. BOX 197, TAHOE CITY, CA 96145; 530/583-4264 OR 800/535-9900, FAX 530/583-7237; WEBSITE WWW. RIVERRANCHLODGE.COM/

For vacation home rentals, contact **Vacation Station,** which offers lakefront, lakeview, and golf course homes and condos and claims to have the largest selection on the North Shore, from basic to deluxe. Three-bedroom/three-bath condos near the Incline Village Championship Course run $145–230 per night. The office is across from Hyatt Regency Hotel Casino. ■ 110 COUNTRY CLUB DR., P. O. BOX 7180, INCLINE VILLAGE, NV 89452; 800/841-7443 OR 775/831-3664, FAX 775/832-4844; WEBSITE WWW.VACATIONSTATION.NET

Cabins, homes, and condos can also be booked through the **North Lake Tahoe Resort Association** at 800-TAHOE-4-U (800/824-6348); website www.tahoefun.org, email info@tahoefun.org.

Dining

ITINERARY SELECTIONS

Ikeda's is ideal for a stop on the way up I-80 to North Lake Tahoe. The Ikeda family has operated here since the 1970s, offering fresh fruit from its own orchards, pies, and specialty food items like chutneys and sauces from family recipes. Order hamburgers, salads, or baked goods at the counter to go or eat in the small café. Buy food items in the small grocery as well. ■ 13500 LINCOLN WAY, AUBURN, CA; 530/885-4243, FAX 530/885-6215

Awful Annie's is in Old Town Auburn, serving hearty breakfast and lunch dishes like the "Morning Mess" (you can have a big or little mess), which is a delicious omelet concoction; sandwiches; chili; and generous salads. Sit inside or on the deck, sipping the house-special cinnamon orange decaf tea. ■ 160 Sacramento St., Old Town Auburn, CA; 530/888-9857

Timbercreek Restaurant is conveniently located in the Village at Northstar, perfect if you don't feel like cooking in the condo and don't want to drive very far. It's quiet and relaxing inside and has an outdoor patio where you can watch all the Village activity. Restless children can run around and still be in sight. Wide menu choices include appetizers (mostly under $10) like pan-fried crabcakes or grilled artichokes, entrée salads as well as dinner salads, and entrées ranging from $15 for pastas to meats like the chile-rubbed one-pound porterhouse or the Mediterranean seafood paella, priced just under $25. Kids get their own menu. Dinner only. ■ Northstar Village, Truckee, CA; 530/562-1010

Moose's Tooth Café at Old Brockway Golf Course has become popular with locals who aren't even golfers for great menu items like eggs Benedict, buttermilk malt pancakes with mixed berry compote, and maple mustard burger or Danish baby-back ribs (the only dish over $10 on the lunch menu). Come on back for dinner and enjoy roast duck, New York steak, or seafood specials, all under $20. The deck overlooks the putting green and offers a glimpse of the lake. Breakfast, lunch, and dinner. ■ 400 Brassie Ave., Kings Beach, at Old Brockway Golf Course, corner of Highway 267 and Highway 28, CA; 530/546-9495

At the classy **Lone Eagle Grille,** on the Hyatt Lake Tahoe's private beach in Incline Village, you can run right out and dip your toes in the chilly lake or take a moonlit walk on the beach after dinner. Its spacious interior resembles a mountain hunting lodge with high beamed ceilings and massive rock fireplaces. The menu appetizers like baked brie ($9) or crabcakes ($10.50) whet your appetite for entrées like ginger-roasted duck ($18) or North Lake Tahoe clam bake ($25). Lunch, dinner, Sunday brunch. ■ Country Club Dr. at Lakeshore Blvd., Incline Village, NV; 775/832-3250

At **Sunsets On The Lake,** valets are available for your car and your boat. The large heated and glass-enclosed deck is always in demand, and in the summer, the Island Bar is open; a few steps down from the deck, right over the water, it too is glass-enclosed and heated. Grab a chair and sit on the sand beach, sipping a tropical drink, and you could be in Maui, except that's a pine tree, not a palm tree, you're sitting under. Ahi tuna is served as both an appetizer and an entrée. In addition to fish and game specials, the broad menu includes spit-roasted garlic chicken and wood-fired filet mignon, with prices ranging $17–23. Dinner; lunch and brunch seasonally. ■ 7320 North Lake Blvd., Tahoe Vista, CA; 530/546-3640

Valet boat parking is also available at **Gar Woods,** or you can dock it yourself. Next to Sierra Boat Company, the restaurant is named for boat designer Garfield Wood, whose elegant wooden crafts designed in the 1920s can still be seen around the lake. Gar Woods features a contemporary upbeat atmosphere, on several levels, but everyone wants to be on the spacious lakeside deck. Cool deck drinks include the house favorite, the Wet Woody, and the Bent Prop. The moderately priced dinner menu includes such favorites as lime chicken sandwich ($9), surf 'n Caesar (seared rare ahi tuna on Caesar salad, $13), grilled salmon ($19), and roasted prime rib ($21). Be sure to start with the beer batter coconut prawns with mango mustard marmalade ($10). Dinner, happy hour, lunch, Sunday brunch; hours change seasonally. ■ 5000 NORTH LAKE BLVD., P. O. BOX 1133, CARNELIAN BAY, CA; 530/546-3366 OR 800/BY-TAHOE (800/298-2463), FAX 530/546-2184; WEBSITE WWW.GARWOODS.COM, EMAIL GARWOODS@SIERRA.NET

ALTERNATIVES

Big Water Grille (341 Ski Way, Incline Village, NV; 775/833-0606, fax 775/833-0627; email Bigwatergrille@msn.com) sits near Diamond Peak Ski Resort in a spectacular mountain setting with expansive lake views. The decor showcases local artistry, featuring etched glass, Old Tahoe style accents, and a fireplace of native rock. The cuisine focuses on American contemporary dishes with a strong Mediterranean and Pacific Rim influence. Here's more Hawaiiana, Tahoe-style, like the popular appetizer, Hawaiian ahi poke with fried wonton chips ($10), and nightly Hawaiian fish entrées in addition to the main entrées. The owners have been successful restaurateurs for more than 20 years. Their other dinner houses include the Plantation House at Kapalua, Maui, and the Sea Watch at Wailea, Maui. Entrées range $16–24, and the fish specials, like mahimahi or opakapaka, are around $21. Cocktails, dinner.

The kids will love **Rosie's Café** (571 North Lake Blvd., Tahoe City, CA; 530/583-8504), and so will you if you're looking for something casual with a little history thrown in. Bicycles, pinball machines, deer antlers, and Old Tahoe memorabilia create a cozy clutter. Opened in 1981 on a site whose history traces back to the 1800s, Rosie's offers hearty food in a funky atmosphere. Breakfasts and lunches are generally under $10, including omelets, quesadillas, chili, and salads. Dinner entrées include choice of soup or house salad and range from about $14 for veggie stir-fry to $19 for filet mignon or prime rib. The kids' menu features burgers, raviolis, and fish and chips for around $6. Breakfast, lunch, dinner.

If you want tasty, reasonably priced Mexican food, **El Toro Bravo** (10186 Donner Pass Rd., Truckee, CA; 530/587-3557) is the place. Family-owned and -operated in this location for 14 years, it specializes in seafood dishes and offers indoor and outdoor dining as well as takeout. Everything is homemade including the chips. Convenient if you want to eat in the condo one night or join in on happy hour (4–6). Combination dinners range $7.90–9.50 and may include enchiladas, tamales, or chiles rellenos. Lunch and dinner.

Straying Off Course

On Land

North Lake Tahoe is a great area for adventurous people of all ages who like the outdoors. Hiking trails abound, whether it's the easy hike along the Nevada Shoreline, beginning 2.9 miles south of Sand Harbor, or the strenuous trail to the Mt. Rose Summit, a vertical climb of 2,200 feet. The *Trail Map for the North & East Shores of Lake Tahoe* is available from the Lake Tahoe Incline Village & Crystal Bay Visitors Bureau (800/GO-TAHOE).

Experienced mountain bikers like the Marlette Flume Trail, an exciting single track 1,600 feet above Lake Tahoe, but there are easier trails as well as street biking trails. Northstar keeps lifts open during the summer to transport bikers to its 100 miles of trails. At Squaw Valley, bikes are allowed in the cable car that goes up the mountain. Among the many bicycle rental and repair shops, Porter's Ski & Sport operates three convenient locations: 502 North Lake Blvd., Tahoe City, 530/583-2314; 885 Tahoe Blvd., Incline Village, 775/831-3500; and Lucky-Long's Shopping Center, Truckee, 530/587-1500.

Another favorite land-based activity is horseback riding. Vacationers can choose a one- or two-hour ride or a half day, either in a group or privately, by contacting one of the full-service stables, as follows: Northstar Stables (off Highway 267 at Northstar; 530/562-2480), Squaw Valley Stables (1525 Squaw Valley Rd. off Highway 89; 530/583-RIDE), or Tahoe Donner Equestrian (15275 Alder Creek Rd., Truckee; 530/587-9470).

To rise above it all, take the Squaw Valley Cable Car to High Camp, at elevation 8,200 feet, where you'll find five tennis courts, ice skating, and swimming amidst the soaring peaks that put Squaw Valley on the map. The scenic ride ascends 2,000 vertical feet from the valley floor (Squaw Valley USA, 1960 Squaw Valley Rd. off Highway 89; 530/583-6985; website www.squaw.com).

Water Sports

Water enthusiasts will find Tahoe's activities unparalleled. Kayaks, canoes, sailboats, and more are available for rent at various locations around the lake; here's a sampling: Action Watersports (Incline Village; 775/831-4386); North Tahoe Marina (Highway 28, Tahoe Vista; 530/546-8248); Tahoe City Marina (530/583-1039).

Several charter services conduct fishing tours on the lake to seek macki-naw, commonly known as lake trout: Big Mack Charters (Carnelian Bay; 530/546-4444 or 800/877-1462); Kingfish Guide Service departs from 5165 W. Lake Blvd. (Homewood; 530/525-5360 or 800/622-5462).

Rafting on the Truckee River is fun for the whole family. An easy float is from Fanny Bridge in Tahoe City to River Ranch (2–3 hours), which is con-sidered a Class I. Other parts of the Truckee River offer more excitement. Tahoe Whitewater Tours in Tahoe City takes groups and individuals (530/581-2441) or (800/442-7238). Less active visitors can cruise the lake on a historic paddlewheeler, the *Tahoe Gal* (530/583-0141 or 800/218-2464), or take a dinner dance cruise on the Hornblower's *Tahoe Queen* (530/541-3364 or 800/238-2463).

Sights and Entertainment

If sightseeing is more your cup of tea, by all means check out the Ponderosa Ranch (100 Ponderosa Ranch Rd., Incline Village; 775/831-0691), where *Bonanza,* the most popular TV western of all time, was filmed. In the re-created western town, you'll find gunfights, free pony rides, and a pettin' farm. Wind up your hay wagon ride with a hearty all-you-can-eat meal.

To see some of the region's history, visit the Donner Memorial State Park & Emigrant Trail Museum, which features a slide show of the ill-fated 1846 Donner Party (12593 Donner Pass Rd., Truckee, CA 96161; 530/582-7892).

Combine shopping with history by visiting historic downtown Truckee. Many original Truckee buildings remain among the storefront facades and covered wooden walkways. Shops, bars, and restaurants will capture your attention.

Culture has a firm hold on Lake Tahoe, as evidenced by the popularity of the Lake Tahoe Shakespeare Festival, held during July and August. Call 800/74-SHOWS for locations. The Lake Tahoe Summer Music Festival brings jazz, Broadway, opera, pops, you name it, to locations around Lake Tahoe from July through Labor Day weekend. Begun more than 17 years ago, the festival features the Reno Philharmonic Orchestra as well as performances by other musical groups (530/583-3101; website www.tahoemusicfestival.org).

Details, Details

SUITCASE

Autumn is the best time at Tahoe because the crowds have diminished and the weather is perfect. Mornings can be cool, even as low as 27 degrees at

7 A.M., but warming up to 75 degrees by afternoon. Evenings cool down again. Incline is known as the "banana belt" of the North Shore; it can be as much as 10 degrees warmer there. From mid-September to the end of the season, usually late October, discounted rates make Tahoe even more attractive. It's not dressy, but you might want to bring something nice for a special evening or if you attend a glamorous casino show. Soft spikes are more often preferred than required. Be prepared for weather conditions to change rapidly in the mountains. Even though it's summer, leave that rain-suit in your golf bag and pack an extra windshirt. Do bring a swimsuit for the pools and hot tubs.

GETTING THERE

Northstar is halfway (six miles) between Truckee and the north shore of Lake Tahoe on California State Highway 267. It is 40 miles west of Reno, 100 miles east of Sacramento, and 200 miles east of San Francisco. From San Francisco and points west, take Interstate 80 east until you see the exit for Highway 267 near Truckee. Take Highway 267 south approximately six miles and turn right at Northstar Drive. The registration building is immediately to your right.

Truckee-Tahoe Airport is a general aviation airport on Highway 267 not far from Northstar (530/587-4119). Reno/Tahoe International Airport features 24-hour service by most major airlines and is approximately a 45-minute drive from Truckee and North Lake Tahoe via I-80.

CONTACTS

- **North Lake Tahoe Resort Association** 950 North Lake Blvd., Suite 3, Tahoe City, CA 96145; 800/824-6348 or 530/583-3494 (information and lodging), fax 530/581-4081; website www.tahoefun.org
- **Lake Tahoe Incline Village/Crystal Bay Visitors Bureau** 969 Tahoe Blvd., Incline Village, NV 89450; 775/832-1606 (information), 800/GO-TAHOE (800/468-2463, lodging), fax 775/832-1605; website www.gotahoe.com
- **Truckee-Donner Chamber of Commerce** 530/587-8808
- **National Weather Service** 530/546-5253

Chapter 7

The Right Left Turn: Plumas County

The title of this chapter is the answer to your question, "Where's Plumas County?" You're driving out I-80 to the North Shore of Lake Tahoe and make what might be considered a wrong turn, so that you've gone *left* on Highway 89, away from the lake, instead of right. By the time you land in the majestic Mohawk Valley, hear the Feather River rushing by, and see that snow-capped Eureka Peak has jumped off the state seal onto your windshield, your senses may begin to tell you that although you haven't made a right turn, you may not have made a wrong turn either.

If you love golfing in breathtaking surroundings, in a place where the people are friendly, the nights quiet, the accommodations comfortable, and the dining delectable—all of this, and no pang of guilt when the bills come in—then you have in fact made the most right left turn to be found in Northern California. The worst part of this escape is that just a few evenings wandering around the small towns of Johnsville, Portola, Graeagle (that's Gray-eagle, not Graggle), and Blairsden; just a few days learning the secrets of mastering the Graeagle Meadows, Plumas Pines, Whitehawk Ranch, and Dragon courses; and just a few nights looking up at the stars won't feel like enough. As we did, you will start making a list of reasons to return.

"We're very much off the beaten trail and hope to stay that way to a certain degree," says Graeagle Meadows head pro Bob Klein. "It's the Tahoe feel, without the crowds." On the other hand, says Tom Godman, the director of golf at Plumas Pines, "This is still a secret. But all good secrets are meant to be told."

Indeed. So what originally was going to be just a sidebar to the North Tahoe chapter of this book stands tall on its own—albeit with a little less elevation and snow—as a very special golfer's paradise. That's not to say the golfer has to be very special. The golf courses can satisfy players at any skill level and any age. Women golfers will be particularly delighted at how welcome and comfortable they will be made to feel, particularly at the newest 18-holers on the block, Whitehawk Ranch and the Dragon at Gold Mountain.

But that welcome-and-comfortable feeling starts at the gas station when you stop to ask for directions. You see it at the Village Baker, where a grumpy customer tells the staff he hates the country music they're playing so they smile and put on something classical. You see it at the Mohawk Grill, where pizza's not on the lunchtime menu, "But it's not busy right now so just tell me what kind you want." People are just so friendly here, offering you the kind of service-with-a-smile that the priciest of resorts cannot buy because it comes from within. At Plumas Pines, where the award-winning pro shop brings out the shopper in us all, the starter may well offer to make your dinner reservations!

As for dinner, well, don't get us started. Back in the '50s and '60s, a trio of German chefs moved to the area and set up shop at the Iron Door, the Log Cabin, and the Beckwith Tavern. All three establishments are still thriving—the Iron Door so much so that you'd better have a reservation to dine here—and turned out to be the seeds of a little High Sierra gourmet ghetto, tended by chefs who spend winters at Palm Springs restaurants and then summer at the likes of the Graeagle Lodge, eventually opening kitchens of their own.

"Our little town is growing up," says Bret Smith, who grew up in San Francisco but now, with wife Julia, lives in Clio and owns and runs the charming Graeagle Lodge. "And with these golf courses coming in, there's quite a bit of money here. And, people coming up here from the Bay Area are used to getting good food."

Movie star Sharon Stone and her husband had just found some when we visited. They'd dined at the Iron Door two nights in a row during a week-long stay in Graeagle. Tom Cruise and Nicole Kidman were bound to be having some, because they had just bought property at Gold Mountain.

"This area's changing very rapidly," says Feather River Inn general manager Rich Horton. "It used to be that the jeep with the canoe strapped to the top of it was our market, but 460 lots at Gold Mountain starting at $100,000 have been sold. There's a rumor that John Travolta is purchasing property here. You drive to Reno (one hour away) at 6:30 in the morning, and it's a crawl."

You'd think somebody had just found gold, which was how the region became inhabited by miners back in the 1850s. The construction of the Western Pacific Railroad put Portola on the map and allowed the timber industry to become the county's bread and butter. It also brought tourists to the region, and resorts and lodges began sprouting up along the railroad's scenic Feather River Route.

The Ritz of these resorts was the Feather River Inn, a once-elegant property built in 1914 and then rebuilt in 1921 after a fire. In 1915, Harold Sampson designed a 2,900-yard nine-hole course that started at the inn, crossed the railroad tracks once and again, then ended at the inn. Hardly what we today think of as a resort course, the nine still stands, and still offers a test with its tiny but true-rolling greens. It is an inexpensive and unpretentious miniature of the area's larger gems, and standing at the tracks waiting for the train to pass so you can continue your round only serves to offer up a glimpse of the days when the train would stop to deposit that weekend's revelers.

It's a short golf season in Plumas County, opening around the middle of May and closing down sometime in October, and the town of Quincy found a way to cope back in the 1930s, laying claim to the invention of snow golf. The Quincy Golf Course, another 2,900-yarder that played twice yielded a par of 70 for men and 86 for "ladies," was the scene of sunglass-clad, bundled-up golfers playing either colored or dirty golf balls over packed snow. "Putting is difficult, but the pitch shots stay put," noted the local newspaper.

The Quincy Golf Course was gone by 1968, when the first of Plumas County's 18-hole layouts sprang up on the site of an old box factory owned by the California Fruit Exchange. Thousands were employed here in the '20s, '30s, and '40s, before the mill became obsolete in 1956. In 1958, the West family bought the town, and Harvey West Jr. enlisted Ellis Van Gorder to design a golf course that could live in harmony with the Feather River. Graeagle Meadows opened with a sprinkling of condos and homes on its outskirts in 1968 and was without competition until Plumas Pines was built in a few miles north in 1980 as the center of an expansive new housing development. It was yet another 15 years before Dick Bailey's widely acclaimed masterpiece at Whitehawk Ranch was to open—yet another housing development hub, this one even more upscale. Now 18 more holes would be quick to follow, with the Dragon at Gold Mountain.

The first three courses vary in concept. Plumas Pines is probably the tightest design, with houses lining much of the front nine; busy Graeagle

Meadows is a temptation to the long hitter, with wide-open vistas and some parallel fairways; and upscale Whitehawk Ranch seems almost like a nature walk, with its 10-minute tee times and sprawling layout. But they are similar in that they are relatively flat, walkable layouts where the player is generally looking up and around at great vistas of pine-covered ridges and snow-topped peaks under a bright blue canvas.

At the Dragon, though, the player is usually looking down at the scenery, beginning at the highest point on the course, the first tee. Only one hole among the 18, hole number 3 ("Simplicity"), lacks a big mountain vista. But the fourth hole, "Faith," makes up for that in a hurry, with a look straight down into the Feather River Canyon at the middle fork.

The 7,000-yard Dragon is unlike its sister courses also in that it would be the center of not a housing development, but an entire community, where nature is king and big, beautiful homes are built in its shadow, not its spite. "A community in harmony with life," is how Peggy Garner, Gold Mountain's co-developer with husband Dariel, puts it.

Nature and the environment, of course, compose the precious local commodity today, and it is well protected. Development is welcomed, yet not overly encouraged, and if there is a minus to all the pluses of the Plumas County golf escape, it is that there are all too few lodging options. With some 156,000 rounds of golf expected to be played and only 400 rooms in the eastern, golfing part of the county, researchers were told that more lodging could increase the golf rounds by as much as 20 percent.

And so Horton was working on restoring the Feather River Inn's glory days by renovating the three-story Swiss Alpine–style main lodge with 25 new rooms complete with private baths, TVs, and telephones. And Gold Mountain was hurrying to prepare 20 to 30 new guest bungalows for visitors, not far from the Frank Lloyd Wright "Nakoma" design clubhouse.

It's a good thing, too. Otherwise, crowds might soon turn the right left turn into the wrong left turn, and we might be inclined to keep the nice little secret to ourselves. Now, you, too, know the way.

Itinerary

WARMING UP

Call the Feather River Inn and reserve a room in the main lodge overlooking the golf course for at least two nights or preferably three. Make a mid-morning tee time at the Dragon (not before 9, or you could be delayed by frost) for Day 1, an early-morning time at Whitehawk Ranch and a twilight time at Graeagle Meadows for Day 2, and an early-afternoon time at

Plumas Pines for Day 3. Granted, this is a lot of golf for just three days—because you're also going to want to go around the Feather River Inn course at least once—so try to make this a longer escape than three days. Also, call the Sardine Lake Resort for Day 1 dinner reservations (ask for the second seating) and the Iron Door for Day 2 dinner rezzies.

And consider making the drive, and that right left turn, the evening before Day 1.

day 1

Follow I-80 as if you're heading for North Lake Tahoe, but skip the Highway 89 south exit and look for 89 north. Hopefully it's still light, because the first 20 miles or so of this two-laner meander through a forest along the Truckee River, and the deer love to come out and play at night. The road narrows when it arrives at a series of small towns, beginning with Sierraville, where you'll find yourself in a valley with forever vistas of meadow and mountain, and then goes on through Sattley and Calpine. Soon you'll see signs for our first golf course, Whitehawk Ranch, and then you'll enter the Mohawk Valley and admire more views. Off to the right is a sign for the Dragon at Gold Mountain. If you're arriving the morning of your first tee time, follow it to the clubhouse.

If you were able to make the trip the evening before your first round of golf, proceed up 89 to Highway 70. Turn left and look for the Feather River Inn turnoff coming up quickly on your right. Check in, order a glass of wine, and take a seat on the big front porch to unwind and start getting friendly so you won't look too out of place.

In the morning, have a little breakfast at the inn and then retrace your steps down Highway 89, keeping an eye out for the left turn to the Dragon. You'll take a cart for this round and pick up a yardage book for advice on how to navigate this beauty. Also, choose your tee box wisely, because there is a difference of more than 2,000 yards from the 1-Dragon to the 5-Dragon, and remember to consider the altitude (good for one- to two-clubs difference) when planning a shot.

Architect Robin Nelson is not from the start-em-out-gently school of Donald Ross. His par-5 first hole, "Dragon's Lookout," offers the most fabulous vista on the course and is a fair preview of what's to be required here. The high-elevation tee shot needs to be right to give the long hitter a shot at the green in two, and the green is well protected by trees on the left and bunkers on the right. Our group, a fivesome previewing the course before it officially opened, got a big kick out of "Deception," the relatively short par-four second hole, because the same cluster of fairway bunkers snagged four of our drives. Another favorite was "Charity," the sixth hole, where you need a good drive to hope to carry the junk with your approach shot to a green that slopes severely from back to front.

Enjoy a beverage in the clubhouse after your round and have a bite to eat either here or at the Mohawk Grill, back north on Highway 89 with a left turn onto A-14. The Mohawk Grill is on the right; take your sandwich out onto the deck and don't miss the homemade cookies.

Then head back to the Feather River Inn and either relax with a book on the porch or walk nine holes on the ancient but fun and flat Feather River Inn course. Tonight you are leaving Plumas County to dine at Sardine Lake, one of the more unusual spots in the region. To get there, go south on Highway 89 and make a right at the sign to Gold Lakes Basin (Gold Lake Forest Highway). You'll follow this road about 10 miles to the resort, a right turn at Packer Lake Road. Plan to arrive about an hour before your seating and enjoy cocktails in the gazebo on the lake before your dinner, which will include soup, salad, bread and butter, and a lovely view of the Sierra Buttes.

Sleep fast.

day 11 Rise early, then make a quick stop at the Village Baker in Blairsden for one of its mouthwatering fruit and cheese Danishes, which taste like they're just out of the oven. Eat it on the way to Whitehawk Ranch, south on 89 in Clio. You'll want to arrive about 30 minutes early to warm up at the range, which is conveniently located just outside the pro shop. The friendly staff will move you to the putting green en route to the first tee, where someone will see you off with some advice (friendly, of course) on making your way around the course.

Many people tend to shoot their lowest scores at Whitehawk Ranch, which was beautifully designed by Dick Bailey to be quite a challenge for accomplished golfers playing from the 4-Hawk tees, yet very friendly, in that Plumas County style, to the higher handicap golfer. The fairways are a little wider here than at the Dragon, the greens vastly more welcoming, and, with only 30 bunkers waiting to deter you from the green, what you see is pretty much what you get. There are four sets of tees here, and the average woman player will want to try her skill from both of the forward sets. No surprise, then, that head pro Van Batchelder says, "Most of the time, it's the woman making the reservations to play here. And the guys are happy because the gals are happy." Special highlights here include the dogleg-left second hole, on the floor of the valley with great views all around, and the first few holes on the back nine, which is more remote and, says the head pro, even prettier than the front nine. But all around there are streams, waterfalls, and, especially early in the season, lots of wildflowers for eye candy.

Hopefully it's lunchtime now, and you're ready for fuel and yet another round of golf. So drive back on up Highway 89—isn't this starting to look familiar now?—and turn into Graeagle Meadows on the right. Enjoy lunch in the clubhouse, and then when the twilight bargain hour has set in, start walking. That's what town owner Harvey West Jr. does when he plays, and he's in his 70s.

The signature hole here is "English Gold," the sixth hole, which plays 386 yards from the highest point on the course. You're not quite eye-to-eye with Eureka Peak, but here's looking at it, kid. Head pro Bob Klein's favorite is the 15th hole, a long but downhill left-to-right par-4 ending at a green surrounded by a grove of tall pine trees.

We found this course to be tougher than we expected; it's busier and less manicured than the area's other 18-holers, so there are fewer perfect lies and less fairway roll. The par-3s especially are challenging, and the greens frequently fooled us. That said, we'd have no problem playing here every day for the rest of our lives. You can hit driver all you want without worrying about breaking a window, and there's plenty of sunshine. It's a lovely golf course, especially as evening sets in and the wildlife emerges.

After your round, there'll be no time for dawdling. You'll want to freshen up at the inn and then get back in the car (while it seems like a lot of driving on paper, everything in this escape is much closer than, say, in the Bay Area) to go to the Iron Door. Turn onto A-14 just north of the town of Graeagle and head west to historic Johnsville, an early mining town that still has Gold Rush–era unrestored buildings standing and the kind of cemetery where headstones speak of the history of the place.

There's no place to go wrong on chef Peter Schmid's Continental-style menu, although we were told the pepper steak is a destination meal in itself. Again, soup and salad are included, and we were quite pleased to take a foursome one evening and enjoy cocktails, a bottle of wine, dinner, dessert, and even port in a warm, serene atmosphere for a total of $156—this for the kind of delicious meal that would probably cost another $100 in the Bay Area, maybe even another $200 in Napa, and let's just figure on another $300 in Pebble Beach. Adults, don't miss the Johnsville Special for dessert, strange as it sounds: vanilla ice cream, crème de menthe, and Ovaltine.

If you need a nightcap, you may have one in the Tiger's Den back at the inn; it's been a long day, full of golf shots to remember and to forget. And tomorrow is your day to sleep in.

day III This morning is a time to have breakfast, wander around the shops and galleries in Graeagle, play the Feather River Inn course, or finish that book you were reading on the porch on Day 1. Then, unfortunately, you'll probably have to check out.

The last stop for this particular golfing idyll is Plumas Pines, where you'll be greeted (warmly, of course, but you knew that by now) in a lovely modern clubhouse that's all about golf. The range is just outside, and the award-winning pro shop is a golf supermarket, where men and especially women will be thrilled at the variety of clothing and shoe lines. Last year, for instance, Tom Godman ordered 16 lines of women's shoes. There are also many varieties of golf balls, which you may need for your first round at Plumas Pines.

If you've got the energy, you'll enjoy walking the course. The front nine is quite flat, meandering along the Feather River, and has water in play or in sight on all nine holes. If that's not enough, the houses here encroach more than they do at the other Plumas courses, which makes for more out-of-bounds areas.

We were happy to have played with a couple of regulars, who guided us through some of the trickier spots, for instance "River's Edge," the par-4 second hole. Here you'll probably want to hit iron off the tee to guarantee a safe landing spot in the narrow fairway along the river's edge, then keep your approach shot below the pin on a green that slopes so severely that if you're behind the hole, you might be chipping back uphill if you miss your putt down.

Before you go home, we suggest you enjoy an early meal at the restaurant here and let us know how you like it. It has a great reputation and ambience but lost its chef and was forced to temporarily close in the middle of the season when we visited.

Not that anyone could go hungry in Plumas County, of course.

 NOTES

Time Savers. This is not the escape for those in a hurry.

Money Savers. The Feather River Inn has "rustic" but clean cabin rooms (no TV, no telephone) overlooking the ninth green that go for less than 75 percent of what the lodge rooms cost.

Nongolfers. For an exquisite escape in a serene setting, stay at the Gray Eagle Lodge. You can walk out the door and onto a hiking trail around the Lakes Basin recreation area, go fishing or horseback riding, or just find a tree, roll out a blanket, and read in peace.

Parents. The River Pines, with its big pool and hot tub, and plenty of barbecue areas, is a fun lodging option for families.

High-Handicappers. Consider postponing your round at the Dragon until you're feeling better about your game.

Courses

ITINERARY SELECTIONS

The Dragon at Gold Mountain
P. O. Box 880 (on County Road A-15 in Portola)
Graeagle, CA 96103
877-DRAGON1 or 530/832-4887, fax 530/832-0884
email info@dragongolf.com;
website www.dragongolf.com

SCORECARD
Architect: Robin Nelson, 1998
Course Record: NA
5-Dragon: 7,070 yards
4-Dragon: 6,586 yards
3-Dragon: 6,079 yards
2-Dragon: 5,463 yards
1-Dragon: 4,671 yards
Call two weeks in advance for your tee time, (877) DRAGON1.

The homeowners have first dibs on the Dragon, which was fully open in the summer of 2000 and offering 2-for-1 specials, with green fees starting at $125. The clubhouse and casitas were not expected to open until spring of 2001. Don't even think about cutting corners by forgoing a cart when you play here. Between the altitude and the hills, you'll want to ride for your exploratory round at the Dragon.

TEE TIDBITS | The Frank Lloyd Wright-design "Nakoma" clubhouse looks to be a great place to linger after the round, and the logo is so unique you might want to plunk down a few more bucks for a souvenir. On busy weekends, you might see forecaddies out on the course to assist you in locating golf balls, raking bunkers, and so on. The season runs from around May 1 through about the end of October, but with no firm opening/closing dates. Eureka Peak was known as Gold Mountain back in the 1800s; thus, the Dragon at Gold Mountain. Originally the course was named the Grizzly; Dragon seemed a bit more, well, approachable. Course architect Robin Nelson is also designing an 18-hole putting course and a nine-hole short course here.

The Golf Club at Whitehawk Ranch
P. O. Box 170 (on Hwy. 89 in Clio)
Clio, CA 96106
800/332-HAWK or 530/836-0394, fax 530/836-4504
email whrgolf@psln.com; website www.graeagle.com/whitehawk

The Golf Club is semiprivate, which means the residents get first dibs on tee times, but crowds are not such a hassle in this part of NorCal, particularly at an in-season peak-time (10-minute gaps) green fee of $95, including cart (although some of the green-to-tee distances are long, the course is walkable, but walking won't save you a dime), range balls, and a small yardage guide and map. Twilight and shoulder season fees are lower. Lessons, club-fitting, and repairs are also available, and the practice facilities are commendable: grass tees, practice bunkers, and chipping area. Soft spikes required, and the dress code is politely enforced (a long list of dos and don'ts that amount to no short-shorts, tank tops, or ratty jeans for anyone, and men must have collars on the shirt). Carts must remain on the paths.

TEE TIDBITS | Unlike other area courses, Whitehawk Ranch adheres firmly to its May 1 opening and October 31 closing dates. Wildflowers are plentiful here, and the forest and nature areas are played as lateral hazards to protect the environment. There's a small but jam-packed pro shop and a small but sandwich-packed snack shop. A restaurant is part of the Lodge at White-hawk Ranch, which also has one- and two-bedroom cot-tages. You've got to like the sales pitch of the Whitehawk Ranch development: "Live. Breathe. Golf." The driving range is conveniently outside the pro shop; player assistants quietly move you from range to put-ting green to first tee. A unique feature at Whitehawk is the practice program. Ten bucks will allow you to hit balls and practice as long as you can stand it.

SCORECARD

Architect: Dick Bailey, 1995
Course Record: 63, Sean Farren
4-Hawk: Par 71, 6,928 yards, 72.4 rating for men, 130 slope
3-Hawk: Par 71, 6,422 yards, 70.2 rating for men, 122 slope; 74.3 rating for women, 137 slope
2-Hawk: Par 71, 5,673 yards, 66.8 rating for men, 113 slope; 71.0 rating for women, 129 slope
1-Hawk: Par 71, 4,816 yards, 62.9 rating for men, 105 slope; 64.2 rating for women, 115 slope
Call 800-332-HAWK up to six months in advance for tee times.

Graeagle Meadows Golf Course
P. O. Box 310 (on Highway 89 just south of town)
Graeagle, CA 96103
530/836-2323

Graeagle was the first 18-hole course to open in the area, and it's also usually the first to open every spring. Frost delays, however, hinder starts in April and November. A very walkable course, it's the best deal, with rates starting at $35 on a high-season weekday or $40 on a weekend. Power carts, which are not restricted to paths, cost another $15 per player. The dress code, says head pro Bob Klein, is: "Any spikes, and wear clothes please."

SCORECARD

Architect: Ellis Van Gorder, 1968
Course Record: 63, Dick Lotz
Blue: Par 72, 6,725 yards, 72.1 rating for men, 129 slope
White: Par 72, 6,345 yards, 70.1 rating for men, 128 slope
Red: Par 72, 5,589 yards, 71.0 rating for women, 127 slope
For tee times call 530/836-2323 up to a year in advance.

TEE TIDBITS | The range is grass, but it is a bit inconvenient (downhill from the clubhouse) compared to the likes of Whitehawk, so plan to arrive early for your tee time to hit a few balls. As the area's best bargain, Graeagle is also the busiest of its 18-hole courses, and rounds are not played at an aerobic pace. A third set of tees (blue) was installed just last year, and now the course plays 300 yards shorter from the white tees and a few yards shorter from the red.

Plumas Pines Golf Resort
P. O. Box 1210 (402 Poplar Valley Rd. in Blairsden)
Graeagle, CA 96103
530/836-1420, fax 530/836-0801
email pprgolf@psln.com; website www.graeagle.com/plumaspines

Plumas Pines is a shot-maker's paradise, where walkers can still play a twilight round for well under $30, and $50 will get players around the course with a cart on weekday prime times. There's even a nine-hole rate. The driving range is next to the modern, eye-catching clubhouse. Reservations are taken at any time. The dress code is for golf attire and the spikes of your choosing. Carts are generally allowed on the fairways, 90-degree rule of course, though seldom on the killer ninth hole, known as "Hot Dog Hill," which heads up the hill to a green that slopes sharply back

SCORECARD

Architect: Homer Flint, 1980
Course Record: NA
Blue: 6,504 yards, 71.6 rating for men, 127 slope
White: 5,894 yards, 69.0 rating for men, 120 slope; 74.1 rating for women, 136 slope for women
Red: 5,240 yards, 68.5 rating for women, 126 slope
Call 530/836-1420 anytime for tee times.

downhill. The green is big, which is good in some respects, but not good in that there's all the more chance to land your shot above the hole, in which case you're in for an adventure. Locals either love this hole for the unique challenge or hate it—for the unique challenge.

TEE TIDBITS | On your first visit, you'll want to pick up Tom Godman's cheat sheet, *Advice on playing Plumas Pines Country Club.* The yardages are hard to read on this photocopy, but the suggestions on how to play each hole are precious—especially on hole number 3, "Honker's Haven": "Water, water, everywhere—to the left, to the right, and over the green." We could see water everywhere, we thought, but not behind the green. Lodging is available on the golf course. Allow time to browse the varied, affordable merchandise in the pro shop and to enjoy a meal before or after in the restaurant upstairs. Rental clubs are available at $10 a set. Ride-along spectators have to pay a $12 cart fee. Ask about play-and-stay and play-and-dine packages when you call for a tee time.

Feather River Inn Golf Course
P. O. Box 67 (on Hwy. 70, just west of Hwy. 89)
Graeagle, CA 96103
530/836-2722

It's a whole different scene at this old-time nine-holer next to the Feather River Inn. We brought our own six-pack, carried our clubs, played nine for little more than a buck a hole (it's $18 for 18, and that doesn't include the discounts for seniors, twilight players, and guests of the inn). The course design has a lot of character, and the tiny, ancient greens—still the original, 1915 models—make the perfect shot oh-so-elusive. Carts are available, not that you'd need one. And no need to be picky about attire.

SCORECARD

Architect: Harold Sampson, 1915
Course Record: NA
Yellow/Yellow: Par 70, 5,657 yards, 66.0 rating for men, 105 slope
Yellow/White: Par 70, 5,605 yards, 65.8 rating for men, 104 slope; 70.4 rating for women, 115 slope
Advance tee times are not really necessary here, but you may want to call ahead, (530) 836-2722, to make sure the course isn't booked by a conference group.

TEE TIDBITS | The course is popular with beginners, wedding parties, and business groups, so be prepared to have a little patience. Your nine holes may not zip by as quickly as you'd hope, but there's plenty of scenery to enjoy. Play the yellow tees first and the white tees second, unless you want the extra 52 yards from playing yellow both times. Beer and wine but nothing harder are to be had in the quaint, cozy clubhouse, with an inviting deck overlooking the first tee. Souvenirs and apparel are very reasonably priced, and there's usually a sale to be found. Play-and-stay packages are available at the inn.

ALTERNATIVES

The **Feather River Park Resort** offers nine holes (no tee times) on the ubiquitous Middle Fork of the Feather River. At 2,582 yards and with a par of 35, this is the place to work on your game in a low-budget (around $16 for 18 holes), low-pressure setting. The course is very walkable but also very open, so beware the mis-hit balata. You'll drive by here on your way to Plumas Pines. ■ 8339 HIGHWAY 89 AND A-14, BLAIRSDEN, CA 96103; 530/836-2328

If you're enjoying an extended stay in the area, you may want to consider a visit to Lake Almanor, a popular resort community a couple of hours to the north. Homer Flint, who designed Plumas Pines 20 years ago (as well as Silverado in Napa, Spyglass in Pebble Beach, Kapalua on Maui, and Mauna Lani on the Big Island), has been at work on a new course here called **Bailey Creek** at Lake Almanor. The first nine holes opened in 1999, but nine more were on the way. Like Plumas Pines, Bailey Creek will be the center of a new community. ■ 433 DURKIN DR., LAKE ALMANOR, CA 96137; 530/259-4653

Lodging

ITINERARY SELECTIONS

The **Feather River Inn** has become in recent years a place to get away from it all, though the new rooms in the main building have televisions and phones with modem hookups. There are two ways to stay here: in new rooms in the main building, which start at about $105, or the so-called "rustic" cabins, clean and comfortable but rather run-down and sparsely furnished units that have a living room with fireplace and kitchenette shared by two private rooms and bath. The latter rent by the room, at probably the best prices in the area short of camping—around $100 for the two-bedroom cabin. Some of them are perched on a boardwalk overlooking the ninth green. The inn does not have full restaurant service but serves breakfast in the grill and offers a Friday prime rib dinner and Sunday brunch.
■ P. O. BOX 67, GRAEAGLE, CA 96103 (ON HWY. 70, JUST WEST OF HWY. 89); 530/836-2623

GOLF PACKAGE OPTIONS

The houses on the golf course at **Graeagle Meadows** offer surprisingly first-class accommodations in Mother Nature's finest surroundings. These are two- and three-bedroom townhouses (ask for golf course view, or opt for the more economical forest-meadow scenery), fully furnished (full kitchen, washer and dryer) and with decks for enjoying the birdies and bogeys of others, safely removed from harm's way. Linens are provided, and if you don't want to use the kitchen, the kitchen at the Graeagle Meadows Clubhouse can feed you breakfast and lunch. Two-night minimums start at around $150 a night; don't forget to ask about play-and-stay deals.
■ P. O. Box 310, Graeagle, CA 96103 (on Highway 89 just south of town); 800/800-6282

The similarly appointed units at **Plumas Pines** are an even better deal (starting at $150 for two nights); these include tennis and swimming but no break in your green fee. At Plumas Pines, though, your accommodations might be so close to the golf course that you'll feel like you're playing golf. ■ Plumas Pines Realty (800/655-4440) handles reservations here and for a few units at Whitehawk Ranch.

Opening in the summer of 2000 was the **Lodge at Whitehawk Ranch.** One- and two-bedroom cabins are available starting at around $180 a night, and golf discounts are offered to those staying two nights or longer. Lodge accommodations include use of the pool, hot tub, tennis courts, and fly-fishing pond on the gorgeous Whitehawk Ranch property, plus daily continental breakfast and wine and cheese. ■ 985 Whitehawk Dr. (P. O. Box 175), Clio, CA 96106; 877/945-6343 or 530/836-4985; website www.lodgeatwhitehawk.com

Construction on golf accommodations also was under way at the **Dragon at Gold Mountain** (877/DRAGON1).

ALTERNATIVES

If there's an outdoors-inclined nongolfer in your gang, or if you just want to stay at the most unique, cozy, and complete accommodations in the area, the number one choice is the **Gray Eagle Lodge,** off the Gold Lake Highway in the Lakes Basin Recreation Area. Owner Bret Smith and his wife, Julia, have been remodeling these 10 one-bedroom and eight two-bedroom cabins in a style so harmonious with the surroundings, they feel lush without making you whisper or even hesitate to clomp around in your hiking boots. Outside your door are hiking trails, and if you're so inclined you may be able to fish off your deck. The rates are a steal: for less than $200 a night for two adults, you may have a two-bedroom cabin (it's even less for one bedroom) with full breakfast and a scrumptious dinner at Firewoods. When you call, be sure to tell the reservationist what kind of stay you have in mind so you're assigned the perfect cabin, and do ask about golf packages. Bret is a golf nut himself. No TVs, no phones, no problems—and not open from early October until early June. ■ 5000 GOLD LAKE FOREST HWY., GRAEAGLE, CA 96103; 800/635-8778; WEBSITE WWW.GRAYEAGLELODGE.COM

The stagecoach stopped at the **White Sulphur Springs Bed and Breakfast** in 1852, and much of the original furnishings have remained at this eye-catching, beautifully restored house along Highway 89 near Clio, just across from a huge Mohawk Valley meadow. There are six rooms in the main building, to be had for around $100 a night, plus the Dairy House and Hen House, two adjacent cottages. The three-room Dairy House holds a cozy foursome; the two-bedroom Hen House accommodates up to seven; both cost around $170 per night for four. Rates include a fabulous country breakfast, and if you tell host Don Miller you've got an early tee time, chances are he'll send you off with a brown bag of fortification. The warm mineral-spring Olympic pool is a big draw. ■ 2200 HIGHWAY 89, CLIO, CA 96106; 800/854-1797 OR 530/836-2387; WEBSITE WWW.GRAEAGLE.COM/MARKETPLACE/WHTSSBB

A completely different atmosphere marks the **River Pines Resort,** a lively, fun, and central property with a swimming pool and snack bar that offer daytime respite for nongolfers or a post-round splash. Rooms here are well-priced, large, and comfortable, with telephones and TVs, and there are also housekeeping cottages and suites. (River Pines also has golf villas at Whitehawk Ranch and Plumas Pines.) Next door is the Coyote Grill; just across the street is the road to the Feather River Park Resort and Plumas Pines; and within walking distance are the towns of Graeagle and Blairsden. On Highway 89 just north of Graeagle. ■ 8296 HIGHWAY 89, CLIO, CA 96106; 800/696-2551 OR 530/836-2552

There's also a large assortment of small lodges, cabin complexes, and, of course, campgrounds in the Lakes Basin area, some of them spilling over into Sierra County. Check the websites listed under Contacts or call the Plumas County Visitors Bureau (800/326-2247) and see if it'll send you a copy of its annual guide, which has detailed listings in the back. If you need a room this weekend, just ask the Visitors Bureau to point you in the right direction—remember, folks here are nice.

Dining

ITINERARY SELECTIONS

The **Mohawk Grill** is reached by taking Highway 89 just north of Graeagle and turning left onto A-14. It's open at 8 A.M. for breakfast and closes at about 8 P.M. ■ 1228 JOHNSVILLE RD., PLUMAS PINES; 530/836-0901

It's hard to believe the food could match the view at the **Sardine Lake Resort,** but most people think it comes close. You arrive early and enjoy your cocktail (full bar) at the gazebo on the lake at the foot of the Sierra Buttes, then answer the dinner bell and are treated to elegant decor and service for a meal of fresh seafood or leg of lamb or whatever's the daily special. A bit of a ride—15 miles from Graeagle up and down Gold Lake Road—that's worth it, with full dinners starting at about $15. It's closed Thursdays and from mid-October through mid-May, and reservations are a must, with a choice between 6 P.M. or 8 P.M. seatings. And go figure: They do not take credit cards but accept personal checks. ■ 990 SARDINE RD., OFF GOLD LAKE ROAD, SIERRA CITY; 530/862-1196

While the **Village Baker** is hardly a dining destination, it is a must-stop for the heavenly pastry selection, plus such divine fresh breads that you may want to take a loaf home with you. Ed and Christine Barry keep the place open just about year-round Wednesday–Saturday, 6 A.M.–3 P.M., and until 2 P.M. on Sunday. ■ 340 BONTA RD., BLAIRSDEN; 530/836-4064

The **Graeagle Meadows Clubhouse** is popular even with locals who don't golf. The terrace makes it a great spot for lunch (American grill, salads, and Mexican) with a view, and there's breakfast and a full bar. It's closed December through March, like the course. ■ HIGHWAY 89, GRAEAGLE; 530/836-2348

A more leisurely meal at the **Iron Door** might begin with cocktails at the bar, then move to homemade soup, salad with vinaigrette with garlic and walnuts, and perhaps the pepper steak diablo, the scampi alla gallipolina, the chicken nasi goreng, or the kassler rippchen (port chops over sauerkraut). Chef Peter Schmid will do it all, starting at about $15 per dinner. But save room for dessert, the Johnsville Special. Closed in winter and on Tuesdays. You'll find the Iron Door on Highway A-14 in Johnsville, 10 minutes from Graeagle. ■ 5417 MAIN ST., JOHNSVILLE; 530/836-2376

The setting at sunset is a star at **Plumas Pines Restaurant,** which is open for dinner May through October, Wednesday through Sunday. Expect a selection of pastas, chicken, and steak, and nightly specials. ■ AT THE PLUMAS PINES GOLF COURSE CLUBHOUSE; 530/836-1305

ALTERNATIVES

Your next stop, should you be fortunate enough to stay a third night, is **Firesides** at the Gray Eagle Lodge (5000 Gold Lake Forest Hwy., Graeagle; 530/836-2511 or 800/635-8778). Chef Luis Ramirez winters in Palm Springs and returns for the golf season to prepare trout, duckling, leg of lamb, and seasonal seafood with soup, salad, and the most addictive bread basket to be found. The atmosphere is intimate (try to arrive after the family hour, unless you're participating), and if you don't have to drive back out of the Lakes Basin you might as well enjoy an after-dinner port by the fireplace. Dinner, with the whole shebang starting at about $16, is 6–8 nightly, May–October, reservations required.

If you've had enough fine dining and just want to eat, the **Coyote Bar and Grill** (8296 Highway 89, Clio; 530/836-2002) is your place, year-round. On Highway 89 at the River Pines Resort, the Coyote offers delicious Southwestern cuisine and great margaritas, with quite the selection of tequilas. You will probably have time to sample them all if you do not make a reservation—and the chips and salsa in the bar do not measure up to the quality of the reasonably priced dinner offerings. Closed Monday.

The Grizzly Grill (250 Bonta St., Blairsden; 530/836-1300) is another local favorite. The chef left the Gray Eagle Lodge to open her own place on Bonta Street in Blairsden, and she is cooking up more of the contemporary American cuisine that's so popular here. (The grilled rib-eye steak with gorgonzola butter and cabernet sauce do anything for you? The penne rigati with sautéed rock shrimp?) The Grizzly is open for dinner every night, unlike most area restaurants, and offers small and large portions of its starters and pasta, as well as early-bird specials including soup, salad, and dessert starting at $10.95.

In the town of Portola, just a few miles from the Dragon at Gold Mountain, chef Wolfgang Heuser is preparing German, Austrian, and European specialties at the **Log Cabin** (64 E. Sierra St., Portola; 530/832-5243). The menu is large, so you might want to cut to the chase and order the day's special. Prices start at around $12 for a surprisingly delicious meal that includes soup and salad, in a casual atmosphere. A featured attraction at the Log Cabin is the back bar, made of tamarack wood from the Tetons, brought in on the railroad and put together in 1940. Open all year, but never on Tuesday.

Check with the **Feather River Inn** (Highway 70 at Feather River Inn Road; 530/836-2323), which has been offering only breakfast, a Friday prime rib buffet, and Sunday brunch, with only beer and wine, but may be expanding its offerings.

Straying Off Course

The Lakes Basin Recreation Area, where you'll find Sardine Lake Resort and Gray Eagle Lodge, among others, offers loads of fishing lakes—some accessible only by hiking, biking, or horseback riding in. There's a stable (530/836-0940) and boat landing at Gold Lake, and there are numerous fishing guide services offering outings for salmon, steelhead, and bass. The

Plumas County Visitors Guide and website listed under Contacts is a starting point for anglers, and also for horsefolks—nine locations offer an assortment of horseback riding, chuck wagon barbecues, and boarding.

Leisurely shoppers may enjoy wandering among the red-painted buildings of Graeagle, and Graeagle's Mill Pond is a good spot for a swim, picnic lunch, or jaunt in a paddle boat. Snowshoe Rentals (530/836-2414) rents kiwi kayaks by the hour or day.

Of course you can still pan for gold, and the Plumas Eureka State Park (530/836-2380) offers a supervised program in the summer. An assortment of museums offers more insight into the rich history of the county, including the Portola Railroad Museum (530/832-4131) and the Plumas County Museum (530/283-6320) in Quincy.

Hunting, water sports, and hiking opportunities are too plentiful to mention, and of course there's skiing in winter. No need to exert yourself, however. At the right time of the year, just driving can be a glorious pastime. Plumas County puts on a great color show in autumn, and the Feather River Scenic Byway is most stunning in spring, when the hills turn electric green and nearly 100 waterfalls come onto the scene. Map and guide are available from the Plumas County Visitors Bureau.

Details, Details

SUITCASE

Leave those high heels and ties at home; this is an unpretentious destination where phones start ringing if anyone too glamorous, e.g., Sharon Stone, comes to town. It would be theoretically be okay to wear your golf clothes to dinner, except that you must be sure to have the option of warm clothes for evenings, which were cold when we visited both early and late in the all-too-short golf season here. You will also want to have the option of shorts or long pants for golf. Early in the morning, you will want the latter, but soon you will be wishing you'd had the guts to wear the former. Warmup pants over shorts would probably be acceptable at these courses.

If you still prefer metal spikes, you can wear them at Plumas Pines and Graeagle Meadows, as well as the Feather River Inn, which requires only that you keep your shirt on.

It would be smart to pack a bug repellent in your golf bag; we fortunately just missed the annual pilgrimage of the buffalo gnats. And don't forget hats and sunscreen. While the sun feels great, it is nearer to thee here and so much more deadly.

GETTING THERE

From any direction, take I-80 near Truckee to Highway 89 north. It's 45 minutes to an hour from that junction to the Feather River Inn.

Three airports in Plumas County are open to planes and jets of up to 12,500 pounds, visual approach only. The closest to Graeagle is Nervino Field in Beckwourth (530/832-5042), but there's no car rental. Willits Motors (530/283-4852) in Quincy rents for Hertz and is within walking distance of Gansner Field (530/258-3616), but Willits is closed on Sundays.

CONTACTS

- The **Plumas County Visitors Bureau** is in Quincy to help you, but you can call it or search its website and most likely find what you're looking for (800/326-2247, fax 530/283-5465; www.plumas.ca.us).
- More concentrated information on the Graeagle area is available at the website www.graeagle.com, and the **Eastern Plumas County Chamber of Commerce** includes restaurant and dining listings on its site (800/995-6057; www.psln.com/epluchmb).

- The publisher of the **Plumas visitors guide** has much of its content online (www.plumasnews.com). And clicking on the Sierraville link at the Sierra County home page (www.sierracounty.org) will serve up more information on Lakes Basin area lodging and activities.

Chapter 8

Gambler's Windfall: South Lake Tahoe and Carson Valley

T he ravages of winter in the mountains and the overpopulation of summer by the lake add up to one thing: a golf course deficit at Lake Tahoe's South Shore. And that's added expensive green fees to the bottom lines of all of us who couldn't bear to take a summer vacation to a gorgeous destination without hacking away at a little turf. Has this shortage led to the construction of any new courses? No, in fact it's gone the other way. Glenbrook, a sweet lakeside nine-holer that used to welcome all, has gone private, reserved for homeowners.

There are only two championship 18-hole courses in South Lake Tahoe itself: Edgewood Tahoe Golf Course, the Pebble Beach of the mountains, and Lake Tahoe Golf Course, the gorgeous local equivalent of your neighborhood muni. Take the 40-minute ride around the East Shore and there's Incline, another pricey destination where tee times are so hard to procure on a summer weekend that the course started running Sunday shotguns.

So we have to thank Nevada's Carson Valley, particularly the tiny, golf course rich town of Genoa, for its rescue efforts. With a scenic, low-stress drive of 30–45 minutes, golfers can leave a shortage that will pinch their pennies at South Lake Tahoe and find a glut that makes them kings and queens of Carson Valley.

It will surely feel like the best drive of the day, no matter which of Carson Valley's nine—the Divine Nine, they call them here—championship courses is on the dance card. The weather may be better than it is up the hill, with annual highs averaging only 89 degrees and nighttime lows averaging 19, along with 266 days of sunshine. The courses surely will be firmer, drier, and better conditioned—unless you have the privilege of playing Edgewood in July—because Carson City averages just 31 inches of snow, nearly 100 inches less than Lake Tahoe. Nearby Dayton Valley gets even less than that. Unfortunately, you will not hit the ball quite as far at 4,500 feet as you would at 6,200, but you still may feel like you need one less club than at wherever you call home.

Best of all, the service at Carson Valley courses is top-notch, because it has to be. After all, if you were treated like anything less than one of the kings and queens of the valley at Golf Course A, then what's to keep you from replacing Golf Course A with Golf Course B on your next itinerary? Golf course operators know you will, and so even at the bottom of the pay scale they try hard—often from the moment you arrive. In fact, they even try before the moment you arrive, which is why there is a glut of play-and-stay packages with the lodging properties in the region that may make you wonder, "How do the hotels make a profit?" Sometimes they're making it just by the cocktails you buy in their lounges, the meals you buy in their restaurants, and the money you lose in their casinos.

Says Dayton Valley Director of Golf Jim Keppler, "Most golfers are gamblers, so it's a natural fit." Keppler's course so badly wants your group's business, it will send a free shuttle out to pick up a group of 12 or more and bring them to the course in style—with air-conditioning, TV, and wet bar. With that sort of treatment, in the end you may well forget how many balls you left in the pretty ponds and lakes on this challenging Arnold Palmer–designed layout that's used for PGA Tour qualifying sectionals.

Dayton Valley may rank at the top of the service scale, because it's more remote than the other courses. But even at accessible Empire Ranch, designed to suit the lower budget player with a flat, riverside layout that allows one to walk 27 holes in a day for under $50, you can expect to be greeted at your car and warmly welcomed by the staff.

At Lake Tahoe Golf Course, where there are 370 players a day during the peak times of July and August—and that's more than twice as many as at pricey Edgewood—you'll feel fortunate just to get to the staff, the line may be so long at the check-in counter. There are no intentional slights here, but it can be such a madhouse that the starters barely have time to breathe, much less smile.

Which is not to say that you shouldn't play Lake Tahoe, or you shouldn't stay at South Shore. It is to say that if it's a golf getaway you want, Carson Valley will serve you well. If it's a lakeside getaway you want, you will have to pay the price, quite literally. It costs around $45 to walk 18 holes at Lake Tahoe on a weekday; fair comparisons down in the valley are Empire Ranch and Eagle Valley, at about $20 weekdays to walk 18. And while the locals might find it pricey, Genoa Lakes, for its unique design, pretty setting, and great service, is a steal for South Shore visitors at around $70 on a weekday.

So let's say the golf markup is 100 percent when you climb the mountain from Carson Valley to South Lake Tahoe. At the right time of year, and especially if your traveling group includes the unenlightened (nongolfers), it may well be worth it. There's so much to do, for everyone: the casinos, the lounge acts, the serene, secluded beaches on the west shore, the lively, cocktail-pouring beaches the other side of Stateline. Great places to hike and bike, or just sit and enjoy a cocktail, popcorn, and a view. On shoulder seasons, you might even go down to Carson for a late-morning round of golf at Genoa Lakes or Sierra Nevada, then come back up and ski Heavenly at night, stopping only to gawk at the sunset from one of several fine dining spots with peerless views alongside or overlooking Lake Tahoe.

Yes, if your pockets are full, you're probably saying, "Take me there right now. And while we're at it, let's play Edgewood, *every day!*" Indeed, once you've played this incredible course along the shores of Lake Tahoe, right behind the Lakeside Inn, Horizon, and Harveys, you will wonder what the ski resort did to steal the name Heavenly. Although green fees—$150 at press time, but don't hold us to those—seem high, everything is done at Edgewood to make you feel like you got a bargain. Designer George Fazio, and later his nephew, Tom, created a thinking person's course that is meticulously cared for and is a joy to anyone who loves golf, no matter the handicap.

George started his work in the 1960s, when Brooks Park decided that his family's 100-year-old ranch land would be well suited for a golf course—and not just a golf course. Park was thinking "world-class golf course." That's what Fazio gave him, with the assistance of apprentice Tom, who had just graduated from college. Tom, who now has his own world-class reputation, has been refining the course ever since, and it has played host to several USGA events, including the U.S. Senior Open in 1985, as well as an annual Celebrity Golf Championship that draws the crowds early every summer.

Time your visit right, though, and you'll barely see another soul during your round at Edgewood. The day starts with a tee time separated by a full 12 minutes from those in front and back, all the better to enjoy nature's bounty and vistas. You'll tee off between two cones from locally grown Jeffrey pines—ideally from the proper set of tees, because fairways are narrow and the first-timer will best navigate the course by studying the yardage book that is presented to every player along with golf cart. And by the time you finish, with three holes right next to the lake, you too will be gushing.

So, you see, there's good reason even for golfers to get away to South Lake Tahoe. The best getaway of all to these parts would last 10 days and start with three days in Carson City followed by a week by the lake. If you're sticking to our three-day, two-night format, though, you'll have to choose between the two destinations. Good luck.

For additional assistance, if you have Internet access do click into the golf pages at www.playreno.com (also accessed directly at golf.renolaketahoe.com). This is one of the most cleverly done golf websites anywhere, and it lists all of the courses described in this chapter, with updated green fee information. You can tell the database that you want to play a course in Carson City for between $25 and $35 that's 6,000 to 7,000 yards long, for example, and the database will serve up Eagle Valley and Empire Ranch. It doesn't yet tell you how to break par there, however. Unfortunately, neither can we.

ITINERARY 1:
South Lake Tahoe

WARMING UP

This is a relatively short getaway for an area where there's so much to do; if you're following the itinerary, you'll want to leave the kids with trusted friends or family and get out of town on your own. Later in the chapter you'll find suggestions on how to adjust the itinerary for the whole family.

Book a lakeside room for two nights at the Tahoe Lakeshore Lodge and Spa or another of the nearby South Shore, lakeside hotels (see Inn by the Lake and Lakeland Village descriptions in the Lodging section), preferably not before June or after September. Book a Day 1 tee time at Lake Tahoe Golf Course for as early as you think you can arrive, fuel, and loosen up. Book a Day 2 tee time at Edgewood for as early as you think you can rise. For the sake of one last pretty morning on the lake, book your Day 3 tee time for late morning or early afternoon at Genoa Lakes and be prepared to play in a bit of wind.

Make dinner reservations for Day 1, on the early side, at Cafe Fiore, and Day 2, on the late side, at Evans.

Call the Zephyr Cove Marina at 775/588-3508 and reserve space on the

MS *Dixie II* breakfast cruise for Day 3. Check the Sunday papers and see if there's a show you especially want to see during your visit. Find room in the itinerary and order tickets.

day 1

Get out of the car at Lake Tahoe Golf Course and breathe the crisp, clean air. Be careful; don't exert yourself: you're at 6,300 feet, probably about a mile into the clouds from where you left this morning—the good news is the golf ball will fly farther, the bad news is you'll become more easily fatigued and dehydrated. So fuel up, take some practice shots and putts, and get ready to tee off in the midst of snowcapped peaks and the company of the Truckee River.

Lake Tahoe Golf Course is owned by the state park system, and the land is used for cross-country skiing from the time the course closes—never any later than the last day of October—until it reopens in April, or maybe May. It's a tough call, depending on the late snowfall. Look at the scorecard—you'll see lots of blue winding through the green, usually the Upper Truckee, but also Angora Creek and some ponds that were installed as part of the golf course design. So choose your tee wisely—too long a pick and you won't be able to make some carries you'll need, too short a pick and you'll find water that shouldn't even be in play. The scorecard comes with recommendations: those with single-digit handicaps should take the back, 10–24 the middle, and 25 and up the forward, with women who have better than an 11 handicap offered the middle tees rather than the forward.

Then heed the words of head pro Mike Durst: "The best thing about our golf course is that the front nine is wide open, so you can hit your driver and get loose, but you get to the back nine and playing more conservatively is the way to go. Playing for position is the key on the back nine."

Durst's favorite hole, 16, is a great example. It's a dogleg left with a narrow fairway, measuring 360 off the middle tees, and the smart play is to put a tee shot on the 150-marker, making for a straight shot into a green fronted by a creek and surrounded by trees. Miss the fairway right and there's a hidden pond. Hole number 6 is a highlight, too, 124–185 yards from tee to green, with water winding right across the front of the green.

The good news, says Durst, comes once you reach the greens. "The course is flat, and people actually tend to overread our greens. A good rule of thumb is when you think you see a break, take half of that."

The round finishes with a flair, from the strategic 16th to the pretty 17th, a par-3 over the Upper Truckee (so clear you'll see the golf balls in it) and a beach to a green surrounded by tall pines, to the exhausting 18th, a par-5 with water in play on at least two shots off the tee. The clubhouse will look quite friendly at this point, but you might want to delay your 19th hole until after you check in at your hotel. To get there, exit the golf course and turn left, following the signs to South Shore, which will take you onto Highway 89 north, then Highway 50 east, Lake Tahoe Boulevard. Your hotel is on the left. The Tahoe Lakeshore Lodge and Spa is about three miles down, a left turn at the signal at Bal Bijou Road.

Choosing an accommodation in this area isn't easy: there are many choices, in every budget category; unfortunately, many of them are worthy of much lower budget categories than you'd think from the offerings. Lakeland Village and the Inn by the Lake are solid standbys in the limited category of lakeside lodging; the Tahoe Lakeshore Lodge and Spa has been completely redone inside since it used to be the Tahoe Marina Inn, and it is the only property we could find in the area that had on-site spa facilities, usually a welcome enhancement for golfers. Prices also seemed on the reasonable side.

By now it's late afternoon—let's call it happy hour. Take a walk along the beach to the Riva Grill, just five minutes east at the foot of Ski Run Boulevard, and make yourself comfortable on the deck, where you can enjoy your 19th hole watching passengers come and go on the Hornblower dock ahead, and maybe soak up a little sunshine. You might want to try the local potion, "Wet Woody," which is served by the pitcher. In other words, get Tahoed in.

Dinner tonight is just up Ski Run, on the left-hand side; watch carefully because Cafe Fiore is the town with one stoplight on the Tahoe restaurant scene, a tiny place but with a menu and atmosphere that pack a big punch. For an appetizer, the house specialty is the eggplant crepes stuffed with smoked salmon, and the pastas are exquisite—linguine fra diavolo can beat any shot you've taken today. And don't miss the house-made white chocolate ice cream, made most special by fresh summer strawberries. Fear not to ask for help on the long wine list—130 choices at last look—because the staff here is as perfect as the food.

You've had a long day. How about spending the evening with the remote control, saving the nightlife for tomorrow?

day II   You're rising as early as possible to launch your first shot along the shores of the lake at Edgewood Tahoe, just across the state line past the Horizon hotel and casino. It's probably going to be quite chilly; arrive early and get the blood flowing at the range, fuel up at the snack bar, check out the quality merchandise in the big pro shop. And don't let the altitude go to your head: select the proper set of tees. Edgewood Tahoe is a fair test but much tougher than yesterday's gentle introduction to mountain golf.

Now, stand at the first tee and say, "Wow. Isn't it beautiful?" It's not just the scenery around the course, which offers everything from the crystal waters of Lake Tahoe itself to the snowy peaks of Mount Tallac, but the course itself. There are so many trees, such clever routing and mounding, it's amazing to think that the bustle and, oh yes, hustle of Stateline is right next door. The Fazios are going to let us relax for a moment; the first hole is one of the easiest on the course, with a big wide landing area beyond the threatening bunker on the right side and right of the water on the left. The green, too, is large, which seems like a good thing unless you find yourself a distance away from the hole and get acquainted with the slippery poa annua greens with a three-putt.

On the straightaway par-4 second hole, the yardage guide we were given at check-in became our bible for the day. "From the tee, look at the pin position and then hit your tee shot to the opposite side of the fairway," it began, and then followed with advice on how to approach a short or long pin on the green. Your first time at Edgewood, you'll enjoy the course much more if you see what you might be getting into before you're already in too deep. And unlike most yardage books, which seem to be written by the longest hitter in the house, this one proved useful even for the short hitter in our foursome. That's because Edgewood Tahoe is not all about distance but about placement. Many of the fairways and landing areas are narrow, or the greens are undulating, and so a little local knowledge went a long way, even if a drive didn't.

Pace of play is excellent for a morning round at Edgewood, and you should be making your turn about two hours in—wonderfully, with those 12-minute tee times they insist on, there's no one holding you up in front or pushing from behind. So order up a sandwich and a beverage at the full-service snack bar and forge onward.

The highlights of a round at Edgewood Tahoe are the three finishing holes, where the wind may come into play for the first time if you've started early. But the tests are the 12th, 13th, and 14th, a medium-distance par-3 that is the most difficult 3 on the course, and two par-4s with trouble all around. This stretch is followed by the easiest par-4 on the course, hole number 15, and then you're standing at the 16th tee looking down at Lake Tahoe about 500 yards forward.

The most lauded hole on the course is the par-3 17th with Lake Tahoe along the right side. It's just 107 yards from the forward tees, 140 from the white, 175 blue, and 207 gold. But the wind is bound to be raising the difficulty level of your tee shot, which could find bunkers front or back, or trees left. And 18 is a fun finishing hole, a par-5 that offers the best birdie opportunity on the course to the long hitters, with a pond just short and left of the green (known as Lake Laimbeer after a pro basketball player who splashed there to lose his quest for the Celebrity Challenge) that creates the risk-reward quandary for the gambler.

While you're here, you might as well enjoy lunch at the restaurant. The view is one of the best around, and as long as you stick to the appetizer and salad portion of the menu, we don't think you'll spoil your dinner tonight at Evans or blow your bank account. For a lower budget option, there's the Lakeside Beach at Stateline, described in the Alternatives dining section, but remember, there's no alcohol, not even beer or wine.

Now you're fortified for the afternoon, a three- to four-hour block of time we recommend you spend thusly:

Option 1: If you can't resist the temptation of the casinos, oh so near, stop and play on your way back to your hotel. You can choose one of the monster casinos, or if you'd like to play at some tables where the stakes start lower, there's Bill's Casino, right next to Harrah's, just across from the Horizon and Harvey's. Then before you lose your shirt, go back to the hotel and remove it, donning beach togs and relaxing at the pool or beach.

Option 2: Drive right by the casinos back to the hotel, put on your beachwear, gather the cooler and blanket, and drive the other way along Highway 50, veering right on Highway 89 (at the "Y") and turning into Kiva Beach, on the right. There's a lovely stretch of sand here, with views all around—the snowcaps to the west, the lake to the east, the casinos off in the distance—and also things to do for those who can't just sit and read a book or ponder the depths. Just down the beach is the Tallac Historic Site, where the rich and famous used to vacation in the old days, and a little farther is Camp Richardson, a lively summer spot where The Beacon is the place to go for a drink outdoors or a boat rental.

But don't get too carried away. Before it gets dark, you'll want to go back to the hotel, clean up, and look at least civilized for what is bound to be a very special dinner at Evans. To get there, head back toward Kiva Beach. Evans is on the left side about a mile past the Y intersection. It's another tiny restaurant—owners Evan and Candice Williams call it a café, actually—with a big menu. The menu is chef Aaron Maffit's, the desserts are Candice's. Oh, and then there's the chalkboard, a bit of an unwieldy way to post the day's specials, usually at least a pasta, a pizza, and a soup, and of course the daily fresh seafood. You'll want to see those before you choose from the menu favorites, which may include grilled tenderloin of beef with zinfandel and roasted garlic, served with apple-smoked bacon and roast leek potatoes gratin, or the roast New Zealand lamb chops with wild mushroom-plum pan sauce, parsnip mash, and french fried potatoes. We found treats among the appetizers and wine list, and even shared a dessert. There's a price for it all, but this is your splurge meal of the escape, so enjoy.

Now, perhaps you've made reservations to see a show, or you'd like to head back to the casinos for a little action, or you've had enough for today. We're not going to force you to go out, oh no, not us, we're just here for the golf, right?

day III

If you really have to end your great escape today, you've got to pack up the car before the morning begins with breakfast aboard the MS *Dixie II,* on Zephyr Cove a few miles after you've crossed into Nevada on Highway 50. There are plenty of cruises to choose from on Lake Tahoe, but we liked this one for its daily breakfast cruise, an easy 90-minute jaunt at a time when most folks other than golfers aren't really ready yet to start a day of their vacation (9 A.M.). So we were able to book it a day ahead. The lake is so pristine, the air so cool at this time of day—and the food on the boat isn't bad either. Breakfast comes with unlimited champagne, so watch out—you'll want to have your wits about you at Genoa Lakes.

To get there, head back toward the casinos and make a left onto Kingsbury Grade and go over the hill, following the road down into the Carson Valley. At the bottom of the hill, turn left at the stop sign on Foothill Road and look for Genoa Lakes a few miles down on your right. Drive toward the massive clubhouse and decide whether to walk (U.S. Open qualifying has been held here, which tells you the course can be walked twice in a day) or ride through your round. By now the wind is probably kicking up, so head for the range next to the snack shop to work on your low line drives. You'll hear the pro shop call you to the first tee.

Designers John Harbottle III and Peter Jacobsen start you off easy, with a short par-4 to a rather large green, with not too much trouble en route. It may be, in fact, the only hole at Genoa Lakes with not too much trouble en route. There is a lot of water, and there are wetlands and strategically placed bunkers throughout. Yet, Genoa Lakes is a fun course to play. Tiger Woods observed that it made him "think a little bit" before he reached into his bag when he played here as a 17-year-old in 1993, but he has more to think about than us mere mortals.

"All of the par-4s face different directions, which is one of the features I really like," says head pro Randy Fox. "And there's lots of risk-reward type choices, but with plenty of places to bail out."

It is, in short, a great place for the fearful and the fearless. The seventh hole is the most difficult for the men, a long par-4 into the wind and dog-legging left with lots of trouble on the right. For women, the hardest is the 434-yard par-5 hole number 2—so much for gentle beginnings—because the landing area shrinks dangerously for the second shot and third, with a small, undulating green at the end of it all.

After your round, you will definitely want to scarf at the River Bend Grille; we were shocked at the quality of the food here, where the appetizers and a big salad bar star in the show all afternoon. If you're still going home today—haven't changed your mind yet?—at least you won't go on an empty stomach.

ITINERARY 2:
Carson Valley

WARMING UP

This is a terrific adults-only escape, what with all the free drinks you'll be getting from the Piñon Plaza. The only problem with three days and two nights is that we'll be missing some golf courses. So stay longer, if your liver can handle all that fun.

Book a two-night golf package at the Piñon Plaza Resort. If your group is of any size, they'll be handling your tee times for you and planning some of your meals.

If you're on your own, it's likely that Tee-Time Central can save you some time on your bookings; call 888/236-8725 and find out which courses have been added to its list. Then book a Day 1 early tee time at Eagle Valley's West Course or, if you prefer a gentler challenge, Empire Ranch. If you prefer to lose absolutely no golf balls, consider playing the wide-open Eagle Valley East Course, a good choice for beginners and those with high handicaps. Book a Day 2 tee time, as early as you can stand, at Sierra Nevada Golf Ranch, and a Day 3 tee time, again as early as you can stand, at Dayton Valley. Remember, the afternoon winds can be brutal in the Carson and Dayton valleys.

Also, make a dinner reservation for Day 1 at Adele's and for Day 2 at the Carson Valley Country Club Restaurant. If you'd like to schedule any spa services at David Walley's Hot Springs on Day 3, do so now.

day 1 Ideally you'll be arriving the evening before Day 1, so that you can enjoy some of the pleasures of the Piñon Plaza Resort. It's a small property that energetically courts the golfing business, in part because owner Clark Russell and his sales and marketing director, Jackie Behan, are golf nuts themselves. (If you want to know who's been working harder lately, ask which of the two has been giving the strokes lately.) You'll be able to tell the golfers by the VIP badges they wear. These are signs that tell the bartenders all over the Piñon Plaza and sister property Carson Station in town, "Water me with free drinks." The group packages also come with a welcome party with appetizers, a breakfast buffet at the Whiskey Creek Steakhouse and Saloon, and a prime rib banquet with wine, plus plenty of little goodies. It's not uncommon for golfers to be out in the hallways practicing their putting on the long carpet as the cocktail waitstaff comes through with refills. Clearly, golfers love this place—or if they don't, well, they soon forget.

But do try to get an early start on Day 1 or the wind will penalize you for sleeping in. It's a five-minute ride to Eagle Valley or Empire Ranch, two public courses designed to give more bang for less buck.

There are 36 holes at Eagle Valley, which also has full grass practice facilities, including a practice green almost as big as Lake Tahoe, plus there's a restaurant and one of the more attractively arranged pro shops— with reasonably priced merchandise—to be found at a municipal course. It's a good place to start your visit, because Eagle Valley was the first course in the Carson Valley, and it is the center of the local golf scene— with men's, women's, and seniors' clubs, and a series of inexpensive clinics open to all. At Eagle Valley, affordable golf is the draw—it's possible to play two courses here, even riding the West Course, for around $50.

If you're going to do that, though, consider which order you might like to play the courses. The more popular East Course—the one, manager Mike McGehee says, "Ray Charles could play without getting into any trouble"—is 24 years old, entirely different from the West, the 14-year-old youngster that is the reason we've sent you here in the first place. Just across the street from the East Course, but at a higher elevation, the West Course requires shot placement and thought on most of its holes, which wander through high desert full of cottonwoods and sagebrush. Job's Peak presides off in the distance.

Says McGehee: "If you're going to play the East first, appreciate the fact that it's wide open, the greens are relatively flat, and the bunkers are not the kind you can't get out of. The West is entirely different. The greens are faster, and there are a lot of elevated tees."

The West Course has a wilder feel—there's a pack of coyotes that roams here, and an eagles' nest is visible in spring and fall near the 13th hole. Hole number 13 is the highlight of the round, a par-3 from an elevated tee, over a barranca full of cottonwoods and vegetation. Wrong club means punishment. At least there are four choices of tees on this course; there are only three on the East, which is fine. It's target golf for the most part on the West Course; spray it and play it on the East.

If you'd prefer something in between at equally great prices, Empire Ranch is the alternative, with three nines: Red, Blue, and Yellow. There are subtle differences between the three, which wind through a canyon next to the Carson River. The Yellow—also called the River Course—is longest, at 3,500 yards from the back option of five sets of tees, just 2,509 from the front option, but the Red Course, also known as the Comstock, was far more interesting, with some doglegs and carries and tree placements that made it more brain workout than brawn workout. The Blue, Sierra Course, is considered by the staff to be the most "user friendly," and is a good place for the bigger hitters to cut loose for more reward and less risk. The 100-year flood of the winter of 1996–1997 decimated the course before it barely got going, and recovery was slow, but operators are hoping it should be good for another 95 years or so. The greens were great fun when we visited, smooth and subtle, not too big and not too small.

If you're hungry, no matter whether you played at Eagle Valley or Empire Ranch, the restaurant at Empire Ranch is your stop for a quick sandwich, a little soup, a healthy salad, whatever will keep you going through the afternoon. If you're exhausted, the pool and hot tub at Piñon Plaza may be calling your name. But if you took a cart and not too many swings, swing on into Carson City and take the walking tour of the historical district, where the houses "talk" to you via radio frequencies. Pick up the Kit Carson Trail Map or the free map from the Convention and Visitors Bureau, to know which station goes with which address. There's a suggested one-hour walk that will take you past the Governor's Mansion, and you can easily swing by the State Capitol, State Museum, Railroad Museum, and/or Stewart Indian Cultural Center. The architecture alone is a sight to see, and where else would you learn that Nevada is the source of such products as Odor Check and Kibbles'N Bits?

Okay, now you can have that time at the hot tub or in the casino, but go easy on the free cocktails because you don't want to spoil your stomach for Adele's tonight. A favorite of the local politicos, it seems more fit for the big city than the small Carson one, with an imaginative menu and always a long list of specials recited neatly by a server who's probably been there since it opened 30 years earlier. Be adventurous in your selection; we can tell you that though some of the preparations sound unusual, the rewards seemed worth the risks. Yes, Adele's is expensive, but it's the best place in town.

On the right night of the week, there may be music on the deck calling you to linger at Adele's, or perhaps you're ready to go back to the Piñon Plaza for more fun. You can work off some of those luscious calories by bowling a few frames at the fine, high-tech lanes here, or try to win back the money you just spent on dinner in the casino.

day II Go ahead and scarf on that complimentary breakfast they're offering you at Whiskey Creek in the Piñon Plaza. No continental here—we're talking Joe's Special, pork chop and eggs, sirloin and eggs fuel. This morning we're gone until sunset, so bring along a daypack with your swimsuit and clean clothes for dinner. We're leaving Carson City but not the Carson Valley, heading back to Genoa to the Sierra Nevada Golf Ranch. Take Highway 395 south to Jacks Valley Road, turn right, and go about five miles to the gate. The ranch motif will smack you upside the head right away, with stop signs that say WHOA and restrooms for Cowgirls and Cowboys. A ranch hand will greet you and load your golf bag onto your "mule," and you can even saddle up at check-in in the ranch clubhouse. It's a cute gimmick that doesn't detract from the star attraction.

And that is a beautiful 18-hole John Harbottle course carved into the foothills, with rugged 360-degree mountain views, a variety of water features, 114 bunkers, and a most impeccably groomed course with firm fairways and bent-grass greens. "It's a course people like to come back to," says general manager Ken Kaifas. "I think a lot of people who'd normally get into the competition just enjoy the scenery." The high point, quite literally, is hole number 6, a long par-4 for the men, not so long from the forward tees, at 5,050 feet. But the par-3s are probably most memorable, particularly the 17th, with a cascading waterfall creating a pond that nearly surrounds the green. You've been marveling at the beauty for 16 holes—and now it just got even prettier. How they could name it Hyde's Curse, we'll never know.

The Homestead, the 18th hole, leads you back to the ranch, where you might want to have a bite or a drink at the library-themed Golfers Grill before moving on to an afternoon at David Walley's Spa and Hot Springs. Guys, don't wrinkle your noses up. Head out of the golf course and turn left back onto Jacks Valley Road, which will merge into Foothill. You'll see Walley's at 2001. Yes, there are the usual massage, facial, hand and nail services, and body wrap frills that women tend to like, but behind the building—which also has a workout room—are six mineral pools ranging in temperature from 98 degrees to 104, plus a big freshwater swimming pool at about 85 degrees. There are lounge chairs and friendly faces, and the café is open 10–3 daily. If you time it right and dally long enough to watch the light change over the valley beyond the pools, you may leave Walley's in a daze. It's $20 to spend the day here, a splurge for a splash.

After freshening up, it's time for a lot of food. Leave Walley's, turning left onto Foothill and continuing on to Centerville, where you'll turn left. Centerville becomes Dresslerville and then Riverview, where you'll find the Carson Valley Country Club. Dinner tonight is in the restaurant, one of at least three popular Basque establishments where the specialty is to stuff you to the gills with delicious, mostly meat dishes for not very much money. We chose this one for its golf course views, and because it usually has some fish options for the noncarnivorous. Hopefully you are not too stuffed to make it back to the Piñon Plaza, because there is one round of golf yet to play.

day III   Have your breakfast and take Highway 50 east to Dayton. Turn right on Dayton Valley Drive and right on Palmer Road to get to Dayton Valley Golf Course, in the Carson River Valley between the Virginia Range and the Pinenut Range. It's a pretty ride to a pretty course, designed by Arnold Palmer and Ed Seay to please even the golfers farthest from him on the talent scale, with the back tees playing to 7,218 yards and the front tees at 4,900, and three options in between. The King will punish you if you start your round a bit too cocky about your game, though; remember that Dayton Valley is challenging enough played from the proper set of tees for your game, and not even golfers with single-digit handicaps ought to consider playing the back tees their first time here. And with underground aquifers keeping the fairways and rough so lush, there's not quite the roll you'll find on the hard courses in Genoa.

There are lots of great holes here, even the tough par-4 ninth, where water comes into play on every shot—maybe even your putt if you're not careful. It's a narrow strip of fairway, reluctantly offering up a stingy little landing area for your drive, leading to a relatively small green fronted by water that continues around to the right. If you bail out left, there is thick rough and pot bunkers. It's the hardest hole on the course, according to head pro Jim Keppler, and one of his favorites. Well, he's a pretty good player.

The par-3s are also a special treat here. In fact one of them, hole number 4, may give you a good scare coming in because you can see the bunker terracing from the road. Most of the sand is to intimidate, really, and not to foil; the green is quite big, though it won't seem that way if your ball is drawn to the beach. And where hole number 4 is beach, hole number 7 is ocean. It's an island green that penalizes the right-handed slicer by protecting shots short, long, or left from rolling off. How did The King forget us loyal servants?

By the time you finish, the wind will be doing its thing. You can retire to the clubhouse, where beers are served by the pitcher and the food is just delicious. It's sort of a golf great room, with pro shop blending into restaurant and bar, which makes it one of the more comfortable 19th holes we've found.

The only problem with playing Dayton Valley last is that it may whet your appetite for all of the courses we've missed in Carson Valley. Remember, nobody's forcing you to go home now.

 NOTES

Money Savers. The best bargains in these itineraries are the Carson Valley courses—especially Eagle Valley, Dayton Valley, Empire Ranch. Play at twilight for the best deals, but beware the wind.

Nongolfers. Bring your beach gear.

Parents. You are going to have a hard time making this getaway if your kids are old enough to know what you're doing. Itinerary 1 is easily adjusted to include children, especially if you stay at the Embassy Suites—do save Cafe Fiore and Evans for another time, and consider substituting the likes of Chevy's and the casino buffets.

Time Savers. Look at another chapter. This one's a difficult quickie.

Low-Handicappers. The best challenges come from Edgewood, Dayton Valley, Sierra Nevada, and Genoa Lakes.

Extended Stay. Try to arrive the night before Day 1 and relax. For add-on courses not listed here, see Chapter 6 for descriptions of the North Lake Tahoe possibilities. Sierra Nevada and Genoa Lakes go with either of the two itineraries described in this chapter.

Lazy Golfers. The Golf Store at Lake Tahoe can arrange guaranteed tee times at nine Lake Tahoe/Carson Valley courses and fit you with clubs and shoes. It's inside the Embassy Suites Resort Lake Tahoe, at 4130 Lake Tahoe Boulevard; 530/544-1692.

Health. Former PGA tour player and Lake Tahoe resident George Bayer once said of the game at this altitude, "It's one or two clubs less, and two drinks are like four and four are like eight."

Courses

ITINERARY 1:
South Lake Tahoe

ITINERARY SELECTIONS

Lake Tahoe Golf Course
2500 Emerald Bay Rd. (Hwy. 50)
South Lake Tahoe, CA 96150
530/577-0788, fax 530/577-4469
website www.americangolf.com

Green fees start at around $45 on a midweek summer morning, adding another $20 for weekends and holidays and subtracting about $10 for twilight rounds. That's if you walk—and this course is a delightful, scenic stroll, with benches at most tees and easy access from green to tee everywhere. Cart rental is unfortunately required on summer weekends, at about $20 per player, though they won't make you ride them if you'd rather walk. You can make a tee time for free by calling the pro shop seven days in advance, or pay $10 more per player for the

SCORECARD

Architect: Billy Bell, 1959 and 1963
Course Record: 61, Ron Parsons
Gold: Par 71, 6,741 yards, 70.8 rating, 126 slope
Black: Par 71, 6,327 yards, 68.9 rating for men, 120 slope; par 72 for women, 74.1 rating, 126 slope
Silver: Par 69, 5,703 yards, 66.7 rating for men, 109 slope; par 72 for women, 71.2 rating, 117 slope
Tee times may be made up to seven days in advance by calling the pro shop or up to 60 days in advance for an additional $10 per player by calling the toll-free American Golf line at 888/452-4653.

privilege of making a reservation up to 60 days in advance. Play-and-stays are featured with the Embassy Suites.

TEE TIDBITS | What a treat, a driving range where you can hit toward snowy peaks, usually off the grass, practically next to the first tee. There's also a big putting green and an area nearby to practice chipping and sand shots. You could spend hours here working on your short game without spending a dime—a real Tahoe bargain. If you've got 16 players, you can plan a tournament. Pace of play can be dreadful here, because even at the high rates, beginners like it here. That can also make it dangerous; some of the holes are parallel and narrow. Head pro Mike Durst says if you've gotten through 14 with a good score, the worst is over. Water comes into play on 13 of the 18 holes—maybe even more if you're having a really bad day. No strict dress requirements, just no tank tops or short shorts. If you get your round in before lunch, the clubhouse is a good stop; once the kitchen closes, it's on the quiet side. Pro shop is well stocked, a good place to sale shop before the course closes at the end of October.

Edgewood Tahoe Golf Course

180 Lake Parkway
Stateline, NV 89449
775/588-3566, fax 775/588-8049
website www.edgewood-tahoe.com

Edgewood is super busy in the peak summer months, so consider springing for the extra $25 to make a reservation 90 days out. Look at it this way: you're already paying $175 for a round of golf, which wasn't exactly a childhood dream of any of us. And at least your $175 will cover transportation (cart) and navigation (yardage book). If you really want to save that $25, be sure to jump on the Internet or phone 14 days out at 6:30 A.M. and pray your desired time is open.

SCORECARD

Architects: George Fazio, 1968; Tom Fazio, 1992
Course Record: 64, Lee Trevino
Gold: Par 72, 7,483 yards, 75.7 rating, 139 slope
Blue: Par 72, 6,911 yards, 72.3 rating, 132 slope
White: Par 72, 6,464 yards, 70.4 rating for men, 127 slope; par 73 for women, 76.3 rating, 147 slope
Red: Par 72, 5,555 yards, 71.3 rating for women, 136 slope
Book your tee time by phone or on the website 1–14 days out for free, or 15–90 days out for an extra $25 per player.

TEE TIDBITS | Rental clubs are available at $25.
There's a driving range and two greens for putting practice. The restaurant is open for lunch and dinner only; there's a snack bar sitting out in the sunshine at the turn that makes it tempting to stop. If you can't get a tee time while you're visiting Tahoe, there's nothing to stop you from practicing your putting and lunching at the snack bar, just to take in the atmosphere while you're here—unless of course you'd consider that sadistic. Remember, one of the area's biggest events is the Celebrity Challenge, usually held the first weekend of July. After John Elway and friends finish up here, the phone rings off the hook and tee times are precious. The course is extremely well marked and very walkable. If you don't think you should ride just because you paid to ride, give it a try. Carts are paths-only.

The Golf Club at Genoa Lakes
1 Genoa Lakes Dr.
Genoa, NV 89411
775/782-4653, fax 775/782-5899
website www.genoalakes.com

Off-season and shoulder-season rounds go for the amazing bargain price of about $40, including carts and range balls. Even in summer, there's a Sunday getaway special of an early twilight rate starting at noon, and there are at least four rate tiers, peaking with the weekend prime times at around $100. You're allowed to walk if you'd like, but carts are usually allowed on the fairways—and the staff recommends that you do ride.

SCORECARD

Architects: John Harbottle and Peter Jacobsen, 1993
Course Record: 63, Peter Jacobsen
Gold: Par 72, 7,263 yards, 73.5 rating, 134 slope
Blue: Par 72, 6,738 yards, 71.2 rating, 127 slope
White: Par 72, 6,057 yards, 68.2 rating, 120 slope
Red: Par 72, 5,008 yards, 67.6 rating for women, 117 slope
Tee times are taken up to 30 days in advance or a year ahead for groups of 20 or more.

TEE TIDBITS | Soft spikes are required, and they'll change yours if you need them. There are excellent practice areas for putting, chipping, and sand shots. Rental clubs are available for another $30. Prices drop in the afternoon, but note that the wind rises, which is why it's not very difficult to get a twilight tee time at Genoa Lakes. The staff accepts tee times by phone, fax, email, or snail mail. The 18th is a memorable finishing hole, with a carefully placed drive needed that will clear the lake on the left but not run through the fairway on the right, and a final shot into a large green flanked by sand on the left. You know you're supposed to keep your head down, but don't forget to look up at all the fantastic scenery around and above.

Courses

ITINERARY 2:
Carson Valley

ITINERARY SELECTIONS

Eagle Valley Golf Course
3999 Centennial Park Dr.
Carson City, NV 89706
775/887-2380, fax 775/883-0418
website www.eaglevalleygolf.com

In winter, you can play both courses for $40—the East at $15, the West at $25. Generally the West Course runs at around $40 including the required cart, while the East

SCORECARD

Architects: Jack Snyder, 1978 (East) and 1988 (West)
Course Record: NA
East Blue: Par 72, 6,658 yards, 69.6 rating, 120 slope
East White: Par 72, 6,314 yards, 68.0 rating for men, 117 slope; par 72 for women, 74.2 rating, 131 slope

Course costs about $20 to walk or around $12 after 3 P.M. And if you're 80 or older, you can play the East Course for free any time you want. The East Course is very walkable and seems to have a better drainage system than the West, but carts are generally allowed on the fairways of both courses.

TEE TIDBITS | Wear anything you want here, it's a "greasy hamburger and a Budweiser" kind of place, says the general manager, and that's probably the specialty in the Eagles Landing Grill. The carts used to have GPS systems, a feature that would be especially useful on the sometimes confusing West Course, but those fizzled. New systems were being evaluated as we went to press, and hopefully you'll have one aboard. If you figure out how to play hole number 3 West, please let us know. Range balls go for $3 –6 a bucket. If this is your first stop on the escape, the Eagle Valley range would be a good place to gauge the extra distance you'll be getting at this altitude. The range is open at night. There are also two practice bunkers and a chipping area.

SCORECARD — continued —

East Red: Par 72, 5,980 yards, 72.5 rating for women, 127 slope
West Gold: Par 72, 6,851 yards, 72.0 rating, 138 slope
West Blue: Par 72, 6,245 yards, 69.3 rating, 132 slope
West White: Par 72, 5.819 yards, 67.3 rating for men, 128 slope; 71.8 rating for women, 127 slope
West Red: Par 72, 5,293 yards, 68.9 rating for women, 121 slope
Call Friday after 3 P.M. for a tee time the following Monday through Sunday.

Empire Ranch Golf Course
1875 Fair Way
Carson City, NV 89701
775/885-2100
website
www.empireranchgolf.com

Empire Ranch is a bargain-hunter's delight, a place where you can play 27 different holes at only a dollar a hole if you're willing to walk, or for under $50 if you must have a cart. It's a very walkable course, for nine, 18, or 27. The summer walking rates for 18 holes start at around $20 on a weekday; with cart, rates start at $35. Seniors 55 and up can play on Monday and Wednesday with cart for $30. Winter rates are even lower.

SCORECARD

Architect: Cary Bickler, 1997
Course Record: NA

SIERRA-RIVER (BLUE-YELLOW)
Black: Par 72, 6,763 yards, 71.6 rating for men, 129 slope
Blue: Par 72, 6,370 yards, 70.7 rating for men, 127 slope
White: Par 72, 5,882 yards, 69.0 rating for men, 124 slope
Green: Par 72 5,356 yards, 65.5 rating for men, 116 slope; 71.4 rating for women, 129 slope
Red: Par 72, 4,883 yards, 68.1 rating for women, 119 slope

SIERRA-COMSTOCK (BLUE-RED)
Black: Par 72, 6,603 yards, 70.5 rating for men, 127 slope
Blue: Par 72, 6,214 yards, 69.6 rating for men, 125 slope
White: Par 72, 5,799 yards, 68.6 rating for men, 123 slope
Green: Par 72, 5,315 yards, 65.2 rating for men, 116 slope; 71.0 rating for women, 127 slope
Red: Par-72, 4,719 yards, 67.4 rating for women, 118 slope

TEE TIDBITS | Empire Ranch is a host course for John Jacobs golf schools. Not just a place for birdies, the wetlands all around make this a bird-watcher's paradise. Twilight rates begin as early as 1 P.M. You'll play 18 holes in one of three orders, which is why it is rated three times. The housing development you'll drive through hardly comes into view on the course, which has a remote feel to it. There's a 300-yard driving range and three practice greens, with accessible bunkers. No metal spikes, tank tops, or cutoffs. Rounds can be slow in the morning, windy in the afternoon. A super-friendly staff runs the show.

SCORECARD — *continued*

COMSTOCK-RIVER (RED-YELLOW)
Black: Par-72, 6,840 yards, 71.3 rating for men, 128 slope
Blue: Par-72, 6,392 yards, 70.5 rating for men, 127 slope
White: Par-72, 5,923 yards, 68.7 rating for men, 123 slope
Green: Par-72, 5,409 yards, 65.5 slope; 71.4 rating for women, 128 slope
Red: Par-72, 4,854 yards, 68.3 rating for women, 123 slope
Call seven days in advance. Groups of 20 or more can call up to one year ahead.

Sierra Nevada Golf Ranch
2901 Jacks Valley Rd.
Genoa, NV 89411
775/782-7700, fax 775/782-0252
website www.sierranevadagc.com

Sierra Nevada Golf Ranch cuts its rates in half for twilight play, and that's a fair price cut considering that the wind most likely quadruples during the afternoon hours. Weekend peak season players may spring for $100 or so for a prime time, but these do include practice balls and cart, which comes with a useful GPS course guide. You do not want to play this course without a cart because the elevation changes are drastic, and carts are generally allowed on the fairways. If you'd like to play an early-bird nine holes, there may be a special rate available, and juniors also get a break.

Sierra Nevada also offers a Mega Rate Guest Card, of great benefit to locals and frequent visitors. For $100 you can use the card for one year and receive discounts of as much as 40 percent on the peak season rates. Four rounds of golf will recoup the membership fee.

SCORECARD

Architects: John Harbottle and Johnny Miller, 1998
Course Record: 64, Darryl Eddy
Tour: Par 72, 7,358 yards, 75.1 rating for men, 136 slope; 80.9 rating for women, 154 slope
Championship: Par 72, 6,820 yards, 72.7 rating for men, 131 slope; 77.9 rating for women, 147 slope
Players: Par 72, 6,207 yards, 69.5 rating for men, 127 slope; 74.5 rating for women, 140 slope
Resort: Par 72, 5,684 yards, 67.1 rating for men, 122 slope; 71.2 rating for women, 129 slope
Sierra: Par 72, 5,129 yards, 64.2 rating for men, 108 slope; 68.5 rating for women, 124 slope
Call seven days in advance at 7 p.m. for your tee time, or you can book 8–60 days ahead at an extra $10 per player.

TEE TIDBITS | Sierra Nevada is worth visiting just to practice. There are three driving ranges, plus practice greens and bunkers, in a serene setting with fabulous views. American Golf runs summertime golf schools here, at three and five days. With five sets of tees,

TEE TIDBITS continued | even the average woman player will have a decision to make before she even takes a shot. Set in the foothills, Sierra Nevada drains well and is a good place to play after rain. Follow the orders of the cart, er, "mule" screen to succeed—one of the features of John Harbottle's design is to use bunkers and hazards as aiming points off the tee. If you land in the designated area, your drive will roll into the sunset. Despite the western motif, we recommend traditional golf clothes and soft spikes. Pace of play warning: We had a very slow round here due to the group in front of us, which didn't even bother to rake its footprints in the sand, and we never saw a marshal on a busy midsummer day.

Dayton Valley Golf Club

51 Palmer Dr.

Dayton, NV 89403

775/246-7888 or 800/644-3822, fax 775/246-7894

website www.daytonvalley.com

Dayton Valley is semiprivate, but visitors can expect to get decent tee times by calling two weeks in advance—or using Tee-Time Central as many as three months in advance. Green fees, which include cart and a small bag of range balls, start at around $30 in the off-season and top out at around $75 on a peak weekend. There are players who walk this links-style course, which is relatively flat but has some green-to-tee strolls built in.

SCORECARD

Architect: Arnold Palmer, 1991

Course Record: 64, Casey Martin

Grey: Par 72, 7,218 yards, 74.2 rating, 143 slope

Blue: Par 72, 6,637 yards, 72.1 rating, 134 slope

White: Par 72, 5,897 yards, 68.2 rating for men, 128 slope; 72.3 rating for women, 129 slope

Red: Par 72, 5,161 yards, 68.2 rating for men, 128 slope; 69.0 rating for women, 121 slope

Tee times are available two weeks in advance through the pro shop—up to a year for groups—and three months in advance through Tee-Time Central at 888/236-8725.

TEE TIDBITS | The red-tailed hawk is the mascot, and logo, at Dayton Valley. The course is owned by the Bank of Scotland, and there is talk of another 18 holes being built as this one gains popularity. We counted water in play on 12 holes. So far, no one has volunteered to count the bunkers. Rental clubs are available at $25. Carts generally may roam on the fairways, and rounds can be quick at Dayton Valley. Gabriel Hjerstedt qualified for PGA Tour school here. Casey Martin shot 64 in tour school qualifying but didn't get past the next phase. Jim Keppler says green speed is up to 12.5 or 13 on the Stimpmeter for tour qualifying, so no complaining about the greens being too speedy at 9 or 10. Pin placements are changed five days a week.

ALTERNATIVES

The two other top-notch courses among the Divine Nine of the Carson Valley are **Silver Oak** and **Sunridge.** Both are in Carson City. Sunridge is the longer of the two, playing at 7,054 yards; par at Silver Oak is 71 at 6,564 yards. Both courses offer five tee options. Rates at Sunridge are higher, ranging about $45–75, including cart. Silver Oak green fees start at about $25 for a twilight round and range up to about $50. ■ SILVER OAK: 1 COUNTRY

CLUB DR., CARSON CITY, NV 98703; 775/841-7000 ■ SUNRIDGE: 1000 LONG DR., CARSON CITY, NV 89705; 775/267-4448

The **Carson Valley Golf Course** is also open to the public. It plays much shorter, at 5,836 yards from the back, to a par 71, and its rates rank down there with Eagle Valley's, starting at around $22 to walk 18 holes. ■ 1027 RIVERVIEW, GARDNERVILLE, NV 89410; 775/265-3181

There is one other 18-hole course in South Lake Tahoe that's best left to beginners and the extremely patient: **Tahoe Paradise,** an 18-hole executive course, where rates start at around $32 just to walk. ■ 3021 EMERALD BAY RD., SOUTH LAKE TAHOE, CA 96150; 530/577-2121

Lodging

ITINERARY 1:
South Lake Tahoe

ITINERARY SELECTION

The **Tahoe Lakeshore Lodge and Spa** features 25-mile views from every room, and for those more awed by the sight of a slot machine, it has shuttle service to the casinos nearby. The rooms are big, all with decks or patios, and some have kitchens. There are condos, too, but because these are individually owned we found a wide range of quality not represented by an appropriate range of rates. Rooms start at around $125 a night, condos at around $200 a night. ■ 930 BAL BIJOU RD., SOUTH LAKE TAHOE, CA 96150; 800/448-4577; WEBSITE WWW.TAHOELAKESHORELODGE.COM

GOLF PACKAGE OPTIONS

The **Embassy Suites Resort,** a full-service hotel sans casino right next to Harrah's but on the California side of the line, caters to golfers more than any other Tahoe area property. On the premises is the Golf Store, which will guarantee tee times at any of the Lake Tahoe/Carson Valley courses—and rent you shoes and clubs as well. And the resort's golf-lodging packages come with all sorts of frills: maybe a tee bag full of tees, a shoe bag, a voucher for the Golf Store, plus daily golf with cart and range balls (though not at Edgewood). These start at around $125 per person—and yes they include a suite plus a full daily breakfast and nightly 19th hole manager's reception. It's a fantastic deal. And we thought the king suites here would do quite nicely for a foursome. ■ 4130 LAKE TAHOE BLVD., SOUTH LAKE TAHOE, CA 96150; 530/544-5400 OR 800/988-9895; WEBSITE WWW.EMBASSYTAHOE.COM

The Inn by the Lake is not quite on the lake; it's just across the street. But with lake-view rooms starting at around $100 in the low season (lots of discounts, too—Internet, AARP, for instance), a variety of choices (up to a three-bedroom plus loft), and a very welcoming pool and hot tub area, it's a reliable choice. There are also flexible golf packages starting at about $130 a person. ■ 3300 LAKE TAHOE BLVD., SOUTH LAKE TAHOE, CA 96150; 800/877-1466; WEBSITE WWW.INNBYTHELAKE.COM

Lakeland Village Beach and Ski Resort has 209 units, and many of them are townhomes, some of the bigger (four-bedroom) models right at the water's edge. This is a great family destination—not really for the romantic golfer—because it's full of activity: two pools, two tennis courts, a kids' playground, and a boat dock where you can rent the craft of your choice for an hour or a day. There are basic lodge rooms (stay away from poolside if you want to sleep in), but the fully equipped lakefront townhomes are the real deal here. These start at around $300 a night, sleeping eight in the three-bedroom-plus-loft, but that price may double in peak summer weeks. Golf packages are sometimes available in the fall, at around $200 a person for two nights and two rounds. ■ 3535 LAKE TAHOE BLVD., SOUTH LAKE TAHOE, CA 96150; 800/822-5969; WEBSITE WWW.LAKELAND-VILLAGE.COM

Here's one for the real romantics: how about golf-and-wed packages? Well, they're not there yet at the **Fantasy Inn,** but during the fall, you're promised a golf and romance package that includes a stay in a royal spa room, a bottle of wine, and a round of golf for two, starting at around $110 a night. Every room has a big whirlpool tub for two, his and her shower for two, mood lighting, and, uh, "intriguing mirror treatments." And yes, there's a chapel on the premises. ■ 3696 LAKE TAHOE BLVD., SOUTH LAKE TAHOE, CA 96150; 800/367-7736; WEBSITE WWW.FANTASY-INN.COM

ALTERNATIVES

The Tahoe area is so plugged in, it's easy to make a phone call or click of the mouse to find just the kind of lodging you want. Use the suggestions under Contacts at the end of this chapter to find a house to book or a room at a casino. The biggest and most expensive of the casinos are **Harvey's** (800-HARVEYS), Harrah's (800-HARRAHS), **Caesars** (800 648-3353), and the **Horizon** (800/322-7723), with a wide range in room rates depending on time of year and package. A bit on the smaller side, bargain side is the **Lakeside Inn** (800/624-7980), just beyond the big players at the foot of the Kingsbury Grade. No Tom Jones here, but a more intimate casino atmosphere and rooms starting at around $60 in high season.

And for bed-and-breakfast fans, there's something for you too. The oldest of the best is the **Christiania Inn,** most popular in winter for its location at the base of Heavenly, just 50 yards from the main chair lift. The inn has two rooms and four suites, decorated in antiques and warmed by fireplaces. Breakfast comes to your room, and there's a renowned dining room as well. Rooms start around $100 and the fall romance package is usually a terrific bargain. ■ 3819 SADDLE RD., SOUTH LAKE TAHOE, CA 96150; 530/544-7337; WEBSITE WWW.CHRISTIANIAINN.COM

A newer B&B that bills itself as a luxury accommodation is just up the street from Cafe Fiore. It's the **Black Bear Inn,** with five guest rooms in the main lodge, all with king bed and fireplace, TV, VCR, and phone, and three two-bedroom cottages set in the woods. Rates start at $150 for the rooms, $375 for the full cottage, and everybody gets a full breakfast. ■ 1202 SKI RUN BLVD., SOUTH LAKE TAHOE, CA 96150; 877/BEARINN; WEBSITE WWW.TAHOEBLACKBEAR.COM

Lodging

ITINERARY 2:
Carson Valley

ITINERARY SELECTION

Golf packages at the cozy, friendly 64-room **Piñon Plaza Resort** start at around $100 per person for *two* nights and go up not very astronomically from there. The rooms are big and luxurious, and on the premises are a lounge, restaurant, casino, bowling center, sports book, pool, and outdoor hot tub, among other perks. And right across Highway 50 is the Discount Golf Store, where you can find anything you forgot or just might like to have. There's even an RV park within the Piñon Plaza complex. ■ 2171 HIGHWAY 50 E, CARSON CITY, NV 89701; 877/519-5567; WEBSITE WWW.PINONPLAZA.COM

GOLF PACKAGE OPTIONS

This is the new gold mine. The hotels here court golfers shamelessly, and for around $100 per person you should be able to stay two nights, play two rounds, and receive a variety of little gambling, dining, or drinking perks.

In the heart of Carson City, try the **Ormsby House Hotel and Casino,** the biggest lodging property in town. The Ormsby House has a pool and restaurant, and the best deals are available for Sunday through Thursday. ■ 600 S. CARSON ST., CARSON CITY, NV 89701; 800/662-1890

The smaller, 60-room **Nugget,** also downtown, will customize a package for your golfing gang and set you up for goodies, beginning at around $100 per golfer for two nights and one round. Some rooms have kitchens.
■ 651 N. STEWART ST., CARSON CITY, NV 89701; 800/426-5239

And it doesn't end there. The Carson City visitors contacts at the end of this chapter will lead to package after package.

ALTERNATIVES

The nongolfers in your group might enjoy staying in the historical section of Carson City, in one of the four rooms at the 1879 **Bliss Mansion,** just across from the Governor's Mansion. The mansion was beautifully restored in 1994, and guests are treated to huge rooms and breakfasts, starting at around $175 a night. ■ 710 W. ROBINSON ST., CARSON CITY, NV 89701; 800/320-0627; WEBSITE WWW.SITE-WORKS.COM/BLISSMANSION

The town of Genoa would be a fine place to stay, given the proximity of two wonderful golf courses, and the **Wild Rose Inn** would be a fine place to sleep. There are five rooms, including the upstairs Gables, which is a suite that has a queen bed, day bed, and twin bed and might be suitable for families. It's pretty and peaceful, and the rooms include a full breakfast plus afternoon tea with goodies, all starting at around $125. Innkeeper Sue Haugnes also procures guest discounts at nearby Walley's Hot Springs and the Kirkwood Ski Resort. ■ 2332 MAIN ST., GENOA, NV 89411; 877/819-4225

Walley's Hot Springs also has cabins, starting around $90, and some have two queen beds. There also may be condos for rent by owners of the new Quintus Resort on the property. ■ 2001 FOOTHILL RD., GENOA, NV 89411; 800/628-7831

There seems to be little else in the way of family accommodations in the Carson Valley; for houses and condos, Tahoe is your destination.

Dining

ITINERARY 1:
South Lake Tahoe

ITINERARY SELECTIONS

We recommend that you visit **Riva Grill** on Day 1 for drinks, but it has quite a following for its lunch and dinner menus as well. There's a great selection of salads and sandwiches at lunchtime, along with everybody's favorite bar food (curly fries, steamed clams, crabcakes, sashimi) and a long list of exotic drinks. The dinner menu adds pastas, pizzas, and mouth-watering meats, poultry, and seafood at upscale prices, starting at around $16 an entrée. And how about the Gar Woods Godiva silk torte for dessert? Gar Woods is the flagship restaurant of this two-piece chain. The scene is lively, starting every day at around 11. ■ 900 SKI RUN BLVD., SOUTH LAKE TAHOE, CA; 530/542-2600; WEBSITE WWW.RIVAGRILL.COM

Cafe Fiore is intimate and romantic, a tiny room yet with privacy for each of the, count 'em, seven tables. The place is gaining such a magnificent reputation and enthusiastic following, though, maybe they'll have found a way to add more by now. Dinner is served every night, with entrées starting at around $15. By all means, make a reservation. And with only seven tables (there are more outside in summer), it's nice to know that you can even email for a reservation. ■ 1169 SKI RUN BLVD. #5, SOUTH LAKE TAHOE, CA; 530/541-2908; WEBSITE WWW.CAFEFIORE.COM

Edgewood Tahoe's restaurant is open for lunch and dinner every day, and features a fine menu of soups, salads, and seafood specialties, along with meat choices ranging from New York steak to roast loin of elk. The menu suggests wine varietals for each entrée. It's not just a golf course restaurant—the atmosphere here is elegant and lovely, most highly recommended for a sunset. ■ 180 LAKE PARKWAY, STATELINE, NV; 775/588-2787; WEBSITE WWW.EDGEWOOD-TAHOE.COM

Evans, set in a vintage Tahoe cottage, is not quite as small as Cafe Fiore, but reservations are strongly advised for any night in the peak summer months—with confirmation required before 4 P.M. *on the day* you're dining. Entrées average at around $20, with appetizers $8–9 and salads around $6. And though it may not look like much from the outside, the atmosphere is cozy and romantic, but not stuffy. You can even bring your foursome here after a round—someone on the staff will probably be ready to talk birdies and bogeys. Evans opens for dinner every night at 6. ■ 536 EMERALD BAY RD., SOUTH LAKE TAHOE, CA; 530/542-9111; WEBSITE WWW.EVANSTAHOE.COM

The **MS *Dixie II*** paddlewheeler's breakfast cruise included all the eggs, french toast, sausage, bacon, fruit, and pastries anyone could want and was over in 90 minutes. If you want to make a big night of it, there's a 3.5-hour sunset dinner cruise, with live music and dancing. Menu options include New York steak, Alaskan halibut, and chicken, all of this starting at around $45 a partaker. ■ ZEPHYR COVE MARINA, ZEPHYR COVE, NV; 775/588-3508; WEBSITE WWW.TAHOEDIXIE2.COM

The River Bend Grille serves lunch every day in the clubhouse at Genoa Lakes, at prices averaging around $7 a plate for appetizers like quesadillas or grilled sandwiches, and there's also dinner Wednesday through Saturday. ■ 1 GENOA LAKES DR., GENOA, NV; 775/782-4653

ALTERNATIVES

Guests at the Stateline casino-hotels will discover the **Lakeside Beach Grill** (4081 Lakeshore Blvd., South Lake Tahoe, CA; 530/544-4050) when they explore the private beach to which they're entitled, just down at the edge of Stateline beside Edgewood Tahoe. It's a wonderful, sunny spot, with a glass-enclosed dining deck right on the beach serving amazingly fresh, delicious food out of a tiny kitchen. Breakfast, which starts at 8:30 every morning, is most highly recommended, and don't miss the garlic fries for lunch. Dinner is served Thursday through Saturday, but there's no alcohol, and none may be brought in, though we hear they're working on that. Grill sandwiches run $7–10, and big, fresh salads start at $6 for lunch.

The big casinos all have fabulous upscale dining options. Two favorites are **Friday's Station,** at the top of Harrah's, and **Llewellyn's,** overlooking the lake from the top of Harveys. Friday's Station (775/588-6611) offers luxurious complete meals, starting at around $20, with a killer view, and underwent renovations before the 2000 golf season opened. The menu at Llewellyn's (775/588-2411) is more innovative, and salads and appetizers are à la carte, which will bring up the bill. Consider reservations required at both.

For quick, familiar fare, there's a **Chevy's** just down the street from the casinos (3678 Lake Tahoe Blvd., South Lake Tahoe, CA; 530/542-1741). And if you just want dinner to come to you, we can vouch for the pizza at **Goodfella's** (1007 Ski Run, South Lake Tahoe, CA; 530/544-6609).

And if you need a jump-start in the morning, a good place to stop on your way to Edgewood or the Nevada courses is **Hot Gossip** (530/541-4823), a lively coffee stop with all sorts of exotic caffeine concoctions, healthy fruit smoothies, and delectable baked goods. It's in the little shopping center on Ski Run at Highway 50 and opens well before anybody on any kind of escape would get up.

Dining

ITINERARY 2:
Carson Valley

ITINERARY SELECTIONS

The combination of food and view at the Empire Ranch Golf Course's **Mallard's** will make you wonder why the place isn't open for dinner,

especially considering the mob that comes here from all around for lunch. Maybe it will be by the time you read this. In the meantime, order up a burger and fries and enjoy, or come before your round and have breakfast.
■ 1875 Fair Way, Carson City, NV; 775/885-2100

Adele's offers fine dining in somewhat formal surroundings, yet the atmosphere is low-key and friendly. Sometimes there's live music on the deck off the bar, a good place for cocktails or food on a summer evening. Entrées start at about $15 and include a huge salad. Don't skip the appetizers, though, or miss the chocolate suicide cake. There's lunch on weekdays until 3 and dinner every night except Sunday. ■ 1112 N. Carson St., Carson City, NV; 775/882-3353

Whiskey Creek Steakhouse and Saloon will keep you fed any morning, noon, or night of the week in the Piñon Plaza. Steak is the specialty, but there are also salads and pastas. We found the cocktail menu especially exciting. ■ 2171 Highway 50 E, Carson City, NV; 877/519-5567

The **Carson Valley Country Club Restaurant and Bar** serves lunch every day except Tuesday, when the entire restaurant is closed, and Sunday, when only dinner is served. Dinner is served Wednesday through Monday, but this is not the place for a late-night bite. Service stops at 8:30. Dinners cost about $16 and include barbecued pork, pork à la Basque, baked salmon, and top sirloin, with all the extras. ■ 1029 Riverview Dr., Gardnerville, NV; 775/265-3715

ALTERNATIVES

The other two popular Basque restaurants in Gardnerville are **JT's** and **Overland,** which were once hotels for sheepherders and which still serve up meals to match a sheepherder's appetite at the end of the day, with more food than us golf ball herders can handle in one sitting for under $20 dinner and under $15 lunch. JT's (1426 Highway 395, Gardnerville, NV; 775/782-2074) is open for lunch and dinner daily except Sunday, and Overland (691 Highway 395, Gardnerville, NV; 775/782-2138) is closed on Monday.

Golfers will enjoy the atmosphere at **Silvana's Italian Cuisine** (1301 N. Carson St., Carson City, NV; 775/883-5100). A family-owned and -run restaurant for 25 years, Silvana's is open only for dinner, and only Tuesday through Saturday, and we think that's because the Borcellis want to spend their time on the golf course and not in the kitchen. Pasta entrées start at around $10.

The Piñon Plaza's sister hotel, the Carson Station Hotel Casino, is in the heart of downtown and has a reputation for serving fine food at the **Station Grill and Rotisserie** (1105 S. Carson St., Carson City, NV; 775/883-8400). Choices include wood-oven-baked pizzas and calzones, baby-back ribs and steaks, and a long list of soups and salads, and you can sample the food for free in the bar during the Tuesday through Saturday happy hours from 5 to 7. Prices were great, dinners starting around $10 and stopping at around $15. The Station Grill serves lunch and dinner every day except Sunday and Monday.

Wild Rose Inn proprietor Sue Haugnes suggests a pair of Genoa favorites to her guests. One is **Inn Cognito** (202 Genoa Lane, Genoa, NV; 775/782-8898), which specializes in wild game but also has daily dinner specials at around $15 for steak or baby-back ribs or seafood; entrée prices include relish tray, bread, and salad or soup. There's also a bar. Dinner is served nightly except on Tuesday.

Haugnes also recommends the very French **La Ferme** (2291 Main St., Genoa, NV; 775/783-1004), where chef Yves Gigot offers classic French country favorites such as pâtés, confit, cassoulet, and entrecôte for prices that average around $20 for entrées. Dinner every night, reservations suggested.

DW's (2001 Foothill Rd., Genoa, NV; 775/782-8155, ext. 8953), the restaurant at David Walley's Hot Springs, is a hopping place, particularly for the $20 Sunday champagne brunch, which has an omelet station, fajita station, and even a fruit and cheese corner. Dinner is served Wednesday through Saturday, with prime rib dinners starting at around $20 including salad; seafood, pasta, and poultry specialties also are on the menu, and there's a children's menu available.

Straying Off Course

Let's talk about Itinerary 2 first, because there is not the activity overload in the Carson Valley that's to be found on the South Shore of Lake Tahoe—except that you can quickly find activity overload by taking that short drive up the grade to the blue waters.

There is, of course, quite a bit of gaming action. The Ormsby House in downtown Carson City has the biggest casino (600 South Carson St.); others are to be found at the other large hotels, the Nugget and Carson Station, both on North Carson.

History lovers will enjoy the museums of the Carson City area. The Nevada State Museum, open daily, is a gold mine of information on the old silver mining (600 N. Carson St.). The Stewart Indian Cultural Center has arts, crafts and exhibits (5366 Snyder Ave.); and the Nevada State Railroad Museum is a must for the train buff (2180 South Carson St.). The Capitol Building is a great piece of architecture and has some historical exhibits (101 N. Carson St.). Carson City is on the small side, an easy place to park and walk the day away.

If walking is your thing, there are lots of trails at Spooner Lake, about 15 miles from Carson City on Highway 28, and Washoe Lake State Park, just to the north of Carson City.

One of the nongolfers who visited Carson City was disappointed not to find a bike for rent in town, particularly with the cyclist-friendly Flume Trail off Highway 28, beginning at Spooner Lake. The Carson Valley Bicycle Center out in Gardnerville can help (1504 Highway 395; 775/782-7077).

We were too busy golfing for much nightlife, but we heard that Sharkey's, also out in Gardnerville, is lots of fun for gaming and for dancing on weekend nights (1440 Highway 395; 775/782-3133).

Trout fishing on the Carson River is not bad, but take a 45-minute ride to the rich waters of the Walker River for the very best. There are also German and rainbow trout to be had at Topaz Lake, Jan. 1-Sept. 30 (775/266-3343).

Horseback riding isn't merely history yet, and the Little Antelope Pack Station will have some ideas for you between May and October (800/577-7087).

Seven miles north of Minden on Highway 395, you can learn all about water-skiing at a man-made competition-caliber facility called Sierra Springs Water Ski Lake. Call for information first (775/267-3146).

About five miles north of Minden, you can do some soaring from the Minden-Tahoe Airport. Check with High Country Soaring (775/782-4944) or Soar Minden (775/782-7627) if this thrills you.

Virginia City, just 15 minutes or so from Carson City, is a great destination for history buffs interested in the gold- and silver-mining heydays. It's part mining town, part ghost town, where you can take a ride on the Virginia and Truckee Railroad's original steam engines and try resisting the temptation to drink at the Bucket of Blood. See the listings under Contacts for more information.

Best of all, in the Carson Valley area you can easily get to the Tahoe area, where there does not appear to be anything you can't do. Ready, set, GO!

If you need a yoga class, massage, or facial, try the spa at the Tahoe Lakeshore Lodge (800/448-4577).

For some culture, the Valhalla Arts and Music Festival runs all summer at the Tallac Historic Site, with various live theatrical events plus a Wednesday night classic film series in a lovely setting. Call the Tahoe Tallac Association for more information (916/541-4975).

A favorite activity that goes well with golf is doing not much of anything on a gorgeous beach. We particularly enjoy it when there is cocktail and food service nearby, as at Camp Richardson, on the west shore, and Zephyr Cove, a few miles into Nevada. But also popular along the lake are Baldwin Beach, El Dorado, Nevada Beach, and Regan Beach. The Tahoe-Douglas Chamber of Commerce (775/588-4591) and U.S. Forest Service (916/573-2600) are the experts on what to do, take, and expect.

The bigger marinas—Camp Richardson, Zephyr Cove, Tahoe Keys, Ski

Run, Timber Cove, and Lakeside—can put you in anything from a kayak to a motorboat. They can also send you sportfishing, and maybe even in-line skating. Jet Skis are not so popular at the lake now because of restrictions that allow only the super-expensive models in the water. Camp Richardson and Zephyr Cove also offer horseback riding, and Camp Richardson has a water ski school. For information contact: Camp Richardson (Highway 89, two miles north of Y; 530/542-6570; website www.camprichardson.com); Zephyr Cove (Highway 50 at Zephyr Cove; 775/588-6644; website www.tahoedixie2.com); Timber Cove (Timber Cove Lodge, 3411 Lake Tahoe Blvd.; 916/433-5387); Lakeside Marina (Lakeshore Avenue and Park Avenue near Harvey's; 916/541-6626); Tahoe Keys Marina (near El Dorado Beach; 916/544-8888); Ski Run Marina (foot of Ski Run Blvd.; 800/238-2463).

There are lots of sunset, Emerald Bay, and brunch cruises on Lake Tahoe. You can go via paddle boat, as we did aboard the MS *Dixie II*. Harrah's has its own luxury yacht, limited to 36 guests at a time, the *Tahoe Star* (775/588-1554). The Woodwood sailing yachts (775/588-3000) are gorgeous options for those favoring a more nautical feel; these depart from Zephyr Cove at rates starting at around $20.

You can't help but notice the colorful parasails billowing over the lake if you do make it to an early breakfast at the Lakeside. Most of the marinas listed above can help, and you can check the free tourist guides for discount coupons. And now there are hot air balloon flights, too, from South Lake Tahoe Airport and out over the lake. The company Balloons over Lake Tahoe is the place (916/544-7008).

The biking and hiking options are endless. The Tahoe Rim trail circles the lake for 150 miles, and the Desolation Wilderness is awesome. Outdoors enthusiasts can find two valuable sources of information. The Tahoe Vacation Planner is available free by calling 916/544-9140, and it has trail descriptions for walking and riding. And the U.S. Forest Service (916/573-2600) is quartered at 870 Emerald Bay Rd., South Lake Tahoe.

Here's a way to combine Tahoe's greatest vistas with a little exercise and a meal: you can take the mile ride up the mountain on the Heavenly Aerial Tram and have lunch or dinner at the Monument Peak Restaurant, 2,000 feet above the lake, and also take a hike along the Tahoe Vista Trail. The tram rides run all winter for snow bunnies, but hikers will prefer the time from about the first of June until the end of the summer season in October (775/586-7000; website www.skiheavenly.com).

Of course, if you're visiting at the right time of year, it is entirely possible to golf one of the Carson Valley courses by day and ski Heavenly at night. Go ahead, knock yourself out. When you make your tee time, do ask if there's a discount on the lift ticket, which can run upwards of $40.

If after all this activity you still have your putting stroke on the brain, see if you can find Fantasy Kingdom. This old miniature golf course was on Highway 50 just between Harrah's and Raley's before the extensive redevelopment began on the South Shore in the summer of 2000, and the owners weren't sure where they'd relocate when the bulldozers came in.

Details, Details

SUITCASE

Bring shorts, bathing suits, sandals, and hats for all the usual beach activities, and don't forget the cooler and the beach blanket.

Golfers will need traditional golf attire and nonmetal spikes for virtually every course except Eagle Valley, where they won't throw you out for wearing T-shirt, bathing trunks, and metal spikes on the course. Shorts will feel fine during the golf season months, although if you're playing early in the morning on Edgewood or Lake Tahoe, slacks and a windshirt might feel better. Hats, sunscreen, and summer gear might be wanted in summer on the Carson Valley courses.

Nights are generally on the cool and casual side; golf attire is fine for men, and women will need nothing fancier than a sundress. Have a sweater or jacket handy at all times, especially in the air-conditioned casinos.

GETTING THERE

Itinerary 1: South Lake Tahoe
From the Bay Area, South Bay, and Sacramento, take I-80 to Highway 50 east toward South Lake Tahoe. Lake Tahoe Golf Course will be on the left, about 95 miles along the way.

Lake Tahoe Golf Course is also the perfect first destination if you're flying in, because the airport is right across the street. It's a large airport with regular commercial flights, so do call for information on requirements (530/542-6180). Enterprise will rent you a car.

Itinerary 2: Carson Valley
Follow the directions for South Tahoe, but continue through South Lake Tahoe and into Nevada on Highway 50 east. Highways 50 and 395 will merge; stay left into Carson City and remain with Highway 50 east, going to the right toward Dayton. About a mile and a half down on the right, you'll see the Piñon Plaza. If you're heading straight for Empire Ranch, keep going and watch for the golf course sign on the right. If you're head-

ing straight to Eagle Valley, keep going and watch for the Centennial Park Drive sign; make a left to the course.

The Minden-Tahoe Airport is the destination for private planes. There's no tower, the weight limit is 30,000 pounds single-axle and 50,000 pounds double-axle, and in any case you should call ahead to 775/782-9871. Car rentals are available through Enterprise, 775/782-8277.

CONTACTS

■ The best tool for golfers looking strictly for golf package information is the **Reno-Sparks Convention and Visitors Authority.** The website is so comprehensive and accessible, sometimes we wonder why we wrote this chapter at all (800/367-7366; website www.playreno.com or golf. renolaketahoe.com).

■ The **Lake Tahoe Visitors Authority** produces a travel planner annually with valuable information on South Shore accommodations, including touch-or-click vacation planning, depending on whether you're on the phone or online (800/AT-TAHOE; website www.virtualtahoe.com).

■ The **Carson City Convention and Visitors Bureau** extols the virtues of the area's historical attractions and provides lists of lodging and dining options. The website has a chart with golf course nuts and bolts (1900 South Carson St., Suite 200, Carson City, NV 89701; 800/NEVADA-1; website www.carson-city.org).

■ If what you really want to do is sit down at your computer and book accommodations, plus maybe a flight

into Lake Tahoe or Reno and a rental car, click on www.tahoe.com. This site, put up by Tahoe-Carson Area Newspapers, allows you to see detailed information about lodging properties, including the current low price.

■ Another site with online lodging features (www.tahoechamber.org, click on "visitor center") is operated by the Tahoe Douglas Visitor Center (775/588-4591). You can stop by its offices, on Highway 50 at Round Hill on the Nevada side, and pick up lots of paperwork, including maps and coupon books, and book your lodgings while you're there.

■ The Nevada Commission on Tourism has a huge, good-looking website. Click into the Reno-Tahoe region to find the specific information you want: www.travelnevada.com.

■ If you're hankering for hangin' and steamin' history, you may want to make Virginia City your home base. The Convention and Tourism Authority tells you everything you need to know: 775/847-7500; website www. virginiacity-nv.org.

Chapter 9

Thar's Golf in Them Thar Hills: Calaveras County

From gold to golf. From mining to wining and dining. Just a mere slip of a letter here and there, and many of the once-booming and now almost snoozing towns of Calaveras County are suddenly, finally discovering that having a past doesn't mean you can't have a future too. The next rush for this cranny of the sprawling Sierra Nevada Mother Lode may come in the form of tourism, and the panhandlers of the 2000s most likely will come via Ford Explorer, not stagecoach, carrying not picks and shovels but putters and 3-woods.

"There's been a change in spending patterns for the rich, from driving Mercedes to SUVs, and now instead of going into downtown San Francisco for recreation, they're going to the Sierras," notes Stephen Kautz, president of Kautz Ironstone Vineyards in Murphys. "We've got rafting, spelunking, the Calaveras Big Trees. Bear Valley ski resort is 35 miles up the road. And people think of the wine country as Napa and Sonoma, but we have it and you don't have to fight the crowds to do it."

Not yet, anyway. Though only 75 miles from Sacramento and 135 miles from either San Francisco or San Jose, the former gold country remained largely undiscovered as a escape destination at the time that two ambitious golf course developments were undertaken within 15 miles of each other in the mid-1990s. Visitors came to Calaveras County for the Frog Jumping Festival, held annually in Angels Camp during the third week of May. Or they stepped back in time on the streets of Columbia, where cars are not permitted in order to authenticate a re-creation of the times of the Gold Rush, and tried to imagine Calaveras County in its truly jumping days. They may even have sought to enjoy the splendors of nature, with the ancient sequoias, the awesome Stanislaus River, and snowy Bear Valley all springboards to outdoors recreation opportunities galore.

But the openings of Saddle Creek Golf Club and Greenhorn Creek in 1996, following the newly transformed Kautz family vision for turning Ironstone into a blend of cultural center, tourist attraction, and corporate retreat, expanded the possibilities for Calaveras County. Residential developments were planned around each course, along with cottages to bring players to stay for a few days. Naturally, the two courses compete, but the "Battle of the Creeks" is a mostly friendly one, with cooperative marketing ventures and even an annual contest among the course staffs for a trophy—naturally, a gold pan. Last time we checked, Greenhorn had won it, but—true to the legacy of lawlessness from the Gold Rush days—Saddle had stolen it.

Of course, where there's a "Battle of the Creeks" there's also a comparison of the Creeks. And it is somewhat surprising. There is perhaps only one similarity: in 1999, each course was sold to a respected developer (Saddle Creek to Castle and Cooke, Greenhorn to Grupee) with experience in golf course management. At the time we were researching our Calaveras chapter, the Greenhorn development (whose new owners were hoping to turn it into the Meadowood of the Sierra) was far ahead of the Saddle Creek development. Greenhorn had a small but serene and elegant clubhouse overlooking the first tee, houses overlooking its fairways, and charming, comfortable, fully equipped guest cottages open and busy nearby. The restaurant, Camps, was attracting nongolfers for its exquisite lunches and gourmet dinners. Saddle Creek had a large trailer functioning as its pro shop and restaurant, with only a large deck offering salvation for groups needing post-tournament respite, and the new owners (who also operate two of the top resorts in the world, on the Hawaiian island of Lanai) were hurrying to ready their own golf cottages—in a prime location near the tee of the tough and pretty second hole—for visitors in the next season.

If location is everything, it is Greenhorn Creek that has it. Copperopolis, home to Saddle Creek, has never recovered from the demise of copper mines that produced 19 million pounds of ore in the 1860s. Even though the Old Corner Saloon still stands, all but abandoned, two fires have destroyed the town since it held the principal mine in the west in 1862. The lively Lake Tulloch Resort is just down the road, and there are restaurants in nearby strip malls, but there's no main street for the wanderer without making that winding 15-minute drive to Angels Camp or a longer one to Jamestown or Sonora.

Greenhorn Creek is right next door to Angels Camp, where the gold industry continued to flourish into the 20th century and gave way to tourism only recently. In fact, there are five mines on the golf course property alone, and you may see some of the entrances as you traipse around looking for an errant shot. Though Main Street is short, it has its share of restaurants and shops, and there's even a small movie theater. Another 15 minutes or so away (precisely, nine miles east) is Murphys, "Queen of the Sierra," with a busy Main Street offering one of the more entertaining free activities in the area—just walking along and reading the signs describing the town's characters and events of old. There are also art galleries and shops, and 14 restaurants (and counting). If you want to hang out for a cocktail, there's always life at the place locals call "The Hodle," the Murphys Hotel, where the saloon door still bears scars of the old days in the form of bullet holes. If you're misdirected enough not to want to golf, you'll find something to do nearby—or be happy doing nothing right here at one of the town's charming yet not stuffy bed and breakfasts. And if it's a hot summer's day, you will be much more comfortable on the golf course at 1,380 feet at oak-dotted Greenhorn than at Saddle, at 900 feet and without much shade. You will in fact be so much more comfortable, you will forget that only a 15-minute drive separates the two courses.

On the other hand, however, it's the golf that brought us here, right? So under no circumstances are you to make the Calaveras County jaunt and get too cozy at Greenhorn Creek to play Saddle Creek. On our first few visits, the comparison of the two developments ended with the golf courses—Saddle Creek prevailed, for its setting among wildflowers and wetlands, its views of green meadows and snow-capped peaks, and the sheer caliber and condition of its championship course, with 18 holes played from any of five sets of tees between 4,488 and 6,828 yards. From the nerve-testing par-4 second hole, where the tee looks out at a lot of water to the right and a narrow fairway left, to the thirst-inducing ninth, with an approach shot that must carry a canal and dodge bunkers, Saddle Creek offers great fun, challenge, and beauty. As course marshal Mac McCool said, "How we lucked into something like this in the middle of nowhere, I'll never know."

And at first, the best we could say about Greenhorn Creek was that it wasn't in the middle of nowhere. Oh, and there was also the historical tour—in the early days, the GPS system on the golf carts pointed out the old placer mines, the Chinese oven, and the sacred Miwok land along the way. But the greens we first saw were diseased, and the narrow, confusingly laid out course had an unfinished look about the bunkering that was especially noticeable on the par-3s. Happily, that is all changing—though, unhappily, the GPS had to be abandoned because of technical difficulties here in the hills—and Greenhorn Creek is giving Saddle Creek a run for great golf honors as well as that gold pan. Robert Trent Jones Jr. was called in to put a stamp on the design originated by one of his father's former associates, Don Boos of Murphys, with input from Patty Sheehan of the LPGA Tour and Dick Lotz of the Senior PGA Tour. The redesign would primarily add and reshape bunkers and rebuild the third green. And the new management clearly has made a commitment to course care and conditioning; the greens were perfect the last few times we visited, and though a few of the holes will be forever quirky—don't get us started on the fourth hole, with that rock wall on the right side of the landing area— it's a quirkiness that tends to add interest as the course is played over and over again. That—and the policy of allowing carts in fairways most of the year, which sprawling Saddle Creek refuses to do—make it perhaps the more appealing of the two courses to prospective homeowners.

There's yet a third jewel to the Calaveras crown, a precious one that only gained some luster and some traffic with the arrival of the Creeks. That would be Forest Meadows Golf Course, the first 18-hole layout built in the area, a unique par-60 of under 4,000 yards designed by Boos with Robert Trent Jones Jr. and opened in 1971. "Don't discount this course because of its length and rating," says head pro Norby Wilson. "Golfers who play Forest Meadows say that like Pebble Beach or Cypress Point, one of its greatest challenges is its quality and beauty. It's a top-notch course."

The course, which has one par-5 and four par-4s, is in a unobtrusive housing and condominium development among pines, oaks, and cedars, on a ridge overlooking the Stanislaus River Canyon that makes the 15th hole one of the most unforgettable par-3s you will ever play. On a clear night, the vista here reaches for hundreds of miles, as far as Castle Air Force Base and the top of the Dardanelles. On a clear day, it's distracting, to say the least. "My golf balls always seem to want to go out there (into the canyon) when I play that hole," says Stephen Kautz. "I think they must be enjoying the view too."

Forest Meadows offers special perks, like a year-round golf pass, to residents, but a change in ownership to the sole proprietorship of Lou Papais indicated that it would be reaching out to visitors with a remodeled restaurant, new bar, and play-and-stay condominium packages. Already the cart paths, which were atrocious or nonexistent when we visited, have been paved. Wilson says, though, that as many as a third of the players here enjoy the walk, and when we caught up to him on a late November day for an update he said the sun was shining and golfers were wearing shorts.

Four miles east of Murphys, Forest Meadows is right at the snow line, so the course gets a few dustings during the winter that disappear the next day and, with superb drainage, only briefly mar the course conditions.

With so much to do in the area, vacationers might like to hear that par-60 makes for a three-hour round, but, alas, Forest Meadows is too tough and too busy to be played in much less than four hours. It is, however, a worthwhile trip up the hill from Saddle Creek and Greenhorn Creek, and the coming of the Creeks in the '90s has definitely had implications to the north.

Says Wilson, "We just got our first stoplight two years ago."

See, they're ready for your SUVs in Calaveras County.

|tinerary

WARMING UP

Call lots of friends—the accommodations and activities make this a fun escape for any number of golfers divisible by four, particularly those with SUVs. Plan for your visit to begin later in the week, since most area restaurants seem to be closed on Tuesdays and some even Wednesdays, but not on the weekend if you like smaller crowds. And do not be dismayed if your escape is on the heels of a storm; all of the Calaveras County courses have superb drainage and are playable in all but the worst weather. With summers so hot, that makes this locale a particularly great spring escape.

Now, make a Day 1 morning tee time (or tee times, if you've come up with a high number divisible by four) at Saddle Creek, a Day 2 morning tee time at Greenhorn Creek, and a Day 3 morning tee time at Forest Meadows. If you'd like to visit the Black Sheep and Milliaire wineries, both highly recommended for their delicious potions and delightful hospitality, call and make appointments for either the afternoon of Day 1 or the afternoon of Day 2. Also, call Ironstone Vineyards or check the website to find out of there are any special events happening at the amphitheater or culinary center at the time of your visit. Make a Day 2 dinner reservation at Camps.

day 1 Load up the SUV and head for Saddle Creek for your first round. This isn't a dreadful drive from anywhere during the morning rush hour (the rush isn't coming here, it's going), but give yourself about two hours from the Bay Bridge to Saddle Creek. Notice how you'll start breathing a little easier as you draw closer to the mountains, even though the altitude is making the air thinner. It's the landscape, transformed from flat and boring to rolling and interesting. Quick Stops give way to hay stops, and when you see the old Copper Hotel, you'll know you're somewhere else entirely than wherever you've been. If you do need a modern-day quick stop for caffeine, however, notice the small shopping center on your right when you make the turn onto Copper Cove Road. Here you'll find the Espresso Stop, which specializes in kick starts—even iced ones on hot days.

When you arrive at the first tee, the starter will tell you about the on-path yardage markers and the "savannah rule" designed to keep you out of protected wetlands. He may also mention snakes, in case you need further discouragement from fetching wayward golf balls. And if you want any advice about what to do while you're visiting, he'll tell you that too. More likely, you'll want a suggestion on where to tee off: there are five options at Saddle Creek, including two choices for the average woman player that offer quite different looks for some of the tees.

If you're visiting on a blissfully quiet day, the starter may have been your last chance for human companionship for a few hours; Saddle Creek is laid out in a sprawling fashion, making the most of the acres and vistas without parallel fairways or crowded green-to-tee areas. Memorable holes include the second, one of the most gorgeous and challenging par-4s in Northern California, and the devilish fifth, which looks like a lamb on the scorecard but can be a lion due to a sharp, short dogleg that makes for a mostly blind tee shot.

If the new clubhouse is open, you will probably want to linger after your round. In the meantime, head back to O'Byrnes Ferry Road, turn right, and proceed for about five minutes to Lake Tulloch Resort, where you'll enjoy a 19th-hole beverage and snack or lunch on a deck overlooking the pool and lake. It's a quiet stop on a weekday, bustling on the weekend when the water recreationists make their splash.

Next you'll go back the way you came from Saddle Creek, continuing on O'Byrnes Ferry Road to Highway 4 and turning right to Greenhorn Creek. Follow the signs to the golf course and get checked in to your cottage. Don't get too cozy, however. There's much to do in Calaveras County.

For starters, follow Highway 4 farther east, to Murphys; park in town and take a stroll along Main Street. Make sure you stop to read the plaques, so you'll see the spot where the Murphy brothers were thought to have first pitched their tent and learn the story about the baker who shot himself with the gun he had rigged to his register while making change for a little girl. And scout the menus along the way—at the very least, Grounds, Cafe Soleil, Murphys Grille, Murphys Hotel, and the Enchanted Cottage—to find out which are open and get an idea where you want to dine.

Milliaire (276 Main) and Black Sheep (other end of Main at Murphys Grade Road) are along the strip, so this may be a good time to visit the wineries if you've made an appointment. Be sure to taste the dessert wines at Milliaire and the powerful zins at Black Sheep. Certainly stop in at Malvadino (behind Murphys Hotel), where you are welcome any time. It's the smallest of the county wineries and the only one specializing in the Mission varietal. Or you may just want to stop in the bar at the Murphys Hotel (457 Main St.) and mix with the locals before dinner.

And by now you've hopefully decided between all of the scrumptious options on Main Street in Murphys, because it's dinnertime. Then it's rest time, because there's so much more to do tomorrow.

day 11 Send a scout into Angels Camp to the B of A Cafe (1262 South Main St., on your right) to bring coffee, juice, and heavenly scones, muffins, and pastries back to the cottage. Then you're ready to start and end the day at Greenhorn Creek.

You'll notice it's probably six or seven degrees cooler here than it was at Saddle Creek, and that's simply a matter of altitude, an extra 500 feet or so. You'll also notice it's narrower. Greenhorn Creek was built on property owned by Barden Stevenot, a fifth-generation Calaveras County native and founder of the Stevenot winery and Canadian Gold Mine. On the first hole was the old Selkirk Homestead; along the right side of the second you'll see a waste area that was placer-mined by the 49ers. This is not a hazard by the rules of golf, but you will want to stay out of there.

We almost got lost between the third and fourth holes the first time we played, probably because of the Miwok Native American historical site that was discovered during course routing. Many people would like to get lost for the entire fourth hole, which has always been somewhat controversial in that it requires a short and accurate tee shot to set up a second shot over the rock wall and between the trees onto the fairway dogleg right. From there, it's pretty easy. But we have yet to witness a birdie here.

Other points of interest along the way include the Chinese oven along the tricky fifth hole and the watery grave all around the sixth hole. The par-3s are all pretty and playable, and the par-5s are good birdie opportunities for the player with decent length. Hole number 18 is one of the best finishing holes anywhere—a great spot for high drama, with an oak tree in the middle of the fairway and a lake fronting the green, with the trellised deck of the clubhouse overlooking it all.

Of course you will probably want a cocktail after that, but to make the most of this trip, wash your hands, comb your hair, and head on over to Ironstone Vineyards, where the Kautz family is growing much more than wine. Ironstone is just a mile off Main Street in Murphys (look for the signed turnoff next to the Murphys Hotel)—you'll probably be there in 15 minutes, and you can taste a little wine, pick out a bottle, and order up a delicious lunch for a song at the deli counter.

If it's a beautiful day, you may want to take your lunch outside to the picnic grove and sit amid the azaleas and ducks. Then you can tour the grounds, getting an eyeful of the amphitheater, which holds 3,500 for concerts, and the museum and gallery, where the world's largest crystalline gold leaf specimen, all 44 pounds of it, is kept securely in its own little room. If the timing is right, take the 45-minute official tour, so that you'll get to see most of the seven-story complex with a knowledgeable guide. That should include a stop in the Grand Music Room, where the 1927 organ from the old Alhambra Theater of Sacramento has been installed and restored. You've got to hear this to believe it; just hope there's not a meeting or luncheon tying up the room the day you visit.

From Ironstone, it's time to go underground, to one of the three Calaveras County caverns, and switch gears from golf and grapes to stalactites and stalagmites. Ah, but which cavern—Mercer, Moaning, or California? Well, Mercer Caverns (Sheep Ranch Road; 209/728-2101) is on the way to the Stevenot Winery, so if you have a hankering for yet another tasting of the grape (and a history lesson of sorts), you may want to take the 208 steps down into the limestone. You'll see the sign on Main Street in Murphys. The drive to Moaning Cavern (Highway 4 back toward Angels Camp to Parrots Ferry Road, on your left; 209/736-2708) will take you past the Chatom Vineyards (209/736-6500), another great grape stop (on Highway 4 on your left), and it's a grander tour where you can opt to rappel down among formations that will remind you of food. We took the spiral staircase, test enough. California Caverns (Cave City Road, about nine miles east of San Andreas; 209/736-2708) is the biggest time commitment, requiring closer to 90 minutes than the 45 Mercer and Moaning can do with, and it's a bit off the beaten path around Murphys. However, the passageways go for miles, and walking tours explore a variety of rooms instead of one large grotto. California Caverns also offers Intro Spelunking and Downstream Circuit for the extreme cavers, but we're guessing that they're buying other books than this one.

Finally, Stevenot (three winding miles out of downtown Murphys, via Sheep Ranch Road) is worth a late-afternoon visit just to see the "Alaska House," the 1906 tasting room on the property in the midst of what used to be "Macaroni Flats." Yep, the Italian district. The Stevenots planted grapes in 1970 and produced their first wine in 1994, starting with white zinfandel and then phasing it out for chardonnay and barbera, among others. It's a lovely picnicking spot with deli items for the hungry, and there are tours.

Now you're ready to return to Greenhorn Creek, where you can kick back and enjoy what's left of Day 2. We'd like to tell you what to have or not have for dinner at Camps, but you can't possibly have room for everything that's good and it's doubtful that they serve anything that isn't. Order what you like, have a bottle of local wine, and save room for dessert.

day III

It's up and at 'em, packing the car up and heading for Grounds for breakfast. If you want to eavesdrop on the locals, sit in the busy front room; if your gang needs a little more privacy, head for the back. L.A. transplants (including River Klass and wife Nannette, an artist whose paintings are on the walls) opened Grounds, which serves three meals a day from three very different and eclectic menus. Be adventurous and try the potato pancakes; if you just want fried eggs and toast, the Murphys Hotel is open for breakfast as well.

Then it's back to Highway 4 east to Forest Meadows (look for the Golfers Welcome! sign on your right) for what you think is going to be a quick round of golf, but, no! You'll spend four hours, kicking yourself all the way for not having a better score on what should, by the scorecard anyway, be such an easy course! It's a very different-looking 18 than the ones you've just played, with the higher altitude offering different kinds of trees and terrain, but there's great variety among the par-3s and the greens are terrific. When you get to the 12th tee, you'll get your first glimpse of the spectacular vista that awaits you at hole number 15—but, heck, 13, 14, and 15 are all pretty fantastic.

Your next order of business is to continue on Highway 4 toward Arnold, where you'll pick up a sandwich at the Big Trees Market (2182 Highway 4, in the Meadowmont Center) in town. Then go on to Calaveras Big Trees State Park, where, if you didn't walk the course this morning, you're going to have to go hike the four-mile loop through the untraveled South Grove— if you did walk the course this morning you can take the short (one mile), easy (any shoes will do) stroll to enjoy the giant sequoias of the North Grove. We recommend a nature walk like the one we had with ranger Craig Mattson, but even on your own you can pick up a guidebook at the trailhead so that you'll know why the big stump looks so much like a dance floor and why there's that big hole in the Pioneer Cabin Tree. There's no famous tree or biggest tree here among the 150 giant sequoias, but there is a good story in the North Grove. It's a story of conservation, because logging was long the primary industry in Arnold and some very big logs were never taken.

Once you've finished exploring the park—and no doubt getting an idea of what you'll do when you come back and have more time—you probably will try to talk yourself into staying in Arnold for the night. The Yellow Dog Inn, right next to the Meadowmont nine-holer, is calling your name, and the Snowshoe Brewing Co. is serving your brew.

Or maybe you'll just have to get back in your SUV and head home. It's a pretty good guess that it'll all still be here when you decide to make the trip again.

NOTES

Time Savers. Greenhorn Creek makes a nice and easy overnight trip—just be sure that Camps is open for dinner the night you plan to stay.

Money Savers. If you opt for any of the bed and breakfasts in the area, inquire about discounts on green fees at Calaveras courses. At par-72, 5,169 to 6,599 yards, and under $40 with cart, Mountain Springs is one of the best bargains in this book.

Nongolfers. Drop the golfers off, keep the car and enjoy a morning of wine-tasting or antiquing or cave touring or even hiking.

Parents. Leave the kids at home until you can come back here and rent a houseboat for the week. In the meantime, bring grownups on this escape.

Low-Handicappers. If you feel entitled to 18 holes and 6,000 yards a day, replace Forest Meadows with Sonora's quirky Mountain Springs Golf Course.

Extended Stay. Consider adding a round at Mountain Springs and one at La Contenta, a great little overnight escape by itself.

Courses

ITINERARY SELECTIONS

Saddle Creek Golf Club

P. O. Box 613 (1001 Saddle Creek Dr.)
Copperopolis, CA 95228
209/785-3700 or 888/852-5787, fax 209/785-8890
website www.saddlecreek.com; email info@
saddlecreek.com

Saddle Creek is semiprivate, but the homeowners have yet to make their presence loudly known. It's still quite easy to get a tee time here, except on any of the days when the NorCal PGA asserts its rights to its official "home" course for a tournament. Regular weekday green fees begin at around $50, plus cart fee, and weekend fees at around $60, but there's a long list of exceptions and bargains, including for juniors, seniors, "ladies," Quad County residents, NCGA members, and twilight play, so inquire away.

SCORECARD

Architect: Morrish and Associates, 1996

Course Record: 65, Les Phillips

PGA: Par 72, 6,829 yards, 73.0 rating for men, 134 slope

Championship: Par 72, 6,434 yards, 71.1 rating for men, 130 slope

Middle: Par 72, 6,049 yards, 69.4 rating for men, 125 slope; 74.0 rating for women, 130 slope

Saddle: Par 72, 5,326 yards, 70.2 rating for women, 122 slope

Forward: Par 72, 4,471 yards, 65.4 rating for women, 111 slope

Tee times may be made up to 14 days in advance, or up to 60 days in advance for an additional $5 per player.

TEE TIDBITS | Metal spikes aren't permitted here, but flat-soled tennis shoes are. They'll change your metal spikes for $10—or rent you a pair of shoes for $5. Denim is not allowed, and shorts supposedly should be knee length, but, ladies, it's not likely that anyone will challenge your standard four-inches-above-the-knee golf shorts. Walking is a workout but possible (except in the highest heat of summer) and permitted, and pull carts are allowed but not rented. Until the clubhouse is finished, it's unlikely you'll want to linger here. But if you're hungry, the sandwiches are quite good. The practice area is excellent, although the grass tee boxes sometimes are reserved for members only.

Greenhorn Creek Golf Course

P. O. Box 1419 (676 McCauley Ranch Rd.)
Angels Camp, CA 95222
209/736-8110, fax 209/736-8119
website www.greenhorncreek.com

Greenhorn Creek is semiprivate, and members get a two-week head start on tee times, which makes the weekends busy. Play-and-stay packages do have some priority, though, and offer the best bargain to visitors. Green fees start at around $40 weekdays for walkers, with carts about another $15. As at most new courses, you won't be able to wear metal spikes here, but with the exception of some confusing routing Greenhorn Creek is fairly level and walkable on all but the very hottest days. There's a range with grass stalls and a practice green where chipping is permitted. Golf attire is required.

SCORECARD

Architects: Don Boos, 1996, and Robert Trent Jones Jr., 1999
Course Record: 64, Earl Cross Jr.
Gold: Par 72, 6,849 yards, 72.7 rating for men, 130 slope
Blue: Par 72, 6,213 yards, 70.0 rating for men, 124 slope; 76.0 rating for women, 133 slope
White: Par 72, 5,691 yards, 67.3 rating for men, 119 slope; 73.2 rating for women, 127 slope
Red: Par 72, 5,181 yards, 70.1 rating for women, 119 slope

TEE TIDBITS | Schedule your visit carefully if you want the full Greenhorn experience, because the fine restaurant may not be open for dinner on Mondays and Tuesdays, or for lunch either on Mondays. The pro shop is on the small side but well-stocked, and the bar is cozy. LPGA Hall of Famer Patty Sheehan consulted on the original design. Though in the midst of a housing development, homes border only six holes—and only on one side of any fairway. There are five gold mines on the property; the biggest of them is called the Tough Nut and is under the 12th green. Owners Fritz and Phylis Grupee also own Brookside Country Club in Stockton.

Forest Meadows Golf Resort

P. O. Box 70 (14 miles east of Angels Camp on Highway 4)
Murphys, CA 95247
209/728-3439, fax 209/728-3430
website www.forestmeadows.com or www.forestmeadowsprop.com

Forest Meadows residents love the year-round golf pass here, which gives them great privileges without a great initiation fee. The rest of us can play 18 holes for around $25 on a weekday, $35 on a weekend, carts not included and not really necessary if you're in half-decent shape. There's also a tennis court, swimming pool, and hiking trails in the resort, which makes the golf packages worthy of inquiry.

TEE TIDBITS | There's no driving range or practice area to speak of. Greens are swift and nicely maintained. They don't require soft spikes at Forest Meadows, but, naturally, they do like them. The first hole is the hardest on the course, the only par-5. The wire sculptures that show the hole diagram make for a nice touch at each tee. Walkers here are in for a pretty little hike. The course drains extremely well, so don't let a little snow scare you away. Duffers Cafe on the Green was serving breakfast and lunch daily, plus dinners on Friday and Saturday, when we visited, but new owner Lou Papais was planning a redesign.

SCORECARD

Architect: Robert Trent Jones Jr., 1971

Course Record: 51, Mike Lane

Back: 3,886 yards, 58.3 rating for men, 95 slope; 62.2 rating for women, 95 slope

Forward: 3,221 yards, 58.0 rating for women, 90 slope

Tee times are taken two weeks in advance, at 209/728-3439.

ALTERNATIVES

A little farther east on Highway 4, past Forest Meadows at 4,000 feet, privacy and a four-hour round can routinely be found at **Sequoia Woods Country Club,** a par-70 Bob Baldock design that welcomes members of other country clubs. ■ 1000 CYPRESS POINT DR., ARNOLD, CA 95223; 209/795-1378

Still farther east on Highway 4, and even higher, the oldest course in Calaveras County appears on your left when you reach Arnold. That would be **Meadowmont,** built in an old apple orchard and opened in 1962 with nine holes meandering through a meadow frequented by Reas Creek. A nine-holer that plays 18 at 5,800 yards from two sets of tees, Meadowmont was up for sale when we last visited. In the meantime, you could play 18 for about a buck a hole. ■ 1684 HIGHWAY 4, ARNOLD, CA 95223; 209/795-1313; WEBSITE WWW.MEADOWMONTGOLF.COM

In the busier and slower realm, visitors may want to cross the river into Tuolumne County and play 18 at beautiful, intriguing, and lovingly cared for **Mountain Springs.** The hard-to-find course is very hilly—only about 15 percent of the players walk, and many of those may spring for a cart at the turn—and very difficult to navigate your first time out, partly because Robert Muir Graves wasn't able to finish what he started because funds ran short. They say it's a lot more fun the third time you play it than the first time, so encourage the starter to group you with one of the many regulars—though even they may not have figured out how to make par on hole number 9. The scorecard tip sheet will help. New owners have big plans here; keep an eye out for a golf school and hotel. Call two weeks in advance for a tee time. ■ 17566 LIME KILN RD., SONORA; 209/532-1000; WEBSITE WWW.MOUNTAINSPRINGSGOLF.COM

Lodging

ITINERARY SELECTION

The **Cottages at Greenhorn Creek** can be configured in three different ways: as guest rooms, with one or two queen beds plus bathroom, cable TV and minibar, or as either a one-bedroom or two-bedroom cottage with full living room and dining room. Prices without golf range $65–195 a night, depending on configuration and day of the week; golf packages start at around $70 per person. ■ P. O. BOX 1419 (676 MCCAULEY RANCH RD.), ANGELS CAMP, CA 95222; 800/736-6203, FAX 209/736-8119; WEBSITE WWW.GREENHORNCREEK.COM

GOLF PACKAGE OPTIONS

The **Lake Tulloch Resort** teams up with Saddle Creek, just up O'Byrnes Ferry Road, to offer play-and-stay packages that begin at around $85 per person for weekday nights. These include deluxe lake-view rooms and golf with cart. Lake Tulloch also has a chalet with kitchen, two bedrooms, two baths, and private boat docks that sleeps six, starting at around $275 a night. ■ 7260 O'BYRNES FERRY RD., COPPEROPOLIS, 95228; 888/785-8200; WEBSITE WWW.TULLOCHRESORT.COM

At **Forest Meadows,** there are lovely fairway-view homes of two, three, and four bedrooms for your gang, starting at around $150 a night. There are also some condos that can be had for less than $100. Play-and-stay packages are in the works, so do inquire. ■ P. O. BOX 70 (14 MILES EAST OF ANGELS CAMP ON HIGHWAY 4), MURPHYS, CA 95247; 209/728-3433, FAX 209/728-3430; WEBSITE WWW.FORESTMEADOWSPROP.COM

Mountain Springs in Sonora has teamed with the **Best Western Sonora Oaks** for years, but discounts good for a $30 all-inclusive (cart, range balls) round may be available anywhere you stay in the area, so if you have your eye on another property be sure to ask about golf. ■ 19551 HESS AVE., SONORA, CA 95370; 209/533-4400

Worth special note: On 10 wooded acres just down Lime Kiln Road from Mountain Springs is a lovely new English Tudor style bed and breakfast, **Sterling Gardens.** The owners used to live in Italy; rooms with a full gourmet breakfast for two cost around $100. ■ 18047 LIME KILN RD., SONORA; 800/510-2225; WEBSITE WWW.STERLINGGARDENS.COM

ALTERNATIVES

The most sumptuous and romantic accommodations in Calaveras County are a pair of bed-and-breakfasts right in the town of Murphys.

First, the **Dunbar House, 1880,** would be tough to beat. Innkeepers Bob and Barbara Costa have restored the house Willis Dunbar built for his bride to an inviting retreat. You arrive at the big white front porch and are escorted to your room, where appetizers and wine are soon to arrive. Depending on your choice of wood—we loved the Sugar Pine room upstairs, with the balcony practically in the elm trees in the front yard, but there's not a bad room in the house—you may have a private sun porch or a clawfooted tub or a whirlpool bath, but all the rooms have surprising touches like TV, VCR, and even CD player. Breakfast, served in your room, in the dining room, or in the gardens, is almost too much. Rates begin at about $135. ■ 271 JONES ST., MURPHYS, CA 95247; 800/692-6006; WEBSITE WWW. DUNBARHOUSE.COM

The success of the Dunbar House no doubt inspired Pam Hatch, the innkeeper who recently made the **Redbud Inn** the first new inn built in Murphys in 136 years. There are 14 rooms and suites with 14 different themes (at almost as many different rates, starting at just under $100), and you're welcome to walk through in the afternoon when many of the rooms may be empty. If you do, you'll become in engaged in a game of "This would be my room," changing your mind with every open door. As at the Dunbar House, your stay will include before-dinner wine and hors d'oeuvres, and a full breakfast in the dining room. A warning, though: This is a nonsmoking inn, including the balconies. ■ 402 MAIN ST., MURPHYS, CA 95247; 800/827-8533; WEBSITE WWW.REDBUDINN.COM

It's hard to beat the convenience of the **Murphys Hotel** in the heart of town. The Murphys Hotel offers comfortable rooms and mini-suites for well under $100 a night. You may want to ask for a room off Main Street, though, if you're a light sleeper. ■ 457 MAIN ST., MURPHYS, CA; 800/532-7684; WEBSITE WWW.MURPHYSHOTEL.COM

In Angels Camp, there's a good place to sleep on Main Street outside of town, the **Angels Inn Motel,** which has a swimming pool and even offers some rooms where pets are allowed. Angels Inn Motel also has a restaurant, and VCRs in every room. Rates start at around $50. ■ 600 N. MAIN ST., ANGELS CAMP, CA 95221; 209/736-4242 OR 800/225-3764, EXT. 328

An entirely different ambience permeates the 1911 arts and crafts **Cooper House Bed and Breakfast,** perched on a hill off Main Street amid lush gardens. There are three suites—Zinfandel, Chardonnay, and Cabernet—and they all come with a wonderful breakfast made by the proprietor of the B of A Cafe. In fact, if it's a weekday and you're the only guests, she may just send you down the street for your breakfast. Rooms start at under $100. ■ 1184 CHURCH ST., ANGELS CAMP 95221; 209/736-2145 OR 800/225-3764, EXT. 326

For something completely different, there is the option of houseboats on New Melones Lake. The hit of the fleet these days is the *Eclipse* with the

"No Way" hot tub, sleeping 14 at a price of around $2,000 for a summer weekend, with discounts in the off-season and shoulder season. ■ P.O. Box 1389, Angels Camp, CA 95222; 209/785-3300; website www.houseboats.com

And if you do succumb to temptation and decide to spend a night in Arnold, in the shade of the Calaveras Big Trees, the **Yellow Dog Inn** is a wonderful hideaway for golfers, perched as it is on a Meadowmont fairway. There are four rooms here of the romantic variety, beginning at around $80 and including breakfast at a local café. ■ 1320 Pine Dr., Arnold, CA 95223; 209/795-1980; website www.yellowdoginn

Dining

ITINERARY SELECTIONS

No one recommended that we eat at the **Lake Tulloch Resort,** and when we told people the next day what a fine meal we had, the response was generally, "Oh really?" We dined on the penne, a menu staple served with sausage in a spicy tomato sauce, and the salmon special, which was baked crispy on the outside and tender inside. The wine list was a highlight, with lots of older wines fairly priced. There's a view of the lake from every table, every day, for breakfast, lunch, and dinner (also Sunday brunch). ■ 7260 O'Byrnes Ferry Rd., Copperopolis; 209/785-8200

Your Day 1 dining options in Murphys cover a lot of cuisine. We had an excellent meal at the then-new **Murphys Grille,** which offers California/Persian selections at good prices. It also stays open on the nights when the other area restaurateurs must be having their weekly bridge club. ■ 380 Main St., Murphys; 209/728-8800

The **Murphys Hotel** is always open—always seemingly busy—serving continental cuisine. Breakfast, lunch, dinner. ■ 457 Main St., Murphys; 209/728-3444

Cafe Soleil serves lunch and dinner and offers lunches to go, in something they call "Mediterranean-inspired California fresh." Lots of salads, plus duck, lamb, and pastas on the dinner menu. There's also a retail wine store here. Open Tuesday through Saturday. ■ 409 Main St., Murphys; 209/728-2875

And **Grounds** is on the itinerary for breakfast, but that certainly doesn't mean you shouldn't have lunch or dinner here as well. The menu is that varied, the atmosphere that appealing, and the prices that reasonable for this kind of food. Open every day for breakfast and lunch. Dinner is served Wednesday through Sunday. ■ 402 Main St., Murphys; 209/728-8663

The **B of A Cafe** is open for breakfast at 8 A.M. every morning. It also serves lunch daily and offers a Basque feast for dinner Friday, Saturday, and Sunday nights. ■ 1262 S. Main St., Angels Camp; 209/736-0765

The deli at **Kautz Ironstone Vineyard** will give you a great price on soup-and-sandwich and salad-and-sandwich combinations, and you'll be given a long list of garnishes (from chipotle mayo to avocado) from which to select. It is open daily from 11 A.M. until the winery closes. ■ 1894 SIX MILE RD., MURPHYS; 209/728-1251; WEBSITE WWW.IRONSTONEVINEYARDS.COM

Even though **Camps** is in the clubhouse of a golf course, think of it is a country club dining room and dress accordingly. Also, be prepared to spend accordingly. Each course is à la carte; there's no food fest here in terms of quantity, but the quality of the food and the atmosphere are unmatched in the gold country. (And don't worry—they don't serve it in finger-food portions either.) In the Greenhorn Creek clubhouse overlooking the 18th green. ■ 675 McCAULEY RANCH RD., ANGELS CAMP; 209/736-8181

The **Big Trees Market** in Arnold provides for your picnic lunch with a bakery, deli, Chinese takeout, and liquor. The market opens daily at 8 A.M. ■ 2182 HIGHWAY 4 IN MEADOWMONT CENTER, ARNOLD; 209/795-3868

ALTERNATIVES

There's a great pizza joint on Main Street in Murphys, just across from the Murphys Hotel. **The Peppermint Stick** (4454 Main St., Murphys; 209/728-3570) serves the staples of life—ice cream and pizza ($15 or so for the biggest)—and offers free delivery.

If you're hankering for Chinese food, **Sun China** (386 Main St., Murphys; 209/728-1294) has been on Main Street forever, open every night, serving up Chinese specialties to eat in or take home.

In Angels Camp, **Cruscos** (1240 S. Main St.; 209/736-1440) is doing a fine business serving pastas for lunch and dinner, Thursday through Monday, with a top dinner price of about $16.

If you're going to overnight in Arnold, the popular spot is the **Snowshoe Brewing Company** (2050 Highway 4, Arnold; 209/795-2272), for great burgers and bar cuisine.

Straying Off Course

The wineries of Calaveras County, which seem to be specializing in zinfandel but also are producing tasty alternatives, have conveniently for us tourists formed an association. For information about all of them, contact the Calaveras Wine Association (800/225-3764, ext. 25, or online at www.calaveraswines.org). If you're really a wine buff, inquire about the Passport weekend every June. A pretty stop not mentioned in the itinerary is Rios Vineyards, on Pennsylvania Gulch Road in Murphys (209/728-1020), which was considering expanding its tasting hours beyond the weekend and offering fly-fishing clinics at its pond.

The Big Trees Carriage Company (209/728-2602) will take you on a 3.5-hour historic wagon tour that includes tastings at three wineries and a gourmet lunch.

History buffs who want to make their own tour might start at the Calaveras County Museum in San Andreas (209/754-1058).

The most exciting way to learn about the Gold Rush, however, is to simply relive it, which is possible in Columbia State Historical Park. Beginning in the 1940s, the town was preserved and restored, and now it's a place to ride the stagecoach, pan for gold, see costumed artisans demonstrate the skills of the day, browse for antiques, and enjoy live theater and saloon music. There are fine restaurants and comfortable inns in town. The chamber of commerce is the place to start for information (209/536-1672; website www.sierra.parks.state.ca.us).

There are far too many outdoors activities in Calaveras County to list. If you want to ski the day after you golf, Bear Valley is but 39 miles northeast of Murphys (209/753-2301; website www.bearvalley.com).

If fishing is your thing, the trout season starts in April and runs into November, and many specimens are to be found in the Stanislaus River Forest.

Rafting is exciting in the spring, and at least three companies have permits to guide you on the Stanislaus River. Call the Visitors Bureau (800/225-3764) for contacts.

More water sports are happening at both Lake Tulloch, which offers boat rentals at the Lake Tulloch Resort (888/785-8200), and at New Melones Lake and Marina (209/785-3300; website www.houseboats.com). New Melones is the third-largest reservoir in California, with 12,500 surface acres of water and seven miles of the Stanislaus River, so there's fishing, water-skiing, and boating (rental crafts) of every kind.

Details, Details

SUITCASE

Bring your coolest golf clothes for summer, and don't forget the swimsuit—you'll be able to use the pool, and even work out if you like, at Greenhorn Creek. Pack soft spikes, and if you plan to visit any the caverns bring sneakers or hiking shoes. Golf attire is appropriate for dinners, but nights can be quite cool here in all but the hottest months so do bring a pair of slacks and a sweater. Lots of sunscreen, some bug repellent, and, for allergy sufferers, medication and Kleenex will be welcome additions to the putter and driver.

Wine lovers should also bring a cooler on a summer visit, to protect any purchases you might make along the way.

GETTING THERE

From San Francisco and the East Bay, take I-580 to I-205 to I-5 north and choose either Highway 120 or Highway 4 east from Stockton (we prefer Highway 4 for some inexplicable reason). At Copperopolis, turn left off 120 or right off 4 onto O'Byrnes Ferry Road and follow the signs to Saddle Creek.

From Sacramento, it's Highway 99 south to Highway 4, and from San Jose and points south you'll hop on I-680 to head for I-580 and then the 4- or-120 decision.

Golfing pilots can land at Calaveras Community Airport in San Andreas. Greenhorn Creek will pick you up with a little notice.

CONTACTS

- Look for information about **Columbia and Calaveras Big Trees State Parks** at the website www.sierra.parks. state.ca.us/.
- The **Calaveras Visitors Bureau** can help in just about every department (800/225-3764; website www.visitcalaveras.org).
- The town of **Murphys** has a website touting its attractions for visitors, including where to stay and where to dine (www.murphysqueenofsierra.org).
- If you're on your way to or from **Yosemite,** the website www.yosemite-gold.com has information about lodging and dining along the highway corridors.

- Sonora and Jamestown are among neighboring Tuolumne County's gems, and the **Tuolumne County Visitors Bureau** has a comprehensive presence on the Internet as well as a free guide available for the phoning (800/446-1333; website www. thegreatunfenced.com).
- The **Calaveras Publishing Co.** links to all county business that have websites (www.calaveraspubco.com).

Chapter 10

In the Shadow of Diablo: Livermore Valley

nybody who undertakes this Livermore golf escape will be able to say that he came, he saw, and he Wente-ed. Follow the plan and you'll eat, drink, and golf Wente, and be perfectly merry, maybe even marry (they do weddings, you know). The oldest, biggest winery in Livermore, under the direction of siblings and golf nuts Carolyn, Phil, and Eric Wente, is such a force in the development of tourism in the Tri-Valley area (which includes Dublin, Pleasanton, and San Ramon), you may even soon be sleeping Wente.

So raise a glass to the Wentes. What's happening in the Livermore wine region is a good thing for tourists, and especially for golfers who prefer to confine their long drives to the fairways. Just 35 miles east of San Francisco and 18 miles from Oakland, no more than an hour from San Jose or Sacramento, under smog-free skies with temperatures averaging no less than 36 degrees (January) and no more than 89 (July), are three championship golf courses: Las Positas, Poppy Ridge, and Wente Vineyards. The last two sprang up in the last half of the '90s, fueled by an explosion in industry and the influx of huge companies like Peoplesoft, Providian, and AT&T.

"In 1985, people thought of Livermore as a dry dusty cow town, or as the home of the Lawrence Livermore Lab, or as a place you drive through on your way to Yosemite," says Phil Wente, a single-digit handi-cap golfer who's behind the Wente land development ventures. "The business parks were not even there yet. But now we've got 160 software companies, 155 biomed research firms. The economic boom in this val-ley is unbelievable right now. And these companies want quality of life to offer employees. That's what led to the golf and restaurants and all of the things to come."

The Wentes were a solid force through a 10-year process that led to the South Livermore Valley Plan, which established an urban limit line and makes vineyard planting a condition of housing development. The results have been an increase in new vineyards—even though the Liver-more Valley have yet to be recognized, worldwide, for its wines in any manner that approaches the accolades awarded to the Sonoma and Napa Valleys—and the opening of two wonderful golf courses in the midst of grapes, not houses.

"Everybody said you don't build golf courses for profit, you have to have some real estate attached," Wente said. "But look at Poppy Ridge. Poppy Ridge showed that if you build it, they will come."

Poppy Ridge, where three very similar nines meander every which way over elevation changes and under one lonely oak tree, has been doing about 75,000 rounds a year since its 1996 opening at Greenville and Tesla Roads, in the heart of Livermore's wine country. A Northern California Golf Associ-ation members course offering public play, it is the little sister to Poppy Hills, though it is nothing like the Pebble Beach gem. There is one tree at Poppy Ridge, an oak, and no way to count the trees at Poppy Hills. In fact, while Poppy Hills once suffered by comparison to Cypress Point, the course it replaced in the AT&T Pebble Beach National Pro-Am rotation, Poppy Ridge immediately was disparaged for not being enough like Poppy Hills.

"That's the trouble with comparing golf courses," says Paul Porter, presi-dent of Poppy Holding Inc. "Actually, the NCGA first had a club agreement with Spyglass, which was a Robert Trent Jones Sr. course, and then Robert Trent Jones Jr. did Poppy Hills and his brother Rees did Poppy Ridge, so the comparisons are all in the family.

Porter notes that Rees Jones was attracted by the idea of building golf holes that wouldn't be next to swimming pools. "It's not often that a golf course doesn't have real estate attached, but that changes the look of the golf course," Porter said. "The goal of the area is to turn it into a little Napa, and what's happening means that we're going to have vineyards on three sides of the course. It's going to be beautiful here for many years to come."

At Poppy Ridge, there are wide-open vistas in every direction, with peeks at Mount Diablo, the Altamont Pass, the town of Pleasanton. But the

Course at Wente Vineyards is at the top of the leaderboard when it comes to beauty. With 12-minute tee times and happy to attract only 42,000 or so rounds a year (at higher green fees than Poppy Ridge), Wente doesn't just offer views of vineyards, it puts you in the vineyards. Unlike wide-open Poppy Ridge, there are few areas of the course where other players come into the picture, or within earshot, and it's quite possible you'll remember almost every hole after you've played the course once.

Jean Wente—Carolyn, Phil, and Eric's mom—was the real golf nut in the family. Her parents were members at Monterey Peninsula Country Club, and she was one of the founding members of Castlewood Country Club. Her trophy collection includes, Phil suspects, a few "women's invitational salad bowls." Later a member at Cypress Point, even at 74 she was playing golf three or four times a week, thrilled with the family's new venture. Daughter Carolyn, who's in charge of the sales-marketing-retail end of things and lives in the house parked above the back nine, has a handicap in the 20s, and Eric, who is in charge of the wine, gets a few strokes from Phil, who dipped under 10 after the Course at Wente came to be.

You'll see where playing the Course at Wente regularly would improve anyone's game—not to mention psyche. Former head pro George Price advised players, "Expect to have a very memorable experience from the time you arrive to the time you leave, because that's what you're going to get." No one plays the course very regularly (except the Wentes), however; there are no men's or women's clubs, because the plan is for this to be a resort course, with bungalows to come up in the area west of the first tee. Phil Wente said the plan is to put in an elevator shaft to take guests from the wine caves up to the top of the ridge, where they'll find upscale cottage-style accommodations in the $200 or so range. "I don't think people think about a $200 room in Livermore yet, so that will take some marketing and development," he said. "The earliest would be spring of 2002."

Well, folks didn't used to think of a $100 round of golf (Wente's weekend rate) in Livermore either. For some 20 years, Las Positas pretty much had the market cornered, pleasing the locals with green fees that stayed under $20 for Livermore residents, on a course with lots of character and a reputation solid enough that it regularly hosts Northern California PGA playing-ability tests. This layout, designed by Robert Muir Graves, opened in 1972, at about the same time the adjacent freeway came to town. And like Poppy Ridge and Wente, the surroundings had everything to do with the construction of the course: Las Positas is right next to the Livermore Airport and is part of a three-project development that also includes a sewer plant. The golf course was planned to dispose of the effluent water from the plant and to provide additional runway land should the airport ever need it. That did happen in 1990, so the front nine at Las Positas was rebuilt on newly added land, and the current back nine is the old front nine.

What with the airport, the sewer plant, and the freeway, you might think Las Positas must be a dog track. That is absolutely not the case. It is a tight, challenging 18 for players at every level, with a-well received nine-hole course and excellent practice facilities as well. "I would consider this golf course a very fun golf course to play," said head pro Dan Lippstreu, who has seen all kinds take the Las Positas test. "It's not a monster." Some parts of the course are so isolated from the freeway that you'll forget it's there; only on three holes would you be best served by resting your vocal cords and golfing in sign language.

And you'd be best served by starting your Livermore golf escape right here.

Itinerary

WARMING UP

This is a quiet golf itinerary, best undertaken by adults who enjoy adult grape beverages. It's a convenient itinerary for the nongolfer, because once you are at the Purple Orchid, the wineries and golf courses are no more than 10 minutes away, so it would be easy to drop off a golfer and while away the hours pleasurably. It is wonderful for a couple, or for a foursome or two of good friends. It would even be fun to assemble four foursomes and have the entire Purple Orchid Inn to yourself.

So call the Purple Orchid Inn and reserve your room(s) for two nights. Inquire whether the inn could help you with tee times for Day 2 at Wente (after breakfast) and Day 3 at Poppy Ridge (late morning). If not, call the golf courses as far as 30 days in advance and make your reservations. We put Wente on Day 2's schedule because it is so luxurious; you will really feel like you're on vacation. Poppy Ridge is not quite all that and will help bring you back to reality (gently of course). If you'd like a golf lesson in the olive field behind the Purple Orchid Inn, be sure to inquire in advance; there's no counter where a pro is standing by at all times. Also, if you'd like to schedule a spa service, reserve now.

If you're dining at the Pleasanton Hotel on Day 1, make a reservation. Also, make a Day 2 dinner reservation at Wente Vineyards, and inquire about any special events (wine-maker's dinners, concerts, cooking classes) that might be scheduled during your stay.

And, at 5 A.M. seven days before the first day of your escape, make your Day 1 morning tee time at Las Positas.

day 1   When you pull up to—or land at—Las Positas, you'll see a big, modern clubhouse complex, with the restaurant to your right and the pro shop to your left. Just beyond the pro shop is the first-rate executive course, which winds through the front nine of the championship course; the first tee of the big course is just outside the clubhouse window, where the staff can watch the customers continually be confounded by this beastly opening hole.

"Number 1 is a nightmare," admits longtime head pro Dan Lippstreu. "Women really hate that hole, and men don't like it much either."

Looking at the card, it seems harmless enough: just 304 yards from the most forward of the four tee sets, just 372 from the tips. But take a good look at the diagram the course so kindly posts on the tee. If you hit the ball left, you may splash. If you hit the ball right, you may splash. And if you miss the short landing area or the carry, you may splash. Most aggravating of all, due to some mounding in front of the hidden *agua,* you may not even see the splash. So players often spend a lot of time looking, oh so hopefully, for their very first shot of the day.

Cruelty on the part of Robert Muir Graves? Could be. Or maybe he was just divulging a hint on how to best tackle Las Positas. The course has trees and water, and sneaky fairway bunkers that Lippstreu says, "You think you can carry but you can't, because they wander—they're teasers." It is not a grip-it-and-rip-it exercise, jammed as it is so efficiently into its purposeful piece of land. The risks generally outweigh the reward for that philosophy. No, Las Positas is a shot-maker's friend, a thinking player's partner. Pay close attention to the diagrams at the tee and the Kirby markers in the fairways, and keep your putter warm, and you may finish the day with a fine score.

Particular holes worth noting are the challenging ninth, which comes back to the clubhouse alongside hole number 1 and thus has some similar characteristics—the water about 100 yards short of the green makes it imperative to hit an accurate tee shot. "After you play that one, you're going to say 'Wow,'" says Lippstreu. "It's an exciting hole. I like it." Then there's hole number 5—"the most controversial hole," Lippstreu says— which takes a 90-degree right turn around a large lake. On the average, two balls in a foursome splash, making the lake a nice little money-maker for the city of Livermore.

The finishing hole is a fine one, a long par-5 doglegging to the left to an undulating green flanked by bunkers. Your score on this hole may make it tempting to stop at the practice area as you head for the clubhouse and the 19th hole at Beeb's, the former flagship of the popular Heroes and Legends chain of sports bars serving big portions of good food at golf courses in the East Bay. Have a little something to eat with your cocktail so that you'll have the strength to taste a little wine before you check in at the Purple Orchid.

Now hop back onto I-580, heading east, and exit at North Livermore Avenue toward Central Livermore. Follow North Livermore about 2.5 miles, turning into Retzlaff Vineyards on your left, unless it's a weekday and it's already past 2 P.M. Watch carefully: One minute you're passing industry and low-income housing, the next you're in the wine country.

If it's after 2 P.M. on a weekday, go a little farther up the road, to Concannon, just past Retzlaff and also on the left. Concannon is not to be missed, but Retzlaff is a good first course to your gourmet escape in the Livermore Valley because of its rustic ambience, friendly service, and unique wines. Pepper trees line the dirt road in to the small tasting room, and it's not uncommon for Gloria Retzlaff Taylor to pop in and give advice on the rest of your stay. Even if you're just making a day trip to the Livermore Valley, this 14-acre winery is the place to make you forget where you were and look forward to where you're going.

From Retzlaff, you may want to make another stop, so take your pick of wineries along Tesla Road but save Stony Ridge for Day 2. Along Tesla Road (which is what South Livermore Avenue becomes) are Concannon, which has a really fine, big tasting room and pours very good wines including its signature Petite Syrah; Ivan Tamas, perhaps the liveliest tasting room; and a Wente Estate tasting room, plus Cedar Mountain and Garre, two wineries that have tasting rooms open only on weekends. When you come to Cross Road, veer left and go about two miles to the Purple Orchid Inn.

After you check in and get settled, take a look around. Karen Hughes got lost one day delivering a prescription to a home-care patient and fell in love with this piece of property. While she was there, a pickup truck pulled up and the man who got out asked her if she wanted to buy the place. They wrote the contract on the back of her home-care progress notes. It was obviously lovingly designed and furnished; the hand-carved doors, all done by Alicia Trout, a Reed Springs, Missouri, artist, are something to behold. Golfers will appreciate the one adorning the Double Eagle Suite.

We're betting you're not going to want to leave the inn tonight. Instead, you'll get comfy, meet other guests as you indulge in the wine and cheese happy hour, spend a little time in the hot tub, pick out a movie, and maybe be hungry enough to order a pizza or some Chinese food to arrive via Takeout Taxi. The menus are right next to the movies.

If you're up for the 25-minute drive to Pleasanton, you probably will want to go back to I-580 heading west, exiting at Santa Rita Road/Tassajara and turning right onto Tassajara, which will become Santa Rita and then Main if you stay straight. The Pleasanton Hotel is at 855 Main, hard to miss because it has been restored to rival its 1860s Victorian splendor. Billed as "the only hotel in town without guest rooms," it still has the look of a Wild West hotel that should have saloon doors banging back and forth. Inside, the decor is sedate and ornate, and it really is quite a nice, special place serving "California freestyle" cuisine with Italian and Asian influences.

If you got this far, you may as well take a few moments to walk it off along Main Street before you go back to the Purple Orchid and rest up for . . .

day II . . . Breakfast! No doubt you've already been asked what kind of fuel you require in the morning; you'll smell the coffee as soon as you leave your room. And even if your tee time is before the breakfast hour, the staff will not mind putting some nibbles out early for you to grab. If you're wise, you've scheduled your tee time late enough to gorge on the morning feast that comes with a stay at the Purple Orchid— it'll get you through your 18 holes at Wente.

Head back down Tesla, turn left at Wente, right on Marina, and left on Arroyo to get to Wente Vineyards. You'll pass some vineyards and catch a glimpse of the course on the left, then turn into the estate and drive past the restaurant, on your right, to the club drop.

Here, the exquisite service begins and you're king or queen for the day. The fee you'll pay at check-in includes virtually everything but whatever you'll eat or drink, so take a look at the yardage guide, putt, hit some balls, and take in your surroundings as you await the call to the first tee. After you maneuver your golf cart up, up, up, you'll be greeted by the starter, who'll tell you to watch out for snakes and stay out of the vineyards, keep your cart on the path, and have a good time. If you have a hard time pay- ing attention, you can blame the view—the Del Valle Reservoir off to the right, Cresta Blanca range off to the left, and a wide-open fairway below.

"One of the nice things Greg Norman did was not put any fairway or greenside bunkers on this hole," says George Price. "There's OB right (cabernet grapes) and left (Arroyo del Valle)—why throw a lot more haz- ards out there?"

Right on, Shark. The golfing great's favorite hole, though, is hole num- ber 2, a short par-4 with a huge risk-reward factor. It's the only hole on the course with trees lining both sides of the fairway—at the tee, you may feel them on top of you—and if you have the self-restraint to hit an iron off the tee for position, you'll make par most of the time. Norman, playing from the very back and usually vacant tees, hit driver to just in front of one of the bunkers in front of the green. That's why he's Greg Norman.

Another characteristic of this course that's unique to the designer is the shape of the fairway bunkers. Most of them are unreachable from the tee and serve as targets. And when you get to the green, look back—you'll be able to appreciate a great vista, without any bunkers in sight!

Vistas are grand, and if you get so wrapped up in the challenge of each distinct hole, you're missing a Wente specialty. Look around—etch each hole in your memory and you may be able to sit down after the round and remember each one.

Don't sit down too long, however; you'll return to Wente this evening. Instead, head over to Stony Ridge, back over on Tesla Road, and sample a few wines before you sit down to lunch. The sampling list is long, long, long at Stony Ridge, so you may want to confine your tasting to their premium wines or recent prize-winners—just ask the friendly face behind the counter for suggestions. As for suggestions on the menu, well, you probably can't go wrong. Do sit out on the deck if it's remotely weatherable on the day you visit.

By now it's probably mid- to late afternoon, because you've probably been in no hurry. It's a good time to have that massage at the Purple Orchid, explore another winery or two, or take a hike and walk off lunch. Maybe even nap time or pool time. Get yourself nice and relaxed for the special evening to come.

As for dinner at Wente Vineyards, just remember that this restaurant was a dining destination long before the first dirt was moved on the golf course. The setting is fabulous—if the climate is suitable and the bee population is low, that would be the deck; if not, the dining room is serene and large enough to provide each table with some intimacy. And there will be no mistakes on the menu—order whatever dishes you love, and they will come out of the kitchen better than you've ever had them. Portions are satisfying, not ridiculously huge, so be brave enough to start with an appetizer, move on to a salad, then an entrée, and dessert. With wine and gratuity, you will not possibly leave without spending at least $40 a person at lunchtime, $60 a person at dinner—and that's assuming your wine intake is low and low-budget. But you will surely not feel cheated, and you will look forward to returning soon. Most of all, you will look forward to the time when you can walk to your bungalow from here.

day III By now you know better than to miss breakfast at the Purple Orchid, so hopefully you've made your tee time for late morning at Poppy Ridge. Not too late, mind you, unless you like to magnify your challenge. Remember that the winds tend to stir in the afternoon. You'll be assigned to play two of the nines; if you'd like to add the third, you may inquire about availability and fee as you check in. Poppy Ridge discourages requests for particular nines, however—and did from the get-go.

"One of the big requests to Rees Jones during the design process was to make it so that the nines were well balanced," says Paul Porter. "Merlot is harder off the first tee, but otherwise they really are pretty well balanced."

Porter's favorite holes are holes 17 and 26—the construction names for the eighth hole on the Zinfandel and eighth hole on the Chardonnay, home of the lone oak. But all three nines and all 27 holes share an overall character that reminds world travelers of the Scotland links style.

"It has that windblown look, with the fescue grasses we planted," says Porter. "And the greens are open, so you can keep the ball low and run it in. There's a lot of variety and quite a few bunkers."

Quite a few, as in 114: an average of more than four per hole. We suggest you close your eyes to those and look around and enjoy all of the scenery—Mount Diablo, the Altamont Pass—and maybe you'll see some of the golden eagles who call the course home. Best of all, when you reach the final green of the day, you can look up and see the inviting clubhouse deck. We've found the food here to be much better than the usual golf course fare, so relax over a drink or one final glass of Livermore Valley wine with an appetizer or sandwich before you head home from this glorious escape.

And if you're not quite ready for it to end and never got into Pleasanton on Day 1, consider making a stop on Main Street for a stroll before you go home. Your visit may go on and on into the evening.

 NOTES

Money Savers. Oddly—at least in this book—you may find area lodging to be cheaper on weekends than on weekdays. The hotels along the I-580 corridor cater to business travelers and offer attractive weekend deals to fill their rooms.

Nongolfers. Shoppers and outdoors enthusiasts will enjoy this escape. Culturally it is of little interest.

Couples. With a stay at the Purple Orchid, this is a wonderful Valentine.

Parents. What with the wine-tasting and the romantic lodging options, we'd leave the kids at home for this one.

Time Savers. This is an easy overnight escape from the three Northern California population centers (Bay Area, Sacramento, and San Jose). For the sake of convenience, spend your first day at Wente, the night at Purple Orchid, and then play Poppy Ridge before you go home the next day.

High-Handicappers. Play from the shorter tee options and you will have fun at any and all of the courses on this itinerary.

Extended Stay. Nearby courses that could be easily added to this itinerary include Canyon Lakes and The Bridges in San Ramon and Boundary Oak in Walnut Creek.

Courses

ITINERARY SELECTIONS

Las Positas Golf Course
917 Clubhouse Dr.
Livermore, CA 94550
925/455-7820, fax 925/455-7838

What with the fine nine-hole executive course and the reasonably priced 18-hole championship course, no wonder this complex is always hopping. Rates on the big course start at $17 on a weekday at twilight, $25 for a regular weekday round, and you can also opt to play just nine holes of the big course at a discounted rate. There are junior rates and monthly membership plans, and every Monday is senior citizen day, $22 with proof of age. Fees do not include cart rental, but few will actually need them on this walker-friendly layout. Call one week in advance of the day you want to play, starting at 5 A.M. And if you live in Livermore, you can get a jump on weekend tee times by appearing at the pro shop at 6 A.M. on Friday, eight or nine days before the Saturday or Sunday you want to play.

SCORECARD

Architect: Robert Muir Graves, 1972 and 1990
Course Record: 66, James Hay and Scott Watson
Blue: Par 72, 6,677 yards, 72.1 rating for men, 127 slope
White: Par 72, 6,331 yards, 70.8 rating for men, 123 slope
Gold: Par 72, 5,709 yards, 68.2 rating for men, 116 slope; 72.4 rating for women, 124 slope
Red: Par 72, 5,270 yards, 70.1 rating for women, 120 slope
Tee times may be made up to seven days in advance by calling 925/443-3122.

TEE TIDBITS | Nonmetal spikes may be required by the time you visit. There's a wonderful short-game practice area, with a bunker, near the 18th green. Driving range is grass most of the year, mats in winter. The 2,000-yard par-31 executive course (58.1 rating from the whites, 90 slope) is of the same quality as the big course and does 40,000 rounds a year. Generally, prices for two nines equal the green fee for 18 on the championship course. Beeb's is the busiest sports bar in the East Bay, and it's no wonder why. The menu is large, the food is good, and the beer selection plentiful. Plus there's a full bar and plenty of TV screens. Even though the course is next to the busy I-580 freeway, only three holes will test your vocal cords. The rest of the well-groomed and well-marked course is quite serene and pretty.

The Course at Wente Vineyards
5050 Arroyo Rd.
Livermore, CA 94550
925/456-2475, fax 925/456-2490
website www.wentegolf.com

Wente's complete package makes this course such a great tournament venue that it can get very, very busy, even with green fees of $80 (including cart, yardage book, range balls, repair tool, and deluxe treatment) on weekdays and $100 on weekends. Generally, you can make a tee time 30 days in advance, but for a special occasion you can pay an extra $25 per player for an extra 30 days advance notice. The major flaw in the Wente design is that the course is barely walkable, and you'll pay the same price if that's what you decide to do. Pull carts are permitted, though unwieldy on the hills, and the staff will give you a ride up "Lombard Street" to the 10th tee.

TEE TIDBITS | Carts stay on paths at all times, on all holes. The pro shop is small but packed, and there's usually a sale table out on the deck. Plan to arrive no less than 45 minutes before your tee time if you'd like to take some practice shots; the range is an uphill cart ride away, and it's worthwhile to do some putting on the green next to the clubhouse. That's Carolyn Wente's house overlooking the course. One of Jean Wente's three children, she loves cooking and golf. Don't make a day trip here without stopping in at the Visitors Center to taste the latest releases. The Grill has great casual cuisine (fries to die for), and the deck puts you just behind the 18th green for a relaxing finish to your round. It stays open until 8 P.M. in summer months. Twilight bargains begin at 3 in the summer, 1:30 in the winter. There's usually a sale table in front of the well-stocked pro shop. Tee times are 12 minutes apart here, and the starter up at the first tee carefully adheres to those. If you're lucky, you'll neither wait nor be pushed, but plan on a 4.5-hour round due to the carts-on-paths-only policy.

SCORECARD

Architect: Greg Norman, 1998
Course Record: 68, Dan Arroyo and Greg Norman
Black: Par 72, 6,949 yards, 74.5 rating, 142 slope
Gold: Par 72, 6,693 yards, 73.5 rating, 139 slope
Blue: Par 72, 6,235 yards, 71.3 rating for men, 130 slope; par 76 for women, 76.4 rating, 136 slope
White: Par 72, 5,718 yards, 69.0 rating for men, 126 slope; 73.6 rating for women, 130 slope
Red: Par 72, 4,975 yards, 69.4 rating for women, 122 slope
Call 30 days in advance at 7 A.M. for your tee time.

Poppy Ridge Golf Course

4280 Greenville Rd.
Livermore, CA 94550
925/455-2035, golf shop 925/447-6779,
fax 925/455-2020
website www.ncga.org

Poppy Ridge is a public course but with some 175,000 members. It joined Poppy Hills in 1995 as the newest of two Northern California Golf Association courses, and, as such, it is a great bargain for any player who belongs to an associate club and receives a monthly handicap card. Twilight rates often are available, but generally an NCGA member can play for $35 on a

SCORECARD

Architect: Rees Jones, 1995
Course Record: 65, Hank Kuehne and Ryan King
Black: Par 72, 7,121 yards, 74.6 rating, 139 slope
Blue: Par 72, 6,693 yards, 72.4 rating, 131 slope
White: Par 72, 6,150 yards, 70.4 rating for men, 124 slope; 75.6 rating for women, 135 slope
Red: Par 72, 5,200 yards, 70.2 rating for women, 120 slope
Tee times are accepted 30 days in advance and must be secured with a credit card.

weekday and bring a guest for $45. Nonmembers must pay $55. The Friday–Sunday and holiday rates accelerate by $5 for NCGA members, $10 for guests, and $15 for nonmembers. And, unfortunately, this is another of those so-called walkable courses that is really only for the fit at heart. The elevation changes and green-to-tee distances, in some cases utterly ridiculous, make walking a tough workout, especially with pull carts prohibited. Carts cost $24 each.

TEE TIDBITS | Nonmetal spikes and golf attire are required. Check the handicap charts in the clubhouse and be sure to choose the correct set of tees—there are four options. The course distances and ratings are based on averages of the three courses, which are all quite similar. Indeed, one of the criticisms of Poppy Ridge has been that it has no memorable holes. The Merlot nine is a favorite here; it plays a bit tougher than the Chardonnay and Zinfandel nines, and if the wind is blowing at you on the first tee you'd better put on your thinking cap for the next two hours. Pace of play has generally been quite poor at Poppy Ridge; opening all three nines every day, as opposed to just two in the early days, has helped ease the crowding. Designers aced the clubhouse, which, though not large enough for many weddings and tournaments, houses an excellent pro shop and restaurant. The deck overlooks the three finishing holes and offers great vistas beyond.

ALTERNATIVES

Folks retire to Walnut Creek just to become eligible for **Boundary Oak's** favorable rates and tee-time policies for residents, especially senior residents. Operated by former Senior Tour long driver Bob Boldt, Boundary Oak is one of the finest municipal complexes in Northern California, from course conditions to 19th hole. There's a daily tip sheet to tell you how fast the greens are rolling, and remember that all of the putts break toward downtown. Green fees start at a little more than $20 on a weekday. ■ 3800 VALLEY VISTA RD., WALNUT CREEK, CA 94598; 925/934-4775; WEBSITE WWW.BOUNDARYOAK.COM

Canyon Lakes is an upscale daily fee course designed by Ted Robinson where carts are mandatory and included in the green fees that start at around $65. Opened in 1987, the course has lots of water and trees, and at the end of each hole are those undulating Ted Robinson greens. Reservations are accepted seven days in advance. ■ 640 BOLLINGER CANYON WAY, SAN RAMON, CA 94583; 925/735-6511

The area's newest upscale daily fee course, a bit more pricey than Canyon Lakes, is **The Bridges Golf Club** at Gale Ranch, a Graves/Pascuzzo design with Johnny Miller consulting that opened in 2000. It's a links-style course inspired largely by a Miller favorite, Royal Dornoch in Scotland, and caddies are available. Par is 73 from the back tees, which measure 7,200 yards. ■ 9000 S. GALE RIDGE RD., SAN RAMON, CA 94583; 925/735-4253; WEBSITE WWW.THEBRIDGESGOLF.COM

Players who are members of private courses may want to inquire with their professional about playing **Ruby Hill,** which is on the Pleasanton side of Vineyard Avenue. It's a Jack Nicklaus course that's the center of a chichi housing development; it has a reputation for being as tough as the Golden Bear himself. ■ 3404 W. RUBY HILL DR., PLEASANTON, CA 94566; 925/417-5850

If it's nine holes you're looking for, there are two other esteemed short courses in the Livermore area besides Las Positas. One is **Pleasanton Fairways Golf Course,** a par-30 with a reputation for being tougher than its brethren. An extensive practice and training complex connect to the course, which is owned and operated by co-author Cori Kenicer's cousins. ■ ALAMEDA COUNTY FAIRGROUNDS, PLEASANTON, CA 94566; 925/462-4653

The other nine-holer belongs to the City of Livermore and has undergone recent renovations. That would be **Springtown Golf Course,** a 1963 Billy Bell design measuring nearly 3,000 yards and playing to a par of 35. ■ 939 LARKSPUR DR., LIVERMORE, CA 94550; 925/455-5695

This escape also segues nicely into the Central Valley getaway detailed in Chapter 11. Diablo Grande is only about 30 minutes away.

Lodging

ITINERARY SELECTION

Purple Orchid owner Karen Hughes is such a golf nut that she's offered her guests golf lessons with a local pro that might take place in the olive field behind the inn. "With the olive trees 20 feet apart, you can definitely see how straight you can hit the ball," she says. There's also a four-stage golf cage, a bunker, and a putting green. Naturally, she'll cater to golfing guests—making your tee times, cleaning your shoes, packing little snacks, and hosting a daily wine and cheese reception where you can brag/moan about your game. The Purple Orchid has eight uniquely designed and luxuriously furnished yet friendly bedrooms, with Jacuzzi tubs, fireplaces, and views. There's a pool and hot tub outside, and spa services are available. Rates start at around $150, including breakfast and the daily happy hour. ■ 4549 CROSS RD., LIVERMORE, CA 94550; 925/606-8855; WEBSITE WWW.PURPLEORCHID.COM

GOLF PACKAGE OPTIONS

There weren't any play-and-stay options at press time, but check with Wente on the progress of the plan to build cottages and turn the winery into a full-scale resort.

ALTERNATIVES

The **Queen Anne Cottage** on 8th will thrill those charmed by history and period architecture. The Cottage Rose was built in 1875; it has been restored and filled with antiques plus a modern bathroom and kitchen. Rooms in the main house, built at around 1900, present a similar mix of the old and new, with antiques mingling with TVs, VCRs, and whirlpool tubs. There's a waterfall and rock spa for soaking in the garden. Rooms start around $125. ■ 2516 8TH ST., LIVERMORE, CA 94550; 925/606-7140; WEBSITE WWW.QUEENANNEON8TH.COM

Another lodging option with some character is **Evergreen,** a bed and breakfast billed as "modern yet rustic" just five minutes away from Pleasanton's Main Street. Each room has private bath, telephone, TV, and fridge, and some sound well suited to honeymooners. The Hideaway, for instance, has its own entrance and outdoor deck, with a king canopy bed and hot tub. And the Grand View has a fireplace and huge bathroom with private hot tub. Rooms start at around $135. ■ 9104 LONGVIEW DR., PLEASANTON, CA 94588; 925/426-0901; WEBSITE WWW.EVERGREEN-INN.COM

If your idea of a escape includes as little driving as possible, the **Plum Tree Inn** in downtown Pleasanton may be your place. Rates start at $125 for two, including a full gourmet breakfast, for any of five antique-furnished suites with private entrance and bath. There's also a large room with twin beds. The Plum Tree Inn is just two blocks from the shops and restaurants of Main Street. ■ 262 W. ANGELA ST., PLEASANTON, CA 94566; 925/426-9588; WEBSITE WWW.PLUMTREEINN.COM

Breaking ground in the spring of 2000 was an upscale 34-room inn on Main Street in Pleasanton, next to the Pleasanton Hotel that's not a hotel but a restaurant. Maybe they'll call the new lodging property the Pleasanton Restaurant.

And though the local inns have charm, for this escape you might want to consider one of the chain hotels that are sprouting up uncontrollably with the emergence of a Silicon Valleyette along the I-580 corridor. The new **Courtyard by Marriott** (925/243-1000) offers rooms for as low as $59 on weekends, when all the business travelers are gone, and there's an indoor pool and spa to make you feel very unlike a business traveler. Other chains with properties in the area include Radisson, Hilton, Crowne Plaza, Holiday Inn and Holiday Inn Express, Comfort Inn, and Hampton Inn.

Dining

ITINERARY SELECTIONS

You'll almost need to time your round at Las Positas to end after the peak lunch hour at **Beeb's,** or you'll have trouble getting a table. The restaurant, a classic sports bar with great nachos and appetizers and burgers and sandwiches, has a tremendous following apart from the golf course traffic. It opens at 6:30 in the morning and serves food until 9 P.M., except on those cold and rainy winter nights when it closes earlier. Portions are ample, and here's a clue: half orders are human-size. ■ 915 CLUBHOUSE DR., LIVERMORE; 925/455-7070

Takeout Taxi options range from pizza to Chinese to fine dining. Your hosts for the night most likely will have menus and can order for you. ■ 925/277-1990

If you're able to drag yourself back out from the Purple Orchid on your first night there to dine at the **Pleasanton Hotel,** you'll be selecting from an eclectic menu with whispers of Asia, Italy, and even the Hawaiian Islands. Sounds weird, tastes delicious, and is reasonably priced for a meal of this quality. Entrées start at around $14 for dinner; Sunday brunch has a grand reputation, and there's also lunch daily. ■ 855 MAIN ST., PLEASANTON; 925/846-8106; WEBSITE WWW.PLEASANTONHOTEL.COM

Everyone in Livermore who doesn't take lunch at Beeb's seems to opt for **Stony Ridge,** and it's no wonder. The menu is full of Mediterranean specialties and unique sandwiches—all with suggested matching wines. Sandwiches go for about $6—an appetizer or two plus two sandwiches and a bottle of wine can be had for only about $30—and you can taste that wine for free before you buy. Lunch is served 11–3 weekdays, until 4 on Saturday and Sunday. ■ 4948 TESLA RD., LIVERMORE; 925/449-0660; WEBSITE WWW.STONYRIDGEWINERY.COM

The **Wente Vineyards Restaurant** offers the beautiful, delicious food of chef Kimball Jones for dinner nightly, lunch Monday–Saturday, and brunch Sunday. The dining room has a formal feel; if that makes you uncomfortable, beg for a table on the terrace. And inquire about special events; there are frequent wine-maker dinners here, featuring wines from Wente competitors, and there are the summer concerts, which make for an entirely different kind of evening. ■ 5050 ARROYO RD., LIVERMORE; 925/456-2450; WEBSITE WWW.WENTEVINEYARDS.COM

ALTERNATIVES

If you visit on a Friday or Saturday, consider **Elliston Vineyards** (463 Kilkare Rd., Sunol; 925/862-2377) for dinner. The fixed price includes wine with each of three courses, plus dessert. Call for reservations.

A little farther up Tesla Road from Stony Ridge is another winery with a café, **Garre,** serving lunch only (7986 Tesla Rd., Livermore; 925/371-8200; website www.garrewinery.com). Garre serves lunch every day, but at press time the winery offered tours and tastings only on weekends. The menu includes soups, an antipasto platter, a seafood sampler, and sandwiches.

Pleasanton's Main Street doesn't discriminate when it comes to taste. Restaurants and cafés of all ethnic ingredients line the drag, and there's outdoor dining available at most. Take a walk to find the likes of: **Alberto's Cantina** (Mexican), **Blue Agave Club** (Mexican haute cuisine), **Panda** (Northern Chinese), **Sassy's** ("comfort" food), **Strizzi's** (Italian), and **Stacey's Cafe** (pastas and seafood, with a funny menu courtesy of one of the owners, *Dilbert* comic strip creator Scott Adams).

A couple of the favorites of those in the local wine trade are **Faz** (5121 Hopyard Rd., Pleasanton; 925/460-0444), a pretty place with Mediterranean appetizers and entrées in the $10 and up range, and **Girasole** (3180 Santa Rita Rd., Pleasanton; 925/484-1001). Girasole serves what it describes as "fresh Italian with a California attitude," which sounds like one or two of the wine makers in the Livermore Valley.

There's even a place for the beer-lovers, the **Hopyard American Alehouse and Grill** (3015 Hopyard Rd. #4, Pleasanton; 925/426-9600; website www.hopyard.com). In one of the industrial centers that line Hopyard Road, the Alehouse serves bar classics like fries and nachos and ribs, burgers too of course, at probably no more than $10 for all the food you can handle with your beer.

And if you're thirsting for a margarita and classic Mexican food in a longtime Livermore favorite, try **Casa Orozco** (325 South L St., Livermore; 925/449-3045). Specialties start at around $10 a plate, margaritas at around $13 a pitcher.

Straying Off Course

Doing nothing at all is a perfectly acceptable option at the Purple Orchid Inn. You may also want to consider doing nothing at all while receiving a massage. The inn has a small day spa (925/606-8855) with a variety of packages, the ultimate of which is of course the Ultimate Day of Beauty, about four hours of services plus lunch and use of the estate's common areas. There's also waxing.

Pleasanton's Main Street might entertain a leisurely stroller for a few hours. This was once a major Wild West stop en route to the gold country, and some of the structures are unchanged, but the overall flavor has turned genteel. On the first Wednesday of summer months, there's a street party on Main with music, wine-tastings, and art. The Pleasanton Downtown Association can offer information (925/484-2199).

Wente Vineyards (925/456-2400) presents a spectacular summer concert series, and there are occasional cooking classes and even a cooking-and-golf clinic.

Other vineyards also keep things lively in the valley with concerts and barbecues. For an entrée, contact the Livermore Valley Winegrowers Association—it can set you up with a winery map and phone numbers (1984 Railroad Ave., Suite A, Livermore, CA 94550; 925/447-9463; website www.livermorewine.com).

If you prefer to do your wine-tasting in a more passive manner, Vino Ventures (888/414-7273; website www.vinoventures.com) will start you off with lunch and a tasting and then take you to three more wineries, for around $50 a person. Stops vary depending on day of the week.

If you prefer to do your wine-tasting in a more active manner, Livermore Cyclery (2288 1st St., Livermore; 925/455-8090) can set you up with bikes and directions. This is also a good place to stop for suggestions about exploring the Del Valle Reservoir, an outdoors-lover's paradise for hiking, fishing, boating, swimming, and cycling.

Details, Details

SUITCASE

Due to the Livermore Valley's propensity for wind and heat, a hat may be the most important item you'll pack. It can get super hot here in the summer, so if you don't like to sweat while you golf, consider planning your visit at other times of the year, when the weather tends to be a bit milder than other areas. Or try to secure early-morning tee times.

Don't forget your swimsuit for the Purple Orchid hot tub and pool, and bring your bike if you'd enjoy exploring the wineries or backroads that way. And though golf clothes will be suitable for mostly everything, it would be a fine idea to dress up to match what surely will seem like a special dinner at Wente.

Metal spikes are unlikely to be necessary on this trip and may well be forbidden at all three courses by the time you read this.

GETTING THERE

From all points west and south, take I-580 east to Livermore and exit on Airway Boulevard. You'll see Las Positas on the right, next to the airport. From Sacramento and points east, you'll probably take I-680 south to I-580, heading east to the Airway Boulevard exit.

Air travelers, it doesn't get much better than this. Land at the Livermore Airport, tie down at the gate, unpack your clubs, and walk next door to Las Positas. Or, arrange for a van to pick you up and take you to Wente for the day. Class D planes are welcome 7 A.M.–9 P.M., and Class E can land any time. Enterprise (925/449-3600) will come and meet you with a rental car.

For commercial service from out of the area, fly into the full-service Oakland Airport.

CONTACTS

■ The **Tri-Valley Convention and Visitors Bureau** publishes a visitors guide with winery, lodging, and dining information, most of which is also contained in its website (260 Main St., Pleasanton, CA 94566; 888/874-9253; website www.trivalleycvb.com).

Chapter **11**

For Golfers Only: The Central Valley

ll of the other golf escapes in this book can entice the traveler
with great restaurants or shopping or surroundings, and the best
have them all and even more. In the mood for some wine-
tasting? Need a massage? Just want to sit on the deck and
watch the waves crash? Well, this is not the escape for you—
not yet, anyway. But if it's a great golfing experience you
seek, you've come to the right chapter.

In most cases, if there's nothing but a golf course in an area, we don't
recommend that you spend three days there. But the Central Valley escape
described here rates its stars on the strength of two fantastic golf courses—
well, actually three, if we're giving Diablo Grande's Legends and Ranch
courses their due. Diablo Grande's sprawling, oak-dotted pair of courses in
the Diablo foothills plus Stevinson Ranch's flat, Scottish-style layout over
450 acres of wetlands equal one great weekend or midweek excursion for
the golfer who loves the game. If you want to come home talking about
how to play the 18th hole next time and not which appetizer you'd order if
you had it to do all over again, this is the trip for you.

And the theme of this "For Golfers Only" escape is vision. That's what you'll need to navigate your way around these courses successfully for the first time, and that's the gift that belongs to two men who dreamed of putting golf courses in what seems to most Northern Californians—with all due respect to the hard-working folks in Patterson and Stevinson—to be the middle of nowhere.

Patterson, Stanislaus County, is one of those places where folks keep busy watching the grass grow—literally. Turf is big business in this town of 10,000, which didn't even have a McDonald's until Donald Panoz came to town. Panoz, the son of a prizefighter, shagged range balls when he was a kid growing up in West Virginia. He went to work as a pharmaceutical salesman, then decided he could probably make more money if he bought the company. And so he built Elan into a worldwide force.

Men like the red-haired Panoz, full of energy and always on the lookout for new empires to build or conquer, don't rest on their laurels. While the rest of us might have celebrated our success by living a life of leisure on the nearest golf course, Panoz decided to build one. Well, more than just a golf course. He started in 1989 in Braselton, Georgia, with Chateau Elan, a 2,400-acre resort that comprises three championship golf courses (two designed by world-renowned architect Denis Griffiths and another, the Legends, by Gene Sarazen and Sam Snead), a nine-hole pitch-and-putt, a winery, an inn, a spa, tennis courts, and equestrian facilities.

J. Morton Davis, a New York investment banker, realized that Panoz would be looking for new horizons at about the time Chateau Elan opened, so he introduced him to a rancher in Patterson's Oak Flat Valley, about six miles west of the I-5 freeway, which takes travelers from Mexico to western Canada. Heber Perrett had always thought of his rolling, 30,000 acres of heaven as an all-too-well-kept secret that would be better shared with vacationers in search of a place of peace and beauty, and as Panoz sat out on Perrett's porch, he saw that. That, and much more.

In fact, he turned to one of his assistants and said, "What do you see here?" The man saw trees and hills and cattle. Panoz saw golf courses, a winery, a resort, and a development of 2,000 residential sites. A deal was struck, and soon a 25-year plan was under way for an escape much like Chateau Elan—but with, eventually, *six* golf courses to keep visitors from going home, or at least from wanting to.

What Panoz didn't see, however, was opposition to his plan from some in the local community who agreed only with Panoz's perhaps unfortunate choice of a name. Diablo Grande came to be seen as a big devil of a project from antidevelopment, pro-environment factions who hung their hats on the issue of water. Where would it come from? What would it cost farmers in the valley? And why should anyone but Panoz pay any price? As grapes began growing in hillside vineyards and two spectacular championship golf courses opened (the Ranch by Griffiths in 1996 and the Legends, a one-of-a-kind joint venture by Sarazen and Jack Nicklaus, in 1998), lawsuits stalled the rest of the project and paperwork filled the 18,000-square-foot clubhouse that had once been Heber Perrett's home. In 1999, a settlement was achieved to allowed work to begin on the four-star resort and conference center necessary to make the golf courses profitable, with a target date for a spring 2001 opening. But more red tape intervened, and by the end of 2000 ground had still not been broken. Maybe someday, golfers will be able to have their golf and eat dinner too—even have that massage if they want.

In the meantime, with the largest population center (Livermore) 40 minutes away, about half of Diablo Grande's visitors were making a day trip out of two rounds here sandwiched around, most likely, one of the restaurant's terrific sandwiches. The staff wasn't waiting for any four-star hotel to arise before they began practicing their four-star service; after all, all of the red tape served to drive up the price of the rounds (morning green fees range from $55 winter weekdays on the Ranch up to $100 on summer weekends on the Legends), so they made sure to remind the customer that it was he or she who was doing Diablo Grande an honor, and not vice versa.

But players invariably came away marveling at the challenge and the beauty of both courses—with the less-heralded Ranch Course surprisingly playing to a higher degree of difficulty than the Legends, which is a favorite of the women players who stick to the front tees and thus reduce those fabled Nicklaus carries. The Legends has also been a favorite of publications like *Golf Digest,* which rated it 12th best in the state in 1999 and ignored the Ranch Course altogether.

"The Ranch has a couple of holes I don't really care for, but the Legends doesn't have a single hole that I don't like," said one of the club's early members, David Alves of Gustine, an avid golfer who joined with his favorite golf partner, wife Diane. "I just think the conditions are great, especially late in the day when it's really quiet. And what I really enjoy is winter, when the valley's in fog and you can drive 20 minutes and be in the sunshine up here."

Nature's gifts truly are beautifully packaged here, with oaks in the middle of some fairways and wildflowers covering the hillsides in spring. Birds, deer, coyote, and even the occasional mountain lion roam the land, with Panoz occasionally there to watch from his new home high on a hill towering over the property.

"Everything Mr. Panoz is trying to do is about bringing nature back—not cutting down trees, but bringing nature back," said head pro Shane Balfour, who takes responsibility for making sure the operation is first-class. "He even moved trees out of the fairways; he didn't cut them down."

They may have to be defensive about such things in Patterson, but that hasn't been the case for George Kelley in Stevinson, another of those towns you won't even find in your AAA guide. The community was, he says, "dumbfounded" when he devised a plan to turn 450 acres of old pasture that had never been worthy of farming or development into a golf course that would achieve Signature status in the Audubon Society's golf course conservation program.

In an area where land was divided into parcels too small to farm and too big to maintain, where the joke is that everybody has a home that's mobile and two cars that aren't, and where the term "rural ghetto" is not all that unkind, Kelley's proposal to put an upscale golf course on a plot of useless soil was seen as a way to create jobs and attract tourists who otherwise wouldn't stop for anything but gas on the way to Yosemite National Park.

It also didn't hurt that Kelley's Irish ancestors had settled in Stevinson more than 100 years earlier and built a large dairy business over 10,000 acres just north of the golf course property. In the late 1890s, a mule team hand-dredged a canal that stretched for 26 miles to provide water for the region, but the way the canal traversed through the property that is now Stevinson Ranch—at a 45-degree angle—made the land difficult to use for farming. Plus, the sandy soil was not useful for deep-root crops.

But it was ideal for turf grass, Kelley would learn in his years on the golf circuit. He picked up the game in Golf Heaven, when his parents decided that their four sons needed more of an education than they could get in Merced County and bought a home in Pebble Beach so that they could attend Robert Louis Stevenson. Kelley didn't particularly want to go there, but the Kelleys also bought a family golf membership at Pebble Beach ($450 a year in those days, and not all that long ago), so he immersed himself in golf and played the game constantly until he discovered girls.

He spent some years as a touring pro, qualifying for and playing in U.S., British, and Australian Opens, and finishing fourth one year in the Dutch Open. It was during that time that Kelley fell in love with the Scottish links style of golf course architecture.

"On the European Tour in '75, there was a drought, and most courses we played did not have irrigated fairways, so you had to learn to hit the bump and run shots and be more creative in your shot-making," Kelley said. "They don't spend as much money obsessing with the color of green there. You could play the Old Course at St. Andrews with a putter, and I just love that. It makes the game playable for everybody.

"I've always been attracted to that sort of design. And I had a piece of property with not a lot of trees on it and it just called out for a Scottish design."

Kelley lined up a fellow golf nut, former San Francisco Giants owner Bob Lurie, to back his project, and then began interviewing architects.

He'd pick one up at the Oakland Airport, drive the two hours to the property, take him to lunch and drive him back. And after he met perhaps 20 of the top golf course designers in the world, John Harbottle flew in from Tacoma, Washington.

"And I just knew," Kelley said.

Harbottle, whose mother Patricia Lesser Harbottle won the U.S. Women's Amateur in 1965, was thrilled with that sandy soil disdained by farmers, and he shared Kelley's vision for a Scottish-style links course. What's more, he actually appreciated that Kelley wanted to share the signature on the course and had already done much of the advance work.

"Playability for the average golfer was a priority,'" Harbottle said. "But if you know George, you know that he wanted to build a course that would test even the best golfers in the world. And it was nice to work on a course that blends all that.'"

All that—and a proactive approach to conservation. Even before Harbottle came on the scene, Kelley had flown in Ron Dodson, the president and CEO of Audubon International. Dodson, one of those rare environmentalists who appreciates golf as an outdoors experience, helped Kelley select turf grasses and create wetlands that have not merely preserved existing species.

"Now there are 85 species of birds, most of which are nesting on the property, where before there wasn't a decent water hole for any bird to land on,'" said Dodson. "Before, there were just a lot of dead trees and scrubby stuff, and it was biologically not too productive. Now, we have a lot more lakes and biologically diverse wetlands."

Kelley's only disappointment has come from the same community that initially welcomed his project. He miscalculated, he says, in thinking that the Stevinson area was ready to embrace an upscale, championship golf course.

"I always thought I'd be filling a void for the locals, but I was wrong," Kelley said. "People here are very price-sensitive and really couldn't afford to pay what we needed. But the flip side of that is we're a bargain to people from the Bay Area. What's evolving is that we're becoming a destination. Most golf resorts are very, very expensive, and I think there's a niche for an affordable escape. That's our market."

And that's music to the ears of the Northern California golf traveler.

|tinerary

WARMING UP

Make a tee time at Diablo Grande's Ranch Course for the afternoon of Day 1 and the Legends Course for the morning of Day 2. Make a hotel

Yosemite National Park

A trip to Yosemite National Park probably doesn't belong on any itinerary other than its own. There are so many lodging, dining, and activity options that you can easily enjoy a week among the many splendors of the park.

One of these is not as famous as it ought to be. That's the Wawona Golf Course, which opened in 1918 just across from the historic Wawona Hotel. And if you're saying, "That's just a nine-hole pitch-and-putt," well, just come on up and watch the thing bite your behind. Par is 70, the 18-hole length is 6,015 yards, and many pro golfers have crawled away after a round at the Wawona. Fairways are tight and tree-lined, greens are small and tricky, and the rolling hills make the course not just another walk in the park. It's an incredibly beautiful spot, though. In fact, if you take a deep breath and enjoy the views of the mountains that provide the backdrop for the first tee shot and the final approach, the sound of the creek that flooded the course in 1997, and the fragrances of the trees that are everywhere, you will wonder why people bother to hike when they can be here chasing the little white ball around.

There are two schools of thought on when to visit. One is that the waterfalls are at their gushiest in spring in Yosemite Valley, but remember that Wawona is under snow all winter and sometimes the course can't open until May. The other is that autumn brings a show of colors in the mountains, and so the Wawona offers some appealing golf packages in October, when the course is at its greenest until the snow falls.

If you go, the golf shop number is 209/375-6572. Rooms at the Wawona Hotel (209/252-4848 for all park lodging) run about $100 a night in season, without bath, and another $25 or so with bath. Hotel guests do not get a break in green fees or tee-time scheduling, but sometimes there are discount coupons at the gate. There's no range, but manager Barry Ferris has installed a warmup net, and there are greens where you can putt and chip. The shop does a busy lunch business; there's a general store with wine, cheese, and snacks a block away; and the Wawona dining room offers an elegant, peaceful, and delicious night of civilization.

reservation for one night at the Best Western Del Lago Inn in Patterson. Call Stevinson Ranch and make a late afternoon tee time for Day 2, if the days are long enough, and for late morning on Day 3.

day 1

It's early spring, and many of the courses in Northern California are still drying out from the winter rains. But in the Central Valley, wildflowers are sprouting wings of gold and purple, and the courses of Diablo Grande and Stevinson Ranch await the spring-fever afflicted golf nut.

You'll bid your nongolfing friends farewell for this escape. They'll be tending to their lawns, watching baseball games or—horrors—doing their spring cleaning, while you make your way from home to I-5. As the traffic begins to thin and cars and trucks fall into the orderly pattern of slow traffic on the right, speed demons on the left, you'll begin to breathe a little more deeply. Then, the closer you get to Patterson, California, the more you'll begin to ask, "Where the heck am I?" You'll exit I-5 and, until the Oak Flat Road is finished, make a tour of Patterson that you really don't need, passing some of those places where they watch the grass grow and wondering what you've gotten yourself into.

But when you make that turn onto Oak Flat Road, allow yourself to have the eyes of Heber Perrett and Don Panoz for a few minutes. Try to imagine what Perrett saw when he decided to put his ranch here, and then what Panoz saw when he decided the land should become home to golf courses and vineyards. Imagine visitors driving up to the Perrett home: it is exactly what you're doing as you take your gear to the bag drop, where the staff will set you up with a cart you should accept if this is your first time here.

The friendly greeting here hints at the standards at Diablo Grande, where the player is king or queen for a day (or, in our case, two). Hear more of the same in the pro shop, as you check in for your round on the Ranch Course, and then enjoy lunch overlooking the statue of Gene Sarazen that presides at the Legends Course putting green.

You'll want to hit a few balls, of course, and try a few putts. There's a small green adjacent to the first tee on the Ranch Course that makes an ideal quick stop before the round. You can visit Sarazen tomorrow.

Don't let the beauty of the tall grasses and old oaks deceive you; there's lots of pretty trouble on the Ranch Course, which opens with a relatively easy par-4 and then gets serious. The eighth through 11th holes meander around the hilltop snack shack and restrooms; use all of these facilities beyond need, because you'll see nothing like them after 12 takes you back to nature with "Mustang," an incredible, 583-yard par-5 from the white tees (649 from the very back) but, curiously, a boring par-4 from the forward reds. Women, live dangerously here and play the rear red tees for an extra challenge. The Mustang is also daunting to the average player at 583 yards from the whites. Three long and precise shots, one of them over a deep canyon, are required to reach a well-bunkered green. Once you get there, don't forget to enjoy the view of Mikes Peak, the highest point at Diablo Grande. There's a short red tee here that sidesteps the canyon carry, but live a little and play the back one. Hole number 3, "The Morgan," is another lovely terror, with lots of oaks in play, a fairway doglegging left, and lots of trouble on the right off the tee. We haven't quite figured this one out yet, but we can't wait to go back and try it again.

When you've finished 18, enjoy 19 in the bar, taking advantage of the local knowledge and hospitality of the staff and members for restaurant suggestions and directions. (With the 25-year development plan under way here, we're offering no guarantees that our routes are still best.) Tonight you're headed for Las Gaviotas, Patterson's version of a five-star restaurant. As you drive out of the course on Oak Flat Road, turn left on Ward and right on Sperry. Now you're heading east, toward downtown Patterson. At the second stop sign, Highway 33, turn left, and look for Las Gaviotas on your left. Don't worry—most nights, you'll be overdressed in traditional golf attire.

Linger over the menu with a beverage and chips and salsa, and then go ahead and overeat. There are the usual choices, plus a selection of fish and shrimp specialties, but none of your mundane greasy spoon Mexican fare. It's good stuff.

From here, you'll head back the way you came and check in at the Best Western Villa Del Lago Inn, which you passed on the way in.

day 11 Check out in the morning and return to Diablo Grande for breakfast and practice. Now you're bowing to Sarazen and heading for the Legends Course. We dare you to resist the temptation to compare it to the Ranch Course and guess that you'll judge them as different but equally wonderful. It's more sprawling, and a tougher walk, with several especially beautiful holes and one you'll probably think about long after.

Okay, okay, that's hole number 3, a par-4 that brings into play a big oak in the center of the fairway, a windmill, and/or a water tower, depending on your choice of tees. It's not uncommon to play the fourth hole and hear clanging to the rear as balls rattle off one structure or another. Head pro Shane Balfour advises that the wise choice is to hit your tee shot to the right, over the bunker, rather than test your nerve over the wetlands and around the windmill left. Get away with four here and you'll feel like you put one over on old Gene and Jack. The five finishing holes are beauties to behold, particularly the par-5 15th, where the good drive will produce a dilemma: go for the green behind the lake or lay up and bank on a more accurate approach shot onto this green.

Loser buys lunch—in the restaurant this time, if you're finished before 3—or dinner, if you got a late start in the morning. If the days are long enough, though, you'll want to drive back to Highway 33 and head south to Stevinson Ranch for at least a late-afternoon nine. Turn left onto Highway 140 and then proceed about 10 miles to Van Clief, turning left and proceeding to the course entrance on the right.

As you enter, you'll see the Cottages on the right. Drive on up to the inviting, ranch-style clubhouse and check in for your cottage and your golf, picking the brain of the cottage manager in the pro shop for restaurant suggestions. Take some time to practice your putting, adjusting to the even quicker, bigger greens here before you tee off on this little bit of Scotland in a town you've never before had a reason to visit.

After your first nine or 18, you'll want to head for Marty's, a Newman institution about 15 minutes from the Cottages. To get there, you'll go back to Highway 140 the way you came, drive back to Highway 33, turn right, and head 3.5 miles north to Newman and Marty's, on the right. Here you'll have a steak to your heart's desire, *and* soup *and* salad *and* antipasto *and* dessert, all included in the $10–15 price of your entrée. Add a couple of drinks, a couple of glasses of wine, and a tip, and you still may not have spent $50 for dinner for two. A really good dinner for two.

If you feel you need to work off a bit of that meal before working out the remote control at the Cottages, you'll want to stop at Ma Fish's on the way back. Ma Fish's, which is on 3rd Street less than half a mile outside the gate at Stevinson, has a pool table, a bar, and not much else but a bit of the local flavor. Or, go back to the Cottages, change into your swimsuit, and enjoy the outdoor hot tub before entering dream land.

day III You'll have to pack up the car in the morning, then park it at the clubhouse and return your keys. Enjoy the breakfast buffet or order some healthier fare at the bar if eggs are not your thing. Allow for some time shopping in the pro shop, where the threads are fine and the prices reasonable. Take some time to practice here; it's not often that you'll find a practice bunker and chipping area at your disposal.

Today you may want to walk 18. Stevinson is beautifully laid out, with no Grand Canyons to cross from green to tee, and it's flat enough for even the reluctant hiker. If you don't like to carry your bag, a pull cart will get you around just fine, or spring for the luxury of a caddie. Stay left on the first hole and you're already ahead of the game—many balls are lost in the wetlands to the right. Pay heed to the Savannah Rule, especially in summer snake season, and play a ball lost in the tall grasses as if it were lost in a lateral hazard. Drop two, hit three.

The holes are handicapped separately for men and for women; for example, the par-3 fourth hole, Eden, which measures 110 yards from the forward tees and 148 from the middle, is rated the ninth hardest hole on the course for women but only 13th hardest for men. Hole number 9 is rated third-hardest hole for women, but it is the hardest hole on the front nine for men. It's a stretch at 437 yards from the middle tees, but from the back it's 472 yards, with wetland hazard on the right and a tree guarding the right side of the green. The clubhouse is a welcome sight after you putt out on this undulating, bunker-guarded green. It's a good time for refreshment.

If you're playing Stevinson for a second time already, notice how ingrained the holes already have become in your golfing processor. They're distinctive and memorable, and you've no doubt already got a favorite. And an equally diverse set of holes. Owner George Kelley is especially partial to Home Cape, the par-5 18th that measures 512 yards from the middle of five tee options and starts with a tee shot that needs to be played diagonally across a long lake and proceeds with a second shot that must either lay up short of a canal or play across the canal to a parallel fairway on the left.

"There's so much strategy and so much going on that people don't realize," Kelley said. "It's one of the best examples of risk-reward I've ever seen. We had a Pepsi Tour event here, and Ron Ewing had a three-shot lead going to 18, with $10,000 on the line, and he lost and didn't even go to a playoff."

That happened when Jeff Sanday killed his drive, busted a 3-wood onto that parallel fairway just short of the green, and chipped in for an eagle 3 while Ewing played it safe off the tee with an iron, went into the canal with his second shot, and ultimately 3-putted for 7.

"That's what can happen on that hole," Kelley said.

You may prefer the lake-guarded 17th or Eden, the short par-3 fourth hole that requires a precise shot over a lake. But, as the builders intended, Stevinson is to be enjoyed and not feared by the average player. Most of the greens are approachable in bump-and-run style, and the course is kept firm with minimal watering and regular winds. Another player-friendly feature is the extended bent-grass collar around most greens, serving as a bailout area from hazards. The "Savannah Rule," allowing you to play the tall grasses as lateral hazards is also hospitable, but the grasses themselves are not. You may lose many balls and find others that don't belong to you. Don't forget to do some bird-watching during your round—many of the 85 species spotted here are also nesting on the property.

Surely there's time for one more Western meal, this time right here at the SR Grille and Outdoor Patio, before you ride off into the sunset.

 NOTES

Time Savers. If you only have one day and one night, either try to play both courses at Diablo Grande and then follow the Day 1 dining and sleeping itinerary, or drive to Stevinson Ranch, follow the Day 1 dining and sleeping itinerary, and then golf the next day.

Money Savers. This escape was made for you just the way it is.

Nongolfers. This trip is all about golf. So stay home or walk along for the scenery.

Courses

ITINERARY SELECTIONS

Diablo Grande

10001 Oak Flat Rd.
Patterson, CA 95363
209/892-4653, fax 209/892-7403
website www.diablogrande.com

The most economical way to experience Diablo Grande is to play both courses in one day at $100 on a weekday, $120 if you dare to try to beat the darkness on a winter weekend or holiday, $150 on a summer weekend or holiday. Fees include carts and range balls, with no discount for walkers. There are also 4-for-3 specials generally in effect. Standard rates on the Ranch Course range from $55 on a winter weekday to $80 on a summer weekend or holiday; add $15 to play the Legends Course.

TEE TIDBITS | Blue jeans are discouraged, soft spikes encouraged (but not required), halter tops, sweat pants, and short shorts prohibited. Shirts should have collars and sleeves. If there's anything you need, the pro shop is well stocked with fashionable threads for men and women, along with oft-forgotten items like socks and hats. Practice facilities include range, bunkers, and greens, and instruction is available. Putting practice is highly recommended for these fast, subtle bent-grass greens. The layout on the Legends Course is a bit friendlier to walkers; both are walkable, but we recommend that you ride if you're playing both in a day. Carts are not allowed on the pristine fairways here, except in cases where special permission is granted, so you'll get plenty of exercise anyway.

SCORECARD

RANCH COURSE
Architect: Denis Griffiths, 1996
Course Record: 67, Casey Boyns
Black: Par 72, 7,243 yards, 75.1 rating, 141 slope
Blue: Par 72, 6,915 yards, 73.5 rating, 136 slope
White: Par 72, 6,378 yards, rated 71.4 for men, 129 slope; par 73 for women, rated 77.5, 135 slope
Red (playing the 12th hole from the back reds): Par 72, 5,291 yards, 71.4 rating for women, 123 slope
Red (playing the 12th hole from the forward reds): Par 71, 5,026 yards, 69.5 rating, 120 slope

LEGENDS COURSE
Architects: Gene Sarazen and Jack Nicklaus, 1998
Course Record: 61, Jeff Sanday
Gold: Par 72, 7,112 yards, 74.3 rating for men, 143 slope
Blue: Par 72, 6,680 yards, 72.3 rating for men, 133 slope
White: Par 72, 6,057 yards, 69.8 rating for men, 127 slope; 74.5 rating for women, 134 slope
Red: Par 72, 4,905 yards, 68.1 rating for women, 120 slope
The courses take tee times over the Internet and phone, up to 7 days in advance with a credit card guarantee. Cancellation should be made at least 48 hours in advance, but in case of inclement weather the staff here tends to be kind.

Stevinson Ranch

2700 Van Clief Rd.
Stevinson, CA 95374
Information 877/752-9276, tee times 209/668-8200,
fax 209/668-6909
website www.stevinsonranch.com

Green fees here start at $20 twilight on weekdays and go up to $60 in weekend/holiday prime time, and juniors can play for $10 after noon. Fees do not include carts ($12 a rider, or $24 for a four-bag cart available by special request) or range balls (starting at $2.50 for a small bag). But the course layout, and its flatness, are friendly to walkers. The play-and-stay packages, starting at around $80 a person for one night and one round including cart, are the way to go from most parts of the Bay Area. An extra-special touch at Stevinson Ranch is that you can have a caddie, for $25 plus tip, if you request one when you make your tee time.

SCORECARD

Architects: John Harbottle III and George Kelley, 1996
Course Record: 64, Earl Cross
Black: Par 72, 7,205 yards, 74.3 rating for men, 140 slope
Gold: Par 72, 7,060 yards, 73.9 rating for men, 137 slope
Blue: Par 72, 6,646 yards, 72.0 rating for men, 130 slope
White: Par 72 for men, 6,093 yards, 69.3 rating, 122 slope; par 73 for women, 75.5 rating, 131 slope
Green: Par 72, 5,461 yards, 71.9 rating for women, 124 slope
Tee times are taken by phone and on the website, 14 days in advance, and must be guaranteed by credit card.

TEE TIDBITS | Soft spikes are required at Stevinson Ranch and golf attire requested. Bring some mosquito repellent for windless summer days, especially during corn harvest. The first-class chipping and bunker practice area is free, as is the big putting green, which should not be ignored before a round on these slick, well-cared-for greens. There are also golf schools here, run by the renowned John Jacobs chain, and a nice, big outdoor pavilion where barbecues can be catered for tournament groups. The course may play harder or easier than rated on a given day depending on the temperamental breezes that can blow with abandon across these wide-open fairways.

Lodging

ITINERARY SELECTIONS

Check with **Diablo Grande** to find out if its hotel has opened yet. If so, you might not need any of the following information.

In the meantime, the **Villa Del Lago Inn** will take good care of you. The hotel opened in May of 2000 with pool, sauna, spa, and exercise room—and yet to come, an RV park and a putting green. Rooms are well-appointed, with two-line phones, hair dryers, and in-room movies. Rates start at $69 a night, with discounts available for NCGA members. There were also golf packages available at press time, with a room for a night and a round of golf on both courses for $129 per person, double occupancy.

Figure it out: That's practically free lodging. On weekends, the price goes up by about $50. ■ 2959 Speno Dr., Patterson, CA 95363; 209/892-5300

The **Cottages at Stevinson Ranch,** just inside the course gates, are ideal for two—sleeping together or separately—but we wouldn't recommend stowing an extra passenger. The nicely furnished living room and bedroom each have a TV with remote, and there's a microwave and fridge. Room-and-golf packages here start at around $80 per person. If you have a roommate, just remember to shower fast; only 15 minutes of hot water is promised. ■ 2700 Van Clief Rd., Stevinson, CA 95374; 888/606-7529; email info@stevinsonranch.com

ALTERNATIVES

You'd be perfectly comfortable at the **Holiday Inn Express** in Westley, the next exit north on I-5 from Patterson (4525 Howard Rd., Westley, CA 95387; 209/894-3055). The quiet, comfortable rooms start at around $50. There's also a similarly priced **Days Inn** (7144 McKraken Rd., Westley, CA 95387; 209/894-5500). At either of these chains, you'll find chances good that they'll give you some sort of discount. Start with AAA and go down the list.

If you're looking for that place to open your own romantic bed and breakfast, here it is.

Dining

ITINERARY SELECTIONS

You won't find a great restaurant on this escape—residents drive as far as San Francisco for a special occasion. You won't find an expensive restaurant on this escape—a twosome can wine and dine beyond their fill for $20 plus tax and tip at all of the restaurants except one. You won't need a reservation anywhere, with the possible exception of the busy Sunday brunch at the Restaurant at Diablo Grande. And if you can time it right, there's no need to eat anywhere but at the golf course restaurants. Both offer much more and much better than the minimal 19th hole peanuts and beer.

The cozy, elegant ambience in **Diablo Grande**'s bar will suffice for most, and the food's the same as that served in the restaurant. But poolside tables are prime locations for the Sunday brunch, and if you're lucky enough to be here on a night when dinner is served, you'll also want to opt for the main dining room. Lunch runs until 3 every day except Sunday, when brunch ends at 2. Dinner is served Friday and Saturday nights. ■ 10001 Oak Flat Rd., Patterson; 209/892-2497; website www.diablogrande.com

Las Gaviotas opens every morning at 8 A.M. and stays open until around 10, and here's a twist: You can order from the lunch or dinner menus at any time of the day. Nothing is expensive; a dinner tab for plenty of food and drink for two most likely won't top $30. ■ 525 S. 2ND ST., PATTERSON; 209/892-6219

It's a step up to **Marty's Inn,** for a complete steak or pasta dinner with all the trimmings. ■ 29030 HIGHWAY 33, NEWMAN; 209/862-1323

In Stevinson itself, the **SR Grille and Outdoor Patio** offers terrific burgers, soups, and chilis, along with other Western-style fare, and though dinners have been served only on weekend nights, there's something cooking almost any other time of any other day of the week. ■ STEVINSON RANCH, 2700 VAN CLIEF RD., STEVINSON; 877/752-9276

ALTERNATIVES

For a great steak and some of the local flavor, try **Mil's Bar and Grill** (100 S. Del Puerto Ave., Patterson; 209/892-2100) in Patterson. Mil's opens at 5 A.M. every day and shuts down around 9, except on Sunday when the doors close in the afternoon.

Stevinson is just 14 miles south of Turlock, where there are plenty of dining options. You just exit the course on 3rd Avenue, turn right at Highway 165, which folks here refer to more as Lander Avenue, and look for the neon. Among the favorites of the local golfing set are **Trax Bar and Grille** (10 E. Main St., Turlock; 209/668-8729), serving pastas, poultry, meat, and seafood entrées, **Papachinos** (217 S. Golden State Blvd., Turlock; 209/668-8095), serving fusion cuisine, Greek and Western style, and the pasta chain **Strings Italian Cafe** (1501 Geer Rd., Turlock; 209/669-9777). There are several Mexican stops around, too, and you might want to ask which is currently the favorite of Stevinson's George Kelley.

Folks say the **Branding Iron** (640 W. 16th St., Merced; 209/722-1822) is worth the ride from Stevinson, about 20 miles west to Merced. It's the lone price exception in this chapter, with filet mignon running $20, but you still can't drop a C-note on dinner for two. The dining tradition in this part of the state means big, huge steak dinners with all the prelims and postmortems, folks, so golf up an appetite. Open for lunch Monday–Friday and dinner every night.

Straying Off Course

The best nongolfing activity available here is a day trip to Yosemite National Park, which is about an hour and 45 minutes east of Stevinson

Ranch. The smart nongolfer will drop the golfer off at Stevinson on the afternoon of Day 2 and not return until the afternoon of Day 3, particularly during the ideal days of spring, when Yosemite Valley's waterfalls are gushing. A side trip here is highly recommended, and not just for the nongolfer—a well-kept secret is that the Sierra's oldest golf course is here at Wawona. (See Yosemite National Park, page 230.)

One sidelight of the trip makes a convenient stop on the way to or from Stevinson Ranch, and that is a tour of the Hilmar Cheese plant (209/667-6076). Hilmar produces 500,000 pounds of cheese daily and has a new visitors center with deli and gift shop.

There's also a great nature experience just 15 minutes down the road from Stevinson, at San Luis Wildlife Refuge (209/826-3508). There's great bird-watching here without anyone yelling "Fore!" and if you're lucky you'll spot members of one of the largest herds of tule elk in the West. Extensive online information, including trail suggestions, is available at www.gorp.com in the California pages.

Also, George Kelley points out that the Gustine–Los Banos area has been known as a sportsman's paradise for some time because of the duck-hunting in the area. If bagging ducks is your bag, you may want to call Stevinson Ranch for more information about that.

In that vein, if you have always wanted to see a bullfight, here's your chance. A search on the web for information on Stevinson and surroundings found www.mundo-taurion.org as a source for the USA Bullfight schedule, and Gustine and Stevinson are hotspots for such activities.

Details, Details

SUITCASE

Your bags will be light if you decide to make this trip in the least desirable of seasons, summer. It will be so hot that the staff at Diablo Grande will be visiting you with wet towels during your rounds, so pack shorts and light, collared shirts—and don't expect to wear anything twice.

Fall, spring, and even winter are the ideal times to make this trip. In the autumn, you may notice some colors, and in the spring the hills around Diablo Grande are full of wildflowers. The superior drainage systems at all three courses make this a wintertime destination when most other Northern California courses are unworthy of a escape.

But if you do visit in any season but summer, you will have to be prepared for warm weather and for cold. It tends to be warmer in these parts than it is in, say, the Bay Area, but the winds can cool you off fast. Bring along a couple of windshirts with your golfing attire (include a pair of shorts most any time of year) and you'll be set.

If you still love to wear metal-spiked shoes, you'll have to bring two pairs of shoes. Stevinson Ranch requires soft spikes.

And remember, this is not an escape for your tuxedo. It is down-home, not upscale, and the most elegant thing you'll do is golf, which means there'll be no stopping to change between the 19th hole and the 20th.

GETTING THERE

Diablo Grande has hopes of offering air traffic access someday; for now, it's difficult enough to reach via freeway. If you're coming from the north, take I-5 to the Patterson exit and head east on Sperry Avenue, 2.1 miles to Ward Avenue. Turn right on Ward and go 2.8 miles south to Oak Flat Road. Turn right on Oak Flat and proceed six miles to Diablo Grande.

Coming from the south, take I-5 to the Crows Landing Road exit and make a right on Fink Road. Take an immediate left onto Ward Avenue and head north 1.8 miles to Oak Flat Road. Turn left on Oak Flat and proceed six miles to Diablo Grande.

You can fly your own plane into the Gustine Airport, which has a 3,000-foot runway but no control tower, and be picked up by the Stevinson Ranch crew to enjoy one of their overnight packages or just a round of golf. It's about 15 minutes from airport to first tee. The nearest airport with a control tower is Merced, which is 25 minutes away. They'll pick you up there too, but if the weather's so bad that you need a control tower you might not be all that interested in golfing when you land.

CONTACTS

■ The **Modesto Convention and Visitors Bureau** (800/266-4282; website www.modestocvb.org) can be of some assistance to travelers in the area. Check out its colorful Internet homepage.

Golden Gate Golf:
San Francisco

San Francisco's golf courses are inextricably linked with the city's history and culture. You might have to holler "Fore!" at clueless tourists before you tee off on hole number 17 at Lincoln Park Golf Course, but they're just drawn to the irresistible view of the graceful Golden Gate Bridge and San Francisco Bay. When grand exhibits arrive at the California Palace of the Legion of Honor, like the Georgia O'Keeffe paintings presented in spring 2000, cars are parked all the way down the hill on 34th Avenue and sometimes into the parking lot at Lincoln Park. The golf course wraps around the museum, a grand neoclassical structure that houses 4,000 years of ancient and European art.

Lincoln Park's claim to fame is its scenic layout and fabulous views. Locals have long complained that the admittedly modest green fees go into the general fund for other city services instead of being spent on the courses that generated the revenue. Consequently, maintenance has never been a strong point, its greens are constantly maligned, and it has no driving range. But Lincoln remains a sentimental favorite.

San Francisco is still getting used to having the Presidio's historic golf course available for public play. The former army base was originally established by the Spanish as a military post in 1776. Grand old eucalyptus and cypress trees line the fairways of this long, challenging course. The original nine holes were built in 1895 and expanded to 18 holes in 1910. It was used exclusively as a private club for members and the military until 1994. With the transition from military to civilian use, responsibility for the course passed to the National Park Service. The Presidio is part of the Golden Gate National Recreation Area (GGNRA), which is the largest urban national park in the world, covering 28 miles. The GGNRA follows the Pacific shoreline north and south of the Golden Gate, creating a vast coastal preserve. It includes Fort Mason and Muir Woods, Alcatraz and the Presidio, plus other beaches and smaller parks in the area. In 1995 the National Park Service awarded the concession contract for operating the golf course to Arnold Palmer Golf Management.

Palmer Golf made many improvements to Presidio Golf Course and presented San Francisco with a first-rate golf course, and green fees to match, just a short taxi ride from downtown. The showcase clubhouse held its grand opening in summer 1999.

In early 2000, San Francisco's Recreation and Park Commission cemented a deal with Palmer Golf to lease venerable Harding Park Golf Course, after Palmer's promise to invest some $11 million to restore the course to its tournament-quality glory days. Details were still being finalized at press time, but Palmer Golf seeks to bring the PGA Tour Championship to Harding Park by 2002. Reaction was mixed. Harding suffers from the same dearth of city funds that Lincoln does, so privatization would bring much-needed improvements, but players lament the inevitable hike in green fees and proposed year-long closure of the course. Proposed renovations include replacing turf area and all the existing buildings, plus adding a double-decker driving range and additional parking space. Stay tuned.

Palmer representatives Brad Beanblossom and Bill Hunscher have been the company's liaisons on the Harding project. Beanblossom says that once the Harding renovation is underway, probably mid-2001, the city is expected to turn its attention to Lincoln Park and seek a private partner to fund and execute massive improvements to the course and clubhouse. Look for Palmer to be in the running for the contract. So in just a few years, San Francisco could boast three upscale daily fee courses and become a regular PGA Tour stop.

San Francisco a golf destination? That would only add to the accolades the city regularly receives. *Condé Nast Traveler*'s "Reader's Choice Awards" recently gave San Francisco the highest score of any city in the United States. The readers of *Travel & Leisure* also voted San Francisco the highest scoring city in the country, and *Money* named San Francisco the "Best Big City" in its annual survey of the Best Places to Live.

Even some of San Francisco's most sacred institutions have a golf connection, like the magnificent Grace Cathedral atop Nob Hill, headquarters for the Episcopal Church in California. The man in charge, Bishop William Swing, is the son of a touring golf professional and has played in the AT&T Pebble Beach National Pro-Am numerous times. Swing says, "If a player misses the dimension of friendship that goes along with the game of golf, he or she is just missing the best aspect of the game." You might see the Bishop hitting balls at the practice range at Presidio Golf Course.

San Francisco's tolerance for diverse lifestyles defines the city as much as its breathtaking natural setting, world-famous landmarks, and lively history. After the Barbary Coast days of rowdy saloons during the Gold Rush, North Beach was settled by Italian pioneers like A.P. Giannini, founder of Bank of America. And who could forget the 1960s' "summer of love," when hippies with flowers in their flowing hair brought the world's attention to the Haight-Ashbury? Skyscrapers rose to dwarf early landmarks like Telegraph Hill and the Ferry Building, and San Francisco became a financial powerhouse, gateway to the emerging markets of the Pacific Rim and Asia.

San Francisco enters the 21st century in the midst of a building boom that is reshaping the city's image. The Embarcadero from the Ferry Building to Fisherman's Wharf has been transformed into a wide palm tree–lined boulevard along the bay, including a pedestrian promenade and new trolley cars. South of Market Street (SOMA) has become the latest hot spot with the opening of Sony's 350,000-square-foot entertainment/retail complex called Metreon. The four-story complex includes 15 movie theaters, the first and only Microsoft store in the world, a Discovery Channel store, eight restaurants, and more. Next to the San Francisco Museum of Modern Art, the new W San Francisco Hotel and its upscale restaurant XYZ are modern, sophisticated, and *hip*. About five blocks away is Pacific Bell Park, the new downtown ballpark that is home to the San Francisco Giants.

For all its stunning big-city attributes, San Francisco is a comfortable city to visit. Its major attractions are easily reached from a central downtown location, as are the miles of waterfront along the bay, which can help balance out a busy city lifestyle. As Robin Williams, one of San Francisco's most famous residents, said in a recent *San Francisco Examiner* interview, "This is a user-friendly city. In a way, it seems small. You walk around the corner, go to the store, talk to people. It's the combination of the people and the place, that's what I like about it most. I jog on the Marina, no one bothers me. Had a woman come up the other day and say, 'It's true, you do run here.' She couldn't quite believe it. Like I was Bigfoot."

One day's golf outing should be outside the city, and we suggest playing at Tilden Park Golf Course in Berkeley. In addition to the golf course, the Charles Lee Tilden Regional Park contains a botanic garden, picnic grounds, trails, and amusement rides for children. Winding Grizzly Peak

Boulevard climbs through Berkeley's northeastern edge, along the crest of the hills behind the city to elevations of almost 1,600 feet. The golf course sits in a forested setting high above the University of California campus.

Tilden is a busy, popular course that ranges from 6, 294 yards to 5,399 yards. Recent work has included remodeled greens, new cart paths, and a practice facility with a three-tiered driving range. The hilly course has few flat fairways, and its elevated tees, particularly on the back nine, yield scenic views of the unspoiled park land.

On this itinerary, you'll experience what San Franciscans love about their city: all the excitement and glamour of a world-class destination with its rich diversity and dreamy vistas, yet so close to the wild beauty of nature. The itinerary golf courses are all in pristine park settings surrounded by ocean, bay, and forests.

With all that, perhaps San Francisco as a golf destination isn't such a far-fetched idea after all.

Itinerary

WARMING UP

Since this is our only city golf itinerary, we're suggesting that you stay right downtown in order to have the most authentic city experience possible. A word about downtown. It can be noisy and expensive. Parking is outrageous, and your room may overlook a gravel rooftop. Did we mention the panhandlers? If these things upset you, this isn't the itinerary for you. Others will find that the exciting tempo of downtown far outweighs anything else.

It pays to be flexible with your planning. Many downtown hotels price rooms according to occupancy levels. For instance, you could be quoted a "rack rate" of $369, but depending on your date of arrival, the rate could be as little as $229 for the same room because the hotel shows low occupancy for that date. Also, always ask if any "specials" or discounts are available, typically corporate rates, AAA, or AARP.

How did we select restaurants in a city that the readers of *Bon Appetit* named "Favorite American City for Dining Out"? They had to serve wonderful food and be convenient to the itinerary lodging or golf courses. Outside of the city, we gave you places with great views of San Francisco, usually on the water. In the East Bay, Chez Panisse is the hands-down favorite.

San Francisco would be a great getaway for one or more couples, including a mix of nongolfers, because there is so much to do. Planning ahead is essential, so make all reservations ahead. The itinerary courses are all popular public courses very much in demand, especially on weekends, so follow the protocol to get the tee times you want.

The hotel concierge can be your best friend. When you book your room, enlist the concierge's assistance in making tee times and restaurant reservations. Also ask about any Broadway shows or museum exhibits during your stay. Pacific Bell Park is one of the hottest tickets in town.

Summer and holiday times are usually busy. Also, large conventions at Moscone Center can fill up the downtown hotels and monopolize taxicabs and restaurant reservations for days, so avoid those times if possible.

day 1 Go directly to Presidio Golf Course and enjoy a round of golf at this historic course. It's just minutes from downtown and south of the Golden Gate Bridge. The setting is pure San Francisco, with city views of colorful Victorians, the shiny dome of Temple Emanu-El, and the University of San Francisco's twin spires. Fresh coastal breezes blow in from the Pacific, and sometimes you can hear the mournful wail of the foghorns from the bay. Countless military officers played the Presidio back when it was the military's pride and joy, including historical leaders like Teddy Roosevelt and Dwight Eisenhower.

The Tudor-style clubhouse you see across from the ninth green belongs to the private Presidio Golf Club, established in 1905, whose members retained their own clubhouse and pro shop when the transfer to the Park Service took place. When Arnold Palmer Golf Management took over, they switched the nines around so that hole number 18 would finish in front of the new clubhouse, which is where you will check in for your round.

Assistant general manager Brad Gocha says that low-handicappers who select the blue tees based on the length of 6,477 yards will be surprised to find that Presidio plays much longer than it looks. For one thing, the hilly terrain diminishes roll, as does the typically damp and windy climate. So 150 yards uphill becomes a 5-iron instead of an 8-iron. The course plays long for everyone, with many uphill par-4s. Take extra clubs for the uphill approaches.

Palmer representative Brad Beanblossom admits that it's challenging to operate a premier golf course in the middle of a national park. While the golfers are clamoring to get rid of the daisies or fix the greens, course superintendents have to work within the constraints of Park Service restrictions. In 1999 an infestation of nematodes, a microscopic organism, was literally eating up the grass on the greens. The only known effective chemical cure was prohibited by the Park Service. Beanblossom says that no chemicals, herbicides, or pesticides are allowed on the course. Consequently, Presidio has become one of the most environmentally sensitive golf courses in the country, and a showcase for cutting-edge alternative treatments. As the nematode infestation worsened, Palmer Golf chose to convert to new bent-grass greens, pleasing golfers who like the more consistent putting surface.

Give yourself enough time to warm up on the practice range before you tackle this hilly, tree-lined course. The elevated tee on hole number 1 faces a dogleg-right hole with the driving range to your right, so range balls often collect on the fairway. In an ongoing effort to make the 100-year-old course more user-friendly, Palmer has moved up some of the forward tees, most notably on par-5 hole number 2, a difficult hole with a blind elevated green that is well-bunkered.

The par-3s aren't easy. Hole number 4 is considered the signature hole, a short par-3 with an "island green" surrounded by bunkers. Gocha says when the course was private, the bunkers were all connected to each other. Hole number 7 is another difficult par-3 because it is long. The tee shot on par-3 hole number 13 faces a large tree mid-fairway that partially obstructs your view of the uphill green.

When you're playing hole number 10, expect to encounter players from the parallel fairway of hole number 18, the tall trees between the two notwithstanding. On hole number 14 you'll be approaching the smallest green on the course. Take extra clubs into the uphill greens on holes 16 and 17, and hit it straight on the narrow, tree-lined par-5 18th hole. Take a minute to enjoy the lush, aromatic forested path to the 18th tee.

The Presidio Café inside the new clubhouse is a beautiful 19th hole that often has a fire going. Have a bite while you add up your score.

From Presidio, take a right on Arguello and follow it around to Geary Boulevard, where you want to turn left and head east to Union Square, the heart of the downtown theater and shopping district. Here you'll find sidewalk flower stands and the famous cable cars, as well as elegant department stores (Neiman-Marcus, Saks Fifth Avenue, Nordstrom, Macy's), fancy designer boutiques, and the venerable Gump's, known for its jade collection. Check into the Hotel Monaco at 501 Geary, a landmark American beaux arts building built in 1910 and completely renovated five years ago as part of the Kimpton Hotel & Restaurant Group. The glamorous lobby with high-ceilings and fanciful murals is warm and welcoming. Once you're settled in, it's time to explore the exciting sights just outside your door.

Head for Grant Avenue via the Bush Street entrance, guarded by a pair of fierce-looking Fu dog statues who welcome you into the oldest Chinatown in North America, dating back to the days of the gold rush. If you venture off touristy Grant Avenue onto narrow back streets and alleyways, you'll find that Chinatown is a vibrant community still honoring traditional ways.

On Grant Avenue just before Chinatown, be sure to visit Don Sherwood Golf & Tennis World. There are two floors of golf merchandise and equipment, plus a testing area with two nets and video swing analyzer. Sherwood's promises to meet any price, and it ships anywhere. When you exit the store on Sutter Street, walk down the block to Relax the Back at 217 Sutter and try out their fancy recliners, which massage your back every which way.

Check out the show boards at the TIX Bay Area booth on the Stockton Street side of Union Square Garage, which sells half-price tickets on the day of performance. A block away on Powell Street, you can catch a cable car to Fisherman's Wharf. Shoppers won't be able to resist the wonderful stores around Union Square.

Walk back to the Hotel Monaco to freshen up before your dinner at Farallon, one block away on Post Street. At Farallon, the imaginative seascape decor is as divine as the food.

day II This morning, walk a few blocks to Sears Fine Food for the best old-fashioned breakfast in town. Sears was founded in 1938 by Hilbur and Ben Sears, a retired circus clown who built a reputation serving delicious Swedish pancakes from an old family recipe.

After breakfast, retrieve your car for the drive to Lincoln Park Golf Course. Drive up Geary heading west, and after you cross Park Presidio Boulevard turn right on any cross street and go one block to reach Clement Street. Follow Clement out to 34th Avenue and turn right at the golf course.

Park in the shady lot to your left and walk across the street to the simple, old-fashioned clubhouse to check in. The orange spires of the Golden Gate Bridge peek through the dense trees. There's no driving range, but you can practice chipping and putting. Lincoln is hilly but short at 5,416 yards from the back tees, so it's certainly walkable. There are no water hazards and few bunkers. Course conditions weren't the greatest at press time, so you may find bare spots and bumpy greens.

Head golf professional Lance Wong says this may change if the city pursues its stated intention to give Lincoln the massive makeover that Harding will receive. In the meantime, Palmer Golf has made some improvements since taking over operation of the golf shop and the restaurant in 1997, but course maintenance is still the city's domain. Palmer redid the cart paths and added blue tees, where there were only two tees before. Forward tees were moved up some. Holes 2 and 12 were switched in order to even out par to 34 and 34, and to speed up pace of play, since there always seemed to be a bottleneck at the difficult uphill par-3 when it was the second hole. The clubhouse was improved with some new paint, and the grill upgraded to a sports bar. Lincoln is already busy, especially with city residents who receive priority and discounts, and Wong expects play to increase at Lincoln and all area courses with Harding Park closed for renovation.

Lincoln Park is part of San Francisco history just as the Presidio is. The course was built in 1908 and the clubhouse in 1913. The grand California Palace of the Legion of Honor sits atop the hill, almost in the middle of the course, and the holes meander around it. The Legion of Honor was given to the people of San Francisco by Mr. and Mrs. Adolph B. Spreckels on Armistice Day in 1924 to honor the Californians who died during World War I. Recently renovated and expanded, it is a replica of Napoleon's *Palais de la Legion d'Honneur* in Paris and contains museum exhibits from ancient art to 20th century.

The first two holes at Lincoln lead up to the prestigious boulevard, El Camino del Mar, which is the main thoroughfare through the swanky Sea Cliff neighborhood. Cross that to reach hole number 3, a par-3 that plays to a wooded green. The ocean is to your right. Big hitters try to carry the gully on par-4 hole number 4, leaving just a chip shot to the green. The museum overlooks the fifth fairway to the right of the uphill green. The sixth tee is a bit elusive, tucked away around the back of the museum after you cross the road again. Watch out for cars. Hole number 7 runs along Clement Street from a blind tee shot where everything kicks to the right. Go for the green on hole number 10, a fairly short par-4 with the grounds of the nearby museum out of bounds, as defined by a cement wall. Another blind shot to the green on hole number 11. You'll need a big tee shot for hole number 13, 500 yards from the back tees and the only par-5.

From hole number 16 you can see Baker Beach and the Golden Gate Bridge, but the best views are from signature hole number 17, one of the most scenic golf holes anywhere. Panoramic views of the Pacific, the Golden Gate Bridge, sailboats on the bay, and the Marin headlands are truly dazzling from both the tee and the green. It's a downhill par-3 from an elevated tee. Nongolfers tend to park on adjacent El Camino del Mar and walk across the fairway on their way to a wooden lookout platform, heedless of the golf in play. The magnificent view draws people like a magnet, and unfortunately some have been hit by golf balls. Marshals try to enforce safety concerns, and Wong laments that the course is prohibited from installing warning signs.

After playing Lincoln, it's hard to resist a visit to the California Palace of the Legion of Honor, just up the hill. It contains more than 20 galleries exhibiting ancient art, medieval tapestries, and famous paintings from the 16th to the 20th century including two masterpieces by El Greco and a collection of Impressionist works. An original cast of Rodin's *Thinker* welcomes visitors and is part of the museum's extensive collection of Rodin sculpture.

You're probably ready to return to your hotel and relax a little, perhaps take advantage of the steam room and sauna in the fitness center, or even wander around some of the shops you may have missed the day before. Then it's time to sample the Asian fusion menu and exotic atmosphere of the E & O Trading Company, just a short walk from your hotel. Afterward, perhaps a nightcap atop the city's tallest building, the 52-story Bank of America Building at 555 California St., crowned by the Carnelian Room with its panoramic 360-degree view. It's about five blocks from E & O. You could walk or take a cab.

day III You could have breakfast at the Grand Café in the hotel or order room service before you check out. Today we recommend you head east to Tilden Park Golf Course in Berkeley. From San Francisco take the Bay Bridge to Highway 24, then take the Fish Ranch Road exit, on the east side of the Caldecott Tunnel, and drive a mile north to Grizzly Peak Boulevard. Grizzly Peak Boulevard climbs into the Berkeley Hills to Tilden Park, where you'll see hiking trails and miniature train rides for children in the park grounds.

Tilden is part of the East Bay Regional Park System, and the golf course has been operated by American Golf Corporation for 30 years. American Golf has invested more than $3 million in improvements in the last several years, part of which went to the new Tilden Tiers three-tiered driving range and the elaborate Learning Center. In 1998, *San Francisco Magazine* named Tilden Park the "Best Place to Play Golf in the Bay Area," so you can imagine that it's busy.

You won't see any houses at all around this parkland course, which plays to par 70 from 6,294 yards to 5,399 yards. The first three holes are up and down, playing through pine, eucalyptus, and redwood trees. PGA head golf professional Trisha Hinze says hole number 1 is rated the toughest starting hole in Northern California. You can't see the green. Beginners will find a welcome "beginner tee" with yellow markers on that hole as well as on others throughout the course, which take about 200 yards off hole number 1 and less on shorter holes. The beginner tee is an on-course tool enabling players of different handicap levels to play together and is also a good on-course instruction tool.

The rocks on the left side of the second fairway add a little character for those who want to cut the corner. On hole number 6, Hinze recommends playing it safe and hitting an iron because of trees on the left and a creek on the right of the narrow fairway. On the back nine, she advises long hitters to be careful from the white tees of hole number 12 because you can't see the second creek at about 225 yards out. Trees come more into play on the back nine, as well as some elevated tees that create outstanding views. From the 14th tee, the view spans four parallel fairways. Hole number 16 is a long par-3 where tee shots tend to go toward the hillside. There's trouble to the right on this memorable uphill hole with two traps in front of the green.

Surprisingly, Hinze says, "we sell a lot of sweatshirts in July." The fog comes blowing over the Berkeley Hills, and July can be one of the foggiest months. It rarely burns off before noon and sometimes not at all, then may come in again about 4 P.M. Players driving in from Walnut Creek or other sunny climes only a short drive away can find very different weather conditions. Also, Tilden sits at a higher elevation so sometimes it can be foggy down below and clear at Tilden. Go figure. Dress in layers. After golf, sit on the outdoor patio of the Grizzly Grill and watch players on the two greens below you.

When you leave Tilden, stop to visit the University of California campus, which encompasses more than a thousand acres including archives, art and science museums, a botanical garden, and the Campanile, a 307-foot tall bell tower at the center of campus that chimes on the hour and plays music regularly. Instead of taking Grizzly Peak Boulevard, exit the golf course onto Centennial Drive, which will take you past Memorial Stadium onto Gayley Road, which turns into Hearst Avenue. The campus is east of Oxford Street, between Hearst Avenue and Bancroft Way.

Just be sure you don't miss dinner at Chez Panisse. Owner Alice Waters is credited with creating "California Cuisine" at her landmark restaurant, which opened in 1971.

 NOTES

Extended Stay of the Pampering Kind. Stay at the Claremont Hotel in the Berkeley Hills, not far from Tilden Park, and book treatments at the luxurious spa. Watch the sunset from the Terrace Bar overlooking the bay and San Francisco.

Extended Play South. Play at the Poplar Creek Golf Course, previously San Mateo Golf Course, which opened in 2000 after a complete renovation. It's about 40 minutes south of San Francisco at Coyote Point Recreation Area. Dine at Kincaid's, which is about a mile north of the course on the roadway that goes along the bay.

Extended Play North. Play at San Geronimo Golf Course in rural Marin County. It's set into the hills of Novato and will be a pleasant, relaxed round. The weather will be warmer too. Go to Sausalito for great bay and city views while you dine, and stay right on the water at the Inn Above Tide.

Extended Play Funky. The nine-hole Gleneagles International Golf Course is a favorite of many San Francisco golfers.

Practice, Practice, Practice. Mission Bay Golf Center is a popular downtown practice facility that is lighted at night; it's not far from Pacific Bell Park.

Money Savers. Take advantage of weekday and twilight golf rates. You might save some money parking your car yourself in a downtown garage rather than with the hotel's valet parking service. For a more budget-oriented getaway, forgo downtown and stay in one of the motels along Lombard Street in the Marina District, where you can walk to casual neighborhood restaurants.

Painkiller. If that old golf injury flares up when you're playing in San Francisco, just call Julie Wong at Pro-Active Therapy. She's past president of the San Francisco chapter of the Executive Women's Golf Association and specializes in treating golf injuries at her physical therapy clinic.

Courses

ITINERARY SELECTIONS

Presidio Golf Course
300 Finley Rd., P. O. Box 29603
San Francisco, CA 94129
415/561-4661
website www.presidiogolf.com

Presidio allows 90-degree cart use unless otherwise posted, but carts are required to stay on cart paths on the par-3 holes. On Tuesdays and Thursdays, they give the course a rest, and it's cart paths only. You'll pay around $75 for 18 holes plus $15 per person double occupancy for golf carts. Carts are equipped with the GPS "Par View," which has a color monitor, keeps score, and can send and receive messages. Twilight and early bird rates are available. Soft spikes are required. The dress code is simply golf attire.

There's a full driving range with alternate grass tee and artificial turf

SCORECARD

Architect: Robert Johnston, 1895
Course Record: 64, Alwyn Pirtle
Green: Par 72, 6,477 yards, 72.2 rating for men, 136 slope
White: Par 72, 6,141 yards, 70.8 rating for men, 131 slope; 76.1 rating for women, 136 slope
Red: Par 72, 5,785 yards, 69.2 rating for men, 127 slope; 74.2 rating for women, 131 slope
Tee time reservations are accepted up to 30 days in advance, 24 hours a day, by calling 415/561-4653. Internet reservations available: www.presidiogolf.com.

stations, plus practice bunkers and putting green. Golf clinics are offered by PGA and LPGA instructors as well as individual instruction.

TEE TIDBITS | The new 7,500-square-foot clubhouse is stunning, done in a Mission-style architecture to reflect the Presidio's Spanish history, while following design elements of Bay Area architect Bernard Maybeck by the use of natural materials and colors. Check out the memorabilia and historical photos from the century-old golf course and from Arnold Palmer's golf career. The pro shop is well-stocked. Presidio Café is open for breakfast and lunch, with wood-beamed cathedral ceiling and stone fireplace opening onto a heated trellised patio. The upscale menu features several large salads, notably the three-pepper seared tuna, sandwiches, and burgers, plus blackened rib-eye steak, pasta, and fresh seafood. Prices are under $15.

Next on Palmer's list of improvements is a new facility at the first tee/driving range area that would house the starters, food service, and restrooms.

Lincoln Park Golf Course
34th Avenue and Clement Street
San Francisco, CA 94121
415/221-9911, fax 415/221-1519
website www.lincolnparkgc.com

Lincoln Park Golf Course allows carts on the fairways unless the course is wet, and it isn't fussy about your spikes or your clothes. It's walkable but somewhat hilly. There's no driving range, but you can practice chipping and putting. Instruction is given in an informal, open practice area. Green fees are under $30 plus $22 for carts. They offer twilight rates and early morning "back 10 holes" rates. San Francisco residents with a resident card receive discounts.

SCORECARD

Architects: Tom Bendelow, 1908; Herbert Fowler added nine new holes and redesigned the others in 1922, and Jack Fleming did another redesign in the 1960s.
Course Record: 60, Tom Susko and Ken Harrington
Blue: Par 68, 5,416 yards, 66.0 rating for men, 109 slope
White: Par 68, 4,948 yards, 65.1 rating for men, 107 slope
Red: Par 70, 4,732 yards, 66.0 rating for women, 105 slope
For tee times call 415/750-GOLF. Tee times are accepted seven days in advance for registered San Francisco-resident cardholders, six days in advance for all others. The reservation line opens at 7 p.m.

TEE TIDBITS | At press time, Arnold Palmer Golf Management operates the pro shop and the Lincoln Park Sports Grill, which was redone in 1999 to provide a fresh, open setting, outdoor patio, and a brand-new menu. The Sports Grill is open for breakfast and lunch and offers a full bar with satellite TV and a billiards room. It's casual and kind to your budget. Breakfast will run under $7, and most lunch items are under $10. Sandwiches are named for local golf heroes and heroines, e.g., Dorothy Delasin, Ken Venturi, Johnny Miller. Watch for changes at Lincoln similar to Harding Park by 2001 or 2002.

Tilden Park Golf Course
Grizzly Peak and Shasta Road
Berkeley, CA 94708
510/848-7373

Tilden allows walking, soft spikes are optional, and there are no restrictions on attire. Carts may go on fairways at 90 degrees. On the weekend you'll pay around $55 including cart. Carts are equipped with "Pro Shot." Other rates available include twilight, sunset, early bird back nine, seniors, and juniors. Monthly passes are also available. Members of American Golf Players Association receive discounts at any American Golf facility, including Tilden.

The three-level Tilden Tiers Driving Range has 70 stalls, all mats, and includes lights and heaters. It was named one of the top 10 new ranges in the United States by *Range Magazine.* Tilden is user-friendly with a definite bent toward teaching and learning. The yellow beginner tees allow new players to play from shorter distances so they can be out on the course without holding up play. The new Nike Golf Learning Center offers a big variety of lesson programs for players of all abilities, including summer junior golf camps.

SCORECARD

Architect: William Park Bell, 1937
Course Record: 64, Randy Haag
Back: Par 70/71, 6,294 yards, 69.9 rating for men, 120 slope; 76.0 rating for women, 133 slope
Middle: Par 70/71, 5,823 yards, 67.8 rating for men, 116 slope, 73.4 rating for women, 127 slope
Forward: Par 70/71, 5,399 yards, 71.1 rating for women, 122 slope
Tee-time reservations may be made up to seven days in advance. Tilden Park guarantees single player reservations. Call 510/848-7373. A credit card may be required during peak times.

TEE TIDBITS | The casual Grizzly Bar & Grill is open for breakfast and lunch. Part of it is a sports bar with large-screen TV and several smaller ones.

Tilden was named one of the "Top Ten Women-Friendly Courses in the U.S. and Canada" by *Golf for Women* magazine in 1999 and made the list again in 2000. Back and middle tees are rated for both men and women. Tilden hosts American Golf's annual "Women-in-Golf Day" each spring, offering free instruction and playing tips.

ALTERNATIVES

San Mateo Golf Course reopened July 2000 as **Poplar Creek Golf Course,** after a complete renovation that included new cart paths and the addition of water features. The lovely new clubhouse is double the size of the old facility. The four tee boxes range from 6,042 yards to 4,768 yards, with three tees rated for women. Daily pin placement locations, six in all, are depicted on the scorecard. PGA professional Gary Monisteri and his amateur-champion wife, Eva Monisteri, operate the golf shop. ■ 1700 COYOTE POINT DR., SAN MATEO, CA 94401; 650/522-4653

Formerly private **San Geronimo Golf Course** became available for public play in 1996, and golfers enjoy the meandering course in rural Marin County. Water hazards come into play on more than half the holes. The front plays longer but the back is more difficult, especially hole number 11 where trees and a barranca before the green require thoughtful play. New homes are under construction along the 12th fairway. The clubhouse was completely remodeled and has a full bar and dining facilities. Green fees are $55 plus $24 for carts. ■ 5800 Sir Francis Drake, San Geronimo, CA 94963; 415/488-4030

Gleneagles International Golf Course is one of Jack Fleming's designs (1963). Fairways are tight and tree-lined and greens are fast. Serious golfers find Gleneagles a great place to hone their game because of the uneven lies and the wind. Nine holes from the back tees plays 3,000 yards. The bar in the funky clubhouse has a surprisingly sophisticated store of aged Scotch, a tribute to its name. Insiders say Gleneagles is a hidden gem. Its only drawback is being alongside housing projects with a notoriously high crime rate. Just be aware, and follow the suggested route: exit from Highway 101 on Paul Avenue, then onto Mansell Street, which goes through McLaren Park. As you come down the hill, go left onto Sunnydale and look for the course on your left. Green fees are under $25 for 18, less for nine, and carts are available. ■ 2100 Sunnydale Ave., San Francisco, CA 94134; 415/587-2425

Mission Bay Golf Center has 66 hitting stalls in a two-tiered practice facility, lighted at night, where the top level is also covered and protected from the wind. Two putting greens plus bunker and chipping practice area. The Beginner Value Program for only $99 allows over 20 hours of supervised practice, plus the Mission Bay Golf School has a wide range of individual and group lessons and clinics. The Golf Mart has a wide range of equipment and apparel at reasonable prices, and the casual self-service restaurant stays open until 9 P.M. on weeknights. It's well-kept and convenient, especially for downtown office workers. ■ 1200 6th St., San Francisco, CA 94107; 415/431-7888

The only way you'll get on **Olympic Club** is to have a member take you or to get invited to a swanky golf event. Do whatever it takes. The Lake Course is consistently rated among the top courses in the country and has hosted four U.S. Opens (1955, 1966, 1987, 1998). Wind and fog often come into play on both the Lake Course and the shorter Ocean Course. Golfers love the trademark long, skinny grilled hamburgers tucked into hot dog buns. The nine-hole par-3 Cliffs Course opened in 1994. ■ 524 Post St. (downtown club) off Skyline Blvd. (golf course), Daly City, CA 94102; 415/587-8338

Lodging

ITINERARY SELECTION

Enter the lobby at the **Hotel Monaco** and your attention is immediately drawn upward to the hand-painted ceiling domes and two-story French Inglenook fireplace. The "celestial lady" wall mural holds court above the grand marble staircase. Opulent but not overdone, this newly restored hotel provides the perfect getaway mood in a great location. The 201 rooms and suites have romantic canopy beds, striped wallpaper, luxurious fabric covers, and marble baths.

One of the reasons Hotel Monaco is one of the hottest hotels in San Francisco is the added value guests receive. At the afternoon wine and cheese reception in the large "living room," you may have a complimentary chair massage or tarot card reading. Also complimentary are the nightly shoeshine service, morning coffee/tea service, weekday Town Car service within a six-block radius, and fitness club facilities. Dogs are allowed, with complimentary dog walking, but they do charge for the doggie massage. Best of all, general manager Nanci Sherman is a golfer, as are many of her staff, so golfing guests will feel right at home. When you make your reservation, ask for chief concierge Jacques Rachal, who will be happy to make tee times and arrange the rest of your stay. The hotel's Grand Café serves breakfast, lunch, and dinner in a colorful, ornate atmosphere. Room rates start at $289. Valet parking is $24. ■ 501 GEARY BLVD., SAN FRANCISCO, CA 94102; 415/292-0100 OR 800/214-4220, FAX 415/292-0111; WEBSITE WWW.MONACO-SF.COM

ALTERNATIVES

The Claremont Resort & Spa opened in 1915 as a "country getaway" and today is considered a Bay Area landmark, nestled in the Berkeley Hills with a spectacular view of San Francisco and the bay. The majestic castle-like structure amidst 22 acres of landscaped gardens contains 279 guest rooms and a separate European-style health and beauty spa, which will soothe and relax you after golf. In 1998 the Claremont was purchased by KSL Recreation Corporation, which owns La Quinta Resort and Club, PGA West, the Doral Golf Resort, and others. The spa is also open to nonhotel guests as a "day spa" and includes outdoor swimming pools and hot tub. Rates range $275–850. Parking is $14. ■ 41 TUNNEL RD., BERKELEY, CA 94705; 510/843-3000 OR 800/551-7266, FAX 510/848-6208; WEBSITE WWW.CLAREMONTRESORT.COM

The romantic **Inn Above Tide** is next to the ferry boat landing in Sausalito. Built in the late 1960s prior to waterfront development restrictions, it is the only Sausalito hotel in the area directly on San Francisco Bay. When it was converted to an inn in 1996, owners made sure that all 30 luxurious rooms faced the bay. Most have gas jet fireplaces and private decks, and some have hot tubs. Rates include continental breakfast and afternoon wine and cheese and range $215–535. ■ 30 EL PORTAL, SAUSALITO, CA 94965; 415/332-9535 OR 800/893-8433, FAX 415/332-6714

The Hotel Rex is a 94-room Union Square hotel whose clubby atmosphere was inspired by literary artists of the 1920s and '30s. Dark wood-paneled walls lined with bookcases surround deep cushioned armchairs set around tall columns in the inviting lobby. Browse in the antiquarian bookstore. The lobby bar is open until 11 P.M. The rooms are done in warm tones of gold and orange, with wooden armoires used as closets. Rates range $175–675. Continental breakfast is available in the lobby for an additional charge of $10.95. Valet parking is $25. ■ 562 SUTTER ST., SAN FRANCISCO, CA 94102; 415/433-4434 OR 800/433-4434, FAX 415/433-3695; WEBSITE WWW.THEHOTELREX.COM

The Inn at Union Square has 30 rooms and has been a popular downtown choice for more than 20 years. It's tiny, quaint, and charming. The narrow hallways are mirrored and well-lit, and rooms are brightly furnished in floral prints with marble baths. Rates include continental breakfast and afternoon wine and hors d'oeuvres, served on each of the six floors in a sitting room with a wood-burning fireplace. You can sign up for a complimentary chair massage. The inn is a completely smoke-free hotel, and, what's more unusual, the staff does not accept tips. It is in the middle of the block between other buildings, so don't expect a view from the lower floors. Room rates range from $180 to $350 for the Howell Suite, which has a hot tub. Valet car parking is $23. ■ 440 POST ST., SAN FRANCISCO, CA 94102; 800/288-4346 OR 415/397-3510, FAX 415/989-0529; WEBSITE WWW.UNIONSQUARE.COM, EMAIL INN@UNIONSQUARE.COM.

Thirty-one story **W San Francisco** is so New York–cool, you'll think you should be rooting for the Yankees instead of the Giants. Although designed for business travelers with the latest in telecom equipment, it also delivers stylish comfort in the form of goosedown comforters and special bath products for all 418 guest rooms. Telephones have a special button for "Whatever, Whenever." W and its signature restaurant, XYZ, form the cornerstone of the trendy SOMA neighborhood. Rooms do have city and bay views on higher floors, and corner rooms are the best. The indoor heated pool is open 24 hours. Rooms range $369–429. Parking is $33. ■ 181 3RD ST., SAN FRANCISCO, CA 94103; 877/946-8357 OR 415/777-5300, FAX 415/817-7800; WEBSITE WWW.WHOTELS.COM

If you want to go all out and splurge for a stay at a San Francisco legend, the **Westin St. Francis** at Union Square is the place. Heads of state and visiting VIPs have been staying at the majestic St. Francis ever since it opened in 1904. The cable car line is right out in front. Elegant decor, majestic columns, balconies, and crystal chandeliers bespeak its glorious past while a recent $55 million restoration brought new furniture and state-of-the-art improvements, including a health club with full spa services, notably, La Stone Therapy. The 1,194 luxuriously appointed guest rooms are contained in the main building and the tower, which has the best view rooms. Choose from several fine restaurants or the elegant

Compass Rose, where afternoon tea is served. Room rates range from $279 all the way up to $2,500 for a specialty suite. Valet parking is $30. ■ 335 POWELL ST., SAN FRANCISCO, CA 94102; 415/397-7000 OR 800/WESTIN-1, FAX 415/774-0200; WEBSITE WWW.WESTIN.COM

For more casual, affordable lodging, stay in one of the many motels along Lombard Street, which is also Highway 101, the main route to the Golden Gate Bridge. You'll be centrally located to the golf courses, and it's an easy walk to the shops and restaurants of the Marina district. You can get a double room in the busy summer months for just under $100 with free parking. Double-paned windows muffle some of the traffic noise, but ask for a room that is not facing Lombard Street. The nicest motels are the **Chelsea Motor Inn** (2095 Lombard St., San Francisco, CA 94123; 415/563-5600, fax 415/567-6475) and its sister properties, the **Cow Hollow Motor Inn & Suites** (2190 Lombard St., San Francisco, CA 94123; 415/921-5800, fax 415/922-8515) and the **Coventry Motor Inn** (1901 Lombard St., San Francisco, CA 94123; 415/567-1200, fax 415/921-8745).

Dining

ITINERARY SELECTIONS

At **Farallon** the menu changes every day, but the undersea-fantasy decor remains blissfully the same. The ethereal jellyfish chandeliers, shell-shaped booths, and seductively lit columns combine to create a romantic mood throughout the thoughtfully designed space with several choices of intimate seating areas. The winding staircase, covered with blue-black "caviar beads," leads to cozy upstairs tables. "Imaginative" and "creative" also apply to the food, prepared in an open kitchen and specializing in seafood dishes like seared Alaskan halibut with white truffle potato puree, or roasted Florida red grouper with cumin-infused butter bean puree. Oysters on the half shell and caviar are popular appetizers, and the house-cured salmon gravlax is delicious. Prices run $24–29. Lunch and dinner. ■ 450 POST ST., SAN FRANCISCO; 415/956-6969, FAX 415/834-1234

Sears Fine Food claims to be "world famous for our 18 little pancakes," so you know that breakfast is its specialty, and it has been since the doors first opened in 1938. On Union Square, Sears is so San Francisco you can hear the "clang clang" of the Powell Street cable car passing by. This comfy homestyle restaurant has simple tables covered with pink tablecloths under plastic, fluorescent lighting, and old-fashioned counter seating. The 18 Swedish pancakes are $5.50, $7.50 with bacon or sausage. The rest of the large menu is also reasonably priced, as is the lunch menu, a recent innovation. Everything's under $10 except the New York steak sandwich ($12.95). Healthy low-fat items are marked with a heart symbol. Breakfast and lunch. ■ 439 POWELL ST., SAN FRANCISCO; 415/986-1160, FAX 415/765-0957

The Asian fusion menu at **E & O Trading Company** suits the decor, that of a 19th-century Southeast-Asian trading house, right out of a James Michener novel. It's like an Asian brewpub. Antique Chinese birdcages hang from the ceiling, and bamboo and burlap touches surround the dragon bar. Among the "Small Plates" the Indonesian corn fritters with chili soy sauce are divine, as are the chicken, beef, and prawn satays, served by plate or by stick. E & O (Eastern and Oriental) makes its own home-brewed ales and refreshing sodas. Don't miss the old-fashioned cream soda with natural vanilla extract, or the classic root beer. Entrées run from $13 to $23 for the delicious Malay rack of lamb served with sweet curry sauce. Live jazz music plays Thursday through Sunday nights near the entrance. Lunch and dinner. ■ 314 SUTTER ST., SAN FRANCISCO; 415/693-0303; WEBSITE WWW.EOTRADING.COM

For more than 25 years, **Chez Panisse** has defined "California Cuisine," Alice Waters's innovative style that relies on the best quality, fresh organic produce, meats, and other ingredients, expertly and simply prepared. Entrée items are rarely repeated because only the freshest ingredients are used. The unpretentious small wooden building and pleasant, down-to-earth staff belie the restaurant's fame. Downstairs the main dining room features a prix fixe menu of 3–5 courses each day, with the week's listings printed on one page. Here's one night's menu: soft-shell crabs with Italian squash, parsley, garlic, and new olive oil; cannelloni with squash blossoms, ricotta, and Chino Ranch corn; Liberty Ranch duck with roasted artichokes, olives, and bay leaves; peach ice cream *capelli* with blackberries.

Prices are around $70 on weekends. Reservations are a must, and it can take one to two months to get a table. The casual café upstairs accepts only same-day reservations and serves an expanded, à la carte menu. The food is every bit as good. Dinner. ■ 1517 SHATTUCK AVE., BERKELEY; 510/548-5525

ALTERNATIVES

From **Kincaid's** waterfront setting (60 Bayview Place, Burlingame; 650/342-9844, fax 650/342-9857), you can watch the planes from San Francisco International Airport taking off and landing over the bay. There's a lively bar area. The restaurant has windows all around and is arranged on two levels so every table has a view. Big comfy booths line the walls. It's comfortable, relaxed, and friendly. Kincaid's expansive menu specializes in fresh fish from around the world, and its signature preparation is grilled over applewood. Toasted herb pan bread accompanies the entrées. Meat dishes are also very good, such as the tender rock-salt-roasted prime rib or pan-seared venison. Entrées run under $25. Lunch and dinner.

Sausalito has several special spots from which to view San Francisco. We recommend brunch from the big deck of the **Alta Mira Hotel & Restaurant** (125 Bulkley Ave., Sausalito; 415/332-1350). Looking out at the bay with its little islands, the city, and the bridges, you could almost be in the south of France or on the Italian Riviera. At the **Spinnaker Restaurant** (100 Spinnaker Dr., Sausalito; 415/332-1500), the floor-to-ceiling windows all the way around make you feel like you're riding the waves yourself. Watch the moon rise over the bay and the city skyline light up from the *très chic* deep red and mauve surroundings of **Ondine's** (558 Bridgeway, Sausalito; 415/331-1133, fax 415/332-0795).

For old-fashioned North Beach hospitality, visit the cozy retreat that is **Buca Giovanni** (800 Greenwich St., San Francisco; 415/776-7766, fax 415/776-8084; website www.bucagiovanni.com). Jimmy Rizzo makes sure customers have a good time while chef-partner Mike Alfieri prepares traditional Italian dishes that will satisfy the heartiest appetites. In addition to fresh homemade pastas, their signature dish is rabbit, prepared several ways. Founder Giovanni Leone was known for his rabbit stew, and Mike's version is delicious. Entering the restaurant, you're greeted at the wine lounge, then time stands still a little when you walk downstairs to the intimate dining room and dine to the music of Jimmy's favorite crooners, like Frank Sinatra or Jerry Vale. Desserts are homemade too, and don't miss Grandma Alfieri's amaretto and walnut cheesecake. Share your golf stories with Jimmy and Mike, who take to the links whenever they can.

Ton Kiang Restaurant (5821 Geary Blvd., San Francisco; 415/387-8273) is close to Lincoln Park and would be a great place to stop before or after golf for the best dim sum in San Francisco. Dim sum is a delightful form of Chinese cooking that presents an amazing variety of creatively prepared delicacies served on small plates—little dumplings, pot stickers, crispy duck buns, shrimp balls, and much more. There's also a full menu of Hakka-style cuisine, and you can combine dim sum items and main dishes in your order. The large, brightly lit restaurant has little atmosphere, but the staff is friendly and the food very good. For dim sum, the cost is $26 for any nine items for two people. Most entrées, including seafood, beef, and traditional Hakka casseroles, are under $10. Ton Kiang is open daily from mid-morning to 10 P.M.

If you want to see what the "new San Francisco" is all about, dine at **Dine** (662 Mission St., San Francisco; 415/538-3463, fax 415/538-3466). The trendy, casually dressed SOMA crowd fills the high-ceilinged dining room and the rising din reverberates off the wooden floors, brick walls, and other hard surfaces. Nevertheless, Chef Julia McClaskey, previously of the Universal Cafe, turns out superb meals with certain sure winners like the pork tenderloin wrapped in pancetta and the hazelnut-crusted Chilean sea bass. For dessert, try the silky smooth butterscotch *pots de crème.* In a poignant sign of the times, the menu pleads "Please no cellular phones." Compare golf tips with general manager Maureen Donegan. Entrées run under $25. Dinner.

If you're staying in the Marina district along Lombard Street, walk two blocks north and you'll run into Chestnut Street. There's a wide choice of neighborhood restaurants, such as **Café Marimba** for Mexican food (2317 Chestnut St., San Francisco; 415/776-1506), **Yukol Place** for Thai cuisine (2380 Lombard St., San Francisco; 415/922-1599), **Andiamo,** for casual dining, Italian-style (3242 Scott St., San Francisco; 415/440-2600). Owners Vince and Marika will make you feel like family. Their next-door pizza place, **Blue Moon,** offers takeout and delivery (3244 Scott St., San Francisco; 415/775-2583). Don't miss old-fashioned **Lucca Delicatessen** (2120 Chestnut St., San Francisco; 415/921-7873), a Marina tradition for sandwiches, salads, homemade pastas, and minestrone soup. Takeout only.

Straying Off Course

Sightseeing Excursions

If it's your first visit to San Francisco, a city tour by Gray Line San Francisco (350 8th St., San Francisco; 415/558-7300) is an excellent way to get oriented. Free walks hosted by City Guides (415/557-4266) or San Francisco Heritage (415/441-3004) will take you through various neighborhoods. Also free are the historical walking tours through Golden Gate Park hosted by the Friends of Recreation and Parks (415/263-0991).

Shirley-Fong Torres (Wok Wiz; 415/981-8989) offers Chinatown tours that meet at her cooking school at 654 Montgomery St., between Montgomery and Kearny. Grace Ann Walden, *San Francisco Chronicle* restaurant columnist, leads Mangia North Beach food tours of North Beach (415/397-8530). Take a bay cruise with Blue & Gold Fleet (Pier 41, Fisherman's Wharf, Powell Street at the Embarcadero; 415/705-5555) or Red & White Fleet (Pier 43½, Fisherman's Wharf; 415/447-0591).

On Your Own

San Francisco is such a compact city that you can discover it on your own. Walk from Union Square to Chinatown, North Beach, or SOMA. You can catch a cable car to sights that are out of walking range. Pick up a guide to the Barbary Coast Trail (available at the Visitor Information Center), which is a self-guided walking tour covering more than three miles along city streets, where bronze plaques identify historical buildings.

In addition to shopping at Union Square, check out the Tix Bay Area (251 Stockton St., San Francisco; 415/433-7827; website www.theatrebayarea.org), which sells half-price tickets on the day of performance to selected events and full-price tickets in advance, and Don Sherwood Golf & Tennis World (320 Grant Ave., San Francisco; 415/989-5000) for equipment and apparel.

You'll find the stunning San Francisco Museum of Modern Art (151 3rd St.; 415/357-4000; website www.sfmoma.org) in SOMA, as well as Metreon (101 4th St.; 415/369-6000), the Sony Entertainment Center with theaters, IMAX, restaurants, and shops.

Nearby is Pacific Bell Park (24 Willie Mays Plaza, San Francisco). Tickets for San Francisco Giants' games may be purchased in person at the park, by telephone (510/762-BALL or 415/972-2000), or via the Internet (sfgiants.com or Tickets.com/BASS online at tickets.com).

For more highbrow entertainment, there's the San Francisco Opera (War Memorial Opera House, 301 Van Ness Ave.; 415/864-3330). The San Francisco Ballet Box Office (415/865-2000) is also at the Opera House. The San Francisco Symphony performs at Davies Symphony Hall (201 Van Ness Ave.; 415/864-6000). One sight you don't want to miss is San Francisco's newly renovated City Hall (400 Van Ness Ave.; 415/554-4000), reopened in 1999. The historic landmark was brought up to seismic readiness while retaining and enhancing its historic detailing. It's now become the *in* place to host special events. And don't forget the California Palace of the Legion of Honor in Lincoln Park (415/750-3600).

There's no better way to see the city than by following the blue-and-white seagull signs along the scenic and historic highlights, called the 49 Mile Scenic Drive.

You may be tempted to stop at any of the trails along the Golden Gate National Recreation Area (415/556-0560), the vast coastal park that contains Presidio Golf Course. At the north end of town, near the Golden Gate Bridge, Crissy Field is being restored to its pre-military-base condition as a series of trails and sandy beaches along the bay, where dogs chase driftwood and windsurfers race the waves. Just across Marina Boulevard and several blocks up Baker Street sits the Palace of Fine Arts, which looks like a majestic Grecian temple, alongside a serene lagoon. Swans gracefully glide by, and waterbirds dip and dive around the soaring fountain.

After all that golf and touring, a physical therapy treatment at Julie Wong's clinic, Pro-Active Therapy (1489 Webster St., Webster Tower, Suite 210, San Francisco; 415/346-8373) will soothe any aches and pains.

Details, Details

SUITCASE

San Francisco's fog is the stuff of legends. Poet Carl Sandburg said the fog comes in "on little cat feet." Sometimes it does. But whether it blasts in or tiptoes, you're bound to encounter fog in San Francisco in the summer, so plan ahead and bring more than just a windshirt. Try a parka. Well, at least dress in layers. Because with the fog usually comes wind, although generally it's calmer in the morning. Mysteriously, as soon as you cross the bridges to points north or east, or head south toward the peninsula, the fog clears and sunshine and blue sky return. Inland temperatures can be as much as 20 degrees warmer in the summer months.

The climate is mild year-round with fresh, smog-free air. San Francisco's sunniest weather is usually in the fall, and Indian summer can extend well into October. Spring days are usually clear and warm as well. Be prepared for the changeable climate and bring a jacket. For this itinerary you'll need soft spikes and comfortable walking shoes for museums and shopping. Bring a swimsuit, workout clothes, and dressier clothes for an evening out on the town.

GETTING THERE

To reach Presidio Golf Course from downtown, take Geary Boulevard to Arguello Boulevard. Turn right on Arguello and go one-half mile up Arguello through the Arguello Gate. Continue right on Arguello about 100 yards until you see the new clubhouse, then turn left into the parking lot.

From Marin take the Golden Gate Bridge/Highway 101 south. After the toll plaza stay in the right lane and take the 19th Avenue exit. Go through the tunnel and take the first right, onto Lake Street. Make a U-turn heading east on Lake to Arguello (about 12 blocks). Make a left on Arguello and go through the Arguello Gate. Continue right on Arguello about 100 yards until you see the new clubhouse, then turn left into the parking lot.

From the peninsula, take I-280 until it turns into 19th Avenue. Turn right on Lake Street and travel east to Arguello Boulevard. Make a left on Arguello and go through the Arguello Gate. Continue right on Arguello about 100 yards until you see the new clubhouse and turn left into the parking lot.

From east of San Francisco, take Interstate 80 and the Bay Bridge into the city. Exit at Fell Street and proceed down Fell to Stanyan. Take a right on Stanyan and turn left on Fulton. Turn right on Arguello Boulevard and go through the Arguello Gate. Continue right on Arguello about 100 yards until you see the new clubhouse on your left, then turn into the parking lot.

The closest airport is San Francisco International Airport, which is undergoing a major renovation and expansion, so give yourself extra time to get in and out during the construction phase.

CONTACTS

- **Francisco Visitor Information Center** 900 Market St. at the corner of Powell and Market Streets, lower level, Hallidie Plaza; 415/391-2000
- The online resource service of the **San Francisco Convention & Visitors Bureau** includes local and state maps, events calendar, and capsule descriptions (P.O. Box 429097, San Francisco, CA 94142-9097; toll-free number for lodging reservations 888/782-9673 within North America or 414/974-4499 elsewhere; website www.sfvisitor.org). Write to request visitor and lodging guides. The cost is $3 for postage and handling.

- **San Francisco Fast/Fax** will fax visitor info (800/220-5747 in the United States and Canada or 617/960-9216 elsewhere).
- **Marin County Convention & Visitors Bureau** Avenue of the Flags, San Rafael, CA 94903; 415/499-5000, fax 415/499-3700; website www.marincvb@marin.org
- **Berkeley Convention & Visitors Bureau** 2015 Center St., Berkeley, CA 94704; 510/549-7040 or 800/847-4823

Chapter 13

Coast is Clear: Half Moon Bay

K nown as the "quiet side" of the San Francisco Peninsula, the coast side is bounded by mountains to the east and the vast Pacific Ocean to the west. Most visitors reach it either by taking windy, scenic Highway 1 south from San Francisco or by coming "over the hill" on 11-mile-long Highway 92 from San Mateo to Half Moon Bay. Both Highway 1 and Highway 92 follow original trails of the Costanoan Indians. When Captain Gaspar de Portola founded San Francisco's Mission Dolores in 1776, the mission found the coast side ideal as grazing land for cattle, horses, and oxen. Today, livestock still grazes on the land, and some farms date back to the 1800s. The coast side attracts artists, surfers, and those seeking a slower-paced lifestyle.

Since geographic circumstances prevented easy access, the region has remained somewhat isolated. Yet Half Moon Bay is a desirable weekend escape because it's midway between the major population centers and major airports of San Francisco and San Jose. Moves are afoot to improve access along the controversial section of Highway 1 known as Devil's Slide, and talks continue about widening Highway 92.

"Build it and they will come" may be true in some circles, but on the coast side they seem to be coming before the work is even done, and Half Moon Bay may soon catch up to the rest of San Mateo County in sophistication and prices. Certainly the two world-class golf courses at Half Moon Bay Golf Links have done much to bring the area to the attention of both sophisticated travelers and upscale homeowners. Homes around the golf course have recently sold for over $1 million.

The Links Course opened in 1973, surrounded by the Ocean Colony residential community. When the Ocean Course opened in 1997, that paved the way for Vestar-Athens to build a luxury hotel in 2000 to be managed by Ritz-Carlton and transform sleepy Half Moon Bay into a fancy golf destination. The grand six-story hotel has 261 rooms, including bungalow rooms along the 18th fairway of the Links Course.

During 2000 the Links Course underwent renovation with extensive drainage work and changes to the course. The new back nine opened April 14, and in September the front nine closed for similar work. Updated scorecards and yardage books in 2001 reflect the course's new rating after the opening of the completed front nine. Although much work has been done on the course, there still is no driving range.

One of the reasons Arthur Hills was chosen to redo the Links Course is the success of his drainage and irrigation work in his design of the Ocean Course. The hollows created by new drainage areas have left the Links fairways with far more undulations than before. All the fairways were regraded, and the bunkers were rebuilt. Some were removed, and the new ones tend to be deeper and smaller. All the tees were rebuilt; there are now four sets of tee boxes on each hole, and some of the forward tees were moved up. From the back tees, hazards now appear that weren't there before, as exemplified on hole number 14.

When the Ocean Course opened, it was hailed as the epitome of a links-style course since much of it runs along ocean bluffs with few trees to block the wind and fog, which can roar in on a typical coast side day. While the perimeter holes garner the best ocean views, the interior holes meander along a rolling setting with side-by-side fairways. You can see the ocean from every hole, but the three finishing holes are directly on the water and provide a dramatic finish.

The new Ritz-Carlton has the best view of all atop the bluffs between the finishing holes of both the Links Course and the Ocean Course. Touted as a "grand seaside lodge," it is certainly the best place to watch the sunset.

Although the hotel project and Ocean Course were approved years ago, developers still fought their way through the bureaucratic process to eventual completion. Building on the oceanfront is always a controversial issue for coastal communities. The issue of leaving nature untouched or allowing even limited use also affects the lands "over the hill."

Discussions continue on use of the vast Crystal Springs Watershed, a pristine wilderness comprising 37,000 acres of land with seven lakes and including the Crystal Springs Golf Course. At issue are the public's right to access for walking, hiking, and biking within the property versus the San Francisco Water Department's concern for preserving the quality of the water supply. The land is owned by the City of San Francisco, under the jurisdiction of the Water Department. To golfers, it seems like there is also plenty of room for another 18 holes and they've been lobbying for years, but to no avail.

Crystal Springs is adjacent to Interstate 280 in Burlingame. From the elevated tee of hole number 6 at Crystal Springs Golf Course, the clear blue lake waters of the Crystal Springs Reservoir resemble the fjords of Norway. The spectacular view appeals to wedding parties, and PGA professional Roger Billings says that Crystal Springs has sodded and irrigated an area behind the tee where wedding ceremonies can be conducted in a gazebo setting. Fortunately there's a gate onto a gravel road that goes back into that area, so guests don't have to traipse across the fifth fairway to reach the site.

Crystal Springs is the most convenient course for western San Mateo County, enhanced by its pristine setting amid protected wilderness and abundant wildlife. It's been certified by the National Audubon Cooperative Sanctuary Program. The course was laid out in 1924 and retains its natural setting with no homes around it. Interstate 280 borders the last few holes, but traffic noise is muffled by dense trees. There are three tee settings, and it plays 6,515 yards from the back tees. Although the course has wonderful water views, in fact water comes into play only on one hole, par-4 hole number 15.

The battles fought over use of the Crystal Springs watershed property and of the coast along Half Moon Bay reflect the needs of a growing population that is running out of room in Northern California and turning its attention to previously inaccessible spaces.

For now, Half Moon Bay is still a typical coastal retreat with art galleries and quaint inns. That will probably change as home prices rise and affluent homeowners demand more upscale business and services so they don't have to go "over the hill." The little beach towns to the north, like Princeton-by-the-Sea and Moss Beach, may remain untouched for a longer time until real estate prices catch up.

Walking and biking trails around Moss Beach will lead you to the Moss Beach Distillery, known for its spectacular ocean views and the legend of the Blue Lady, which was recently featured on the NBC TV series *Unsolved Mysteries*. The romantic story took place in the 1920s when a young wife, who always dressed in blue, and her handsome lover met for secret rendezvous at an inn next to the distillery. The Blue Lady died in a violent auto accident, and it's said that her ghost haunts the beach. Mysterious noises and pranks that have occurred at the Moss Beach Distillery have been attributed to the ghosts of the tragic pair, a theory corroborated by Bay Area psychic Sylvia Brown, who has communicated with the spirits in a series of séances held at the distillery. On a foggy night with the waves breaking below, the place certainly has atmosphere.

Pescadero, 25 miles south of Half Moon Bay, resembles a New England town with old frame houses and steepled churches, notably the Pescadero Community Church, a California Registered Landmark built in 1867 and the oldest church in San Mateo County on its original site. Pescadero was once on the main road along the coast, traveled by stagecoaches, so its main street is called Stage Road.

It remains to be seen whether the coast side, and Half Moon Bay in particular, follows the lead of other coastal communities like Carmel or Sausalito and becomes a tourist haven. For now, there are more housewares shops than T-shirt shops on Main Street. Stay tuned.

Itinerary

WARMING UP

Golfers will enjoy having two great golf courses in one place, and this itinerary would also be fun for nongolfers. It's a compact, easy weekend where everything is close by and you can settle in comfortably, yet it feels like you are far away from home. It would be a good romantic getaway and would also be fun for a few couples. We're suggesting a stay at the Ritz-Carlton because of its great location, and while it was not completed by press time, we can see enough to know it will be gorgeous.

Ask the hotel to book tee times when you make your reservation. Certainly book as far ahead as possible for these popular courses. At Crystal Springs you can call seven days in advance. Reservations come in as soon as the pro shop opens at 6 A.M., especially for weekend play. For Half Moon Bay, it's three weeks in advance. We suggest morning tee times in both locations. Playing Crystal Springs on the first day, you'll want to be finished and on your way to Half Moon Bay on Highway 92 by midafternoon to be ahead of the commuter traffic. In the case of Half Moon Bay Golf Links, morning tee times are preferable because it tends to be less windy. Wind is more of an issue on the wide-open Ocean Course. Remember the mantra at Half Moon Bay: "When it's breezy, hit it easy."

Make dinner reservations ahead. If you'll be there on a weekend, call the Bach Dancing and Dynamite Society to see if there's a concert on Saturday night or Sunday afternoon. You can reserve ahead or just drop in.

You would need reservations for sportfishing excursions, but be aware that these trips generally depart around 7 A.M. and return in midafternoon, so it would be difficult to do on the same day as you play golf. Whale-watching trips depart about 10 A.M. and last three hours, but since the whale season is December to March, you wouldn't be back in time to complete a round of golf before dark.

Even small inns have meeting rooms, so this could be a good opportunity for a company retreat in a relaxing environment with golf nearby. They call it "coastal conferencing."

day 1 Take bucolic I-280 from San Francisco or San Jose to Crystal Springs Golf Course for your morning tee time. From points east, Highway 92 across the San Mateo Bridge will bring you to I-280. Nongolfers could go into the town of Burlingame and browse its attractive shops and restaurants.

Crystal Springs retains its original 1924 design even though a few holes on the front nine were altered in 1964 when I-280 was built alongside. The hilly layout meanders through a forested setting and you can expect side-hill lies. Most days it's sunny like the rest of the peninsula, but fluffy coastal fog sits atop the lush hills like frosting on a cake, and when it spills over and tumbles down, the temperature drops in a hurry. Deer, singly or in groups, wander the course, napping and nibbling, and barely flinch when a golf ball whizzes by.

Leave yourself enough time to warm up at the newly remodeled driving range, which is also lit at night. Recent changes to the course include a new tee on hole number 1, which now has a middle tee and a forward tee about 30 yards ahead, beyond the cart storage facility. The new tee box is to the left side and forces tee shots to angle right and away from cars on the road, which had been in danger from errant hook shots. Hole number 5 is an uphill par-4 and the number one handicap hole. Take an extra club to the uphill green when the wind is up. When the pin is on the left side, the bunker comes even more into play. You're rewarded by the view at the tee of signature hole number 6, which is a dogleg left par-4 overlooking the Crystal Springs Reservoir. Hole number 9 borders the driving range, so expect to search for your ball among the range balls.

Roger Billings advises first-time players at Crystal Springs that the front nine is more difficult than the back nine and more up-and-down. Thus it tends to play longer, not yardage-wise but time-wise, as much as a half-hour longer than the back nine, which moves along fairly quickly. So don't be discouraged after the first nine.

The existing narrow tee box at hole number 10 is built into the hillside and will be redone, but in the meantime, new middle and forward tees have been added at the bottom of the hill. As with hole number 1, the forward tee will remain in the new location while the middle tee will rotate back to its old position, mainly for the purpose of spreading out wear and tear. Other changes include replacement of most of the cart paths around tees and greens and drainage work so the course won't be as spongy in the winter.

The shorter back nine rewards accuracy—many of the fairways are narrower. Hole number 13 is a fun par-3 with an elevated tee that makes the green look closer than it is. Try to resist the temptation to floor it going down the steep cart path. Hole number 14 is a sharp dogleg left. There's a chance for birdie on hole number 16, a relatively short par-5. After golf sip a cold one on the deck of the remodeled Crystal Café.

We suggest you hasten to Half Moon Bay, via Highway 92, because the commuter traffic from Silicon Valley starts to back up by late afternoon. Return to I-280 and, in just a few miles, take the exit to Highway 92 west. The scenic road passes through the watershed property and climbs up to the crest where Highway 35/Skyline Boulevard intersects, then descends down toward the coast and Highway 1.

Shortly before you reach Highway 1, you'll pass Obester Winery on your left. If you don't have time to taste the wine, at least pick up a bottle of the black fig vinegar; it's yummy for dipping bread and makes salad greens come alive. Turn left when you reach Highway 1 and head south for three miles until you reach the entrance sign. Proceed directly to the Ritz-Carlton to check in and relax a little. Then go into the town of Half Moon Bay, only five miles north, to walk along Main Street before dining at Pasta Moon.

day II For breakfast you'll have the choice of room service, the hotel restaurant, or Caddy's at the golf course. Today you'll be playing the Links Course. Hopefully, by the time you read this, the new front nine will have opened, so you can experience the entire course. Non-golfers can enjoy guest activities at the Ritz, and the Spa and Fitness Center sounds like a great place to spend the day.

At the Links Course, walking is not permitted, but carts can follow the 90-degree rule onto fairways. This may be adjusted for newly sodded areas. The greens are much faster than those on the Ocean Course as they are poa annua, while the Ocean has bent-grass tees and greens. Locals grin watching players who practice on the two poa annua greens close to the clubhouse and then head for the Ocean Course.

While extensive work will be done on the front nine by the time you read this, the character of the original design won't change. A few holes were redesigned where, over the last 25 years since the course was built, trees had come into play or bunkers needed to be moved. Everyone is hoping that Mr. Hills will trim that bunker that sits up on the right side of the green on hole number 3. The ridge captures balls headed for the pin and makes for a difficult shot hitting over the steep bunker wall to get out. On hole number 4 the word is that the bunker around the landing area on the right will come out. Long-hitters still try to cut the corner, which was probably easier before the trees got so high and the homes were built. At hole number 8, a downhill par-5, players are used to aiming for the white house on the right side. Houses surround the Links Course, but you'll see not a one on the Ocean Course. When you come up to the tee of hole number 9, it's something of a shock for old-timers to see how the new Ritz-Carlton obstructs what used to be the best ocean view on the Links Course next to hole number 18. The next shock is to hear that the going price for prime ocean-view lots along the ninth fairway is a million bucks.

First impressions of those who played the new back nine when it opened in April were that it's tougher than before. In general, some bunkers have been removed, others added or downsized to be smaller and deeper; greens are smaller; and fairways that used to be fairly flat are now undulating. That's evident right off the bat on hole number 10. It's harder to get a good lie, and the course seems to play longer because when the ball hits those mounds, it stops rather than releasing as it would do on flatter terrain.

One of the most controversial changes on the new back nine was the removal of a grove of eucalyptus trees between the 11th tee and the 15th green. Hole number 11 now has a new tee box more to the left than before, closer to the lake, which has been enlarged and now comes into play more from the back tees than it did before. On hole number 12 the left-side fairway bunker comes into play more, and the green is much smaller. Also, new mounding rises behind the green and extends to behind the blue tees of hole number 13, which makes for a more attractive backdrop.

Players appreciate the curbs on the new cart paths, especially on par-3 hole number 13, where the path goes between a reed-filled pond and the curb stops errant tee shots that might otherwise roll right into the water. The dramatic change on hole number 14 is that from the back tee the new fairway bunker on the right has created a narrow landing area between it and the left-side bunker on this severe dogleg right. The lake on hole number 15 was enlarged all the way around. Hole number 16 is still a difficult par-4 with a wide barranca in front of the green, but the forward tees were moved up by 80 to 100 yards to make it easier to reach the green in regulation. The Ritz-Carlton's mountain-view bungalow rooms sit behind the 16th green. At hole number 17 the ocean comes into view, and hole number 18 is a downhill par-4 with the waves crashing against the rocky cliffs to your right and the new Ritz perched overlooking the green. The barranca before the green has been narrowed, which extends the playing area so you can lay up. Additional bunkers make for a difficult approach to the green.

After golf stop for lunch at Caddy's. It's an attractive spacious restaurant with great selections. Grab a table in the bar area if you're in a hurry. The late afternoon menu has lots of choices too.

In the afternoon after golf, you have several options. We're suggesting dinner at Mezza Luna in Princeton-by-the-Sea, north of the golf course. On the way, if it's a Sunday afternoon, you could listen to some music at the Bach Dancing and Dynamite Society at Miramar Beach, then go next door to the Miramar Restaurant to watch the sunset over cocktails and the generous appetizers. For something more active, you could take a horseback ride on the beach at Sea Horse Ranch or rent bikes in Half Moon Bay. You could also retire to your room at the Ritz, check out the spa and chill out until dinner at Mezza Luna. The new Navio's at the Ritz, not open at press time, promises romantic oceanfront dining.

day III If you liked the breakfast at Caddy's, try it again, or see what the Ritz has to offer, before you walk over to the Ocean Course. One of the services the Ocean Course's higher green fee buys is being escorted to the first tee by a charming greeter who will give you tips that could save a few strokes. No extra charge for the exciting view of whales just off the coast from December to March.

Dramatically different from the Links Course, the Ocean Course has no houses around it, and it's also treeless, so there is no shelter from the Pacific winds, which can rule your game. Arthur Hills created a links-style course whose rolling, wide-open holes are bordered by native grasses and thick rough from which you can retrieve missed shots. You can see the ocean from every hole. Players say it reminds them of courses in Scotland or Ireland.

The Ocean Course starts off with a sharp dogleg right to a downhill green. Hole number 2 requires lots of carry over a barranca, and by the time you're done with hole number 3 and its postage-stamp green, you'll realize that what you're dealing with here is target golf, where accurate shot-making will pay off. The cart path that goes between hole number 2 and hole number 18 doubles as a public-access path to the beach, so don't be surprised to see sightseers strolling the path, heading for the stairway down to the driftwood-laden beach. It's clearly marked on the entry road with a parking lot set aside for beachgoers.

The only water to overcome is the lake on par-3 hole number 7, which encroaches slightly onto hole number 5 as well. Similar to Hills's redesign of the Links Course, fairways here also display subtle undulations. However, the greens are generally much larger on the Ocean Course. The three closing holes provide a memorable finish. At the elevated 16th tee, the view stretches for miles along the coast to the north, with native grasses and plants bordering the fairway. After the sublime view, the hole itself is challenging enough, with a creek before the green. Hole number 17 is a par-3 that's all carry, even from the 75-yard forward tees. The tee shot on hole number 18 is an uphill carry on this long par-5 along the cliff's edge to a big, long green that sits on a high bluff overlooking the Pacific. The Ritz rises above the green like some mystical castle, complete with towers and turrets.

Do stop in for afternoon tea after your game.

NOTES

Extended Stay South. Head down the coast to Pescadero. Have lunch at Duarte's Tavern, which used to be the town saloon and barber shop in 1894 and now serves old-fashioned hearty food. Then visit the elephant seals at the Año Nuevo State Reserve. If you want to stay overnight, try the fancy lodge or economy tents at Costanoa.

Money Savers. Take advantage of midweek and twilight rates. Dine at Barbara's Fish Trap or Ketch Joanne Restaurant.

If You Have Only One Day and One Night. Go directly to the Ritz and stay there, enjoying the dining and the spa. Play one course the day you arrive and the other the next day.

Extended Stay for Romantics. Go to Moss Beach and stay at Seal Cove Inn, where you can walk to the Moss Beach Distillery and perhaps catch a glimpse of the Blue Lady.

Courses

ITINERARY SELECTIONS

Crystal Springs Golf Course
6650 Golf Course Dr.
Burlingame, CA 94010-6598
540/342-0603
website www.courseco.com,
email csgolf@pacbell.net

Crystal Springs is only 10 miles from San Francisco Airport. It has three sets of tees. Soft spikes are not required, but shirts and golf shoes must be worn on the golf course at all times. Carts use the 90-degree rule. Roger Billings says that they recently decided to go to a seasonal rate structure with reduced winter rates December–March.

SCORECARD

Architect: Herbert Fowler, 1924
Course Record: 62, Charlie Leider
Championship: Par 72, 6,515 yards, 71.7 rating for men, 124 slope
Middle: Par 72, 6,236 yards, 70.4 rating for men, 121 slope
Forward: Par 72, 5,813 yards, 73.3 rating for women, 128 slope
Tee times can be made up to seven days in advance with a major credit card. Call 650/342-0603 starting at 6:00 A.M.

Another change at Crystal Springs is the requirement of a cart on weekends before noon. That is, the fee includes a cart. You can still walk, but you will pay the full fee, which on the weekends is around $80. From noon to 3 P.M. it's $65 to walk. Crystal also offers staggered twilight rates, with carts not allowed after 5:30 P.M., and rates for seniors and juniors. Currently Crystal hosts 14 local high school golf teams.

TEE TIDBITS | The uncovered practice range was completely redone and now has all new mats and a large putting green. Dede Braun and John Abendroth run the learning center, which has two hitting areas on one end of the range and video swing analysis equipment. The USGA and University of California Extension maintain a putting green for the testing of different species of bent grass, monitored on a monthly basis. The Crystal Café offers full breakfast and lunch, full bar, and evening libations and appetizers either inside or on the covered veranda overlooking the practice range.

Half Moon Bay Golf Links
2000 Fairway Dr.
Half Moon Bay, CA 94019
650/726-4438

At Half Moon Bay Golf Links, metal spikes are not permitted. Appropriate golf attire must be worn, which means no tank tops, T-shirts, cutoffs, or jeans. The upscale clubhouse has men's and women's locker room facilities, and a fine selection of clothing and equipment is for sale in the well-stocked Golf Shop. There is no driving range. The practice facility consists of chipping and putting greens and a practice bunker. Professional golf instruction is offered, with nine- or 18-hole playing lessons available. Twilight rates and replay rates are available at both courses.

The Links Course
Since the Links Course is a work in progress, things are subject to change. Currently carts are permitted on the fairway at 90 degrees, but that could change with tender new fairways needing a chance to mature. Walking is not permitted. Green fees will probably increase by the year 2001 at both courses. The Links Course is longer and more challenging than the Ocean Course, and

SCORECARD

THE LINKS COURSE
Architects: Francis Duane with Arnold Palmer
Course Record: NA
Championship: Par 72, 7,131 yards, 75.0 rating for men, 135 slope
Regular: Par 72, 6,434/6,459 yards, 71.8 rating for men, 130 slope
Forward: Par 72, 5,745 yards, 73.3 rating for men, 128 slope
Reserve tee times by calling 650/726-4438 three weeks in advance with a valid credit card.

THE OCEAN COURSE
Architect: Arthur Hills, 1997
Course Record: 64, Aaron Oberholser
Championship: Par 72, 6,732 yards, 71.8 rating for men, 125 slope
Regular: Par 72, 6,339 yards, 69.9 rating, 120 slope
Forward: Par 72, 5,109 yards, 71.6 rating for men, 119 slope
For tee times call 650/726-4438 three weeks in advance with a valid credit card.

residents prefer it because of its more traditional layout. It has one of the highest course ratings in Northern California. Weekend green fees are $115, including cart.

The Ocean Course

The Ocean Course is the one that first-timers want to play the most because of its dramatic terrain. It was selected as one of *Golf Digest*'s "Top 10 Best New Upscale Public Courses." Carts must remain on paths, but walking is permitted. Expect to pay around $135 on weekends including cart.

> **TEE TIDBITS** | Caddy's serves both courses in fine style, from the cozy bar area done in light wood to the spacious restaurant, serving breakfast, lunch, and "lighter fare." Create your own omelet for $7.25. For lunch, the homemade clam chowder is perfect for a blustery day. The spicy seared ahi tuna sandwich and the bleu bacon burger are both delicious, as are the pasta specials. Prices are under $12. Tee times can be made for both courses by calling 650/726-4438 three weeks in advance with a valid credit card.

ALTERNATIVES

Without a driving range at Half Moon Bay, golfers either go to Crystal Springs, which is about 20 minutes away, or they continue on Highway 92 to Foster City and **Mariners Point**. Mariners Point has a two-tier driving range plus 21 grass stalls and is lighted year-round, as is the nine-hole par-3 course. The 18-hole grass putting course costs $5. Soft spikes are required. Located on the bay, Mariners Point can be quite windy.

Lessons are available at the Jim McLean Golf Academy with two indoor video learning centers and video swing analysis. There's a strong junior program. The Grill at Mariners Point serves delicious, innovative meals at lunch, dinner, and Sunday brunch. Full bar. ■ MARINERS POINT GOLF LINKS AND PRACTICE CENTER, 2401 E. 3RD AVE., FOSTER CITY; 650/573-7888

Lodging

ITINERARY SELECTION

The elegant **Ritz-Carlton** stands out as the only major beachfront resort between San Francisco and Monterey. Its 261 rooms have oversized marble baths and luxurious amenities, and guests enjoy the spa and fitness center, six tennis courts, and outdoor fireplaces and hot tubs amidst landscaped gardens. Its dramatic setting above the Pacific means great views. Room rates range $295–2,500. Guests can make one phone call to book room and tee times. ■ 1 MIRAMONTES POINT RD., HALF MOON BAY, CA 94019; 650/712-7000 OR 800/241-3333, FAX 650/712-7070; WEBSITE WWW.RITZCARLTON.COM

GOLF PACKAGE OPTIONS

Half Moon Bay Lodge is the closest hotel to the golf courses, after the Ritz. The tile-roofed two-story hotel offers 81 spacious rooms with one king or two queen beds, refreshment bars, and coffeemakers. Private balconies or patios overlook the Links Course. Heated pool and hot tub. Standard rooms run $175, but the nicest rooms are the deluxe fireplace king rooms for $205. Rates include an expanded continental breakfast. Weekday rates for golf packages are the best, but on the weekends it's $405 for two on the Links Course or $445 for two on the Ocean Course. They also offer a single rate of $290/$310 if two players each want to have their own room.
■ 2400 S. CABRILLO HIGHWAY, HALF MOON BAY, CA 94019; 650/726-9000, FAX 650/726-7951

The Beach House, opened in 1996, is a beautiful 54-room lodge on the ocean side of Highway 1 with wonderful views and the beachside trail right outside your door. The rooms are called "ocean lofts," with defined living room and bedroom areas. All have wood-burning fireplaces, kitchenette with burners, microwave, and refrigerator, as well as a five-disc CD player and two TVs. Heated pool and hot tub. The Anchorage Restaurant next door provides room service, or it's an easy walk. Room rates range $185–280 and include expanded continental breakfast. Golf packages are around $200 per person, double occupancy, for a mountain-view room, including 18 holes with cart, slightly more for an ocean-view room. ■ 4100 COAST HIGHWAY 1, HALF MOON BAY, CA 94019; 650/712-0220 OR 800/315-9366, FAX 650/712-0693; WEBSITE WWW.BEACHHOUSE.COM

ALTERNATIVES

Costanoa has lodgings to suit all price ranges and is a trendsetter in the concept of "upscale camping." It's in Pescadero in a wilderness area that abuts 30,000 acres of parkland. The posh lodge rooms are the only ones with private bathrooms. Then there are the tent accommodations, similar to what you might find on an African safari, ranging in comfort (and price) from deluxe to economy, where you provide your own linens or sleeping bag. Rates include breakfast, and any other gourmet treats you might want are available at the fancy General Store. From economy tent accommodations to premium lodge rooms, the rates range $65–275. ■ 2001 COSTANOA RD. AT HIGHWAY 1, PESCADERO, CA; 650/879-1100; WEBSITE WWW.COSTANOA.COM

Seal Cove Inn offers 10 sumptuously decorated guest rooms in a grand

English Manor–style hotel in secluded parklands amidst wildflowers and cypress trees that look to the ocean. The elegant living room and dining room are furnished with antiques, as throughout the inn. Each room has a sitting area before a fireplace with French doors opening to a small private deck or garden. Owner Karen Brown Herbert is best known for her *Karen Brown's Country Inn Series,* guidebooks to the most charming country inns in Europe and California. Seal Cove Inn is her crown jewel. By the way, you can walk to the Moss Beach Distillery for dinner. Rates range $200–300 and include breakfast. ■ 221 CYPRESS AVE., MOSS BEACH, CA; 650/728-4114, FAX 650/728-4116; WEBSITE WWW.SEALCOVEINN.COM

If you want to stay in a B&B in Half Moon Bay, try the **Mill Rose Inn.** The white building trimmed in blue is a few blocks from downtown and surrounded by gardens, resembling an English country inn. Six cozy rooms are furnished with antiques and lace, and some have clawfoot tubs. An enclosed hot tub sits in the garden, and the Bordeaux Rose suite has a whirlpool tub. Rates run from $165 to $285 and include breakfast delivered to your room, afternoon wine and cheese, and dessert table. ■ 615 MILL ST., HALF MOON BAY, CA; 650/726-9794 OR 800/900-ROSE, FAX 726-3031; WEBSITE WWW.MILLROSEINN.COM

The contemporary **Cypress Inn** sits right on Miramar Beach with the beach trail at your doorstep. The collection of native folk art from the Oaxaca region of Mexico livens up the lobby area and the 12 guest rooms. Eight are in the main house, four in the adjacent Beach House building. Most rooms have decks and fireplaces. Rates range $175–275 for Las Nubes (Clouds), the room with its own hot tub. Included are a lavish full breakfast, afternoon tea, wine and hors d'oeuvres, and dessert. The dessert, coffee, and sherry in the evening are so good that you can skip dessert at dinner. ■ 407 MIRADA RD., HALF MOON BAY, CA; 650/726-6002 OR 800/83-BEACH, FAX 650/712-0380; WEBSITE WWW.CYPRESSINN.COM

Dining

ITINERARY SELECTIONS

Pasta Moon is a local favorite for good reason. It's crisp and sophisticated yet small-town friendly, with great house-made pastas, sometimes creatively combined with fresh local seafood. Full bar and extensive wine list. You'll enjoy talking golf with owner Kim Levin and executive chef Matthew Kurze. Pasta Moon offers wine-tasting dinners, matching a several-course meal with wines from a certain region of Italy. Entrées are under $20. Lunch and dinner. ■ 315 MAIN ST., HALF MOON BAY; 650/726-5125

You can't dine any closer to the ocean than at **Miramar Beach Restaurant.** Sunset is a prime attraction, so the restaurant gives patrons a year-round "Sunrise & Sunset Table," showing the exact time of day for each. Enjoy a sunset cocktail, and you can make a meal out of the generous appetizers like crabcakes or smoked salmon quesadilla. Entrées are a little pricey. Lunch and dinner. ■ 131 MIRADA RD., HALF MOON BAY; 650/726-9053, FAX 650/725-5060

Mezza Luna, which means Half Moon, sits on a sunny corner in Princeton-by-the-Sea with tall arched windows all the way around. The varied menu features steaks, seafood, and Italian dishes with special preparations, like the delicious half-moon-shaped pasta stuffed with fresh salmon in a tomato cream sauce. Live music is featured on Friday and Saturday nights. Full bar. Entrées are under $20. Lunch and dinner.
■ 459 PROSPECT WAY, PRINCETON-BY-THE-SEA; 650/728-8108 OR 650/728-8606, FAX 650/728-8201; WEBSITE WWW.MEZZALUNABYTHESEA.COM

ALTERNATIVES

Rustic **Duarte's Tavern** (202 Stage Rd., Pescadero; 650/879-0464) was once a rowdy saloon and is now known for hearty, old-fashioned cooking, funky and fun. Fans come from all over for the legendary artichoke soup, crab cioppino, and the traditional fruit pies, especially the yummy olallieberry. Duarte's is one of the few places you can still get abalone. Breakfast, lunch, dinner.

For fresh fish served in a rustic atmosphere at budget prices, go to Pillar Pt. Harbor at Princeton-by-the-Sea, where the fishing boats come in. **Ketch Joanne Restaurant & Harbor Bar** (17 Johnson Pier, Pillar Pt. Harbor, Princeton-by-the-Sea; 650/728-3747) is open every day for breakfast, lunch, and dinner, and you'll see an eclectic mix of local fishermen and folks out for the evening. Four couples can fill up the big wooden booth at the entrance. For all the bare decor, the bar is stocked with top labels. Prices are under $15 for entrées that include a salad. You can't miss **Barbara's Fish Trap** right on the water, painted bright orange and gold, with fishnets and seashells hanging from the ceiling of its covered patio entryway, (281 Capistrano Rd., Princeton-by-the-Sea; 650/728-7049). It's a little more touristy but still casual, and the portions are generous. Favorite dishes are the calamari, fish and chips, and the fish of the day sandwich. Entrées include chowder or salad and are under $20.

The Moss Beach Distillery (Beach Way and Ocean Blvd., Moss Beach; 650/728-5595) was once a notorious roadhouse and is now recognized for its great views, especially at sunset. Grab a chair (or two) on the patio, cuddle up in the big blankets, and watch the waves crash on the beach below, with perhaps a thought for the tragic Blue Lady. Steamed mussels and/or clams is a great appetizer with toasted garlic bread. It's a casual, comfortable atmosphere where the view is more of a draw than the food. Lunch, dinner, Sunday brunch, bar and patio menu, and full bar.

Straying Off Course

Browse the galleries, shops, and cafés along Main Street of historic Half Moon Bay, built in 1900. Cunha's Country Store (448 Main St.; 650/726-4071) is a traditional general store with wooden floors, crammed with grocery items on the main floor and household five-and-dime type items upstairs. The Flower Market (650/712-9439) is held the third Saturday of each month from May through September outside at the corner of Kelly and Main. The entire block is used. Growers bring their freshly cut flowers, live plants, and even artwork. Prices are much less than what you're used to, and the flowers will stay fresh for weeks. In the winter the Flower Market is held at La Piazza at Main and Miramontes Streets.

Attend jazz and classical music concerts Saturday nights and Sunday afternoons at the Bach Dancing and Dynamite Society right on Miramar Beach, a tradition since the 1960s. Call 650/726-4143 for the schedule. Stop in at the Dunn Mehler Gallery (650/726-7667) next door, which features sculpture, ceramic, and glass creations.

Pillar Point Harbor is a full-service marina where you can arrange for sportfishing or whale-watching. Commercial fishing boats occupy most of the boat slips, but recreational boats are launched as well, and you can reel in your own "catch of the day" from the public fishing pier.

At Capt. John's (650/726-2913) you can charter a boat, take a trip to the Farallon Islands, or go fishing for salmon. Huck Finn's Sportfishing Center (650/726-7133) schedules year-round rock-fishing trips, as well as seasonal salmon-fishing and whale-watching trips.

Annual Events
Around the corner from Pillar Point at the outer breakwater lie world-class surfing beaches where the annual "Maverick's Men Who Ride Mountains" contest is held. No specific date is set, instead a window of time from November through March is established and surfers are on a 24-hour notice system, summoned when the big waves are near. Maverick's was a secret spot until it hit the cover of *Surfer* magazine. If you're lucky enough to hit the right day, you'll see the world's best surfers battling the monster wave known as "Maverick's," which can be over 30 feet high. The winning surfer gets $30,000, contributed by sponsor Quiksilver.

The Half Moon Bay Pumpkin Festival (650/726-9652) is held in mid-October and has put Half Moon Bay on the map as "Pumpkin Town USA" in its 28 years of operation. There's the Great Pumpkin Weigh-Off, arts and crafts, a pumpkin-carving contest, pumpkin-pie-eating contest, games, and entertainment. Downtown Half Moon Bay is closed off for the festive two-day event.

Outdoors

At Sea Horse Ranch (650/726-2362) you can ride horseback on your own on trails or beaches, or take guided tour rides. See ancient redwoods up close on hiking trails at the Purisima Creek Redwoods (650/691-1200) in Half Moon Bay, or see marine life up close in the natural tidepools at Fitzgerald Marine Reserve (650/728-3584) in Moss Beach. Visit the Año Nuevo State Reserve (650/879-2025) in Pescadero, which is a 1,500-acre protected breeding site for the northern elephant seal. More than 2,000 come ashore annually to give birth to their pups. Guided walks are led December–March.

Stop by Obester Winery (12341 San Mateo Rd., Half Moon Bay; 650/726-9463) for some award-winning local wine and the unusual black fig vinegar. San Mateo Road is also Highway 92.

Details, Details

SUITCASE

It's best to dress in layers on this itinerary. The coast side weather typically is foggy in the summer months, wet and windy in the winter, although between storms in February and March you can find sunny, mild days. Spring is usually clear but windy. Generally September, October, and November bring the best golf weather. It rarely goes above 70 degrees anytime. When temperatures go over 100 degrees in the valley during the summer, golfers flock to the coast.

Even though Crystal Springs is "over the hill" from the coast, it catches some of the same weather patterns. Mornings tend to be calmer, with the wind picking up in the afternoon, so early morning tee times are preferable at both locations.

You'll need soft spikes at Half Moon Bay and at Mariners Point. Bring a swimsuit for the hotel pool and workout clothes for the Ritz. One of the greatest pleasures of a seaside getaway is just walking along the beach. A three-mile paved walkway runs along the beach past Pillar Point Harbor and the Beach House. Take some good, comfortable shoes for beach walking and hiking and definitely pack a windbreaker with a hood and a warm layer for underneath, useful for any outdoor activity including golf.

GETTING THERE

Crystal Springs is adjacent to Interstate 280 in Burlingame, approximately 12 miles south of San Francisco. On I-280 heading north or south, take the Black Mountain Road exit heading west until you come to the stop sign at Golf Course Drive. Turn right onto Golf Course Drive and proceed approximately one-half mile to the clubhouse.

Both San Francisco International Airport and San Jose International Airport are a convenient distance to this destination, as is Half Moon Bay Airport (650/573-3701) for small aircraft.

If you decide to play Half Moon Bay Golf Links on the first day instead, go directly to Half Moon Bay via Highway 92 west to Highway 1. Half Moon Bay Golf Links is three miles south of the intersection of Highway 1 and Highway 92. You'll turn right onto Miramontes Point Road, pass an RV park, and drive for a mile or so to the clubhouse until you see the new two-level parking garage and the clubhouse behind it. After dropping off your bags, you can either park in the garage or in the lot to the right of the clubhouse.

CONTACTS

■ **Half Moon Bay Coastside Chamber of Commerce and Visitors Bureau** 520 Kelly Ave., Half Moon Bay, CA 94019; 650/726-8380, fax 650/726-8389; website www.halfmoonbaychamber.org, email info@halfmoonbaychamber.org/

Chapter 14

Chips Galore: Silicon Valley

Can a vacationing golfer find happiness in the "Tech Capital of the World?" Newcomers to Silicon Valley may see it primarily as a money-making machine, with the profusion of "dot-coms" and 20-something millionaires. Housing prices are out of sight and luxury car dealerships can't keep enough in stock. It follows that the best golf courses in Silicon Valley are the private ones, with membership fees to match, some as high as $300,000. Municipal courses have served the public well for many years but are getting increasingly more crowded and hard to get on, almost taking all the fun out of it.

If you can't play at Los Altos Hills, or Stanford, or CordeValle, or some other fancy private course, what are the golfing choices in Silicon Valley? Surprisingly, there are some excellent options. Demand outpacing supply has spurred the development of new courses south of San Jose in Morgan Hill and Gilroy.

Longtime California residents can't believe the changes in what used to be the bucolic Santa Clara Valley and neighboring areas like Morgan Hill and Gilroy. Up until the 1950s, the valley was a flourishing agricultural area with vast orchards and food processing businesses. It was the land of lawn sprinklers and barbecues. Then it seemed that almost overnight the region launched myriad companies based on computers, electronics, software, research, and all areas of the technology industry, and nothing's been the same since.

The term Silicon Valley was coined by the late Don Hoefler of *Electronic News,* who began using the phrase in trade journal articles in the early 1970s to describe the area that housed so many interrelated technology companies. In the '70s, Intel scientists invented the 4004 microprocessor, the first computer on a chip; Hewlett-Packard introduced the first handheld calculator; and Steve Wozniak and Steve Jobs started Apple Computer from their garage. When personal computers became commonplace and the Internet opened up new worlds, the big money followed. Venture capitalists set up shop on Sand Hill Road in Menlo Park to finance technology ventures and became the subject of a 1999 book by David Kaplan entitled *The Silicon Valley Boys.*

More hands-on than ivory tower, Stanford University professors played a prominent part in the technological innovations, from as far back as 1927 when Fred Terman taught electronics courses at Stanford and later became a mentor to David Packard and William Hewlett. Silicon Graphics founder James Clark was a Stanford professor, and Sun Microsystems was founded by four Stanford grad students. You can take campus tours or ride to the top of the Hoover Tower for a panoramic view of Stanford University.

Silicon Valley is generally considered to run along the peninsula from San Mateo south, and San Jose is the largest city in the region, often described as the "Capital of Silicon Valley." That's a far cry from where it stood in the 1960s when Dionne Warwick sang "Do You Know the Way to San Jose?"

Land soon became more valuable for office parks than for agricultural use. Downtown San Jose was redeveloped and now has a sports arena, a convention center, and a luxurious Fairmont Hotel for all those visiting VIPs. As land and housing prices have escalated, residents and newcomers seeking more affordable housing and services look south to Morgan Hill, Gilroy, and even Hollister. Golf course development has followed the movement to the wide open spaces, and now visitors who would like to do business on the golf course or extend a business trip to play golf over the weekend have several premium, daily-fee courses to choose from. The new golf courses are still mostly "stand-alone" courses, not a resort destination among them. But the hotels, restaurants, and services are not far behind.

One of the most exciting newcomers is Coyote Creek Golf Club, within San Jose city limits but so close to Morgan Hill that it's more closely identified with Morgan Hill. It's on the site of the old Riverside Golf Course. The new Jack Nicklaus Signature Course opened in 1999, with an early California ranch–style clubhouse. The first Siebel Classic in Silicon Valley,

This being high-tech Silicon Valley, the golf carts at Cinnabar Hills are equipped with Global Positioning Systems that can order your lunch and keep score for your group, with a color screen that displays a graphical overview of the golf course. This elaborate system has to be set up properly for the combination of nines you will be playing that day, and those among us who are "high-tech challenged" can ask for assistance from the attendants.

a Senior PGA Tour event, was scheduled for March 2001, bringing national attention to Coyote. The local hospitality industry intended to roll out the welcome mat for visitors.

The course is easily seen off the right side of Highway 101 heading south, and if you look to the left, you'll see the eight holes on the other side of the freeway. A tunnel goes under the freeway connecting the two sides—way too far to walk, so golf carts are mandatory. The course is fairly flat on the west side and more hilly on the east side, with generally long carries and target greens that don't allow for much error or even bump and run shots.

The old Riverside Course was redone by Nicklaus and opens in spring 2001 as the Coyote Creek Valley Course, with the intention of supporting more rounds and being more affordable. Coyote Creek plans to introduce a Nicklaus-Flick Golf Academy, which will offer traditional instruction programs as well as golf schools for several days.

When you ask valley residents for their favorite public course, Cinnabar Hills is at the top of the list. The three nines—Mountain, Lake, and Canyon—sit on top of the world in a truly scenic setting that resembles more private club than public course. Unless you play on a Monday in winter when green fees are only $50, peak rates reflect the value, but you'll get your money's worth. Any combination of nines you play will be in good condition, challenging, and memorable. The grand clubhouse has great food and a fascinating collection of golf memorabilia, collected over the years by partner Lee Brandenburg. Cinnabar was the first public course to open in San Jose in 30 years.

While neither Coyote Creek nor Cinnabar Hills has houses around it, Eagle Ridge Golf Club in Gilroy is just the opposite. Most people associate Gilroy with two things: the outlet stores and garlic. Indeed, garlic has been a source of identity and pride for Gilroy ever since 1979 when the Gilroy Garlic Festival started and Gilroy became internationally acclaimed as a sort of garlic haven. Garlic packing and processing is a multimillion-dollar business, and garlic specialty stores have sprung up to meet consumer demand.

But now there's another reason to put Gilroy on your list of places to go, and that's Eagle Ridge Golf Club. Center of an 1,800-acre master planned community of 890 homes, Eagle Ridge is clearly a draw for real estate sales, but the course is no pushover. Players will find difficult shot-making down narrow corridors with lots of bunkers. But with six tee options to choose from (three rated for women) there should be a spot for players of every level. Johnny Miller designed the course in collaboration with the architects Fream & Dale—Golfplan.

New home construction is booming all around the course, but when you play hole number 11 you'll get an idea of what it will be like when the construction has finished, because completed, occupied homes line the fairway. Those home sites were the first done because they are near the sewer and water hookups. A guard at the entrance to Eagle Ridge will give you a pass for golf course parking for the day. Many of the visitors are coming not for the golf, but to look at the model homes.

Cinnabar Hills and Coyote Creek are only about 15 minutes apart, and Eagle Ridge is just down Highway 101 in Gilroy. As Morgan Hill and Gilroy become bedroom communities for those commuting into San Jose, more businesses will open to serve the needs of these growing towns. The Senior Tour event will heighten awareness of the area as a golf destination and bring tourism infrastructure to support those spectators who, once they see the area, are likely to return. The future of golf in Silicon Valley is south, and the good news is that you don't have to go all the way to Monterey to find great courses. Save the Monterey Peninsula for a special occasion getaway.

Itinerary

WARMING UP

Book tee times ahead and make your hotel reservation. Stay-and-play packages were still in the talking stages at press time, but ask at the golf courses and the hotels to see if they have been implemented. None of the courses has lodging adjacent, so this is a "design-your-own" itinerary. Morgan Hill is the most convenient location for lodging and dining, although, depending on traffic, central San Jose is another option. This is another destination where hotel rates are generally cheaper on the weekends, as the area caters mostly to business travelers during the week.

This is a good escape for serious golfers, maybe not so much fun for the nongolfers. There is lots of driving around between golf, lodging, and dining, and it's an area full of traffic bottlenecks. Coyote Creek is convenient to the freeway, but Cinnabar Hills and Eagle Ridge are more remote. If all you want is basic amenities, you could make this a no-frills getaway by staying at one of the budget motels along Condit Road in Morgan Hill.

The area doesn't hold any great cultural or historical attraction. Shopping probably provides the best diversion. Basically the nongolf activities aren't very close to the golf, unless you go to the outlet malls in Gilroy while your partner is at Eagle Ridge, or go to Stanford Shopping Center while your partner is playing at Palo Alto, Stanford, or Shoreline. You could easily spend all day in either place since there is a big selection of stores. Also University Avenue in Palo Alto has interesting stores. You just don't want to plan activities that are too far away from your golf/lodging base because the traffic in and around Silicon Valley is so bad that to be stuck in it will take all the fun out of your trip.

day 1

Plan to spend the day at Cinnabar Hills Golf Club and play all 27 holes if you can possibly do it. It's about 30 minutes south from downtown San Jose and will take about two hours from San Francisco. If it's a weekend, you can have a full breakfast in the main clubhouse starting at 7 A.M., otherwise it's snack bar service on weekdays.

The roads leading up to Cinnabar Hills wind through rolling foothills, past the Calero Reservoir (which offers boating), until you reach the top of the hill and look over the entire valley. IBM has a large office facility on Bailey Road, and Cisco Systems reportedly plans to build a $1 billion campus on 400 acres nearby on Bailey Road, which will employ approximately 20,000 new workers over a 10-year period, with accompanying new home construction. But Cinnabar Hills is not surrounded by any buildings and probably won't ever be.

The three distinct nines, the Canyon, Lake, and Mountain, are each in play every day, but the combination you will play depends on the time of day and the day of play. The combinations are determined months in advance. You can request a certain combination when you call for tee times, and if it is available you can play it. None of the combinations is considered long, and John Harbottle III's design allows for players of different skill levels to either go for it or choose a safer route on most holes. Environmentally sensitive areas are marked by green stakes.

The greens are big, tiered, and fast on all the nines.

Warm up at the grass-tee driving range, chipping green, or putting greens. Normally the cart rule is 90 degrees, except in wet weather, and we already warned you to ask the cart attendants to set up your GPS for the nines you will be playing that day. The multitask golf carts are also equipped with club cleaners, ball washers, and sand-and-seed mix.

The Lake nine is the flatter side of the course and derives its name from the four-acre lake and two creeks that come into play on most holes. This nine is just to the left of McKean Road as you enter the grounds. The Lake nine starts with a par-5 uphill dogleg left hole number 1. Hole number 4, "the Witch's Nose" is an uphill par-4 with trouble to the right, and is tricky rather than long. The course requires lots of layup shots, especially on hole number 7, where there are creeks and wetlands to be carried before you reach the green, which is pretty much surrounded by the large lake.

The secluded Canyon nine is the most dramatic, with lots of mounding and great variety. Hole number 2 starts from an elevated tee requiring that you carry the lake in front of the green on the second shot. It's not readily apparent that the lake extends almost all the way to the cart path on the right, so if you try to cut it on the right, the little finger of water you can't see from farther back catches the ball every time. The signature hole number 8 is a downhill par-3 with a lake to the left and a target green set against a wooded backdrop. Golf artist Jim Fitzpatrick's painting of hole number 8 hangs in the expansive clubhouse lobby.

Play slows down at par-5 hole number 6, which plays left to right along a creek that requires giving some thought to laying up in order to reach the green. In summer when the ground is hard, you can run the ball up nicely to feed into the hole. You can barely see the putting surface from the very steep fairway at uphill par-4 hole number 7, and the flag looks like it's waving in the clouds, but a stunning full-valley view awaits you from the top. Canyon hole number 9 is the signature hole, and it's a beauty from the elevated tee with big wide fairway, a dogleg left par-5 with small deep bunkers to the right of the green.

The rolling hills of the Mountain nine yield fine views. Par-5 hole number 1 requires carry over a barranca to a wide fairway with bunkers. On hole number 4 you'll need a good tee shot to clear the wetlands. The best views are from the tee of hole number 5. The par-4 hole rolls out amidst natural rock formations and five fairway bunkers, then more bunkers to the large green. The Mountain-Lake combination has the highest course rating of the three combinations. Striped barber poles at 150 yards out on all nines help you line up your shots. Look for the red-tail hawks that claim Cinnabar as their territory and inspired the club's logo.

Enjoy the spacious clubhouse after your round, which offers lunch, a full bar, and an appetizer menu starting at 3 P.M. You could have entrée items, the most expensive of which is the New York steak dinner, or hamburgers and not have to go anywhere else for dinner, or just choose appetizer fare.

Continue on to check in at the Inn at Morgan Hill, about 20 minutes south, where the complimentary cocktail hour is just beginning. From Cinnabar turn right on McKean Road and stay on it for one mile to Bailey

Road. Turn right on Bailey and stay on it for three miles to Monterey Road. Turn right onto Monterey and then left onto Cochrane Road to reach Highway 101 south. It's about five miles to the inn.

The very generous selection 5–7 P.M. includes full bar including local wines (Guglielmo) and beers and a buffet of hot and cold items like sausages, egg rolls, fresh vegetables with dip, a big fruit platter, and cheese and crackers. The buffet is offered in the small dining area off the main lobby, which is also where breakfast is served. Sit there or in the adjacent lounge area with comfy leather couches, or, if it's a nice evening, head for the outdoor patio around the pool and hot tub.

If you want to have dinner on the way to the Inn at Morgan Hill, stop at popular Encore in Morgan Hill, which serves upscale California cuisine.

day 11 The inn's complimentary breakfast is just as generous as the cocktail hour. It offers eggs, pancakes, breakfast, fresh fruit, yogurt, cereal, and breakfast pastries. You'll be well fortified for your round at Coyote Creek Golf Club. From the inn, get back on Highway 101 heading north and exit at Coyote Creek Golf Drive, crossing over the freeway. It's about six miles. You'll see the course on your left.

Coyote Creek Golf Club is the hot spot in South Bay golf, with its Jack Nicklaus Signature Course and the Coyote Creek Valley Course. Both courses share the same pro shop and clubhouse. The Siebel Classic will put Coyote on the map, when Senior PGA Tour players come to town.

Coyote Creek is a Castle & Cooke golf property, and the new clubhouse design was influenced by owner David Murdoch's penchant for bookcases, leather furniture, and a "library look." The painted murals on walls and ceiling were done by his private artist. Murdoch's trademark rose garden is planted in front of the restaurant patio. Coyote looks like a private club with its large covered entryway and circular drive.

The Nicklaus course has five sets of tees, but whatever tees you choose, expect a lot of carry and little forgiveness around the target greens. Carts are mandatory because the course crosses under the freeway. The west side holes are flat, with water and stone bridges and a little creek running through the terrain. The holes across the freeway are hilly. The odd circumstance of having a freeway run through the middle of the golf course doesn't seem to deter proponents of the Tour event, who are delighted with the easy freeway access for spectators and transportation. It can be distracting on some holes, but as one player put it, "I don't mind seeing those cars one bit. It makes me think how lucky I am to be down here playing golf while they're stuck in traffic."

Be aware that what they call "native area" crosses many of the fairways, so get out those lofted clubs. In many cases the best approach is to lay up. The first hole is on the west side. Cross under the freeway and bear left up the hill to reach the second hole, which has views across the freeway and the valley. Hole number 5 is typical of most of the par-3s, which are mostly carry over native area with little fairway to work with. The bunkers to the left of the green are some of the deepest on the course. Most people want to play hole number 8 again because the tee shot, weaving through all those oak trees, looks harder than it is. Then it's time to return to the other side, where hole number 9 comes back to the valley.

At hole number 12, the cars streaming by on Highway 101 to your left don't look very close, but a severe hook shot could reach the freeway. Hole number 14 is the only par-3 on the back nine. The signature hole number 17 starts with an elevated tee and plays to a target green surrounded by water. There's even more water on hole number 18, which has three lakes cascading into one another with waterfalls, and the green sits to the right behind the water. Although most of the greens aren't wrapped by water as much as the last two holes, it's fair to say that there's not much room for error in approach on any of them

Bob Mejias, general manager and director of golf, says that Coyote Creek is typical of Jack Nicklaus's courses. "It's not real demanding off the tee, but Nicklaus designs courses to accentuate the second shot. So everything you do off the tee should be something that will put you in position to have the opportunity to hit an accurate golf shot to the green."

After golf, have lunch in the clubhouse. It's an attractive bar and restaurant area with Southwest-style menu items and an outdoor patio. Then relax with some wine-tasting in nearby Morgan Hill at several family-owned-and-operated wineries that go back for generations.

Guglielmo Winery is on East Main Avenue. Go east on the Dunne Avenue exit from Highway 101 and turn left on Condit Road, then right on Main, and the winery will be about a quarter mile down the road. The tasting room is in an old-fashioned small building with a friendly, cozy atmosphere. Premium varietal wines under the Guglielmo Private Reserve label have won awards.

From Guglielmo you can come back down Condit Road and turn right on San Pedro Avenue to reach Pedrizetti Winery, which has an attractive, high-ceilinged Mediterranean-style tasting room that looks like it belongs in the Napa Valley. A separate tasting bar for events opens up to the vine-trellised patio. The Pedrizetti family has owned and operated the winery for more than 50 years. You won't need an appointment at either winery, and there is no tasting fee.

You could go back to the Inn at Morgan Hill, maybe take a swim or a hot tub, before dining at the Golden Oak Restaurant, a 66-year-old converted winery on Condit Road, a short drive away.

day III Enjoy the generous breakfast and perhaps the workout room. In summer, a swim in the pool would be nice. Then it's off for your tee time at Eagle Ridge Golf Club in Gilroy. Take Highway 101 south. Exit at Masten/Fitzgerald Avenue heading west. Turn left onto Santa Teresa Avenue and head south. Eagle Ridge is about four miles from Masten/Fitzgerald and the first road after 1st Street.

New home signs announce Eagle Ridge before you see the golf course. In the foothills west of Gilroy, this bustling new community reflects the transformation of Gilroy into a sort of San Jose suburb. Eagle Ridge Golf Club was designed by Golfplan's Ron Fream and David Dale, together with Johnny Miller. Six tee boxes span the distance from 7,005 yards at the back tees to 5,012 yards from the forward tees.

We may as well tell you that this beautiful course is just full of bunkers, and some are huge. Superintendent Frank Zamazal, usually accompanied by his dog, Tamara, says there are four acres of bunkers in all, which are high-maintenance because many have to be hand-raked. You'll particularly want to stay away from the "riveted bunker" to the right of the sixth green, patterned after the one on hole number 11 at St. Andrews. It's about five feet deep.

On hole number 4, the first par-5, aim right to avoid a grand old oak tree down the left center of the fairway and the bunkers all along the left. Hole number 5 is somewhat deceptive when you look back from the green and realize how much room you really had. Long hitters will probably lay up to avoid the water hazard. Hole number 8 is a par-4 that goes back up the canyon past the clubhouse and is considered the signature hole with its mountain backdrop. Walkers will find a short but quite steep climb up to the ninth tee. The course climbs more after hole number 12, which runs along Santa Teresa Avenue and requires both tee shot and approach shot to carry water. There are more steep walks from hole number 12 to the 13th tee and again between hole number 14 and hole number 15.

Hole number 14 looks like a piece of green ribbon from the elevated tee of hole number 15, a beautiful short par-4. Hole number 18 is a dramatic finishing hole. The 411-yard par-4 rolls down to a large barranca on the way to the multitiered green. We hear the barranca may be tamed to become a more playable area.

As general manager during the opening stages, Scot Hathaway watched Eagle Ridge develop. He says don't be intimidated by what you see because there's always a bailout area, and the bunkers don't come into play as much as it looks like they would. Your enjoyment of Eagle Ridge has a lot to do with selecting the proper set of tees for your skill level.

After golf, relax on the clubhouse deck before heading over to Joe's Ristorante for dinner, just a few miles away.

✐ NOTES

Extended Stay in Gilroy. Stay at the Forest Park Inn, then shop at Prime Outlets, where they have more than 100 outlet stores, or go wine-tasting on the scenic Hecker Pass Road, which is also Highway 152, leading to the coast.

Extended Play. Play at Santa Teresa Golf Club, a popular municipal course in San Jose. The additional nine-hole, par-three layout allows up to five players so a family can have a fun outing. Stay overnight at the San Jose Fairmont and dine at 71 Saint Peter. Visit the Tech Museum of Innovation across the street from the Fairmont, which has been called "a theme park for your brain."

Money Savers. Check out the winter golf specials, which usually last until March 31.

Extended Play for Conventioneers. Play golf at Santa Clara Golf and Tennis Club, walking distance to the Santa Clara Convention Center and the Westin Hotel. David's Restaurant at the golf course is a popular lunch spot with local businesspeople as well as golfers. The San Francisco 49ers' headquarters are across the street. Across from the convention center there's a pedestrian entrance to Paramount's Great America, a theme park that boasts "the most coasters and thrill rides in Northern California."

Extended Play for Academics and Shoppers. Stay at the Stanford Park Hotel and explore Stanford University and Stanford Shopping Center, just across the street. The Duck Club in Stanford Park Hotel is a fine restaurant, or you could try some of Palo Alto's great restaurants along University Avenue. Two municipal courses are nearby, Palo Alto Golf Course and Shoreline Golf Course. Tiger Woods, Notah Begay, Casey Martin, and other young Tour players honed their skills at Stanford University Golf Course, which is private, but the driving range is open to the public.

Traffic. Commute traffic to and from Silicon Valley is very heavy morning and evening, whether you choose Highway 101 or I-280. Take potential delays into consideration in your planning. Also south of San Jose the freeway changes from three lanes to two, which creates a slowdown for a few miles.

Courses

ITINERARY SELECTIONS

Cinnabar Hills Golf Club
23600 McKean Rd.
San Jose, CA 95141
408/323-5200, fax 408/323-9512
website www.cinnabarhills.com

Cinnabar Hills gives you the option of walking the course for a reduced green fee during the week before twilight hours, but on weekends the cart is included in the $100 green fee. If you want to play another nine or even 18 after your round, the additional fee will be the twilight rate. The Early Bird Special rate of $60 includes a cart for all times before 7:30 A.M. on Fridays only. The course offers twilight rates and junior rates. Soft spikes are required.

TEE TIDBITS | The grass tee driving range, putting greens, and chipping area are convenient to all three nines. The grand 25,000 square-foot clubhouse has a resort feel. Leave enough time to explore the fully-equipped golf shop and the Brandenburg Historic Golf Museum, an expansive collection displayed in glass cabinets in the lobby. There are historical golf photos, old tournament programs, Billy Casper's wedge (1973), Richard Nixon's driver, and the original green member's jacket worn by President Dwight D. Eisenhower when in residence at Augusta National in the 1950s.

Cinnabar has one of the biggest clubhouse dining areas, including patio seating, and serves large groups well. Full breakfast service is only on weekends, but lunch is served daily, appetizers after 3 P.M. The varied menu offers several large entrée salads, hearty sandwiches like Philly cheese steak or gyros, burgers, pastas, and even fish and chips. Most items are under $10.

SCORECARD

Architect: John Harbottle III, 1997
Course Record: NA

MOUNTAIN-CANYON
Hawk: Par 72, 6,641 yards, 72.2 rating for men, 135 slope
Cinnabar: Par 72, 6,269 yards, 70.5 rating for men, 131 slope
Quicksilver: Par 72, 5,713 yards, 67.8 rating for men, 125 slope
Oak: Par 72, 4,859 yards, 68.1 rating for women, 118 slope

LAKE-MOUNTAIN
Hawk: Par 72, 6,653 yards, 73.1 rating for men, 135 slope
Cinnabar: Par 72, 6,397 yards, 70.8 rating for men, 130 slope
Quicksilver: Par 72, 5,850 yards, 68.2 rating for men, 124 slope
Oak: Par 72, 5,010 yards, 68.1 rating for women, 120 slope

CANYON-LAKE
Hawk: Par 72, 6,688 yards, 72.5 rating for men, 134 slope
Cinnabar: Par 72, 6,318 yards, 70.7 rating for men, 130 slope
Quicksilver: Par 72, 5,827 yards, 68.2 rating for men, 125 slope
Oak: Par 72, 4,959 yards, 68.4 rating for women, 121 slope

For tee times call 408/323-5200 or 408/323-7880 two weeks in advance.

Coyote Creek Golf Club

1 Coyote Creek Dr.
San Jose, CA 95037
408/463-1400
website www.coyotecreekgolf.com

Coyote Creek requires a cart, but not the new Valley course. Weekend rates are around $90. Usually carts can go on the fairways at 90 degrees. Twilight rates and junior rates are available, and seniors can play on Mondays for $60. Green fees are expected to be just above $40 to walk the Valley course. Coyote is a soft-spike facility and requires appropriate golf attire, which means a collared shirt for men and no jeans, tank tops, T-shirts, or cutoffs are permitted. Coyote is poised to be a significant teaching facility. The new full length driving range is double-ended, with a practice hole and chipping and putting areas. Coyote is fast gaining a reputation for its friendly staff.

SCORECARD

Architect: Jack Nicklaus, 1999
Course Record: NA
Black: Par 72, 7,027 yards, 75.5 rating for men, slope 141
Blue: Par 72, 6,633 yards, 73.4 rating for men, 130 slope
White: Par 72, 6,420 yards, 72.4 rating for men, 128 slope
Gold: Par 72, 5,907 yards, 70.2 rating for men, 123 slope; 74.4 rating for women, 132 slope
Red: Par 72, 5,184 yards, 70.4 rating for women, 124 slope
For tee times call 408/463-1400 three weeks in advance.

TEE TIDBITS | The comfortable clubhouse has a well-stocked pro shop, locker rooms, and a free shoe-cleaning service. An intimate dining room and bar area opens onto a patio facing the rose garden. Menu selections for both breakfast and lunch favor a Southwestern theme, like chicken San Jose or The Yucatan, a New York strip steak with south of the border spices. Prices are under $10.

Eagle Ridge Golf Club

2951 Club Dr.
Gilroy, CA 95020
408/846-4531

Walking is permitted at Eagle Ridge and it does rent pull carts, but it's a tough climb in several places. On the weekends it's around $95 including cart. Twilight rates apply, and seniors get a discount on Thursdays. Carts must stay on paths. The practice range has both grass and mats and offers short game and bunker practice. The sloped putting green will prepare you for the course.

Eagle Ridge is a soft spikes facility and insists on appropriate golf attire. Shorts must be mid-thigh length or longer.

SCORECARD

Architects: Johnny Miller and Fream & Dale—Golfplan, 1999
Course Record: 70, Brian Shayne
Black: Par 72, 7,005 yards, 74.0 rating for men, 138 slope
Blue: Par 72, 6,665 yards, 72.2 rating for men, 136 slope
White: Par 72, 6,290 yards, 70.4 rating for men, 131 slope
Yellow: Par 72, 5,959 yards, 68.9 rating for men, 129 slope; 74.5 rating for women, 133 slope
Green: Par 72, 5,546 yards, 72.2 rating for women, 128 slope
Burgundy: Par 72, 5,102 yards, 69.6 rating for women, 119 slope
Tee times can be made 30 days in advance by calling 408/846-4531.

TEE TIDBITS | The Monterey Colonial-style clubhouse is a traditional white building with green trim including the railings around the outside deck. It contains well-appointed locker rooms and a somewhat cramped pro shop, but the dining room is spacious and open for breakfast and lunch. You can build your own burger starting at $6.75 and adding items for 50 cents each. Entrées are just under $15.

Golfers may find the main road to be a little congested once all the homes are finished and occupied. Homeowners will receive golf benefits.

ALTERNATIVES

Santa Teresa Golf Club has long been one of the South Bay's best public courses. It's so popular that tee-time reservations are alternately taken, one from the counter, one from the telephone. It can be a long round on weekends. With the flat front nine and hilly back nine, Santa Teresa is like two different golf experiences. There are three tee settings, the back at 6,742 yards. Groups of more than four can play on the Short Course, built in 1996, as long as they keep up. It's a fun nine-hole par-3 of 922 yards, played first-come, first-served. There's a driving range. Green fees are $44 plus $24 for carts. The Short Course is $14. Twilight and back nine rates are available, and students and seniors play for less during the week.
■ 260 BERNAL RD., SAN JOSE, CA 95119-1899; 408/225-2650

Santa Clara Golf & Tennis Club offers 18 holes designed by Robert Muir Graves, seven lighted tennis courts, and a 35-station lighted golf practice range. It's a long rolling course that can be windy. Many of the holes play parallel and you can be out of bounds on another fairway. It's managed by American Golf and next to the Santa Clara Convention Center and the Westin Santa Clara. David's Restaurant on site is popular for breakfast, lunch, and dinner. Rates are $36 plus $24 for carts. Residents of the city of Santa Clara get discounts, as do Westin guests. ■ 5155 STARS & STRIPES DR., SANTA CLARA, CA 95054; 408/980-9515

Palo Alto Golf Course just completed a major renovation with replacement of greens and fairways and drainage work. A back set of tees was added so there are now four sets of tees. Some yardage was changed but not dramatically. It offers a night lighted driving range and full service restaurant. Green fees are $35 plus $22 for carts. ■ 1875 EMBARCADERO RD., PALO ALTO, CA 94303; 650/856-0881

Shoreline Golf Links is part of a busy park area that includes the Shoreline Amphitheatre and a nearby sailing lake for small boats and windsurfing. The course can be windy too. Lakes come into play on many holes and attract waterfowl. Be careful what you step in. Since it's built on landfill, new drainage work had to be done on both nines, scheduled for spring 2001 completion. There is a night lighted driving range. Michael's Restaurant opens out to a patio overlooking the pond and is much better than usual grill fare. Green fees are $42 plus $22 for carts. The City of Mountain View operates the course, so residents receive discounted fees. ■ 2940 N. SHORELINE BLVD., MOUNTAIN VIEW, CA 94043; 650/969-2041

Deep Cliff Golf Course is an 18-hole executive course, great for new players who aren't yet ready for a regulation course or for more experienced players seeking to practice. The scenic little course winds through a canyon with little streams and trees. It's fairly flat. Plan on carrying or pulling your bag, because they don't have power carts. It can be slow on weekends. Green fees are $33. ■ 10700 CLUBHOUSE LANE, CUPERTINO, CA 95014; 408/253-5357

Find a CEO or otherwise well-connected friend to take you to member-only **CordeValle Golf Club,** which opened in 1999. Robert Trent Jones Jr. designed a spectacular course in a secluded valley with a luxurious club-house that includes full fitness center and spa, cigar room, meeting rooms, and a gourmet dining room. Bungalow-style suites accommodate overnight guests. CordeValle even enticed Joe Root, popular director of golf at Mauna Kea Resort, to leave the balmy shores of Hawaii to run the golf operation. CordeValle has its own winery, Clos LaChance. Typical members would be Silicon Valley executives who want to relax, entertain clients, and do some business in a private, resort-like setting. ■ 1005 HIGHLANDS AVE., SAN MARTIN, CA 95026; 408/278-7280

Lodging

ITINERARY SELECTION

You can see the **Inn at Morgan Hill** from Highway 101, off of Tennant Avenue, but it's set back far enough to escape the noise. Although the California Mission–style architecture suits the historical aspect of Santa Clara Valley, the interiors and amenities are up-to-date and thoroughly modern. The 100 oversized guest rooms have TV and VCR, refrigerators or wet bars, coffeemakers, microwaves, irons, and ironing boards. Many rooms have fireplaces and whirlpool baths. Rates include full buffet breakfast and plentiful hors d'oeuvres and drinks 5–7 P.M. Room rates run $129–319 during the week. Manager Rich Higdon offers a $109 rate to golfers on the weekends. Golf packages are in the works. ■ 16115 CONDIT RD., MORGAN HILL, CA 95037; 408/779-7666 OR 800/645-3450, FAX 408/779-8757; WEBSITE WWW.INNMH.COM

GOLF PACKAGE OPTIONS

The Westin Santa Clara is a 500-room luxury hotel connected to the Santa Clara Convention Center. The new sundeck has poolside cabanas fully equipped with Internet access. Westin guests are entitled to pay resident green fees at next door Santa Clara Golf & Tennis Club. Room rates start around $325 but can go down by 50 percent on the weekends.
■ 5101 GREAT AMERICA PARKWAY, SANTA CLARA, CA 95054; 408/986-0700

The 541-room **San Jose Fairmont Hotel** hosts VIPs, foreign dignitaries, and high school proms. It's big, lavish, and so downtown, if that's what you're looking for. The 24-hour multilingual staff will tend to your every need. A golf package with Cinnabar Hills is proposed, but check the website, www.fairmont.com, for updates. Room rates range $150–350 for a standard room with one king or two double beds, depending on the hotel's occupancy level. ■ 170 S. MARKET ST., SAN JOSE, CA 95113; 408/998-1900, FAX 408/287-1648

ALTERNATIVES

Forest Park Inn is conveniently located on Gilroy's main street, with Lyon's Restaurant next door. The attractive entryway crosses over a tranquil fishpond lined with bamboo. Guest rooms are comfortable and well lit, with little atmosphere. There's a pool and tennis court. This is the closest lodging to the Gilroy Outlets, and to Eagle Ridge, and the inn may offer a golf package by the time you read this. Rates run from $60 up to $99 for a suite with fireplace and hot tub. ■ 375 LEAVESLEY RD., GILROY, CA 95020; 408/848-5144, FAX 408/848-1138; WEBSITE WWW.FORESTPARKINN.COM

The Stanford Park Hotel sits back from El Camino Real in Menlo Park, just across from Stanford Shopping Center. Elegant but not pretentious, this hotel is a favorite of visiting executives to Silicon Valley. Try to get a room around the beautifully landscaped courtyard or the serene pool and hot tub area in the back of the property. Guest rooms have recently been redone in luxurious fabrics, and some feature fireplaces and vaulted ceilings. The circular drive leads to the spacious lobby and to the Duck Club Restaurant, worthy of a visit. In the evenings, live piano music from the Lounge serenades the lobby area as well, just about the time they're setting out the coffee, tea, and cookies. Room rates range $280–495. ■ 100 EL CAMINO REAL, MENLO PARK, CA 94025; 650/322-1234

The Holiday Inn Express Hotel & Suites is an upscale Holiday Inn that opened in 1999 and more closely resembles an Embassy Suites Hotel, conveniently located at the Dunne Avenue exit off Highway 101. The 62 rooms and 22 suites sit around an attractive central atrium and are conveniently equipped with high-tech features like Internet access, Nintendo 64, and DVD players (in the suites only). Rates run $119–189 and include an expanded continental breakfast. The hotel is working on a golf package. ■ 17035 CONDIT RD., MORGAN HILL, CA 95037; 408/776-7676, FAX 408/776-1577

Between the Inn at Morgan Hill and the Holiday Inn Express are several hotels along the 16000 block of Condit Road that would be ideal for a budget golf getaway. You can find a room for under $100 that includes continental breakfast and a swimming pool. The nicest in this category is the **Best Western Country Inn** (408/779-0447 or 888/434-1444), next door to the Golden Oak Restaurant. Hotel guests get a 10 percent discount at the restaurant. The **Comfort Inn** opened in 1999 (408/778-3400). **Executive Inn Suites** has some rooms with hot tubs (800/626-4224 or 408/778-0404). If you want to pay around $60 with no frills, go to the **Microtel Inn & Suites** (888/771-7171 or 408/782-5000).

Dining

ITINERARY SELECTIONS

Encore Café has been pleasing customers since 1996 at its offbeat location next to a laundromat. The upscale California cuisine menu changes with the seasons. Chef Kathleen Lynch was sous chef and pastry chef at the Los Gatos Brewing Company when Encore owner Jennifer Colasuonno was general manager. Menu favorites are rack of lamb and Indian salmon bake, and of course, Lynch's award-winning tiramisu. Entrées range $15–27. Lunch and dinner. ■ 207 W. MAIN AVE., MORGAN HILL; 408/782-2505

The Golden Oak Restaurant was an operating winery 66 years ago, then was used as the tasting room for San Martin Winery until 1985, when it was converted into the present-day restaurant after approximately $1.5 million of renovations. The tree-shaded building features high ceilings, several banquet rooms, and a piano bar lounge. It's a traditional continental menu, not for the lactose intolerant. Rich cream sauces accompany fettuccine Alfredo, tortellini gorgonzola, and chicken Dijonnaise. Entrée prices are under $20 and include soup or salad. Lunch and dinner. ■ 16695 CONDIT RD., MORGAN HILL; 408/779-8085; WEBSITE WWW.GOLDENOAKRESTAURANT.COM

Drive only a mile or so from Eagle Ridge to **Joe's Ristorante Italiano,** owned by Joe and Elviar Bertolone since 1981. On the corner in a shopping center, it's open and friendly with lazy ceiling fans and Italian music. Joe will tell you what's best tonight. Try the homemade pasta or the house special scaloppini à la Marsala. Portions are generous and include minestrone soup or salad. Entrée prices start at $7 for spaghetti and meatballs

and stay under $20. The pizza is good too. Lunch, dinner, Sunday brunch.
■ 1360 1st St., Gilroy; 408/842-1446, fax 408/842-9780

ALTERNATIVES

71 Saint Peter (71 N. San Pedro St., San Jose; 408/971-8523, fax 408/938-3440; website www.71saintpeter.com) is in the popular San Pedro Square area of downtown San Jose. The brick walls, wooden beams, and candlelit tables create a cozy, intimate atmosphere. Some tables are out on the sidewalk. Say hello to owner Armand Tiano, who's also a golfer. Some of the top choices on the creative menu are seafood linguine and grilled lamb. Entrée prices range $15–22. Lunch and dinner.

A local tradition, **David's Restaurant** at Santa Clara Golf & Tennis Club (5151 Stars & Stripes Dr., Santa Clara; 408/986-1666, fax 408/727-0927) is right next door to the Santa Clara Convention Center and across the street from San Francisco 49ers headquarters. Sometimes golfers have trouble getting a seat midday because it's so popular with local business people. David's is convenient and reasonably priced, serves generous portions, and includes soup or salad with the entrées. The lunch menu is longer than the dinner menu. At dinner, David's seafood platter of seasonal fresh fish is popular, as is the grilled filet mignon with peppercorn sauce. Prices range $15–20. Breakfast, lunch, dinner.

The Duck Club Restaurant in Stanford Park Hotel (100 El Camino Real, Menlo Park; 650/330-2790) is open until midnight so you can come early or late. Stop in the lounge for the homemade potato chips, unusually light. Naturally, Governor Stanford's roast duck would be the signature dinner entrée. It's a delicious half duck with crispy skin. The foie gras melts in your mouth and the crabcakes are divine. Five Onion Soup was featured in *Bon Appetit Magazine* and appears on the lunch and dinner menus. Look for a creative twist to traditional favorites like eggs Benedict, prepared with smoked salmon, crabmeat, or vegetarian. You can have roasted duck confit on your Caesar salad. Dinner entrées run $16–30. Ask for a seat on the small patio at an umbrella table when the weather is nice. Breakfast, lunch, dinner.

University Avenue in Palo Alto has some wonderful stores and, on the side streets, some great restaurants. Try **Spago** (265 Lytton Ave.; 650/833-1000), another Wolfgang Puck creation, a worthy successor to the original in L.A. **Evvia** (420 Emerson; 650/326-0983) serves Greek food with a new and lighter touch. **Zibbibo** (430 Kipling St.; 650/328-6722) is a Mediterranean-style restaurant and a popular hot spot, much like Lulu, its sister establishment in San Francisco, although not as cavernous. The **Mandarin Gourmet** (420 Ramona St.; 650/328-8898) offers reliably good upscale Chinese food.

For an old-fashioned milk shake or burger and onion rings, go back to the '50s-like **Peninsula Fountain & Grill** (566 Emerson St.; 650/323-3131), not far from the wonderful **Whole Foods Market** (774 Emerson; 650/326-8676), which has a big selection of healthy takeout items.

Sinaloa Café (19210 Monterey Rd., Morgan Hill; 408/779-9740) is a casual, popular local spot for old-fashioned Mexican food without any fancy trimmings, just plain and simple. Everything is under $10. You can create your own burrito for $3.50. The six deluxe dinner combinations are a good value. Homemade crispy tortilla chips and two choices of salsa— hot and very hot—pique your thirst for that margarita. Lunch and dinner.

Straying Off Course

Near the Golf Courses in the Itinerary
Wine-tastings at Guglielmo Winery (1480 E. Main Ave., Morgan Hill; 408/779-2145, fax 408/779-3166; website www.guglielmowinery.com) and Pedrizetti Winery (1645 San Pedro Ave., Morgan Hill; 408/779-7389, fax 408/779-9083) are a good way to while away an afternoon in Morgan Hill. If you have more time, follow scenic Hecker Pass Road (Highway 152) west of Gilroy to the coast and stop at wineries along the way.

The many county and state parks in the area offer hiking and biking. The biggest is Henry W. Coe State Park (408/779-2728), 79,000 acres 14 miles east of Highway 101 in Morgan Hill. The highest point is 3,560 feet.

Boating is popular at Anderson Reservoir (408/779-3634), off Highway 101 in Morgan Hill, the county's largest reservoir, with a boat launch area and picnic area. Calero Reservoir and Park (408/268-3883), near Cinnabar Hills, offers power-boating and water-skiing. The Equestrian Center (408/268-2567) has trail rides on more than 2,000 acres.

You can find some bargains at the more than 100 outlet stores of Prime Outlets in Gilroy (408/842-3729). Exit Highway 101 at Leavesley Road.

The Annual Gilroy Garlic Festival (408/842-1625), traditionally held the last weekend in July, draws thousands of visitors. Chefs create outrageous garlic-flavored dishes, even desserts, to celebrate "the stinking rose." There's lots of entertainment and arts and crafts booths.

San Jose and North
Entertainment activities abound. There are outdoor concerts in the summer at various venues, like Villa Montalvo (15400 Montalvo Rd., Saratoga; 408/741-3421), former home of U.S. Senator James Phelan, now a park and center for fine arts. Shoreline Amphitheatre (1 Amphitheatre Parkway, Mountain View; 650/967-4040) always has an all-star lineup.

Sports fans like the San Jose Arena, which seats 20,000 and is home to the San Jose Sharks ice hockey team. The arena doubles as an entertainment venue where such stars as Luciano Pavarotti have performed. For walking tours call 408/999-5823.

Kids love Paramount's two theme parks, Raging Waters (Tully Road at Capitol Expressway, San Jose; 408/654-5450) and Great America (Great America Parkway and Mission College Blvd., Santa Clara; 408/988-1776), which is across the street from the Santa Clara Convention Center.

The history of the area is reflected in the Mission Santa Clara de Asis (408/554-4023), founded in 1777 as the eighth in the chain of missions built from Mexico to Sonoma. It's on the grounds of Santa Clara University at 500 El Camino Real, and the mission church is open daily.

There's an odd mix of museums in the area, from the Rosicrucian Egyptian Museum & Planetarium (1342 Naglee Ave., San Jose; 408/947-3600), which houses the largest public collection of Egyptian artifacts in the West, to the Tech Museum of Innovation (201 S. Market St., San Jose; 408/795-6100), where it's fun to explore the spirit of innovation through the interactive exhibits and displays and to visit the IMAX Dome Theatre. Learn all about computer chips at the Intel Museum (2200 Mission College Blvd., Santa Clara; 408/765-0503). The bizarre building spree that created the Winchester Mystery House (525 S. Winchester Blvd., San Jose; 408/247-2101; website www.winchestermysteryhouse.com) is a mystery to most, but the dramatic 160-room Victorian mansion is beautiful and evokes all sorts of questions.

Open-air Stanford Shopping Center (adjacent to Stanford University off El Camino Real, Palo Alto; 800/772-9332; website www.stanfordshop.com) has more than 140 stores, many restaurants, and numerous coffee shops. It's considered one of the best shopping centers in the country. You can shop the boutiques or department stores like Macy's, Neiman-Marcus, Bloomingdale's, and Nordstrom. There's even a European-style open market.

Visit Stanford University Campus on a walking tour (650/723-2560) or take an elevator ride to the top of the 285-foot Hoover Tower (650/723-3563) for a different view. The Rodin Sculpture Garden (650/723-3469) contains the largest collection of the famous artist's bronze sculptures outside of Paris.

Details, Details

SUITCASE

Locals will tell you they go to the coast to play golf in the summer, when a 30-degree temperature drop between the valley and the coast is not unusual. Inland temperatures can soar to over 100 degrees, and in some of the valleys it can be suffocating. For summer play, book an early tee time or play at twilight, and bring a hat and sunscreen.

Casual attire is appropriate in Morgan Hill. You'd want to dress up a little if you're dining at the elegant Stanford Park Hotel in Palo Alto or if you're at the ritzy Fairmont Hotel in downtown San Jose. Soft spikes are required most everywhere, and you'll want a swimsuit and workout clothes.

GETTING THERE

To reach Cinnabar Hills, from San Jose take Highway 101 south or Highway 85 south, exit Bernal Road. Turn right on Bernal (west) until you get to Santa Teresa Boulevard (stoplight, one mile). Turn left on Santa Teresa Boulevard, go until you get to Bailey Avenue (stoplight, three miles). Turn right on Bailey Avenue, go until it dead-ends into McKean Road (stop sign, two miles). Turn left on McKean Road. Cinnabar Hills will be on your left-hand side in one mile.

From Gilroy, take Highway 101 north, exit Cochrane Road. Turn left on Cochrane (west) and go until you get to Monterey Road (stoplight). Turn right on Monterey Road and go to Bailey Avenue (stoplight, 5.5 miles). Turn left on Bailey Avenue and go three miles until it dead-ends into McKean Road (stop sign). Turn left on McKean Road. Cinnabar Hills will be on your left-hand side in one mile.

San Jose International Airport is the closest major airport, and small aircraft can use the San Martin–South County Airport of Santa Clara County (408/683-4741).

CONTACTS

- **Gilroy Visitors Bureau** 7780 Monterey, Gilroy, CA 95020; 408/842-6346; website www.gilroyvisitor.org
- **Morgan Hill Chamber of Commerce** 25 W. 1st St., Morgan Hill, CA 95037; 408/779-9444, fax 408/779-5405; website www.morganhill.org/mhcc
- **San Jose Convention & Visitors Bureau** This is San Jose's official website and connects visitors with current info on events in the area. 333 W. San Carlos St., Suite 1000, San Jose, CA 95110; 408/295-9600; website www.sanjose.org
- **Santa Clara Chamber of Commerce & Convention-Visitors Bureau** 1850 Warburton Ave., Santa Clara, CA 95050; 408/244-9660 or 800/272-6822, fax 408/244-9202; website www.santaclara.org

Chapter 15

Where the Sun Usually Shines: Santa Cruz

There are so many reasons why sunny Santa Cruz makes for a great golf destination, beginning with the mild climate. But there are so many reasons why sunny Santa Cruz makes for a great anything destination, beginning with the mild climate, that we dare you to try to make this a golfers-only escape. There are world-class beaches to suit the great weather, fun family attractions and amusements for the kids, and plenty of fresh seafood and produce for chefs who know just what to do with them. Imagine telling your nongolfing loved ones, "Sorry, gotta go to Santa Cruz for the weekend. Just a little golf for the regular foursome, you understand. But don't worry, I'll bring back a suntan for you." Well, sorry, golf nuts, that's not going to go over very well. Everyone in the family loves to visit Santa Cruz, especially in the summer, and so the golfers in the bunch are just going to have to get used to some company for this escape.

And when you think about it, the sprawling Santa Cruz County area sets up beautifully for accommodating a variety of vacation agendas all within one car. There's enough to do in Santa Cruz, between beaches and mountains, Boardwalk and boardsailing, to please child, teen, and grownup while the golfer gets dropped off nearby for 18 holes that will surely take four hours, going on five. The dangers for the golfer are twofold: finding room in the car for the clubs amid bikes, beach chairs, and cooler, and resisting the temptation to leave the clubs at home and pack nothing but the swimsuit.

Don't do it. We're here to tell you that if you succumb to the lure of the surf, you'll be missing some fabulous golf, including some of the best public golf courses anywhere in Northern California and, in Pasatiempo, one of the most renowned and elite semiprivate courses in the nation. The golf boom began here in the '20s as an extension from what was developing in Monterey and Pebble Beach, but today Santa Cruz stands on its own as a worthy golf destination, distinguished by its ample selection of fabulously fun, beautiful, challenging, and friendly 18s—all of them with, of course, that famous weather, which makes it sunnier than Monterey, warmer than San Francisco, and cooler than San Jose. Pajaro Valley head pro Bob Bowker likes to call it "the banana belt," because even with 300 days of sunshine it never gets uncomfortably hot or ungolfingly cold. The lay of the land and soil structure at all of the courses we will visit in this chapter make for excellent drainage, so that the Santa Cruz County courses are often playable when others are sopping from winter storms. And with the overall agricultural richness of the area—many of the flowers you buy at the grocery store or nursery sprouted in the fields here—its golf courses tend to be colorfully accessorized in flower beds and bushes, luring birds and bees while uplifting the greened out golfer.

If you're a student of golf history, you no doubt think that Pasatiempo was the first and is, thus, the oldest of the Santa Cruz County courses. In fact, about 20 miles south of the land that would become Pasatiempo in 1929, Pajaro Valley opened as a nine-hole golf course in 1922. In 1953, when Charlie Leider's father and uncle acquired the course, that nine was remodeled and a second nine was added, and in 1969 the whole 18 was renovated once more. In 1999, Leider had returned to take back the course after 31 years of management by the Lombardo Group, and yet another renovation was launched to add yet another nine. First, the clubhouse got a facelift. That included a spiffy new restaurant, with a new head chef, and a remodeled pro shop, which already had a strong reputation for selection and affordability among the locals. Next, ParView's GPS system was installed on the carts.

And if you prefer walking, Pajaro Valley is your course. Its fairways roll gently through 75-year-old cypresses and Monterey pines, and there are views of the Elkhorn Slough National Preserve just to the southwest. In the traditional, walkable style, greens generally transition easily to tees, of which there were three sets at press time. Bowker and Leider, however, have big plans for Pajaro Valley. "I came back down here to fulfill my dream to build a great golf course here," said Leider. An additional nine holes is on architect David Pfaff's drawing board, with perhaps additional tee options to alter the dimensions of a course that measured up only to 6,234 yards at its fullest.

That's not to say that Pajaro Valley has been easy or boring. As Bowker puts it, "It's not too easy. It has a few blind spots but no strange holes, and it doesn't beat your brains out." The par-4 second hole, for example, offers a testy approach shot, with water to the far right of a small green bounded on the left and right sides by bunkers, and the third hole is a pretty 130- to 189-yard par-3 with water in front of the tee yet plenty of safety beyond.

But if the new holes are true to the design, they will be the pride of Pajaro, venturing as they do onto the surrounding hillsides and opening up new views of the slough—not to mention new tests of the equipment in your bag. Most of the players here are local, and Leider vows to keep the golf affordable for all, however spiffy and new the most ancient of the Santa Cruz area courses becomes. He also promises that the 90 or so adjacent housing units that will be built to justify course improvements will not encroach on the natural beauty that makes playing Pajaro Valley a truly enjoyable walk in the park.

So the area's first nine-holer is about to become the area's first 27-holer. That must mean that the first 18-holer was Pasatiempo, yes? No, we're not there yet. The granddaddy of the Santa Cruz area 18s is in the heart of Aptos—and unless you want to let on that you're a tourist, that'll be AP-toss, not AP-toes.

Though it's within one monster drive of the ocean, Aptos Seascape oddly offers little in the way of wet, sandy views. Indeed, after you park in front of the modern clubhouse and make your way around the back, you'll wonder if Treescape wouldn't have been a more appropriate name. But if you'd visited in 1926, when the course opened, you'd have entered through a grand gate that told you you were at the Rio Del Mar Country Club. Maybe back then, you might have even been told who designed the course, but today that information appears to be irretrievably lost; a local historian commissioned to dig up the architect's name struck out, so a mystery remains. The grand gate closed during World War II, and the course was transformed into victory gardens. The Seascape Corporation bought it in about 1948 and changed its name, though the trees were already obscuring whatever views the Rio Del Mar Country Club might have offered, and when the Seascape Resort, Racquet Club, and Golf Club were broken up and sold in 1987, American Golf arrived on the scene to transform the property into largely what it is today.

Today, Seascape is the antithesis of a country club. It does offer private memberships, but it is always busy—indeed, an intricate progressive rate structure and $15 replay fee keep golfers on the course until dark,

Boulder Creek

We're not sure how Jack Fleming ended up in these parts in 1961, but the designer best known for his work in and around San Francisco worked some magic with Boulder Creek Golf and Country Club. In a tiny town in the Santa Cruz Mountains, on Highway 9 right next to Big Basin Redwoods State Park, Boulder Creek Golf and Country Club is close enough to San Francisco and San Jose to make for a wonderful day trip, except once you get there you'll want it to be more.

There are fully equipped condos on the scenic course, a 4,400-yarder that has a par of 65 for men, 67 for women, winding around ponds and redwoods, and there's a swimming pool and tennis courts along with a casual and comfortable but excellent restaurant. There are more dining choices in town, but Boulder Creek's economical package deals encourage the getting-away golfer to stay on the property. Its friendly length makes it appealing to the new and evolving golfer, but beware Boulder Creek's popularity with conferences; when a convention tournament has commandeered the course, it has it by the, er, boulders and doesn't let go until everybody to the rear screams uncle. Repeatedly. At the right time of year, you can stay two nights and play three rounds of golf (with extras like lunch and cocktails) for around $150 a person.

■ 831/338-2111, fax 831/338-7862; website www.webfairway.com/bouldercreek

especially in busy July and August. It is probably even busier than its neighbor up in the hills, municipal De Laveaga, even though Seascape costs a little more. On weekends, even a lot more.

"People love this golf course," says general manager Bruce Pluim. "It's fun to play, and it fits a lot of people's games. The 40-handicapper is not going to lose a lot of balls here—there are only one or two holes with a little bit of a forced carry—and the greens are very challenging." At their swiftest, you can make that very, very challenging.

"It's always been known as a fun golf course, so the improvements we've been making were just to enhance everybody's experience," Pluim said.

Those $1.7 million improvements included moving the pro shop out of the basement and into a big, bright space overlooking the first tee, and modernizing the restaurant with Bogey's Bar and Grill, offering huge, tasty sandwiches, salads, burgers, and seafood. Progress also spread to the golf course, which underwent a John Harbottle redo of the 36 bunkers on the course, all of them around the greens, none of them in the tree-lined fairways. The par-5 13th hole was slightly shortened to a par-4, making the course a par-71 that measures only about 6,000 yards from the back tees, with a 69.4 rating and 125 slope. Upgrades to the irrigation and drainage systems also were on the boards.

Another change hardly cost any money at all, and it's open to debate whether it helped heal or merely camouflage one of the few blemishes on the Aptos Seascape complexion. That was reversing the nines, so that the former first hole, a long par-5 off an elevated tee that offered a scenic but daunting start, is now hole number 10. And hole number 1 is the former hole number 10, a friendly little par-4 that drives home the best bit of advice to playing Aptos Seascape. (That is, stay below the hole.)

Your round now ends on a superb finishing note, the par-5 18th, with a characteristically tree-lined but comfortably wide fairway leading to one of the more narrow greens on the course, fronted by a big bunker and backed by the clubhouse and usually a landscaped display of bright color. But the reason for the swap was to accelerate play, which can be excruciating slow—a side effect to the overall friendliness of the Seascape Aptos golf course. It just doesn't do enough to scare golfers away.

De Laveaga head pro Dave Loustalot looks at it this way: "Seascape is like a bas relief of De Laveaga. At Aptos, the fairways are more like a bowl, so if you miss, the ball comes back. At De Laveaga, the fairways are more like a bowl upside-down." So if you miss at De Laveaga, you never see the ball again. The first time we played there, there was a stop at the turn to fish more golf balls out of the trunk for the back nine.

That's not to say that De Laveaga—and we're going with De laveeAYEga on this one—is not utterly lovable. Its location, in the middle of what wealthy naturalist and humanitarian Jose Vicente de Laveaga intended to be the Golden Gate Park of Santa Cruz when he bought 500 parkland acres here in 1892, puts it literally atop the other area courses, in a world of its own. It's an exceptionally maintained and run city-owned course that has been operated since it opened (1970) by the Loustalot family, a NorCal institution when it comes to golfing genes—though head pro Dave Loustalot says if genes counted for all that much, he'd be a better player. "I'm the nongolfer in the family," says Dave. "My dad (Gary) played the Tour in the '50s, my uncle Vic was a pro in the '60s, and my younger brother Mike and older brother Tim are both good players. I played in high school and didn't really like it. But I got a job at Kapalua when I was 21, and everybody said we needed a club pro in this family, so here I am. We grew up here, this is home, we treat this like family, and the customer sees that most of the time."

Tim was the latest of the Loustalots to hold the course record of 62, which is 10 under par on the 6,010-yard course that plays so much harder than it is long. There are only two sets of tees at De Laveaga, 6,010 or 5,331, and no plans to add any others.

"It just doesn't have the length for another set," Loustalot said. "But just because it's a 6,000-yard golf course doesn't mean it's easy. Patience is very important on this golf course. It gets to the point where people just get tired of thinking about every shot, then they get to the (345-yard, par-4) 12th and just say screw it, I'm hitting driver. People start making bad choices. And if you're in trouble off the tee here, you're really in trouble."

Specifically, you're probably down in a barranca, beyond hope of redemption until the next hole. Play here once and you'll wonder how on earth Bert Stamps could thread a golf course through the rough spots that surround De Laveaga's 18 holes. Play here twice and you'll really begin to appreciate the wildness that makes De Laveaga unique. Hole number 12 is Dave Loustalot's favorite, and it is a fair representation of what makes the course what it is, doglegging gently right around an apex of bunkers not entirely visible from the tee to a green that, like a few others at De Laveaga, shifted in the 1989 Loma Prieta quake. Hole number 15 will get your attention as well, a medium-long par-3 to a green fronted by a bunker and an oak tree.

As at many Northern California courses, the Monterey pines at De Laveaga all are dying of the pitch pine canker disease, and work has been in progress to replace them with cedars, oaks, cypress, and redwoods before they fall. The Loustalots also would like to replace the course's reputation for being too wet to play after winter storms: extensive work has been done on irrigation and drainage to make that go away.

The subject of reputation brings us finally back to Pasatiempo Golf Club, which gets skipped in the natural segue from Aptos Seascape to De Laveaga. Pasatiempo is the course most likely to bring golfers a-calling to Santa Cruz County, as it has since back in the '20s, when Marion Hollins bought a large parcel of land she felt might make for a suitable follow-up to Cypress Point.

Hollins, the 1921 U.S. Women's Amateur champion, collaborated with Alister MacKenzie on his 1927 Cypress Point design, and he credited her with the inspiration of the famous 16th hole there. She persuaded him to work his magic again in the hills above Santa Cruz in 1929, and he incorporated her design philosophy, which she called "strategic golf." Hollins thought there should be alternate, safer lines of play on every hole other than just the direct line, to comfort and challenge the shorter hitter.

But Pasatiempo is unmistakably a MacKenzie course. "Anybody who knows what that means won't be surprised to find very difficult, undulating greens," says head pro Shawn McEntee. "That's his trademark, and you see that at Augusta National and Cypress." Any renovations at the semiprivate course, which hosted the 1986 U.S. Women's Amateur and still holds U.S. Amateur and Open qualifying rounds, are undertaken with the goal of staying true to the original design, although changes in the game have forced modifications like altering the first hole from an easy par-5 to a long par-4.

The small but shifty greens, though, can be exasperating. It is generally not wise to attack the pin, unless you know a bit about the tendencies of the green around it. Better to play safe, to the middle or short of the hole. After one round here, it becomes clear how Juli Inkster, who grew up on the course and worked at the range, became such a phenomenal iron player. If she could hold the greens at Pasatiempo, many of them seemingly built to reject any golf shot, then she would indeed go to the LPGA Hall of Fame.

"MacKenzie's thoughts at the time were always more fairway bunkers, more fairway bunkers, but men now drive right over the top of those," McEntee says. "There are subtle trees, pines and cypresses, and some difficult bunkering around the greens, but that's another one of his signatures. You don't hear people say of a MacKenzie course that it's demanding off the tee. This is about iron play, bunker play, and the putter."

The course record, 63, has stood since Ken Venturi was a collegian. And Bobby Jones, who had already seen Cypress Point and was here to tee it up with Hollins, Glenna Collett, and British Amateur champion Cyril Tolley on opening day (Sept. 8, 1929), was so impressed with this work that he enlisted MacKenzie's expertise to create Augusta National.

It is no coincidence that all three courses have stood the tests of time and Tiger Woods, so that Cypress and Augusta are considered among the top 10 courses in the world, and Pasatiempo joins them on most of the longer lists—perhaps so relegated only because it is hidden here off the beaten path, not quite in San Francisco and not quite in the golf mecca of Pebble Beach.

But so what if the rest of the world hasn't yet discovered Santa Cruz. Some 30,000 commuters make their way along a winding highway through the mountains every day so that they can play, eat, and sleep here after a day's work in the Silicon Valley. Some three million sunseekers pack up their cars to play, eat, sleep, and pour $525 million annually into the economy here after weeks of work somewhere hotter, colder, or foggier. And if many of those are packing golf clubs, chances are good they're not alone.

|tinerary

WARMING UP

For this particular itinerary, round up the family—and maybe even another one just so there are baby-sitters to cover the golfers in the group. Book a two-bedroom condo at Seascape Resort. Do you want a serene ocean view, or would you rather be able to sit on your deck and have a view of your kids at the pool? Seascape is huge, so consult frankly with the reservationist over the location of your unit. Generally, the south bluff seems livelier and more family oriented, while the north bluff has a more detached and romantic feel to it.

Now, for your tee times. No less than one week before you go, book a Day 1 afternoon tee time at Aptos Seascape, a Day 2 early morning tee time at De Laveaga and a Day 3 late morning tee time at either Pasatiempo, if you're splurging, or Pajaro Valley, if you're feeling less confident in your game. Keep in mind that tee times from late morning on at Pasatiempo are easier to come by than at the other three courses because of the prices, so it might be possible to book the other three courses and then substitute the more famous course at the last minute.

Also, it can't hurt to make a Day 1 dinner reservation at seemingly always busy Palapas.

day I

Drive immediately to Seascape Resort, check into your condo, and get everyone settled. Once they're comfortably in the pool or hot tub or at the beach, take the car and play a round of golf at Aptos Seascape. It's the logical choice for today, as convenient as it is— and as inexpensive as it becomes later in the day.

Aptos Seascape is also a terrific appetizer for your Santa Cruz golfing escape, being perhaps the kindest of all of the options here. Take it easy on the first hole; the putt from behind the flagstick is frightening, and if you fly the green by very much you're in the road. And do your scoring on the front nine; by most schools of thought, the back nine is a bit tougher. A favorite hole of the regulars is hole number 17, a par-4 with a blind tee shot. Split the tree-lined fairway and you'll set up an undaunting approach shot to a tree encircled green.

If there's time, enjoy a beverage in the clubhouse before returning to Seascape and taking the gang across the street to Palapas Restaurant y Cantina. At first glance, the menu may seem startlingly pricey for a Mexican restaurant, but those on a budget can opt for a patio table and fill up on the ample appetizers, a pitcher or two of margaritas, and plenty of chips and salsa. No budget? Go for any of the fresh seafood dishes. But watch it on those margaritas—the idea is for everyone else to sleep in the next morning while you awaken a chauffeur to steal you away to your next golf stop.

day II

Now that you've warmed up on Aptos Seascape, it's time to test your nerves at De Laveaga, which is back north on Highway 1 to the Morrissey Boulevard exit. Take the first right to the stop sign, turn left, and take the next right to Upper Park Road and the course. This should take no time at all, except that one can never count on taking no time at all to go anywhere in the Santa Cruz area, and this stretch between Aptos and Santa Cruz is particularly nightmarish for those 30,000 commuters. With an early morning tee time, you will get their drift. Finally, resistance to widening the freeway is beginning to crumble, so maybe by the time you read this you will be able to make it to De Laveaga with time to hit a few balls and enjoy an eye opener at the Lodge. We didn't.

If you're like most folks, i.e., right-handed, the first hole will clue you in on the nuances of De Laveaga. The friendly starter will probably have to tell you where to hit your drive on this dogleg right par-5: stay left, she'll say, but not so far left that you land in the road. Of course, since you're not entirely warmed up yet, you'll probably hit it right, where there's a tree-lined canyon waiting to gobble up your golf ball. And if you don't play it smart and left on your next shot, you'll probably hit a tree and lose that one too. Relax, hole number 2 is a short par-4 with a wide fairway—but stay out of the canyon on the right again. If you're walking unassisted, it might be worth printing out the instructions on the De Laveaga website. Though sometimes you're better off just not knowing. And don't get too adventurous in retrieving lost balls: poison oak runs rampant in the park.

If your nongolfing loved ones have timed it right, they'll be cheering your arrival to the 18th green—another of those tilted by the Loma Prieta quake—and ready to buy you lunch on the deck at the Lodge. It's a big menu with plenty of options for everyone, and the picnic tables and umbrellas make it a nice place to linger.

From here, you may want to check out another kind of golf entirely— disc golf. There's a 27-hole course in the park, just about a quarter mile past the clubhouse off Upper Park Boulevard. Disc golf is much harder than golf if you've played golf but not disc golf. The object is to throw the disc, more commonly known as a Frisbee, through airways, not fairways, into a basket. If you need to know more, check out the website www. discgolf.com before you go.

This is your big chance to visit the Mystery Spot, an inexplicable natural phenomenon in the redwoods, just up Branciforte Road from the golf course. Instruments won't work here, and you'll feel strange variations in gravity and perception that just have to be experienced to be believed. Kids love it, adults can't explain it, and coupons can be found on the website (www.mystery-spot. com) to reduce the $5 for adults, $3 for kids price of admission.

Next, it's back in the car and on to the Santa Cruz Beach Boardwalk, not to be missed by anyone who was ever a child. Just head west on Highway 17 and follow the signs to the Beach Boardwalk. The classic 1911 Looff Carousel and 1924 Giant Dipper Roller Coaster were declared historic landmarks in 1987, but they're still in fine working order for a few minutes of fun. The Giant Dipper is not to be missed if you're anywhere in the area, with speeds of up to 55 mph and a rickety clitter clatter that only adds to the thrill. For the few moments when you'll have enough presence of mind to look around, there are even some exhilarating views. And there are about 30 other rides, plus laser tag, an arcade, and even miniature golf. For $20 you can ride all day, or there are various packages. We visited once on a retro Wednesday, when the prices were rolled back 30 years or so for the evening. Certainly, check the website, www.beachboardwalk.com, or call 831/426-7433 before you go.

Now, how tired are you? Probably too tired to walk over to the Municipal Wharf, so just return to the car and go find a parking place right out there on the pier. Take a short walk, just long enough to find a restaurant (there are probably 10 options, most of them serving up fresh seafood, of course, though there's also Italian, and one or two may be offering a $9.95 midweek Maine lobster special) that meets with the group's approval, and enjoy a meal and the view of the ocean and sunset. Scontriano's Dolphin has a special kids' menu, and Gilda's boasts of family dining "in a relaxed and casual atmosphere." The whole list is available in advance, at the website www.santacruzwharf.com. And after dinner, just follow your ears to the nightly concert presented by the sea lions at the wharf.

Home to Seascape, James. If the adults need a nightcap, it might be a good time to visit the bar at Sanderlings and regroup.

day III Everyone's feeling pretty pooped by now, so head for Sanderlings for breakfast out on the deck overlooking the ocean. We're going to recommend this stop for the family escape simply because of the dinner we had here one night: award-winning clam chowder to die for and real crabcakes, with delicious desserts that weren't house-made but were yummy, and a nice wine list. The dining room emptied of children by about 8 and became quite the romantic little spot; it's probably a little bit too pricey, anyway, at an easy $100 for two, to make for an appropriate dinner spot with little ones. Breakfast, though, is a treat to be shared, especially since checkout chores are next.

But the fun's not done. Load up those nongolfers and situate them on the beach at Capitola-by-the-Sea, a happening little town with lots of action on the beach and off it. An ideal dropoff spot is at the little park just in front of Capitola Beach, where there are benches and showers for washing off sand, and Cafe Lido stands by next door with Italian fuel. On the beach, there are some cafés practically alongside the sand castles, and there are shops to shade the sun-weary. In other words, the nongolfers will hardly notice that you're gone.

And now, if you're feeling pretty good about your game, you're off to Pasatiempo for your splurge of the summer, to walk in the footsteps of Bobby Jones, Marion Collins, Babe Didrickson. But you've got to take your car first and go back to Highway 1 and take it to Highway 17, exiting at Pasatiempo Drive. Turn left at the overpass and left again at the Pasatiempo Inn, then right at Pasatiempo Drive through the gate and to the clubhouse. Here's hoping that you've been paired up with someone who's familiar with the course; it's bound to enhance your enjoyment. You'll start making your way back down toward the ocean for the first two holes, and then you'll come back up with one of the toughest par-3s anywhere—and that tells you all you need to know about the great golfing skill of head pro Shawn McEntee, who says this is probably his favorite hole on the course. When you get to hole number 6, you may be able to pick out the Alister MacKenzie house, about 100 yards short of the green on your left. MacKenzie loved Pasatiempo so much that he lived here and died here; now, a club member appreciatively lives in the house and cares for his ghost. The parties would do a Scotsman proud.

MacKenzie's favorite hole here was the par-4 16th, and he said it was his favorite "two-shot" hole anywhere. And sorry folks, that's not because it's easy. There's a blind tee shot over an indicator flag, with barranca left and OB right. And then there's that approach shot, which some say might as well be blind, to a green with trouble all around it and three tiers on it. By now, you're not surprised at any of this. Pasatiempo is tough and unique, not to be missed unless you're really struggling with your game or finances.

In the latter cases, you've opted out of Pasatiempo on Day 3 and gone south, to Pajaro Valley. You'll have to take Highway 1 again, about 15 miles, turning left on Salinas Road and proceeding to the golf course, less than a mile down on your right. For less than half the price of a round at Pasatiempo, and way less than half the aggravation, you will take a walk that ought to take you no more than four hours or so at this friendly, pace-conscious place. We'll spare you the play-by-play, since the course is slated for a vast redesign any day now. Just know that it was a nice course to begin with, which only bodes well for whatever is to come.

Pasatiempo and Pajaro Valley both offer appealing 19th holes, but we're guessing that you're wanted by the sun worshippers back in Capitola. So play your 19th hole at the beach with the rest of the gang, and then load up and make your way through the usual horrendous traffic nightmare home. At least you'll probably be going against the commute as you leave sunny Santa Cruz County.

 NOTES

Money Savers. Avoid Santa Cruz in the summer.

Nongolfers. Only Lake Tahoe can possibly equal Santa Cruz when it comes to its abundance of summertime activities for those yet to discover the great game.

Couples. You don't have to bring kids on this escape to have fun—Santa Cruz can be plenty romantic. Stay at the Inn at Depot Hill in Capitola-by-the-Sea, dine at the Bittersweet Bistro and Hollins House, take a wine-tasting cruise on the *Chardonnay II* and be kids yourselves at the Santa Cruz Beach Boardwalk.

Time Savers. This can be a relaxing one-night escape in the middle of the week. Book a room at the Inn at Depot Hill, which offers a limited number of deeply discounted rounds for two at Pasatiempo, and enjoy your evening browsing the Capitola Village shops and dining at any place that catches your fancy.

Low-Handicappers. Don't under any circumstances miss Pasatiempo. If you only have time for three rounds of golf, drop Aptos Seascape or Pajaro Valley from the itinerary instead.

Extended Stay. Book a house or condo at the beach.

Courses

ITINERARY SELECTIONS

Aptos Seascape Golf Club
610 Clubhouse Dr.
Aptos, CA 95003
831/688-3214, fax 831/688-3587

Green fees that reach above $65 on weekends without cart begin declining every day at twilight, then drop again at super twilight and again at sunset, so you might get away with playing Aptos Seascape for as little as $15. Just be sure to call seven days in advance at 7 A.M. for your time slot—or spring for an extra $5 per player and go for an advance reservation up to 30 days ahead. A family perk is the student rate, $25 any time. The course is so walkable, there's no need to spring for a cart at $16 per player unless you must.

SCORECARD

Architect: Unknown, 1922
Course Record: 62, Jeff McMillan and Ken Woods
Black: Par 71, 6,029 yards, 69.4 rating for men, 125 slope; par 72 for women, 75.6 rating, 133 slope
Gold: Par 71, 5,813 yards, 68.4 rating for men, 123 slope
Silver: Par 71, 5,514 yards, 67.0 rating for men, 120 slope; par 72 for women, 72.6 rating, 5514 slope
Tee times may be made up to seven days in advance, or up to 30 days in advance for an additional $5 per player.

TEE TIDBITS | Collared shirts are required, but non-metal spikes have been merely "encouraged." There's a small range near the first tee, and there's also a good place to practice chipping and bunker shots nearby. The practice greens give you a good idea of what's in store, so don't be lured into Bogey's for a burger instead of putting before your round. The food is excellent and the clubhouse has a cozy, friendly ambience.

De Laveaga Golf Course

401 Upper Park Rd.
Santa Cruz, CA 95065
831/423-7212, 831/423-7214 pro shop, fax 831/458-1309
website www.delaveagagolf.com

De Laveaga is a busy public course, so remember to make that 7 P.M. call seven days in advance of your tee time. Visitors have to pay for the big break residents receive on green fees, $9 more at $35 on a weekday and $45 on a weekend. While the GPS in the carts is a luxury you'll be glad you had, the course is very walkable.

SCORECARD

Architect: Bert Stamps, 1970
Course Record: 62, Tim Loustalot and Steve Pacheco
White: Par 72, 6,005 yards, 70.4 rating for men, 133 slope; 75.0 rating for women, 132 slope
Red: Par 72, 5,322 yards, 67.6 rating for men, 127 slope; 71.2 rating for women, 124 slope
Call seven days in advance at 7 P.M. for your tee time.

TEE TIDBITS | Twilight bargains begin at 3 in the summer, 1:30 in the winter. There's usually a sale table in front of the well-stocked pro shop. The double-deck, lighted range has 40 stations and is open until 9:30 on summer nights. While it may be cool in the morning, it is almost always delightful after noon. Metal spikes weren't yet forbidden at press time. The restaurant, a destination on its own yet not at all clubbish, opens daily at 7 A.M., but lunch ends at 2:30. Rounds can be slow, because you know how golfers hate to give up on a ball that goes in the woods. Just remember—at De Laveaga it's probably gone.

Pajaro Valley Golf Club

976 Salinas Rd.
Watsonville, CA 95076
831/724-3851, fax 831/724-9394
website www.pvgolf.com

Pajaro Valley is a public course, but it has at least two echelons of annual memberships. Members have a one- to two-day head start on coveted weekend tee times, so if that's what you seek, call first thing Monday morning (6 A.M.). Weekends do include Friday. Weekday rates are generally around $40 on this easily walkable course, where nonmetal spikes are required. Rates fall for twilight, sundown, winter, and juniors. If you're interested in a lodging package, inquire about Pajaro Dunes' beach houses.

SCORECARD

Architect: Floyd McFarland, 1922
Course Record: 65, Charlie Leider
Blue: Par 72, 6,233 yards, 69.9 rating for men, 122 slope
White: Par 72, 6,005 yards, 69.1 rating for men, 119 slope; 74.5 rating for women, 127 slope
Red: Par 72, 5,696 yards, 72.3 rating for women, 123 slope
Public tee times are taken a week in advance, except for weekend tee times, which are taken on Monday of the week you want to play.

TEE TIDBITS | Pajaro Valley is especially popular with women golfers, probably because of its traditional, walkable style of design and overall friendly feel. From pro shop to snack shop, hospitality reigns. Plans to add nine holes also call for a redesign of the entire course, including five sets of tees on each hole. Charlie Leider promises if the new housing planned for the course is going to encroach on the golf, he'll scrap it. Leider played on the PGA Tour and still holds the course record.

Pasatiempo Golf Club

20 Clubhouse Rd.
Santa Cruz, CA 95060
831/459-9155, fax 831/459-9157
website www.pasatiempo.com

Pasatiempo's members have dibs on prime tee times, so the course is generally booked up until 11 A.M. or so on weekends and holidays before the public comes calling. And with various member days during the week, your best bet is to plan to play here late in the morning. Green fees are $115 Monday–Friday and $125 on weekends and holidays. Add $17 per player for a cart, which you should use on your first visit. Add $20 per player if you want to make your tee times farther than a week out (up to 90 days in advance). For a midweek overnight golf escape to Pasatiempo, check with the Inn at Depot Hill.

SCORECARD

Architect: Alister MacKenzie, 1929
Course Record: 63, Brian Pini, Ken Venturi, and Forrest Fezler
Blue: Par 70, 6,445 yards, 72.9 rating for men, 138 slope
White: Par 70, 6,128 yards, 71.4 rating for men, 134 slope
Red: Par 72, 5,629 yards, 73.6 rating for women, 135 slope
For weekday play, reservations are taken seven days in advance beginning at 7 A.M.; for weekend play, call Monday at 10 A.M. before the weekend you want to play. For a $20 per player surcharge, reservations may be made up to 90 days in advance.

TEE TIDBITS | Pasatiempo translates into "passing of time," and the unusual logo shows a little guy in a sombrero snoozing under a palm tree. Nothing about Pasatiempo made us snooze. The high green fees at Pasatiempo are somewhat misleading. They don't include range balls—and if you want to hit a few, give yourself ample extra time, because the range is at the bottom of a hill. And they don't include the cart fee. Remember, you're paying for the privilege of playing a lovingly preserved MacKenzie original. Try that at Cypress Point or Augusta National. Collars and nonmetal spikes required. We really enjoyed our 19th hole stop at the MacKenzie Bar and Grill. The margaritas were excellent and enhanced our perverse pleasure in watching others agonizingly approach and putt the ninth green.

ALTERNATIVES

Spring Hills in Watsonville, just a few miles south of Santa Cruz, is worthy of consideration for its surroundings and its relatively easy access. Presided over by a 1911 farmhouse-turned-clubhouse, the course was built in 1965, designed by Hank Schimpeler in the short-but-tight template that seems to prevail all around the Santa Cruz area. It's likely that the first hole, a big dogleg right to an elevated green, will utterly confuse you, but it's not typical of the next 17. For the most part, what you see is what you get on this gently rolling, very walkable and playable—if not all that well groomed—course between Highways 1 and 101. Par is 71, 6,015 yards from the back, 5,883 from the middle, and 5,397 from the front. The area's least expensive course is also one of the busiest, and weekend prime time rounds can be torturously slow. On the plus side, tee times can be made up to a month in advance. ■ 501 SPRING HILLS DR., WATSONVILLE, CA 95076; 831/724-1404

For a more modern and deluxe experience, consider traversing the pass to Gilroy to play Eagle Ridge, which is described in detail in the Silicon Valley chapter.

Lodging

ITINERARY SELECTION

Seascape Resort is the happening place to stay during the summer season. With three pools and a putting green, a fine restaurant, and a lively lounge—not to mention Seascape's generous portion of the 17 miles of sandy beach below—you'll certainly never feel alone here. Rates have been on the rise (to start at more than $200 a night), and there are 285 units, yet it can be difficult to get in on a peak weekend. Reserve in advance and be sure to ask about package deals. The resort often offers golf specials with both Aptos Seascape and Pajaro Valley, or it may have access to preferential tee times. ■ 1 SEASCAPE RESORT DR., APTOS, CA 95003; 800/929-7727; WEBSITE WWW.SEASCAPERESORT.COM

GOLF PACKAGE OPTIONS

Other than Boulder Creek (see page 310), none of the golf courses in the Santa Cruz chapter has a close tie with a lodging property. Seascape Resort and the Aptos Seascape course are separately owned, and De Laveaga is a municipal course. Pajaro Valley occasionally offers packages with Seascape Resort and discounts to Pajaro Dunes vacation home dwellers. The Inn at Depot Hill sells discounted certificates for Pasatiempo, which had no official lodging packages in effect at press time.

ALTERNATIVES

The **Inn at Depot Hill** is *the* place to stay for couples looking to get away from it all while staying right in the middle of it all. The 12 large, beautifully furnished rooms and suites in this former train station are all decorated differently—there's something to suit all tastes and maybe even offend some, so take a good look at the brochure or website for detailed descriptions. Some have hot tubs, gardens, and/or patios; all have fireplaces, hidden TVs, VCRs, stereos, and fresh flowers. A full gourmet breakfast (peaches-and-cream-stuffed french toast; blueberry-filled pancakes with sauce l'orange) is served, in your room if you like, and appetizers and wine are served at happy hour. Before bed, there's even dessert. Just down the hill is the village of Capitola-by-the-Sea, with shops and galleries and restaurants galore, but you may never want to leave your room. Rates start at around $165. ■ 250 MONTEREY AVE., CAPITOLA-BY-THE-SEA, CA 95010; 800/572-2632; WEBSITE WWW.INNATDEPOTHILL.COM

Another romantic option, where you almost surely will not want to leave your room, is the remotely located **Inn at Manresa Beach,** an 1867 restored replica of Abraham Lincoln's Springfield home. Jocks Susan Van Horn, a tennis player and triathlete, and Brian Denny, who played on the pro tennis circuit, have settled down here with their kids and three tennis courts—two of them clay, one of them grass. Weekend guests get the bonus of Saturday and Sunday tennis clinics with Brian, while enjoying the decor selected by Susan, with the help of a little feng shui. Rooms here are modern, many with hot tubs and all with luxurious, adjustable massage beds, fireplaces, and TV-VCR units that beg for a selection from the shelves in the hallway. In two mid-March weekends, there were five proposals here. The hosts don't golf, but they will help you make a tee time and send you off with a dynamite breakfast. All this, starting at $150 or so. ■ 1258 SAN ANDREAS RD., LA SELVA BEACH, CA 95076; 888/523-2244; WEBSITE WWW.INDEVELOPMENT.COM

The more centrally located **Pleasure Point Inn** offers bed-and-breakfast accommodations on the water in Santa Cruz, just south of the harbor. This 1920 beachfront home has four rooms, starting at around $125, and offers hot tubs, fireplaces, expanded continental breakfast, and, for your 19th hole, appetizers and wine at happy hour. ■ 2-3665 E. CLIFF DR., SANTA CRUZ, CA 95062; 800/872-3029

The **Inn at Pasatiempo** can hardly be beat for its convenience to Pasatiempo Golf Course, which is practically next door, and the Hollins House, as well as downtown Santa Cruz. There are 54 recently refurbished units, many with sitting areas and fireplaces. Be sure to ask for one over-looking the tranquil pool and gardens, not the busy highway out front. Rates start at around $120 and include a continental breakfast at your door. ■ 555 HIGHWAY 17, SANTA CRUZ, CA 95060; 800/834-2546

Naturally there are lots of rental houses and condos in an area this sprawling. Some of the very best—and very best deals—are a few miles south of Santa Cruz, at Pajaro Dunes, which is just four miles west of Watsonville and the Pajaro Valley Golf Club. Two companies in particular offer uniquely designed and furnished beachfront condos and homes, some as large as five bedrooms. Units start at around $200 a night and are discounted by the week. Try the **Best of Pajaro Rental Agency,** 101 Shell

Drive, Watsonville, CA 95076; 888/641-6100; website www.bestofpajaro.
com; or **Pajaro Dunes Beach Rentals,** 2661 Beach Rd., Watsonville, CA
95076; 800/564-1771; website www.pajaro-dunes.com.

Dining

ITINERARY SELECTIONS

Palapas Restaurant y Cantina offers a surprising range of fresh seafood
and traditional Mexican entrées, some as high as $20. But appetizers are
large enough to satisfy many appetites, and the chips and margaritas are
filling enough. It's open seven days a week, beginning at lunch, and reservations are suggested. ■ 21 SEASCAPE VILLAGE, APTOS; 831/662-9000

The **De Laveaga Lodge** opens for breakfast at 7 (served all day on Saturday and Sunday) and often offers a golfer's special: bloody Mary, screwdriver,
or salty dog and two eggs, bacon, hash browns, toast and jelly, for under $10.
Lunch is served 11:30–2:30. Reservations recommended for Sunday mornings. ■ DE LAVEAGA GOLF COURSE, 401 UPPER PARK RD., SANTA CRUZ; 831/423-1600

Sanderlings at Seascape is open daily for breakfast, lunch, and dinner,
and the weekend brunches are very popular. There's also a full bar. ■
SEASCAPE RESORT, 1 SEASCAPE RESORT DR., APTOS; 831/688-6800; WEBSITE WWW.INFOPOINT.
COM/SC/LODGING/SEASCAPE/SAND.HTML

ALTERNATIVES

Golfers will surely want to dine at the **Hollins House** at Pasatiempo (20
Clubhouse Rd., Santa Cruz; 831/459-9177; website www.hollinshouse.com).
It's a graceful early-California style white mansion that served as Marion
Hollins' original golf course clubhouse, and it requires little exertion of the
imagination to see the orchestra playing to the dining and dancing 1920s
jet-setters in what is now the main dining room. On summer evenings, or
for Sunday brunch almost any time of year, guests can sit at tables on the
lawn, overlooking the front nine and, beyond, Santa Cruz and the ocean.
Oh, you want food? It's a continental-style menu specializing in seafood,
with entrées starting around $13 and Sunday champagne brunch under
$20. Closed Monday and Tuesday, open for dinner and Sunday brunch.

At **Shadowbrook,** romance is served up nightly (1750 Wharf Rd., Capitola; 831/475-1511; website www.shadowbrook-Capitola.com). You take the
cable car down to dine in one of the many rooms in this sprawling
redwood complex along Soquel Creek. The restaurant has been in business

for more than 50 years, opening as a room for 50 but annexing and expanding along the way to seat 210 yet retain its feeling of intimacy. Recent improvements include renovations to the bar, which now serves lunch on weekdays, plus appetizers and light meals nightly. Sunday brunch is a highlight—reservations virtually required—and dinners offer mouthwatering entrées like ravioli with grilled lamb sirloin, petite filet and prawns, and teriyaki-glazed salmon, starting at around $13 a plate. There's a kids' menu too, but that's not the reason Shadowbrook is regularly named to the all-romance restaurant team.

Bittersweet Bistro (787 Rio Del Mar Blvd., Rio Del Mar; 831/662-9799; website www.bittersweetbistro.com) is another adult dining option, though its hours are ever expanding and it is probably a comfortable place to take the kids during lunch or the late-afternoon "bistro" hours. For dinner, there's a feeling of serenity even at the busiest times, which are most times when chef Thomas Vinolus is in the kitchen putting the freshest ingredients of the day to heavenly use. Entrées start at around $15, the seafood is exquisite—wild sturgeon saltimbocca highlighted the long list of daily specials when we last visited—and the wine list is interesting and well priced. And with a name like Bittersweet Bistro, you surely are smart enough to save room for dessert. Closed on Monday.

As at its sister restaurant, Shadowbrook, you'll want to go to the **Crow's Nest** as much for the atmosphere and setting as the fresh seafood (2218 E. Cliff Dr., Santa Cruz; 831/476-4560; website www.crowsnest-santacruz.com). The two floors and three decks showcase the Santa Cruz Harbor in all its glory, with sweeping views of the Monterey Bay beyond. The Crow's Nest is open every day starting at 11:30, and if you visit on a Wednesday don't be surprised at the wait: The Crow's Nest is the best place in town to watch the Wednesday night sailboat races and the sunsets every night. The upstairs grill is especially comfortable for families.

There are many, many more restaurant options in and around Santa Cruz County; we've had great success asking the locals for their favorites, and the CVC website offers many links.

Straying Off Course

Okay, let's get this straight right now. There's no skiing in Santa Cruz, no winter sports at all in fact. But when it comes to activities, well, let's all just take a deep breath and . . . ready . . . set . . . go.

There are beaches for campfires, for camping, for fishing, kayaking, surfing, learning to surf, skating, swimming, swimming nude, whale-watching, people-watching and dog-watching, and the CVC can tell you which are best for what. Two of the more popular attractions are admiring the windsurfers at Davenport Beach and looking for whales beyond, and waiting for the surfers to catch a wave at Steamer Lane, which is right below the Mark Abbott Lighthouse and surfing museum. The museum, on West Cliff Drive, is open every afternoon but Tuesday (831/429-3429).

Beach volleyball is regularly in progress at the main beaches at Capitola and Santa Cruz.

Wednesday evening, the Santa Cruz Harbor is the place to be for the weekly sailboat races.

There are charters to take you fishing, sailing, and whale-watching. Or for a more civilized experience of wind and water, there's the 70-foot yacht *Chardonnay II,* which offers wine-maker sails, brewmaster sails, and even a taste of Santa Cruz sail for around $40 for two hours (831/4223-1213; website www.chardonnay.com).

If you'd prefer to find out what's going on in and under the water without actually going there, try the new Seymore Center at Long Marine Lab, which has exhibits, aquaria touch tanks, and the skeleton of an 85-foot blue whale.

Club Ed runs surfing and windsurfing schools right on Cowell Beach near the Santa Cruz Wharf (831/459-9283; email ed1@cruzio.com).

Hikers most likely will be drawn to the 18,000 acres of redwood forest at Big Basin, where the trail to Berry Falls is a particularly popular draw. Nature lovers may be inspired by the sights of the Elkhorn Slough to learn to kayak. Elkhorn Slough is one of 17 estuarine reserves in the United States, home to all sorts of land, air, and sea animals. Kayak Connection offers tours and rentals every day from two locations, one at Santa Cruz Harbor (831/479-1121) and the other next to Elkhorn Slough (831/724-5692; website gate.cruzio.com).

The beaches here are surrounded by agriculture, and some gardens, farms, and ranches welcome visitors to do what is most succinctly expressed as "u pick." At any rate, you will want to stop at some roadside produce stands on your way home.

Of course, one of the popular crops is grapes. There are 23 wineries in and around Santa Cruz County, mostly of the mom-and-pop come-on-in variety, but there are also larger producers like Bonny Dune, Bargetto, and Ventana. The CVC's *Visitors Guide* has listings, and the Santa Cruz Mountains Winegrowers Association is another good place to start for a map and information about tasting room hours and the quarterly Passport weekend promotion (831/479-9463; website webwinery.com/SCMWA/).

For those whose favorite outdoors activity is shopping, there are two particularly wonderful possibilities. The Pacific Avenue mall in Santa Cruz is thriving since it was rebuilt after the 1989 Loma Prieta earthquake. It's full of shops and galleries and restaurants. And Capitola-by-the-Sea has a great selection of unique items for sale in a pleasant beachside ambience.

Outdoors, schmoutdoors, you want a massage. Two highly recommended day spas can fix what ails you. The Sanctuary Day Spa is right across from the Seascape Resort (16A Seascape Village, Aptos; 831/688-7727; website www.thesanctuaryspa.com). And Well Within Spa, which has indoor and outdoor hot tubs, is in downtown Santa Cruz (417 Cedar St.; 831/458-9355; website www.wellwithinspa.com).

The arts and nightlife are everywhere (check out the website www.shakespearesantacruz.org for details on the annual late-summer Shakespeare Festival), but the most famous nightspot in Santa Cruz has to be The Catalyst, nearly 25 years old and still going strong. Everyone from Arlo Guthrie to The Band to Chris Isaak has performed here over the years, and today you can buy show tickets on the Internet (1011 Pacific Ave., Santa Cruz; 831/423-1338; website gate.cruzio.com/~catalyst).

Of course you can always just relax and do nothing, which probably would make you the most unusual visitor to Santa Cruz County.

Details, Details

SUITCASE

Despite the chamber of commerce hype about the weather, it can be foggy in the Santa Cruz area, particularly from Capitola south, so you'll want to bring along a windshirt or sweatshirt. But if you're golfing on a summer morning, wear shorts and gut it out for a few holes. You'll be glad you did when the sun breaks through. And mostly everything is casual here; dining in golf attire, you'll look as sharp as most and sharper than many.

Of course you will want your swimsuit for the pool and/or hot tub, and hats and visors are strongly recommended. And you probably will have no need for metal spikes on this trip.

GETTING THERE

From all points north and east, go south to Highway 880, which becomes Highway 17 south. Exit at Highway 1 south and continue nine miles to the San Andreas/Larkin Valley Road exit. Turn right onto San Andreas, and make another right at the flashing stop sign for Seascape Boulevard. The resort will appear between you and the ocean.

The Watsonville airport accepts any plane, up to 106,000 pounds dual-tired and 69,000 pounds single-tired, any time, and Hertz car rental is available on the airfield. In the lobby are direct-dial phones to Enterprise, as well as to a local Ford dealership that offers rentals. And here's a bonus: there's a driving range at the airport!

CONTACTS

- The **Santa Cruz County Conference and Visitors Council (CVC)** produces a free visitors' guide full of essential information on lodging, dining, and all of the area activities. It is the place to consult to erase any of your question marks (701 Front St., Santa Cruz, CA 95060; 800/833-3494; website www.scc-cvc.org).

- There's additional information about Santa Cruz and surrounding counties online at www.infopoint.com and gate.cruzio.com, which both link to most of the businesses that have a presence on the World Wide Web.

Chapter 16

Mission Possible: Hollister and San Juan Bautista

Long before there was golf in the Hollister area, there was motorcycle riding. It all started during the July Fourth weekend in 1947, when nearly 4,000 bikers converged on the small, unsuspecting agricultural community. Newspaper reports greatly exaggerated the goings-on, which attracted *Life* magazine photographers to the scene. The resulting image published in the magazine depicting an inebriated biker perched on his motorcycle, beer bottle in hand, struck the public's imagination and soon achieved star status, portrayed on film by the great Marlon Brando in *The Wild One*. "The Biker" was born.

Now, more than 50 years later, the Hollister Independence Rally has become a tradition. The first weekend in July more than 50,000 motorcyclists arrive for the well-organized event, where San Benito Street is closed to traffic so vendors can tout their wares and crowds can ooh and aah at the shiny motorcycles. One resident said, "It's a sight to see, all that chrome lined up block after block in downtown." After a day or two of reveling, the swarm of thousands departs just as quickly as it descended, and Hollister breathes a collective sigh of relief.

Hollister and surrounding San Benito County have long been mainly agricultural but became known as a golf destination when Ridgemark Golf and Country Club opened in 1972. Turkey rancher Sonny Paullus's dream to convert his old turkey farm into a golf course became feasible when new well drilling techniques produced a consistent water supply, and by 1972 the first 18 holes opened. The turkey farm provided the fertilizer for the project. The bittersweet opening day was also the birthday of Paullus's son, Mark, who had lost his life in a car accident two years before. In his honor, they named the golf course Ridgemark.

Homes were built around the course, membership grew, and soon another golf course was called for, which opened in March 1987. Ridgemark is semiprivate, and with the additional course, they were able to alternate courses each day so one course would always be designated for members only. Each 18-hole course combined nine new holes with nine holes of the original course. The first tee of the original course became the first tee of the Gabilan Course, and the first tee of the Diablo Course was the 10th hole of the original course.

The "new holes" are numbers 7–15 on the Diablo Course and the front nine of the Gabilan Course. Building the second 18 holes meant working around the newly constructed homes, and you'll notice when you play Gabilan, particularly, that there are many instances of crossing streets in the subdivision to reach the next tee. Residents, golfers themselves, are watchful of wandering golf carts, but sometimes you find yourself reaching for a nonexistent turn signal or wishing for a rear-view mirror.

Ridgemark's primary appeal has remained constant. It offers a great weekend getaway with two resort-style golf courses in a friendly, comfortable atmosphere. The 32 rooms are spacious, the food and drink are plentiful and convenient, and the price is right. PGA/LPGA head professional Kathy Wake sets the tone when she says, "We just want our guests to relax and have a good time."

Enter "Boom Boom." Popular PGA Tour player Fred Couples and golf architect Gene Bates collaborated to create San Juan Oaks Golf Club, which opened in 1996, just 15 minutes from Ridgemark. The championship course has five sets of tee boxes ranging from 4,770 yards to 7,133 yards, with all tees rated for both men and women. *Golf Digest*'s 1998 Readers Survey named San Juan Oaks the only course in California to rank in the Top 10 for both service and value.

San Juan Oaks also drew national attention because it is a no-smoking golf course, the first in the country. People shook their heads and felt sorry for any course marshal who would try to enforce such a rule. In fact, says former PGA head professional Bruce Lewis, they have had little problem. Smoking areas are designated at the turn and outside the clubhouse. Lewis explains that since native grasses are such an integral part of the area, fire prevention is important. In 1998 Lewis was flying over

Ridgemark on his way to San Jose Airport and saw a fire below, which happened to be on a remote part of the back nine. Fortunately, his superintendent activated the computerized sprinkler system in time, and helicopters took buckets of water from the lakes to squelch the fire.

Lewis initiated the popular Junior Club Boom Boom for players 7–16 years old. For their monthly events red stakes that look like big firecrackers are put at the 150-yard marker, an easier distance for most juniors. Increasingly, families are finding that playing the holes from 150 yards out, even when the "firecracker tees" aren't in place, is a great way to enjoy the course with children.

San Juan Oaks makes the most of its location in historic San Juan Bautista and reflects the area's rich heritage in its design. Note the mission-bell logo. San Juan Oaks fashioned its clubhouse after the Mission architecture, particularly the colonnade of arches facing the plaza. The Old Mission San Juan Bautista was founded June 24, 1797, by Father Fermin de Lasuen, successor to Father Junipero Serra. It is the 15th of the 21 missions established by the Franciscan fathers and is the largest.

The wide chapel with colorfully painted main altar and *reredos* behind the altar attracts sightseers, but it also hosts an active parish church with scheduled services held in English and in Spanish. The mission and several other buildings around the large plaza together constitute the San Juan Bautista State Historic Park. The mission was damaged several times by earthquakes occurring along the San Andreas Fault, which runs along the base of the hill below the cemetery, and walls collapsed during the 1906 earthquake that nearly destroyed San Francisco.

The mission buildings and plaza form the centerpiece for the town of San Juan Bautista, which still retains an authentic Spanish-Mexican atmosphere. Restored adobe buildings now house shops and restaurants, mostly on 3rd Street. It's a great town for strolling and musing about a bygone era. Although Hollister is the county seat, San Juan Bautista holds more attraction for tourists. Both towns pretty much shut down at night, although several restaurants offer Western music on weekends.

San Benito County made national news in early 2000 with President Clinton's decree expanding Pinnacles National Monument, 40 miles from Ridgemark, by 8,000 acres beyond the existing 16,000 acres. The park is known for its distinctive spires, crags, sheer rock walls, and subterranean caves. Conservationists want to protect rural San Benito County, but as Silicon Valley workers seek more affordable housing, Hollister is no longer considered remote, and large-scale development is even being proposed.

Ridgemark and San Juan Oaks offer very good golf halfway between San Jose and the Monterey Peninsula. On business in Silicon Valley? Drive down for the day. On your way to Monterey? Here's an opportunity to average out the cost of a pricey Monterey golf weekend by playing either course on the way down or back, particularly on the weekdays when green fees drop to $50 and below. Even with all the new courses north and south, Hollister and San Juan Bautista together remain a great bargain destination.

Itinerary

WARMING UP

Ridgemark is a fun getaway for a group of friends, for guys, gals, or couples. It's reasonably priced, and you don't have to drive after dinner. General manager Ron Taborski says that an average group size is 8–10 rooms, or a group of 20 people. They get a lot of private club members and groups that return year after year.

Reserve a golf package, including tee times, with one phone call to Ridgemark. Then make tee times at San Juan Oaks. Try to call as soon as the pro shop opens, especially for weekends. You may need dinner reservations if it's a weekend.

This destination revolves around golf, with not a lot of nongolf activities or family activities. However, it's also the kind of getaway where you can make your own fun, so if you do go with a group, creative nongolfers may organize a bridge game or some other diversion.

day 1 When you arrive at Ridgemark, you'll see how convenient it is, with the golf, pro shop, clubhouse, and lodging all easily accessible. Depending on the time of day, you could check in to your room or just leave your bags in the car and check in at the pro shop for your round. At this semiprivate course, an easy system accommodates members and public players. Each course is open to the public one day, then only to members the next day, so you'll have a chance to play both courses in two days. Both courses have lots of mature trees and are scenic layouts.

Leave yourself time to warm up at the recently expanded practice facility and heed the advice of PGA/LPGA head professional Kathy Wake, who suggests that the way to enjoy yourself on any golf course is to take the pressure off the scorecard by playing the yardage of the hole and selecting a club you can hit well consistently.

Keep that in mind if today is the day to play the Diablo Course, considered the more difficult of the two courses. It's hillier and has more water and more places to get into trouble. The par-4 first hole is below the lodging registration office, and it's an elevated tee to a wide fairway with a pond to the left. The dogleg-left fairway runs along Airline Highway and

California Missions

In the late 1700s, Spain wanted to secure its territorial claims to the New World and entrusted Father Junipero Serra with establishing a series of Franciscan missions in California. During the years 1769–1823, 21 missions in all were established, spaced about a day's journey apart along what is today Highway 101, or the old El Camino Real in Northern California.

The purpose of the missions was to convert the indigenous population to Christianity, and while that sometimes succeeded, the more lasting result was the creation of some of California's first settlements. When Mexico won independence from Spain, much of the mission land was divided up and the missions fell into disrepair, but most have been restored in recent years. The centuries-old Spanish missions weave in and out of our chapters, reminding us of California's vibrant history.

presents an almost blind shot to the green. Holes 1, 2, and 3 are long par-4s lined with weeping willows. The par-3 fourth hole plays long over water to an uphill green. Some of the lodging units overlook this green. Five-par hole number 7 is the number one handicap hole for both men and women. There's no avoiding the large ravine in front of the tee, which also comes into play on the second shot. A directional flag was recently installed midway up the hill because players were driving up to locate the green before hitting, which slowed down play.

Long hitters can probably drive the green on par-4 hole number 13, but the tiered green on hole number 14 will challenge players to hold the ball. Hole number 15 is a downhill narrow par-3 with a bunker to the right of the green not visible from the elevated tee. Two lakes come into play on par-4 hole number 16, while 17 is a short par-3. The tee shot on hole number 18 is a blind shot over the hill of a long par-5. Repeat players will notice that lots more homes have been built around Diablo, which now tend to define the course. The elevated tees and greens make for an interesting layout, and good shot-making is necessary to score well.

Relax on the outdoor patio, where you can order drinks from the bar window or grill items from the menu until 2 P.M. Now comes the convenient part. You can walk to your room and freshen up before the afternoon activities. We suggest going into San Juan Bautista this afternoon for some sightseeing, about 20 minutes away. Turn left out of Ridgemark onto Highway 25/Airline Highway and left onto Union Road until it intersects with Highway 156. Turn left onto 156 and follow the signs to San Juan Bautista.

Start with the historic Mission San Juan Bautista and the adjacent buildings surrounding the plaza, at Second and Mariposa Streets. Most of the shops are along 3rd Street. You'll find a large supply of dried flowers at County Bounty, handcrafted specialty candles at Terry's House of Candles, good quality Peruvian handicrafts including beautiful ceramics at Inka Market. Reyna's Gallery-Museum specializes in American Indian art and jewelry. Just a few doors down is the San Juan Bakery, where the French bread is delicious and so are the pastries. You may want to pick up something for breakfast. There's a coffeemaker in your room at Ridgemark.

Stay in San Juan Bautista and dine at Jardines. If it's summertime, you can sit outside in the big patio and be serenaded by live music while little chickens scoot around underfoot.

day II The Gabilan Dining Room is open for breakfast in the clubhouse, or you can grab something from the snack bar on your way to the first tee. If you played Diablo yesterday, today it must be the Gabilan Course, which is flatter than the Diablo Course with wider fairways—pretty straightforward. Kathy Wake says Gabilan is "more forgiving."

The first nine of Gabilan was built as part of the second 18 holes in 1987, and as such it weaves in and out of the housing subdivision. Follow signs carefully between greens and tees and stay on the paved cart paths alongside the roads. It can be easy to miss the turn for the tee.

The course starts out with a straight par-4, then a pair of par-5s. The drainage area of hole number 3 comes more into play when it holds water. Dogleg-left hole number 6 slopes left to right, so expect drives to kick right. It seems like a long way on the road to reach hole number 11, and several streets intersect. Hole number 11 used to be the signature hole of the original 18 holes and is the cover photo for the Gabilan scorecard. There's trouble along the right side with two ponds off the tee and dense trees. Cross a little bridge to reach par-3 hole number 12, where your tee shot has to carry the barranca. Holes 13 (par-5) and 14 (par-4) are long straight holes that play parallel to each other. Hole number 18 is a scenic, uphill par-5 with water at tee and green.

After lunch and some relaxation, we suggest you visit Pinnacles National Monument, about an hour's drive away. Turn right out of Ridgemark on Highway 25/Airline Highway heading south, and make a right on Highway 146/Pinnacles Highway. Dramatic spires and crags that rise abruptly from the surrounding landscape are the remains of an ancient volcano. The park covers more than 16,000 acres and offers hiking trails from easy to strenuous, with subterranean caves and rock climbing, if you have the energy.

After a full day in the outdoors, you'll be ready to return to your cozy room at Ridgemark and dinner at the Diablo Dining Room.

day III After breakfast, check out of Ridgemark and go to San Juan Oaks Golf Club, about 15 minutes away. Exit Ridgemark by taking a left turn onto Highway 25/Airline Highway. Go to Union Road and make a left, and follow it toward Highway 156 until you see the sign on your left for San Juan Oaks. The entry drive winds through pastureland for one and a half miles to the clubhouse.

Not to be outdone by Ridgemark's 36 holes, San Juan Oaks plans to build another 18 holes and a hotel, which would be situated to the right of hole number 14 on the hillside and wrap around hole number 18 to the front. Word is that Fred Couples is already contracted to design the course and the application has been submitted, but plans are stalled by a growth moratorium in the county. The new course would be country-club style, and the current course would retain its championship status.

Many of the trademark oak trees on San Juan Oaks have been transplanted from the more than 2,000 surrounding acres, which are part of the same ownership.

San Juan Oaks is set in rolling foothills with five lakes and large bentgrass greens. The front nine plays through a valley and has fairly level to rolling terrain, while the back nine goes above the valley floor to steep holes with expansive rural views. The course is in great condition, and Lewis points out that the fairways are striped in tournament condition every day.

Fairway undulations reflect the underground drainage work that prevents standing water from forming on the course. It's said that Couples's course design is like his game, and since he hits a slice, there are lots of dogleg-right holes. With five sets of tees, a big difference in distance is expected, but low-handicappers say they weren't ready for the difference in playability from the back tees. A dogleg will be more severe, or a tree or water hazard comes into play that wasn't there before, for instance from the second tee. Hole number 2 is named for Nutting's Creek, which crosses about 75 yards in front of the green. Hole number 3 is a sharp dogleg right but fairly short, and holes 4 and 5 go back into the canyon. On par-3 hole number 8 the lake isn't as much of a problem as the large multilevel green, more than 40 yards long. It can be a four- to five-club difference depending on where the flag is. You'll find the toughest green on the course on par-3 hole number 12. It rises about three feet from front to back.

Hole number 13, "The Chute," looks west to San Juan Bautista and is probably the most difficult hole, especially facing the prevailing wind. It plays as a par-5 from the forward tees. Hole number 14 is aptly called "Split the Difference" because the fairway is split by a creek. The left side is narrower while the more wide open right side is elevated above the green with a large oak tee protecting the approach. Hole number 15 is a long uphill double dogleg par-5 that plays as a par-4 from the forward tees. The par-3 hole number 16 is all carry to a long and narrow green bunkered in front.

The tee box of par-4 signature hole number 17 sits high above the fairway with expansive valley and mountain views. Play to the right center and catch a good downhill roll. From what are called "the Fred tees" on hole number 18, the tee shot must carry an area of native grasslands on this dogleg-right finishing hole.

By all means stop and have lunch at the majestic clubhouse, dining indoors at the Adobe Room or out on the patio, before heading home.

 NOTES

Extended Play. This itinerary would be best extended by playing courses from either the Silicon Valley, Monterey, or Pebble Beach chapters.

More the Merrier. Organize a small group to visit Ridgemark, perhaps creating a golf competition with prizes amongst your players.

Time Savers. If you have an early tee time at Ridgemark, give yourself enough time to get through the commute traffic around Silicon Valley.

Courses

ITINERARY SELECTIONS

Ridgemark Golf & Country Club
3800 Airline Hwy.
Hollister, CA 95023
831/637-8151 or 800/637-8151
website www.ridgemarkgolf.com

Ridgemark is casual and relaxed, allowing carts on the fairway at 90 degrees, and there's no rule on spikes. However, carts are required except during twilight. Weekend green fees of around $70 include cart. Ridgemark's dress code is clearly spelled out: shirts with sleeves and collars, no tank tops or T-shirts; shorts must have at least six inches inseam and be hemmed; no short shorts, spandex bike shorts, or cutoffs; slacks preferred, no jeans please.

Ridgemark's signature logo, "The Old Farm," recalls humble origins, but it is way

SCORECARD

THE DIABLO COURSE
Architect: Richard Bigler, 1972
Course Record: 62, Don Meyers
Blue: Par 72, 6,582 yards, 72.3 rating for men, 126 slope; 78.0 rating for women, 132 slope
White: Par 72, 6,068/6099 yards, 70.0 rating for men, 122 slope; 75.2 rating for women, 126 slope
Gold: Par 72, 5,807 yards, 68.8 rating for men, 119 slope; 73.7 rating for women, 123 slope
Red: Par 72, 5,441/5,361 yards, 67.0 rating for men, 116 for women; 71.0 rating for women, 117 slope, 71.7 rating for women, 118 slope

ahead of some newer golf courses by having all four sets of tees rated for both men and women.

TEE TIDBITS | The remodeled practice facility includes a 25-stall grass/mat driving range, green-side bunker with chipping green, and three putting greens, with PGA and LPGA teaching professionals on staff.

The comfortable clubhouse includes two dining rooms, a bar/lounge, and a grill for snacks both inside and outside. Breakfast and lunch are served in the Gabilan Dining Room, dinner and Sunday brunch are served in the Diablo Dining Room. The grill menu offers a selection of large salads; the half Cobb salad is plenty of food at only $5.50. Sandwich selections include classic Rueben, Philly steak, or grilled New York steak on a hoagie roll, all under $10.

Ridgemark is a semiprivate facility with about 450 members. Privileges of membership include making tee times seven days in advance and being allowed to walk the courses.

SCORECARD *continued*

THE GABILAN COURSE
Architect: Richard Bigler, 1972
Course Record: 63, John Bedell
Blue: Par 72, 6,721 yards, 72.7 rating for men, 126 slope; 78.2 rating for women, 132 slope
White: Par 72, 6,336 yards, 71.0 rating for men, 123 slope; 76.0 rating for women, 128 slope
Gold: Par 72, 69.9 rating for men, 119 slope, 73.9 rating for women, 123 slope
Red: Par 72, 5,624/5,512 yards, 67.6 rating for men, 116 slope; 72.1 rating for women, 119 slope, 71.6 rating for women, 118 slope

Tee times for both courses can be made 30 days in advance by calling 831/637-8151.

San Juan Oaks Golf Club
Highway 156 at Union Road
San Juan Bautista, CA 95045
831/636-6113 or 800/GLF-TEES (800/453-8337)
website www.sanjuanoaks.com

San Juan Oaks has lots of rules: no smoking, soft spikes only, and carts on paths. Severely sloped holes, especially on the back nine, make the carts-on-paths policy necessary for safety reasons. San Juan Oaks accommodates players of all skill levels with five sets of tees, all of which are rated for both men and women. Juniors and families enjoy the innovative "firecracker tees." The yardage book is detailed and helpful. It will cost you $90 to play on weekends including cart, but that's optional at $14. Twilight rates are called "Sundowner." Juniors, seniors, and San Benito County residents receive discounts. The dress code is fairly liberal, requiring collared shirts and no cutoffs. Lockers are available for men and women.

SCORECARD

Architect: Fred Couples, 1996
Course Record: NA
Black: Par 72, 7,133 yards, 74.8 rating for men, 135 slope; 80.2 rating for women, 146 slope
Blue: Par 72, 6,712 yards, 72.8 rating for men, 131 slope; 77.9 rating for women, 141 slope
White: Par 72, 6,342 yards, 71.0 rating for men, 125 slope, 75.9 rating for women, 136 slope
Gold: Par 72, 5,785 yards, 68.5 rating for men, 120 slope, 72.8 rating for women, 128 slope
Red: Par 72, 4,770 yards, 63.9 rating for men, 110 slope; 67.1 rating for women, 116
Tee times can be made 30 days in advance by calling 831/636-6113 or 800/GLF-TEES (800/453-8337).

San Juan Oaks runs a classy and stylish operation, more akin to a private club. The 19,000-square-foot adobe-look clubhouse follows the contours of the old mission in its design, with arches opening onto outside corridors. You'll like the selection and presentation of items in the expansive pro shop.

Breakfast, lunch, dinner, and Sunday brunch are served in the grand Adobe Room, which has high-beamed ceilings and a rustic wood-burning fireplace. The regional California cuisine has a Southwest flavor at lunchtime, when the menu features such items as fajita salad with chicken or prawns, Southwestern pork loin, and the border burger with salsa and guacamole. The Clubhouse Specialties come with soup or salad, but most items are under $10.

TEE TIDBITS | San Juan Oaks has an all-grass-tee, full-length 14-acre driving range with target greens, chipping and bunker practice area, and a 10,000 square foot putting green. Instruction takes place in a separate teaching area.

Lodging

ITINERARY SELECTION

Ridgemark Golf & Country Club has 32 one-story rooms that are spacious and well equipped and run along the 18th fairway of the Diablo Course in single-story, gray wooden buildings with shingle roofs. There's one tennis court. The quiet, secluded setting feels safe and relaxing. All rooms have either one king bed or two queens, sliding doors to small patios, and large bathrooms with separate dressing area. A king room is $100 and $115 for the same room with a hot tub. Ridgemark's golf packages are a good value. Two nights lodging plus two rounds of golf per person with cart and $10 in fun money runs $423. You can also get a package that includes one golfer only.
■ 3800 AIRLINE HIGHWAY, HOLLISTER, CA 95023; 831/637-8151 OR 800/637-8151

ALTERNATIVES

You can walk to the mission from the 34-room **Posada de San Juan** in downtown San Juan Bautista. The lobby has high ceilings with a tiled entryway and big fireplace. A small, sunny breakfast room serves continental breakfast, included in the room rate. The two-story building has no elevator. Rooms are attractively furnished with floral prints and gas fireplaces, and the bathrooms feature two shower heads and Jacuzzi tubs. Weekend rates are $105 for a room with two queen beds or $108 for one king with a balcony. Balconies overlook a walkway that runs alongside the hotel up to

the Cutting ⬛ [...] nain street of
town. ⬛ 310 [...] 831/623-2378

Lodging ir [...] out 30 rooms
each, located [...] ou'll usually
see one or tv [...] ﬞﬞﬞﬞﬞﬞﬞﬞﬞﬞﬞﬞﬞﬞﬞﬞ rﬞighway 25/Air-
line Highway on the way to the Pinnacles is a popular motorcycle route.
Room rates are well under $100 a night. The newest is the **Best Western
San Benito Inn** (660 San Felipe Rd., Hollister, CA 95023; 831/637-9248).
You can also try the **Cinderella Motel** (110 San Felipe Rd., Hollister, CA
95023; 831/637-5761), the **Hollister Inn** (152 San Felipe Rd., Hollister, CA
95023; 831/637-1641), or the **Wiebe Motel** (1271 San Felipe Rd., Hollister,
CA 95023; 831/637-5801).

Dining

ITINERARY SELECTIONS

Jardines (pronounced Hardines) is one of the best Mexican restaurants in
San Juan Bautista, serving northern Mexican fare in the big dining room or
outside on the landscaped courtyard, where little chickens run around
underfoot and live music plays on weekends. You might hear a duet of
mandolin and guitar or a Paraguayan harpist. Watch out for the prickly
cactus plants. Combination plates are under $12, and à la carte items like
crab and shrimp tostada or the unusual albondigas soup (large meatballs
with vegetables) run under $10. Regional specialties are served for dinner
on weekends in limited amounts, and include salad and dessert for $13.75.
You might find shrimp fajitas or Huachinango à la Alicia, local red snapper
in a cold cream sauce. The margaritas are great. Lunch and dinner.
⬛ 115 3RD ST., SAN JUAN BAUTISTA; 831/623-4466; WEBSITE WWW.JARDINESRESTAURANT.COM

The **Diablo Dining Room** at Ridgemark offers continental cuisine in a
friendly, comfortable atmosphere, so convenient if you're staying there, or
for an after-golf meal on your way home. Traditional Caesar salad is prepared tableside for two. Great pasta dishes with seafood include fettuccine
with prawns or farfalle Del Mar. Roast prime rib is served Friday and Saturday. You can add sautéed prawns to any entrée for an additional $6.50.
Entrées include soup or salad and are mostly under $20. Dinner and Sun-
day brunch. ⬛ 3800 AIRLINE HWY., HOLLISTER; 831/637-8151

Dine at San Juan Oaks' warm and spacious **Adobe Room** on steaks and
chops from the grill or clubhouse specialties like the slowly roasted baby-
back ribs, grilled salmon, or grilled lamb tenderloins. Some of the same
Southwestern dishes on the lunch menu work well at dinner too, like the

hacienda fajita salad and the spicy breast of chicken Diablo. Entrées include soup or salad and are priced under $17. On Friday nights, the all-you-can-eat buffet features either seafood or prime rib for under $20. Breakfast, lunch, dinner, and Sunday brunch buffet. ■ UNION ROAD AT HIGHWAY 156, SAN JUAN BAUTISTA; 831/636-6127

ALTERNATIVES

Owner Mike Howard calls his **Inn at Tres Pinos** (6991 Airline Hwy., Tres Pinos; 831/628-3320) a "destination restaurant" because you have to go out of your way to go there. Plenty of folks do. The former banquet manager at the Lodge at Pebble Beach, Howard has restored the 1880s-era, Spanish-style inn (there are no rooms, by the way) to an intimate, elegant restaurant, which he personally oversees. House specialties include the delicious Asian penne rigate, with shredded roast duck, fresh seafood, and filet mignon with green peppercorn sauce. Seasonal dishes might be venison or osso bucco. For $2.50 you may add any salad or soup to your entrée. The Inn at Tres Pinos is three miles down Highway 25/Airline Highway from Ridgemark. Dinner.

Progresso Tamale Parlor & Factory (230 3rd St., Hollister; 831/637-3278) has been owned and operated by the Zuniga family for more than 60 years, specializing in homestyle Mexican food. The tamales are still hand-made by cousin Elizabeth Valenzuela, who learned the skill from her mother and who is the only worker in the tamale factory. Articles have been written about the hardworking family that still maintains the old traditions. The wonderful tamales are $4.25, and other individual items, like enchiladas, burritos, or tostadas, are also under $5. Combinations of one or two items run about $10. The Mission-style adobe building with archways and cactus is as authentic as the food. Lunch and dinner.

One hundred years ago, **The Cutting Horse** (307 3rd St., San Juan Bautista; 831/623-4549, fax 831/623-1769) was a house of ill repute. Today it looks like the hacienda of an early California Spanish landowner with western-style decor like pen and ink drawings of Hollywood western stars and wrought-iron chandeliers. Cattle brands decorate the entry and deep, high-backed booths line the walls. This old-fashioned dinner house is known for its steaks and for the generous meals, which include soup and salad and a tasty little decaf cappuccino served in a shot glass after dinner. The steaks are as tender and flavorful as promised, but other menu selections are good too, like veal piccata, fettuccine Alfredo, or the crunchy pesto-crusted pork tenderloin over garlic mashed potatoes. You won't go away hungry. Entrées range $14–33, all inclusive.

Straying Off Course

Sightseeing

San Juan Bautista State Historical Park (200 2nd St., San Juan Bautista; 831/623-4881) contains the Mission San Juan Bautista (2nd and Mariposa Streets, San Juan Bautista; 831/623-2127) and several other buildings around the plaza dating from California's Spanish-Mexican days.

Spend some time browsing the shops in San Juan Bautista, like County Bounty (209 3rd St.; 831/623-4407), for dried flowers; Terry's House of Candles (400 3rd St.; 831/623-2293); and Inka Market (203 3rd St.; 831/623-1465) for Peruvian handicrafts. Reyna's Gallery-Museum (311 3rd St.; 831/623-2379) features American Indian arts and crafts. The San Juan Bakery (319 3rd St.; 831/623-4570) makes delicious specialty breads and pastries.

Outdoor Activities

Pinnacles National Monument (5000 Highway 146, Paicines; 831/389-4485, campgrounds 831/389-4462) is a park of more than 16,000 acres about 40 miles from Hollister. Visitors come to hike the many trails, some of which pass over or through subterranean caverns, and to climb the rock formations. No bicycles are permitted.

Hollister Hills State Vehicular Recreation Area (7800 Cienega Rd., Hollister; 831/637-3874) is a 2,400-acre area set aside for motorcyclists, four-wheelers, picnickers, and campers.

Events

For information on the annual Hollister Independence Rally, call 831/634-0777, fax 831/634-4452, or check the animated website, www.hollisterrally.com.

Details, Details

SUITCASE

Ridgemark sits in a valley sheltered by the Gabilan Mountain Range to the west and the Diablo Mountain Range to the east. Some sea breeze comes in from over the mountains. The weather is usually mild, but it can get really hot in the summer at both Ridgemark and San Juan Oaks, so be prepared with sunscreen and a hat. Casual dress is appropriate for the locations we've included. Bring soft spikes for San Juan Oaks. If you go to

Pinnacles National Monument, you'll want good hiking shoes and a flashlight for the caves. The wildflowers are splendid in the spring.

GETTING THERE

To reach Ridgemark from San Jose and points north, take Highway 101 south, south of Gilroy. Take the San Juan Bautista/Hollister 156 east exit. Continue past San Juan Bautista. At the second set of stoplights, turn right on Union Road. Continue down until you reach Airline Highway. Make a right on Airline Highway. Ridgemark is a half mile down on your right at the four-way stop.

From Highway 101 south (Salinas) take the Highway 156 exit to the San Juan Bautista exit and follow past San Juan Bautista to the second set of stoplights. Make a right on Union. Follow until it ends. Turn right on Airline Highway. Ridgemark is a half mile on your right-hand side at the four-way stop.

From Interstate 5, take Highway 152 west. Turn left onto Highway 156 to Hollister. At the blinking yellow light (approximately five miles) turn left on to Fairview Road. Follow until it ends. Ridgemark is directly across from the four-way stop.

San Jose International Airport is the closet major airport. Hollister Municipal Airport can handle smaller aircraft (831/636-4365).

CONTACTS

■ **San Juan Bautista Chamber of Commerce** 402A 3rd St., San Juan Bautista, CA 95045; 831/623-2454

■ **San Benito County Chamber of Commerce** 615-C San Benito St., Hollister, CA 95023-3988; 831/637-5315, fax 831/637-1007

Chapter 17

Almost Heaven: Monterey Peninsula

Not everyone can afford a ticket into Golf Heaven. Others can afford the ticket but can't gain admission at the heavenly tee times they'd like. Then there are those who've been there and done that.

This chapter is for all of you. We acknowledge that there's no place exactly like Pebble Beach but suggest that every golf course bears some smidgen of resemblance and that there's no place in the world where Pebble Beach casts as large as shadow as on the golf-rich Monterey Peninsula. So we offer two alternative golf itineraries for Almost Heaven. One of them we call Penultimate because the service, course maintenance, lodging, and dining on this itinerary come close to what you'll find at Pebble Beach. The other is the Budget version, where players can get a feel for the coastal conditions Pebble Beach players face, only at a fraction of the price, while sacrificing the luxury lodging and meals for something a bit more sensible. It's probably not a budget in terms of the other escapes in this book, but it certainly is one in light of the $300 rounds, $350 rooms, and $100 dinners at Pebble Beach.

"Pebble Beach attracts golfers to the area, no doubt about it," says Mike

Chapman, the director of golf at the Carmel Valley Ranch Resort course. "And the best thing about it is that everything else seems so much cheaper by comparison."

So the likes of Carmel Valley and Quail Lodge offer up $150 rounds without a blink, and golfers can't help feeling they've gotten a deal. And the Lombardo Group courses, Laguna Seca and Rancho Canada, can sell $80 rounds to visitors to subsidize discount programs for the locals. The visitors go away happy that they've played a first-rate course at what they think is a steal—again, in comparison to the Pebble Beach prices.

Our Penultimate package even has some advantages, we think, over Golf Heaven that have nothing to do with price. Because the getaway is centered, after a first round in the Pebble Beach trees at Poppy Hills, in the Carmel Valley, just a few miles inland, the sun is usually shining when the coast is fogged in. In fact, on a summer day, it might be 10 degrees warmer at Carmel Valley Ranch than it is at Pebble Beach Golf Links.

Also, the golf is generally less penal. Yes, there was some crying about the sadistic design Pete Dye initially provided Carmel Valley Ranch—with railroad ties across the center of one fairway to make your most perfect shot potentially awful—but Dye heard that out in Florida and came back to undo the damage he'd done. Now it's a more fun resort-style course, where a shot down the middle of the fairway is generally rewarded and the greens generally have no more than three tiers. At Poppy Hills, there were complaints initially, but many of those can be attributed to the unfortunate sequence of events that led to the public course replacing magnificent and super-private Cypress Point in the rotation of three for the annual AT&T Pebble Beach National Pro-Am. Now, even the pros enjoy the park-like setting and the bonus birdie chances that five par-5s and five par-3s present.

"We are not an elitist club; we are a great value with a well maintained course, so what is there to complain about," says Poppy Holding President and CEO Paul Porter. "David Duval, who likes this course, says, hey, it just takes a while to learn to play this course."

Not far from the Pebble Beach Company courses, where Pebble Beach is as tough as it is beautiful, Spyglass is even tougher, and Spanish Bay will gobble up golf balls by the sleeve, there are beautiful places to play golf that may make you smile about your score in the end and not just the scenery on the way. We know high-handicappers don't want to hear this, but you need to take some game to the Pebble Beach courses—except gentler Old Del Monte—or be prepared for some humbling. Our Penultimate and Budget escapes, on the other hand, are perfect for all sorts of players.

Another thing nice about golf—and even lodging and dining—on these itineraries is that when you're number two you try harder. From being able to make a tee time with a human, not recorded, voice at Rancho Canada to finding ball washer, club cleaner, water cooler, and towel all right on the cart included with the green fee at Carmel Valley Ranch, there are special touches when the ocean views disappear. Back in the early '60s, former San Francisco City champion Ed Haber opened his golf course at Quail Lodge with the help of Robert Muir Graves's sound design, and suddenly he found himself building a resort around the 18 holes. It quickly developed a starry reputation with its attention to details—imagine, 35 years ago, a newspaper delivered to the door.

"None of us had ever developed a golf course or a hotel before," said Haber, who had the help of friends. "But we created these facilities based on what we liked."

Haber was still working seven days well into his eighties, running to keep up with the competition, which in the Carmel Valley now includes the Carmel Valley Ranch Resort and the newest entrant to the scene, Bernardus Lodge. Bernardus is a small and ultradeluxe spa and food getaway, built by the owner of the Bernardus Winery, a few more miles inland from the four courses that dot five miles along Carmel Valley Road. It is carving its own niche, with sumptuous furnishings and personal touches, like making your area tee times for you.

Bernardus management will proudly tell you that even when the 57 rooms are occupied, the lodge doesn't seem full. They'll say the same across the road, up on the rolling hills that house the 1,700-acre, 144-suite full-service Carmel Valley Ranch Resort. There's a feeling of privacy in the Carmel Valley, a little more serenity than is to be found in lively Monterey or at the always busy courses and dining rooms at Pebble Beach, and a lot more space than there is in the village of Carmel.

It's not Golf Heaven, but our Penultimate and even our Budget itineraries are a long way from golf hell.

ITINERARY 1:
Penultimate

WARMING UP

There is a lot to do on the Monterey Peninsula, and nongolfers would enjoy this getaway. However, golfers should think long and hard before dispensing invitations: those who can afford it may want to play twice a day, with so many courses in such a small area. Then again, with the right partner and a suite at Carmel Valley Ranch Resort, golfers may not want to play at all!

So, call the Carmel Valley Ranch and reserve your suite for two nights. Discuss with the reservation agent what kind of view you'd like. If you'd like to book an in-room massage or a horseback riding trip for the afternoon of Day 2, do so now. Also request a morning tee time for Day 2. Call Poppy Hills 30 days in advance to make a Day 1 late-morning tee time. Call Quail Lodge to make a late-morning tee time for Day 3.

You'll be dining early enough at Baja Cantina and Rio Grill that you probably won't need a reservation, but definitely make one for dinner Day 2 at the Bernardus Lodge. If the weather is good, request a table outside (there is a fireplace and heaters) by the bocce ball court.

day 1

"Just being in the Del Monte Forest, there's such a special feeling of driving in through those gates," observes Paul Porter.

It's true, especially for golfers. Especially for a round of golf that won't even cost $100 for most. Poppy Hills could just as easily be part of the budget itinerary, but it's too great a course to be cast into the bargain basement. You won't be able to tell initially; in fact, when you get out of the car it may seem like there's too much commotion—the John Jacobs School is in session at the range, perhaps, and the putting green is full of players waiting eagerly to get going, and maybe there's even a line at the starter's desk in the pro shop. Not to worry: Take your clubs around to the back, check in, pay the walker's rate if you're the least bit fit, shop a little, relax, and get ready for the best golf course you'll ever play for under $80. (Hopefully you're an NCGA member.)

The NCGA built Poppy Hills a few years ago, when it had a little bit of extra money and came into a piece of land cast off by the Pebble Beach Company. A gorgeous piece of land, we might add, not because of views but because of its tall Monterey pine and cypress trees and nonparallel fairways, allowing the golfer to walk in a park while deer fearlessly graze alongside. Formerly, the NCGA headquarters had been at Spyglass, which was built by Robert Trent Jones Sr.; Jones Jr. designed Poppy Hills, originally with a less traditional feel to it, and work has been done over the years to bring the course's drainage into the 21st century while letting the design regress a bit to a more classic style. Poppy Hills, we are happy to say, is not as difficult as Spyglass, and the rough has to be overgrown in January to give the PGA Tour players a sufficient test. Which is not to say it's easy: The first hole will give players a good idea of what's in store. It's a par-4 with a decent-sized fairway as long as you stay left, but bunkers and a lateral hazard will pain first-tee slicers. The second shot will be a mid- to long iron in to a huge undulating green. Make par and it could be your day. Three-putt and, well, others have been down this road. The greens are big and challenging to read, lots of fun even for high-handicappers.

When you're finished, enjoy some time on the terrace overlooking the 18th green, having a beverage or some of the excellent appetizers the kitchen produces. Then exit 17-Mile Drive for Highway 1 south, turn left at Carmel Valley Road, and proceed about three miles to the Baja Cantina, on your right. (If it's before 4 P.M., drive right on down to Chateau Julien for a quick wine-tasting and perhaps a glass of something to your liking on the flowery terrace. Then come back to Baja.) You should be catching the early dinner hour; relax outside over a margarita and check the specials—if it's Tuesday it must be the lobster.

If it's summer, it should still be light when you make the rest of the drive to the Carmel Valley Ranch Resort, just a few more miles out Carmel Valley Road on your right. As you pass through the gate, you'll see lots of flower beds. The first time we were here, our first impression hit us right in the nostrils, with the scent of flowers wafting through the air. Check-in is one of the highlights. You don't, really. Someone shows you to your room and checks you in on a little hand-held computer. No waiting in line.

If you splurged on one of the suites with a private deck and hot tub, what are you waiting for? If not, put your suit on and find the nearest out-door spa—there are several scattered about the property. Then light one of the fireplaces and settle in for the night. Don't forget to order up some room service breakfast before you start snoring.

day II

Today you'll play "The Ranch," which is no relation to Diablo Grande's fine 18 holes in Patterson, described elsewhere in this book. This property indeed was once a working ranch, and there are still several in the valley. Then Pete Dye came in and got creative with his railroad ties and multitiered greens. After so many comments about Disneyland, Dye came back, and he and wife Alice softened up the layout. By that we don't mean it's soft, we just mean the old one bordered on the unfair. No wonder Dye charged only $1 for the welcome remake.

What players will find here now is top-notch service—from the curb-side bag service to the post-round club cleaning and incredibly friendly staff all along the way—and fantastic views. The front nine seems harmless enough, though the wind can sometimes roar through this relatively open and flat part of the course, and you'll wonder what the cart is for, after all. It seems to come in handy only when you pick up your lunch at the turn—don't miss the pasta salad if there's any left—and are happy to have someplace to put everything. Then you drive back through the tunnel you took to the first tee and keep driving, up to the 10th tee. And then you get to the 11th tee and you're gripping that steering wheel, vowing never, ever to walk this golf course. Hole number 11 is really something, though we haven't figured out how to navigate it successfully to make par on the tiny elevated green there at the end. Maybe blindfolds would help; the view is really something.

When you've finished, the afternoon is all about leisure. Maybe you'd like to play a few more holes. Perhaps this is your chance to visit Carmel

Valley Village to sample wines at the tasting rooms. Or maybe you saw the swimming pool and tennis courts at the turn and have other sports in mind. Then there's horseback riding, or maybe just a massage in the room. Enjoy the ranch, then gussy up for dinner down the road.

You're heading for the Bernardus Lodge, another upscale lodging option in the valley that's less for golfers, more for eaters and veggers (as in, let's go veg out). It's a delightful spot for dinner on a summer evening, with tables in front of the main dining room, Marinus, and more tables out in the courtyard by the big stone fireplace. We liked the coziness of Wickets— and the servers offered us both menus, so how could we go wrong? Guest is king at Bernardus; we liked that. Every morsel was scarfed up, and even dessert was deemed necessary. Not that they didn't give us enough food— it was just too good.

So, you want to know what to do after dinner? You're staying at the Carmel Valley Ranch, remember? Take your little flashlight and get out of here.

day III Enjoy the morning at CVR or mosey on in to Carmel Valley Village for a bit of breakfast. Then it's time to check out and head back toward the ocean, turning left at Quail Lodge.

Somehow it always seems peaceful here, even when the course is full and the driving range—just in front of the pro shop—is hopping. Most days, you'll see something that looks like a golf welcome wagon out there. That's Ben Doyle's cart full of teaching gizmos. Don't laugh; get a lesson. His reputation is mighty. Janet Coles teaches here too. She's the former LPGA pro who found that those who can do can also teach; her book, *Three Shots to Bogey Golf,* is a road map to improvement for women who are too busy to practice every facet of the game.

Lots of players walk at Quail Lodge, with good reason. The course is flat and nicely laid out, without ridiculous walks like the one you may have noticed on Day 1, from the ninth green to the 10th tee at Poppy Hills. It's difficult to characterize this course; through some of it, you feel like you're playing in the back alley between pricey homes, then in other areas you're walking through a tree-filled riverside valley. The greens are neither huge nor small, the fairways neither wide nor narrow. Experienced players do tend to observe that the par-3s, where most of us higher handicap golfers hope to make up ground, are unusually difficult, and there's no denying the beauty of the fourth hole, which takes players off the beaten path, greeting players off the tee with a wide tree-lined fairway that narrows as it approaches the elevated, small green. This approach is one of those shots that keeps the game from getting boring: you can't see how small the green is, or that it slopes from front to back, requiring a shot that lands just in front and rolls on. Most players either underestimate or overestimate, and bogey starts looking good.

Check out Doris Day's house high above the 18th tee—she actually owns that one little piece of the course. Then post your score, check out the pro shop—really, if you've gotten out of Poppy Hills and Carmel Valley without splurging on any of their many fine threads, you deserve to reward yourself here—and enjoy the 19th hole on the deck upstairs. It's not Pebble Beach, but, really, are you complaining?

Travelers who can't bear to leave just yet may stop at the Rio Grill, on the way out of the valley, for an oak-grilled burger, some center-cut pork chops, or perhaps a half-slab of barbecued baby-back ribs. We're not going to rush you.

ITINERARY 2:
Budget

WARMING UP

Let the rates dictate your itinerary, which means you want to go to Monterey during midweek, in the summer months when extended daylight hours will allow more time to take advantage of twilight golf rates. Book tee times ahead and book your condo at Sunbay Suites. With a condo, you'll have a full kitchen to prepare meals and save on eating out, so it would be a good idea to shop before you go and bring food with you. Order tickets ahead of time for the Monterey Bay Aquarium so you can avoid waiting in line to purchase. Tickets are about $16, less for seniors and students. Call 800/756-3737 or purchase tickets online at www.montereybayaquarium.org, or go to BASS outlets in northern California.

Since you have a choice of one- or two-bedroom condos, this itinerary could easily suit one or two couples or even a family. The nongolfers could either lounge around the pool at Sunbay or drop the golfers off at Bayonet and Black Horse, then go into Monterey or Carmel for the day, about 20 minutes away. When you play Pacific Grove Golf Links, the town and beach are close by, so the nongolfers would also have fun.

day 1

Heading south on Highway 101 through Silicon Valley is one of the busiest commutes in the greater Bay Area, but you can avoid the techies' morning rush by leaving midday on your way to Monterey. The communities south of San Jose, such as Morgan Hill, Gilroy, and San Martin, used to be primarily agricultural. Now large housing developments and even golf courses are beginning to make their way across the bucolic hills. Seaside's big sand dunes announce the dramatic shoreline as you approach the Monterey Peninsula.

When the City of Seaside took over ownership of Bayonet and Black Horse in 1997 from Fort Ord in conjunction with the Base Closure Act, civilians soon realized what gems the military had been hiding under all those overgrown cypress and evergreen trees. Houston-based BSL Golf Corporation signed a long-term lease to operate the courses and quickly brought both up to PGA Tour specifications. Course renovations included reshaping bunkers and repositioning tee boxes. Although trimmed considerably, the big gnarly trees still capture errant shots. In 1999 the PGA chose Black Horse to host the First Stage of the PGA Tour Qualifier and Bayonet to host the Second Stage, and in 2000, the reverse.

Big plans are in the works for Bayonet and Black Horse. Construction of a new driving range is scheduled to begin in late 2001, adjacent to the first fairway of Bayonet. Plans call for a new 450-room Hilton Hotel to be built on the site of the old driving range, with timeshare units to follow. The Buy.com Tour Monterey Bay Classic is held at Bayonet, inaugurated in September 2000. So now is the time to play these fine courses while they are still a great value and within the affordable range.

Bayonet is long and difficult, designed in 1954 by then–Fort Ord commander General Robert McClure, who named it after the 7th Infantry "Light Fighter" Division, nicknamed the Bayonet Division. According to local historian Ray A. March, at that time during the Korean War, many professional athletes who had been drafted into the military were stationed at Ford Ord. They had a baseball team that was almost all pros and a football team that played the San Francisco 49ers. The tough Bayonet layout was designed to challenge McClure's physically fit military troops. Keep that in mind when you begin to feel beat up, especially at "Combat Corner."

The infamous "Combat Corner" starts out with hole number 10, a long, uphill par-5. At hole number 11, the course departs from the straight and narrow and introduces several sharp doglegs. Hole number 12 was slightly modified, but otherwise holes 11 through 14 remain the most challenging combination on the course. With the elevated greens at Bayonet, you often can't see where the ball landed until you get up to the green.

Both courses now have four sets of tees. At 7,094 yards from the championship tees, Bayonet has a rating of 75.1 and slope of 139. High-handicappers will find it challenging to reach any of the par-3s with the first shot. The good news is that there is no water on either course.

After golf, continue south two miles past Bayonet and Black Horse until you reach Coe Avenue, where you will take a right going west. Sunbay Suites is one-quarter mile down on the right side. The compact but efficient units each have a full kitchen, cable TV, private phone service, and daily housekeeping. The Sports and Fitness Club offers exercise equipment, indoor and outdoor hot tubs, and heated swimming pool. So you really won't be roughing it. If the nongolfers checked in early and relaxed while you played golf, maybe they'll have dinner waiting for you. Outdoor barbecue grills are available, so save the price of dinner tonight by preparing your own and eating in. Same goes for breakfast.

day II Drive to Monterey for a look at the world-famous Monterey Bay Aquarium (831/648-4888), which opens at 10 A.M., 9:30 during the summer months. From Sunbay get back on Highway 1 south to Monterey; exit at Pacific Grove/Del Monte Avenue in Monterey and follow the signs to Cannery Row/Aquarium. It is the country's top aquarium, featuring more than 100 galleries and displays reflecting Monterey Bay's many habitats, including a three-story kelp forest and the one-million-gallon Outer Bay exhibit, where silvery anchovies spin by in an iridescent rainbow and ethereal jellyfish float rhythmically with the currents.

Take your time at the aquarium, or, for a change of pace, you can walk one block down Cannery Row to A Taste of Monterey (831/646-5446), a wine visitors' center where for $5 you can taste several Monterey County wines in a spacious tasting room/gift shop with a panoramic view of Monterey Bay. Relax at one of the window tables. The tasting fee is refunded if you buy wine.

Then drive a short distance to the charming town of Pacific Grove, also known as "Butterfly Town USA," due to the annual migration of thousands of monarch butterflies. From Cannery Row take Lighthouse Avenue west to Forest Avenue, less than a mile, and turn right for lunch at Peppers Mexicali Café, a casual setting featuring Mexican and Latin American specialties. From Peppers get back on Lighthouse Avenue west to Asilomar Avenue and turn right, about a mile, to Pacific Grove Golf Links, often called "The Poor Man's Pebble Beach." Twilight rate here is only $15, but it doesn't start until 3 P.M. during standard time months and 4 P.M. during daylight saving time. Nongolfers can drop off the players and spend the afternoon strolling around Pacific Grove or hiking the shoreline trail.

The course winds through forested areas to start, but its nickname better suits the back nine, which is laid out in links style over rolling dunes interspersed with thick iceplant as it nears the ocean. Quite a bargain for the price. And if you go for the late-starting-time twilight rate, you'll get to watch the sunset while playing the back nine ocean holes. After that sublime experience, depart the golf course and turn left on Asilomar Drive and go to Sunset Drive, about a mile, to the Fishwife at Asilomar Beach, which fortunately serves dinner until 10 P.M. The Fishwife is known for great food at affordable prices. Return to Sunbay Suites after a full day.

day III Take advantage of the resort-like exercise facilities and swimming pool at Sunbay this morning before having brunch in your condo and checking out, then heading over to Black Horse. Black Horse used to be shorter, more forgiving, and cheaper than Bayonet, until the course renovations were implemented. Now the green fees are the same for both courses, which is still a bargain since they compare well with the more famous Monterey Peninsula courses in terms of scenic beauty, degree of difficulty, and fine conditioning.

Black Horse was opened in 1964 and named in honor of the 11th Cavalry Regiment, nicknamed "Black Horse," which was stationed at the Presidio of Monterey 1919-40. When the City of Seaside and BSL took over in 1997, Black Horse was more extensively renovated and actually redesigned under the direction of PGA Tour architects. Yardage increased from 6,500 to 7,009 from the gold tees, and all of the tee boxes and bunkers were rebuilt, as were fairways 1 and 8, although the basic characteristics of narrow fairways and small greens remain. It's now considered every bit as competitive as Bayonet, and its hilly fairways yield more ocean views.

From the gold tees on hole number 4, you can see all the way to Moss Landing. On several blind tee shots on the back nine, players are guided by a sign: Aim at the Rock. The par-3s are shorter on Black Horse, most about 120 yards from the forward tees. The pink buildings with the red tile roofs behind the 10th green are the Sunbay Suites. Hole number 18 is a beautiful par-5 finishing hole, especially on a clear day.

At the end of your round, drive up Highway 1 north and exit shortly at Highway 156 to Castroville. Turn left at the exit to enter the town of Castroville, known as "The Artichoke Center of the World." And no wonder. All the artichokes grown in the U.S. come from California, the majority from Castroville. Betcha didn't know that Norma Jean Baker, a.k.a. Marilyn Monroe, was Castroville's Artichoke Queen in 1948.

The Giant Artichoke on your right serves up tempting fried artichoke hearts, but keep going on Merritt Avenue (the main street) to the Central Texan Barbecue, where owner Don Elkins, a Willie Nelson look-alike, heaps your plate with slabs of slow-cooked, pit-smoked meats and all the fixings.

 NOTES

Romantics. Stay overnight in a special B&B in Pacific Grove, like the cozy Gosby House Inn near the shoreline, or the Pacific Gardens Inn, nestled in the forest.

Money Savers. Play at Monterey Pines Golf Course, the former U.S. Navy Course, the most reasonably priced course in the county.

Extended Play in the Sun. Seeking escape from the fog? Add Laguna Seca or Carmel Valley's two Rancho Canada courses. And don't miss the Baja Cantina.

If You Have Only One Day and One Night. Play Bayonet or Black Horse on the way down, stay overnight at Sunbay, and play the other course on your way back

Courses

ITINERARY 1:
Penultimate

ITINERARY SELECTIONS

Poppy Hills Golf Course
3200 Lopez Rd.
Pebble Beach, CA 93953
831/625-2035, fax 831/626-5421,
golf shop 831/622-8239
website www.ncga.org

Poppy Hills is probably the best bargain in this book for Northern California Golf Association members—not because the $45 weekday member fee is so low but because it is generally unthinkable to be able to play such a carefully groomed and gorgeously framed layout for under $50, and in Pebble Beach let's make that under $150. Guests of NCGA members may play for $75, Monday–Thursday, while outsiders will have to fork over $115. Weekend rates go up to $50, $80, and $130, respectively. Carts cost $30. Metal spikes are not permitted.

SCORECARD

Architect: Robert Trent Jones Jr., 1986
Course Record: 63, Clark Dennis
Blue: Par 72, 6,822 yards, 74.6 rating, 144 slope
White: Par 72 for men, 6,236 yards, 71.5 rating for men, 138 slope; par 73 for women, 76.5 rating, 140 slope
Red: Par 72, 5,473 yards, 72.1 rating for women, 131 slope
Tee times are accepted beginning exactly 30 days in advance, with a credit card guarantee. And if you can't get the weekend time you want, call the pro shop; it will put you on the waiting list.

TEE TIDBITS | The setup here is convenient—big clubhouse, with restaurant opening into well-stocked pro shop (again, discounts for NCGA members are always in effect). Just outside are putting greens and a small driving range with one of the world's biggest clocks, so you'll be on time for the first tee. The food is good, and so is the view from the terrace. Carts are allowed on fairways only in the driest of seasons. The course is surprisingly walkable, except for the long hike from the ninth green through the tunnel under Lopez to the 10th tee. It can be quite difficult to get a tee time here in season; call as soon as you're eligible.

Carmel Valley Ranch Golf Course
1 Old Ranch Rd.
Carmel, CA 93923
831/626-2510, fax 831/626-2503
website www.grandbay.com

The Ranch used to be a bit more open to visitors, but Grand Bay Resorts is cultivating a new reputation for exclusivity. Rates for hotel guests are about $150, including mandatory cart and recommended range balls, and you can expect to play all day for that if you're nice to the staff. If your round is arranged by one of the other resorts in the area, or by the head pro of your own country club, you can expect to pay $10 to $20 more.

TEE TIDBITS | This is one of the more underrated facilities in the region, with a big pro shop stocked with fine, well-presented merchandise, a large bar and grill with a lovely outdoor deck, and top-notch service all around. Carts are stocked with towel, ball washer, club washer, and water cooler. Mornings and afternoons can be cool, because the course is situated between ridges to the east and west. Carts are allowed on fairways of most holes, making for fast resort rounds and allowing for replays. Lots of deer and birds call this course home. Front nine is fun, especially the pretty second hole, but wait until you see the back—and especially the views from some of the most elevated tees. The 11th tee is the highest point on the course.

SCORECARD

Architect: Pete Dye, 1981, 1996
Course Record: 64, Justin Russo
Blue: Par 70; 6,234 yards, 70.5 rating for men, 132 slope; 77.0 rating for women, 137 slope
White: Par 70, 5,563 yards, 67.5 rating for men, 123 slope; 71.3 rating for women, 125 slope
Red: Par 70, 5,046 yards, 65.2 rating for men, 120 slope; 68.6 rating for women, 120 slope
Gold: Par 70, 4,337 yards, 62.8 rating for men, 114 slope; 64.7 rating for women, 112 slope
Tee times for resort guests and club members only, available at the time you make your accommodations reservation.

Golf Club at Quail Lodge
8000 Valley Greens Dr.
Carmel, CA 93923
831/620-8808, fax 831/626-8481
website www.quail-lodge-resort.com

Quail Lodge is described as semiprivate, but as long as the members and resort guests are taken care of you can usually make a tee time from the outside. Weekend fees for resort guests are about $100 in winter, $125 in summer, including range balls and a cart that's not required and you really don't need, but rise to $165/$145 for nonguests. Juniors can play after 1 Monday–Thursday for $25,

SCORECARD

Architect: Robert Muir Graves, 1963
Course Record: 62, Lennie Clements and Bobby Clampett
Blue: Par 71, 6,494 yards, 72.1 rating for men, 129 slope
Gold: Par 71, 6,139 yards, 70.5 rating for men, 125 slope
Red: Par 72 for women, 5,595 yards, 72.2 rating, 128 slope
Tee times are taken up to a year ahead at the pro shop; credit card required for nonguests.

but that'll be $145 before 1. Twilight fees are generally available at a discount of $50 or even more, after 3 in summer and after 1 in winter.

TEE TIDBITS | Quail Lodge is home to some of the region's top teachers, including former LPGA pro Janet Coles and Ben Doyle, whose cart full of teaching gizmos will grab your eye at the wide, grass driving range just outside the pro shop. Clubs and shoes are available to rent, at $35 and $5, respectively. Course is very walker-friendly. This shop rivals any in terms of quality of women's resort wear. We're guessing it's not only golfers who shop here. Get a scenic lunch and drinks upstairs from the pro shop. Golf dress code is enforced and metal spikes are not allowed. It's okay to come and hit range balls, $5 or so for a large bucket.

Courses

ITINERARY SELECTIONS

Bayonet Golf Course
Black Horse Golf Course
1 McClure Way
Seaside, CA 93955
831/899-7271 (PAR-1), fax 831/899-7169
email bayonetgolf@redshift.com
Bayonet and Black Horse share a pro shop and grill. By 2002, however, expect many changes with construction of the new driving range and the planned hotel.

Most holes have ocean views when it's clear, but the fog can change everything.

Carts are required before noon on Saturdays, Sundays, and holidays. Green fees range from under $40 (weekday twilight) to peak rates of $75 plus $30 cart fees. Ask about special rates for seniors, juniors, and military. Soft spikes and collared shirts are required, no cutoffs.

TEE TIDBITS | Both courses offer excellent rates for military personnel who live within a 50-mile radius of the former Fort Ord. The driving range for both courses will be at the end of the parking lot until construction commences. The Bayonet Bar & Grill serves a full breakfast menu (omelets about $6, Texas flapjacks about $4) and lunch until 4 p.m. Lunch items are all priced under $8 and the full bar stays open after the grill closes.

SCORECARD

THE BAYONET COURSE
Architect: General Robert McClure, 1954
Course Record: 65, Notah Begay
Gold: Par 72/74, 7,094 yards, 75.1 rating for men, 139 slope
Patriot: Par 72/74, 6,817 yards, 73.6 rating for men, 135 slope
Pearl: Par 72/74, 6,496 yards, 72.4 rating for men, 132 slope
Crimson: Par 74, 5,763 yards, 73.7 rating for women, 134 slope
Tee times for both courses may be made 14 days in advance by calling 831/899-7172. For reservations beyond 14 days, there is a $10 fee. Credit card required to make tee times on Friday, Saturday, Sunday, and holidays.

THE BLACK HORSE COURSE
Architect: General Edwin Carns, 1964
Course Record: 64, Ted Oh
Gold: Par 72, 7,009 yards, 74.4 rating for men, 135 slope
Patriot: Par 72, 6,527 yards, 71.8 rating for men, 129 slope
Pearl: Par 72, 6,175 yards, 70.2 rating for men, 125 slope
Crimson: Par 72, 5,648 yards, 72.5 rating for women, 120 slope

Pacific Grove Golf Links
77 Asilomar Blvd.
Pacific Grove, CA
831/648-3177, fax 831/648-3179
Pacific Grove Muni, as it's called, has a loyal following of golfers who

pushno ①

...d low prices,
even though the clubhouse is a little
shabby and needs some TLC. It's a great
value for the Monterey Peninsula. The first
nine opened in 1932 and plays inland
among the pine and cypress forests. The
back nine opened in 1960 and was
designed by Jack Neville in true links style
over sand dunes that run to the sea.
Neville was the original designer of Pebble
Beach Golf Links.

The course is definitely walkable, only
5,732 yards from the blue tees. It's next to
the landmark Point Pinos Lighthouse, built
in 1855. Midweek twilight rates are $15

SCORECARD

Architect: Chandler Egan, front
  nine, 1932, and Jack Neville,
  back nine, 1960
Course Record: 60, Rich Hunter
  and Peter Vitarisi
Blue: Par 70, 5,732 yards, 67.7 rating for men, 119 slope
White: Par 70, 5,571 yards, 66.9
  rating for men, 117 slope; 71.6
  rating for women, 115 slope
Red: Par 70, 5,305 yards, 70.1 rating for women, 112 slope
For tee times call 831/648-3177
  seven days in advance.

plus $26 cart fee, vs. peak rates of $36 plus $26 cart fee. Also available are
nine-hole rates, junior rates, and one-year Play Cards for both residents
and nonresidents. Carts are allowed on fairways (there are no cart paths)
except in wet weather.

There is a driving range, chipping, and putting green. You can wear
either soft spikes or metal spikes, and there is no dress code.

TEE TIDBITS | Pacific Grove Muni is within walking distance to the beach and the shore-
line recreational trail, convenient to the small restaurants and shops and inns of Pacific
Grove, which are less expensive than the more glamorous parts of the Monterey Peninsula. The Grill is adequate but could use better ventilation and a menu update.

ALTERNATIVES

Even though Pebble Beach dominates the landscape, there are plenty of
other places to play in this region. Here's a look at our favorites, listed in
order of budget category from low end to high:

Monterey Pines was formerly known as the U.S. Navy Course and
remains a good value for civilians as well as military personnel. The course
is short (5,675 yards from the back/white tees), fairly flat, and quite walkable. Green fees range from $7 (military rate) to peak rates of $26 for weekends plus cart fee of $18. Note that these are _all day fees,_ for unlimited play
in one day. Monterey Pines is so casual, you can usually get on without
calling ahead. It's off Fairgrounds Road, not far from the Hyatt Regency
Monterey. ■ 1250 GARDEN RD., MONTEREY, CA 93940; 831/656-2167, FAX 831/656-4516

Rancho Canada's East and West Courses are well-cared-for public
courses that represent an excellent value. Turning off Carmel Valley Road,
you come to a T intersection with a sign indicating "Play Pray." Rancho

Canada is to the left and a church to the right. The West Course is more difficult, with the Carmel River coming into play, while the East Course presents a challenging back nine. Both grass and mats are available on the large practice facility, plus there's a chipping and pitching practice area. You'll find friendly service and good food in the spacious clubhouse. Peak rates are $80 (West), $65 (East), with an additional $32 cart fee. Note that twilight rates start at 2 P.M. during daylight saving time. Popular membership programs are well-priced. ■ P. O. BOX 22590, CARMEL, CA 93922 (ON CARMEL VALLEY ROAD, ONE MILE EAST OF HWY. 1); 831/624-0111; 800/536-9459; WEBSITE WWW.RANCHOCANADA.COM

Operated by the same group that keeps Rancho Canada affordable, especially for locals, is **Laguna Seca Golf Club,** known as the "Sunshine Course" for its location in the Monterey-Salinas corridor and bearing the signatures of Robert Trent Jones (Sr. and Jr.). Johnny Miller still holds the course record here, 64. Par is 71 and, more important for bargain hunters, green fees are $65 daily, not including cart, and $35 at twilight. ■ 10520 YORK RD. (OFF HWY. 68), MONTEREY, CA 94920; 888/524-8629; WEBSITE WWW.GOLF-MONTEREY.COM

Then there's the high end of things, the Monterey Peninsula golf scene known only to country clubbers, movie stars, and their friends, of which the most exclusive is **Cypress Point Club.** Cypress was designed by Scottish architect Alister MacKenzie in 1928 and sweeps along the sea in majestic fashion, pleasing to the eye and a treat to play. It's considered his masterpiece. The traditional feel of both the clubhouse and the course represent a step back in time. Cypress was used for the AT&T Pebble Beach National Pro-Am (formerly the Crosby) from 1947 to 1990. In true links style, some of the holes require long carries over dunes or ravines, but none tougher than the famous par-3 16th hole over the sea. You must play with a member. ■ 3150 17-MILE DR., PEBBLE BEACH, CA 93953; 831/624-2223

Seemingly next to Cypress Point along the ocean, actually between Spyglass and the Links at Spanish Bay, is the country club known locally as simply "The Country Club," **Monterey Peninsula.** There are two courses here, one of which, the Dunes, was redone recently by Rees Jones to either the dismay or delight of the members, depending on whom you talk to. The other is the Ocean. Used to be, the Country Club played host to the Crosby, but eventually the membership tired of that and found it's more fun to host a big charity shindig with PGA Tour players the Monday before the main event. Only a member can get you onto these courses, but if you play with one it's only $60 or so. Ladies, remember, skirts must be knee-length. ■ 3000 CLUB RD., PEBBLE BEACH, CA 93953; 831/372-8141

If you know Dirty Harry, you'll surely be invited to play **Tehama,** Clint Eastwood's exclusive country club just off Carmel Valley Road, the other side of Quail Lodge. Bill Murray belongs. Bryant Gumbel does too. It's *invitation only* to see a course reputed to be difficult, hilly and drop-dead gorgeous. ■ 7145 CARMEL VALLEY RD., CARMEL, CA 93923; 831/624-5549

Lodging

ITINERARY 1:
Penultimate

ITINERARY SELECTION

Carmel Valley Ranch Resort gets the nod here primarily because golfers will want to have easy access to the only Pete Dye spread in Northern California, but there are many golfers who visit here and do not care if they sink a putt during the course of their stay. It is, like the Bernardus Lodge described under Alternatives, one of those places that still seems serene and private even when it is full, and that's a tribute to the sprawling design (area of the resort is more than 1,700 acres, twice the size of Quail Lodge) and the friendly, unstressed, unobtrusive service. Let's just say that co-author Susan Fornoff spent her honeymoon here and leave it at that. ■ 1 OLD RANCH RD., CARMEL VALLEY, CA 93923; 831/625-9500; WEBSITE WWW.GRANDBAY.COM

GOLF PACKAGE OPTIONS

Quail Lodge came first among the Carmel Valley golf courses and resorts, but you'd never know it. It's been so well kept over the course of its 30-some years that there is not a shabby plank in its infrastructure. Rooms are on the small size, but they make up for it in luxury, peacefulness, and, most likely, surroundings. There are swimming pools, tennis courts, and two restaurants, plus the wonderful golf course. Golf packages start at around $200 a night in the off season. ■ 8205 VALLEY GREENS DR., CARMEL, CA 93923; 800/538-5916; WEBSITE WWW.QUAIL-LODGE-RESORT.COM

ALTERNATIVES

There are hundreds of places to stay from Monterey at the coast to Carmel Valley inland, and the Monterey County Travel and Tourism Alliance's guide and website are good places to start your search. Generally, you'll have to pay more for a room in the village of Carmel, and sometimes that'll get you little more than easy access to great shopping and dining; many of the hotels are stuck in the '60s and '70s. Best bets are any of the

Four Sisters Inns, including Gosby House and Green Gables in Pacific Grove, and any of our tried and true selections.

For the penultimate itinerary, golfers traveling with a romantic non-golfer will have to consider the new, ultradeluxe, sun-kissed **Bernardus Lodge.** With Quail and the Ranch cornering the market on golf packages, the owner of the Bernardus winery decided to offer upscale travelers a different option: sumptuous dining and spa services. So he lured the chef away from the Highlands Inn, and now foodies are flocking to Marinus and Wickets to sample his light French-inspired artistry and perhaps try their hands at a little bocce or croquet in the courtyard. Only lodge guests, however, may take advantage of the warming pool, sauna, steam room, and superb staff at the spa. Room rates start at around $300 plus the mandatory service charge. For more money, there are a couple of rooms that have hot tubs on their decks. ■ 415 CARMEL VALLEY RD., CARMEL VALLEY, CA 93923; 888/648-9463; WEBSITE WWW.BERNARDUS.COM

At **Stonepine** you'll feel like a guest at the country estate of someone with impeccable taste and the funds to indulge it. No expense was spared in the sumptuous furnishings of this French manor house tucked away amid 330 acres deep in Carmel Valley, sheltered behind massive wrought-iron gates. There are eight luxurious guest rooms upstairs, each designed after a particular style, such as "The Wedgewood Suite." Six other guest rooms in private houses and cottage on the grounds appeal to those seeking privacy. Regardless of the season, coat and tie are required in the guests-only dining room, set with fine china and crystal. Amenities include swimming pool, tennis court, and four golf holes built around a waterfall. The "horsey set" will love the Equestrian Center. Stonepine rates start at about $300 a night and quickly escalate. ■ 150 E. CARMEL VALLEY RD., CARMEL VALLEY, CA 93924; 831/659-2245; WEBSITE WWW.STONEPINECALIFORNIA.COM

Highlands Inn, now a Park Hyatt Hotel, opened in 1917 on a wooded hillside four miles south of Carmel, overlooking the spectacular coastline, and still has the best view around. The style is "rustic elegance," from the open-beamed ceiling of the natural wood lobby with north and south fireplaces to the clusters of buildings nestled among landscaped gardens. The rooms have great ocean views too, but the decor takes second stage. Most have wood-burning fireplaces and full kitchens. Rates start around $350 a night. ■ HIGHWAY 1 (FOUR MILES SOUTH OF CARMEL VILLAGE), CARMEL, CA 93921; 800/682-4811; WEBSITE WWW.HYATT.COM/HIGHLANDSINN

For all its touristy location right on Cannery Row near the Monterey Bay Aquarium, the **Monterey Plaza Hotel and Spa** is *très* upscale. Lots of teakwood and Italian marble. The entire roof was removed to build the new 10,000-square-foot spa and three huge spa-level suites, which are among the priciest accommodations in the area, from $1,200 to

Tennis, Anyone?

With our fine little game to occupy us for four or five hours each day, we confess to giving short shrift to that calorie-burning country club sport, tennis. After all, we would not want to wear ourselves out around the net to the detriment of our touch around the greens. But here on the Monterey Peninsula is a special place for the tennis players we love—and a chance for us to go along on the tennis package, for a change, while scheduling our own golf on the side. That would be **John Gardiner's Tennis Ranch,** where there is a tennis court for every guest cottage (14). The main attractions here are the intimate tennis clinics, but there are two swimming pools plus hot tubs and saunas, and the restaurant's focus is on delicious, healthy cuisine for the active golf, er, tennis player. Most visitors stay here on an all-inclusive tennis package; these begin at $875 per person for the two-day, two-night weekend "tiebreaker," with a credit for nonplayers. But a couple can also stay here and eat three meals a day for $450 a night. ■ **114 Carmel Valley Rd., Carmel Valley, CA 93924; 800/453-6225**

$2,800. If you stay in one of the new suites, it's just you and the spa on the entire fifth floor. The fancy European-style spa has nine treatment rooms and a full fitness center where you can watch the kayakers on Monterey Bay from your treadmill. Rates start at just over $200 a night. ■ 400 CANNERY ROW, MONTEREY, CA 93940; 800/334-3999; WEBSITE WWW. WOODSIDEHOTELS.COM

If your style is between "Almost Heaven" and "Budget," you may want to splurge on the golf itinerary and buckle down on the lodging and dining. In that case, consider some of the homier places in Carmel Valley. **Acacia Lodge** and **Hidden Valley** offer comfortable accommodations overlooking gardens and pool within walking distance of Carmel Village, starting at around $110. ■ FOR RESERVATIONS, CALL 800/367-3336; WEBSITE WWW. COUNTRYGARDENSINN.COM.

There's also the **Los Laureles Lodge,** formerly the Los Laureles Country Inn. A rustic country atmosphere is promised here, where the history of hospitality goes back 100 years. Rooms start at around $125 a night. New owners brought in a chef from Club XIX at The Lodge at Pebble Beach to revamp the restaurant menu and the French country cuisine is getting high marks. ■ 313 W. CARMEL VALLEY RD., CARMEL, CA 93923 JUST OUTSIDE THE CARMEL VALLEY VILLAGE; 831/659-2233; WEBSITE WWW.LOSLAURELES.COM

Lodging

ITINERARY 2:
Budget

ITINERARY SELECTION

Sunbay Suites has studio, one-bedroom, and two-bedroom units, some of which have couches that convert into beds. They are compact but fully equipped and offer daily housekeeping service as well as outside barbecues and access to the Sports and Fitness Center. The best units are upstairs on the back side away from the parking and facing the trees. Sunbay is currently the most convenient lodging to Bayonet and Black Horse; however, there are no restaurants or stores on site. Rates start at $129 a night. Golf packages start at $250 a night including a studio unit and two rounds of golf with cart. ■ 5200 COE AVE., SEASIDE, CA 93955; 831/394-0136 OR 800/285-3131; WEBSITE WWW.SUNBAYSUITES.COM

GOLF PACKAGE OPTIONS

The 575-room **Hyatt Regency Monterey** offers room and golf packages with the adjacent Del Monte Golf Course. The hotel has 26 rustic-style, wood-shingled, three- and four-story buildings set on 22 acres with several swimming pools and tennis courts. The packages include a room with breakfast for two plus cart and golf, which usually runs under $300, but the rate varies according to the day you want and sometimes the package rate may not be available at all. ■ 1 OLD GOLF COURSE RD., MONTEREY, CA 93940; 831/372-1234 OR 800/233-1234

ALTERNATIVES

Gosby House Inn would be a splurge on the Budget itinerary, but well worth it. This National Historic Landmark inn opened in 1887, its 22 spacious guest rooms comfortably furnished in classic Victorian style, most with fireplaces. It's within walking distance to the center of Pacific Grove and to the shoreline recreation trail that winds by Lovers Point. Rates range $90–170 and include full breakfast and afternoon wine and hors d'oeuvres. ■ 643 LIGHTHOUSE AVE., PACIFIC GROVE, CA 93950; 831/375-1287 OR 800/527-8828, FAX 831/655-9621

   Pacific Gardens Inn is an attractive two-story brown-shingled building with flowers in window boxes and gardens. Rooms have wood-burning fire-

Every Dog Has Its Day

Dog lovers can rejoice. Some Monterey Peninsula hotels accept dogs, so you don't have to leave man's best friend moping at home while you're off on a golf getaway. And just so you know, these hotels are not *dogs* themselves, but some of the finest, e.g., The Lodge at Pebble Beach and Quail Lodge.

Perhaps the most famous dog-friendly hotel is The Cypress Inn, owned by animal-lover Doris Day and recently featured in *Architectural Digest* for the stunning renovation restoring its 1929 Spanish Colonial Revival design.

San Mateo acupuncturist and dog lover Joanne Wolfeld shares her recent experience at the Cypress Inn, accompanied by her furry daughter, Coralise, "Queen of the Valley," a purebred keeshond:

"Concierge Kevin Hale opened the double glass doors and said, 'Welcome, what is your name and his name?' 'Her name is Cora,' I replied. Kevin said, 'She is beautiful,' and pointed the way to the front desk where Michelle checked us in and leaned over the desk to say, 'Happy Birthday, Cora.' Then Kevin asked, 'How old is she?' I told him nine years old, and he said, 'She doesn't look nine or act that age.' Later when Cora and I were having tea in the library/bar, Kevin brought a biscuit for Cora and some water, as well as a list of reliable pet-sitters, and a pet-friendly dining list. We chose to dine at Nico.

"We arrived about 6:30 and were offered a seat on the side patio. Immediately the waiter brought Cora a disposable container of water. We ordered from the wonderful Italian/Mediterranean menu, Caesar salad and penne pasta with seafood for me, and a chicken breast for Cora, no sauce. When my entrée arrived, the waiter brought Cora's chicken breast on a disposable plate and asked if he had cut the chicken up in small enough pieces for her. The restaurant had attractive, soft décor, with low lighting and a roaring fire in the fireplace, candles on the tables, and romantic Italian music played at a comfortable level in the background. We both had a lovely evening."

Cypress Inn rates start at $185 for a queen bed and from $275 for a deluxe room. There is a deposit of $20 per pet, each additional pet $12, maximum two pets. There is no regulation on the size of the pet. However, guests must sign a "Pet Check-in Agreement," which emphasizes two main rules: pets cannot be left alone in the rooms, and pets must be on a leash while in the lobby/public areas of the Cypress Inn. This applies to both cats and dogs. ■ **Lincoln and 7th, P. O. Box Y, Carmel-by-the-Sea, CA 93921; 831/624-3871 or 800/443-7443, fax 831/624-8216; email info@cypress-inn.com; website www.cypress-inn.com**

Nico is open for lunch and dinner. ■ **San Carlos between Ocean and 7th, Carmel-by-the-Sea, P. O. Box 6315, Carmel, CA 93921; 831/624-6545**

places, popcorn poppers, and coffeemakers, and suites offer fully-equipped kitchens. It's in a forested setting close to Asilomar Beach, with two out-door hot tubs. Rates from $85 to $175 include continental breakfast and afternoon wine and cheese. ■ 701 ASILOMAR BLVD., PACIFIC GROVE, CA 93950; 831/646-9414 OR 800/262-1566, FAX 831/647-0555; WEBSITE WWW.PACIFICGARDENSINN.COM

Lighthouse Lodge and Suites is really two different properties on Lighthouse Avenue, walking distance to the ocean. Both are a good value. The lodge is a two-story, motel-style structure with comfortable rooms and a heated pool. Full breakfast is served in the morning, and a late afternoon barbecue buffet is like dinner: grilled hamburgers, salads, chips, and drinks. Great for families with hungry kids in wet bathing suits. The suites are more elaborate, and the barbecue is replaced by a sophisticated wine and hors d'oeuvres selection. Rates range from $79 to over $500. ■ 1150 LIGHTHOUSE AVE. (ROOMS) AND 1249 LIGHTHOUSE AVENUE (SUITES), PACIFIC GROVE, CA 93950; 831/655-2111 OR 800/858-1249, FAX 831/655-4922; WEBSITE WWW.LHLS.COM

The two-story **Coachman's Inn** in central Carmel has 30 spacious rooms around a courtyard and is "golfer-friendly." It's become a hideaway for the pros during the AT&T Pebble Beach National Pro-Am, and in the reception area it proudly displays the "Coachman's Cup," which honors the guest PGA Tour professional recording the lowest score during the annual AT&T Pro-Am. Names engraved on the trophy include David Duval, Jim Furyk, Steve Jones, and Grant Waite (2000). Rates are $115–250 including continental breakfast and afternoon sherry, but mention that you're in town to play golf and you may get a better rate, especially during the week. ■ SAN CARLOS AT 7TH, CARMEL, CA 93921; 831/624-6421 OR 800/336-6421, FAX 831/624-3311; WEBSITE WWW.COACHMANSINN.COM

We'll also vouch for the **Horizon Inn,** one of those in-Carmel establish-ments once stuck in the '60s but recently remodeled and still reasonable, with rooms (plus continental breakfast, newspaper, and in-room fridge) start-ing at around $140 in high season, and discounts available on slow nights. ■ 3RD AT JUNIPERO, CARMEL, CA 93921; 800/350-7723; WEBSITE WWW.HORIZONINNCARMEL.COM

Dining

ITINERARY 1:
Penultimate

ITINERARY SELECTIONS

Baja Cantina calls itself a "Grill and Filling Station" and looks like a road-side gas station from the 1930s, displaying the history of automotive racing and oil and gas companies through a vast collection of memorabilia inside and out: metal signs, antique filling pumps, and the like. You can order just a taco, but the full meals like fajitas or combination plates are a good value, and the New York steak is the highest priced menu item at around $20. Baja Cantina's party atmosphere really shines during big events like car races at nearby Laguna Seca or Cinco de Mayo, and there are special menus even in the middle of the week, like Lobster Night on Tuesday, Prime Rib night on Wednesday. Live band on weekends. The food is good and it's a fun place to enjoy with friends. Big patio area. Lunch, dinner, Sunday brunch. ■ VALLEY HILLS CENTER, 7166 CARMEL VALLEY RD. (NEXT TO QUAIL LODGE), CARMEL; 408/625-2252

Wickets and **Marinus** at the Bernardus Lodge appear here as one entry, mainly because the same chef designed both menus and the staff is just so eager to please that you may order from either one. Marinus has a more formal atmosphere, though the tables on the terrace create another atmosphere altogether. Wickets is a more bistro-style environment, with a bar and televisions informalizing the atmosphere. And we expect the most popular tables here to be the few by the big stone fireplace in the courtyard next to the bocce ball court. Entrées start around $20. Breakfast, lunch, dinner, outdoor tables daily. Reservations requested. ■ 415 CARMEL VALLEY RD., CARMEL VALLEY; 831/658-3500

The decor and the name of the **Rio Grill** are Southwestern, but the food is far more adventurous in flavors. Pastas, seafood, steaks, and vegetarian dishes start at around $15 for dinner, and the specialty is anything from the grill and smoker. There is usually an interesting selection of wines by the glass. Lunch and dinner daily. Reservations recommended. ■ 101 CROSSROADS BLVD., CARMEL; 831/625-5436

ALTERNATIVES

Naturally, the fine dining options around the Monterey Peninsula boggle the palate. If you're looking for a particular cuisine or price range, the online information at www.critics-choice.com is a place to start. And there are so many little wonderful restaurants in the village of Carmel, you can just walk the streets and peruse the menus before settling on something that seems right at the time. Also, remember that there's nothing stopping you from trying the wonderful restaurants of the Pebble Beach Company, described in Chapter 18.

We're going to focus on options convenient to the Penultimate itinerary we've laid out. There's quite a lineup of cuisines in sleepy Carmel Valley Village, and you can park your car and look at all the menus until you find something that appeals to you.

Bon Appetit (7 Del Fino Place, Carmel Valley; 831/659-3559) supplies the Continental option, with salads and sandwiches at lunch and pastas, seafood, and grilled rack of lamb at dinner. Entrées start around $12 and don't range too far from there. Closed on Tuesdays, and the dining hour ends at 9.

The quaint, homey Italian favorite is right next door: **Sole Mio Caffe Trattoria** (3 Del Fino Place, Carmel Valley; 831/659-9119). The food is all-Italian, starting with the fresh bruschetta, and pastas start at around $12. The long menu doesn't stop there. Lunch and dinner daily except Monday. Reservations recommended on weekends.

For a little western flavor there are the **Running Iron** (24 E. Carmel Valley Rd., Carmel Valley; 831/659-4633), a popular breakfast and burger spot, and **Will's Fargo Dining House and Saloon** (West Carmel Valley Road; Carmel Valley; 831/659-2774), which specializes in steak starting at $21 including soup or salad and sides. Both are open daily, and both are right on Carmel Valley Road in the heart of the village.

Dinner at **The Oaks at Carmel Valley Ranch** (1 Old Ranch Rd., Carmel Valley; 831/626-2533) makes for a honeymoon highlight. It's a romantic spot with views of the valley, and the menu is a touch on the Cal-Asian side, including some Golden Door low-fat recipes. Entrées start around $15, and reservations are recommended for dinner. Breakfast and dinner daily. The Ranch also offers poolside dining during lunch hours at the Terrace Grill, but with a very limited menu.

There's also fine dining at Quail Lodge, where **The Covey** (8205 Valley Greens Dr., Carmel; 831/624-2888) serves salads for two, with lots of fresh seafood, including locally farmed abalone, and meat-eaters' favorites like grilled tournedos of beef and medallions of veal. Dinner prices start at around $21, but you'll spend much more. Open nightly from 6 P.M.

You'll find ocean views from every table in the glass-walled multilevel restaurant called **Pacific's Edge,** at the Highlands Inn, which overlooks the coastline south of Carmel from Pt. Lobos State Park to Yankee Point (Highway 1, four miles south of Carmel; 831/620-1234). Book ahead if you want table four for that special celebration lunch. Also, the cozy corner looking out at the twinkling lights on the trees is the perfect spot for a romantic dinner. With this kind of atmosphere, you might not even care about the food, but it's just as good as the view. Try the four-course prix fixe menu, which might feature lobster, venison, or seafood. Take some time with the wine list; it consistently wins the "Wine Spectator Grand Award." Entrées run from $23 to $35, and the set menu is $90 per person including wines. Lunch, dinner, and Sunday brunch. Complimentary valet parking for dinner guests as well as hotel guests.

Dining

ITINERARY 2:
Budget

ITINERARY SELECTIONS

Peppers Mexicali Café is famous for fresh Mexican food like homemade salsas, grilled tacos, creative seafood dishes, and homemade tamales, in generous portions, spicy but not overbearing. The light, casual atmosphere has a tropical feel to it. Try the flavored margaritas. Lunch and dinner, entrées $10–15. ■ 170 FOREST AVE., PACIFIC GROVE; 831/373-6892

The Fishwife at Asilomar Beach is just two blocks from the ocean and serves up impressive seafood specials, including salads and pastas, as well as housemade desserts, of which Key lime pie is the most famous. You won't find the rare delicacy, abalone, here but the calamari abalone-style is a close second. It's a casual, unpretentious place and consistently rated by local publications as "Best Valued Restaurant." Lunch entrées are usually under $10 and dinner under $15. Lunch, dinner, and Sunday brunch. ■ 1996 1/2 SUNSET AT ASILOMAR, PACIFIC GROVE; 831/375-7107

The Central Texan Barbecue calls itself a "smoking pit stop," a reference to its smoked meats so well known by locals. The most famous dish is the tender beef brisket, smoked for 18–20 hours. In business for more than 15 years, owner Don Elkins has created a memorable place: two brightly lit rooms with sawdust covering the floor, saddles, boots, beer signs, and license plates on the walls. Beer and wine are served at the four-barstool Rattlesnake Bar. Line up to get your plates and take a seat at a wooden booth or picnic table. Meals are generous and include pinto beans, French bread, salad, and fixings. They're all around $9, with a choice of the brisket, ribs, chicken, homemade sausage, or ham. Sandwiches are $6.50. Lunch and dinner. ■ 10500 MERRITT, CASTROVILLE; 831/633-2285, FAX 831/633-8396

ALTERNATIVES

At the **Mediterranean Market** in Carmel (Ocean Avenue and Mission, Carmel; 831/624-2022) you can get wonderful deli fixings to go and create your own picnic or have sandwiches made up. Full selection of meats, cheeses, salads, and condiments, as well as special hot dishes like Italian sausage and peppers, and wine as well. Take it to the beach or to the park next door.

r.g. Burgers is on lively Alvarado Street in Monterey, which seems to attract a casual, hip crowd (470 Alvarado St., Monterey; 831/647-3100). It offers a good selection of reasonably priced burgers, sandwiches, and salads, as well as beverages including milk shakes and malts. The burgers average $5–6. Lunch and dinner.

Lallapalooza (474 Alvarado St., Monterey; 831/645-9036) is two doors down from r.g. Burgers and known for "big American meals" and an extensive martini bar. It's colorful and fun with "twisted olive" paintings and illustrations decorating the walls. The big American meals range from $8 for a cheeseburger to $24 for filet mignon, with pastas, fresh fish, and big salads somewhere in between. Lots of menu choices. Lunch, dinner, and cocktails.

Straying Off Course

If tennis is your game, Carmel Valley is an excellent destination. All of the lodging properties have access to courts, and John Gardiner's Tennis Ranch has long made its home here. Check the Carmel Valley website for the latest information.

Hikers, bikers, and horseback riders will find some glorious opportunities around the Monterey Peninsula. There's Garland Ranch Park in Carmel Valley (831/659-4488), where hikers and horseback riders can see the entire valley at one point up in the Santa Lucia Mountains. And Point Lobos (831/624-4909), a favorite site for hiking, beachcombing, and sea otter watching, is just three miles south of the village of Carmel. There's also some wonderful hiking and beach strolling farther south, at Big Sur, especially Pfeiffer Big Sur State Park (831/667-2315) and Andrew Molera State Park, which also has equestrian trails (831/667-2315). Just the drive down to Big Sur—with a stop at Nepenthe to lounge and have a sandwich on the open-air deck—makes for a wonderful half-day excursion. Your hotel's concierge or the sources listed under Contacts can help you launch any of these activities.

You can rent horses at a number of places in Carmel Valley, including Holman Ranch (831/659-6054) and Carmel Valley Trail Rides (through the Carmel Valley Ranch Resort).

Of course there is wonderful shopping in the village of Carmel, at the Barnyard near the intersection of Highway 1 and Carmel Valley Road and in the Cannery Row area of Monterey.

Many of the area's fine resort spas are for guests only, including Bernardus, Monterey Plaza, and Carmel Valley Ranch. The Spanish Bay Club has offered spa services to outsiders, though it is slated for a renovation (800/654-9300). And two magnificent properties in Big Sur are open to day visitors, the Allegria Spa at Ventana Inn (831/667-2331; website www.

ventanainn.com) and the Spa at Post Ranch Inn (800/527-2200; website www.postranchinn.com).

Carmel has been an artists' colony for decades. The more than 50 art galleries along Carmel's tree-lined streets and hidden courtyards feature local artists as well as works of art from all over the world. Most are between 5th and 6th Streets, between Lincoln and San Carlos. Take your time browsing through the many galleries; most welcome visitors. If the art scene seems a tad overwhelming, the Carmel Art Association produces a free booklet you can pick up in town that includes a map and categories of art.

Golfers will appreciate Richard MacDonald Galleries (San Carlos between 5th and 6th; 831/624-8200), which represents the work of one of the most collected figurative bronze sculptors at work today. MacDonald's 15-foot bronze monument of a golfer in swing, commissioned especially for the 2000 U.S. Open at Pebble Beach, graced the main spectator entrance. MacDonald's 24-foot high bronze sculpture *The Gymnast* commemorated the 1996 Summer Olympics in Atlanta.

Other than the center at Cannery Row or the tasting rooms in Carmel Valley Village, wine-tasting can make for quite a scattered day here. The Monterey County Vintners and Growers Association can help boil it down. It's got an excellent map and guide (P.O. Box 1793, Monterey, CA 93942-1793; 831/375-9400; website www.montereywines.org).

Readers will have to tell us about the area's nightlife. Outside from a cocktail or two at the Jack London in Carmel, we have generally been too exhausted to have much life left at night.

Details, Details

SUITCASE

We'll give you one little word about the weather: youneverknow. In Carmel Valley, it's generally warmer and sunnier than at the coast, but once the sun drops behind the mountains—or in the morning, before it's emerged—it can be very chilly. Shorts probably will be comfortable, but you will want something warm to wear above. Carmel Valley can get downright hot in late summer. Be prepared for summer fog along the coast and dress warmly. The distant ocean views are beautiful from both Bayonet and Black Horse, but some days you can't see the water at all for the fog. Do not attempt to play the Monterey Peninsula courses in January and February without rain gear close at hand.

On these itineraries you are okay being casual, though for the Penultimate itinerary you may want to get a little more chicly dressed for dinner at the Bernardus Lodge. Bring soft spikes and a swimsuit for the pools and hot tubs, and good walking shoes for extracurricular activities.

GETTING THERE

To start Itinerary 1 at Poppy Hills, take Highway 1 to the Monterey Peninsula and follow the signs to Pebble Beach. After you enter the gates, follow the signs to Poppy Hills Golf Course.

To start Itinerary 2 at the Bayonet and Black Horse courses: From San Francisco, San Jose, or points north, take Highway 101 south and exit at Highway 156 west to Castroville, until it turns into Highway 1. From Highway 1, take the Fort Ord/CSUMB exit, travel east to Moore Blvd., and take a right traveling south until you see the Bayonet/Black Horse entrance on McClure Way, on the right.

Monterey Peninsula Airport serves the major airlines, and private jet passengers are well taken care of at Million Air Monterey; 831/648-4888. Or you can fly into San Jose and rent a car for the 75-minute drive.

CONTACTS

- The **Monterey County Travel and Tourism Alliance** can help start your lodging search, and its website is also helpful (888/221-1010; website www.gomonterey.org).
- The **Monterey Peninsula Visitors and Convention Bureau** (P. O. Box 1770, Monterey, CA 93942-1770; 831/649-1770; website www.monterey.com) annually produces a thorough guide to the area, especially useful in finding lodging. It's available at a fee of about $6.

- Likewise, the **Carmel Business Association** (P. O. Box 4444, Carmel, CA 93921; 831/624-2522) puts out an annually updated lodging guide. It charges $5; you can usually find them around town, though.
- For information and history on **Cannery Row,** there's an attractive, useful website (www.cannery-row.com).
- And if you're following the Penultimate itinerary, you may make good use of the quickly developing **Carmel Valley visitors site** (www.carmelvalleycalifornia.com).

Golf Heaven: Pebble Beach

Whoever said "the best things in life are free" obviously hasn't tried to get a tee time at Pebble Beach Golf Links recently. Green fees just increased to $300 for resort guests and $350 for nonresort guests, who can only make tee times 24 hours in advance. Reservation agents advise guests to make their hotel and tee time bookings 18 months ahead, and even then, the tee time you want may not be available, so you may be put on a waiting list. Room rates start at $375 at the Inn at Spanish Bay, $425 at the Lodge, and $475 at Casa Palmero. You do the math.

In spite of the hefty price tag, Pebble Beach is solidly booked. There are lots of oceanfront golf resorts all over the world with stunning views and challenging layouts. What special magic does Pebble Beach have and how did it come to be *numero uno?*

Some would say the single most important element is the setting at Pebble Beach, the way the bay is formed and how the golf course follows the bay, looking across to Point Lobos and points beyond. It is drop-dead gorgeous. And certainly this is why Pebble Beach began to attract the sort of people who would make it what it is today. People like entertainer Bing Crosby and his celebrity cronies.

The Bing Crosby National Pro-Am was informally called "The Crosby" or "The Clambake." The first one was held in 1947. Crosby decided the format would be three days' play on Cypress Point, Monterey Peninsula Country Club, and Pebble Beach Golf Links, and amateur partners would be included throughout the competition, which is unusual as Pro-Ams go. It was "invitation only."

Crosby personally selected the participants, and the combination of top golf professionals playing with celebrity amateurs, usually from the worlds of sports or show business, was a sure winner.

In 1958 the final round of the Crosby was broadcast live on national television by NBC, and an audience of millions saw first-hand the beauty of Pebble Beach. Aside from television viewers, the opportunity to "celebrity-watch" drew many to attend the tournament. "The Crosby" was a relaxed event where fans could talk and joke with their favorite celebrities. When Bing Crosby passed away in 1977, his widow, Kathryn, continued the Crosby National Pro-Am. By the mid-1980s, however, PGA pros were turning their attention to events that offered larger purses, which AT&T agreed to do for the Crosby in exchange for inclusion in the name of the tournament. Kathryn Crosby expressed concern that the event would change under corporate sponsorship and withdrew the Crosby name. Officials decided that since Pebble Beach Golf Links had consistently been one of the host courses, the new name of the event would be the AT&T Pebble Beach National Pro-Am, effective with the 1986 event.

The tournament continued to be popular and over the years has contributed millions of dollars to charitable organizations. However, long-time fans felt the traditional spirit of the fun-loving "Crosby" was forever changed with the 1998 ruling prohibiting cameras during the tournament. Taking photos with celebrities had always been a highlight. In recent years, comedian Bill Murray and his crazy antics were like a throwback to the early days. When Murray didn't participate in the 2000 AT&T, you had to wonder if the powers-that-be had become concerned that the next gray-haired lady he tossed into a bunker might not come up smiling.

As Pebble Beach became more esteemed in the golf world, playing host to the U.S. Open in 1972, 1982, and 1992, the company's holdings had continued to grow. By 1992, Pebble Beach Company properties included two hotels (the Lodge at Pebble Beach and the Inn at Spanish Bay) and four golf courses—Pebble Beach Golf Links, Spyglass Hill Golf Course, the Links at Spanish Bay, and Del Monte Golf Course, the oldest course west of the Mississippi River still in continuous operation. Del Monte began as a nine-hole layout in 1897, designed by Englishman Charles Maud and associated with the grand Del Monte Hotel, which opened in 1880 in Monterey and later became the Naval Postgraduate School. The golf course was one of the properties in the original holdings of Samuel F. B. Morse, whose vision created the present-day Pebble Beach.

Del Monte is by far the most affordable and most accessible of the Pebble Beach Company's courses. Its traditional layout and rolling parkland terrain make it easy to walk. Some of the holes have been moved at various times during the years, particularly when the freeway was widened and when the adjacent Hyatt Hotel was built. Although many courses closed down during World War II, Del Monte stayed open and was operated by the City of Monterey. For all its longevity, the course is in great condition and hosts many events, including the prestigious Callaway Golf Pebble Beach Invitational, which plays Del Monte in addition to Pebble Beach and Spyglass. Top players from the PGA, the Senior PGA, and the LPGA compete for the same purse in this four-day tournament, which began in 1971. Also, the AT&T Monday Qualifier takes place at Del Monte.

Del Monte's gnarly old oak trees, some as old as the course itself, are holding up better than the Monterey pines, which, as elsewhere on the Monterey Peninsula, are affected by a fungal disease called "pitch canker" that is killing pine trees all over California. There is no known cure, but hope lies in the fact that some Monterey pines remain healthy even within a stand of diseased trees. The Pebble Beach Company has developed a method of cloning the canker-resistant trees so they can eventually replace those that are lost.

It appears that more changes are on the horizon at Pebble Beach. In June 1999, the assets of the Pebble Beach Company were purchased by an investment group spearheaded by Arnold Palmer, Clint Eastwood, Peter Ueberroth, and Richard Ferris. The new owners have close ties to the community and are frequent participants in the AT&T Pebble Beach National Pro-Am. Eastwood was formerly the mayor of Carmel.

Previous owners had sought approval to build a Tom Fazio–designed golf course and new homes within Del Monte Forest, displacing the riding stables and polo fields in exchange for building a new Equestrian Center. The project faced legal action from various groups and would still have to pass the California Coastal Commission. At press time, it's unclear if the project will be pursued by the new owners.

All eyes were on Pebble Beach once again when it hosted the 100th U.S. Open in June 2000. Tickets sold out as soon as they were issued, and hotels were booked as far away as Santa Cruz. The nine-hole Peter Hay Course was closed and put to other uses for the event. It represents the fourth U.S. Open for Pebble Beach.

Whether another golf course is built or not, Pebble Beach will still be "Golf Heaven" to its legions of fans all over the world, and hopes are high that the new owners will see that it remains so.

Itinerary

WARMING UP

The cost of living in Pebble Beach, even for three days, makes this an adult vacation. It can be romantic if you've got the right twosome, or an excellent reward for clients or employees in a group setting, or sheer fun for a regular foursome. All you need to do is make one call: 800/654-9300.

First, reserve two nights at either the Lodge at Pebble Beach or the Inn at Spanish Bay, after you've read the descriptions under Lodging.

Next, arrange a tee time for late morning on Day 1 at The Links at Spanish Bay; for Day 2, line up early morning at Spyglass or, if you'd like to take it a bit easier on your golf stress level, Del Monte; and accept any time you can get at Pebble Beach on Day 3.

Finally, make two special dinner reservations, at Roy's and at Club XIX. If you're staying at the Inn at Spanish Bay, make your Roy's dinner for Day 1 and Club XIX for Day 2. If you're staying at the Lodge at Pebble Beach, switch the order. That way, you don't have to drive—er, we meant, take the Pebble Beach shuttle—away from your home on the first night.

day 1 As you enter the 17-Mile Drive, remember to give your name so that you don't have to pay the $7.50 entrance fee. You'll need that $7.50 if you're staying in Pebble Beach for three days.

As you enter the Resort at Spanish Bay, you'll see the golf course and spa on your right. Park nearby and hand your clubs over. Check in at the pro shop and notice the great selection of clothes and other golf goodies; Spanish Bay has the best pro shop among the Pebble Beach options.

There's no driving range here, but you'll be able to practice chipping, putting, and sand shots in the big practice area behind the first tee. We find the first shot of the day here at Spanish Bay to be one of the more unnerving in golf—the tee is somewhat elevated, putting you in full view of the folks having breakfast or lunch at the Clubhouse Bar and Grill. Just try to remember those folks are only admiring their view of the dunes and ocean—they'll hardly notice you. Yeah, right.

You will want to follow the suggestions in the yardage book as you navigate here for the first time—not so much to avoid any invisible surprises, but to measure yardages and know when it's safe to use a driver off the tee.

The first hole is a gentle one after that tee shot, taking you toward the ocean, with a par-5 of 461 yards from the middle tees that dares the big hitters to go for it right off the bat. The "sensitive" hazard protecting the right side of the small green should discourage most.

The next hole looks so easy on the scorecard, but it's a tricky, short uphill par-4 that demands proper club selection off the tee to put you in a flat, safe landing area for a hard-to-calculate steep approach shot. Now you know what you've gotten into today. The Links at Spanish Bay has its detractors because of its style—placement is everything, and there are many forced carries that may aggravate the novice. But there's also awesome scenery from all but a few holes on the back nine, and some holes that you will remember long after you've reveled in the round at the 19th hole. You will, certainly, want to sit and rest—the wide open last three holes can be quite brutal if the wind is blowing—and have a refreshment on the terrace or in the sunken bar at the Clubhouse. This is a fantastic place to watch the sunset—probably the best in all of the Resorts at Pebble Beach property—and get those goose bumps when you hear the bagpiper start to play.

Now it's check-in time. If you're booked at the Lodge, take 17-Mile Drive over to the ocean and follow the signs from there, enjoying the view all the while you cover the three miles between the two properties. After you get checked in, you'll be having dinner at Club XIX, which is discussed here under Day 2. If you're at the Inn, check in to your room and get comfy for tonight's dinner on the premises, at Roy's.

Roy Yamaguchi's renowned chain got its start in Hawaii, building its fame on flavors of Asia, Europe, and California. Here at Spanish Bay, the window-walled, two-level room is big and usually quite lively; if you're alone, you might enjoy the seats along the bar overlooking the kitchen. You'll be asked if you're celebrating a special occasion when you make your reservation, and if the answer is yes you will get a photograph and some festive decorations. The menu changes constantly; some past favorites have included the fire-roasted artichoke, Asian spring rolls, blackened scallop salad, and any seafood risotto or pasta on the menu.

After dinner, you can go outside and sit by an open-air fireplace over a glass of port, or retire to Traps, a cozy sports bar with fireplace, or just go throw that match into your own fire and get ready for more of this wonderful place.

day 11 Have a little breakfast in your gorgeous room—on the terrace if it's nice, by the fire if it's not—or try the Gallery at the Lodge or the Clubhouse at Spanish Bay. Then the party may be splitting up for the morning.

The real golf nuts are on their way to Spyglass, one of the toughest golf courses, we think (and so the pros are beginning to believe, since it generally produces the highest scores in the annual Pro-Am), in the world. And it's not because it's funky or tricky or unfair. It plays quite long, depending on the elements, and narrow, and generally penalizes the errant with long, thick rough. That said, it is a magnificent course, one that most who play it badly will only wistfully imagine having the talent to master, while those who play it well will be quite satisfied with themselves for days.

The first few holes are the highlights for most. The last few are truly among the hardest finishing holes in golf. Hole number 1 is a par-5 doglegging left to a small green surrounded by bunkers, taking you down nearer to the ocean. You can smell the saltwater and feel the sea breezes on the second hole, a short par-4, and then you're looking out at the surf on hole number 3, a par-3 with an elevated tee that looks out at the Pacific Ocean and down to a wide green that plays more easily than every hole on the course but the 100-yard 15th. Hole number 4 travels along the dunes, and then at the par-5 fifth you're again facing the ocean from the tee of a par-3. Then at the sixth tee, you say good-bye to the ocean and travel up into the Del Monte Forest for the rest of the day.

If you've opted out of this beautiful monster, you're playing Del Monte Golf Course. The history alone makes it a treasure, but the course can stand on its own merits. This parkland course has some gentle hills and is very walkable. There have been some changes over the years, but PGA Professional Neil Allen believes that while architect Charles Maud may not recognize it hole by hole, he would certainly recognize the layout. The holes are mostly straight with some doglegs and parallel fairways. There are no water hazards.

Del Monte looks fairly flat, but there are gradual rises in elevation, which Allen calls "one of the subtleties of the golf course." Like on par-4 hole number 3, where it's not so obvious on approach that you'll need an extra club. Golfers comment on the small greens, many of which are pitched back to front. The biggest elevation change is on hole number 7, a difficult uphill par-4 with a three-tiered green that is one of the bigger greens on the course. The elevated tee of hole number 8 is the high end of the golf course.

One of the most intimidating tee shots is over the ravine on hole number 13. Coming up to hole number 14, it's a short 4-par from the red tees, only 200 yards, but a long par-3 from the blues or whites. Allen says, "In my opinion, holes 10 through 13 are scoring holes." At hole number 15, the trees hang over the approach more than you think, and your goal should be to get an open shot and not go for distance. Hole number 16 is a long par-4 that typically plays into the wind, and the green pitches back to front. Going lateral and playing down the parallel first fairway will work. The finishing hole is straight, but the big oak tree makes it a dogleg, so try to go short or just a little right.

At the end of it all, everyone can meet up and share the 19th hole, lunch at Stillwater's in the Lodge at Pebble Beach or at the Clubhouse at Spanish Bay. Then it's off for an afternoon of leisure—take your pick from the optional activities, or take the shuttle into Carmel and go shopping—before yet another memorable meal. Tonight it's Club XIX, a quiet, cozy, glass-and-brick enclosed patio room where the men will feel most comfortable in jackets for dinner. Generally there are two or three prix fixe dinners on the menu, one of them always vegetarian. The cuisine was inspired by Hubert Keller, of French Laundry (Napa) fame, and everything is a treat. Fresh salmon baked in a corn pancake and topped with caviar and watercress sauce, cassoulet of lobster, duck confit and spring vegetables . . . you get the idea. Do not dine with an eye on the purse strings; a more sensible option would be Stillwater's, described under Dining. You're cutting loose tonight.

Then, it's time for cocktails at the Terrace upstairs before you roll on back to your room.

day III Hopefully this morning you're in no hurry to check out. Take some time to browse the shops, or have a massage, or just relax by the pool. Today you're playing Pebble Beach—at its most beautiful for the day's first or last tee times. Settle in for a long day, because no one ever seems to be in a hurry here and there are all too many players on the course wanting to be able to say they played Pebble Beach when they really have no business doing so. It's not just a pretty course, it's a difficult one, and with carts confined to paths only, Golf Heaven can be hell on a bad golfer. Is there anything we can say to urge you to wait until you've got more than the money to play, but also the game?

If it's your first time, and you've got the money to play, pay a caddie to lug your bags around the Links. He'll be able to tell you who owns that ugly building along the 18th fairway, and who's building that spectacular home next to the fifth tee, and how the course came to be built and the story of Jack Nicklaus' new fifth hole, which looks like it's been there forever. He'll tell you what club to use and show you the putting line, but these things you're permitted to ignore at your peril.

There's nothing like standing over the ball on the first tee, thinking, "Oh my God, I'm playing Pebble Beach," and whacking a perfect shot, mid-fairway with a clear approach to the green. It's a tiny green; get used to it, they all are here. And if you think all the putts break toward the ocean, well, pay closer attention to that caddie. The breaks are subtle on these often quick surfaces, but, at Pebble Beach, just getting to the green is its own reward.

The most famous holes are the seventh, eighth, and 18th. Hole number 7 is a tiny little par-3 to a green surrounded by bunkers and with ocean if you're long or right. The wind plays such a big role in club selection here that pros have been known to pull out a 5-iron with the stormy south winds blowing. Think about it: 100 yards, Tiger Woods, 5-iron.

Hole number 8 is one that management has had a tough time helping the amateurs learn to play. You have to hit your tee shot from out on the point in to the right spot on the bluffs to carry a chasm carved into the course by Mother Nature—and filled with the Pacific Ocean. On the other side of the chasm is one of the smallest greens on the course. It is a favorite hole of the pros for the challenge it presents, pure agony to amateurs who can't carry the ocean even from the optimal point on the cliff. Thankfully, there is usually a marshal here to advise you as you tee off.

As for hole number 18, well, you've all seen it on TV, but there is nothing like the view from the tee. Players have to hope the group in front is dawdling, so they can linger here, looking for seals, otters, and whales while enjoying the sight of the waves crashing on the recently reconstructed (artificial) seawall. Then there's the walk alongside the waves as you complete this long hole, where the green has been driven only by the young and strong, like Tiger Woods and Phil Mickelson. And the wonderful thrill of putting out, under the towering Monterey pine, which might now even be lighting your way, at one of the most famous, most beautiful golf courses in the world.

Of course now you must go to the Tap Room. It's required. Have a bite to eat, a glass of champagne, revel in the experience of not only getting a tee time at Pebble Beach(!) but living to tell about your 18 holes there.

 NOTES

Money Savers. Turn to another chapter—Monterey budget perhaps—and come visit the Pebble Beach Market to get a picnic lunch and sit near the golf course.

Nongolfers. You will enjoy luxuriating in the surroundings, walking on the beach, shopping in Carmel, working out at the spa, sitting by the pool.

Couples. Five-stars romance at either property.

Time Savers. Just come for a one-nighter, playing at Spanish Bay or Spyglass the first day and trying for a last-minute slot at Pebble the second. What a treat.

Low-Handicappers. You will not enjoy another getaway in this book more than this one.

High-Handicappers. Do yourself a favor and omit Spyglass. And if you cannot break 100 yet, save Pebble Beach for better days.

Extended Stay. If you can afford it, do it. Add courses from the Monterey chapter.

Courses

ITINERARY SELECTIONS

The Links at Spanish Bay
2700 17-Mile Dr.
Pebble Beach, CA 93953
800/654-9300, fax 831/644-7956
website www.pebblebeach.com

Guests at the Pebble Beach resorts will have a cart included in their $165 green fee; nonguests will pay $185 without one and have to spring for another $25 not to walk. Carts are allowed on fairways here when the courses are dry. The course is walkable, though, and caddies can be arranged with advance notice at $50 a bag plus tip.

TEE TIDBITS | There's no range, but the short game practice area is excellent and will give you a good grasp of the greens. Expect more roll here than at other area courses; drainage is good and Spanish Bay is the first course to dry out in the spring. The course has a wild look about it, exposed as it is to the ocean and breezes. Co-designers Watson and Tatum were a team for many years at the annual Pebble Beach Pro-Am. Tatum is a former USGA president and, like Watson, a Stanford grad. Spanish Bay tends to be a love-it-or-hate-it course. In case you're wondering, there are no hate-it courses in this book. Golf clothes and soft spikes are required. The worst thing about the course is the turn—nowhere near the upscale resort that is at the center of it all. The Clubhouse Bar and Grill is a great stop, before or after you golf.

SCORECARD
Architects: Robert Trent Jones Jr., Tom Watson, and Sandy Tatum, 1987
Course Record: 67, Tom Watson
Blue: Par 72, 6,820 yards, 74.8 rating, 146 slope
White: Par 72, 6,078 yards, 71.7 rating, 134 slope
Red: Par 72, 5,287 yards, 70.6 rating for women, 129 slope
Resort guests may arrange tee times up to 18 months in advance. Nonguest parties of two or more may make a tee time up to 60 days in advance.

Spyglass Hill Golf Course
Stevenson Dr. and Spyglass Hill Road
Pebble Beach, CA 93953
800/654-9300, golf shop 831/625-8563, fax 831/622-1308
website www.pebblebeach.com

Spyglass still belongs to the NCGA for a day here and a day there, and it is almost as hard to get a tee time here as it is at Pebble Beach. Guest fees of $195 include a cart, which costs another $25 for those nonguests, who have to pay $225 to play. Caddies can be arranged in advance, and pull carts are

SCORECARD
Architect: Robert Trent Jones Sr., 1966
Course Record: 64, Dan Forsman
Blue: Par 72, 6,859 yards, 75.9 rating for men, 143 slope
White: Par 72, 6,346 yards, 73.0 rating for men, 138 slope
Red: Par 74, 5,642 yards, 73.7 rating for women, 133 slope
If you're staying at the resort, you can make a tee time up to 18 months in advance. If not, you get 30 days.

generally allowed. Carts are confined to paths, which makes for a lot of walking on this sprawling course.

TEE TIDBITS | There's a driving range near the first tee, and don't skip the practice greens behind the first tee. The clubhouse doesn't nearly match the quality of the golf course, but the pro shop is full of carefully selected merchandise. There's a small grill to feed and water you at the turn. It can be sunny everywhere else and foggy for those first few holes. Spyglass was originally the home course of the NCGA, until it built Poppy Hills. The NCGA still holds many of its tournaments there. The big old mansion atop the hill houses the offices of the Pebble Beach Golf Academy, which offers schools under the direction of renowned teacher Laird Small. Robert Trent Jones Sr. named the holes in honor of Robert Louis Stevenson, who lived in the area for a time, and his most famous tome, *Treasure Island*. The first hole is Treasure Island.

Del Monte Golf Course
1300 Sylvan Rd.
Monterey, CA 93940
831/373-2700, fax 831/655-8792

It's quite a bit easier to get a tee time at Del Monte, which is actually on the Monterey Hyatt property. Green fees start at around $70 for resort and hotel guests, plus $25 for a cart that few will truly need on this old-fashioned walker-friendly layout. You can rent pull carts. Anyone can make tee times two months in advance. There's no driving range. Soft spikes are recommended but not required.

SCORECARD

Architect: Charles Maud, 1932
Course Record: 62, Ken Venturi and Todd Gjesvold
Blue: Par 72, 6,357 yards, 71.3 rating for men, 125 slope
White: Par 72 for men, 6,052 yards, 70.3 rating for men, 123 slope; par-74 for women, 74.3 rating, 126 slope
Red: Par 74 for women, 5,526 yards, 71.0 rating, 120 slope
Tee times are taken two months in advance.

TEE TIDBITS | The casual Del Monte Bar & Grill recently upgraded and offers a lighter menu with more salads, in addition to burgers, hot dogs, and sandwiches. Open for breakfast and lunch. The best deal in town just might be the Duke's Club, where, for an annual fee of $175, you get discounted green fees and merchandise at Del Monte and its sister course, the Links at Spanish Bay, plus other benefits.

Pebble Beach Golf Links
17-Mile Dr.
Pebble Beach, CA 93953
800/654-9300, golf shop 831/624-3811, ext. 5228, fax 831/622-8795
website www.pebblebeach.com

Guests at the resorts will pay at least $300 for golf and cart. Caddies cost $50 a bag and unlike the other resort courses are sometimes available at the last minute. A warning: Many of them will caddie only if there are two bags awaiting them. Nonguests will pay $325 and will get no cart or caddie; they will not be allowed to use a pull cart. Carts, which must remain on the paths year-round, are another $25. We recommend that you walk this course if you possibly can.

If you're not staying at the resort, you can call 24 hours in advance of the time you would like to play and see if they can accommodate you. Probably not. So you can report to the course at 6:30 A.M. and put your name on the starter's waiting list and pray for some bad luck—just something small, like a flat tire—to befall someone with a reservation.

TEE TIDBITS | Taking time out for the putting green outside the Lodge before your round is all part of the program, whether you're staying here or not. Club rentals here and at all the resort courses are $50, for the best of course. If you're taking a caddie, strip your bag down before you go. Chances are you won't need the entire dozen golf balls. Monterey pines here have been devastated by the pitch canker, and the course has undergone changes because of lost trees. Check with the concierge inside the pro shop if you want to schedule a round elsewhere or find a good pizza place in town; help is not exclusively for resort guests. In winter, Pebble Beach can be the most benign of the Pro-Am courses, because greens are so receptive softened by the rain. For the likes of the U.S. Open in summer, fairways are narrowed and rough is overgrown.

SCORECARD

Architects: Jack Neville and Douglass Grant, 1919
Course Record: 62, Tom Kite, David Frost, and David Duval
Blue: Par 72, 6,719 yards, 74.4 rating for men, 142 slope
White: Par 72, 6,357 yards, 72.1 rating for men, 138 slope
Red: Par 72, 5,197 yards, 71.9 rating, 130 slope
Tee times can be arranged up to 18 months in advance for resort guests, but many groups and tournaments come through, so don't expect to play at the time you want just because you got a two-bedroom suite at the Lodge. Nonguests can call 24 hours before the time they want to play and hope something has opened up.

Lodging

ITINERARY SELECTIONS

There are two places to stay for the ultimate Pebble Beach experience: the **Lodge** at Pebble Beach and the **Inn at Spanish Bay.** Most visitors develop a passionate preference to one over the other over time, but that's not because either place is shabby. Each has a magnificent spa and has two fabulous restaurants, plus other more casual choices for a leisurely lunch or breakfast. There are gorgeous golf course and ocean views to be had at each, fine and friendly service, shuttles to take you back and forth. But each has a slightly different feel to it.

The Lodge began catering to discriminating guests in 1919, but there's certainly nothing old or decrepit about the property. Rooms—and even some restaurants—undergo transformations every few years, and there always seem to be improvements in progress. The main building is elegant yet friendly, beginning with the door staff, who'll truly welcome you, not wonder what you're doing there. Beyond the check-in area is a large lobby area, with couches, a piano, and bar service, and windows overlooking the course and ocean.

The 185 guest rooms (including the new Casa Palmero, a private 24-room estate with its own billiards room, pool, library, and personal service) are scattered about six acres, the very best offering unobstructed views of the 18th hole and ocean. The most basic rooms may be lacking view and fireplace, but there are few of these. Most rooms have a terrace or porch—the huge spa rooms in the Fremont Wing have a private hot tub in the garden terrace outside—and a wood-burning fireplace that will be set up for you daily so that all you have to do is toss in a match. There are even six suites upstairs in the main building, and there's a home, Fairway One, for those seeking the ultimate in creature comforts and privacy.

Unless you're in the wrong spot—next to a loading dock, for instance—the prevailing feel at the Lodge is one of serenity and magic. Until you've stayed there, it will remain a mystery, but once you have, you'll know exactly what the golfers on TV mean when they say, "It's a special place."

At the Links at Spanish Bay, however, the prevailing feel is one of activity. It feels a little bit more hip, shall we say, which is understandable considering the property came along in 1987. All of the rooms are beautifully furnished—although you do have to flip the switch to turn on the gas fireplaces—and all are within the main building. So you could spend three days at the Inn and never go outside, which sounds utterly ridiculous—don't even think of trying it. The lobby always seems to be action-packed, a great place for celebrity-watching, yet the ocean and golf course give off a special kind of magic, especially when the bagpiper is playing at sunset. Goose bump time.

There is really no way to recommend one over the other. Rates start at about $375 at the Inn, about $425 at the Lodge—seasonal specials or packages are not the norm here either—and inch upward for a view, a spa, a full view, a studio, a suite, until finally you're spending about $1,800 for a two-bedroom suite. There's also a service charge of about $18 tacked on, so that you don't have to tip all those people who make your stay so wonderful, from greeter to fire builder to maid to minibar stocker to plant waterer. (A friend stayed in her room at the Lodge one day, sick, and was amazed at all of the service people who came by during the day to do this and that.) ■ FOR RESERVATIONS CALL **800/654-9300**; WEBSITE WWW.PEBBLEBEACH.COM

ALTERNATIVES

Only by staying at the Pebble Beach resorts do players have access to advance (18 months) tee times at the Pebble Beach Golf Links. But ng | 385

nonresort guests can make tee times at the Links at Spanish Bay and Del Monte as much as 60 days in advance and Spyglass Hill as much as 30 days out. If you're willing to try a last-minute getaway and see if you can get on Pebble Beach with 24 hours notice (not likely unless you're a single), see Chapter 17 for other lodging options in the area.

Dining

ITINERARY SELECTIONS

At Spanish Bay

The **Clubhouse Bar and Grill** serves breakfast, lunch, and some afternoon appetizers in a casual setting alongside the first tee at Spanish Bay, and it's a great place to watch the sun set. Lunch offerings include hearty sandwiches, salads, and pastas, averaging around $10.

Roy's is open virtually all day, starting at 6:30 with breakfast and espresso bar, every day. Breakfast and lunch will start at around $10; dinner with wine can easily cost $100 and more for two, if you start it with appetizers and finish it with dessert. Reservations will make your life easier: Spanish Bay, 831/647-7423.

Trap's has a bar menu that includes an exotic selection of mouthwatering appetizers, all courtesy of Roy's. It's open nightly and is another great place to watch the sun set.

At Pebble Beach

The recently remodeled **Gallery,** with a terrace overlooking the first tee with a view also of the 18th green, is the place for golfers. Breakfast and lunch are served from the crack of dawn daily, at better prices than are to be found anywhere else in Golf Heaven. (You can eat for less than $10 a person.)

Club XIX is open daily for lunch 11:30–4, and then reopens for dinner (reservations essential) at 6. By day it's a sunny, quiet spot to while away the afternoon over a lobster salad sandwich, seared scallop salad, and bottle of wine; by night it becomes an experience in the art of dining, where two cannot expect to have a full dinner, drinks, and wine for less than $150.

Then of course there's the famous **Tap Room,** which has changed very little over the years because those who come back annually for the Pro-Am wouldn't stand for it. Open for lunch and dinner, the specialties are for the carnivorous: burgers, New York steak, prime rib, and filet mignon, starting at around $10 for sandwiches. The bar area seems to be shrinking, making the Tap Room more a place to eat—and walk around looking at the golf history on the walls.

ALTERNATIVES

At Spanish Bay, the new **Peppoli** brings a little bit of Tuscany to the Monterey Peninsula. It's named for Peppoli Vineyard, one of the wine estates of the Florence-based Antinori wine family, which has been in the wine business since 1385. Ask for the wine list featuring the best Antinori vintages, including the "Super Tuscans" considered some of Tuscany's finest blends. The restaurant is done in warm earth tones with an open rotisserie, and floor to ceiling windows reveal the ocean view. Don't miss the signature dish, veal scaloppine with baby artichokes. This authentic Italian restaurant is warm and friendly and not all that expensive unless you go for a "Super Tuscan," which will run you way over $100. Entrées range $16–24. Dinner only.

At the Lodge, **Stillwater's** is the place for seafood lovers. It's open daily for breakfast, lunch, and dinner offering, with its second-floor location atop Club XIX, the best view in the Lodge. A seat along one of the windows gives you the entire Carmel Bay in all its glory, plus a bird's-eye view of the golfers finishing up on the 18th green, shaking hands and stopping for pictures, anything to make the glorious round last just a little longer. Oh, almost forgot, the food is terrific—a case full of fresh catches for the day's sushi board and some of the best Dungeness crabcakes anywhere are among the highlights. Prices are on the high side, but only Roy's high, not Club XIX high.

And the **Pebble Beach Market** is a godsend for those times when you're tired of dining and just want to pick up some cheese and crackers and a bottle of wine or chilled champagne to take back to the room without the hefty room service charges, or just sit at a picnic table under a tree outside. It's just across from the Lodge, next to the post office.

If you're willing to leave the Del Monte Forest, see Chapter 17 for some other suggestions. The Inn at Spanish Bay is nearer to Pacific Grove; staying at the Lodge at Pebble Beach makes the village of Carmel most accessible.

Straying Off Course

You may want to improve your game so it will be worthy of the esteemed Pebble Beach courses. In that case, head for the Pebble Beach Golf Academy, where director of instruction Laird Small and instructor Dan Pasqueriello were both named among the Top 100 Teachers in America by *Golf Magazine* in 1999. There's a practice range with target greens and green-side practice area with bunkers.

You can take your pick of private lessons, playing lessons, video graphics, or a one- or two-hour golf school (831/622-1310). Private lessons are $100 per hour, but the one-hour golf school is $60 per person with four or more students. Pebble Beach also offers a Corporate Women's Golf Business Program which tells women players "how and why to use golf for business." You'll meet at Spyglass Hill Driving Range for a full day of instruction, which runs $450 plus $75 green fee for the nine holes of on-course instruction. Two-day golf schools include an overnight stay at the Inn at Spanish Bay.

As glorious as the golf may be at Pebble Beach, it's not all there is.

If you thought there's nothing they could do to improve Pebble Beach, think again. The brand new 22,000-square-foot Spa at Pebble Beach (800/654-8598 or 831/624-3811) has 22 treatment rooms, some with fireplaces; a full-service salon; and a signature product line emphasizing ingredients derived from the "Sea and Forest." Let the "Water Experience" pummel away at your aches and pains with its 16 shower heads. The soothing sage tones and wooden floors create a relaxing environment throughout, including the "conservatory" and the "ionization room." Couples can even have treatments together. The Spa is also open to nonresort guests.

Guests at the Inn at Spanish Bay have always had their own Spa and Fitness Center, the Spanish Bay Club (831/647-7461). Massage and skin-care treatments are offered in addition to manicures and pedicures. The Fitness Center has a full workout area with equipment and classes. The Spanish Bay Club has a heated outdoor swimming pool and whirlpool spa, plus the Tennis Pavilion with eight individually enclosed courts, two lighted for night play. Private and group instruction is available.

There are 12 tennis courts at the Resort at Pebble Beach, and you can set up a game or schedule a lesson. There are eight tennis courts at Spanish Bay, and two have lights.

The Pebble Beach Equestrian Center has a reputation in its field equivalent to that of Pebble Beach in golf.

There's a wonderful pool for sunning and recreation at Stillwater Cove, which is often sheltered from the elements, accessed through the Beach Club. The pool at the Inn is better for lap swimming and exercise classes.

At the Lodge, there's no beach good for strolling, though you can take the shuttle into Carmel and the big wonderful beach there. At the Inn, there's a path that leads out to the dunes, great for a sunset stroll or early morning breath of fresh air.

There are lots of shops to lure in the golfer at Pebble Beach, with golf-related art, clothes, and collectibles. The shops at Spanish Bay are geared more to the general consumer.

Details, Details

SUITCASE

You must come prepared for cold weather, even if you expect it to be glorious. The fog can roll in on a whim, or the wind can come up, and you will feel pretty stupid if you've read this book and are caught in shorts and golf shirt with no warmth in reach. The best times to visit are October through December, when the courses are still fairly dry, the crowds have left, and the weather can generally be expected to be glorious. Still, be prepared for Mother Nature to turn a 90-yard par-3 into a 5-iron hole. At some places on Spyglass and Spanish Bay, and most of Pebble Beach, you are completely exposed to the elements.

We'd also suggest soft spikes, even though the Pebble Beach Company doesn't require them on all of its courses. This way, you won't have to worry about changing shoes if you'd like to have a cocktail. And we would suggest sharp-looking attire for dinner at Club XIX, including a jacket for gentlemen. Lunch is much more casual.

Bring workout gear and swimsuit if you plan to take advantage of the marvelous facilities at both the Inn at Spanish Bay and the Lodge. Both properties have swimming pools, hot tubs, and spa facilities now.

GETTING THERE

From all points take Highway 101 toward Salinas, exiting at Highway 156 to the Monterey Peninsula. This will merge into Highway 1; from here, follow the signs to 17-Mile Drive and your first stop, the Links at Spanish Bay.

Monterey Peninsula Airport serves major airlines, and a free airport shuttle can be arranged through Pebble Beach Company with 24 hours notice. If you're traveling a great distance, fly into San Jose and then rent a car. Private jet passengers are well taken care of at Million Air Monterey (831/648-4888).

CONTACTS

■ If you're staying at the **Inn** or the **Lodge**, your very best contact is the concierge. In fact, the Pebble Beach Golf Links has a concierge all to itself, who will even help you schedule golf at courses outside the resort. Call the resort (one more time, that's 800/654-9300) to be connected.

The contacts listed at the end of Chapter 17 may also prove helpful on this getaway.

Top Itineraries for Special Interests

■ Family Friendly ■

SO MUCH TO DO, EVEN THE KIDS WILL BE HAPPY

Santa Cruz, South Lake Tahoe (Tahoe itinerary), North Lake Tahoe

■ Links with Love ■

SPECIAL DESTINATIONS FOR YOU AND YOUR HONEY

Santa Cruz (with bed and breakfast option), Livermore, Napa, Bodega Bay, Monterey Peninsula (especially Carmel Valley), Pebble Beach, Sonoma, Sea Ranch/Little River, Half Moon Bay

■ Group Getaways ■

IDEAL FOR FOURSOMES AND MORE

Calaveras County, Plumas County, Livermore, Bodega Bay, South Lake Tahoe (especially the Carson Valley itinerary), Santa Cruz, Monterey Peninsula (especially Budget itinerary), Central Valley, North Lake Tahoe, Hollister

■ Nongolfers Rejoice ■

ONE CAN HAPPILY GOLF, ONE CAN HAPPILY NOT

Santa Cruz, Plumas County, Napa, Livermore, Pebble Beach, South Lake Tahoe (Tahoe itinerary), North Lake Tahoe, Sonoma, Half Moon Bay, San Francisco

■ Golf Galore ■

PLENTY TO OFFER GOLF NUTS WHO DON'T MUCH CARE ABOUT OPTIONAL ACTIVITIES

Central Valley, Plumas County, Pebble Beach, Monterey Peninsula, Calaveras County, South Lake Tahoe (Carson itinerary), Sacramento/Foothills, Hollister

■ Golf, Not Gold ■

THE MOST AFFORDABLE OPTIONS

Plumas County, Calaveras County midweek, Monterey Peninsula (Budget), South Lake Tahoe (Carson, especially off-season), Central Valley, Bodega Bay midweek, Santa Cruz (midweek, without Pasatiempo), Sacramento/Foothills, Hollister

■ Short Drive ■

GOLF THAT'S CLOSE TO A MAJOR CITY

San Francisco, Silicon Valley, Sacramento/Foothills

■ Golf and Spa ■

THE PERFECT COMBINATION

Sonoma, Pebble Beach, Monterey Peninsula, San Francisco, Napa, Livermore

■ Good Company ■

ITINERARIES THAT GO HAND-IN-HAND

1. Sea Ranch/Little River Inn with: Bodega Bay, Sonoma
2. Bodega Bay with: Sea Ranch/Little River, Sonoma
3. Sonoma with: Bodega Bay, Napa, San Francisco
4. Napa with: Sonoma, Livermore, San Francisco, Sacramento/Foothills
5. Sacramento/Foothills with: North Lake Tahoe, Plumas County, South Lake Tahoe, Calaveras County, Livermore
6. North Lake Tahoe with: Plumas County, South Lake Tahoe, Sacramento/Foothills
7. Plumas County with: North Lake Tahoe, South Lake Tahoe, Sacramento/Foothills
8. South Lake Tahoe and Carson with: North Lake Tahoe, Plumas County, Sacramento/Foothills, Calaveras County
9. Calaveras County with: Livermore, South Lake Tahoe, Sacramento/Foothills
10. Livermore with: Napa, Sacramento/Foothills, Calaveras County, Silicon Valley, Silicon Valley
11. Central Valley with: Livermore, Sacramento/Foothills
12. San Francisco with: Half Moon Bay, Silicon Valley, Sonoma, Livermore
13. Half Moon Bay with: Silicon Valley, Santa Cruz, San Francisco
14. Silicon Valley with: Santa Cruz, Half Moon Bay, San Francisco, Hollister/San Juan Bautista
15. Santa Cruz with: Half Moon Bay, Silicon Valley, Hollister/San Juan Bautista, Monterey, Pebble Beach
16. Hollister/San Juan Bautista with: Silicon Valley, Santa Cruz, Monterey, Pebble Beach
17. Monterey Peninsula with: Hollister/San Juan Bautista, Pebble Beach, Santa Cruz
18. Pebble Beach with: Monterey, Hollister/San Juan Bautista, Santa Cruz

GOLF COURSE INDEX
featured courses appear in bold

Aetna Springs Golf Course: 67, 78-79
Aptos Seascape Golf Club: 309-311, 314, 318
Auburn Valley Country Club: 102-103

Bailey Creek: 142
Bayonet Golf Course: 352, 357
Black Horse Golf Course: 353-354, 357
Black Oak Golf Course: 102
Bodega Harbour Golf Links: 23-31
Boulder Creek Golf & Country Club: 310
Boundary Oaks: 216
Bridges Golf Club at Gale Ranch, The: 216

Canyon Lakes: 216
Carmel Valley Ranch Resort: 346-351, 355-356
Carson Valley Golf Course, The: 171
Chardonnay Golf Club: 63-65, 72-74, 76-77
Chimney Rock: 63, 66, 78
Cinnabar Hills Golf Club: 287-291, 295
CordeValle Golf Club: 298
Course at Wente Vineyards, The: 205-207, 211-212, 214-215
Coyote Creek Golf Club: 286-288, 291-292, 296
Coyote Moon: 121
Crystal Springs Golf Course: 269-272, 275-276
Cypress Point Club: 359

Dayton Valley Golf Club: 152, 163-164, 170
Deep Cliff Golf Course: 298
De Laveaga Golf Course: 311-312, 314-315, 319
Del Monte Golf Course: 363, 374, 378, 382
Diablo Grande: 225-227, 235
Dragon at Gold Mountain: 132-135, 139

Eagle Ridge Golf Club: 288, 293, 296-297
Eagle Valley Golf Course: 153, 160-162, 167-168
Edgewood Tahoe Golf Course: 151, 153-154, 156-157, 166
Empire Ranch Golf Course: 153, 161-162, 168-169

Feather River Inn Golf Course: 133-135, 137-138, 141-142
Feather River Park Resort: 142
Forest Meadows Golf Resort: 188-189, 193, 195-196
Fountaingrove Resort & Country Club: 41, 50

Genoa Lakes Golf Club: 153, 159, 167
Gleneagles International Golf Course: 253, 256
Golf Club at Quail Lodge, The: 356
Golf Courses at Incline Village, The: 113-114, 121
Graeagle Meadows Golf Course: 131-132, 140
Granite Bay Country Club: 93
Greenhorn Creek Golf Course: 186-188, 191, 195

Haggin Oaks: 98, 101
Half Moon Bay Golf Links: 268, 272-277

Hiddenbrooke Country Club: 78

Laguna Seca Golf Club: 359
Lahontan Golf Club: 122
Lake Tahoe Golf Course: 151-153, 155, 165-166
Las Positas Golf Course: 207-209, 214
Lincoln Hills Club: 92, 98, 102
Lincoln Park Golf Course: 243, 249-250, 254
Links at Spanish Bay, The: 377, 381
Little River Inn Golf Course: 6, 14

Meadowmont: 196
Meadowood: 63, 67, 78
Montalcito: 64
Monterey Pines: 358
Mountain Course: 121
Mountain Springs: 196

Napa Golf Course: 65, 68-69, 75
Nevada County Country Club: 98
Northstar-at-Tahoe: 112, 119
Northwood Golf Course: 48-49, 51

Oakmont Golf Club: 48, 52
Old Brockway Golf Course: 112, 116-117, 120
Olympic Club: 256

Pacific Grove Golf Links: 357-358
Pajaro Valley Golf Club: 308-309, 319
Palo Alto Golf Course: 297
Pasatiempo Golf Club: 308, 312, 316-317, 320
Pebble Beach Golf Links: 373-374, 379-381, 382-383
Pleasanton Fairways Golf Course: 217
Plumas Pines Golf Resort: 132-134, 140-141
Ponderosa Golf Course: 113-114, 122
Poplar Creek Golf Course: 252, 255
Poppy Hills Golf Course: 348, 355
Poppy Ridge Golf Course: 206, 212-213, 215-216
Presidio Golf Course: 243-244, 247-248, 253-254

Quail Valley Golf Course: 98
Quincy Golf Course: 133

Rancho Canada: 358-359
Resort at Squaw Creek: 113, 120-121
Ridge Golf Course, The: 101-102
Ridgemark Golf & Country Club: 329-330, 336-337
Riverside Golf Course: 286-287
Rooster Run Golf Club: 26-27, 29-30
Ruby Hill: 217

Saddle Creek Golf Club: 186-190, 194-195
San Geronimo Golf Course: 252, 255-256
San Juan Oaks Golf Club: 330-331, 335-338
Santa Clara Golf & Tennis Club: 297
Santa Teresa Golf Club: 297

Sea Ranch Golf Links: 6-8, 12-15
Sequoia Woods Country Club: 196
Shoreline Golf Links: 297-298
Sierra Nevada Golf Ranch: 160, 162-163, 169-170
Silverado Country Club and Resort: 66, 75-76
Silver Oak Golf Course: 170-171
Sonoma County Fairgrounds Golf Center: 52
Sonoma Mission Inn Golf & Country Club: 40-41, 47-48, 51
Spring Hills: 320-321
Springtown Golf Course: 217
Spyglass: 377-378
Spyglass Hill Golf Course: 381-382
Stevinson Ranch: 232-234, 236
Stone Tree Golf Club: 52
Sun City Golf Club: 92
Sunridge Golf Course: 170-171

Tahoe City Golf Course: 113, 122
Tahoe Donner Golf Course: 113, 115, 118-119
Tahoe Paradise Golf Course: 171
Teal Bend Golf Club: 93, 98, 102
Tehama: 359
"The Country Club": 359
Tilden Park Golf Course: 245-246, 251-252, 254-255
Turkey Creek Golf Club: 93-95, 100, 103
Twelve Bridges Golf Club: 93-95, 99

Vintners Golf Club: 63, 66-67, 77

Wawona Golf Course: 230
Whitehawk Ranch Golf Club: 132-134, 136, 139-140, 143
Whitney Oaks Golf Club: 93, 96, 97,100-101
Windsor Golf Club: 41-44, 49-50

LODGING INDEX

Acacia Lodge: 362
Angels Inn Motel: 198
Applewood Inn & Restaurant: 48-49, 53-54
Auberge du Soleil: 81

Beach House, The: 278
Bernardus Lodge: 361
Best of Pajaro Rental Agency: 322-323
Best Western Country Inn: 300
Best Western San Benita Inn: 339
Best Western Sonora Oaks: 197
Black Bear Inn: 173
Bliss Mansion: 174
Bodega Bay and Beyond: 31
Bodega Bay Lodge and Spa, The: 28, 31-32
Bodega Bay RV Park: 33
Bodega Coast Inn: 32
Branscomb Gallery: 33

Caesars: 172
Cal-Neva Resort: 117, 123
Carmel Valley Ranch Resort: 360
Chelsea Motor Inn: 259
Christiania Inn: 173
Cinderella Motel: 339
Claremont Resort & Spa, The: 257
Coachman's Inn: 365
Comfort Inn: 300
Copper House Bed and Breakfast: 198
Costanoa: 278
Cottages at Greenhorn Creek: 197
Cottages at Stevinson Ranch: 237
Courtyard by Marriott: 104, 218
Coventry Motor Inn: 259
Cow Hollow Motor Inn & Suites: 259
Cypress Inn: 279, 364

David Walley's Spa and Hot Springs: 174
Days Inn: 237
Delta King Hotel: 98, 104
Downey House Bed and Breakfast Inn: 104
Dragon at Gold Mountain: 143
Dunbar House, 1880: 198

El Bonita: 74, 80
Embassy Suites Resort: 171-172
Evergreen: 218
Executive Inn Suites: 300

Fairfield Inn: 104
Fairway Condominiums: 79
Fantasy Inn: 172
Feather River Inn: 138, 142
Flamingo Resort Hotel: 53
Forest Meadows: 197
Forest Park Inn: 299
Fountaingrove Inn: 52-53
Four Sisters Inns: 361

Gaige House Inn: 54
Glenelly Inn, The: 54
Gosby House Inn: 363
Graeagle Lodge: 132-133
Graeagle Meadows: 143
Grandmere's Bed and Breakfast Inn: 104
Gray Eagle Lodge: 138, 143-144
Gualala Country Inn: 16

Half Moon Bay Lodge: 278
Harvest Inn: 81
Harvey's: 172
Heritage House: 16-17
Hidden Valley: 362
Highlands Inn: 361

Holiday Inn Auburn: 103
Holiday Inn Express: 237
Holiday Inn Express Hotel and Suites: 32, 299-300
Hollister Inn: 339
Horizon: 172
Horizon Inn: 365
Hotel La Rose: 49
Hotel Monaco: 256-257
Hotel Rex, The: 257-258
Hyatt Regency Lake Tahoe: 117, 123
Hyatt Regency Monterey: 363

Inn Above Tide: 257
Inn at Cedar Mansion, The: 55
Inn at Depot Hill: 321-322
Inn at Manresa Beach: 322
Inn at Morgan Hill: 289-290, 298
Inn at Pasatiempo: 322
Inn at Spanish Bay: 383-384
Inn at the Tides, The: 32
Inn at Union Square, The: 258
Inn by the Lake, The: 172

Jack London Lodge, The: 54

Kenwood Inn and Spa: 54

Lakeland Village Beach and Ski Resort: 172
Lakeside Inn: 172
Lake Tulloch Resort: 197
Larkspur Landing Home Suite Hotel: 104
Lavender: 81
Lighthouse Lodge and Suites: 365
Little River Inn: 8-10, 15
Lodge at Pebble Beach: 383-384
Lodge at Whitehawk Ranch: 143
Los Laureles Lodge: 362

MacArthur Place: 55
Meadowood: 80
Mendocino Coast Reservations: 17
Microtel Inn & Suites: 300
Mill Rose Inn: 279
Monterey Plaza Hotel and Spa: 361-362
Murphys Hotel: 198

North Lake Tahoe Resort Association: 124
Northstar-at-Tahoe: 115, 122-123
Nugget: 173

Ormsby House Hotel and Casino: 173

Pacific Gardens Inn: 363-364

Pajaro Dunes Beach Rentals: 323
Piñon Plaza Resort: 160, 173
Plumas Pines Realty: 143
Plum Tree Inn: 218
Posada de San Juan: 338-339
Purple Orchid Inn: 208, 210, 217

Quality Inn: 32
Queen Anne Cottage: 218

Ramekins Cooking School: 49
Rams Head Realty: 17
Redbud Inn: 198
Residence Inn: 104
Resort at Squaw Creek: 123
Ridgemark: 332, 338
Ritz-Carlton: 270, 272, 277
River Pines Resort: 144
River Ranch Lodge: 124
Rocklin Park Hotel: 95, 103

San Jose Fairmont Hotel: 299
Seal Cove Inn: 278-279
Sea Ranch Escape: 16
Sea Ranch Lodge: 7-8, 15-16
Seascape Resort: 313-314, 321
Silverado Country Club and Resort: 69-70, 79
Sonoma Coast Villa: 32-33
Sonoma Mission Inn Golf & Country Club: 40-41,
    46-47, 53
Stanford Inn by the Sea: 16
Stanford Park Hotel, The: 299
Sterling Gardens: 197
Stonepine: 361
Sunbay Suites: 363
Sunnyside Resort: 124

Tahoe Lakeshore Lodge and Spa: 154, 156, 171

Vacation Rentals U.S.A.: 31
Vacation Station: 124
Villa Del Lago Inn: 236-237
Villagio Inn and Spa: 81

Wawona Hotel: 230
Westin Santa Clara, The: 299
Westin St. Francis, The: 258-259
White Sulphur Springs Bed and Breakfast: 144
Wiebe Motel: 339
Wild Rose Inn: 174
W San Francisco: 258

Yellow Dog Inn: 199

DINING INDEX

Adele's: 162, 177
Adobe Room: 339-340

Alberto's Cantina: 220
Alta Mira Hotel & Restaurant: 261

Applewood Inn & Restaurant: 48-49, 53-54
Auberge du Soliel: 83
Awful Annies: 124-125

Baja Cantina: 348-349, 366
Barbara's Fish Trap: 280
Beeb's: 219
Bernardus Lodge: 350
Big 3 Diner, The: 56
Big Water Grille: 126
Bistro Jeanty: 72, 82
Bittersweet Bistro: 324
Blue Agave Club: 220
Blue Moon Pizza: 262
B of A Cafe: 191, 199
Bogey's Bar & Grill: 45
Bon Appetit: 367
Bootleggers Old Town Tavern & Grill: 96, 105
Bouchon: 83
Branding Iron: 238
Breakers Cafe: 34
Buca Giovanni: 261

Café Beaujolais: 18
Cafe Fiore: 156, 175
Café Marimba: 262
Cafe Soleil: 199
Camps: 200
Carson Valley Country Club Restaurant and Bar:
    163, 177
Casa Orozco: 220
Central Texan Barbecue, The: 368
Chadwick's: 94-95
Charlie's Grill: 43-44
Chevy's: 176
Chez Panisse: 252, 260
Clubhouse Bar and Grill: 385
Club XIX: 376-377, 379, 385
Covey, The: 367
Coyote Bar and Grill: 146
Crow's Nest: 324
Cruscos: 200
Culinary Institute of America: 82
Cutting Horse, The: 340
Cypress Inn: 364

David's Restaurant: 301
David Walley's Spa and Hot Springs: 178
Dean and DeLuca: 82-85
De Laveaga Lodge: 323
Diablo Dining Room: 339-340
Diablo Grande: 237
Dine: 261-262
Domaine Chandon: 71, 83
Duarte's Tavern: 280
Duck Club: 28, 33-34, 301
DW's: 178

Edgewood Tahoe: 175
Elliston Vineyards: 220
El Toro Bravo: 126-127
Encore Café: 300

E & O Trading Company: 251, 260
Equus Restaurant: 44, 56
Evans: 158, 175
Evvia: 301

Farallon: 259
Faz: 220
Feather River Inn: 146
Firesides: 145-146
Fishwife, The: 368
Flamingo Resort Hotel: 53
Food Company, The: 18
French Laundry: 83
Friar Tuck's: 106
Friday's Station: 176

Gabilan Dining Room: 334
Garre: 220
Gar Woods: 125-126
General's Daughter, The: 57
Girasole: 220
Girl & the Fig, The: 56
Golden Oak Restaurant: 293
Golden Oak Restaurant, The: 300
Goodfella's: 176
Gourmet au Bay: 28
Graeagle Meadows Clubhouse: 145
Grizzly Grill, The: 146
Grounds: 193, 199

Hollins House: 323
Hopyard American Alehouse and Grill: 220
Horseshoe Bar Grill: 98, 106
Hot Gossip: 176

Ikeda's: 124
Inn at Morgan Hill: 289-290
Inn at Spanish Bay: 385
Inn at Tres Pinos: 340
Inn Cognito: 178
Iron Door: 145

Joe's Ristorante Italiano: 300-301
JT's: 177

Kautz Ironstone Vineyard: 200
Ketch Joanne Restaurant & Harbor Bar: 280
Kincaid's: 252, 260-261

La Ferme: 178
Lakeside Beach Grill: 176
Lake Tulloch Resort: 190, 199
Lallapalooza: 369
Las Gaviotas: 232, 238
L'Augerge du Soleil: 74
Little River Inn: 10
Little River Inn Restaurant: 17
Llewellyn's: 176
Log Cabin: 146
Lone Eagle Grille: 125
Lucas Wharf Restaurant and Bar: 34
Lucca Delicatessen: 262

MacCallum House Restaurant: 18
Mallard's: 176-177
Mandarin Gourmet: 301
Marinus: 366
Marty's Inn: 238
Mezza Luna: 274, 280
Michael's Restaurant: 297-298
Mil's Bar and Grill: 238
Miramar Beach Restaurant: 280
Mixx: 57
Mohawk Grill: 136, 144
Moose's Tooth Café: 117, 125
Moosse Café: 18
Moss Beach Distillery: 280-281
MS *Dixie II*: 154-155, 159, 175
Murphys Grille: 199
Murphys Hotel: 199

Nevada City Grill: 106
Nico: 364

Oaks at Carmel Valley Ranch, The: 367
Ocean Song: 18
Ondine's: 261
Overland: 177

Pacific's Edge: 367
Palapas Restaurant Y Cantina: 323
Palapas Restaurant y Cantina: 314
Panda: 220
Pangaea Restaurant: 18
Papachinos: 238
Pasta Moon: 279
Patterson's: 17
Pelican Pizza and Video: 34
Peninsula Fountain & Grill: 302
Peppermint Stick, The: 200
Peppers Mexicali Café: 353, 368
Peppoli: 386
Pilothouse Restaurant: 98, 106
Pleasanton Hotel: 219
Plumas Pines Restaurant: 145
Pluto's: 262
Progresso Tamale Parlor & Factory: 340

Quail Inn: 52, 57

Restaurant at Meadowood, The: 83-84
Restaurant at Stevenswood Lodge: 17-18
r.g. Burgers: 369
Rio Grill: 366
Riva Grill: 156, 174-175
River Bend Grille, The: 159, 175
Rosie's Café: 126
Royal Oak: 68, 70, 82
Roy's: 376-377, 385
Running Iron: 367
Rutherford Grill: 84

Sanderlings: 316, 323
Sandpiper Dockside Cafe and Restaurant: 34
Sand Trap Bar and Grill: 82
Sardine Lake Resort: 145
Sassy's: 220
Sea Ranch Lodge Restaurant: 18
Sears Fine Food: 249, 259-260
71 Saint Peter: 301
Shadowbrook: 323-324
Shanghai Restaurant and Bar: 96, 105
Silvana's Italian Cuisine: 177
Sinaloa Café: 302
Snowshoe Brewing Company: 200
Sole Mio Caffe Trattoria: 367
Sonoma Mission Inn: 46-47, 53, 56
Spago: 301
Spinnaker Restaurant: 261
Spirit of Sacramento: 106
SR Grille and Outdoor Patio: 238
Stacey's Cafe: 220
Station Grill and Rotisserie: 177-178
Stevenswood: 11
Stillwater's: 386
Stony Ridge: 219
Strings Italian Cafe: 238
Strizzi's: 220
Sun China: 200
Sunsets On The Lake: 125
Susanne Restaurant and Bakery: 95, 103, 105
Syrah: 56-57

Takeout Taxi: 219
Tides Wharf, The: 33
Timbercreek Restaurant: 115, 125
Ton Kiang Restaurant: 261
Trap's: 385
Tra Vigne: 84
Trax Bar and Grille: 238

Union Hotel: 34

Village Baker: 145
V. Sattui: 70-71, 82

Wawona Hotel: 230
Wente Vineyards Restaurant: 219
Wente Vinyards: 212
Whiskey Creek Steakhouse and Saloon: 160, 162, 177
Whitney Oaks Bar and Grill: 97
Wickets: 366
Will's Fargo Dining House and Saloon: 367-368
Wine Train: 84

Yukol Place: 262

Zephyr Cove Marina: 154-155, 159
Zibbibo: 301

INDEX

A

Acacia Lodge: 362
Action Watersports: 127
Adele's: 162, 177
Adobe Room: 339-340
Aetna Springs Golf Course: 67, 78-79
airports: Calaveras Community Airport 202;
　Charles M. Schulz Sonoma County Airport 21,
　59; Gustine Airport 240; Hollister Municipal
　Airport 342; Lincoln Regional Airport 108;
　Little River Airport 21; Livermore Airport 222;
　Minden-Tahoe Airport 179, 182; Monterey
　Peninsula Airport 372, 388; Napa Airport 88;
　Oakland Airport 222; Plumas County 148;
　Reno/Tahoe International Airport 129; Sacra-
　mento International Airport 108; San Francisco
　International Airport 265, 283; San Jose Inter-
　national Airport 283, 304, 342; San Martin-
　South County Airport 304; South Lake Tahoe
　Airport 180; Truckee-Tahoe Airport 129; Wat-
　sonville Airport 326-327
Alberto's Cantina: 220
Allegria Spa at Ventana Inn: 369
Alta Mira Hotel & Restaurant: 261
altitude sickness: 117
American Center for Wine, Food, and the Arts: 87
American River: 107
amusement/theme parks: Great America 303; Rag-
　ing Waters 303; Santa Cruz Beach Boardwalk
　315-316; Six Flags Marine World Theme Park 85

Anderson, Jim: 119
Anderson Reservoir: 302
Anderson Valley: 9, 19
Anderson Valley Brewing Company: 9, 19
Angels Camp: 186-187, 191, 195, 197-200
Angels Inn Motel: 198
Año Nuevo State Reserve: 282
Antique Car Rentals: 86
Applewood Inn & Restaurant: 48-49, 53-54
Aptos: 323, 326
Aptos Seascape Golf Club: 309-311, 314, 318
Armstrong Redwoods State Preserve: 48
Arnold: 193, 196, 199-200
Artichoke Center of the World: 354
Auberge du Soleil: 81, 83
Auburn: 91-96, 101-107, 109, 115, 124-125
Auburn Municipal Airport: 101
Auburn Valley Country Club: 102-103
Awful Annie's: 115, 124-125

B

Bach Dancing and Dynamite Society: 274, 281
Bailey Creek: 142
Bailey, Dick: 136, 139-140
Baja Cantina: 348-349, 366
Baldock, Bob: 65, 75, 196
Balfour, Shane: 232
ballooning: see hot air ballooning
Balloons Above the Valley: 58
Barbara's Fish Trap: 280

ARCHITECTS/COURSE DESIGNERS

Bailey, Dick: 136, 139-140
Baldock, Bob: 65, 75, 196
Bell, Billy: 165, 217
Bell, Brad: 93, 98, 99, 100, 121
Bell, William Park: 255
Bendelow, Tom: 254
Bigler, Richard: 336-337
Bliss, Fred: 27, 29-30, 49-50
Boos, Don: 195
Carns, Gen. Edwin: 357
Casper, Billy: 92
Couples, Fred: 337
Duane, Francis: 276-277
Dunn, John Duncan: 120
Dye, Pete: 346, 349, 355
Egan, Chandler: 358
Fazio, George: 153, 166
Fazio, Tom: 153, 166
Fleming, Jack: 65, 75, 254
Flint, Homer: 140-142
Fowler, Herbert: 254, 275
Fream & Dale: 296
Grant, Douglass: 383

Graves, Robert Muir: 7, 47-48, 51, 112,
　119, 196, 209, 214, 356
Griffiths, Denis: 235
Harbottle, John: 163, 167, 169, 229
Harbottle, John III: 159, 236, 289, 295
Hervilla, Ole: 6
Hills, Arthur: 274, 276-277
Jacobsen, Peter: 159, 167
Johnston, Robert: 253
Jones, Rees: 206, 215
Jones, Robert Trent Jr.: 25, 30-31, 76,
　93, 120-121, 188, 195-196, 206,
　348, 355, 381
Jones, Robert Trent Sr.: 25, 30-31, 381
Kelley, George: 236
McClure, Gen. Robert: 357
McFarland, Floyd: 319
MacKenzie, Alister: 51, 98, 101, 320,
　359
Maud, Charles: 382
Miller, Barry: 64-65
Miller, Johnny: 52, 64-65, 97, 100, 169,
　216, 288, 296
Morrish and Associates: 194

Nash, Greg: 92
Nelson, Robin: 135, 139
Neville, Jack: 358, 383
Nicklaus, Jack: 217, 286-287, 291-292,
　296
Norman, Greg: 214-215
O'Callaghan, Casey: 77
Palmer, Arnold: 78, 163-164, 170, 244,
　276-277
Phelps, Dick: 99
Phillips, Kyle: 25
Pulley, Algie: 76
Robinson, Ted: 41, 44-45, 50, 52, 216
Sampson, Harold: 141-142
Seay, Ed: 163-164
Snyder, Jack: 167
Tatum, Sandy: 52, 381
Van Gorder, Ellis: 140
Watson, Tom: 381
Watson, Willie: 51
Weiskopf, Tom: 122
Whiting, Sam: 51
Williams, Joseph B.: 118

Barbary Coast Trail: 262
baseball: 263
Bayonet Golf Course: 352, 357
beaches: 35, 179, 269-270, 274, 315-316, 325, 369
Beach House, The: 278
Bear Flag Revolt: 41
Bear Valley: 201
Beeb's: 219
Bell, Billy: 165, 217
Bell, Brad: 93, 97, 99, 121
Bell, William Park: 255
Bendelow, Tom: 254
Benziger Family Winery: 46, 58
Berkeley: 245-246, 251-252, 254-255, 260
Bernardus Lodge: 350, 361
Berry Falls: 325
Best of Pajaro Rental Agency: 322-323
Best Western: Country Inn 300; San Benita Inn 339;
    Sonora Oaks 197
Bickler, Cary: 168
bicycling/mountain biking: Bodega Bay 35; Carson
    City, NV 179; Half Moon Bay 274; Lake Tahoe
    127; Livermore Valley 221; Mendocino 19;
    Monterey Peninsula 369; Napa Valley 86;
    Sonoma Valley 58; South Lake Tahoe 180
Big Basin: 325
Bigler, Richard: 336-337
Big Mack Charters: 128
Big Sur: 369
Big 3 Diner, The: 56
Big Trees Carriage Company: 201
Big Trees Market: 200
Big Water Grille: 126
Birds, The: 24
Bistro Jeanty: 72, 82
Bittersweet Bistro: 324
Black Bear Inn: 173
Black Horse Golf Course: 353-354, 357
Black Oak Golf Course: 102
Blairsden: 136, 142, 145-146
Bliss, Fred: 27, 29-30, 49-50
Bliss Mansion: 174
Blue Agave Club: 220
Blue Lady, legend of: 269-270
Blue Moon Pizza: 262
boating/cruises/excursions: Bodega Bay 34-35;
    Calaveras County 201; Chardonnay II 325; Half
    Moon Bay 271, 281; houseboat rentals 198-199;
    Lake Tahoe 127-128, 179-180; Mendocino Coast
    19; Morgan Hill 302; Mountain View 297-298;
    MS Dixie II 154-155, 159, 175; San Francisco
    262; Santa Cruz 325; Spirit of Sacramento 98,
    107; Tahoe Star 180; see also
    canoeing/rafting/kayaking; specific place;
    whalewatching Bodega Bay: general discussion
    23-26; attractions 34-35; climate/what to take
    35; courses 29-31; dining 33-34; getting there
    36; information sources 36-37; itinerary 26-29;
    lodging 31-33; see also specific place
Bodega Bay and Beyond: 31
Bodega Bay Lodge and Spa, The: 28, 31-32
Bodega Bay Marine Laboratories: 33

Bodega Bay RV Park: 33
Bodega Coast Inn: 32
Bodega Dunes State Park: 37
Bodega Harbour Golf Links: 23-31
B of A Cafe: 191, 199
Bogey's Bar & Grill: 45
Boldt, Bob: 216
Bonanza: 120, 128
Bon Appetit: 367
Boonville: 9, 19, 21
Boos, Don: 195
Bootleggers Old Town Tavern & Grill: 96, 105
Bouchon: 83
Boulder Creek Golf & Country Club: 310
Boundary Oaks: 216
Branding Iron: 238
Brando, Marlon: 329
Branscomb Gallery: 33
Breakers Cafe: 34
breweries/distilleries: Anderson Valley Brewing
    Company 9, 19; Moss Beach Distillery 269-270,
    280; Snowshoe Brewing Company 200
Bridges Golf Club at Gale Ranch, The: 216
Buca Giovanni: 261
Buena Vista Winery: 39
bullfighting: 239
Burbank, Luther, Home and Gardens: 58
Burlingame: 260-261, 269, 275-276

C

Caesars: 172
Café Beaujolais: 18
Cafe Fiore: 156, 175
Café Marimba: 262
Cafe Soleil: 199
Calaveras Big Trees State Park: 193
Calaveras Community Airport: 202
Calaveras County: general discussion 185-189;
    attractions 200-201; climate/what to take 201-
    202; courses 194-196; dining 199-200; getting
    there 202; information sources 202; itinerary
    189-194; lodging 197-199
Calaveras County Museum: 201
Calaveras Wine Association: 200-201
Calero Reservoir and Park: 289, 302
California Caverns: 192
California Palace of the Legion of Honor: 250-251,
    263
California Wine Tours: 58
Calistoga: 85
Cal-Neva Resort: 117, 123
Calpine: 135
Campbell Cove: 35
Camp Richardson: 179-180
Camps: 200
Cannery Row: 353, 369, 371
canoeing/rafting/kayaking: American River 107;
    Bodega Bay 35; Graeagle 147; Lake Tahoe 127-
    128, 179-180; Mendocino 19; Santa Cruz 325;
    Sea Ranch 20; Stanislaus River 201; Truckee
    River 128; see also boating/cruises/excursions;
    specific place; whalewatching

Canyon Lakes: 216
Capitol: Carson City, NV 178; Sacramento 107
Capitola-by-the-Sea: 316, 321-322
Carmel: 355-356, 358-370
Carmel Art Association: 370
Carmel Valley Ranch Resort: 346-351, 355-356, 360, 367
Carnelian Bay: 125-126
Carns, Gen. Edwin: 357
carriage rides: 43, 201
Carson City, NV: 162, 167-171, 173-174, 176-179
Carson River: 179
Carson Valley: general discussion 151-154; attractions 178-180; climate/what to take 181; courses 167-171; dining 176-178; getting there 181-182; information sources 182; itinerary 160-165; lodging 173-174
Carson Valley Country Club: 163, 171, 177
Casa Orozco: 220
casinos: 158, 172-174, 178
Casper, Billy: 92
Castroville: 354, 368
caverns: 192, 334
Central Texan Barbecue, The: 368
Central Valley: general discussion 225-229; attractions 238-239; climate/what to take 239-240; courses 235-236; dining 237-238; getting there 240; information sources 240; itinerary 229-235; lodging 236-237; see also specific place
Chadwick's: 94-95
Chana, Claude: 96
Chardonnay Golf Club: 63-65, 72-74, 76-77, 82
Chardonnay II: 325
Charlie's Grill: 43-44
Chateau Montelena: 71
Chateau St. Jean: 45-46
cheese factories: 48, 239
Chelsea Motor Inn: 259
Chevy's: 176
Chez Panisse: 252, 260
child care: 116-117
Chimney Rock: 63, 66, 78
Chinatown: 262
Christiania Inn: 173
Cinderella Motel: 339
Cinnabar Hills Golf Club: 287-291, 295
Claremont Resort & Spa, The: 257
climate/what to take: Bodega Bay 36; Calaveras County 201-202; Carson Valley 181; Central Valley 239-240; Half Moon Bay 282; Hollister 341-342; Lake Tahoe 128-129; Livermore Valley 221-222; Mendocino Coast 20; Monterey Peninsula 370-371; Napa Valley 87; Pebble Beach 388; Plumas County 147; San Francisco 264; Santa Cruz 326; Silicon Valley 303-304; Sonoma Valley 59; South Lake Tahoe 181
climbing: 116, 127, 334
Clio: 136, 139-140, 143-144, 146
Clos LaChance: 298
Clos Pegase: 71
clothing: see climate/what to take
Cloverdale: 9

Clubhouse Bar and Grill: 385
Club XIX: 376-377, 379, 385
Coachman's Inn: 365
Coe, Henry W., State Park: 302
Coles, Janet: 350
Columbia State Historical Park: 201
Comfort Inn: 300
Concannan: 210
cooking schools: 49, 82
Copper House Bed and Breakfast: 198
Copperopolis: 186-187, 194-195, 197, 199
CordeValle Golf Club: 298
Costanoa: 278
Cottage B&B: 55
Cottages at Greenhorn Creek: 197
Cottages at Stevinson Ranch: 237
Couples, Fred: 337
Course at Wente Vineyards, The: 205-207, 211-212, 214-215
course designers: see architects/course designers
Courtyard by Marriott: 104, 218
Coventry Motor Inn: 259
Covey, The: 367
Cow Hollow Motor Inn & Suites: 259
Coyote Bar and Grill: 146
Coyote Creek Golf Club: 286-288, 291-292, 296
Coyote Moon: 121
Coyote Point Recreation Area: 252
Crosby, Bing: 374
Crow's Nest: 324
cruises: see boating/cruises/excursions
Cruscos: 200
Crystal Bay, NV: 123
Crystal Springs Golf Course: 269-272, 275-276
Culinary Institute of America: 82
Cupertino: 298
Cutting Horse, The: 340
Cypress Inn: 279, 364
Cypress Point Club: 359

D

Daly City: 256
David's Restaurant: 301
David Walley's Spa and Hot Springs: 160, 163, 174, 178
Davies Symphony Hall: 263
Day, Doris: 364
Days Inn: 237
Dayton, NV: 163-164, 170
Dayton Valley Golf Club: 152, 163-164, 170
Dean and DeLuca: 82-85
Deep Cliff Golf Course: 298
De Laveaga Golf Course: 311-312, 314-315, 319, 323
Del Monte Forest: 348
Del Monte Golf Course: 363, 374, 378, 382
Delta King Hotel: 98, 104
Del Valle Reservoir: 221
Del Webb Corporation: 92
designers: see architects/course designers
Diablo Dining Room: 339-340
Diablo Grande: 225-227, 231-232, 235, 237
Dine: 261-262

di Rosa Preserve: 74
distilleries: 269-270; *see* breweries/distilleries; wineries/vineyards
dog-friendly hotels: 364
Domaine Chandon: 71, 83
Donner Memorial State Park & Emigrant Trail Museum: 128
Don Sherwood Golf & Tennis World: 249
Doran Park: 35
Downey House Bed and Breakfast Inn: 104
Doyle, Ben: 350
Dragon at Gold Mountain: 132-135, 139, 143
Dresslerville: 163
Druecker, John, Memorial Rhododendron Show: 19
Duane, Francis: 276-277
Duarte's Tavern: 280
Duck Club: 28, 33-34, 301
Dunaweal: 72
Dunbar House, 1880: 198
Dunn, John Duncan: 120
Durst, Mike: 155
DW's: 178
Dye, Pete: 346, 349, 355

E

Eagle Ridge Golf Club: 288, 293, 296-297
Eagle Valley: 153, 160-162, 167-168
Eagle Vines: 64-65
earthquakes: 325
East of Eden: 6
Eastwood, Clint: 359
Edgewood Tahoe: 151, 153-154, 156-157, 166, 175
Egan, Chandler: 358
El Bonita: 74, 80
Elkhorn Slough: 325
Elliston Vineyards: 220
El Toro Bravo: 126-127
Embassy Suites Resort: 171-172
Emerald Bay: 180
Empire Mine State Historic Park: 107
Empire Ranch: 153, 161-162, 168-169
Encore Café: 300
E & O Trading Company: 251, 260
Equus Restaurant: 44, 56
Evans: 158, 175
Evergreen: 218
Evvia: 301
Executive Inn Suites: 300

F

factory outlet stores: 107, 294, 302
Fairfield Inn: 104
Fairway Condominiums: 79
Family Wineries of Sonoma Valley: 46, 58
Fantasy Inn: 172
Farallon: 259
Farallon Islands: 281
Faz: 220
Fazio, George: 153, 166
Fazio, Tom: 153, 166
Feather River Inn: 133-135, 137-138, 141-142, 146
Feather River Park Resort: 142

Feather River Scenic Byway: 147
festivals: Frog Jumping Festival 186; Half Moon Bay Pumpkin Festival 281; Hollister Independence Rally 341; Lake Tahoe Shakespeare Festival 128; Lake Tahoe Summer Music Festival 128; Mavericks Men Who Ride Mountains 281; Music in the Mountains 107; Valhalla Arts and Music Festival 179
Firesides: 145-146
Fish, Bob: 6
fishing: *see* sportfishing
Fishwife, The: 368
Fitzgerald Marine Reserve: 282
Fitzpatrick, Jim: 107
Flamingo Resort Hotel: 53
Fleming, Jack: 65, 75, 254
flightseeing: 86
Flint, Homer: 140-142
Folsom: 93, 107
Folsom Lake Recreation Area: 108
Food Company, The: 18
Forest Meadows: 188-189, 193, 195-197
Forest Park Inn: 299
Fort Bragg: 19
Fort Ord: 352, 357
49 Mile Scenic Drive: 263
Foster City: 277
Fountaingrove Inn: 52-53, 56
Fountaingrove Resort & Country Club: 41, 44-45, 50
Four Sisters Inns: 361
Fowler, Herbert: 254, 275
Fox, Randy: 159
Fream & Dale: 296
Freestone: 35
French Laundry: 83
Friar Tuck's: 106
Friday's Station: 176
Frog Jumping Festival: 186

G

Gabilan Dining Room: 334
Gaige House Inn: 54
galleries: Branscomb Gallery 33; Carmel 370; di Rosa Preserve 74; Fitzpatrick, Jim 107; North Eagle Gallery 45, 58; Reyna's Gallery-Museum 334; Richard MacDonald Galleries 370-371; *see also specific place*
gardens: Chateau Montelena 71; Chateau St. Jean 45-46; John Druecker Memorial Rhododendron Show 19; Kendall-Jackson Wine Center 43-44; Luther Burbank Home and Gardens 58; Mendocino Coast Botanical Gardens/Garden Tour 19; *see also specific place*
Gardiner's, John, Tennis Ranch: 362
Gardnerville, NV: 171, 177, 179
Garre: 220
Gar Woods: 125-126
General's Daughter, The: 57
Genoa Lakes: 153, 159, 167
Genoa, NV: 167, 169, 174, 178
Gibson, Charlie: 42
Gilroy: 287-288, 293-294, 299-302, 304

Girasole: 220
Girl & the Fig, The: 56
Glenbrook: 151
Gleneagles International Golf Course: 253, 256
Glen Ellen: 39-40, 46, 54, 56, 58
Glenelly Inn, The: 54
Goat Rock Beach: 35
Golden Gate National Recreation Area: 243-244, 263
Golden Oak Restaurant, The: 293, 300
Gold Lake: 146
gold panning: 147, 201
golf clinics/lessons: 7, 277, 350, 386-387
Golf Club at Genoa Lakes, The: 153, 159, 167
Golf Club at Quail Lodge, The: 356
Golf Club at Whitehawk Ranch, The: 132-134, 136, 139-140
Golf Courses at Incline Village, The: 113-114, 121
golf packages: 15-16, 31-32, 53, 80, 104, 123, 143, 171-174, 217, 278, 299, 321, 338, 363, 365
Goodfella's: 176
Goodtime Bicycle Company: 58
Goodwin, Jeff: 66
Gosby House Inn: 363
Gourmet au Bay: 28
Graeagle: 132-133, 137, 139-144, 146-148
Graeagle Lodge: 132-133
Graeagle Meadows: 131-132, 137, 140, 143, 145
Grandmere's Bed and Breakfast Inn: 104
Granite Bay Country Club: 93
Grant, Douglass: 383
Grass Valley: 98, 107, 108
Graves, Robert Muir: 7, 14, 47-48, 51, 112, 119, 196, 209, 214, 356
Gray Eagle Lodge: 138, 143-146
Gray Line: 262
Graziani, Ray: 73
Great America: 303
Greenhorn Creek: 186-188, 191, 195, 197
Green, Nicholas: 35
Griffiths, Denis: 235
Grizzly Grill, The: 146
Grounds: 193, 199
Gualala: 5, 12, 16, 18, 21
Gualala Country Inn: 16
Guerneville: 28, 48-49, 53-54
Guglielmo Winery: 292, 302
guided tours: Livermore Valley 221; Napa Valley 86; Old Sacramento 107; San Francisco 262; Sonoma Valley 58
Gustine Airport: 240

H

Haggin Oaks: 98, 101
Half Moon Bay: general discussion 267-270; attractions 281-282; climate/what to take 282; courses 275-277; dining 279-280; getting there 282-283; information sources 283; itinerary 270-275; lodging 277-279
Half Moon Bay Golf Links: 268, 274-277
Half Moon Bay Lodge: 278
Half Moon Bay Pumpkin Festival: 282
Halprin, Lawrence: 7

Haraszthy, Court Agoston: 39
Harbottle, John: 163, 167, 169, 229
Harbottle, John III: 159, 236, 289, 295
Harvest Inn: 81
Harvey's: 172
Healdsburg: 9, 43-44
Healdsburg Carriage Company: 58
Heavenly Aerial Tram: 180
Heritage House: 16-17
Hervilla, Cora: 9-10
Hervilla, Ole: 6, 9-10, 14
Hess: 71
Hewlett-Packard: 286
Hiddenbrooke Country Club: 78
Hidden Valley: 362
High Country Soaring: 179
Highlands Inn: 361
hiking/walking: Big Basin 325; Bodega Head 28; Calaveras Big Trees State Park 193; Golden Gate National Recreation Area 263; Half Moon Bay 282; Jack London State Historic Park 40; Kenwood 58; Lake Tahoe 127; Monterey Peninsula 369; Morgan Hill 302; Napa Valley 86; North Lake Tahoe 116; Pinnacles National Monument 334; Plumas County 146-147; Sea Ranch 20; South Lake Tahoe 180; Spooner Lake 179
Hills, Arthur: 268, 274, 276-277
Hilmar Cheese: 239
Hinze, Trisha: 251-252
Holiday Inn: 32, 103, 237, 299-300
Hollins House: 323
Hollister: general discussion 329-332; attractions 341; climate/what to take 341-342; courses 336-338; dining 339-341; getting there 342; information sources 342; itinerary 332-336; lodging 338-339
Hollister Hills State Recreation Area: 341
Hollister Independence Rally: 341
Hollister Inn: 339
Hollister Municipal Airport: 342
home rentals: 17, 26, 31, 124, 143, 322-323
Hopyard American Alehouse and Grill: 220
Horizon: 172
Horizon Inn: 365
horseback riding: Bodega Bay 35; Carson City, NV 179; Glen Ellen 58; Half Moon Bay 282; Jack London State Historic Park 40, 58; Lakes Basin Recreation Area 146-147; Lake Tahoe 127; Monterey Peninsula 369; Morgan Hill 302; North Lake Tahoe 116
horse-drawn carriages: 43, 201
Horseshoe Bar Grill: 98, 106
hot air ballooning: 58, 86, 180
Hotel La Rose: 49, 54-55
Hotel Monaco: 256-257
Hotel Rex, The: 257-258
Hot Gossip: 176
houseboat rentals: 198-199
hunting: 239
Husch Vineyards: 19
Hyatt Regency: 117, 123, 363

I

ice hockey; 303
Ideka's Fruit Stand: 115
Ikeda's: 124
IMAX Dome Theatre: 303
Incline Village, NV: 113-114, 117, 121, 123-126
information sources: Bodega Bay 36-37; Calaveras
    County 202; Carson Valley 182; Central Valley
    240; Half Moon Bay 283; Hollister 342; Lake
    Tahoe 129, 182; Livermore Valley 222; Mendo-
    cino Coast 21; Monterey Peninsula 371; Napa
    Valley 88; Plumas County 148; Sacramento
    108; San Francisco 264; Santa Cruz 327; Silicon
    Valley 304; Sonoma Valley 60
Inn Above Tide: 257
Inn at Cedar Mansion, The: 55
Inn at Depot Hill: 321-322
Inn at Manresa Beach: 322
Inn at Morgan Hill: 289-290, 298
Inn at Pasatiempo: 322
Inn at Spanish Bay: 376-377, 383-385, 387
Inn at the Tides, The: 32
Inn at Tres Pinos: 340
Inn at Union Square, The: 258
Inn by the Lake, The: 172
Inn Cognito: 178
Intrawest: 115
Iron Door: 145
Ironstone Vineyards: 191-192

J

Jack London Lodge, The: 54
Jack London State Historic Park: 40, 46, 58
Jacobsen, Peter: 159, 167
Jardines: 339
Jenner: 35
Joe's Ristorante Italiano: 300-301
Johnny Belinda: 6
Johnston, Robert: 253
Johnsville: 137, 145
Jones, Rees: 206, 215
Jones, Robert Trent Jr.: 25, 30-31, 76, 93, 113, 120-
    121, 188, 195-196, 206, 298, 348, 355, 381
Jones, Robert Trent Sr.: 25, 30-31, 381
JT's: 177

K

Kalkowski, Dennis: 24-26
Kautz Ironstone Vineyard: 200
kayaking: see canoeing/rafting/kayaking
Kelley, George: 236
Kendall-Jackson Wine Center: 43-44, 58
Kennedy Park: 75
Kenwood: 45-46, 54, 58
Keppler, Jim: 152, 164
Ketch Joanne Restaurant & Harbor Bar: 280
Kincaid's: 252, 260-261
Kingfish Guide Service: 128
Kings Beach: 112, 116-117, 120, 125
Korbel: 28
Kunde Estate Winery: 46, 58

L

La Ferme: 178
Laguna Seca Golf Club: 359
Lahontan Golf Club: 122
Lake Almanor: 142
Lakeland Village Beach and Ski Resort: 172
Lakes Basin Recreation Area: 146-147
Lakeshore Lodge: 179
Lakeside Beach Grill: 176
Lakeside Inn: 172
Lake Tahoe Golf Course: 151-153, 155, 165-166
Lake Tahoe Shakespeare Festival: 128
Lake Tahoe Summer Music Festival: 128
Lake Tulloch Resort: 190, 197, 199, 201
Lallapalooza: 369
Larkspur Landing Home Suite Hotel: 104
La Selva Beach: 322
Las Gaviotas: 232, 238
Las Positas: 207-209, 214
L'Auberge du Soleil: 74
Lavender: 81
lighthouses: Lighthouse Lodge and Suites 365; Mark
    Abbott Lighthouse 325; Point Arena Lighthouse
    and Museum 20; Point Cabrillo Lightstation 19
Lincoln: 92-93, 99-100, 102
Lincoln Hills Club: 92, 98, 102
Lincoln Park Golf Course: 243, 249-250, 254
Lincoln Regional Airport: 108
Links at Spanish Bay, The: 377, 381
Lippstreu, Dan: 208-209
Little Antelope Pack Station: 179
Little River: 6, 8-17, 21
Little River Airport: 21
Little River Inn: 6, 8-10, 14-15, 17
Livermore Airport: 222
Livermore Valley: general discussion 205-208;
    attractions 220-221; climate/what to take 221-
    222; courses 214-217; dining 219-220; getting
    there 222; information sources 222; itinerary
    208-213; lodging 217-218
Livermore Valley Winegrowers Association: 221
Llewellyn's: 176
Lodge at Pebble Beach: 383-384
Lodge at Whitehawk Ranch: 143
Log Cabin: 146
Loma Prieta earthquake: 325
London, Jack: 39-40, 46, 58
Lone Eagle Grille: 125
Loomis: 98, 106
Los Laureles Lodge: 362
Loustalot, Dave: 311-312
Lucas Wharf Restaurant and Bar: 34
Lucca Delicatessen: 262
Luther Burbank Home and Gardens: 58
Lynch, Chris: 113-114, 117

M

MacArthur Place: 55
MacCallum House Restaurant: 18
McClure, Gen. Robert: 357
MacDonald, Richard, Galleries: 370
McEntee, Shawn: 312-313

MOVIE/TELEVISION LOCALES

The Birds: 24
Bonanza: 120, 128
East of Eden: 6
Johnny Belinda: 6

Murder She Wrote: 6
Phenomenon: 92, 96
The Russians Are Coming: 6
Same Time Next Year: 6, 16-17

The Summer of '42: 6
Unsolved Mysteries: 269-270
The Wild One: 329

McFarland, Floyd: 319
MacKenzie, Alister: 51, 97, 101, 317, 320, 359
Mallard's: 176-177
Mandarin Gourmet: 301
Manning, Skip: 7
Mariners Point: 277
Marinus: 366
Mark Abbott Lighthouse: 325
markets: Big Trees Market 200; Mediterranean Market 368; Pebble Beach Market 386; Whole Foods Market 302
Marlette Flume Trail: 127
Marty's Inn: 238
Maud, Charles: 382
Mavericks Men Who Ride Mountains: 281
McLean, Jim, Golf Academy: 277
Meadowmont: 196
Meadowood: 63, 67, 78, 80, 83-84
Mediterranean Market: 368
Mendocino Coast: general discussion 5-8; attractions 19-20; climate/what to take 20; courses 14-15; dining 17-18; getting there 20-21; information sources 21; itinerary 8-13; lodging 15-17; *see also specific place*
Mendocino Coast Botanical Gardens/Garden Tour: 19
Mendocino Coast Reservations: 17
Menlo Park: 299, 301
Merced: 238
Mercer Caverns: 192
Metreon: 245, 263
Mezza Luna: 274, 280
Michael's Restaurant: 297-298
Microtel Inn & Suites: 300
Miller, Barry: 64-65
Miller, Johnny: 52, 64-65, 96, 100, 169, 216, 288, 296
Million Air Monterey: 372
Mill Rose Inn: 279
Mil's Bar and Grill: 238
Minden-Tahoe Airport: 179, 182
Minors Camp: 116

Miramar Beach: 274
Miramar Beach Restaurant: 280
Mission Bay Golf Center: 253, 256
mission history: 333
Mission San Juan Bautista: 333-334
Mission Santa Clara de Asis: 303
Mixx: 57
Moaning Caverns: 192
Mohawk Grill: 136, 144
Mohawk Valley: 131, 135, 144
Molera, Andrew, State Park: 369
Montalcito: 64
Monterey Bay Aquarium: 351, 353
Monterey County Vintners and Growers Association: 370
Monterey Peninsula: general discussion 345-347; attractions 369-370; climate/what to take 370-371; courses 355-359; dining 364, 365-369; getting there 371-372; information sources 371; itinerary 347-354; lodging 360-366; *see also specific place*
Monterey Peninsula Airport: 3712, 390
Monterey Pines: 358
Monterey Plaza Hotel and Spa: 361-362
Monte Rio: 48, 51
Moose's Tooth Café: 117, 125
Moosse Café: 18
Morgan Hill: 286, 289-290, 299-300, 302, 304
Morrish and Associates: 194
Moss Beach: 269-270, 278-279, 282
Moss Beach Distillery: 269-270, 280-281
motorcycles: 329
mountain biking: *see bicycling/mountain biking*
Mountain Course: 121
Mountain Springs: 196
Mt. Rose Summit: 127
Mount St. Helena: 86
MS *Dixie II*: 154-155, 159, 175
Mumm Napa Valley: 70
Murder She Wrote: 6

MUSEUMS

American Center for Wine, Food, and the Arts: 87
Calaveras County Museum: 201
California Palace of the Legion of Honor: 250-251, 263
Donner Memorial State Park & Emigrant Trail Museum: 128
Empire Mine State Historic Park: 107
Nevada State Museum: 178

Nevada State Railroad Museum: 178
Point Arena Lighthouse and Museum: 20
Portola Railroad Museum: 147
Reyna's Gallery-Museum: 334
Rosicrucian Egyptian Museum & Planetarium: 303
Sacramento Railroad Museum: 107

San Francisco Museum of Modern Art: 263
Sonoma County Museum: 58
Sonoma County Wineries Association Wine and Visitors Center: 42
Stewart Indian Cultural Center: 178
Surfing Museum: 325
Tech Museum of Innovation: 303

Murphys: 188-191, 193, 195-201
Murphys Grille: 199
Murphys Hotel: 198-199
Music in the Mountains: 107
Mustard Festival: 86

N

Napa Golf Course: 65, 68-69, 75
Napa Valley: general discussion 63-67; attractions 85-87; climate/what to take 87; courses 75-79; dining 82-85; getting there 87-88; information sources 88; itinerary 67-74; lodging 79-81; *see also specific place*
Nash, Greg: 92
Navarro: 9
Navarro Vineyards: 19
Nelson, Robin: 135, 139
Nelson, Tom: 7, 12
Nevada City: 104-107, 108
Nevada City Grill: 106
Nevada County Country Club: 98
Nevada State Museum/Railroad Museum: 178
Neville, Jack: 358, 383
Newman: 238
New Melones Lake: 198-199, 201
Nicklaus, Jack: 217, 286-287, 291-292, 296
Nico: 364
Norman, Greg: 214-215
North Eagle Gallery: 45, 58
North Lake Tahoe: general discussion 111-114; attractions 127-128; climate/what to take 128-129; courses 118-122; dining 124-127; getting there 129; information sources 129; itinerary 114-118; lodging 122-124
North Lake Tahoe Resort Association: 124
Northstar-at-Tahoe: 112, 115-116, 119, 122-123, 129
North Tahoe Marina: 127
Northwood Golf Course: 48-49, 51
Novato: 52, 252
Nugget: 173

O

Oakland Airport: 222

Oakmont Golf Club: 48, 52
Oaks at Carmel Valley Ranch, The: 367
Oakville Ranch: 72
Obester Winery: 272, 282
O'Callaghan, Casey: 77
Occidental: 34
Ocean Colony: 268
Ocean Song: 18
Old Brockway Golf Course: 112, 116-117, 120, 125
Old Town Auburn: 96, 107, 124-125
Old Town Sacramento: 97-98, 107-108
Olive Press: 46, 58
Olympic Club: 256
Ondine's: 261
Ormsby House Hotel and Casino: 173
Osmosis: 35
outlet stores: 108, 294, 302
Overland: 177

P

Pacific Bell Park: 263
Pacific Gardens Inn: 363-364
Pacific Grove: 353, 363-365, 368
Pacific Grove Golf Links: 357-358
Pacific's Edge: 367
packing/clothing: *see* climate/what to take
paddlewheelers: 98, 107, 154-155, 159, 175
Pajaro Dunes Beach Rentals: 323
Pajaro Valley: 308-309, 319
Palapas Restaurant Y Cantina: 323
Palapas Restaurant y Cantina: 314
Palmer, Arnold: 78, 163-164, 170, 244, 276-277
Palo Alto: 301-303
Palo Alto Golf Course: 297
Panda: 220
Pangaea Restaurant: 18
Panoz, Donald: 226-227
Papachinos: 238
Pasatiempo: 308, 312, 316-317, 320, 322
Pasta Moon: 279
Patterson: 226-227, 231, 235-238
Patterson's: 17
Pebble Beach: 345-346, 354-355, 359, 373-388

PARKS/RESERVES/RECREATION AREAS

Andrew Molera State Park: 369
Año Nuevo State Reserve: 282
Armstrong Redwoods State Preserve: 49
Big Basin: 325
Bodega Dunes State Park: 37
Calaveras Big Trees State Park: 193
Calero Reservoir and Park: 289, 302
Coe, Henry W., State Park: 302
Columbia State Historical Park: 201
Coyote Point Recreation Area: 252
Donner Memorial State Park & Emigrant Trail Museum: 128
Empire Mine State Historic Park: 107

Fitzgerald Marine Reserve: 282
Folsom Lake Recreation Area: 107
Golden Gate National Recreation Area: 243-244, 263
Great America: 303
Hollister Hills State Recreation Area: 341
Jack London State Historic Park: 40, 46, 58
Kennedy Park: 75
Lakes Basin Recreation Area: 146-147
Pfeiffer Big Sur State Park: 369
Pinnacles National Monument: 334, 341

Plumas Eureka State Park: 147
Purisima Creek Redwoods: 282
Raging Waters: 303
Robert Louis Stevenson State Park: 86
Russian Gulch State Park: 19
San Juan Bautista State Historic Park: 331, 341
San Luis Wildlife Refuge: 239
Six Flags Marine World Theme Park: 85
Sonoma Historic State Park: 58-59
Sugarloaf Ridge State Park: 58
Yosemite National Park: 230, 238-239

Pebble Beach Golf Academy: 386-387
Pebble Beach Golf Links: 345-346, 348, 373-374, 379-380, 382-383
Pebble Beach Market: 386
Pedrizetti Winery: 292-293
Pelican Pizza and Video: 34
Peninsula Fountain & Grill: 302
Peppermint Stick, The: 200
Peppers Mexicali Café: 353, 368
Peppoli: 386
Perkins, Brent: 102
Pescadero: 270, 278, 282
Pfeiffer Big Sur State Park: 369
Phelps, Dick: 98
Phenomenon: 92, 96
Phillips, Kyle: 25
Philo: 9, 19
Pillar Point Harbor: 281
Pilothouse Restaurant: 97, 107
Pinnacle Beach: 35
Pinnacles National Monument: 334, 341
Piñon Plaza Resort: 160, 173
Placer County: 91-92
Pleasanton: 210-211, 217-218, 220-221
Pleasanton Fairways Golf Course: 217
Pleasanton Hotel: 219
Plumas County: general discussion 131-134; attractions 146-147; climate/what to take 147; courses 139-142; dining 144-146; getting there 148; information sources 148; itinerary 134-138; lodging 142-144
Plumas Eureka State Park: 147
Plumas Pines: 132-134, 140-141, 143
Plumas Pines Realty: 143
Plumas Pines Restaurant: 145
Plum Tree Inn: 218
Pluto's: 262
Point Arena Lighthouse and Museum: 20
Point Cabrillo Lightstation: 19
Ponderosa Golf Course: 113-114, 122
Ponderosa Ranch: 128
Pope Valley: 78-79
Poplar Creek Golf Course: 252, 255
Poppy Hills Golf Course: 348, 355
Poppy Ridge Golf Course: 206, 212-213, 215-216
Portola: 133, 146-147
Posada de San Juan: 338-339
Presidio Golf Course: 243-244, 247-248, 253-254
Price, George: 207, 211
Princeton-by-the-Sea: 274, 280
Pro-Active Therapy: 253
Progresso Tamale Parlor & Factory: 340
Pulley, Algie: 76
Purisima Creek Redwoods: 282
Purple Orchid Inn: 208, 210, 217

Q

Quail Inn: 52, 57
Quail Lodge: 356
Quail Valley Golf Course: 98
Quality Inn: 32
Queen Anne Cottage: 218

Quincy: 133
Quincy Golf Course: 133

R

rafting: *see* canoeing/rafting/kayaking
Raging Waters: 303
railroad museums: Nevada State Railroad Museum 178; Portola Railroad Museum 147; Sacramento Railroad Museum 107; Virginia and Truckee Railroad 179
Ramekins Cooking School: 49, 58
Rams Head Realty: 17
Rancho Canada: 358-359
Redbud Inn: 198
Reno/Tahoe International Airport: 129
Residence Inn: 104
Resort at Squaw Creek: 113, 120-121, 123
Restaurant at Meadowood, The: 83-84
Restaurant at Sonoma Mission Inn: 56
Restaurant at Stevenswood Lodge: 17-18
restaurants: *see* dining guide; *specific place*
Retzlaff Vineyards: 210
Reyna's Gallery-Museum: 334
r.g. Burgers: 369
Ridge Golf Course, The: 101-102
Ridgemark Golf & Country Club: 329-330, 332, 336-338
Rio Del Mar: 324
Rio Grill: 366
Rios Vineyards: 200-201
Ritz-Carlton: 270, 272, 277
Riva Grill: 156, 174-175
River Bend Grille, The: 159, 175
River Pines Resort: 144
River Ranch Lodge: 124
Riverside Golf Course: 286-287
Riverview: 163
roads/routes: *see specific place*; transporation
Robert Louis Stevenson State Park: 86
Robinson, Ted: 41, 44-45, 50, 52, 216
Rocklin: 103, 105
Rocklin Park Hotel: 95, 103
Roederer Estate Winery: 9, 19
Rombauer: 72
Rooster Run Golf Club: 26-27, 29-30
Roseville: 104
Rosicrucian Egyptian Museum & Planetarium: 303
Rosie's Café: 126
Royal Oak: 68, 70, 82
Roy's: 376-377, 386
Ruby Hill: 217
Running Iron: 367
Russian Gulch State Park: 19
Russian River: 35, 48-49, 53-54
Russian River Wine Road Association: 58
The Russians Are Coming: 6
Rutherford: 81, 83
Rutherford Grill: 84

S

Sacramento International Airport: 102, 108
Sacramento Railroad Museum: 107

Sacramento vicinity: general discussion 91-94; attractions 107; climate/what to take 108; courses 99-103; dining 105-106; getting there 108; information sources 108; itinerary 94-98; lodging 103-104
Saddle Creek Golf Club: 186-190, 194-195
St. Helena: 80-81, 84-85
Salmon Creek Beach: 35
Same Time Next Year: 6, 16-17
Sampson, Harold: 141-142
San Andreas: 201
Sanctuary Day Spa: 326
Sanderlings: 316, 323
Sandpiper Dockside Cafe and Restaurant: 34
Sand Trap Bar and Grill: 82
San Francisco: general discussion 243-246; attractions 262-263; climate/what to take 263; courses 253-256; dining 259-262; getting there 263-264; information sources 264; itinerary 246-253; lodging 256-259
San Francisco International Airport: 265, 283
San Francisco Museum of Modern Art: 263
San Francisco Opera: 263
San Geronimo Golf Course: 252, 255-256
San Jose: 286, 295, 297, 299, 301, 304
San Jose Arena: 303
San Jose Fairmont Hotel: 299
San Jose International Airport: 283, 304, 342
San Juan Bautista: 331, 333-334, 337-341
San Juan Oaks Golf Club: 330-331, 335-338
San Luis Wildlife Refuge: 239
San Martin: 298
San Martin-South County Airport: 304
San Mateo Golf Course: see Poplar Creek Golf Course
San Ramon: 216
Santa Clara: 299, 301, 304
Santa Clara Golf & Tennis Club: 297
Santa Cruz: general discussion 307-313; attractions 324-326; climate/what to take 326; courses 318-321; dining 323-324; getting there 326-327; information sources 327; itinerary 313-318; lodging 321-323
Santa Cruz Beach Boardwalk: 315-316
Santa Cruz Mountains Winegrowers Association: 325-326
Santa Rosa: 44, 49-50, 52-58
Santa Teresa Golf Club: 297
Sardine Lake Resort: 135, 145

Sassy's: 220
Sattley: 135
Sausalito: 252-253, 257, 261
Schneider, Noni: 99
Schramsberg: 68, 72
Schulz, Charles M. Sonoma County Airport: 21, 59
Sea Horse Ranch: 282
Seal Cove Inn: 278-279
Sea Ranch: 5-8, 14-18, 20
Sea Ranch Chapel: 20
Sea Ranch Escape: 16
Sea Ranch Golf Links: 6-8, 12-15
Sea Ranch Lodge: 7-8, 15-16, 18
Sears Fine Food: 249, 259-260
Seascape Resort: 313-314, 321
Seaside: 357, 363
Seay, Ed: 163-164
Sebastopol: 31
Sequoia Woods Country Club: 196
71 Saint Peter: 301
Seymore Center at Long Marine Lab: 325
Shadowbrook: 323-324
Shanghai Restaurant and Bar: 96, 105
Shoreline Amphitheatre: 302
Shoreline Golf Links: 297-298
Sierra City: 145
Sierra Nevada Golf Ranch: 160, 162-163, 169-170
Sierra Springs Water Ski Lake: 179
Silicon Valley: general discussion 285-288; attractions 302-303; climate/what to take 303-304; courses 295-298; dining 300-302; getting there 304; information sources 304; itinerary 288-294; lodging 298-300; see also specific place
Silvana's Italian Cuisine: 177
Silverado Country Club and Resort: 66-70, 75-76, 79, 82
Silverado Trail: 63-64, 66, 70, 78
Silver Oak Golf Course: 170-171
Sinaloa Café: 302
Six Flags Marine World Theme Park: 85
Ski Run Marina: 180
Smith, Christie: 48
Snowshoe Brewing Company: 200
Snyder, Jack: 167
soaring: 179
Sole Mio Caffe Trattoria: 367
Sonoma Cattle Company & Napa Valley Trail Rides: 58

SPAS

Allegria Spa at Ventana Inn: 370
The Bodega Bay Lodge and Spa: 31-32
Calistoga: 85
The Claremont Resort & Spa: 257
David Walley's Spa and Hot Springs: 160, 163, 178
Inn at Spanish Bay: 370, 389
Kenwood Inn and Spa: 54

Lakeshore Lodge: 179
Meadowood: 80
Monterey Plaza Hotel and Spa: 363
Osmosis: 35
Purple Orchid Inn: 220-221
Ritz-Carlton: 272, 277
Sanctuary Day Spa: 326
Silverado Country Club and Resort: 68
Sonoma Mission Inn Golf & Country

Club: 40-41, 46-47, 53
Spa at Pebble Beach: 389
Spa at Post Ranch Inn: 370
Tahoe Lakeshore Lodge and Spa: 154, 156, 171
Third Court Salon and Day Spa: 8, 11, 19
Villagio Inn and Spa: 81
Well Within Spa: 326

Sonoma Cheese Factory: 48
Sonoma Coast Villa: 32-33
Sonoma County Fairgrounds Golf Center: 52
Sonoma County Museum: 58
Sonoma County Wineries Association Wine and
    Visitors Center: 42, 57
Sonoma Historic State Park: 58-59
Sonoma Mission Inn Golf & Country Club: 40-41,
    46-47, 51, 53
Sonoma Valley: general discussion 39-42; attrac-
    tions 57-59; climate/what to take 59; courses
    49-52; dining 56-57; getting there 59; informa-
    tion sources 60; itinerary 42-49; lodging 52-55;
    see also specific place
Sonora: 196-197
South Lake Tahoe: general discussion 151-154;
    attractions 180-181; climate/what to take 181;
    courses 165-167; dining 174-176; getting there
    181; information sources 182; itinerary 154-
    159, 164-165; lodging 171-173
South Lake Tahoe Airport: 180
Spago: 301
Spanish Bay Club: 369
spelunking: 192, 334
Spinnaker Restaurant: 261
Spirit of Sacramento: 98, 106
Spooner Lake: 179
sportfishing: Bodega Bay 34-35; Carson City, NV
    179; Fort Bragg 19; Gold Lake 146; Half Moon
    Bay 270-271, 281; Lake Tahoe 116, 128; Santa
    Cruz 325; Stanislaus River 201
Spring Hills: 320-321
Springtown Golf Course: 217
Spyglass Hill Golf Course: 377-378, 381-382
Squaw Valley: 120-121, 123
Squaw Valley Cable Car: 127
Squaw Valley Stables: 127
Squaw Valley USA: 112-113
SR Grille and Outdoor Patio: 238
Stacey's Cafe: 220
Stamps, Bert: 319
Stanford Inn by the Sea: 16
Stanford Park Hotel, The: 299
Stanford Shopping Center: 303
Stanford University: 286, 289, 294, 303
Stanislaus River: 201
State Capitol: Carson City, NV 178; Sacramento 107
Stateline, NV: 166, 175
Station Grill and Rotisserie: 177-178
Sterling: 71-72
Sterling Gardens: 197
Stevenot Winery: 192
Stevenswood: 11, 17-18
Stevinson: 228, 238
Stevinson Ranch: 232-234, 236-237
Stewart Indian Cultural Center: 178
Stillwater's: 386
Stonepine: 361
Stone Tree Golf Club: 52
Stony Ridge: 219
Strings Italian Cafe: 238
Strizzi's: 220

Sugarloaf Ridge State Park: 58
Sullivan, Terry: 64
The Summer of '42: 6
Sunbay Suites: 363
Sun China: 200
Sun City Golf Club: 92
Sunnyside Resort: 124
Sunol: 220
Sunridge Golf Course: 170-171
Sunsets On The Lake: 125
surfing: 35, 281, 325
Susanne Restaurant and Bakery: 95, 103, 105
Syrah: 56-57

T

Tahoe: see North Lake Tahoe; South Lake Tahoe
Tahoe City: 122, 124, 126; Golf Course 113, 122;
    Marina 127
Tahoe Donner Equestrian: 127
Tahoe Donner Golf Course: 113, 115, 118-119
Tahoe Keys Marina: 180
Tahoe Lakeshore Lodge and Spa: 154, 156, 171
Tahoe Paradise Golf Course: 171
Tahoe Star: 180
Tahoe Vista: 125
Tahoe Whitewater Tours: 128
Takeout Taxi: 219
Tallac Historic Site: 158, 179
Tatum, Sandy: 52, 381
Teal Bend Golf Club: 93, 98, 102
Tech Museum of Innovation: 303
Tee-Time Central: 160
Tehama: 359
tennis: 10, 116, 127, 297, 362, 387; see also specific
    place
theater: 248-249, 263, 302
"The Country Club": 359
Third Court Salon and Day Spa: 8, 11, 19
Thompson, August: 48
Tides Wharf, The: 33
Tilden Park Golf Course: 245-246, 251-252, 254-255
Timber Cove: 180
Timbercreek Restaurant: 115, 125
Tix: 263
Ton Kiang Restaurant: 261
Trap's: 385
Tra Vigne: 84
Trax Bar and Grille: 238
Tres Pinos: 340
Tributary Whitewater Tours: 107
Truckee: 118-119, 121-123, 125-129
Truckee-Tahoe Airport: 129
Try Adventures Aloft: 86
Turkey Creek Golf Club: 93-95, 99-100, 103
Turlock: 238
Twelve Bridges Golf Club: 93-95, 99

UV

Ukiah: 21
Union Hotel: 34
Union Square: 248, 257-258
Unsolved Mysteries: 269-270

WINERIES/VINEYARDS

Anderson Valley: 9, 19
Benziger Family Winery: 46, 58
Buena Vista Winery: 39
Calaveras Wine Association: 200-201
Chateau Montelena: 71
Chateau St. Jean: 45-46
Clos LaChance: 298
Clos Pegase: 71
Concannan: 210
Domaine Chandon: 71, 83
Dunaweal: 72
Elliston Vineyards: 220
Family Wineries of Sonoma Valley: 46, 58
Fountain Grove: 41
Guglielmo Winery: 292, 302
Hess: 71

Husch Vineyards: 19
Ironstone Vineyards: 191-192
Kautz Ironstone Vineyard: 200
Kendall-Jackson Wine Center: 43-44, 58
Kenwood: 45-46
Korbel: 28
Kunde Estate Winery: 46, 58
Livermore Valley Winegrowers Association: 221
Monterey County Vintners and Growers Association: 371
Mumm Napa Valley: 70
Napa Valley: 64-65, 70-72, 84-88
Navarro Vineyards: 19
Oakville Ranch: 72
Obester Winery: 272, 282

Pedrizetti Winery: 292-293
Retzlaff Vineyards: 210
Rios Vineyards: 200-201
Roederer Estate Winery: 9, 19
Rombauer: 72
Russian River Wine Road: 35, 58
Santa Cruz Mountains Winegrowers Association: 325-326
Schramsberg: 72
Sonoma County Wineries Association Wine and Visitors Center: 42, 57
Sterling: 71-72
Stevenot Winery: 192
V. Sattui: 70-71
Windsor Vineyards: 43, 58
Wine Train: 74, 84

Vacation Rentals U.S.A.: 31
Vacation Station: 124
Valhalla Arts and Music Festival: 179
Vallejo: 78, 85
Valley Wine Tours: 58
Van Gorder, Ellis: 140
Villa Del Lago Inn: 236-237
Village Baker: 145
Villagio Inn and Spa: 81
vineyards: *see* wineries/vineyards
Vintners Golf Club: 63, 66-67, 77
Virgina and Truckee Railroad: 179
Virginia City, NV: 179
V. Sattui: 70-71, 82

W

Wake, Kathy: 332
Walker River: 179
walking: *see* hiking/walking
Walley's Spa and Hot Springs: *see* David Walley's Spa and Hot Springs
Walnut Creek: 216
Watson, Tom: 381
Watsonville: 319-321
Watsonville Airport: 326-327
Watson, Willie: 51
Wawona Golf Course: 230
Weiskopf, Tom: 122
Well Within Spa: 326
Wente Vineyards: 205-207, 211-212, 214-215, 219
Westin Santa Clara, The: 299
Westin St. Francis, The: 258-259
Westley: 237
Whale Watch Bar: 10-11
whalewatching: Bodega Bay 34-35; Half Moon Bay 271, 281; Mendocino Coast 19; Santa Cruz 325

what to take: *see* climate/what to take
Whiskey Creek Steakhouse and Saloon: 160, 162, 177
Whitehawk Ranch: 132-134, 136, 143
White Sulphur Springs Bed and Breakfast: 144
Whitewater Connection: 107
Whiting, Sam: 51
Whitney Oaks Golf Club: 93, 96, 97 100-101
Whole Foods Market: 302
Wickets: 366
Wiebe Motel: 339
The Wild One: 329
Wild Rose Inn: 174
Williams, Joseph B.: 118
Will's Fargo Dining House and Saloon: 367-368
Winchester Mystery House: 303
Windsor Golf Club: 41-44, 49-50
Windsor Vineyards: 43, 58
windsurfing: 297-298, 325
Wine Country Golf Camp: 52-53
Wine Plane: 86
Wine Train: 74, 84
Wolf House: 39-40, 46
Wong, Lance: 249
Wright, Frank Lloyd: 134
Wright's Beach: 35
W San Francisco: 258

XYZ

Yellow Dog Inn: 199
Yosemite National Park: 230, 238-239
Yountville: 63-64, 66-67, 81-83, 85, 87
Yukol Place: 262
Zephyr Cove Marina: 154-155, 159
Zephyr Cove, NV: 175, 180
Zibbibo: 301

About the Authors

The golf and travel writing credentials of Susan Fornoff and Cori Kenicer include Kenicer's work for magazines, including *Private Clubs, Luxury Golf, Fortune,* and *Golf for Women,* and Fornoff's career as golf writer for the *San Francisco Examiner* (now *Chronicle*) and *Examiner Magazine.* Kenicer was born and raised in the San Francisco Bay Area, where her family's business focused on golf course development. She lives in San Francisco with husband George, an accomplished golf photographer. Fornoff was born in Baltimore and lives in Alameda, California, with husband Marc Squeri, her favorite companion in golf, life, and Scrabble. The Kenicers and Fornoff/Squeri dream of someday following all of the itineraries in this book, just for the fun of it.

AVALON TRAVEL
publishing

BECAUSE TRAVEL MATTERS.

AVALON TRAVEL PUBLISHING knows that travel is more than coming and going—travel is taking part in new experiences, new ideas, and a new outlook. Our goal is to bring you complete and up-to-date information to help you make informed travel decisions.

AVALON TRAVEL GUIDES feature a combination of practicality and spirit, offering a unique traveler-to-traveler perspective perfect for an afternoon hike, around-the-world journey, or anything in between.

WWW.TRAVELMATTERS.COM

Avalon Travel Publishing guides are available at your favorite book or travel store.

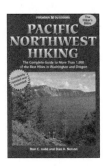

For Travelers With Special Interests

Guides

The 100 Best Small Art Towns in America • Asia in New York City
The Big Book of Adventure Travel • Cities to Go
Cross-Country Ski Vacations • Gene Kilgore's Ranch Vacations
Great American Motorcycle Tours • Healing Centers and Retreats
Indian America • Into the Heart of Jerusalem
The People's Guide to Mexico • The Practical Nomad
Saddle Up! • Staying Healthy in Asia, Africa, and Latin America
Steppin' Out • Travel Unlimited • Understanding Europeans
Watch It Made in the U.S.A. • The Way of the Traveler
Work Worldwide • The World Awaits
The Top Retirement Havens • Yoga Vacations

Series

Adventures in Nature
The Dog Lover's Companion
Kidding Around
Live Well

 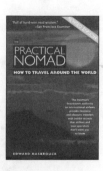 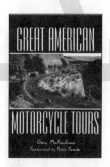

MOON HANDBOOKS
provide comprehensive coverage of a region's arts, history, land, people, and social issues in addition to detailed practical listings for accommodations, food, outdoor recreation, and entertainment. Moon Handbooks allow complete immersion in a region's culture—ideal for travelers who want to combine sightseeing with insight for an extraordinary travel experience.

USA

Alaska-Yukon • Arizona • Big Island of Hawaii • Boston
Coastal California • Colorado • Connecticut • Georgia
Grand Canyon • Hawaii • Honolulu-Waikiki • Idaho
Kauai • Los Angeles • Maine • Massachusetts • Maui
Michigan • Montana • Nevada • New Hampshire
New Mexico • New York City • New York State
North Carolina • Northern California • Ohio • Oregon
Pennsylvania • San Francisco • Santa Fe-Taos • Silicon Valley
South Carolina • Southern California • Tahoe • Tennessee
Texas • Utah • Virginia • Washington • Wisconsin
Wyoming • Yellowstone-Grand Teton

INTERNATIONAL

Alberta and the Northwest Territories • Archaeological Mexico
Atlantic Canada • Australia • Baja • Bangkok • Bali • Belize
British Columbia • Cabo • Canadian Rockies • Cancún
Caribbean Vacations • Colonial Mexico • Costa Rica • Cuba
Dominican Republic • Ecuador • Fiji • Havana • Honduras
Hong Kong • Indonesia • Jamaica • Mexico City • Mexico
Micronesia • The Moon • Nepal • New Zealand
Northern Mexico • Oaxaca • Pacific Mexico • Pakistan
Philippines • Puerto Vallarta • Singapore • South Korea
South Pacific • Southeast Asia • Tahiti
Thailand • Tonga-Samoa • Vancouver
Vietnam, Cambodia and Laos
Virgin Islands • Yucatán Peninsula

www.moon.com

Rick Steves

Rick Steves shows you where to travel and how to travel—all while getting the most value for your dollar. His Back Door travel philosophy is about making friends, having fun, and avoiding tourist rip-offs.

Rick's been traveling to Europe for more than 25 years and is the author of 20 guidebooks, which have sold more than a million copies. He also hosts the award-winning public television series *Travels in Europe with Rick Steves*.

RICK STEVES' COUNTRY & CITY GUIDES

Best of Europe
France, Belgium & the Netherlands
Germany, Austria & Switzerland
Great Britain & Ireland
Italy • London • Paris • Rome • Scandinavia • Spain & Portugal

RICK STEVES' PHRASE BOOKS

French • German • Italian • French, Italian & German
Spanish & Portuguese

MORE EUROPE FROM RICK STEVES

Rick Steves' Europe 101
Europe Through the Back Door
Mona Winks
Postcards from Europe

WWW.RICKSTEVES.COM

ROAD TRIP USA

Getting there is half the fun, and Road Trip USA guides are your ticket to driving adventure. Taking you off the interstates and onto less-traveled, two-lane highways, each guide is filled with fascinating trivia, historical information, photographs, facts about regional writers, and details on where to sleep and eat—all contributing to your exploration of the American road.

*"Books so full of the pleasures of the American road,
you can smell the upholstery."*
~ BBC radio

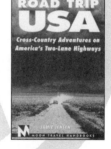

THE ORIGINAL CLASSIC GUIDE
Road Trip USA

ROAD TRIP USA REGIONAL GUIDE
Road Trip USA: California and the Southwest

ROAD TRIP USA GETAWAYS
Road Trip USA Getaways: Chicago
Road Trip USA Getaways: New Orleans
Road Trip USA Getaways: San Francisco
Road Trip USA Getaways: Seattle

www.roadtripusa.com

TRAVEL ✦ SMART®

guidebooks are accessible, route-based driving guides. Special interest tours provide the most practical routes for family fun, outdoor activities, or regional history for a trip of anywhere from two to 22 days. Travel Smarts take the guesswork out of planning a trip by recommending only the most interesting places to eat, stay, and visit.

"One of the few travel series that rates sightseeing attractions. That's a handy feature. It helps to have some guidance so that every minute counts."

~ San Diego Union-Tribune

TRAVEL SMART REGIONS

Alaska
American Southwest
Arizona
Carolinas
Colorado
Deep South
Eastern Canada
Florida Gulf Coast
Florida
Georgia
Hawaii
Illinois/Indiana
Iowa/Nebraska
Kentucky/Tennessee
Maryland/Delaware
Michigan
Minnesota/Wisconsin
Montana/Wyoming/Idaho
Nevada

New England
New Mexico
New York State
Northern California
Ohio
Oregon
Pacific Northwest
Pennsylvania/New Jersey
South Florida and the Keys
Southern California
Texas
Utah
Virginias
Western Canada

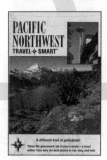

Foghorn Outdoors

guides are for campers, hikers, boaters, anglers, bikers, and golfers of all levels of daring and skill. Each guide contains site descriptions and ratings, driving directions, facilities and fees information, and easy-to-read maps that leave only the task of deciding where to go.

"Foghorn Outdoors has established an ecological conservation standard unmatched by any other publisher."
~ Sierra Club

CAMPING Arizona and New Mexico Camping
Baja Camping • California Camping
Camper's Companion • Colorado Camping
Easy Camping in Northern California
Easy Camping in Southern California
Florida Camping • New England Camping
Pacific Northwest Camping
Utah and Nevada Camping

HIKING 101 Great Hikes of the San Francisco Bay Area
California Hiking • Day-Hiking California's National Parks
Easy Hiking in Northern California
Easy Hiking in Southern California
New England Hiking
Pacific Northwest Hiking • Utah Hiking

FISHING Alaska Fishing • California Fishing
Washington Fishing

BOATING California Recreational Lakes and Rivers
Washington Boating and Water Sports

OTHER OUTDOOR RECREATION California Beaches
California Golf • California Waterfalls
California Wildlife • Easy Biking in Northern California
Florida Beaches
The Outdoor Getaway Guide For Southern California
Tom Stienstra's Outdoor Getaway Guide: Northern California

WWW.FOGHORN.COM

CiTY·SMaRT™

The best way to enjoy a city is to get advice from someone who lives there—and that's exactly what City Smart guidebooks offer. City Smarts are written by local authors with hometown perspectives who have personally selected the best places to eat, shop, sightsee, and simply hang out. The honest, lively, and opinionated advice is perfect for business travelers looking to relax with the locals or for longtime residents looking for something new to do Saturday night.

A portion of sales from each title
benefits a non-profit literacy organization in that city.

CITY SMART CITIES

Albuquerque	Anchorage
Austin	Baltimore
Berkeley/Oakland	Boston
Calgary	Charlotte
Chicago	Cincinnati
Cleveland	Dallas/Ft. Worth
Denver	Indianapolis
Kansas City	Memphis
Milwaukee	Minneapolis/St. Paul
Nashville	Pittsburgh
Portland	Richmond
San Francisco	Sacramento
St. Louis	Salt Lake City
San Antonio	San Diego
Tampa/St. Petersburg	Toronto
Tucson	Vancouver

www.travelmatters.com

User-friendly, informative, and fun:
Because travel *matters*.

Visit our newly launched web site and explore the variety of titles and travel information available online, featuring an interactive *Road Trip USA* exhibit.

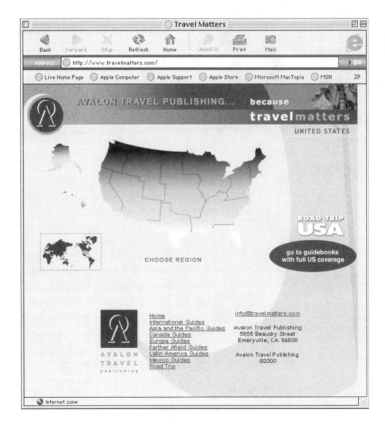

www.ricksteves.com

The Rick Steves web site is bursting with information to boost your travel I.Q. and liven up your European adventure. Including:
- The latest from Rick on what's hot in Europe
- Excerpts from Rick's books
- Rick's comprehensive Guide to European Railpasses

www.foghorn.com

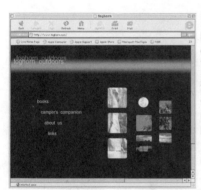

Foghorn Outdoors guides are the premier source for United States outdoor recreation information. Visit the Foghorn Outdoors web site for more information on these activity-based travel guides, including the complete text of the handy *Foghorn Outdoors: Camper's Companion*.

www.moon.com

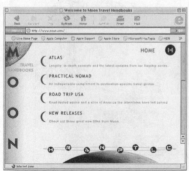

Moon Handbooks' goal is to give travelers all the background and practical information they'll need for an extraordinary travel experience. Visit the Moon Handbooks web site for interesting information and practical advice, including Q&A with the author of *The Practical Nomad*, Edward Hasbrouck.